Multicultural
Counseling
Competencies

MULTICULTURAL ASPECTS OF COUNSELING SERIES

SERIES EDITOR
Paul Pedersen, Ph.D., *Syracuse University*

EDITORIAL BOARD

Volumes in This Series

1. **Increasing Multicultural Understanding: A Comprehensive Model**
   by Don C. Locke

2. **Preventing Prejudice: A Guide for Counselors and Educators**
   by Joseph G. Ponterotto and Paul B. Pedersen

3. **Improving Intercultural Interactions: Modules for Cross-Cultural Training Programs**
   edited by Richard W. Brislin and Tomoko Yoshida

4. **Assessing and Treating Culturally Diverse Clients: A Practical Guide**
   by Freddy A. Paniagua

5. **Overcoming Unintentional Racism in Counseling and Therapy: A Practitioner's Guide to Intentional Intervention**
   by Charles R. Ridley

6. **Multicultural Counseling With Teenage Fathers: A Practical Guide**
   by Mark S. Kiselica

7. **Multicultural Counseling Competencies: Assessment, Education and Training, and Supervision**
   edited by Donald B. Pope-Davis and Hardin L. K. Coleman

Multicultural Counseling Competencies

Assessment, Education and Training, and Supervision

edited by

Donald B. Pope-Davis
Hardin L. K. Coleman

Multicultural Aspects of Counseling Series 7

SAGE Publications
International Educational and Professional Publisher
Thousand Oaks London New Delhi

For information address:

SAGE Publications, Inc.
2455 Teller Road
Thousand Oaks, California 91320
E-mail: order@sagepub.com

SAGE Publications Ltd.
6 Bonhill Street
London EC2A 4PU
United Kingdom

SAGE Publications India Pvt. Ltd.
M-32 Market
Greater Kailash I
New Delhi 110 048 India

Printed in the United States of America

Library of Congress Cataloging-in-Publication Data

Pope-Davis, Donald B.
    Multicultural counseling competencies: assessment, education and training, and
supervision / editors, Donald B. Pope-Davis and Hardin L. K. Coleman
        p. cm. — (Multicultural aspects of counseling series; v. 7)
    Includes bibliographical references and index.
    ISBN 0-8039-7221-0 (acid-free paper). — ISBN 0-8039-7222-9 (pbk.: acid-free paper)
    1. Cross-cultural counseling.   2. Counselors—Training of.
I. Coleman, Hardin L. K.   II. Title.   III. Series.

BF637.C6P595   1996
361.3'23—dc20   96-25239

97 98 99 00 01 02 03 10 9 8 7 6 5 4 3 2 1

Acquiring Editor:	Jim Nageotte
Production Editor:	Diana E. Axelsen
Production Assistant:	Karen Wiley
Typesetter/Designer:	Marion Warren
Indexer:	Virgil Diodato
Print Buyer:	Anna Chin

Contents

Foreword   ix
    Derald Wing Sue

Acknowledgments   xiii

PART I: Assessment of Multicultural Counseling Competence

---

1. Outcome of Training in the Philosophy of Assessment:
   Multicultural Counseling Competencies   3
       Gargi Roysircar Sodowsky, Phoebe Y. Kuo-Jackson,
       and Gary J. Loya

2. Portfolio Assessment of Multicultural Counseling
   Competence   43
       Hardin L. K. Coleman

3. How "Multiculturalism" Obscures Race and Culture
   as Differential Aspects of Counseling Competency   60
       Janet E. Helms and Tina Q. Richardson

PART II: Multicultural Education and Training

4. Sex Matters: Gender and Sexual Orientation in
   Training for Multicultural Counseling Competency   83
   Ruth E. Fassinger and Beth Sperber Richie

5. Multicultural Counseling Training: A Competency Model and
   National Survey   111
   Joseph G. Ponterotto

6. Course Development in Multicultural Counseling   131
   *Charles R. Ridley, Dorothy L. Espelage, and Karen J.
   Rubinstein*

7. A Systemic Multicultural Curriculum Model: The Pedagogical
   Process   159
   Luis A. Vázquez

8. Toward Defining a Multicultural Training Philosophy   184
   Mark M. Leach and Michael A. Carlton

9. Using the Multicultural Change Intervention Matrix
   (MCIM) as a Multicultural Counseling Training Model   209
   Amy L. Reynolds

10. A Multicultural Immersion Experience: Filling a Void in
    Multicultural Training   227
    *Donald B. Pope-Davis, Cynthia Breaux, and William
    M. Liu*

11. Cultural Ambience: The Importance of a Culturally
    Aware Learning Environment in the Training and
    Education of Counselors   242
    Alberta M. Gloria and Donald B. Pope-Davis

PART III: Multicultural Supervision

12. Multiculturalism as a Context for Supervision: Perspectives,
    Limitations, and Implications   263
    Gerald L. Stone

13. Multicultural Counseling Supervision: Central Issues,
    Theoretical Considerations, and Practical Strategies   290
    Michael D'Andrea and Judy Daniels

14. Facilitating Multicultural Competency in Counseling
    Supervision: Operationalizing a Practical Framework   310
    Madonna G. Constantine

15. The Supervision Relationship in Multicultural Training   325
    Rocío P. Martínez and Elizabeth L. Holloway

16. Postmodern Supervision: A Multicultural Perspective   350
    Roberto Cortéz González

17. Cross-Cultural Supervision: Issues for the White Supervisor   387
    Margaret L. Fong and Suzanne H. Lease

Author Index   406

Subject Index   416

About the Contributors   431

Foreword

Ever since the political turmoil of the 1960s, racial/ethnic minority groups have become increasingly vocal in their demands for social justice, fairness, and the preservation of civil/human rights. Recognizing that prejudice, stereotyping, racism, and sexism often manifested themselves in discriminatory behavior toward minority populations, many well-meaning political leaders advocated "non-discriminatory" policies and practices. Unfortunately, a conceptual confusion occurred in which "differential treatment" became equated with "discriminatory treatment." It became a common belief that one was not discriminating if "everyone was treated the same" and that treating people differently (especially on the basis of race or gender) was to discriminate. Such an orientation was also consistent with universalistic notions of "people are people" and that we are all "human beings." Although such statements are valid at some levels, the institutionalization of this belief was often used as a rationalization for continuing to do things in the "same old ways." There was no need to change programs, policies, and practices because they could be universally applied to everyone, regardless of race, creed, or color.

At the same time, however, minority group members challenged the monocultural views of society, emphasizing the importance of recognizing different world views, different cultural values, and different life experiences. Instead of calling for "equal treatment" per se, the culturally different in our society demanded "equal access and opportunities" that often dictated "differential treatment." Indeed, minority groups begun to equate "equal treatment" with discriminatory treatment whenever it denied equal access and opportunities. To this very day, many of us fail to understand the distinction between *equal treatment* and *equal access and opportunities.*

Just as our society has wrestled with these thorny issues, so has the mental health profession. For years, the professions of counseling and psychotherapy have operated from certain universal assumptions: (a) Human beings are "human beings" regardless of race, ethnicity, culture and gender; (b) theories of counseling and psychotherapy are culture-free and can be applied to everyone; and (c) the therapeutic skills and strategies used in "good counseling" work for everyone. Racial/ethnic minority groups, however, challenged these assumptions vocally. They accused counselors of being "handmaidens of the status quo," "transmitters of society's values," and "instruments of oppression."

Racial/ethnic minorities were being denied equal access and opportunities to counseling services because of the monocultural assumptions made in mental health practice. These accusations became glaring when a preponderance of minority utilization studies revealed that ethnic minority clients consistently underutilized traditional mental health facilities and prematurely terminated at rates significantly higher than their White counterparts. Counselors and mental health professionals began to realize that the explanations for these findings resided in the monocultural practices used by counselors to treat their culturally different clients, and in institutional policies and practices which were culturally biased because they failed to acknowledge the different life experiences of their minority constituents.

In 1982, a group of multicultural counseling psychologists (Sue et al.) published a major position paper advocating the need for the development of multicultural counseling competencies and outlining a conceptual framework for their development. In that publication, the authors challenged the universal notion of counseling practice and identified culture-specific attitudes, knowledge, and skills in working with a culturally diverse population. While acknowledged by many as making a major contribution to the counseling field, the competencies failed to generate major changes in training programs and counselor practice. The most frequent explanations given were (a) the multicultural competencies were not specific enough; (b) instruments to measure them had not been developed; and (c) help was needed to translate these competencies into the areas of education and training, assessment, and supervision. With the updated publication of the revised competencies through the Association for Multicultural Counseling and Development (Sue, Arredondo, & McDavis, 1992) and the 1993 American Psychological Association *Guidelines for Providers of Psychological Services to Ethnic, Linguistic, and Culturally Diverse Populations,* and with the development of numerous multicultural counseling competency inventories, we have made tremendous progress in overcoming the first two barriers.

Multicultural Counseling Competence: Assessment, Education and Training, and Supervision, edited by Donald B. Pope-Davis and Hardin L. K. Coleman, represents the next giant step to implementing multicultural standards in the counseling profession. Logically organized and with a list of impressive contributors, the text is divided into three sections: Assessment of Multicultural Counseling Competence, Multicultural Education and Training, and Multicultural Supervision. This is also a book which is not only well grounded in the theory and research of multicultural counseling, but is also a practical guide to how graduate schools of counseling and clinical psychology, social work, and other helping professions might infuse multicultural competence into their faculty and students, curriculum, fieldwork, and supervision. The text provides a good balance between recognizing that change is both individual and institutional; that multicultural competence is more than just an intellectual exercise and must also deal with sociopolitical realities; and that while theory and philosophy of multiculturalism are valued, the "how to" of implementation must be considered as well.

Pope-Davis and Coleman have made a major substantive contribution to the counseling profession with the publication of this text. They have accepted the challenge of cultural diversity and are serving the roles of pioneers in seeking both individual and institutional multicultural competence. I believe they, and their contributors, will be immensely successful in providing our profession with meaningful models, methods, and practices to move us along the path to multiculturalism. Both seem to truly understand that different models, different methods, and different practices need to be developed if we are to provide equal access and opportunities to everyone regardless of race, culture, ethnicity, and gender.

Derald Wing Sue, Ph.D.
California School of Professional Psychology—Alameda
and California State University, Hayward

References

American Psychological Association. (1993). Guidelines for providers of psychological services to ethnic, linguistic, and culturally diverse populations. *American Psychologist, 48,* 45-48.

Sue, D. W., Arredondo, P., & McDavis, R. J. (1992). Multicultural counseling competencies and standards: A call to the profession. *Journal of Multicultural Counseling and Development, 20,* 644-688.

Sue, D. W., Bernier, J. E., Durran, A., Feinberg, L., Pedersen, P., Smith, E. J., & Vasquez-Nuttall, E. (1982). Position paper: Cross-cultural counseling competencies. *The Counseling Psychologist, 10,* 45-52.

Acknowledgments

We wish to thank those people on whose shoulders we stand: Those who have struggled to make the field of multicultural counseling what it is today; our graduate advisors, Teresa LaFromboise and John Krumboltz, respectively; and our students and clients, from whom we are constantly learning.

*We dedicate this book to our families for
their support and patience:*

*To my eleven siblings; my parents, Dolores and Donald, Sr.; and
especially my wife, Sara.*

Donald B. Pope-Davis

*To my siblings, Bill and Lovida; my parents, Lovida, Sr.,
and William, Jr.; and especially my wife, Gail.*

Hardin L. K. Coleman

PART I

Assessment of Multicultural Counseling Competence

1

Outcome of Training
in the Philosophy of Assessment

MULTICULTURAL
COUNSELING COMPETENCIES

Gargi Roysircar Sodowsky

Phoebe Y. Kuo-Jackson

Gary J. Loya

The three sections of this chapter develop the concept of multicultural counseling competencies (MCC) from (a) philosophical, (b) etic, and (c) emic perspectives, respectively. This framework follows Ridley, Mendoza, and Kanitz's (1994) recommendation that multicultural training should first have a philosophical basis. Then the broad philosophical base needs to develop a narrower focus, operationalizing specific proficiencies. In keeping with the pyramidlike broad-to-narrow framework of training, the first section presents a philosophical rationale for the motivation of practicing professionals who seek training in MCC.

The second section, taking a narrower focus, deals with the perspective of comparability or "modified etic" that lies behind competent multicultural assessment of minority clients. In this section, mainstream assessment conclusions are modified to reflect the differences of minority clients' adapta-

3

tion. This section gives guidelines for a hands-on assessment workshop that uses a group feedback process.

The third section, narrowing further the focus of the chapter, utilizes a culture-specific, emic theoretical approach to study the case of a Japanese American client in the context of her Japanese American family members who are acculturating across three generations. In this section, the MCC objectives are to conceptualize problems in culture-specific ways, to build a facilitative cross-cultural dyadic process, and to move toward goal-oriented problem resolutions. In this section, the question is, "How does one work with this Japanese American woman?" rather than "How does one work with Japanese Americans?"

Internal-External Motivations for Multicultural Counseling Competencies: Issues of an Integrated Professional Identity

Ridley et al. (1994) state that either internal motivation or external motivation can be a philosophical basis for implementing multicultural training (MCT) at an institution of higher learning. An example of internal motivation would be a moral concern for equitable services, and an example of external motivation would be the necessity of meeting the accreditation requirements of the American Psychological Association (APA; see American Psychological Association, 1986). We apply the Ridley et al. paradigm to understand why counseling practitioners would seek retraining in MCC. Many practitioners went to school when MCT was not offered or was available through an optional course. In addition, recent graduates or advanced graduate students, after taking a general multicultural counseling course, may seek a focused opportunity to develop MCC via a practice-oriented training method that is outcome oriented.

Ridley et al. suggest that external motivation for MCT is less powerful than internal motivation. We agree fundamentally that internal and external motivations have different sources, especially because institutional policies and professional mandates control external behavior. However, we believe that individual counselors and advanced trainees, with their development of a professional identity, may integrate their internal and external motivations into a deeply felt personalized investment in acquiring MCC. At the outset of training, learning the guidelines set out by APA (American Psychological Association, 1992) and the American Counseling Association (ACA; American Counseling Association, 1988) and receiving training in professionally accredited programs could be external reinforcers of change. With continued training, however, the identification with one's chosen profession transforms enforced conformity into personal commitment to one's profession. An appropriate analogy could be how a child while growing up internalizes the values of its parents, or how individuals voluntarily endorse the religion or worldviews of their cultural group. Therefore, the external mandates of APA's Office of Ethnic Minority Affairs (1993), "Guidelines for Providers of Psychological Services to Ethnic, Linguistic, and Culturally Diverse Populations" could become personally meaningful for the individual counselor, with the mandates growing into intuitive concerns for the counselor. Thus, owing to the maturation of professional identity, the counselor grows from an ambivalent subscriber to a multicultural activist. Table 1.1 provides a summary of the APA guidelines (1993) for psychological services for minorities, so that participants in the workshop presented in Section 2 learn the ethics of MCC.

Professional identity is the force that integrates external and internal motivators. Motivations can be discretely external (caused by rewards, punishments, positive as well as negative political correctness, etc.) or internal (caused by cultural self-awareness, politically based ideology for equity, personal experience of racial or ethnic minority status, etc.). Internal and external motivations can become complementary dynamic parts of one's professional identity like the yin and yang principles or the scientist-practitioner role of the psychologist, the two forces reciprocally strengthening each other. Thus, a counselor's professional identity facilitates regard for the exhortations of minority advocates (e.g., Katz, 1985; Pedersen, 1988) and the ethics of MCC (e.g., APA, 1993; Sue et al., 1982) not as something adversarial but rather as a stimulant that brings forth the potential humanitarian values of the practitioner.

The view that counseling professionals and trainees are guided by both external and internal motivations was supported by research findings that are summarized below. In a study of MCC of students and practitioners in counseling psychology, school psychology, and clinical psychology in Nebraska (Sodowsky, 1996), 40% of the subjects ($n = 197$), expressed through open-ended statements a strong desire and willingness to obtain MCT training opportunities. It is to be noted that only 15% ($n = 90$) of all the subjects had taken a course in multicultural/cross-cultural counseling/psychology. Nearly half of the subjects requesting MCT suggested an increasing professional responsiveness to multicultural counseling even in a midwestern state that does not have a sizable racial and ethnic minority population. The subjects were responding anonymously, confidentially, and in an open-ended

Table 1.1 Guidelines for Working with Ethnic, Linguistic, and Culturally Diverse Populations

---

Knowledge About Diversity

1. Psychologists are cognizant of relevant research and practice issues as related to the population being served. This includes the acknowledgment that ethnicity and culture affect the behavior of clients; considerations of the validity of the use and interpretation of test instruments; recognition of the limits of the psychologist's competencies and expertise; and seeking educational and training experiences to enhance understanding of minority clients.

Psychological Client-Counselor Processes

2. Psychologists recognize ethnicity and culture as significant parameters in understanding psychological processes. This requires an awareness of how both their own and their client's cultural background, experiences, attitudes, values, and biases influence psychological processes and therapeutic interventions.

Client's Collective Culture

3. Psychologists respect the roles of family members and community structures, hierarchies, values, and belief systems within the client's culture.

Client's Religion and Beliefs

4. Psychologists respect clients' religious and/or spiritual beliefs and values, including attributions and taboos, because they affect worldview, psychosocial functioning, and expressions of distress. This may involve familiarity with indigenous beliefs and practices, as well as the incorporation of religious/spiritual leaders/practitioners relevant to the client's cultural and belief systems into psychological interventions.

Client's Language

5. Psychologists interact in the language requested by the client and, if this is not feasible, make an appropriate referral. Clients may be offered a translator who has a nondual relationship with the client and who possesses cultural knowledge with an appropriate professional background. Relevant test data are also interpreted in terms understandable by the client.

---

manner. They were under no pressure to impress the investigator. It could be hypothesized that many psychology professionals in this study were not externally motivated by reasons of societal demographic changes or personal economic survival.

Regarding their needs for MCC, subjects' significant themes appeared to be a need for more professional experiences with minority individuals; for more general awareness about issues related to culture, race, ethnicity, minority status, and cultural value systems; for more MCT; for more self-awareness regarding their own cultural contexts; and for more information about specific areas in racial and ethnic minority cultures (e.g., working with

Table 1.1 Continued

Client's Experience of Racism

  6. Psychologists consider the impact of adverse social, environmental, and political factors in assessing problems and designing interventions. In doing so, types of intervention strategies to be used are matched with the client's level of need.

Psychologist's Advocacy Role

  7. Psychologists attend to as well as work to eliminate biases, prejudices, and discriminatory practices. Thus they are cognizant of relevant discriminatory practices at the social and community level.

Psychologist's Client Notes Address Cultural Factors

  8. Psychologists should document culturally relevant factors in client records. These may include, but are not limited to, factors associated with client's acculturation, extent of family support, level of education, and intimate relationships with people of different backgrounds.

Client's Economic and Political Conditions

  9. Psychologists know that culture, ethnicity, race, and socioeconomic and political factors have a significant impact on the psychosocial, political, and economic development of ethnic and culturally diverse groups.

Client's Cultural Identity

  10. Psychologists facilitate clients' understanding, resolution, and maintenance of their own sociocultural identifications.

Client Variables' Interactions

  11. Psychologists understand the interaction of culture, gender, and social orientation on client behaviors and needs.

NOTE: A summary of "Guidelines for Providers of Psychological Services to Ethnic, Linguistic, and Culturally Diverse Populations," 1993, *American Psychologist, 48*(1), 45-48.

adolescents from a particular group, understanding family structures in different groups). Some subjects honestly indicated a lack of certainty regarding the improvements they needed because they rarely worked with racial and ethnic minority clients, but realized, nonetheless, that they needed to develop MCC.

In this study, nearly half of the subjects' acceptance of the need for MCC indicated their strong professional identity. First, counselors are trained to be open to learning new illnesses and treatments, interpersonal skills, receptivity to supervision and consultation, and about change agency. Second, APA and ACA ethical standards require counselors to demonstrate specific professional competencies and to provide effective services that are accessible to all. Licensure requirements are intended to enforce quality control for multicultural practice. Thus, professional conditions create in counseling professionals a disposition to seek retraining or new training. An accompanying corollary is that many counselors are earnestly requesting training in MCC, perhaps more so than professionals in other fields whose organizational guidelines do not require human relations competence and diversity skills.

On the basis of the subjects' self-reported wishes and needs, the following examples are proposed as some of the internal and external motivations of counselors seeking MCT and MCC:

Wanting to engage in self-exploration in the contexts of one's culture and one's ethnic and racial identity in order to identify value biases as well as ethnic and racial prejudices

Wanting to learn how to articulate one's cultural values and one's ethnic and racial attitudes

Wanting to know institutional barriers that minority clients face when they seek services and being determined to assist in alleviating, removing, or reducing those obstacles

Being willing to seek training from more experienced multicultural counselors

Realizing the importance of always collecting cultural information, whether it is applied or not applied to the treatment process; and realizing that one does not know how to collect such information

Being willing to invest the necessary effort to learn how to work with racial and ethnic minority clients

Realizing that formal training is necessary for the competent collection of cultural data about a client

Wanting to learn how to organize cultural information into a meaningful conceptualization of the client's ideographic experience

Wanting to learn how to use cultural information meaningfully, in a manner that would prove beneficial to the client

Wanting to learn how to use cultural information meaningfully, in a manner that would weaken broad-based stereotypes about a group

Two motivations, (a) self-exploration in the contexts of one's culture and racial and ethnic identity and (b) seeking a politically based ideology for equity, are addressed below because both are characterized by internal and external motivations and are crucial to the development of MCC.

Self-Exploration in the
Contexts of Culture, Race, and Ethnicity

A desire to explore one's identity as a person who has been socialized in a culture, race, and ethnicity is characteristic of counselors who are committed to developing MCC. The processes involved in cultural self-exploration afford one the opportunity to develop awareness of one's collective-self, which is of particular importance in facilitating the dyadic process of a multicultural counseling relationship.

In the self-exploration of their own cultural and racial identity, counselors are involved in an openness to critical self-examination of the cultural aspects of their identity, such as discovering their cultural value orientation (i.e., worldviews); their racial attitudes in endorsing stereotypes and discrimination and in enacting individual racism; and their identification with and sense of belonging to a reference group, such as an ethnic group or a lifestyle preference group. The discovery and acceptance of such socialization contexts, wherein lie meanings and explanations, help counselors to increase their level of comfort with clients' belief systems, racial and ethnic behavioral norms, and physical attributes quite different from those of the counselor.

The increase in the thresholds for openness and comfort level subsequently help in developing a counseling style of flexibility when working with culturally different clients labeled as "very different and difficult" (i.e., labels from mainstream theoretical frameworks and middle-class life experiences). It is also helpful to develop a style of tolerance for working in contextually unfamiliar situations (e.g., clients referring to the mystical Hindu phenomenon of reincarnation, or to their membership in undefined or undefinable extended kinships).

Thus, (a) cultural, racial, and ethnic self-examination; (b) comfort level with obvious differences of others; (c) a flexible interpersonal approach; and (d) tolerance for cultural mysteries are counselor variables that become components of the multicultural counseling relationship. Sodowsky, Taffe, Gutkin, and Wise (1994) expanded the three general multicultural counseling competency domains of knowledge, beliefs/attitudes, and skills, as suggested by D. W. Sue and his colleagues (Sue et al., 1982; Sue, Arredondo, & McDavis, 1992), by adding another essential competency, the multicultural counseling relationship, a human factor in counseling that redresses issues of inequity and lack of empowerment for minorities at the personal client-counselor level of interaction. See summaries of competencies suggested by Sue et al. (1992) and Sodowsky et al. (1994) in Tables 1.2 and 1.3.

Table 1.2 Multicultural Counseling Competencies (Sue et al., 1992)

	Counselor's Awareness of Own Assumptions, Values, and Bias	Understanding the Worldview of the Culturally Different Client	Developing Appropriate Counselor Interventions, Strategies, and Techniques	Total
BELIEFS	1. Culturally self-aware 2. Aware of biases' influence 3. Realize personal limitations 4. Comfortable with client's racial, ethnic, cultural, and belief differences	1. Contrast own beliefs with client's in nonjudgmental fashion 2. Aware of stereotypes and preconceived notions about the different ways of racial and ethnic minority groups	1. Respect client's religious or spiritual beliefs/values 2. Respect indigenous helping practices and networks 3. Value bilingualism	9
KNOWLEDGE	1. How counselor heritage affects definition of normality/abnormality 2. How oppression, racism, discrimination, and stereotypes affect counselor work, allowing counselor to acknowledge individual racism 3. How counselor's social impact and communication style differences affect clients and how to anticipate their impact	1. Have information of particular group one is working with (e.g., life experiences, cultural heritage, and historical background of culturally different client) 2. Culture's affect on personality, choices and preferences for counseling approaches 3. Sociopolitical influences that impinge on minority life (e.g., poverty, racism, powerlessness)	1. How generic counseling skills may clash with cultural systems 2. How institutional barriers hinder minority usage of mental health services 3. Potential bias in assessment instruments 4. Minority family structure, hierarchies, values, and beliefs 5. Discriminatory practices in society	11
SKILLS	1. Seek out educational, consultative, and training experiences to enrich understanding of culturally different populations, recognizing the limitations of your competencies 2. Understand self as a racial and cultural being and actively seek a nonracist identity	1. Understand relevant research and latest findings on cross-cultural mental health issues, disorders, and service 2. Become actively involved with minorities outside the counseling setting so one's perspective is more than an academic or helping exercise	1. Able to engage in a variety of verbal and nonverbal helping responses 2. Able to exercise institutional intervention skills on behalf of client 3. Consult with traditional healers or religious leaders 4. Interact in client's language 5. Aware of cultural limitations in assessment and testing instruments 6. Seek to eliminate biases, prejudice, and discriminatory practices 7. Educate clients in goals, expectations, rights, and counselor orientation	11
Total	9	7	15	31

SOURCE: A summary of D. W. Sue., Arredondo,, & McDavis's (1992) expanded construct of multicultural counseling competencies.

Table 1.3 Multicultural Counseling Competencies (Sodowsky et al., 1994)

Multicultural Counseling Skills	*Multicultural Awareness*	*Multicultural Counseling Relationship*	*Multicultural Counseling Knowledge*
Specific multicultural counseling skills	Proactive multicultural sensitivity and responsiveness	Client mistrust because of racial differences	Culturally relevant case conceptualization and treatment strategies
General counseling skills	Advocacy within institutions	Counselor comfort level with minority clients	Keeping current with the literature and research on client preference
Use of nontraditional assessment methods	Extensive multicultural interactions and life experiences	Counselor's countertransference and defensive reactions	Having information about sociocultural factors of different minority groups
Counselor self-monitoring	Problem solving in unfamiliar setting	Stereotypes in counselor conceptualization of client	Innovative conceptualization and treatment
Tailoring therapy to the needs of the client	Enjoyment of multiculturalism	Counselor acceptance of diverse worldviews and styles of communication, enhancing counseling process	Examination of cultural biases
Retention of minority clients	Increased minority caseload	Making non-normative comparisons	Being abreast of current issues
Understanding own philosophy	Working understanding of major racial, ethnic, and cultural minority groups	Counselor self-examination	Considering heterogeneity of a minority group
Differentiated use of structured and nonstructured therapy	Understanding of immigrant legalities		Informed referrals and consultation
	Familiarity with nonstandard English		Self-monitoring and self-correction
	Seek consultation, workshops, training		Application of sociopolitical history
			Assessing client's acculturation adaptation

SOURCE: A summary of Sodowsky, Taffe, Gutkin, & Wise's (1994) construct of multicultural counseling competencies

The counselor process of focusing on oneself, rather than only on the client or on others, takes one to the core of one's intrapersonal needs and relationship dynamics and brings to the conscious awareness unknown counselor defenses and projections. Thus, counselors who follow the axiom, "Counselor, know thy cultural-self" may be more competent in developing a facilitative multicultural relationship because these counselors are as sensitive to their own cultural, racial, and ethnic feelings and thoughts as they are to those of their clients'.

Several researchers (Kelly, 1990; McRae & Johnson, 1991; Midgette & Meggert, 1991; Pedersen, 1988; Sabnani, Ponterotto, & Borodovsky, 1991; Sue & Sue, 1990) have called for the need to increase the awareness of trainees' cultural-self. MCC involves more than simply acquiring knowledge and skills to work with diverse cultural groups and awareness of the beliefs of these groups. It necessitates "deep-cultural self-empathy," a process that involves a profound understanding of the internal, "gut-level" responses to one's own culture and to the cultures of others.

According to Rogers (1951), counselor empathy involves being sensitively immersed in another individual's subjective world. Moreover, understanding another person's experiential world requires an active and continuous process in which attention is focused solely on the feelings of the other, to the exclusion of all other stimuli. On the other hand, in the MCC context deep-cultural self-empathy is conceived as empathy that is directed toward one's core cultural, racial, and ethnic attitudes, needs, and dynamics, which are often below the threshold of consciousness due to overfamiliarity and one's socialization. Thus, through continuous self-focus and deep introspection, counselors can become more sensitive to their cultural-self. Such deep-cultural self-empathy or sensitive understanding of one's cultural-self will, in turn, facilitate accurate empathy with clients who are culturally different.

Unrecognized counselor emotions include internalized racist reactions that are made credible by the affirmation of many preceding generations of elders and current peers, as well as unintentional individual racist behaviors. Without deep-cultural self-empathy, these racist reactions often remain unrecognized. However, critical incidents, such as being involved in cultural sensitivity training or being guided by a supervisor to assess feelings of discomfort when faced with a culturally different client, may also elicit these feelings forward into awareness (Midgette & Meggert, 1991). Counselors who are not sensitive to their own reactions or who are resistant to critical self-examination may superficially process these emotions and consequently remain incognizant of their cultural-self. Such counselors may not develop the competency to form a multicultural counseling relationship.

The need to develop deep-cultural self-empathy is further exemplified by the fact that many individuals are unable to articulate the values of the culture they endorse. Thus, restricting the training of multicultural competencies to purely cognitive and behavioral levels, such as knowledge and skills, allows individuals to distance themselves from their internalized racist attitudes (Helms, 1984; Ponterotto, 1988; Sue & Sue, 1990) and cultural value orientations (Ihle, Sodowsky, & Kwan, 1996), both of which have strong emotional and ideological roots. For example, training programs that are other-oriented in terms of trainees acquiring only cultural knowledge, skills, and awareness of the attitudes of others remain underdeveloped for the reason that professional growth for multicultural helping services needs to start from within individuals, from the core of each individual's conscience that distinguishes between what is morally just and unjust in interracial and cross-cultural existence. MCC thus demands that one accept the challenge of a personal journey to one's hidden racial constructs and spontaneous affective reactions toward others who are different.

There are various avenues by which one can engage in cultural self-exploration. For example, various racial, ethnic, and minority identity models have been proposed in the multicultural literature (Atkinson, Morten, & Sue, 1993; Cross, 1971; Helms, 1984; Jackson, 1975; Phinney, 1990; Ponterotto, 1988; Sabnani et al., 1991; Sodowsky, Kwan, & Pannu, 1995; Thomas, 1971). These identity models propose, among other constructs, one multiculturally universal construct, presumably an etic construct, which is that all racial and ethnic minority groups in the United States share experiences of oppression as a result of living in the dominant White American culture. One common etic aim of these identity models is to heighten the awareness that all individuals in the United States, White Americans as well as racial and ethnic minorities, have their race and ethnicity defined by society in sociopolitical and racist terms rather than in phenotypic or biological terms. In fact, in a multiracial and multiethnic society such as that of the United States, it may be difficult to identify many pure racial and/or ethnic groups in explicit biological or cultural terms. This may become even more difficult in the immediate future because of the rapid increase of interracial and interethnic marriages and births in U.S. society (Sodowsky et al., 1995). For example, what it means to be White and what it means to be Black have societal constructions that are usually propagated by the mass media. It is, therefore, necessary for all individuals, regardless of race and ethnicity, to go through a self-definitional process that involves, on the basis of personal experiences, a subjective definition of who one is culturally, racially, and ethnically.

A multicultural counselor evolves "from being culturally unaware to being aware and sensitive to his/her own cultural heritage and to valuing and respecting differences" (Sue & Sue, 1990, p. 167). On the cognitive front, the process involves awareness through knowledge of one's own culture and knowledge of the culture's interface with other cultures. Such conscious awareness will inevitably tap into one's sensitivity. Often, negative emotions such as anger and guilt will flow to the surface of one's consciousness. Trainees need to be readily receptive to these negative emotions and subsequently to process them in order to gain cultural self-awareness and self-empathy. For example, a White therapist may feel the collective guilt of the oppression (e.g., slavery of Africans and the incarceration of Japanese Americans) caused by his or her racial group to members of racial and ethnic minority groups. In Helms's (1984) White racial identity model, White individuals may deal with their feelings of guilt in the Pseudo-Independence Stage by adopting a pro-minority, paternalistic attitude toward Blacks. Such individuals believe that they can help Black Americans by helping them to change and adapt to the existing White establishment. As another example, a racial minority therapist might feel anger toward a White client because the counselor sees the client as a privileged individual, one who has windows of cultural and institutional opportunities open to him or her. Such feelings are dysfunctional, unethical, and counterproductive in the counseling, help-giving profession. They operate insidiously to subvert the multicultural counseling relationship. To illustrate, the minority counselor may construe the problems of White clients as being due to a lack of personal effort, especially because they are not subjected to various barriers that are commonly shared by minority individuals. This parallels the phenomenon of blaming the victim, which many minority clients experience from White counselors.

Negative or hostile emotions therefore need to be processed and resolved by the therapist in order for a facilitative multicultural counseling relationship to develop. It is not until one can resolve these emotional conflicts that one can emerge as an individual who is sensitive to what it means to be a person with a culture, race, and ethnicity. Thus, the primary goal of engaging in cultural self-exploration is to gain a confident and secure sense of oneself as a person with various contexts. This allows the individual to appreciate fully what it means to be a cultural being in a pluralistic society. Because one has gone through the subjective self-definitional process, one can step outside of oneself to observe and evaluate oneself objectively. When one has gone through the long subjective journey to objectivity, one is less likely to be vulnerable to personal biases when responding to individuals from diverse cultural backgrounds.

In summary, self-exploration constitutes a fundamental component in MCC. Individuals who are internally motivated by self-exploration are more likely to commit themselves to the time and energy involved in acquiring MCC. Gilbert Wrenn (1962, 1987) proposed that we should engage in "unlearning something each day" and that guarding ourselves against cultural encapsulation involves taking necessary risks. The idea of "unlearning" is taken here to mean that an individual does not automatically assume that others are operating from the same cognitive set or worldview. It is the idea of holding in check an automatic thought, behavior, or emotion that would otherwise be assumed as a natural response that is "etic" or common to all individuals, regardless of their respective culture, race, or ethnicity.

Political Ideology vis-à-vis MCC

A politically based ideology is fundamental to the history of multicultural counseling. The issues of minority status addressed by early multicultural literature (e.g., Atkinson, Morten, & Sue, 1979; Cross, 1971; Wrenn, 1962) were consolidated and succinctly stated in the Education and Training Committee of APA's Division 17 (Sue et al., 1982) position paper: "It is not enough to study solely different cultural groups in the United States without understanding the sociopolitical history that minorities have undergone" (p. 47). During the ensuing years, increasing pressure was placed on the profession, emphasizing the need for trainers to address the status quo politics of mainstream counseling (e.g., Katz, 1985; Pedersen, 1988). Seeing insufficient progress, a renewed call for action was presented to the ACA by Sue et al. (1992), who synthesized the literature on the importance of a multicultural perspective and provided a more detailed enumeration than the 1982 position paper of the necessary competencies of a multicultural counselor. The Office of Ethnic Minority Affairs of APA (APA, 1993) provided a sociocultural framework for addressing in a systematic fashion the cultural expectations, diversity of values, interactional styles, acculturation, language differences, and sociopolitical concerns of the culturally different. In the guidelines, there is a strong recognition of the knowledge and skills necessary for multicultural assessment and intervention. (Refer to Table 1.1.)

The underlying premise for the development of a multicultural counseling perspective derives from the position that "counseling and psychotherapy are handmaidens of the status quo and transmitters of society's values [that] lead many minorities to believe that the mental health profession is engaged in a form of cultural oppression" (Sue et al., 1982, p. 46). The oppression of traditional counseling approaches is implicit in its assumption that an "etic" or universal application of Western psychological theories to all people is appropriate. Counseling implications deriving from the racial, ethnic, and cultural contexts of the client have not been considered as important in the traditional paradigm. Rather, a focus on imposing the cultural norms of the dominant society on minority clients has until recently been the explicit objective of intervention techniques and goals in counseling. Without an understanding of the cultural milieu and sociopolitical history of a minority client, appropriate interventions for the personal growth and empowerment of a minority cannot be implemented, and institutional racism on the individual is implicitly practiced (Sue et al., 1982).

In addressing the sociopolitical realities of counseling, Sue et al. (1992) identified the importance of the worldviews of both counselor and client in an equitable counseling process and contextualized counseling as a process intimately linked to the "larger events of our society" (p. 479). Inasmuch as the social and cultural composition of counselors has been primarily White middle-class, it is not surprising that biases in the formulation of research, theory, and practice reflect their cultural and racial preferences and socialization (Katz, 1985; Pedersen, 1988). Notwithstanding the presumed humanitarian values of counselors, the ethnocentric principles and models of the prevalent "Great White Father Syndrome" (Vontress, 1971) approach to counseling practice has been the historical norm.

Burn (1992) states, "respecting the autonomy or self-governing capacity of a client is critically important, as is the need for the cultural background of the client to influence and direct the course of counseling" (p. 580). The crucial issue here is that social consciousness and a strong political component are the inherent foundation of multicultural counseling, just as psychodynamic and humanistic principles set the origins of mainstream forms of counseling. In short, advocacy and political activism on behalf of minority populations need to be incorporated into one's counseling philosophy, and the level of that personal investment significantly affects one's MCC. Atkinson and Thompson (1992), in discussing the need for counselors to develop their own political consciousness, stated: "attaining a commitment to dismantling oppression as it affects all groups, reminds us of the need for psychology professionals to 'leave their desks' and assume direct responsibility as change agents rather than simply functioning as purveyors of conventional services in the context of troubled environments" (p. 371).

Ridley et al. (1994) also argue for community and organizational intervention and social policy making. They ask the counselor to include local people as stakeholders of the multicultural movement, inviting them to define multiculturalism in local terms. Thus, counselors propagate multiculturalism from locality to locality and from outreach to outreach. It is suggested that proactive approaches to individual involvement in the community could include active participation in local ethnic and racial organizations, with individuals serving local interests in the capacity of consultants, advisors, and/or facilitators of support groups (Atkinson et al., 1993). Also, becoming politically active in advocacy roles within established governing bodies in the community and working for the implementation of programs specifically based upon a multicultural perspective would expand the inclusion of minority concerns within the framework of community planning and development (Atkinson et al., 1993).

Opportunities and commitments for multicultural advocacy must also be integrated into university program development. Ponterotto, Alexander, and Grieger (1995) suggest that the discussion of the interaction of issues related to race, racism, oppression, ethnicity, and culture are examples of multicultural issues that are appropriate for exploration in counselor supervision, and that the creation of a Multicultural Affairs Committee (MAC) to monitor a counseling training program's efforts toward multiculturalism would be desirable. A model for the suggested MAC has been in existence in the Department of Educational Psychology of the University of Nebraska-Lincoln (UN-L) for 23 years (Department of Educational Psychology, UN-L, 1973, 1989, 1993). The faculty and students of the counseling psychology program of this department have historically played a strong role in the formation, membership, and continued growth of the Ethnic Minority Affairs Committee (EMAC).

EMAC is an advocacy and support group within the Department of Educational Psychology, UN-L. Members include students and faculty from the five graduate programs in Educational Psychology; those interested in multicultural issues are encouraged to join, regardless of their racial, ethnic, and cultural background. All of the authors of this chapter are members of EMAC. The primary mission of EMAC is to assist the department in carrying out its commitment to increasing the representation of American racial and ethnic minority groups and international students in the graduate programs and on the faculty. EMAC is actively involved with racial and ethnic minority student and faculty recruitment and retention, multicultural curriculum development, faculty and course evaluations with regard to curricular responsiveness to multicultural issues, research networking among members, and racial and ethnic minority student advocacy.

The application to graduate programs within the Educational Psychology Department, UN-L, includes a form giving a prospective minority student the option to have his or her application reviewed by EMAC. Members of EMAC evaluate the minority applicants using EMAC-developed multicultural criteria, which are different from general graduate admissions criteria of psychology programs. EMAC makes recommendations to the respective program faculty and the departmental Graduate Committee regarding minority students they judge will enhance the diversity of the department and will match the multicultural research and practice interests of the department. EMAC has influenced the departmental application and admissions process to place a definite emphasis on recruiting qualified racial and ethnic minority students. The faculty members of EMAC have also obtained college and university assistantships and scholarships from the department for most of the admitted minority students. Briefly, EMAC facilitates the entry of minority students and faculty into the department, acts as a source of minority student and faculty support, incorporates training on multicultural issues (e.g., multicultural workshops from local as well as national leaders), provides a collaborative peer-review sounding board for in-process research, is productive in multicultural research publications and presentations, and advocates for minority rights and equity campus-wide and within the city of Lincoln.

In summary, in order for counselors to be multiculturally competent, they must be willing to integrate a component of political advocacy for minority populations into their professional identity. In other words, the humanitarian, "people person" motivations that are typically characteristic of counselors must be augmented by a commitment to racial, ethnic, and cultural minority people that extends "beyond the doors" of the counseling clinic.

The Etic Perspective in Assessment

Assessment Biases When Using a
Universalistic Perspective

Assessing a client's concerns is a universal practice in counseling. However, counselors need to be aware of the biases of mainstream American assessment that does not take into consideration the contexts of cultural socialization, ethnicity, worldview, racial identity, and ethnic identity. Counselors need to keep in mind cultural differences in motivation (not all minority test-takers are motivated to perform well in ability and aptitude tests), English language proficiency, and task-relevant test-taking behaviors of those taking standardized tests. Political disparities among racial and ethnic groups in the United States cannot be overlooked; first among them is the uneven distribution of power, privilege, and opportunity, both as a current condition and as a historical legacy. Assessment therefore needs to account for the contributions of minority status, political oppression, and low socioeconomic status on individual differences in test performance.

One of the dangers of assessment is to equate the individual who deviates significantly from the normal curve with the disturbed and to "blame the victim" in the process of assigning responsibility to the client who has a significantly deviant score. Another ubiquitous pitfall is stereotyping, for which blatantly prejudiced persons are not the only ones at risk. Then there are the interactive and complex sociocultural influences to which ethnic groups in a pluralistic society are exposed, producing complex patterns of acculturation and ethnic identity for individual minority members. Mainstream assessment may thus be less appropriate for racial and ethnic minority individuals than for White middle-class, educated people.

There are two types of assessment methodology, structured and unstructured. In structured situations, such as clients' responses to objective personality measures and symptom rating scales, minority clients are explicitly compared to White American normative data. Some items in widely used assessment devices such as the MMPI-2 (1989) and some criteria of the *DSM-IV* (American Psychiatric Association, 1994) refer to behaviors, beliefs, and feelings that are not pathological in certain minority cultures. For instance, a belief in evil spirits is commonly held by traditional Puerto Ricans, Mexicans, and Hmong refugees. Therefore, this apparently normal cultural phenomenon challenges the apparent validity of test items or intake questions, inferring pathology from spiritualistic experiences. There is considerable empirical evidence, although some is equivocal, of mean differences in terms of test norms and epidemiological prevalence rates between White and racial and ethnic populations and among racial and ethnic minority populations (e.g., Malgady, Rogler, & Costantino, 1987). Thus, the majority yardstick may not be appropriate for the racial and ethnic minorities. However, most instruments do not have separate norms for minority populations.

In a study of MMPI-2 performances of Asian American and White American students, less acculturated Asian Americans had higher scores than acculturated Asian Americans, who in turn had higher scores than White Americans (Sue, 1996). Sue (1996) argues that Asian Americans are under greater stress than White American students because of culture conflict, adjustment to a new environment, language problems, and minority status—these being even more true of the unacculturated. Or, the ethnic differences may result from cultural response biases of Asian Americans (e.g., a preference for the True response in the True/False scoring format, indicating an acquiescent response style). Thus, MMPI-2 may be invalid for Asian Americans.

In unstructured situations, such as counselors doing routine intake interviews, minority clients are implicitly compared to the counselor's White American perception of pathology. Also, the counselor tasks of judgment, clinical inferences, and interpretations are subject to human biases, stereotyping, and faulty information processing. Many first-generation Asians in the United States show flat affect, restricted emotional responses, and the stress-related physiological symptoms of headaches, backaches, and stomachaches. Thus, large numbers of Asians could be inaccurately perceived as depressed, psychosomatic, and psychologically unsophisticated. To avoid such inaccurate assessment interpretations, the counselor needs to disentangle culturally patterned behavior from pathological behavior—for example, being able to distinguish between culturally diverse people who speak in spiritualistic terms and those who report being possessed because they are actually schizophrenic.

An overpathologizing bias has been found in clinicians when they assess African American clients. African American clients with depressive symptomatology have been tended to be misdiagnosed as schizophrenic (Neighbors, Jackson, Campbell, & Williams, 1989). One study showed that two thirds of bipolar Hispanic clients were previously misdiagnosed as schizophrenic (Mukherjee, Shukla, Woodle, Rosen, & Olarte, 1983). White American therapists rated Chinese American clients as anxious, awkward, confused, and nervous, whereas Chinese therapists perceived the same clients as alert, ambitious, adaptable, honest, and friendly. In addition, White therapists rated the Chinese clients as more depressed, more inhibited, less socially poised, and having lower capacity for interpersonal relationships than did the Chinese therapists (Li-Repac, 1980). These findings suggest that judgments about psychological functioning depend at least in part on whether or not therapists are of the same ethnic background as their clients and that clinicians are themselves subject to biases. Because people learn to express distress in culturally acceptable ways—such as Asians expressing physiological symptoms or Mexican Americans being stricken by *mal puesto* (being hexed), *embrujado* (bewitchment or possession by spirits), *mal de ojo* (evil eye), or *susto* (magical fright)—similar symptoms may hold different meanings in different cultures (see Brislin, 1993, for further explanation of culture-specific symptom expressions). Thus, cultural modes of symptom expression can lead to inaccurate assessment when clinicians do not understand the client's culture.

Assessment From a Cultural Perspective

Counselors need to identify White American constructs of mainstream assessment. For instance, good decision making in White American culture may be typified by an ability to make independent personal decisions without being unduly influenced by others. On the other hand, good decision making may be understood in Asian cultures as an ability to make a decision that is best for the family and the family's honor. Thus, the counselor breaks away from White American culture-bound paradigms by addressing in assessment specific multicultural constructs, such as racial identity; ethnic identity; worldviews; acculturation; acculturative stress; and immigrant variables including generational status, religion, and family influences (for the latter information see Sodowsky et al., 1995; Sodowsky & Lai, 1996).

Assessment encompasses the appraisal of a person's characteristics in quantitative (tests and measures) and/or qualitative (clinical intake and diagnosis) terms. At this point, the field of multicultural assessment of psychological disturbance largely relies on qualitative procedures. It has not reached the point of consistent quantification of its observations, judgments, and inferences. Thus, the diagnostic activity and clinical intake of the counselor play a prominent role. Because White American assessment procedures should not be routinely generalized to different cultural groups, multicultural tests could be increasingly used. To be sure, there are multicultural scales that measure specific psychological aspects, such as intelligence (the SOMPA, Mercer & Lewis, 1977; the BITCH Test, Williams, 1972), racism (Modern Racism Scale, McConahay & Hough, 1976; New Racism Scale, Jacobson, 1985), racial identity (BRIAS, WRIAS, Helms, 1990), acculturation (ARSMA, Cuellar, Harris, & Jasso, 1980; MMRS, Sodowsky, Lai, & Plake, 1991; AIRS, Sodowsky & Plake, 1992; BAS, Szapocznik, Scopetta, Kurtines, & Aranalde, 1978), ethnic identity (Ethnic Identity Search and Commitment, Phinney, 1990; Internal and External Ethnic Identity, Sodowsky et al., 1995; SL-ASIA, Suinn, Rickard-Figueroa, Lew, & Vigil, 1987), psychodynamic needs (TEMAS, Malgady, Costantino, & Rogler, 1984), acculturative stress (HSI, Cervantes, Padilla, & Salgado de Snyder, 1991; CADC, Sodowsky & Lai, 1996), and depression (VDS, Kinzie et al., 1982). However, these instruments currently retain an auxiliary role. They provide valuable information that contributes to, but does not determine, decisions regarding treatment and interventions, which are the most important justifications for assessment. Nonetheless, the multicultural instruments are particularly useful for cultural, ethnic, and racial conceptualizations of client problems.

The ideal qualitative approach would be to use an "imposed" etic or cross-cultural comparability approach as well as an emic or culturally indigenous, ideographic approach (Draguns, 1996). What is imposed etic? It is the multicultural methodology of applying specific multicultural constructs (e.g., acculturation, ethnic identity) in assessment across diverse cultures, thus allowing for modified universality and cross-cultural comparability. The question that arises is, "How can the emic as well as the etic perspectives be used simultaneously?" The following is an example of such an assessment process.

The counselor captures the unique qualities of the person in a cultural context (e.g., the Asian individual's personalized experience of "loss of face" [i.e., shame] because a private issue has become public knowledge). The counselor also places the individual in relation to other comparable phenomena (e.g., social self-esteem), regardless of the different contexts of occurrence for different people. These two sources of information are respectively brought to bear upon the assessment of an individual, thus providing cultural information as well as comparative/normative data.

Emic assessment is characterized by inclusion of cultural uniqueness, anthropological descriptions, and indigenous concepts and explanations (e.g., fatalism). Culture-bound syndromes (e.g., amok, *susto;* also see *DSM-IV* Appendix I for a listing) and knowledge of culture specific modes of assessment (e.g., methods of *curanderos,* who are Mexican American native healers) fall into the domain of emic assessment. Understanding the structure and meaning of relationships in one's family and among one's kin in a collectivistic society, and understanding abnormal behavior and experiences in social and historical contexts and time frames (e.g., Thomas's, 1970, concept of negromachy) are parts of emic assessment. On the other hand, etic assessment is exemplified by the World Health Organizations's (1983) epidemiological studies on depression; multicultural comparisons with the MMPI; cross-cultural comparisons with acculturation, ethnic identity, and worldview instruments; archival studies; and a universal panorama of abnormal behavior across cultures, such as psychoses. Client assessment is made comprehensive by both emic and etic data.

An Assessment Workshop

Most practicing counselors and graduate students are familiar with the content and format of an Intake Interview. This training exercise relies heavily on an Intake Summary that is based on the Intake Interview. Because peer feedback is an integral component of training exercises, a small group (maximum of 4 group members) format is recommended.

Step 1. Each participant is provided with minimal information about a hypothetical racial or ethnic minority client, such as the following narrative:

Jimmy Jones is a 12-year-old African American boy who is referred for clinical evaluation. Jimmy is referred because of apathy, indifference, and inattentiveness to classroom activities. Teachers have reported that Jimmy does not pay attention, daydreams often, and frequently falls asleep in class. It is suggested by the school counselor that Jimmy is harboring repressed rage that needs to be ventilated and dealt with. His inability to express anger directly has, according to the school counselor, led him to adopt passive-aggressive means of expressing hostility, such as inattentiveness, daydreaming, and falling asleep. It is recommended that Jimmy be seen for therapy to discover the basis of the anger.

Jimmy is currently residing in Omaha, Nebraska, with his mother, Mary, his half-brother, Terence, his sister, Juanita, and his grandmother, Grace. His aunt, who is 8 months pregnant, has recently moved into the home with her 3-year-old daughter. Jimmy's biological father currently resides in Omaha, but is described as being uninvolved.

Each participant is asked to originate information independently that is typically contained in an Intake Summary (i.e., Client Identification, Client Background Information, Presenting Problems, Diagnosis, Case Conceptualization, Treatment Recommendation, and Treatment Goals). Each participant should be encouraged to develop the Background Information and Presenting Problems of a hypothetical client based on the participant's preconceived attitudes and assumptions of the client's culture and race or ethnicity. On the basis of this generated information, the participant will provide the Case Conceptualization, Treatment Recommendations, and Treatment Goals that follow. Each participant should provide his or her group members with a copy of his or her Intake Summary.

Each group member should read the Intake Summaries of fellow group members. Then, focusing only on one's own Intake Summary, each participant presents his or her assumptions about the client and the client's cultural, racial, and ethnic group. A discussion of the participant's imagined Intake Summary ensues among the group members. The following outline may be helpful in guiding the group members' discussion of an Intake Summary:

1. How are the client's behaviors characterized?

2. How is the family composition described? How is the client's family characterized?
3. How is the client's communication style characterized?
4. How are the client's interactions with parents, siblings, relatives, peers, school/work relationships described?
5. How is the client's attitude toward therapy described?
6. How do the lifestyle, social environment, and values of the counselor differ from those of the client?
7. With what private feelings and reactions does the counselor respond (countertransference) to the client?
8. On what strengths and weaknesses of the client does the Intake Summary focus?

Group members should facilitate the counselor's self-exploration by discussing the counselor's cultural, racial, and ethnic beliefs and responses that were most obvious to them when reading the Intake Summary. After all Intake Summaries have been discussed, the group members as a whole should discuss their discoveries of their multicultural knowledge, skills, attitudes, and client-counselor relationship issues and their respective feelings about these self-discoveries.

Step 2. To remind the counselors of MCC proficiencies, as specified by APA (1993), by Sue et al. (1992), and by Sodowsky et al. (1994), the counselors are provided with Tables 1.1, 1.2, and 1.3 (see above). Table 1.4 provides guidelines for family assessment, because many racial and ethnic minority clients come from collectivistic cultures. The family in a collectivistic culture is the primary reference group that provides a bearing on what is right or wrong and transmits the norms of the larger cultural minority group. Many minority individuals are also influenced by members of an extended family network. The family assessment guidelines in Table 1.4 are an example of structured qualitative assessment that could be done in multicultural counseling. The counselors are also informed of the impact of racial and ethnic similarity on the counseling process, minority utilization of mental health services, relative effectiveness of directive versus nondirective styles of therapy, the role of cultural values in treatment, and appropriate counseling as therapy models.

Each counselor rereads and evaluates the section of his or her Intake Summary that consists of Diagnosis, Conceptualization, Treatment Recommendations, and Treatment Goals along the following MCC guidelines.

1. To what extent do the Diagnosis, Case Conceptualization, and Treatment Goals indicate the presence of (a) multicultural knowledge and (b) multicultural awareness?
2. To what extent do the Treatment Recommendations indicate the presence of (a) multicultural skills and (b) a multicultural counseling relationship?
3. To what degree can my cultural values, professional biases, and racial and ethnic prejudices and stereotypes be inferred from my Diagnosis, Case Conceptualization, Treatment Recommendations, and Treatment Goals?
4. What is the potential for the development of a multicultural counseling relationship between the counselor and the client? Or is the client likely to terminate therapy early, participate unwillingly, or resist or refuse to comply with the Treatment Goals?
5. What do I do well as a counselor? Can my counseling strengths be utilized to improve my MCC?

Step 3. On the basis of the above self-analysis, each participant revises his or her Diagnosis, Case Conceptualization, Treatment Recommendations, and Counseling Goals. A revised copy of each Intake Summary is given to all members in the small group.

Step 4. The concluding activity deals with establishing goals to develop MCC in diverse aspects of one's professional life. Ridley et al.'s (1994) multicultural training Instructional Chart can be used for a concluding group activity. All participants are provided with a copy of the chart. Each participant undertakes the task of completing the chart by filling in as many blanks as possible with practical and doable suggestions for incorporating MCC into all aspects of their professional life. For example, the first box on the chart could be filled in by asking the question, "What advocacy behaviors could I show at my place of work that would demonstrate my awareness of minority-related sociopolitical issues?" A possible behavior might be to display, where appropriate, current newspaper and magazine clippings and cartoons dealing with society's multicultural insensitivities. These gentle but pointed reminders would educate and help one's associates to be more alert to incidents of possible cultural and institutional racism. All boxes may not be applicable to every professional situation, but the goal would be to use this chart as a tool to stimulate thinking about specific ways to incorporate MCC into all aspects of one's professional life.

Goals Achieved in the Workshop

The goals that are achieved in this Assessment Workshop are as follows:

Table 1.4 Guidelines for Family Assessment

Family Composition
> Who are the members of the family system?
> Who are the key decision makers?
> Is decision making related to specific situations?
> Is decision making individual or group oriented?
> Do family members all live in the same household?
> What is the relationship of friends to the family system?
> What is the hierarchy within the family? Is status related to gender and age?

Primary Caregiver(s)
> Who is the primary caregiver?
> Who else participates in the caregiving?
> What is the amount of care given by mother versus others?
> What ecological/environmental issues impinge upon general caregiving
> (i.e., housing, jobs, etc.)?

Family's Response to Disobedience and Aggression
> What are the parameters of acceptable child behavior?
> What form does the discipline take?
> Who metes out the disciplinary action?

Family Perception of Child's Problem
> Are there cultural or religious factors that would shape family perceptions?
> To what/where/whom does the family assign responsibility for their child's
> problem?
> How does the family view the role of fate in their lives?
> How does the family view the roles of institutional, cultural, and
> individual racism in their lives?
> How does the family view their role in intervening with their child?
> Do they feel they can make a difference or do they consider it hopeless?

Family's Perception of Health and Healing
> What is the family's approach to medical needs?
> > Do they rely solely on Western medical services?
> > Do they rely solely on indigenous/culture-specific approaches?
> > Do they rely solely on holistic approaches?

---

1. All participants are given the opportunity to apply MCC variables to identify culturally consistent Diagnosis, Case Conceptualization, Treatment Recommendations, and Treatment Goals.
2. All participants are given the opportunity to integrate MCC with a case application and with their general assessment competencies.

Table 1.4 Continued

Do they utilize a combination of these approaches?

Who is the primary medical provider or conveyer of medical information?
Family members? Elders? Friends? Folk healers? Family doctor? Medical specialists?

Do all members of the family agree on approaches to medical needs?

Family's Perception of Help Seeking and Intervention

From whom does the family seek help—family members or outside agencies/individuals?

Does the family seek help directly or indirectly?

What are the general feelings of the family when seeking assistance—ashamed, angry, demand as a right, view as unnecessary?

With which community systems does the family interact (educational/medical/social)?

How are these interactions completed (face-to-face, telephone, letter)?

Which family member interacts with other systems?

Does that family member feel comfortable when interacting with other systems?

Language

To what degree:
Is the counselor proficient in the family's native language?
Is the family proficient in English?

If an interpreter is used:
With which culture is the interpreter primarily affiliated?
Is the interpreter familiar with the colloquialisms of the family members' country or region of origin?
Is the family member comfortable with the interpreter? Would the family member feel more comfortable with an interpreter of the same sex?

If written materials are used, are they in the family's native language?

Interaction Styles

Does the family communicate with each other in a direct or indirect style?

Does the family tend to interact in a quiet manner or a loud manner?

Do family members share feelings when discussing emotional issues?

Does the family ask you direct questions?

Does the family value a lengthy social time at each counseling session, unrelated to the counseling goals?

Is it important for the family to know about the counselor's family? Is the counselor comfortable sharing that information?

---

3. All participants are given the opportunity to develop awareness of their cultural values, professional biases, and prejudices and stereotypes regarding racial or ethnic minority clients.

4. All participants are given the opportunity to evaluate their weaknesses in MCC.

5. All participants are given the opportunity to establish goals for continued professional development.

The Emic Perspective in
Assessment: A Case Study

Selected multicultural variables such as the existential construct of world-views or the social psychological construct of ethnic identity can only be assumed to be universal across cultures and are, in fact, an "imposed" etic, being only a marginal improvement to traditional American psychological constructs, such as self-efficacy, which is also assumed to be generalizable. Etic constructs allow for group comparisons, giving useful information about similarities and differences among different cultural groups, but do not tell us adequately about an individual client coming from a particular cultural group. A perspective specific to a culture group, the emic perspective, that points to within-group differences may be more helpful in individual counseling. Understanding a client from a particular group and the uniqueness of that client within that group are crucial assessment features for maintaining an effective counseling process. Thus, this third section dealing with a particular client case has an emic perspective. MCC proficiencies of conceptualizing a client's issues, formulating treatment methods, and targeting counseling goals are framed within the value structure, behavioral patterns, and experiential domain of a particular cultural group.

Although cultural and environmental issues should be included in the assessment of the client, it should not be forgotten that the client is an individual. Kelly (1955) cautioned, "in the final analysis, a client who is to be genuinely understood should never be confined to the stereotype of his [her] culture" (p. 833, brackets added). Ivey, Ivey, and Simek-Downing (1987) summarized personal-environmental assessment by stating, "clients who come for counseling and therapy are individuals first, last, and always. However, each individual must be considered in relationship to her or his environment" (p. 163).

Ivey et al. (1987) identified the development of culturally and individually appropriate goals as being important for effective therapy. Treatment goals that are relevant and effective are "the result of an effective assessment coupled with an awareness of your personal constructs and theoretical orientations" (Ivey et al., 1987, p. 168). As with the conceptualization of the presenting problem, it must be remembered that "each client will require a uniquely individual treatment plan" (Ivey et al., 1987, p. 168). In the case discussion that follows, counselor personal constructs and understanding will be congruent with the theoretical orientation of acculturation and the guidelines for multicultural counseling competencies.

Case Discussion

Tomika is a 55-year-old nisei (second-generation Japanese American) homemaker who was adopted by her older cousin and his wife at the age of 3. Her cousin, Makoto san, was the proud, silent, first-born of a Fukushima landowner. He confided his deepest thoughts to Tomika, including his disenchantment with her adoptive mother, Sumie san. Makoto found Sumie domineering and disrespectful. Sumie, the adoptive mother, was a picture bride (bride-to-be whose picture was sent to the prospective bridegroom's family). Her marriage to Tomika's cousin, Makoto san, had been arranged by a go-between retained by Makoto's family. Sumie, too, was issei (first-generation Japanese American) like Makoto san, but was educated in Massachusetts as an elementary school teacher. Sumie was a stubborn, critical woman who believed that "idle hands are the devil's tool."

Tomika spent most of her childhood cleaning, cooking, and washing for her family. On the eve of Tomika's wedding, Sumie told her that she had been adopted for her and her husband's financial security in old age. Tomika had lived with her adoptive parents in a plantation pump camp along with other contract laborers and their families. The pump camp consisted of a small cluster of one-room, clapboard shanties constructed near the mechanical irrigation pump in the middle of a sugarcane field.

Tomika came to counseling because of a lingering depression that began shortly after the institutionalization of her adoptive mother. There were long pauses of silence during the session, and Tomika cried a lot. Tomika currently lives in the suburbs with her husband, son, and son's yonsei (fourth-generation Japanese American) girlfriend. Tomika is a former school librarian who resigned after the birth of her son. Her days are spent grocery shopping, laundering, cooking, and landscaping the yard. Her husband, a labor mediator, works late, so she feeds her son and his girlfriend first and waits for her husband's return before eating. When Tomika's husband arrives home, she reheats his supper. He reads the paper and falls asleep in front of the television. Tomika's son is a gun collector, a hobby she finds "frightening." She dislikes the idea of guns in her home, but does not wish to confront him about it because he receives many of these guns as bonuses from his "sacho" (boss; president of his company).

Tomika says, "I feel like a hired help. I never know how much food to prepare. They come and go as they please." Her son becomes very angry and sarcastic whenever she asks him where he is going or when she might expect him back. She says she asks him in case there is an emergency and she needs to reach him. She says that she no longer speaks much to her son or his girlfriend for fear of *yurikaishi* (literal translation: earthquake aftershock). She is afraid that her son and his girlfriend will put her out on the streets when she is old. She says her son and his girlfriend often sit in the backyard and discuss how they would remodel and relandscape.

Tomika's internist recommends a vacation from her family, so she can relax. Tomika has hypertension and walking pneumonia, but she says her "boys are helpless without her."

Theoretical Conceptualization

The following quote seems appropriate as the counselor attempts to integrate a limited amount of background information about Tomika.

> Acculturation is a multifaceted phenomenon composed of numerous dimensions, factors, constructs, or subcomponents—not all of which have been clearly identified or specified. Values, ideologies, beliefs, and attitudes appear to be important components of acculturation as are cognitive and behavioral characteristics such as language, cultural customs, and practices. There is also evidence that acculturation is dynamic, yet domain specific, and multidimensional. (Cuellar et al., 1980, p. 209)

Tomika seems to have acculturated to a greater extent outside of the family (e.g., working as a librarian, house in the suburbs). This may be a good example of the domain specificity of acculturation, in that Tomika's acculturation adaptation to American values regarding home and family is not strong. The clash between traditional ethnic and American values in immigrant families is an important source of intergenerational stress between children and parents because of their differing acculturation adaptations. Padilla, Wagatsuma, and Lindholm (1985) found that generational status was a significant predictor of stress within the Japanese family.

The Japanese values of family solidarity and a group orientation can create stress when two or three generations within a Japanese family adjust to the individuality characteristics of the White American culture. This stress can be experienced by the second- and third-generation individuals because of the disparity between the values of the immigrant home and those of the White American culture. This may be what is occurring between Tomika and her son and the son's girlfriend, who, as young Japanese Americans, are likely to be strongly acculturated.

Role conflicts are another source of acculturative stress. Tomika may be experiencing role conflicts between her traditional Japanese female role and the role expectations of her highly acculturated family members. Unfamiliar norms of behavior and ambiguous cues in a bicultural environment may be confusing and stressful and could lead to intrafamilial role conflicts in the self, again due to differing types of acculturation.

Padilla, Alvarez, and Lindholm (1986) found that those who immigrated at an older age and second-generation individuals like Tomika experienced the most stress, lower self-esteem, and higher externality; whereas younger immigrants and third-/later-generation individuals (like Tomika's son and his girlfriend) had the least stress, higher self-esteem, and higher internality. Second-generation individuals like Tomika may experience significant amounts of stress as a result of being caught between the cultural values of their parents and of the White American society. Tomika's clearly defined roles centering around the family are blurring. Her self-concept may be affected by this role confusion and ambiguity. Indeed, the idea of self-concept from a traditional Asian perspective may now be seen as simply a conglomeration of various roles and relations to the group.

Sue and Sue (1990) suggest that Asian Americans are more likely than people from other ethnic groups to present somatic concerns. This may be a reflection of the fact that physical complaints are usually perceived as legitimate in Asian cultures and that psychological complaints may be perceived as shameful or unacceptable. This may explain the possible somatic manifestation of Tomika's depression and anxiety in the form of hypertension and chronic pneumonia, and may also indicate that she is experiencing enough psychological discomfort to risk the stigma of admitting to "mental health problems."

At this point, it is important to keep in mind the APA Office of Ethnic Minority Affairs (1993) guidelines. The guidelines stress that the counselor should gain knowledge of the client's culture and not rely on the client to tell everything he or she knows about that culture. The counselor needs to seek out information in order to work within the client's framework and level of need. The guidelines also recommend documentation. Suggested examples of what to document are number of generations in the country, number of years in the country, fluency and understanding of English, level of education, acculturation stress experienced, and community resources. Documenting culturally relevant factors helps the counselor look at the whole picture, so that the counselor can keep in mind the culture of the client, what aspects the counselor needs to be careful of and what aspects the counselor needs to respect.

Conceptualization Specific to the Client

Tomika, a 55-year-old second-generation Japanese American, is experiencing great stress due to several long-standing and far-reaching acculturation factors in her life. These factors include minority-majority culture conflicts (Leong, 1986; Sodowsky et al., 1991), the role of the family in Asian societies in the United States (Leong, 1986; Sodowsky & Lai, 1996), the traditional socialization of second-generation Asian children by first-generation parents (Atkinson, Maruyama, & Matsui, 1978; Sodowsky et al., 1995), the issues of ascribed credibility and achieved credibility in Asian relationships (Sue & Zane, 1987), the value of *amae* that determines the mother-son interdependent relationship (Pedersen, 1987), and acculturative stress as it relates to generational and personality dimensions (Berry, 1980; Padilla et al., 1985; Sodowsky et al., 1995; Sodowsky & Lai, 1996). Each concept will be briefly related to Tomika, and some relevant counseling strategies and goals will be suggested.

Culture Conflicts

Due to Tomika's many domestic duties and her self-perception as "hired help" in her own family, she resembles the "traditionalist" Asian woman (Sodowsky et al., 1995) who has adjusted to cultural conflicts by rejecting the White American culture's individualistic orientation concerning relationships. However, there has been a cost. Leong (1986) says, "Caught between the Western standards and the traditional cultural values of their parents, the Asian-Americans [may begin] to experience mental health problems related to these cultural conflicts generated by the acculturation process, as well as interpersonal conflicts" (p. 198). Tomika may have received some implicit messages from her adoptive father about women like Sumie, her adoptive mother, who are educated and assertive ("domineering and disrespectful"). The conflict is complicated even more by the fact that the male members of her family enjoy and benefit from her remaining in the traditional homemaking role, yet do not value her role and resent her attempts at involvement in their lives (e.g., husband is disengaged; son becomes angry when she wants information about his schedule).

What brought Tomika to counseling may be related to her familial obligation to care for her mother and Tomika's resultant depression when she felt that she was not living up to that expectation (i.e., the mother's institutionalization). Indeed, Tomika's depression and somatic complaints (chronic hypertension and walking pneumonia) have brought her to seek counseling.

Role of the Family

An important client variable in counseling Asians is the role played by the family in Asian cultures in the United States (Leong, 1986; Sodowsky et al., 1995; Sodowsky & Lai, 1996). Leong (1986) warns that "besides facilitating mental health, the family could serve as a potential source of mental health problems" (p. 198). Indeed, at this point in Tomika's development several familial relationships seem to be the catalysts for her anguish. Those relationships include the ones with her son, her adoptive mother whose institutionalization she may regret, and possibly with her husband.

In short, Tomika's son, a third-generation Japanese American, exhibits more assimilated behaviors (Sodowsky et al., 1995) than does his mother, whose behaviors seem to reflect the concept of "rejection" of the dominant culture (Sodowsky et al., 1995). This second-/third-generation family dynamics (in fact, Tomika could also be considered first-generation because she immigrated at age 3) under one roof lead to conflicting role expectations for mother and son. Tomika performs traditional homemaker duties as her husband, son, and also her son's fourth-generation live-in girlfriend seem to expect of her. Tomika expects traditional behaviors from her son, namely, that he show respect by telling her his whereabouts and when he will be home. He does not conform to this expectation, however, and Tomika, in keeping with her gender role, is not confrontational. In fact, Tomika is afraid that her son and his girlfriend will put her out on the street, which is a far worse fate than what she accorded her adoptive mother, which was institutionalization. Evidently, Tomika's husband is not very involved in this dilemma. In counseling it will be helpful to understand how he perceives everyone's roles in the household.

Socialization of Asian Children in the United States

Tomika grew up in a fairly traditional Japanese American home: Her adoptive father was a contract laborer and her adoptive mother, although educated in Massachusetts to be a teacher, reportedly stayed at home, unhappy and critical. Because of her traditional socialization and low socioeconomic status, it is assumed that Tomika, like other second-generation Asian children, was "taught to hide emotions" and witnessed a patriarchal family system "with communication and authority flowing vertically from top (father) to bottom (wife, then children)" (Atkinson et al., 1978, p. 77). Because Tomika was socialized in this way, it is very difficult for her to express her feelings and needs to her family members. In fact,

Tomika's tears in counseling may appear to her as an embarrassing display of affect.

Ascribed and Achieved Credibility

Sue and Zane (1987) discuss ascribed (culturally given, not earned) authority in traditional Asian cultures as it relates to family dynamics: "The youth is subordinate to the elder, the woman to the man, the naive person to the authority" (p. 40). Therefore, the elderly, men, and authority figures would generally represent ascribed credibility, with possibly some achieved credibility being perceived in certain relationships (i.e., a respected family doctor). How might this relate to Tomika? As a young mother, she had ascribed status over her younger son; now that he is an adult, she is still his elder and his mother, but he is a man. Therefore, Tomika would have lost her ascribed credibility or status in the family, and she perceives no avenues for gaining any achieved (or earned) credibility.

The Concept of *Amae*

Pedersen (1987) refers to *amae,* a traditional Japanese concept. It means "the relationship between a mother and her eldest son. While the son is young and dependent, he is being prepared for the time when his mother will be old and dependent" (p. 20). Throughout her life, Tomika has displayed some version of *amae.* As a young girl (her adoptive parents had no sons to rely upon), she was told by her adoptive mother that they adopted her for their future financial security. With the birth of her own son, Tomika had quit working as a school librarian in order to raise her son traditionally. However, it seems that the security inherent in *amae* has stopped in this family. Tomika seems to have no confidence that she will be taken care of; in fact, she worries that she will be put "out in the street" while her son and his girlfriend remodel the house.

In fact, Tomika's depression may have begun with the institutionalization of her mother; possibly because Tomika could no longer fulfill her *amae* responsibilities. This apparent lack of "filial piety" on her part may have aroused guilt and a reciprocal concern for her own future if she perceives that her son, too, will not take care of her. She feels helpless as she begins to note all the differences between her values and those of her son.

Acculturative Stress

"Acculturative stress will be highest when the cultural distance is greatest and when the insistence that the journey be taken is strongest" (Berry, 1980, p. 22). Indeed, in this family, the three members, mother, son, and father, are at a considerable cultural distance from one another, with Tomika herself being the farthest removed from the White American culture. Applying Berry's (1980) model of acculturation adaptation varieties to Tomika, her son, and her husband, it can be hypothesized that Tomika has chosen rejection, or a "self-imposed withdrawal from the larger society" (Berry, 1980, p. 13). Her son, like many third-generation Asians, finds assimilation adaptation most acceptable. He does not retain a strong Japanese identity, and may experience a strong sense of belonging with a White American identity. Tomika's husband, presumably, has sought integration adaptation because he seemingly has a successful career as a labor negotiator (adapting to a White American institutional culture), while he remains married to a traditional Japanese American woman and is comfortable with an ethnic home ambience.

In this family, where different acculturation adaptations abound, there are conflictual role expectations. As Padilla et al. (1985) claim, "Such Japanese mores as family solidarity and group orientations can be experienced as difficulties not only by immigrants but also by second- and third-generation individuals because of the disparity between the values of the home and those of the dominant culture" (p. 296). This disparity is more stressful to second-generation Tomika than to a third-/later-generation Japanese as a result of Tomika being caught between the cultural values of her parents and of the White American society, whom her son represents.

In addition to this generational dimension of acculturative stress, Tomika's stressors could include personality dimensions. Padilla et al. (1985) outline how three key personality dimensions (Introversion, Self-Esteem, and Locus of Control) can be potential sources of stress for Japanese Americans. Tomika appears to be an introvert who exhibits low self-esteem and an external locus of control. All three of these tendencies are more stressful than their alternatives. As the authors claim, "Self-esteem is a highly significant predictor of stress, and acculturation level and generational status are also good predictors of stress" (p. 301).

Treatment

Culturally consistent counseling strategies, goals, and counselor-client dyadic processes that would be helpful for Tomika are enumerated below.

1. In order to help Tomika identify the differences between the traditional ethnic culture in which she was raised and the White American culture that her son and husband reflect, she will be asked how facets of both cultures affect her life.

2. To instill hope, the counselor will give Tomika a gift (Sue & Zane, 1987) by normalizing rather than minimizing her somatic symptoms. For example, the counselor will inform her that although her depression, hypertension, and pneumonia are very real and physical, they are probably reactions to stresses in her life. If she can cope effectively with stress by learning some strategies in counseling, her somatic complaints might be reduced, and she will not have to leave her family for a vacation unless she wants to.

3. Affective expressions will not be a salient feature in the counseling.

4. In order to give Tomika a voice in her relationship with her son, it will be necessary to elicit her husband's help. Tomika could be guided to explain the mother-son conflicts to the husband and get him to intervene on her behalf. The husband's traditional role in the family will be reinforced so that he feels empowered to address his adult son. The son would be more likely to listen to his father than to his mother because the father is still the patriarchal figure. In addition, the husband, having integrated the behavioral ways of both the ethnic culture and the White American culture, might empathize with the differences of both his son and his wife. Being a professional union negotiator, he could use his skills as a mediator to preserve the family's integrity.

5. Tomika may elicit her husband's aid to make the son understand his effect on his mother when he and his girlfriend discuss relandscaping and remodeling, and when they refuse to tell Tomika where they are going or when they will be home.

6. It might be wise to leave the girlfriend out of the family discussions. Even though she lives with the family, she is not kin. The son might communicate to her what he believes is relevant to her after the mediation process.

7. In order to enhance her sense of achieved credibility, Tomika could be asked to monitor and list all the ways she takes care of her family (cooking, cleaning, gardening, shopping).

8. Tomika can be encouraged to enlist her husband's help so that he can have a new understanding of his wife's essential domestic functions in the household. She could have her husband price her services in the community to estimate her economic contributions.

9. Tomika could be encouraged to tell her husband to remind their son and his girlfriend of the ways in which Tomika makes their lives easier, more comfortable, and certainly less expensive.

10. Tomika could be encouraged to begin teaching her son's girlfriend how to cook special Japanese dishes that are still the son's favorites.

11. Tomika could be encouraged to learn some specific skills from her son's girlfriend.

12. Tomika could be encouraged to reframe her domestic tasks as ways in which she can support her family.

13. Tomika can empower herself by learning how to monitor her daily accomplishments.

14. Tomika needs to be supported as she tries to develop a stronger relationship with her son's girlfriend.

15. Tomika can be encouraged to discuss her past experiences in caring for her mother. As much as the client is able without withdrawing, she can be encouraged to express her feelings about her mother, along with any regret she may feel about where her mother is now. This may include any negative feelings she may harbor, such as anger or grief.

16. Encourage Tomika to discuss with her husband how secure their financial future is and what their plans are if one spouse were to die suddenly. This may alleviate some of Tomika's fears about becoming homeless.

17. Assign a bibliotherapy task for Tomika (a former school librarian) that helps her understand about general stress and cultural stresses, and about related acculturation and generational differences in Asian immigrants. A good author to begin reading might be Amy Tan.

18. Teach Tomika stress-reduction techniques such as muscle relaxation or thematic imagery; reinforce coping techniques she already uses (such as gardening).

Counseling Goals

1. To make the covert cultural (traditional vs. White American) characteristics overt so that the client can gain increased understanding of cultural differences and a greater sense of control and informed decision making

2. To help Tomika successfully cope with her psychological and family stressors by learning stress-reduction strategies in counseling

3. To monitor Tomika's somatic complaints as counseling progresses, and possibly consult with her internist if the complaints worsen

4. To keep intact the structure of the family's relationships, the family's importance for Tomika, and Tomika's nurturing role

5. To help Tomika understand some possible sources of her emotions

6. To empower the client to control her affect if it embarrasses her in her family life

7. To be congruent in the counseling relationship regarding affect so that Tomika can see that it is safe to emote in counseling

8. To make Tomika's covert assumptions of *amae* more overt

9. To help Tomika assess how some acculturated version of *amae* could best fit into her son's life now

10. To use Tomika's husband as the patriarchal mediator and authority

11. To encourage Tomika to find new ways of fostering a relationship with her son and his girlfriend

12. To help Tomika learn to cope with stress in diverse ways

Client-Counselor Process Issues

1. Based on research on Asian Americans, general counseling goals will be to maintain relatively structured, direct counseling sessions with low apparent ambiguity. However, if the client can work well with less structure, then those needs will be accommodated. In studies by Atkinson et al. (1978), the counselor was rated as more credible and approachable when employing the direct counseling approach.

2. There are at least two client variables that may enhance the counseling process: (a) Tomika's language skills are excellent; and (b) she voluntarily sought counseling. According to researchers, "Japanese-Americans were twice as likely to come into therapy for reasons of personal growth than were Japanese clients" (Leong, 1986, p. 198). In other words, Tomika may be a motivated client.

3. The counselor may perceive Tomika to be persecuted by a thankless son who is extremely sexist. These personal feelings and attitudes are important for the counselor to be aware of, but the counselor will not disclose them to Tomika because she might be offended by them, which could only add to her conflicts. Counselors might seek adequate supervision to process these personal biases regarding the dynamics of this Asian family system and the traditional Asian ethnic worldview.

4. The counselor will need to explore the potential meaning of new behavior to members of Tomika's own community, particularly attending to the ways that violations of traditional gender roles may affect family and community relationships. It will be important not to cause any *yurikaishi* as a result of counseling.

5. The counselor first needs to be fully cognizant of his or her acculturation attitude preferences. For instance, the counselor may value integration or assimilation, but may not press his or her agenda on the client. The counselor

will need to elicit from Tomika her ideas about which adaptations she considers to be the most desirable and practical/realistic.

6. If the counselor is a feminist, he or she would need to monitor feelings of animosity toward the males in Tomika's life and to understand their cultural perspectives as well (it may even be necessary to enlist the male family members' help and/or cooperation at some point). The counselor would need to be careful not to become overzealous and try to rescue Tomika from her family.

Conclusion

There are three necessary features in multicultural assessment. First, there is a philosophy that counselors need to form through training a personal commitment to multicultural counseling competencies. Second, cross-cultural comparability or "modified" etic takes into consideration the differences of minority clients' adaptation, thus making normative assessment conclusions possible. Third, the etic approach is complemented by an emic or ideographic qualitative method that captures the unique qualities of a person in an indigenous cultural context. An etic-emic integrated assessment system is ideal.

References

American Association for Counseling and Development. (1988). Ethical standards (Rev. ed.). *Journal of Counseling and Development, 67,* 4-8.

American Psychiatric Association. (1994). *Diagnostic and statistical manual of mental disorders* (4th ed.). Washington, DC: Author.

American Psychological Association. (1986). *Accreditation handbook* (Rev. ed.). Washington, DC: APA Committee on Accreditation and Accreditation Office.

American Psychological Association. (1992). Ethical principles of psychologists and code of conduct. *American Psychologist, 47,* 1597-1611.

American Psychological Association. (1993). Guidelines for providers of psychological services to ethnic, linguistic, and culturally diverse populations. *American Psychologist, 48,* 45-48.

Atkinson, D. R., Maruyama, M., & Matsui, S. (1978). Effects of counselor race and counseling approach on Asian Americans' perception of counselor credibility and utility. *Journal of Counseling Psychology, 25,* 76-83.

Atkinson, D. R., Morten, G., & Sue, D. W. (Eds.). (1979). *Counseling American minorities: A cross-cultural perspective.* (3rd ed.). Madison, WI: Brown & Benchmark.

Atkinson, D. R., Morten, G., & Sue, D. W. (Eds.). (1993). *Counseling American minorities: A cross-cultural perspective.* (4th ed.). Dubuque, IA: Brown & Benchmark.

Atkinson, D. R., & Thompson, C. E. (1992). Racial, ethnic, and cultural variables in counseling. In S. D. Brown & R. W. Lent (Eds.), *Handbook of counseling psychology* (2nd ed., pp. 349-382). New York: John Wiley.

Berry, J. W. (1980). Acculturation as varieties of adaptation. In A. M. Padilla (Ed.), *Acculturation: Theory, modes, and some new findings* (pp. 9-25). Boulder, CO: Westview.

Brislin, R. W. (1993). *Understanding culture's influence on behavior.* New York: Harcourt Brace Jovanovich.

Burn, D. (1992). Ethical implications in cross-cultural counseling and training. *Journal of Counseling and Development, 70,* 578-583.

Cervantes, R. C., Padilla, A. M., & Salgado de Snyder, N. (1991). The Hispanic Stress Inventory: A culturally relevant approach to psychosocial assessment. *Journal of Consulting and Clinical Psychology, 3,* 438-447.

Cross, W. E., Jr. (1971). The Negro-to-Black conversion experience: Toward a psychology of Black liberation. *Black World, 20,* 13-27.

Cuellar, I., Harris, L. C., & Jasso, R. (1980). An acculturation scale for Mexican American normal and clinical populations. *Hispanic Journal of Behavioral Sciences, 2,* 199-217.

Department of Educational Psychology, University of Nebraska-Lincoln. (1973). *The Ethnic Minority Affairs Committee (EMAC) mission statement.* Lincoln, NE: Author.

Department of Educational Psychology, University of Nebraska-Lincoln. (1989). *The Ethnic Minority Affairs Committee (EMAC) brochure.* Lincoln, NE: Author.

Department of Educational Psychology, University of Nebraska-Lincoln. (1993). *The Ethnic Minority Affairs Committee (EMAC) brochure* (Rev. ed.). Lincoln, NE: Author.

Draguns, J. G. (1996). Multicultural and cross-cultural assessment: Dilemmas and decisions. In G. R. Sodowsky & J. Impara (Eds.), *Multicultural assessment in counseling and clinical psychology.* Lincoln, NE: Buros Institute of Mental Measurements.

Helms, J. (1990). Toward a model of White racial identity development. In J. E. Helms (Ed.), *Black and White racial identity: Theory, research, and practice.* Westport, CT: Greenwood.

Helms, J. E. (1984). Toward a theoretical explanation of the effects of race on counseling: A Black and White model. *The Counseling Psychologist, 12,* 153-165.

Ihle, G. M., Sodowsky, G. R., & Kwan, K.L.K. (1996). Worldviews of women: Comparisons between White American clients, White American counselors, and Chinese international students. *Journal of Counseling and Development, 74,* 306-312.

Ivey, A. E., Ivey, M. B., & Simek-Downing, L. (1987). *Counseling and psychotherapy: Integrating skills, theory, and practice.* Englewood Cliffs, NJ: Prentice Hall.

Jackson, B. (1975). Black identity development. *MEFORM: Journal of Educational Diversity and Innovation, 2,* 19-25.

Jacobson, C. K. (1985). Resistance to affirmative action: Self-interest or racism. *Journal of Conflict Resolution, 29,* 306-329.

Katz, J. H. (1985). The sociopolitical nature of counseling. In Cross-cultural counseling [Special issue]. *The Counseling Psychologist, 13,* 615-624.

Kelly, G. (1955). *The psychology of personal constructs.* New York: Norton.

Kelly, G. D. (1990). The cultural family of origin: A description of a training strategy. *Counselor Education and Supervision, 30,* 77-84.

Kinzie, J. D., Manson, S. M., Vinh, D. T., Toland, N. T., Anch, B., & Pho, T. N. (1982). Development and validation of a Vietnamese-language depression rating scale. *American Journal of Psychiatry, 139,* 1276-1281.

Leong, F. T. L. (1986). Counseling and psychotherapy with Asian Americans: Review of the literature. *Journal of Counseling Psychology, 33,* 196-206.

Li-Repac, D. (1980). Cultural influences in clinical perception: A comparison between Caucasian and Chinese-American therapist. *Journal of Cross-Cultural Psychology, 11,* 327-342.

Malgady, R. G., Costantino, G., & Rogler, L. H. (1984). Development of a Thematic Apperception Test (TEMAS) for urban Hispanic children. *Journal of Consulting and Clinical Psychology, 52,* 986-996.

Malgady, R. G., Rogler, L. H., & Costantino, G. (1987). Ethnocultural and linguistic bias in the mental health evaluation of Hispanics. *American Psychologist, 42,* 228-234.

McConahay, J. B., & Hough, J. C. (1976). Symbolic racism. *Journal of Social Issues, 32,* 23-45.

McRae, M. B., & Johnson, S. D. (1991). Toward training for competence in multicultural counselor education. *Journal of Counseling and Development, 70,* 131-135.

Mercer, J. R., & Lewis, J. F. (1977). *SOMPA (System of Multicultural Pluralistic Assessment).* New York: The Psychological Corporation.

Midgette, T. E., & Meggert, S. S. (1991). Multicultural counseling instruction: A challenge for faculties in the 21st century. *Journal of Counseling and Development, 70,* 136-141.

Minnesota Multiphasic Personality Inventory 2 (MMPI-2). (1989). Minneapolis, MN: NCS Assessments.

Mukherjee, S., Shukla, S., Woodle, J., Rosen, A. M., & Olarte, S. (1983). Misdiagnosis of schizophrenia in bipolar patients: A multiethnic comparison. *American Journal of Psychiatry, 140,* 1571-1574.

Neighbors, H. W., Jackson, J. S., Campbell, L., & Williams, D. (1989). The influence of racial factors on psychiatric diagnosis: A review and suggestions for research. *Community Mental Health Journal, 25,* 301-311.

Padilla, A. M., Alvarez, M., & Lindholm, K. J. (1986). Immigrant and generational status as predictors of stress in students. *Hispanic Journal of Behavioral Sciences, 8,* 275-288.

Padilla, A. M., Wagatsuma, Y., & Lindholm, K. J. (1985). Acculturation and personality as predictors of stress in Japanese and Japanese-Americans. *Journal of Social Psychology, 125,* 295-305.

Pedersen, P. B. (1987). Ten frequent assumptions of cultural bias in counseling. *Journal of Multicultural Counseling and Development, 15,* 16-24.

Pedersen, P. B. (1988). *A handbook for developing multicultural awareness.* Alexandria, VA: American Counseling Association.

Phinney, J. S. (1990). Ethnic identity in adolescence and adults: A review of research. *Psychological Bulletin, 108,* 499-514.

Ponterotto, J. G. (1988). Racial consciousness development among White counselor trainees: A stage model. *Journal of Multicultural Counseling and Development, 16,* 146-156.

Ponterotto, J. G., Alexander, C. M., & Grieger, I. (1995). A multicultural competency checklist for counseling training programs. *Journal of Multicultural Counseling and Development, 23,* 11-20.

Ridley, C. R., Mendoza, D. W., & Kanitz, B. E. (1994). Multicultural training: Reexamination, operationalization, and integration. *The Counseling Psychologist, 22,* 227-289.

Rogers, C. R. (1951). *Client-centered therapy.* Boston: Houghton Mifflin.

Sabnani, H. B., Ponterotto, J. G., & Borodovsky, L. G. (1991). White racial identity development and cross-cultural counselor training: A stage model. *The Counseling Psychologist, 19,* 76-102.

Sodowsky, G. R. (1996). The Multicultural Counseling Inventory: Psychometric properties and some uses in counseling training. In G. R. Sodowsky & J. Impara (Eds.), *Multicultural assessment in counseling and clinical psychology.* Lincoln, NE: Buros Institute of Mental Measurements.

Sodowsky, G. R., Kwan, K. L., & Pannu, R. K. (1995). Ethnic identity of Asians in the United States: Conceptualization and illustrations. In J. G. Ponterotto, J. M. Casas, L. A. Suzuki, & C. M. Alexander (Eds.), *Handbook of multicultural counseling* (pp. 123-154). Thousand Oaks, CA: Sage.

Sodowsky, G. R., & Lai, E. W. M. (1996). Asian immigrant variables and structural models of cross-cultural distress. In A. Booth (Ed.), *International migration and family change: The experiences of U.S. immigrants.* Hillsdale, NJ: Lawrence Erlbaum.

Sodowsky, G. R., Lai, E. W. M., & Plake, B. (1991). Moderating effects of sociocultural variables on acculturation attitudes of Hispanics and Asian Americans. *Journal of Counseling and Development, 70,* 194-204.

Sodowsky, G. R., & Plake, B. (1992). A study of acculturation differences among international people and suggestions for sensitivity to within-group differences. *Journal of Counseling and Development, 71,* 53-59.

Sodowsky, G. R., Taffe, R. C., Gutkin, T. B., & Wise, S. L. (1994). Development of the Multicultural Counseling Inventory: A self-report measure of multicultural competencies. *Journal of Counseling and Development, 41,* 137-148.

Sue, D. W., Arredondo, P., & McDavis, R. J. (1992). Multicultural counseling competencies and standards: A call to the profession. *Journal of Multicultural Counseling and Development, 20,* 644-688.

Sue, D. W., Bernier, J. E., Durran, A., Feinberg, L., Pedersen, P., Smith, E. J., & Vasquez-Nuttall, E. (1982). Position paper: Cross-cultural counseling competencies. *The Counseling Psychologist, 10,* 45-52.

Sue, D. W., & Sue, D. (1990). *Counseling the culturally different: Theory and practice* (2nd ed.). New York: John Wiley.

Sue, S. (1996). Measurement, testing, and ethnic bias: Can solutions be found? In G. R. Sodowsky & J. Impara (Eds.), *Multicultural assessment in counseling and clinical psychology.* Lincoln, NE: Buros Institute of Mental Measurements.

Sue, S., & Zane, N. (1987). The role of culture and cultural techniques in psychotherapy: A critique and reformulation. *American Psychologist, 42,* 37-45.

Suinn, R. M., Rickard-Figueroa, K., Lew, S., & Vigil, P. (1987). The Suinn-Lew Asian Self-Identity Acculturation Scale: An initial report. *Educational and Psychological Measurement, 47,* 401-407.

Szapocznik, J., Scopetta, M. A., Kurtines, W., & Aranalde, M. A. (1978). Theory and measurement of acculturation. *International Journal of Psychology, 12,* 113-130.

Thomas, C. W. (1970). Different strokes for different folks. *Psychology Today, 4,* 49-53, 80.

Thomas, C. W. (1971). *Boys no more.* Beverly Hills, CA: Glencoe Press.

Vontress, C. E. (1971). Racial differences: Impediments to rapport. *Journal of Counseling Psychology, 18,* 7-13.

Williams, R. L. (1972). The BITCH Test (Black Intelligence Test of Cultural Homogeneity; the BITCH-100: A Culture-Specific Test). St. Louis, MO: Author, Washington University.

World Health Organization. (1983). *Depressive disorders in different cultures: Report on the WHO collaborative study on standardized assessment of depressive disorders.* Geneva: Author.

Wrenn, C. G. (1962). The culturally encapsulated counselor. *Harvard Educational Review, 32,* 444-449.

Wrenn, C. G. (1987). The culturally encapsulated counselor revisited. In P. Pedersen (Ed.), *Handbook of cross-cultural counseling and psychotherapy* (pp. 323-329). New York: Praeger.

2

Portfolio Assessment of Multicultural Counseling Competence

Hardin L. K. Coleman

When I teach a course on multicultural counseling, the most difficult moment comes when I am about halfway through the course material. By this point the students have become comfortable enough with me and each other to start expressing their evaluative feelings and beliefs about what they are learning. It would be much easier to design such a course if there were complete agreement among the students about what was good in the class, and what was not good. The students' responses to the course fall into four general categories. The first includes those who do not see the point of the course. Members in this group are critical of the course in several ways. Some suggest that the material I am presenting has too weak an empirical base to be of much use. Others argue that we are all really the same and that culture should not make any difference in how one approaches the counseling process.

AUTHOR'S NOTE: Parts of this chapter also appear in an article of the same name in *The Counseling Psychologist*.

The second group is awestruck by the information and incredibly appreciative of the opportunity to learn and talk about cultural issues. They admit to an ignorance about cultural factors and their effect on the counseling process. This group also feels intimidated about working with people from different cultures. Many students in this group worry about appearing racist to their clients and to their classmates. The third group is aware of their feelings and thoughts about cultural issues. They are delighted to have the opportunity to get feedback from others and to learn skills to work with people from different cultures. They get frustrated that we spend so much time on the issues related to awareness of cultural differences and not enough time on skill development. The last group gets frustrated that we have not gone farther, faster, and deeper into issues related to specific cultural groups or specific techniques that are effective with specific problems faced by members of specific groups (e.g., How does that theory apply to a depressed female immigrant from Puerto Rico vs. one from Guatemala?).

Members from each group will have this course recorded on their transcript along with a grade. Will all the students have developed the same type and level of multicultural counseling competence? How can each participant be fairly evaluated on the range of knowledge, beliefs, and skills associated with multicultural counseling competence? As their evaluator, do I compare the participants to each other or to a predetermined standard? Is success in the course measured by how much participants have changed, by their performance on course-related exercises, or by their ability to work with culturally diverse clients? Should the process and standards of evaluation be the same or different from those used to evaluate counselors in the field? In short, how do you assess multicultural counseling competence?

Ponterotto, Rieger, Barrett, and Sparks (1994), in their review of the current methods used to assess multicultural counseling competence, report several very important findings. The first is that most approaches to the assessment of multicultural counseling competence are based on the Division 17 report prepared by Sue et al. (1982). This conceptualization of multicultural counseling competence suggests that it involves a combination of (a) awareness, (b) knowledge, and (c) skills. Second, Ponterotto et al. (1994) indicate that all the current instrumentation designed to assess this type of competence could benefit from further examination of their psychometric properties. Third, they encourage the field as a whole to develop increasingly precise definitions of multicultural counseling competence to facilitate the development of effective assessment tools. Fourth, they call for outcome studies both to demonstrate the validity of assessment tools and to improve our understanding of multicultural counseling competence. Finally, they suggest that this understanding would be facilitated by the development of qualitative methods of assessing multicultural counseling competence.

Although the study of multicultural counseling competence has improved significantly over the past 20 years in terms of theoretical development and methodological rigor, it has not received the same attention as has general counseling competence. There is a long history of research that has focused on which counseling theories and techniques are effective with majority clients. This research has produced a sophisticated understanding of which skills, attitudes, and beliefs an individual needs to be considered a generally competent counselor (Cormier & Cormier, 1991; Giles, 1993; Holloway, in press). As Ponterotto et al. (1994) have indicated, that clarity has not evolved in the field of multicultural counseling competency. The purpose of this chapter is to outline an assessment procedure that can serve to improve our understanding of what multicultural counseling competence is, how it is acquired, and how it can be evaluated.

Previous attempts to develop and assess multicultural counseling competence have used several different approaches. The first has focused on quantitative methods using pen-and-paper instruments. The second, and more common, approach to the assessment and development of this competence has used idiographic methods such as individual tutelage within clinical supervision. A third approach has been pedagogical, using multicultural counseling courses in degree programs, continuing education workshops, or in-service programs for practicing professionals. As Coleman and Wampold (1993), Ponterotto et al. (1994), and Ridley, Mendoza, and Kanitz (1994) have suggested, there is a need for an assessment method that can both address the broad range of behavior that comprises multicultural counseling competence, and be relevant to different training and clinical contexts. In addition, effective assessment can facilitate the development of multicultural counseling competence and determine whether an individual has reached a particular standard of multicultural counseling competence. Such an assessment method would be useful both for helping counselors to develop multicultural counseling competence and as a measure of multicultural counseling competence.

Over the past decade, frustration with the irrelevancy and inequitable outcomes of standardized assessments tools has motivated educators to search for an assessment method that would both stimulate improvement in learning and teaching, and provide an accurate assessment of what a student really knows. Wiggins (1989) categorizes this as a search for a true test of performance. By *true test,* Wiggins means a test that requires students to produce an example of their competence in a given area (e.g., write a grammatically correct essay), rather than a test that requires students to identify examples of competence in that area (e.g., answer a multiple-choice question that asks students to identify the correct grammatical constructions). Recently, educators have begun to use portfolios as a way to evaluate what both students (Paulson, Paulson, & Meyer, 1991) and teachers (Collins, 1992; Wolf, 1994) know and can do. Educators have found that using a portfolio approach to assessment has allowed them not only to determine what an individual has learned about a particular topic or skill, but also to demonstrate how that individual's knowledge or skill has changed over time. Portfolios have also been useful in encouraging individuals (a) to be more self-reflective about their learning, (b) to take greater ownership of the learning process, and (c) to show what they have learned to others. In essence, portfolios are an effective way of helping students and teachers determine the important information and skills that are necessary to acquire within a particular context and then demonstrate the degree to which an individual has acquired that information and skills. If transferable, the success of this method would have a beneficial effect on development and evaluation of multicultural counseling competence.

What Are Portfolios
and What Do They Do?

One way to conceptualize a portfolio is to think of what artists have to do to convince a gallery to show their work. Artists must assemble a collection of the work they have completed, describe what each piece means, how it fits into their general approach, how it fits into their genre, and what effect they feel it will have on an audience. An artist's portfolio, therefore, not only shows what the artist knows, but how the artist can put that knowledge into practice over a range of situations. In the field of postsecondary education, this is the process by which many universities make decisions concerning faculty tenure. They ask the applicant to demonstrate competence across several domains, most often research, teaching, and service. In the general counseling field, the process by which an applicant receives a license or a Diplomate often requires, beyond performance on standardized tests and completion of courses, case examples that serve to demonstrate the applicant's general clinical competence.

Arter and Spandel (1992) define a portfolio as "a purposeful collection of student work that tells the story of the student's efforts, progress, or achievement in a given area(s)" (p. 36). As this definition suggests, a key component in the development of a portfolio is the goal. The skills and/or knowledge that a portfolio represents and to whom it is being shown greatly affects what goes into the portfolio. Navarrete (1990) points out that a portfolio must have a clear purpose to give meaning to the contents. Collins (1992) emphasizes the importance of differentiating between the *goal* (what will be demonstrated) and the *function* (how will be it used) of the portfolio.

According to Collins (1992), portfolios can accomplish a wide range of goals. They will allow their developers to demonstrate what they know in a way that reflects the complexity of a particular topic and how the developer has integrated skills with knowledge. Portfolios will provide a stimulus for discussion about what they know with their colleagues and/or supervisor. Portfolios will allow people not only to show that they have mastered certain facts, but also that they understand what those facts mean. They also provide a way to integrate information collected over several content domains, they can replace formal and decontextualized examinations, and they can serve as documentation for how effective particular educational processes are at developing competence in students.

Wiggins (1989) suggests that portfolios can provide a perspective on student change over time as the student demonstrates increasing sophistication with particular skills. The primary value of this form of evaluation is that it can look at the change within the learner as well as between the learner and some hypothetical norm. It can, therefore, be a valid assessment process for both novices and experts. Portfolios also stimulate self-reflection, because the learner is responsible for deciding the goal and content of the assessment and is involved in determining the criteria by which he or she will be evaluated (Hansen, 1992; Herbert, 1992; Herman, 1992; Paris & Ayres, 1994).

How Do They
Do What They Do?

The first step in developing a portfolio is to determine its purpose or goal and how it will be used. Once that goal is determined, the developer can go on to the second step, which is to identify what evidence will be most effective at demonstrating the acquisition of the goal (Collins, 1992). For each piece of evidence learners submit, they are encouraged to make a statement about what it is, and why and how it demonstrates their knowledge. This is what Collins calls a caption and Fox (1981) calls a competence statement. Furthermore, learners are encouraged to prepare a statement about how the portfolio as a whole reflects what they have learned and/or want to learn. This process facilitates both the learner's sense of ownership over the material, and his or her willingness to reflect about the skill or knowledge he or she is attempting to demonstrate (Paulson et al., 1991). Both Holloway (in press) and Skovholt and Ronnestad (1992) have suggested that this process of self-evaluation fosters the ability to be self-reflective, which is an important factor in the development and maintenance of counselor competence.

The creation of a portfolio is context-dependent. The purpose and use of a portfolio will be determined by the learner in relationship to his or her audience, whether that be an instructor, a supervisor, a prospective employer, clients, or colleagues. This quality of portfolios serves to make them excellent tools for the portfolio assessment of multicultural counseling competence, which, as both Ridley et al. (1994) and Atkinson, Thompson, and Grant (1993) have indicated, needs to be responsive to context.

In their paper on multicultural counseling training, Ridley et al. (1994) point out that training programs develop idiosyncratically. They advocate this process approach over the expert-oriented approach to developing an effective multicultural counseling program. They also indicate that one weakness of existing instruments designed to assess multicultural counseling competence is that they are either too responsive to context, or not well developed enough to be adequate outcome measures for multicultural training programs. Using portfolios would allow the instructor and learners to create a performance-based assessment of what was learned in a course or program that is responsive to the needs of the learner and the focus of the particular course or program.

Given that the 1982 position paper by Sue et al. continues to be the major conceptualization of multicultural counseling competence in the field, the goal of an authentic assessment in this area would most likely be to demonstrate the learner's multicultural awareness, knowledge, and skills. Ridley et al. (1994) suggest this would include the following learning objectives: (a) display of culturally responsive behaviors, (b) ethical knowledge and practice concerning multicultural counseling and training issues, (c) cultural empathy, (d) ability to critique counseling theories for cultural relevance, (e) development of an individualized theoretical orientation that is culturally relevant, (f) knowledge of normative characteristics of cultural groups, (g) cultural self-awareness, (h) knowledge of within-group differences, (i) multicultural counseling concepts and issues, and (j) respect for cultural differences.

With the development of the counselor's competence, the areas of competence and the type of evidence used to show the competence would change. In the same fashion a novice clinician's portfolio would look very different from that of a clinician with years of experience with culturally diverse clients. Each learner, however, could use this assessment process to reflect on and demonstrate his or her existing or emerging competence in particular areas as they are relevant to the learner's context.

Advances in technology will allow for the creation of interactive portfolios. Using scanners and laser disk production, learners would be able to transfer written work as well as audio- and videotape productions to a format that would be accessible in a CD-ROM format (Campbell, 1992). This would allow evaluators to make point-in-time assessments or comments about a particular counseling interaction or about the portfolio as a whole. Given the storage capacity of a CD, a learner could review initial attempts at competence in a particular domain as well as later attempts and then comment on the change.

Given the current understanding of multicultural counseling competence, a portfolio would have to demonstrate the individual's state of competence over three domains: awareness, knowledge, and skills. These domains of competence would be demonstrated within the four major modalities that are commonly taught in clinical training programs and practice sites, namely, individual, group, family, and consultation. A portfolio would also reflect the interaction between multicultural awareness, knowledge, and skills, and the context in which the competence is being displayed.

Table 2.1 presents examples of types of evidence individuals could present that would represent their multicultural counseling competence in a given modality or context. What evidence a counselor would produce would vary with the context in which the portfolio would be used. As the outcome of an introductory course, competence in awareness and/or knowledge in several modalities and one context may be sufficient. As the outcome of a practicum course, one would expect demonstration of competence in the skill domain. If a portfolio is being used as part of a job application, as it is for some school counselor positions in the state in which I work, the issues related to context would become the organizing principle in the evaluation of the portfolio. If the document is being used to measure the progress of a trainee or the accomplishments of an experienced clinician, that purpose, interacting with the context, would influence the type of evidence produced for the portfolio. That flexibility and context specificity are what makes the portfolio approach to evaluation of multicultural counseling competence so exciting.

A major challenge in creating a portfolio is choosing appropriate evidence. Despite the injunction that the evidence should fit the purpose of the portfolio, most people are more concerned about the quality of their evaluation than about demonstrating what they do or do not know, which is more often the purpose of the evaluation. To facilitate this process, I encourage students to use Sue et al.'s (1982) hypothesis that competence has three levels—awareness, knowledge, and skills—and, furthermore, to think of competence

Table 2.1 Demonstrations of Multicultural Counseling Competence Within Specific Treatment Modalities and Treatment Settings

	Awareness	*Knowledge*	*Skills*
Modalities:			
Individual	Can recognize a cultural concern	Can describe the cultural etiology of a pattern of behavior	Can address a cultural concern within counseling (e.g., recovery skills)
Group	Includes culturally relevant materials in handouts	Can design a culturally relevant intervention	Can resolve a within-group conflict that is cultural in its etiology
Family	Aware that parental role is different in each culture	Knows the parental role within particular cultures	Adjusts interventions to be culturally relevant
Consultation	Can identify culture norms within an organization	Knows how different cultures react to different organizational styles	Can facilitate a discussion about cultural norms in a culturally diverse and homogeneous organizations
Case Management	Aware that context can influence help-seeking behavior	Knows what type of interventions are culturally appropriate	Adjusts interventions fit the cultural norms of clients
Settings:			
School	Aware that guidance activities need to include culturally diverse materials	Can design guidance activities that are culturally relevant	Has equivalent success with minority and majority students
Hospital	Aware of the relationship between culture and health beliefs	Can design programs that maximize access to treatment by culturally diverse clients	Has successfully implemented such a program

as a contextual phenomena. In other words, the setting in which one displays one's awareness, knowledge, and skills will help determine the criteria for competence.

The examples in Table 2.1 serve to highlight the progressive nature of multicultural counseling competence. It is this progressive nature of multicultural counseling competence that influences students' choice of what to put in their portfolios. Students completing their first course in multicultural counseling would have a lot of empty cells. They may just be aware of the effect cultural factors have on the counseling process, or have some knowledge as to how culture affects particular psychological processes, but not have the skills to put that awareness or knowledge into action with an individual from another culture—let alone with a group or family. Depending on the course expectations, the purpose of a portfolio may be to demonstrate awareness and knowledge in several counseling modalities. Evidence that one could produce for a course would be a theory of multicultural counseling competency, or a culture specific group intervention with at-risk adolescents within a school setting.

In clinical practicum, the expectations of demonstrating one's ability to apply awareness and knowledge with clients would be much higher than in a classroom setting. In fact, the criteria for competence would change over the course of the practicum experience. Whereas the portfolio would be a reasonable expectation for students in a course to complete as their final project, students in a clinical project may be asked to complete one at the beginning as a way of establishing their baseline competence and determining their goals for the practicum. Achievement of those goals would, therefore, be the criteria for evaluation at the end of the experience (see Caffarella & Caffarella, 1986, for a discussion of techniques of self-directed learning). In the practicum settings, the criteria for competence would be specific to the context in which the practicum is being held. A community mental health counselor would, for example, be expected to have more family skills than a college counselor.

Choosing evidence for demonstrating multicultural counseling competence should be directed by the nature of the setting, the counselor's goals, and the evaluator's expectations. Using portfolios is an excellent way of forcing the counselor to create clear and realistic goals, and the evaluator to create clear and realistic expectations. To follow the outline of portfolio development suggested by Tierney, Carter, and Desai (1991), the first step is to meet with the student or counselor to discuss and negotiate the goals of the portfolio. In that discussion, the participants—for the purpose of clarity I will focus on the supervisor-counselor relationship—would establish the purpose of the portfolio. In the case of a counselor just starting out in the field, the goal may be to establish a baseline competency in providing one-on-one clinical services to culturally diverse individuals. The focus of the portfolio would be on collecting data that would form the base of a formative evaluation. The next step in the process would involve developing guidelines and procedures for demonstrating the competency, determining the appropriate material to be used as demonstrations, and the criteria for evaluation. This is an important step in the process as it will have a direct impact on the evaluation of the portfolio. In this step, the counselor and supervisor would agree on what type of evidence would be helpful in demonstrating the counselor's competence, such as videotapes of counseling sessions, case conceptualizations, progress notes of sessions, or outcome measures of the counseling. The time line for establishing competence would also be agreed upon then. An important part of this step is to choose appropriate criteria.

Criteria for competence could be clients' rating of the counselors' effectiveness using a combination of general counseling effectiveness scales such as the Counselor Effectiveness Rating Scale (Atkinson & Carskaddon, 1975). The Multicultural Counseling Awareness Scale-Form B: Revised Self-Assessment (Ponterotto, Sanchez, & Magids, 1991), and the Multicultural Counseling Inventory (Sodowsky, Taffe, Gutkin, & Wise, 1994) are excellent self-assessment tools that counselors can use to identify their current level of multicultural counseling competence. The counselor would then produce evidence, such as a videotape, that reflected that level of competence. The Multicultural Awareness-Knowledge-and-Skills Survey (D'Andrea, Daniels, & Heck, 1991) could be used for the same purpose and also by teachers of multicultural counseling courses to demonstrate their competence in teaching this material. Another source of information for evaluation would be the self-evaluative comments that counselors would use to analyze the evidence by which they choose to demonstrate their competence in a particular domain or context.

In clinical supervision, portfolios are useful both in establishing training goals and in evaluating their acquisition. At the start of a practicum or evaluation year, supervisees present portfolios that demonstrate their current level of multicultural counseling competence. In consultation with the supervisor, the individual supervisees establish goals for the period of evaluation. As supervisees engage in their clinical work, they can demonstrate progress toward the acquisition of those goals. At the end of the evaluation period, the supervisee can present a final portfolio for evaluation. Such a procedure serves to make the criterion of success explicit for both the supervisor and supervisee. It also provides a useful tool for encouraging growth and development beyond just reaching an acceptable criterion of competence.

Having determined the materials that will be in the portfolio and the criteria by which competence will be judged, the counselor would create the portfolio within the agreed-upon length of time and then submit it to the supervisor. Following Tierney et al.'s (1991) outline, the supervisor would then review the portfolio and the counselor's self-evaluative comments. The supervisor would then use this information to determine the degree to which the counselor met, exceeded, or failed to meet the criteria of competence that the counselor and supervisor had agreed on at the beginning of the process. The Cross-Cultural Counseling Inventory-R (CCCI-R; LaFromboise, Coleman, & Hernandez, 1991) could be used by the reviewer of the portfolio to guide this evaluation process. A strength of the portfolio approach to assessment is that these judgments would be made on a range of behavior rather than a slim slice of behavior, such as a videotape with a single client, which is the more common approach to assessing multicultural counseling competence.

Creating fair and useful criteria for evaluation is very difficult in the counseling field. We know that mere knowledge is not enough to become a skilled and effective counselor, and we know that having all the traditional counseling skills does not make one competent to work with culturally diverse clients. To cope with the difficultly of creating useful evaluation criteria, we tend to focus on issues of accountability rather than competence (Coleman, James, Hellman, & Tuescher, 1995). We count how many times a counselor does a certain behavior (hours of client contact, number of psychological evaluations, types of clients seen) rather than actual evidence of competence. We look at résumés rather than case reports, or at courses taken rather than videotapes of sessions.

One reason that we use information we can quantify to determine competence is that much of what we believe is competence is very subjective. Coleman et al. (1995) spent 2 hours working with a group of school counselors to identify examples of counseling competence. These counselors consistently pointed to characterological and subjective variables as exemplars of competence. Wiggins (1991) argues that it is just that subjective, or aesthetic, understanding of competence that we should use to evaluate the evidence students present.

Because we also provide grades to students, that idiosyncratic perspective is problematic. In lieu of true objective standards or trustworthy subjective ones, it is the congruence between the evidence students present concerning their competence and their self-evaluation that is a useful source of information for the evaluation. A student who presents a videotape in which there is no evidence of addressing cultural information yet states that this shows something about his or her multicultural counseling competency is demonstrating a lack of awareness. A student who presents a cognitive-behavior program for adolescent substance abusers and says that it is culturally relevant because all the group members and the leader will be from the same cultural group is showing some awareness, but not a thorough knowledge of what it means for an intervention to be culturally relevant.

Working with discrepancies between the evidence a student presents and the student's self-evaluation is one source of information for evaluations. Another is the discrepancies between the student's self-evaluation and scores on some of the objective measures that have been created to assess multicultural counseling competency (see Ponterotto et al., 1994). As trained psychologists, we also need to let our "sense" of competence influence our evaluations of students, particularly within the clinical settings. We should also be willing to prepare formal written feedback to our students, using the framework in Table 2.1, so that they can both dispute our comments and use them to focus on the areas in which they need to grow.

The final step in the process involves returning the portfolio to the counselor with feedback on his or her strengths and weaknesses. This feedback would form the basis of the next round of portfolio development. At this point, both supervisor and counselor will have a baseline understanding of the counselor's competence and will be able to focus on areas of growth in new domains and contexts, and areas that need improvement, such as those in which the counselor did not meet the predetermined criteria of competence.

There is a need for empirical investigations to validate the effectiveness of this approach and to determine whether the costs, in terms of time, are worth the benefits of a deeper understanding of this type of counseling competence. The outcome of such investigations would serve to improve our understanding of what multicultural counseling competence looks like and to help establish criteria for competence. We are currently aware of the domains of competence and the contexts in which these competencies are demonstrated. Careful examination of the examples of competence that counselors develop using the portfolio approach would help establish standards of practice in the field. By examining what counselors actually do that is effective with culturally diverse clients, we can generate more precise hypotheses concerning multicultural counseling competence that would form the basis of controlled process/outcome investigations.

OK, Let the Other Shoe Drop

As excited as one can get about the use of portfolios to assess a learner's existing or emerging competence in a particular domain such as multicultural counseling competence, there are several issues that are consistently presented as obstacles to their widespread use. The first is that the development and review of a portfolio can take much more than the 20 to 30 minutes required by most pen-and-paper instruments (Maeroff, 1991; O'Neil, 1992). Particularly at the start of setting up such an assessment approach there is much anxiety and confusion related to the change. There is also some question as to how portfolios can be used within a training program, as part of the job-seeking process, and as a research tool. Ultimately, these are questions that need to be addressed through systematic investigation. Those who have used portfolios with teachers (Stone, 1995; Wolf, 1994) have found that they are useful in stimulating self-reflection and, if used within a group setting, fostering conversation about one's activities among other professionals. In my own setting, I have had school counselors asked by potential employers to provide a portfolio of their competence. These employers have been particularly impressed by the multicultural component of the portfolio. I have also had students use their portfolios to prepare for interviews. I, and other colleagues (Kim Tuescher, personal communication, April 21, 1995), have used student portfolios as the basis for writing letters of reference. Specifically, in terms of multicultural counseling competence, the benefit is in terms of collecting a body of examples of that competence that can be used as exemplars of practice in this area. Whether the time it takes to create a portfolio is worth those benefits is a question that needs to be addressed within particular contexts and through empirical investigation.

A major concern about portfolios has to do with developing reliable methods for their scoring or evaluation (Maeroff, 1991; Navarrete, 1990; O'Neil, 1992). As others have suggested (Ponterotto et al., 1994; Ridley et al., 1994), greater specificity in an assessment tool is often gained at the loss of generalizability of the results. Maeroff suggests that assessment be perceived as an integral component of instruction. Evaluation, therefore, comes in two forms. The first involves feedback on the degree to which a learner has improved his or her performance over time, thus focusing on emerging competence. This type of evaluation would be considered formative. The second involves feedback on the degree to which the learner has approached an acceptable and predetermined standard of behavior, thus focusing on achieved competence. This type of evaluation would be considered summative. The portfolio approach requires that the instructor have both a sense of the learner's progress and a sense of the standards that are accepted by the profession (Atkinson, 1994) or a strong sense of what quality counseling looks like (Wiggins, 1991) . As in clinical supervision, using direct feedback on performance by an acknowledged expert can have a positive effect on learning and self-esteem. It does not, however, produce reliable evaluations from a psychometric perspective.

Collins (1992) points out that methodology for scoring and evaluating portfolios is still emerging. She argues that any methods must recognize and value the holistic nature of the performance. She advocates the use of expert judgment in the evaluation of the portfolios. This process would allow the instructor to engage in the formative feedback process as the portfolio is being developed and then arrange for the final product to be evaluated by two or more expert raters. This is a common process in art schools, where the students' work is critiqued by artists in the field who have not had an active role in the students' development or in the evaluation of faculty for tenure or merit raises. Navarrete (1990) advocates developing a systematic approach to scoring portfolios that would ensure reliability. She suggests the following approach to the evaluation of portfolios: (a) develop scoring criteria for raters, such as the Cross Cultural Counseling Inventory-R (LaFromboise et al., 1991); (b) maintain objectivity by comparing ratings given to other learners' work in the same area; (c) check for interrater reliability regularly by having more than one supervisor rate the portfolio; (d) use objective terminology to describe the learner's performance; (e) keep consistent and continuous records of the learner's progress; and (f) use multiple measures to assess the learner's performance.

Using a systematic approach to evaluation with two or more raters who are checked for interrater reliability would address one major psychometric concern in the use of portfolios. Messcik (1994) raises the question as to what constitutes validation in portfolio assessments. On the one hand, it is clear that the skills and knowledge being demonstrated are real and valid. The issue is whether or not they (a) fully represent a particular construct, in this case multicultural counseling competency; or (b) achieve particular criteria. Again, the use of expert raters in the evaluation process could address both these concerns.

In the realm of multicultural counseling competence, this could be achieved through the inclusion of the instruments that have been constructed to measure various aspects of this type of counseling competence. Some of these instruments could be used by the creator of the portfolio as evidence of competence in a particular domain or context. Others would be useful as a summative evaluation by the expert raters.

Conclusions

As portfolio assessment of multicultural counseling competence is implemented into training programs and clinical settings, there are a number of empirical and practical questions that need to be answered. Not the least of these is whether portfolios are reliable and valid measures of competence and whether the time spent creating a portfolio is worth the effect on practice. Nevertheless, portfolios do appear to offer many exciting possibilities as a method for assessing multicultural counseling competency. They allow for the assessment of a broad range of behaviors within the context in which those behaviors are being developed and produced. Portfolios are useful in providing both formative and summative evaluations. They are useful in the assessment of both novices and experts. They can be both structured and unstructured, but they can also be evaluated in a systematic and psychometrically sound manner. They can be used to determine whether a learner has achieved particular standards of performance, they can provide evaluative feedback to instructors as to which competencies students are developing, and they can serve to identify further what skills or knowledge have functional use within a particular context. In short, the use of portfolios to assess multicultural counseling competency appears to hold great promise in helping to improve our understanding of this particular domain of counseling competence.

References

Arter, J. A., & Spandel, V. (1992, September). Using portfolios of student work in instruction and assessment. *Educational Measurement: Issues and Practice,* pp. 36-44.

Atkinson, D. R. (1994). Multicultural training: A call for standards. *The Counseling Psychologist, 22,* 300-307.

Atkinson, D. R., & Carskaddon, G. A. (1975). A prestigious introduction, psychological jargon, and perceived counselor credibility. *Journal of Counseling Psychology, 22,* 180-186.

Atkinson, D. R., Thompson, C. E., & Grant, S. K. (1993). A three-dimensional model for counseling racial/ethnic minorities. *The Counseling Psychologist, 21,* 257-277.

Caffarella, R. S., & Caffarella, E. P. (1986). Self-directedness and learning contracts in adult education. *Adult Education Quarterly, 36,* 226-234.

Campbell, J. (1992). Laser disk portfolios: Total child assessment. *Educational Leadership, 49*(8), 69-70.

Coleman, H.L.K., James, A., Hellman, S., & Tuescher, K. (1995). *Portfolio assessment of school counselor competence.* Manuscript under review.

Coleman, H.L.K., & Wampold, B. E. (1993, August). *An integrated curriculum: Course examples.* Paper presented at the American Psychological Association Annual Meeting in Toronto.

Collins, A. (1992). Portfolios for science education: Issues in purpose, structure, and authenticity. *Science Education, 76*(4), 451-463.

Cormier, W. H., & Cormier, L. S. (1991). *Interviewing strategies for helpers* (3rd ed.). Monterey, CA: Brooks/Cole.

D'Andrea, M., Daniels, J., & Heck, R. (1991). Evaluating the impact of multicultural counseling training. *Journal of Counseling and Development, 70,* 143-150.

Fox, D. B. (1981, August). *Academic credit for experiential learning in psychology: Learning by doing.* Paper presented at the annual convention of the American Psychological Association.

Giles, T. R. (Ed.). (1993). *Handbook of effective psychotherapy.* New York: Plenum.

Hansen, J. (1992). Literacy portfolios: Helping students know themselves. *Educational Leadership, 49*(8), 66-68.

Herbert, E. (1992). Portfolios invite reflection from students and staff. *Educational Leadership, 49*(8), 58-61.

Herman, T. L. (1992). What research tells us about good assessment. *Educational Leadership, 49,* 74-78.

Holloway E. L. (1995). *Supervision: A systems approach.* Thousand Oaks, CA: Sage.

LaFromboise, T. D., Coleman, H.L.K., & Hernandez, A. (1991). Development and factor structure of the Cross-Cultural Counseling Inventory-Revised. *Professional Psychology: Research and Practice, 22,* 380-388.

Maeroff, G. I. (1991). Assessing alternative assessment. *Phi Delta Kappan, 73*(4), 272-281.

Messcik, S. (1994). The interplay of evidence and consequences in the validation of performance assessments. *Educational Researcher, 23*(2), 13-23.

Navarrete, C. (1990). *Informal assessment in educational evaluation: Implications for bilingual education programs.* Washington, DC: National Clearinghouse for Bilingual Education: Office of Bilingual Education and Minority Languages Affairs.

O'Neil, J. (1992). Putting performance assessment to the test. *Educational Leadership, 49*(8), 14-19.

Paris, S. G., & Ayres, L. R. (1994). *Becoming reflective students and teachers with portfolios and authentic assessment.* Washington, DC: American Psychological Association.

Paulson, F. L., Paulson, P. P., & Meyer, C. A. (1991). What makes a portfolio a portfolio? *Educational Leadership, 48*(5), 60-63.

Ponterotto, J. G., Rieger, B. P., Barrett, A., & Sparks, R. (1994). Assessing multicultural counseling competence: A review of instrumentation. *Journal of Counseling and Development, 72,* 316-322.

Ponterotto, J. G., Sanchez, C. M., & Magids, D. M. (1991, August). *Initial development and validation of the Multicultural Counseling Awareness Scale.* Paper presented at the annual meeting of the American Psychological Association, San Francisco.

Ridley, C. R., Mendoza, D. W., & Kanitz, B. E. (1994). Multicultural training: Reexamination, operationalization, and integration. *The Counseling Psychologist, 22,* 227-289.

Skovholt, T. M., & Ronnestad, M. H. (1992). *The evolving professional self: Stages and themes in therapist and counselor development.* New York: John Wiley.

Sodowsky, G. R., Taffe, R. C., Gutkin, T. B., & Wise, S. L. (1994). Development of the Multicultural Counseling Inventory: A self-report measure of multicultural competencies. *Journal of Counseling Psychology, 41,* 137-148.

Stone, B. (1995, April). *Portfolios for teacher evaluation: Are they effective?* Paper presented at the meeting of the American Educational Research Association, San Francisco.

Sue, D. W., Bernier, J. E., Durran, A., Feinberg, L., Pedersen, P. B., Smith, E. J., & Vasquez-Nuttal, E. (1982). Position paper: Cross-cultural counseling competencies. *The Counseling Psychologist, 10,* 45-52.

Tierney, R., Carter, M., & Desai, L. (1991). *Portfolio assessment in the reading-writing classroom.* Norwood, MA: Christopher-Gordon.

Wiggins, G. (1989). A true test: Toward more authentic and equitable assessment. *Phi Delta Kappan, 70*(9), 703-713.

Wiggins, G. (1991). Standards, not standardization: Evoking quality student work. *Educational Leadership, 47*(5), 17-25.

Wolf, K. (1994). Teaching portfolios: Capturing the complexities of teaching. In L. Ingvarson & R. Chadbourne (Eds.), *Valuing teachers' work: New directions in teacher appraisal* (pp. 112-136). Victoria: Australian Council for Educational Research.

3

How "Multiculturalism" Obscures Race and Culture as Differential Aspects of Counseling Competency

Janet E. Helms

Tina Q. Richardson

Most of the traditional counseling and psychotherapy theoretical orientations favored in the United States claim to honor the unique psychological characteristics of clients, but, in fact, ignore the differential psychological consequences to clients (and therapists) of being continuously socialized in a variety of sociodemographic groups. Some proponents of multicultural counseling as it pertains to members of one demographic group or another have attempted to provide frameworks for translating sociode-

---

AUTHORS' NOTE: A version of this chapter was presented as one of the untitled discussions for the "Symposium: Multicultural Counseling Competencies—Assessment, Education, and Training Issues," at the American Psychological Association (APA) Convention, August 13, 1994, Los Angeles, CA.

mographic variables into psychological constructs and integrating them into the counseling process (e.g., Helms & Cook, in press; Sodowsky, Taffe, Gutkin, & Wise, 1994; Sue, Bernier, et al., 1982).

Still other mental health theorists, researchers, and practitioners minimize the need for special multicultural interventions because, for them, all counseling is "multicultural" to some extent (e.g., Fukuyama, 1990; Pedersen, 1988). Therefore, for these theorists, practitioners seemingly need only to attend better to "whole clients" rather than particular diversities, if they wish to be multiculturally competent.

Thus, almost a decade and a half since Sue, Bernier, et al. (1982) first proposed a catalog of cross-cultural competencies, there is still considerable debate concerning what client characteristics should be the focus of efforts to enhance counselors' multicultural competence (Helms, 1994a; Locke, 1990). Perhaps equally important are the nascent questions concerning whether the same kinds of therapist competencies are required to attend responsively to each of the characteristics covered under the rubric of multiculturalism.

The controversy stems in part from the lack of precise psychological conceptualizations of multiculturalism and related terms as well as the absence of relevant theoretical models for interpreting the role of such factors in the counseling process as broadly defined (Helms, 1994a; Helms & Cook, in press). Consequently, the tendency has been to impose the same set of multicultural competencies on clients regardless of their cultural characteristics. For the most part, "cultural" in such instances typically means whatever the advocate would have it mean at the moment.

In this chapter, we will emphasize race and culture as critical differential aspects of human diversity in the United States, although our perspective may have similar implications for other aspects of diversity as well. Moreover, we will suggest that race and culture are not synonymous constructs, and that each may have different implications for the counseling process as well as the therapist's level of competence within that process (Helms, 1994b; Helms & Cook, in press).

Our perspective is that multicultural competence does not require a unique set of skills per se, but rather requires a specific type of philosophical orientation—an orientation in which responsivity to the relevant sociopolitical dynamics of race and principles of cultural socialization are integrated into the counseling process regardless of the client's ostensible sociodemographic characteristics (Richardson & Molinaro, in press). In making our case, we will (a) discuss the origins of the current multicultural competencies movement as we see it, (b) redefine relevant constructs, and (c) discuss the implications for treatment and training of a multicultural approach that is defined by psychological attributes of counselors and clients.

Origins of Multicultural Competencies

According to Helms (1994a), the contemporary interest in assessment and implementation of multiculturalism and multicultural competencies in the counseling and psychotherapy process has its roots in the racial civil rights movement of the 1960s and early 1970s. As activists within the mental health fields began to pay better attention to the mental health needs of racial and ethnic minority groups (henceforth, visible racial and ethnic groups or VREGs; Cook & Helms, 1988), the dearth and inadequacy of theoretical models for guiding appropriate interventions became evident.

For example, S. Sue, Ito, and Bradshaw (1982) recognized the prevalence of the "deficit model" for "diagnosing" the mental health of African, Asian, Indigenous, and Latino/Latina Americans. Under this model, all of the visible racial and ethnic groups except Asian Americans were assumed to have serious identity and self-esteem deficits due to societal racism. Thus, commentaries on the therapy-related sociopolitical implications of race during that era reveal a focus on the psychological damage or societal "disadvantage" to members of disempowered racial and ethnic groups and their consequent need for interventions intended to foster self-empowerment (Gunnings & Simpkins, 1972; Sue & Sue, 1990).

As detailed elsewhere, the deficit model had many negative implications for members of visible racial and ethnic groups, including the following: (a) the overemphasis on the alleged impairments of VREGs virtually eliminated recognition of the strengths, competencies, and skills of members of these nondominant racial or ethnic groups; (b) the VREG person was the exclusive focus of remediation efforts as opposed to the societal systems that were presumably responsible for the person's deleterious circumstances; and (c) White Americans, regardless of their level of psychological impairment, became the standard for defining mental health.

Nevertheless, an asset of the deficit model was that it represented a subtle shift in the conceptualization of mental health problems. Pathology was no longer defined exclusively by the character of individual VREGs, but could be elicited by the societal systems in which VREGs were expected to function effectively. In the mental health professions, this shift is still evident in the relatively large number of studies of mental health treatment and service delivery systems (e.g., Sue, McKinney, Allen, & Hall, 1974;

Snowden & Cheung, 1990). Such studies of service utilization, differential diagnosis, and premature attrition are based on usually implicit assumptions of possible racial or ethnic cultural discrimination within mental health systems.

Moreover, if counseling competence is considered to pertain to those activities in which the counselor engages during the counseling process, then the deficit model did contribute to a particular definition of competence. The model viewed conditions in the environment external to the counseling process per se as being responsible for racial and ethnic cultural symptomology. Therapists were more often considered to have the best interests of clients at heart, even if they were also assumed to be ignorant of what was in the VREG client's best interests. That is, discrimination occurred within the broad society and perhaps within the extraneous mental health environment(s) in which a particular counselor-client interaction occurred, but it presumably did not occur in the one-to-one counseling relationship.

Consequently, one of the first sets of multicultural competencies to be defined was the capacity of the counselor to teach skills and assist VREG clients in negotiating societal systems (Gunnings & Simpkins, 1972). In other words, facilitation of client empowerment was defined as a critical aspect of competent counselor behavior. This theme remains a strong aspect of present-day multicultural-competence perspectives.

Equally important but overshadowed themes were the differential influences of the race-related psychological and cultural characteristics of therapists and clients on the quality of the therapy process. With respect to race specifically, early theorists (e.g., Jones & Seagull, 1977; Vontress, 1971) proposed counseling process models by which clients' manifestations of internalized racism could be interpreted (e.g., Sue & Sue, 1990). Furthermore, although relevant research was rare, these early theorists and researchers seemed to understand that underlying the construct of race—or rather racial-group classification—were psychological factors (e.g., attitudes, behavioral styles). The expression of these psychological factors were presumed to have implications for the diagnosis of clients' intrapersonal dynamics within and outside of counseling or therapy and therapists' manifestations of countertransference issues during counseling or therapy, as well as for the quality of the dynamics of the overall therapy process itself.

However, speculation about competent use of race in the counseling process, conceptualized as quality of psychological functioning as it pertains to racial classification, is a fairly recent phenomenon (Helms, 1984; Helms & Cook, in press). Thus, clearly stated competencies for integrating racial dynamics other than empowerment or sociopolitical dynamics as previously discussed do not exist.

For the most part, the early racial process models dealt with the mental health issues of Black Americans. As the multicultural mental health movement broadened its focus to encompass the mental health concerns of sociodemographic groups in addition to African Americans, various socially defined racial groups (e.g., Asians and Blacks), ethnic groups (e.g., various Native American communities or nations), and cultural groups (e.g., Latino/as and women) came to the forefront of the multicultural movement. Attention to the group-related dynamics within the psychotherapy process of these additional groups was justified because their mental health needs also had been neglected in some manner in traditional Western applied psychology. However, though the numbers and varieties of cultural groups in need of mental health services increased, group-specific models for explaining the counseling process as it pertained specifically to members of the relevant groups did not. Instead, the same sort of imprecise admonitions against "counselor insensitivity" that had been used to promote better services for Black clients were also applied to the new groups (see Ridley, Mendoza, Kanitz, Angermeier, & Zenk, 1994, for a discussion).

Be that as it may, the pluralistic approach to multiculturalism has had some long-lasting beneficial effects. Perhaps the most enduring contribution of this expanded definition of multicultural competence was the promulgation of language diversity (use of languages other than "standard" English) as a potential impediment to successful counseling (Sue & Sue, 1990). In fact, nondominant language usage is probably the primary operational definition of culture in counseling and other mental health professions to this day. Nevertheless, one could make an argument in support of the equivalent importance and relevance to the counseling process of other psychological dimensions such as personality styles (Sue, 1977), worldviews (Ibrahim, 1991; Ivey, Ivey, & Simek-Morgan, 1993), or cultural value orientations (Carter, 1991).

With respect to counseling competencies, insufficient attention was given to the possibility that competent counseling might require attention to race and culture as separate domains for all clients, but not necessarily the same type or amount of attention. Nor was competency defined in terms of the many dimensions on which members of racial and ethnic cultural groups might be similar or dissimilar. Presumably, these oversights stemmed from the tendency to use simplistic definitions of race (e.g., disempowerment, demographic categories) and culture (e.g., language).

Moreover, theorists' narrow conceptualization of race as a demographic category or life condition specific to certain groups, primarily Blacks, meant that as practitioners began to "treat" other aspects of human diversity (e.g., ethnic group, gender, sexual orientation), they had no conceptual models for assessing the extent to which existing race-based models should or should not be generalized to other dimensions subsumed under the rubric of multiculturalism. In addition, they had no explicit conceptual framework for managing "racial" dynamics for "cultural" clients or "cultural" dynamics for "racial" clients.

Redefinitions

Helms and Cook (in press) have proposed a counseling and psychotherapy conceptual framework for using both race and culture as aspects of the counseling process. In their framework, they use the prefix *socio* to refer to societal classifications of people (e.g., sociorace, sociogender, socio-economic class) that are used as the justification for differential treatment or implementation of certain socialization practices. They use the prefix *psycho* (e.g., psychorace, psychogender, psycho-economic class) to refer to the person's internalization of societal principles relevant to the person's socially ascribed groupings. Thus, psychological characteristics are the subjective experience of racial or cultural socialization, including relevant attitudes, expectations, values, rituals, interpersonal skills, and more. Helms and Cook contend that therapists and clients bring such characteristics to their interactions, and these psycho-salient characteristics may influence the success of the process as much as any other aspect of the people involved therein.

According to Helms (in press), differentiating sociodemographic categories from principles of socialization (e.g., exposure to or implementation of racism) and subjective experiencing of these principles (e.g., internalized racism) permits examination of the psychological effects of relevant social categories without reifying assumptions that such categories are necessarily innate or immutable aspects of the human condition. She contends that if separate domains of sociodemographic and psychodemographic characteristics can be identified, then relevant competencies can also be specified.

From this perspective, for example, racial classifications derive from consensual societal criteria rather than from biological or genetic determinants (e.g., Yee, Fairchild, Weizmann, & Wyatt, 1993). Personal or individual reactions to racial classifications (e.g., racial identity, skin color negativity) occur in response to being treated as though one's racial classification had objective innate meaning. Thus, in these instances, relevant competencies would include specific knowledge of the kinds of reactions that might occur in response to dominant or nondominant racial group socialization. They would also include the capacity to "diagnose" reactions.

Also, Helms and Cook (in press) provide some distinctions among the constructs of *race, ethnic groups,* and *culture* on both sociodemographic and psychological dimensions that might be useful for developing diagnostic or assessment competencies. They propose that *race*—or, more accurately, *socioracial classifications*—are sociopolitical and economic classification systems used to allocate societal resources differentially. They suggest that persons come to understand the position of their (socio)racial group in the societal sociopolitical and socioeconomic hierarchies by means of information communicated about their group vicariously (e.g., media) and directly (e.g., incidents of racial discrimination), as well as by societal laws, customs, and traditions.

Psychological race, according to Helms and Cook (in press), develops in response to the contemporary sociopolitical racial system and the socialization that results from it. Thus, just as members of groups that benefit from racial discrimination may come to view themselves as superior to groups that do not so benefit, members of groups that do not benefit may come to think of themselves or other members of their group as inferior.

Specification of the type of competencies necessary for effectively and appropriately managing psychological race and counselor-client racial dynamics never has been satisfactorily addressed in the applied psychology literature. Nevertheless, it seems that racial competence requires that the therapist be capable of assessing (a) the client's race-related socialization, (b) the client's internalized experience of such socialization, and (c) the implications of each of these components on the quality of the client's functioning. Moreover, the therapist should be able to assess the impact of sociorace and psychorace on his or her own quality of functioning with each client. Such self-assessment should include an analysis of the therapist's own expectations and stereotypes as they pertain to clients of the same racial, ethnic, and social class categories as the client with whom the therapist is working.

Nowadays, racial and quasi-ethnic identity models are available for guiding the therapist's self-exploration and assessment of client racial dynamics (e.g., Helms, 1990, 1992). However, strategies for assessing environmental manifestations of the relevant socialization principles are rudimentary at best.

Ethnic group is a manner of classifying people according to their ancestral origins and/or the presumed origins of at least one of their potential cultures.

However, the concept is rarely used to denote the specific content of a culture (i.e., group-related behaviors and mental processes). Because ethnic group is typically used as a euphemism for racial classification in society as well as in the mental health professions, various theorists (Betancourt & Lopez, 1992; Helms, 1994a) have recommended that the terms *ethnic, ethnic group,* or *ethnicity* be used when one can specify specific cultural content dimensions to which the terms allude, but not as proxies for socioracial categories.

Implicit in the concept of ethnicity is the notion that race and culture are not synonyms. Nor are ethnic cultures in this country necessarily hierarchical as are racial classifications; rather, they are the day-to-day strategies originally adopted by a group of people to ensure its survival in the environmental context in which it found itself (Helms, 1994b). Using this more specific definition, spoken language would be an aspect of cultural content, but skin color per se would not. People of different skin colors can share the same culture and cultural (as well as biological) origins.

Moreover, ethnic groups may be assessed at sociodemographic as well as psychodemographic levels. Teaching or exposing a person to a group's language is a socioethnic socialization practice. Capacity to speak the language—or language competence—is a psychoethnic reaction to such socialization. In this regard, special competencies for particular groups (e.g., Spanish language competence for treating Spanish-speaking clients) occasionally have been discussed in the relevant literature, but only with respect to a narrow range of ethnic cultural groups.

For example, until recently (Landrine & Klonoff, 1996) African Americans were never the focus of empirical studies of psychoculture or acculturation, whereas Latino\Latina and Asian Americans were virtually never the focus of psychoracial studies (Canabal, 1995; Kohatsu, 1992). To the extent that ethnicity is attributed to some groups but not to others and race is attributed to some groups but not to others in the applied literature, it is likely that counselors and mental health professionals will lack the competence to address the differential psychological and socialization issues of race and ethnicity for clients regardless of their visible manifestations of these two sets of attributes.

Culture—at least subjective culture—means the internalized values, beliefs, and rituals that, among other things, define any group or collective. Thus, a person might have internalized a variety of cultures including racial, ethnic, gender, occupational, and so forth. Each of these cultures might consist of different content (e.g., socialization principles). Various theoretical models exist for focusing attention on one aspect of subjective culture rather than another. For example, Hofstede's (1980) factor-derived and Kluckhohn and Strodtbeck's (1961) value-orientations models both have been recommended for use in assessing client dynamics and providing a focus for culture-specific counseling interventions (Carter, 1991).

Hofstede's model emphasizes normative "personality" characteristics of groups. Briefly, Hofstede's (1980) dimensions are as follows: (a) individualism, favoring of individual desires, needs, and attributes over analogous dimensions of the group; (b) masculinity, preference for agentic or male-dominated rather than expressive or female-dominated aspects of the culture; (c) uncertainty avoidance, avoidance of situations in which the outcome is ambiguous because norms are unclear; and (d) power distance, valuing of a hierarchical social structure.

Kluckhohn and Strodtbeck's (1961) model emphasizes sets of values that guide human behavior. Their motivational model assumes that the answers to five basic life questions guide a person's and her or his group's quality of functioning in the world. The questions (and possible answers) are as follows: (a) What is the nature of humankind (basically evil, basically good, or both)? (b) What is the nature of social relationships (lineal, collateral, hierarchical)? (c) What is a person's relationship to nature (mastery, harmony, subordination)? (d) What is the nature of time (past, present, future)? (e) In what type of activity does one engage (doing, being, becoming)?

Either of these models might be used to determine what aspects of culture are salient for a client and/or his or her relevant cultural groups, as well as how culture is expressed within a particular group. Also, the various aspects of the potentially group-related cultures might be differentially salient and important to the individual client (and therapist) and, consequently, the counseling process. Helms (1994b) uses the term *metaculture* to mean the dominant culture(s) or the culture to which everyone within a society is expected to conform. In the United States, the metaculture is the so-called American culture.

People who do not, will not, or cannot conform to the metaculture are often the targets of not necessarily volitional ethnocentrism. For example, for some bilingual people (e.g., Spanish-English), the expectation that they perform as well in their second language (i.e., English) as native speakers of the language do may be a stressful consequence of ethnocentrism. Thus a culturally responsive counselor must be capable not only of assessing the salience of clients' cultures and the ways in which cultures are manifested for each client (and therapist), but also the societal acculturative stressors and forces that may result when the client does not conform to the metaculture.

Multicultural Competencies

Insofar as we can tell, most contemporary conceptualizations of multicultural competence come from a seminal paper originally proffered by Sue, Bernier, et al. (1982) and later updated by Sue, Arredondo, and McDavis (1992). They provided a list of competencies divided into three categories: attitudes, knowledge, and skills. Sue, Bernier, et al.'s competencies have become a landmark in the field because they initially awakened theorists', researchers', and practitioners' attention to the reality that traditional Western approaches to counseling and psychotherapy minimized the unique contributions of clients' and therapists' sociodemographic and psychodemographic characteristics to the therapy process.

Most measures of multicultural counseling competencies (e.g., Coleman, 1994; LaFromboise & Foster, 1992; Ponterotto, 1994) use Sue, Bernier, et al.'s competencies as their framework. In addition, the American Psychological Association (1993) has provided a set of service guidelines that provide some suggestions for addressing issues of culture during the helping process.

The advantage of having access to a specific set of competencies is that they permit one to think about multiculturalism in more "culturally diverse" ways. For example, Ponterotto's (1994) and Coleman's (1994) versions of multicultural competence suggest that it is an active process in which the practitioner continuously engages him- or herself, rather than a passive memorization task. One cannot merely memorize cultural competence, but must learn and demonstrate it through a variety of active self-involving strategies and procedures. They each offer some creative and innovative modifications of existing methodologies as a means of enhancing such self-involvement.

Sodowsky et al. (1994) and D'Andrea (1994) illustrate the importance of varied life experiences in shaping multicultural competence. It appears that teaching the therapist and client to recognize and appreciate the socialization forces that occur in their respective cultural contexts might be the best strategy for promoting multicultural competence in counseling and psychotherapy as well as for life more broadly defined. Whereas a universalistic interpretation is not necessarily inherent in Sue, Bernier, et al.'s (1982) statement of their competencies, most developers of measures and/or operational definitions of multicultural competencies have tended to interpret them in the same way for virtually all sociodemographic groups.

Thus, heretofore, multicultural competence seems to have come to mean that the same skills, awarenesses, and knowledges are required to treat every aspect of human diversity—gender, immigration status, social class, race, ethnic group, sexual orientation, ad infinitum. It is probably the case that many of these sociodemographic domains do require a flexible perspective, but it is not clear that counselors will have to attend to each of these aspects of diversity with all or even most clients. In our experience, issues of race, ethnic culture, and ethnicity generate more consistently strong, negative, and unpredictable responses from counselors-in-training (and our professional colleagues) than virtually any other aspects of personhood.

Because multicultural specialists have relied on all-inclusive or pluralistic conceptualizations and operational definitions of "culture" while ignoring "race," it is not surprising that most of the existing multicultural competencies inventories do so as well. Equally not surprising is the fact that teaching people the importance of being multiculturally competent counselors is much easier than teaching them how to be so (Johnson, 1987).

Nonetheless, perhaps an advantage of having a variety of researchers and theorists examining multicultural competencies, even from ambiguous perspectives, is that such information makes it easier to see some of the issues that need to be resolved before mental health academics can adequately teach, learn, demonstrate, and measure multicultural competence. A first step in increasing and improving the specificity of the construct of multicultural competencies is to move back a step or two and seriously consider what we intend the construct to mean. In our rush to develop an all-inclusive construct, "multiculturalism" has become essentially a meaningless construct.

Multiculturalism, in our opinion, should refer to the integration of dimensions of client cultures into pertinent counseling theories, techniques, and practices with the specific intent of providing clients of all sociodemographic and psychodemographic variations with effective mental health services (Richardson & Molinaro, in press). Consequently, multicultural competence in counseling and psychotherapy should refer to the capacity to read the various cultural dynamics of clients (and therapists) and to react to each of these aspects of cultures in a manner that best suits the client's mental health needs and the therapist's relevant skills.

Yet being a competent multicultural counselor might be much more difficult than one might suppose, because cultural dynamics are so subtle. Of the various dimensions described by Hofstede (1980) and Kluckhohn and Strodtbeck (1961), individualism-collectivism might be particularly useful for illustrating the complexity of being multiculturally competent in a universalistic manner. Considerable empirical information exists to the effect that not only can cultures be differentiated on the basis of individualism-collectivism, but also that the behaviors of people socialized in one type of cultural environment rather than the other can be discriminated.

Consider, for example, the constructs of "time competence" and "emotion competence." In individualistic cultures, a cultural content dimension that Hofstede (1980) found was most strongly reflected in (presumably) White American and European cultures rather than other cultures of the world, was that time is a quantity to be managed and conserved. Thus, Diaz-Guerrero (1979) found that Americans rush time whereas Mexicans prolong it. Moreover, in collectivistic cultures (e.g., among African, Asian, Indigenous, and Latino/Latina Americans), time is expressed via processes or events (e.g., rites of passage, acts of nature).

Nevertheless, in most therapist training programs, therapists are taught that a 50-minute session is sacrosanct. But what if the client isn't finished? The individualistic cultural approach, which most counselors and therapists have been taught, is to change the client to fit the 50 minutes by restructuring her or his therapy expectations. However, a multiculturally competent therapist might shift time orientations to be congruent with the client's *demonstrated* orientation.

Or consider the construct of emotional expression. Although emotions may be universal, cultures differ in the extent to which particular emotions can be expressed in various settings. The cultural rules that govern displays of emotions are called "cultural display rules" (Ekman, 1992). Matsumoto (in press) showed that different cultural display rules pertain for members of the following self-designated socioracial groups: Asian, Black, Hispanic/Latino, and White Americans. For example, he found that Whites differed from Asians in the extent to which they believed that contempt was an appropriate public emotion and from Blacks and Latinos with respect to disgust.

Be that as it may, few psychologists have attempted operationally to define and assess culture in a manner that moves beyond mere racial or ethnic group classifications. Many use the term *multiculturalism* as a euphemism for every conceivable dimension on which people could possibly be classified—or, with the possible exception of race, whatever particular dimension is of interest to some advocate. Therefore, when multicultural advocates charge therapists and other applied psychologists to become multiculturally competent, it is impossible to tell what psychologists are expected to do or to know. In the absence of clear conceptual models focused on the counseling process (in this case), it is impossible for even the willing trainee to discern what is expected of her or him in order to be deemed competent. A clear conceptual model would provide guidelines for assessing which types of diversity are equally salient and important (Ridley et al., 1994).

Implications for Therapy Research

So far, we have discussed a variety of conceptual holes in the multicultural competence movement in counseling and psychotherapy. Perhaps our discussion of the lack of adequate empirically based information by which to fill these holes was more subtle. Nevertheless, we think that it is important that multicultural specialists extend the debate over the content of multicultural competence to include empirical investigations of proposed dimensions.

Also, we think that it might be possible to begin to conduct empirical investigations of conceptual issues in the area of multicultural competence even if such investigations are not guided by formal theoretical or conceptual frameworks. Related to this point, Helms (in press) has advised that models might be developed whose specific purpose is to define the measurement and assessment issues of a domain even in the absence of a specific theory-driven question or theoretical orientation.

Thus, with respect to racial, cultural, and social class constructs, Helms (in press) speculated that measurement and assessment of relevant variables could occur at at least two levels of observation, socio-domains and psycho-domains. *Socio-domains* refer to behaviors and observable processes that occur at the environmental or interpersonal level with respect to the person (i.e., client or therapist, in this case) being observed. *Psycho-domains* refer to person-level or intrapsychic domains of observations (e.g., psychorace). According to her empirical framework, the quality of human functioning can be assessed and perhaps manipulated at each of these levels either separately or in combination.

Tables 3.1 and 3.2 show some examples of how the domains of race and culture might be operationally defined at the two proposed levels of specificity. The variables used as possible examples of operational definers should be self-explanatory, because we have discussed most of the relevant racial and cultural factors in other sections of the present chapter. In addition, the content of Tables 3.1 and 3.2 is intended to be thought-provoking rather than exhaustive. Although our intention is not to do so, generalizing the empirical framework to other aspects of diversity ought to be possible as well. Moreover, with respect to multicultural competence per se, the proposed observational levels may be examined at different levels of the counseling process as well.

For example, the counseling process in general might be (perhaps simplistically) conceptualized as consisting of the following four components: (a) client, (b) counselor, (c) process or interaction, and (d) outcome. Examination of the socio-domain with respect to culture might involve a focus on the

Table 3.1 Some Indicators of the Person-Level of Observation as It Pertains to the Counseling Process

Indicator	Counseling Example
Psychoculture	
Language Proficiency (Sue et al., 1991)	Counselor's ability to communicate in the language in which the client expresses emotions; client's competence in the language of his other family
Value Orientation (Kluckhohn & Strodtbeck, 1991)	Counselor and client levels of individualism-collectivism
Cultural Competence (LaFromboise et al., 1990)	Client's skill in performing age-appropriate social roles or duties in the culture of origin; therapist's skill in performing according to her or his theoretical orientation
Psychorace	
Racial Identity (Helms, 1994b)	Client's and counselor's manner or internalizing racial socialization and its impact on cognitions
Racism Coping Strategies (Meijer, 1993)	The client's and therapist's style (e.g., distancing, reappraisal) of reacting to negative race-related events in his or her life
Perceived Racial Climate (Thompson & Jenal, 1994)	Client's and/or counselor's perceptions of the level and quality of racial tensions in the environment

nature of familial socialization practices for the client, the cultural socialization messages implicit in the therapist's professional training, patterns of verbal or nonverbal interactions within the process, and changes in one or more of these aspects with respect to outcome (see Table 3.2).

Similarly, with respect to the psycho-domain, client's and therapist's value orientations could be assessed; the types of interactions resulting from congruent or incongruent therapist-client matches could be the focus of process studies; and remediation of psychological symptoms under varying conditions of therapist-client match might be a suitable psychological outcome variable.

Examples of how Helms's empirical framework might be implemented are not readily available. However, Thompson and Jenal's (1994) study of the types of counseling interactions that occur when Black and White therapists avoid discussing racial issues with Black women clients provides an example of how race might be studied at a socio-observational level in therapy dyads. Also, the study could easily have been modified to reflect both levels.

In Thompson and Jenal's study, therapists were instructed to avoid discussing race with their clients. Thus, they were perhaps simulating a race-

Table 3.2 Some Indicators of the Environmental-Level of Observation as It Pertains to the Counseling Process

Indicator	Counseling Example
	Sociocultural
Ethnic Culture's Socialization Practices	A cultural group's rules and definitions of mental health may shape therapy participants' help-seeking behaviors and expectations
Linguistic Community of Origin	Client's and therapist's capacity to communicate with one another effectively is influenced by their shared linguistic backgrounds
	Socioracial
Degree of Racial Segregation-Integration	Lack of opportunity to acculturate or be assimilated into the dominant group makes it less likely that the therapist or client will know, be competent in, or value its mental health practices
Objective Racial Climate	Discriminatory practices directed toward members of client's racial group may influence life options available to client
History of Intergroup Conflict	Counselors from a group with a history of negative treatment of the client's group may be rejected, even if the group's mistreatment happened long ago

related environmental or interpersonal socialization practice, avoiding the discussion of race. Therefore, the research manipulation occurred at the socio-observational level. If the extent to which clients and/or therapists were comfortable with the avoidance of racial discussions had also been assessed, then the psycho-observational or person-level factors would also have been included in Thompson and Jenal's design.

On the other hand, Carter and Helms (1992) investigated the self-reported intentions of counselors and reactions of clients in counseling dyads differing in levels of measured racial identity expressions. Their study illustrates how racial constructs might be investigated at the psycho-observational level, but not the socio-observational level. If they had analyzed the participants' actual behaviors during the counseling simulation, as Thompson and Jenal (1994) did, then the socio-observational level would also have been present in their study. Perhaps it is too demanding to expect any researcher to attend to both of the observational domains and each of the four counseling components within them. However, it might be useful for counseling and psychotherapy researchers to begin at least to think about how relevant constructs might be measured or manipulated.

In any case, the investigator's particular counseling interests probably determines which aspect of multicultural competence is the focus of his or her manipulation or assessment as well as which type of observational domain will be subjected to operational definition. Unfortunately, considerable creativity may be needed to find and/or create measures and research designs that are suitable for this more complex manner of examining racial and cultural parameters of multicultural competence.

Implications for Teaching Multicultural Competence

Nevertheless, while we are awaiting better focused models of multiculturalism and more relevant empirical investigations of such models, existing models and perspectives might be used to assist counselors and counselors-in-training to discover and apply a variety of perspectives in ways that acknowledge their own diversity as well as that of their clients. Diaz-Soto and Richardson (in press) have described their training approach for teaching practitioners to develop awareness, knowledge, and skills in responding effectively to racial and cultural dynamics in the counseling process.

The course is structured around Sue, Bernier, et al.'s (1982) three cross-cultural competency components that, for their purposes, are defined as follows: (a) awareness, the process of examining the content and validity of personal and societal attitudes, opinions, and assumptions about societal racial and cultural groups including one's own; (b) knowledge, acquisition and accurate comprehension of facts and information about the relevant racial and cultural groups; and (c) skills, the capacity to use awareness and knowledge to interact effectively with clients and colleagues regardless of their racial classification or cultural origins. Although the components of competence are not mutually exclusive, it might be useful to highlight some of the salient themes and interventions pertaining to each of them.

To enhance awareness, students are encouraged to experience the socio-racial and sociocultural impact of traditional counseling and mental health practices on individuals who violate the traditional racial and cultural assumptions implicit in the relevant socialization practices. Self-examination and analysis of person-environment stressors, as they involve the racial and cultural self, are addressed as an aspect of the awareness enhancement process. Various cultural socialization (Katz, 1985; Kluckhohn & Strodtbeck, 1961; LaFromboise, Trimble, & Mohatt, 1990) and racial consciousness models (Helms, 1994b; Ponterotto, 1988) are used to foster awareness and to explore the psychological consequences of socioracial and sociocultural socialization.

As previously mentioned, internalized psychoculture refers to attitudes, values, beliefs, and rituals acquired as a result of being socialized in a particular sociocultural group. Racial consciousness models describe intrapersonal and interpersonal interpretations of racial dynamics. To obtain maximum student involvement in the learning process, it is generally advisable to use models that reflect the sociodemographics (in this case, especially racial and ethnic categories) of the participants in the course. Thus, when the course consists of primarily White, individualistically oriented participants, the instructor should make sure that the focus of racial and cultural exploration is not limited to groups of color or nondominant cultural orientations. Instead, White participants are given the opportunity to examine their own psychoracial and cultural development, even if it is uncomfortable for them and/or the instructor (Meijer, 1993; Tatum, 1994).

To a large extent, enhancement of knowledge and awareness occur concurrently. However, Diaz-Soto and Richardson (in press) advise that ensuring the accuracy of the racial and cultural knowledge with which students leave the course requires that the instructor clarify key concepts and expose students to new information. With respect to clarification, involving students in redefining and/or defining concepts such as "culture," "multiculturalism," "diversity," "affirmative action," and others, is an essential experience for students to engage in as a group. Provision of accurate information should include factual historical and contemporary experiences of relevant societal groups, ideally through the eyes of members of the relevant groups. It should also include information about differential historical patterns of treatment of clients of various races and cultures as well as the customary patterns and styles of utilization of mental health services of members of the client's relevant sociodemographic groups (Snowden & Cheung, 1990; Sue, Fujino, Hu, Takeuchi, & Zane, 1991).

Lectures, reading assignments written from the perspectives of various socioracial and cultural groups, media presentations, class discussions, and group presentations by class members can serve as effective strategies for teaching knowledge and awareness. Helms (1990) discusses several models that have been used to match teaching materials to trainees' levels of racial and cultural development. Ponterotto (1988) and Tatum (1994) can be used to help prepare students and their instructors for the strong emotional issues that occur when one focuses on race and culture as mental health concerns.

Finally, it is worth noting that active participation in an interactive course with race and culture as its focus will most likely translate into some type of behavioral change, not always for the better. Following an intensive 14-week course, many participants in Diaz-Soto and Richardson's (in press) courses inevitably voluntarily share with the class the pain associated with their attempts to make behavioral changes, even if they only have had access to monoracial or monocultural environments.

Yet students are aware that brief self-improvement interventions are not sufficient for building their own confidence in their multicultural competencies. So are we. From our perspective, multicultural competence will only become a meaningful concept when academics, theorists, researchers, and practitioners turn their attention to addressing the age-old (paraphrased) question, "Which competencies work best for what aspects of diversity?"

References

American Psychological Association. (1993). Guidelines for providers of psychological services to ethnic, linguistic, and culturally diverse populations. *American Psychologist, 48*(1), 45-48.

Betancourt, H., & Lopez, S. R. (1993). The study of culture, ethnicity, and race in American psychology. *American Psychologist, 48*(6), 629-637.

Canabal, I. (1995). *Latino group identities and collective and personal self-esteem.* Unpublished doctoral dissertation, University of Maryland, College Park.

Carter, R. T. (1991). Cultural values: A review of empirical research and implications for counseling. *Journal of Counseling and Development, 70,* 164-173.

Carter, R. T., & Helms, J. E. (1992). The counseling process as defined by relationship types: A test of Helms's interactional model. *Journal of Multicultural Counseling and Development, 28,* 181-201.

Coleman, H. (1994, August). *Assessment of multicultural counseling competencies—Using a portfolio approach.* Paper presented at the Annual Convention of the American Psychological Association, Los Angeles.

Cook, D. A., & Helms, J. E. (1988). Visible racial/ethnic group supervisees' satisfaction with cross-cultural supervision as predicted by relationship characteristics. *Journal of Counseling Psychology, 35,* 268-274.

D'Andrea, M. (1994, August). *Multicultural counseling competencies and the call of conscience.* Paper presented at the Annual Convention of the American Psychological Association, Los Angeles.

Diaz-Guerrero, R. (1979). The development of coping style. *Human Development, 22,* 320-331.

Diaz-Soto, L., & Richardson, T. Q. (in press). Theoretical perspectives in multicultural applications. In R. Martin (Ed.), *On equal terms: Approaches to dealing with race, class, and gender in the classroom.* New York: SUNY Press.

Ekman, P. (1992). Facial expression of emotion: New findings, new questions. *Psychological Science, 3,* 34-38.

Fukuyama, M. A. (1990). Taking an universal approach to multicultural counseling. *Counselor Education and Supervision, 30,* 6-17.

Gunnings, T., & Simpkins, G. (1972). A systemic approach to counseling disadvantaged youth. *Personnel and Guidance Journal, 50,* 29-35.

Helms, J. E. (1984). Towards a theoretical explanation of the effects of race on counseling: A Black and White model. *The Counseling Psychologist, 12,* 153-165.

Helms, J. E. (1990). *Black and White racial identity: Theory, research, and practice.* Westport, CT: Greenwood.

Helms, J. E. (1992). *A race is a nice thing to have: A guide to being a White person or understanding the White persons in your life.* Topeka, KS: Content Communications.

Helms, J. E. (1994a). How multiculturalism obscures racial factors in the therapy process: Comment on Ridley et al. (1994), Sodowsky et al. (1994), Ottavi et al. (1994), and Thompson et al. (1994). *Journal of Counseling Psychology, 41,* 162-165.

Helms, J. E. (1994b). Racial identity and other "racial" constructs. In E. J. Trickett, R. J. Watts, & D. Birman (Eds.), *Human diversity* (pp. 285-311). San Francisco: Jossey-Bass.

Helms, J. E. (in press). The triple quandary of race, culture, and social class in cognitive ability testing. In D. Flanaghan, J. L. Genshaft, & P. L. Harrison (Eds.), *Beyond traditional intellectual assessment: Contemporary and emerging theories, tests, and issues.* New York: Guilford.

Helms, J. E., & Cook, D. A. (in press). *Using race and culture in counseling and psychotherapy: Theory and process.* Fort Worth, TX: Harcourt Brace Jovanovitch.

Hofstede, G. (1980). *Culture's consequences.* Beverly Hills, CA: Sage.

Ibrahim, F. A. (1991). Contribution of cultural worldview to generic counseling and development. *Journal of Counseling and Development, 70,* 13-19.

Ivey, A. E., Ivey, M. B., & Simek-Downing, L. (1993). *Counseling and psychotherapy: Integrating skills, theory, and practice.* Englewood Cliffs, NJ: Prentice Hall.

Johnson, S. D., Jr. (1987). Knowing that versus knowing how: Toward achieving expertise through multicultural training for counseling. *The Counseling Psychologist, 18,* 41-50.

Jones, A., & Seagull, A. A. (1977). Dimensions of the relationship between the Black client and the White therapist. *The American Psychologist, 32,* 850-855.

Katz, J. H. (1985). The sociopolitical nature of counseling. In Cross-cultural counseling [Special issue]. *The Counseling Psychologist, 13,* 615-624.

Kohatsu, E. L. (1992). *The effects of racial identity and acculturation on anxiety, assertiveness, and ascribed identity among Asian American college students.* Unpublished doctoral dissertation, University of Maryland, College Park.

Kluckhohn, F., & Strodtbeck, F. (1961). *Variations in value orientations.* Evanston, IL: Row, Peterson.

LaFromboise, T. D., & Foster, S. L. (1992). Cross-cultural training: Scientist-practitioner model and methods. *The Counseling Psychologist, 20,* 472-489.

LaFromboise, T. D., Trimble, J. E., & Mohatt, G. V. (1990). Counseling intervention and American Indian tradition: An integrative approach. *The Counseling Psychologist, 18,* 628-654.

Landrine, H. A., & Klonoff, E. (1996). *African American acculturation: Deconstructing race and reviving culture.* Thousand Oaks, CA: Sage.

Locke, D. C. (1990). A not so provincial view of multicultural counseling. *Counselor Education and Supervision, 30,* 18-25.

Matsumoto, D. (in press). Ethnic differences in affect, intensity, emotion judgments, display rules, and self-reported emotional expression. *Motivation and Emotion.*

Meijer, C. (1993). *White racial identity development and responses to diversity in an Introduction to Psychology course and curriculum.* Unpublished doctoral dissertation, University of Maryland, College Park.

Pedersen, P. B. (1988). *A handbook for developing multicultural awareness.* Alexandria, VA: American Counseling Association.

Ponterotto, J. G. (1988). Racial consciousness development among White counselor trainees: A stage model. *Journal of Multicultural Counseling and Development, 16,* 146-156.

Ponterotto, J. G. (1994, August). *Competency assessment—Moving beyond multicultural awareness.* Paper presented at the Annual Convention of the American Psychological Association, Los Angeles.

Richardson, T. Q., & Molinaro, K. (in press). Counselor self-awareness: A prerequisite for multicultural counseling. *Journal of Counseling and Development.*

Ridley, C., Mendoza, D. W., Kanitz, B. E., Angermeier, L., & Zenk, R. (1994). Cultural sensitivity in multicultural counseling. A perceptual schema model. *Journal of Counseling Psychology, 41,* 125-136.

Snowden, L., & Cheung, F. K. (1990). Use of inpatient mental health services by members of ethnic minority groups. *The American Psychologist, 45,* 347-355.

Sodowsky G. R., Taffe, R. C., Gutkin, T. B., & Wise, S. L. (1994). Development of the Multicultural Counseling Inventory: A self-report measure of multicultural competencies. *Journal of Counseling Psychology, 41,* 137-148.

Sue, D. W. (1977). Counseling the culturally different: A conceptual analysis. *Personnel and Guidance Journal, 55,* 422-425.

Sue, D. W., Arredondo, P., & McDavis, R. J. (1992). Multicultural counseling competencies and standards: A call to the profession. *Journal of Multicultural Counseling and Development, 26,* 64-84.

Sue, D. W., Bernier, J. E., Durran, A., Feinberg, L., Pedersen, P., Smith, E. J., & Vasquez-Nuttall, E. (1982). Position paper: Cross-cultural counseling competencies. *The Counseling Psychologist, 10,* 45-52.

Sue, D. W., & Sue, D. (1990). *Counseling the culturally different: Theory and practice* (2nd ed.). New York: John Wiley.

Sue, S., Fujino, D. C., Hu, L. T., Takeuchi, D. T., & Zane, N. W. S. (1991). Community mental health services for ethnic minority groups: A test of the cultural responsiveness hypothesis. *Journal of Counseling Psychology, 59,* 533-540.

Sue, S., Ito, J., & Bradshaw, C. (1982). Ethnic minority research: Trends and directions. In E. E. Jones & S. J. Korchin (Eds.), *Minority mental health* (pp. 37-58). New York: Praeger.

Sue, S., McKinney, H., Allen, D. & Hall, J. (1974). Delivery of community health services to Black and White clients. *Journal of Consulting and Clinical Psychology, 42,* 794-801.

Tatum, B. (1994). Talking about race, learning about racism: The application of racial identity development theory in the classroom. *Harvard Educational Review, 62,* 1-24.

Thompson, C.E.F., & Jenal, S. T. (1994). Interracial and intraracial quasi-counseling interactions when counselors avoid discussing race. *Journal of Counseling Psychology, 41,* 484-491.

Vontress, C. E. (1971). Racial differences: Impediments to rapport. *Journal of Counseling Psychology, 18,* 7-13.

Yee, A. H., Fairchild, H. H., Weizmann, F., & Wyatt, G. E. (1993). Addressing psychology's problems with race. *American Psychologist, 48,* 1132-1140.

PART II

Multicultural Education and Training

4

Sex Matters

GENDER AND SEXUAL ORIENTATION IN TRAINING FOR MULTICULTURAL COUNSELING COMPETENCY

Ruth E. Fassinger

Beth Sperber Richie

Multiculturalism has been termed the "fourth force" in counseling, implying a powerful paradigm shift that radically alters the way we think about clients and approach our work with them (Pedersen, 1991). Much of this paradigmatic change focuses on increased attention to the cultural forces that shape and interact with the developing individual, implying a dynamic, reciprocal relationship between intrapsychic forces and environmental influences related to one's cultural milieu. Moreover, the burgeoning literature in multicultural counseling is just beginning to attend to the interactive effects of multiple cultural identities and multiple sources of oppression in conceptualizing mental health issues and problems (e.g., Board of Ethnic Minority Affairs, Task Force on Delivery of Services to

Ethnic Minority Populations, 1991; Reynolds & Pope, 1991). It is crucial that we begin to train counselors to think complexly, rather than categorically, about the many manifestations of culture they will experience with their clients, as well as the many cultural assumptions that have shaped their own lives.

This chapter posits that sex—what sex one is as well as the sex of one's intimate partners—constitutes a primary organizing principle used by people in their interpretation of daily experiences and in their construction of attitudes and worldviews. As such, sex functions as a pervasive (often nonconsciously perceived) cultural force that powerfully affects one's attitudes, the bases of knowledge to which one is exposed and has access, and the interpersonal modes and skills one develops in response to others in the environment. In training for multicultural counseling competency (MCC), it is critically important that we examine the myriad effects of growing up in a society in which sex *matters*—where one's sex (male, female) and preferences for intimacy (lesbian/gay/bisexual, heterosexual) necessitate active awareness and struggle with strong societal assumptions that a particular sex is better than another (sexism) or that a particular orientation toward intimacy is better than others (heterosexism/homophobia). Like the fish, experientially constricted by its total inability to imagine anything other than a wet world in which to live, we too are bound by gendered, sexist, heterosexist, homophobic assumptions (or "nonconscious ideologies," Bem & Bem, 1970) that are so pervasive and non-obvious that we are unable to imagine our world being anything other than what it always has been. Treating sex as a cultural variable that has both unique and additive effects vis-à-vis other cultural variables, and viewing cross-gender and cross-orientation counseling situations as legitimate cross-cultural experiences, allows us to scrutinize these nonconscious ideologies carefully and translate our increased awareness into more sensitive intervention and more effective counselor training.

In conceptualizing gender and sexual orientation as components of a potential cross-cultural therapeutic relationship, it is easy to fall into conceptual traps. One (client-as-problem) is that the presenting difficulty to be resolved is rooted in the cultural uniqueness of the client, and that effective counseling simply requires extensive knowledge of that client's cultural milieu (as a woman or as a lesbian/gay/bisexual person) in order to understand predictable personality traits, behavioral choices, abilities, interests, and life roles. The corollary trap to the view of the client-as-problem is one that presumes that any difficulties that arise in the therapeutic process result from the biases, prejudices, and ignorance of the counselor, who has failed to develop an appropriate attitudinal stance or knowledge base for understanding the client accurately (counselor-as-problem). It must be remembered, however, that a counseling relationship is a dynamic, interactive exchange between two gendered, sexually oriented people, and each brings to the relationship her or his own cultural location, with all its attendant attitudes, beliefs, and interpersonal style. A focus on the relationship (rather than either individual to the exclusion of the other) can help to avoid guilt and blame, and can place the focus more appropriately on improving the therapeutic connection between two people that is the very foundation of counseling.

Although a detailed analysis of gender and sexual orientation in society and in counseling is beyond the scope of this chapter, it is our intention to frame these issues in the context of multiculturalism, and to demonstrate their relevance to MCC training. Thus, in this chapter, we examine nonconscious ideologies related to gender and sexual orientation, and explore their potential effects on the attitudes, knowledge, and skills (see Sue & Sue, 1990) needed for effective multicultural counseling. We also make suggestions regarding ways in which MCC training can and should incorporate gender and sexual orientation.

Nonconscious Idealogies Regarding Gender and Sexual Orientation

Widely held assumptions regarding gender and sexual orientation can be manifested both in individuals (e.g., attitudes, beliefs, choices) and institutions (e.g., policies, procedures, implicit hierarchies, and social codes). When prevailing ideologies are rooted in oppression and advantage one cultural group over another, the negative effects of those ideologies become the "isms" (e.g., sexism, heterosexism/homophobia) that a multicultural perspective seeks to eradicate. Particularly alarming in terms of mental health is that the negative ideologies regarding particular groups of people come to be internalized by individuals who are themselves members of those groups, thus producing a "double whammy" of both external and internalized oppression with which the individual must contend. The multiple layers of therapeutic difficulty caused by negative nonconscious ideologies therefore can be daunting: (a) There are individuals needing help who are oppressed (b) by other people as well as (c) by institutions; (d) they also are struggling with having internalized much of the oppression they have experienced; and (e) they are seeking a uniquely interpersonally intimate form of help that, (f) as an institution, is itself grounded in the negative ideologies inherent in the larger culture; delivered by other individuals who are themselves products of (g) the dominant culture and, (h) for many, oppressed groups within that dominant culture, as well as (i) engaged in their own ongoing struggles with their particular location(s) in that culture. Given such complexity, it should cause little surprise that ideologies, both conscious and nonconscious, and in both counselors and clients, powerfully affect the therapeutic relationship.

Ideology and Gender

Gender is a crucial determinant of people's life experiences, roles, behavior, opportunities, and orientation to the world around them (e.g., Cook, 1993; Deaux, 1985; Gilbert, 1992; Sherif, 1982). Gender role ideologies show variation within and among cultural groups, but within patriarchal societies such as ours, "constructed power" (Brod, 1987, cited in Gilbert, 1992) based on gender results in marked differences in social roles that put women at a considerable disadvantage relative to men. Although constrictive stereotypes based on traditional gender role ideology certainly have deleterious effects on men as well as women (Davenport & Yurich, 1991; Gilbert, 1992), our focus here is on their disproportionately negative impact on women.

Prevailing gender role ideologies in present U.S. society dictate that "[m]en tend to define themselves and their lives primarily through independent, goal-directed, assertive activity, and women through interdependent, nurturing relationships with others" (Cook, 1993, p. 229). This ideology carries along with it pervasive stereotypic expectations regarding personality traits (e.g., women should be gentle and expressive while men should be strong and instrumental), social roles (e.g., women are best suited to homemaking and child-rearing while men are suited to paid work outside the home), behaviors (e.g., women take care of others while men direct others), and even physical characteristics (e.g., women should be small and graceful while men should be large and powerful). Even where we have moved beyond these traditional stereotypic expectations, other modern stereotypes have developed to take their place: for example, the myth of the "Superwoman" who works outside the home but retains all of her traditional homemaking and child-rearing roles and fulfills all of her roles with stunning aplomb.

Unfortunately, gender-related bias in psychological research has prevented much movement beyond these stereotypes, in part because that research is embedded in the very beliefs it seeks to illuminate. Gilbert (1992) summarized the characteristics of psychological research that lead to bias in regard to gender. The first of these Gilbert refers to as "context stripping," in which social phenomena are isolated from the context in which they typically occur, a legacy of the positivist tradition in science that others have noted as well (Hoshmand, 1989). This approach to science renders the possibilities of multiple identities and knowledge based on connection un- thinkable (Belenky, Clinchy, Goldberger, & Tarule, 1986; Reynolds & Pope, 1991). Yet, newer approaches that emphasize the construction of reality based on an individual's culture, gender, and worldviews (Tavris, 1991) have much to offer in fostering consideration of salient contextual influences in attempting to understand human functioning.

Related to the problem of context stripping, two additional characteristics noted by Gilbert (1992) as fostering bias in research are the focus on individual, intrapsychic variables to explain behavior, and the preoccupation in psychology with exploring sex differences rather than similarities (also see Hare-Mustin & Maracek, 1988). These are interactive problems, because in examining and documenting differences the focus has been on individual and internal characteristics that appear to be determined biologically and intrapsychically, rather than by environmental and external forces such as life experiences, resources, and power (Tavris, 1991). The former tend to be unchanging, whereas the latter alter and shift with particular circumstances. This may explain why most gender differences have not appeared consis- tently over many years of study (despite prevailing societal stereotypes to the contrary), as they are likely to be largely determined by situational rather than dispositional factors (Tavris, 1991).

The final characteristic noted by Gilbert (1992) in biasing research is the positioning of White heterosexual men as the standard against which others are measured in terms of healthy psychological functioning, a bias resulting, in part, from the preponderance in the psychological literature of studies developed and conducted by White, Western, heterosexual, middle-class men on samples similar to themselves (Espín, 1993; Tavris, 1991). There has been a tendency in theory and research to generalize from this population to all others, and to judge characteristics of the "others" to be deficient or deviant when they differ from the accepted "norm" (Fitzgerald & Nutt, 1986; Gilbert, 1992; Tavris, 1991; Yoder & Kahn, 1993). It is worth noting that there never has been a similar threat to men that the current burgeoning literature on women will be generalized and assumed to apply to men as well (Tavris, 1991). We might ask ourselves why this is so, and what it implies about the relative valuing of knowledge regarding men and women in current scientific scholarship.

The bias inherent in positioning men as the psychological norm also reminds us of the importance of viewing women not only according to their gender, but incorporating culture, race, socioeconomic status, geography, age, sexual orientation, acculturation, and other variables into conceptualizations of women's lives and functioning in order to capture their multiple identities (Comas-Diaz & Greene, 1994; Yoder & Kahn, 1993). In a society characterized by the oppression and marginalization of many groups, it is easy to fall into the trap of assuming that the lives of White, Western, heterosexual, middle-class women studied by other White (etc.) women apply somehow to *all* women, and of judging differences in other groups of women (e.g., lesbians, women of color, working-class women) as deficient or deviant in relation to a new (but perhaps equally oppressive) women's norm (Comas-Diaz & Greene, 1994; Enns, 1993; Espín, 1993; Yoder & Kahn, 1993). Unfortunately, such ideological errors permeate the literature and obscure accurate knowledge about subgroups of women (Comas-Diaz & Greene, 1994).

It is also an unfortunate reality that societal ideologies regarding gender are reflected in the mental health system as well. Virtually all psychotherapy systems are based on White, Western, male, middle-class values (Enns, 1993; Espín, 1993; Katz, 1985). The cultural components of counseling described by Katz (1985) include many values that can be detrimental to the female client. For example, the focus on the individual and on intrapsychic factors in counseling minimizes a woman's connection to others and ignores the environmental (sexist) context in which she lives. The intolerance of passivity or inaction counters the gender role socialization of many women. The traditional counseling situation in which the expert therapist makes decisions and interpretations and shares them with the vulnerable client, especially in those situations in which the therapist is male and the client is female, parallel the social order in which men make decisions about and pass judgment on women's lives (Fitzgerald & Nutt, 1986; Good, Gilbert & Scher, 1990). Moreover, typical goals in counseling often include changing individual behavior and adapting to the societal status quo, which may not necessarily represent a healthy standard to which women should adapt (Broverman, Broverman, Clarkson, Rosenkrantz, & Vogel, 1970; Gilbert, 1992).

Research also has documented the role of therapists (both male and female) in the perpetuation of traditional gender role socialization (Fitzgerald & Nutt, 1986; Nickerson & Kremgold-Barrett, 1990). The classic Broverman studies (Broverman et al., 1970) dramatically demonstrated the view of many clinicians that behavior seen as normal and desirable for an adult female was very different from behavior seen as critical to general healthy adult functioning, creating a double bind for a woman that forced her to choose between being viewed as a normal female (and therefore unhealthy) or a healthy adult (and therefore an abnormal female). Other research since the Brovermans' groundbreaking work has documented sex bias in therapy (see Gilbert, 1992; Nickerson & Kremgold-Barrett, 1990), the most notable of which was carried out by the American Psychological Association. The report of the APA Task Force on Sex Bias and Sex Role Stereotyping in Psychotherapeutic Practice (American Psychological Association, 1975) surveyed 2,000 female psychotherapists regarding their knowledge of incidents of biased psychotherapeutic practice. Results (based on responses from several hundred participants) suggested that biased treatment resulted from the two underlying problems of values in therapy and psychologists' knowledge regarding women. The report further documented evidence of four general areas of biased treatment: (a) a tendency to foster traditional gender roles; (b) a devaluation of female clients; (c) an emphasis on the use of sexist psychoanalytic concepts and; (d) the sexualization of female clients, including having sexual intercourse with them. The report also called for actions to be taken, including education and training in women's issues and psychological processes. The report led to subsequent development of guidelines for counseling and psychotherapy (American Psychological Association, 1978; Division 17 Committee on Women, APA, 1979), as well as numerous books, articles, and chapters on the appropriate therapeutic treatment of women, and, more recently, men as well (see Gilbert, 1992).

Recent work has maintained that although analogue, anecdotal, and survey evidence for gender bias in therapy abounds, there has been little effort to address whether and how gender bias affects the outcome of therapy with women (Hyde, 1991; Nickerson & Kremgold-Barrett, 1990; Unger & Crawford, 1992). One concern raised repeatedly is that in most therapeutic situations environmental factors and cultural experiences are disregarded, and an individualistic focus is imposed in a way that causes many clients to believe that they are personally responsible for their problems (Gilbert, 1992; Katz, 1985; Unger & Crawford, 1992). Similar concerns also have been voiced in regard to racial/ethnic cultural groups in counseling (e.g., Sue & Sue, 1990), again demonstrating that gender is comparable to other cultural variables in the considerable influence it exerts on the counseling process.

Ideology and Sexual Orientation

In examining nonconscious ideologies in regard to sexual orientation, two decades of attitudinal research demonstrate quite clearly that prevailing societal notions assume heterosexuality as normative (Atkinson & Hackett, 1995; Fassinger, 1991; Garnets & Kimmel, 1991). Under this ideological assumption, all other preferences regarding intimate behavior must be viewed as deficient or immature at best (something that the lesbian/gay individual will "grow out of" in time), and deviant or abhorrent at worst (lesbian/gay people are sick, maladjusted perverts, and the AIDS epidemic represents divine retribution). There is a voluminous literature documenting societal heterosexism, homophobia, and discrimination, including persecution in the areas of education and employment, gay and lesbian families, health care, the legal/justice system, religious institutions, and violence against lesbian/gay/bisexual people (see Atkinson & Hackett, 1995; Diamant, 1993; Fassinger, 1991; and Garnets & Kimmel, 1991, for summaries of this literature).

Moreover, the literature clearly documents the difficulties that lesbians and gay men face in recognizing, accepting, integrating, and managing their stigmatized identities (Atkinson & Hackett, 1995; Fassinger, 1991; Garnets & Kimmel, 1991; Gonsiorek & Rudolph, 1991). Issues that have been discussed in this literature include invisibility, isolation, lack of information, lack of role models, negative attitudes from others, lack of family and social support, uninformed or biased helping professionals, religious prohibitions, workplace discrimination, lack of legal supports, and internalized homophobia. The internalization of oppressive attitudes and beliefs is particularly salient in considering counseling and counselor training, for at least two important reasons. First, the internalization of negative affect and ideas regarding same-sex preferences and lifestyles implies that fear, distrust, and (temporary) self-hatred are predictable reactions to recognizing one's stigmatized identity, and therefore can be viewed as normative coming out responses rather than individual pathology; the implications for diagnosis and intervention are quite obvious. Second, the internalization of homophobic ideologies suggests that inappropriate therapeutic behavior arising from unresolved intrapsychic conflicts can occur not only in heterosexuals who are uninformed or prejudiced regarding sexual minority issues and people, but also in lesbian/gay/bisexual professionals who have not engaged in a personal process of confronting their internalized heterosexism and homophobia.

Unfortunately, as is the case with ideologies concerning women, negative societal attitudes regarding lesbians and gay men are reflected in the mental health system as well (Atkinson & Hackett, 1995; Fassinger, 1991). Formal statements made by the American Psychological Association (Conger, 1975) declare that "homosexuality per se implies no impairment in judgment, reliability or general social and vocational capabilities" (p. 633), and that psychologists bear a responsibility to "take the lead in removing the stigma of mental illness long associated with homosexual orientations" (p. 633).

However, results of an recent APA study of bias in therapy with lesbians and gay men (Committee on Lesbian and Gay Concerns, 1990; Garnets, Hancock, Cochran, Goodchilds, & Peplau, 1991) suggest that the extent to which these tenets are carried out in actual practice is quite variable. The APA report documents a national survey study modeled after the 1975 Task Force study on sex bias (APA, 1975, discussed above), in which psychologists were asked to supply descriptions of specific critical incidents of "biased" and "sensitive" therapeutic practice of which they were aware.

Of the 2,544 psychologists who responded, 1,481 provided critical incidents, which were categorized into six broad areas: (a) *Assessment,* including believing that homosexuality is a form of pathology, attributing a lesbian/gay client's problems to sexual orientation, failing to recognize the effects of internalized oppression, and presuming heterosexuality or discounting a lesbian/gay self-identification; (b) *Intervention,* including focusing on sexual orientation when it is irrelevant, discouraging a client from being lesbian/gay, trying to change a client's sexual orientation, demeaning or trivializing lesbian/gay experience, abruptly terminating clients upon disclosure of homosexuality, making the renunciation of homosexuality a condition of treatment, and disclosing clients' sexual orientation inappropriately; (c) *Identity,* including lacking understanding of lesbian/gay identity development, not considering how identity development is affected by internalized homophobia, and underestimating the consequences of the client's disclosure of homosexuality to others; (d) *Intimate relationships,* including minimizing or trivializing the importance of same-sex intimate relationships, being insensitive to the realities of lesbian/gay relationships and using heterosexual frame of reference, being unsupportive of same-sex relationships, and not referring to couples/family therapy when appropriate; (e) *Family,* including presuming poor parenting based solely on sexual orientation, being insensitive to the effects of prejudice on lesbian/gay families, being unsupportive in disclosing sexual orientation to family; (f) *Therapist expertise and education,* including providing services to lesbian/gay clients despite lack of knowledge or training, relying on the client for education, actively discriminating against lesbians/gay men, and teaching information that is inaccurate or prejudiced.

Although it is important to note that the APA report documented incidents reflecting sensitive clinical treatment as well as those reflecting bias, the pervasive existence of bias led the researchers to conclude that "psychologists vary widely in their adherence to a standard of unbiased practice with gay men and lesbians" (Garnets et al., 1991, p. 964), that "bias and misinformation persist among some psychologists" (p. 970), and that "despite

APA's formal, repeatedly stated nondiscriminatory policies, understanding, acceptance and adherence to those goals are seriously lacking" (p. 971). The report further suggests that, in addition to developing guidelines for appropriate treatment, a "key step" is to "ensure that all psychologists receive adequate training" (p. 970) in lesbian/gay issues. The call for attention to training professionals who are competent in providing services to sexual minority clients could not be more clear.

Nonconscious Ideologies and Counseling Competency

In examining the ways in which nonconscious ideologies regarding gender and sexual orientation are likely to affect one's competency as a counselor, we borrow a framework from Sue and Sue (1990), who proposed three broad areas defining a "culturally skilled" counselor, based on and encompassing the *attitudes, knowledge, and skills* required for effective counseling. The first refers to counselors' awareness of their own assumptions, values, and biases, and includes awareness of their own culture and culturally induced beliefs and attitudes as well as a respect for differences and willingness to recognize their limitations without feeling threatened. The second refers to counselors' understanding of the worldview of the culturally different client, and includes specific knowledge of the client's social/political/cultural location and its attendant barriers, as well as thorough knowledge of counseling. The third refers to counselors' developing appropriate intervention strategies and techniques for working with diverse clients, and includes a varied behavioral repertoire regarding communication and arenas of intervention as well as an awareness of the impact of one's therapeutic style.

Gender and Counseling Competency

In applying this framework to gender issues in counseling, the component regarding *attitudes* suggests that pervasive societal sexism and gender socialization may limit both the female client's and the counselor's vision of what is possible for the client. This may be particularly salient in career counseling, where the differential impact of socialization and sexism on women and men is most apparent (Cook, 1993). For example, counselors might unwittingly encourage female clients into traditionally female careers, which tend to be lower in status and pay than those that are traditionally male, and that also may represent underutilization of the abilities of the female client (see Betz & Fitzgerald, 1987, and Fitzgerald, Fassinger, & Betz, 1995, for a fuller discussion of these issues). Other attitudinal issues that bear examination are notions concerning the repression of female sexuality (and concomitant blame for sexual assault and abuse when they occur), stereotypes of attractiveness and body image for women, myths regarding female biological and reproductive processes, restricted notions of appropriate vocational and life roles for women, and masculinist assumptions regarding female psychological processes (e.g., viewing a relational identity as pathological). In terms of *knowledge* in working with female clients, both internalized and institutional sexism render it unlikely that many counselors will have been exposed to accurate, adequate information regarding women. For effective work with female clients, Atkinson and Hackett (1995) recommended basic knowledge competencies in the following areas:

1. gender-fair models of mental health
2. biological sex differences
3. sex bias in psychological theories
4. the psychology of women (including subgroups of women such as lesbians and women of color)
5. social conditions such as discrimination and sexual harassment
6. women and work
7. multiple role conflicts and issues
8. health care
9. social services
10. laws
11. violence against women

In examining these areas of knowledge more closely, it becomes apparent that prevailing ideologies that minimize and marginalize women's concerns prevent important issues from being addressed in training. For example, issues that contain biological or physiological elements (e.g., sexuality, contraception, abortion, pregnancy, childbirth, AIDS, eating disorders) are outside the realm of most psychological training programs, and yet these issues are regularly brought to therapy by female clients and have obvious psychological impact (Fitzgerald & Nutt, 1986).

Accurate knowledge of women has clear implications for appropriate assessment and diagnosis. Overreliance on quantitative evaluation such as psychodiagnostic tests (e.g., intelligence tests, personality inventories, pathology indices, career-related measures) may not address bias that may be inherent in available instruments, may ignore the effects of environmental forces such as sexism on clients, and may lead to a focus on the presenting problem as being located exclusively within the individual (Katz, 1985). As but one example of possible diagnostic bias, it has been documented that women are more likely than men to receive prescriptions for psychotropic drugs, they receive those prescriptions at a higher rate than men, and they tend to remain on those drugs for longer periods of time (Unger & Crawford, 1992). Such patterns raise disturbing questions about the ways in which the problems presented by female clients are judged and treated by mental health professionals.

In terms of intervention techniques and *skills* for working with women clients, it is likely that therapists will have been schooled in fairly traditional approaches to therapy, and may not have considered ways in which accepted theories and strategies may negatively affect female clients. For example, psychological models of personality and pathology that are focused on biological determinism (vs. social learning) can be debilitating in their assumptions regarding the immutability of psychological processes and manifestations (Fitzgerald & Nutt, 1986). Similarly, person-centered explanations of therapeutic issues can ignore the larger social context of the client, and may inhibit therapists from advocating for necessary structural change (Fitzgerald & Nutt, 1986). Collective rather than individual approaches, however, which utilize women's connective and relational capacities, may have much to offer in providing for mutual support and a contextual view of individual problems (Enns, 1993; Kaschak, 1992). Unfortunately, group and systems approaches to treatment often are considered secondary or adjunctive to individual psychotherapy in many training programs, and may not be taught or required.

Similarly, feminist and—more recently—gender aware therapies are seldom even acknowledged in counselor training, despite their usefulness in working with female (and male) clients. Both emphasize the impact of societal conditions on the individual, and both call for mental health professionals to take strong advocacy roles in bringing about social change. Gender aware therapy (Good et al., 1990) includes guiding principles that encourage therapists (a) to view gender as a crucial variable in the therapy relationship; (b) to consider problems brought into therapy in their societal context; (c) to advocate against sexism in all its forms; (d) to develop a collaborative and primarily egalitarian therapeutic relationship; and (e) to encourage clients' freedom to choose behaviors and attitudes that are congruent for them, regardless of whatever role constrictions they may have learned are "appropriate" for their gender.

A skill area of critical importance in working with female clients is understanding and being able to work with the impact of their multiple roles and identities, as well as multiple layers of environmental oppression (Comas-Diaz, 1994; Reynolds & Pope, 1991). In addition, the impact of internalized oppression must be considered in exploring a woman's ideas of womanhood and gender roles, and in sorting out identity conflicts related to multiple roles and self-definitions (Comas-Diaz, 1994). Accurate assessment and diagnosis must include an exploration of contextual issues (e.g., acculturation, racism, socioeconomic realities, intergenerational relationships) that the client faces, and alternative assessment tools, such as gender role analyses, that explicitly take such variables into account should be used by therapists to form a more comprehensive, integrated picture of the client (Enns, 1993; Fitzgerald & Nutt, 1986).

Sexual Orientation and Counseling Competency

In applying the Sue and Sue (1990) framework to issues of sexual orientation, the *attitudinal* component suggests that pervasive societal homophobia and heterosexism are likely to lead to an assumption of universal heterosexuality as normal, and an implicit belief that a same-sex relational orientation is a phase to be outgrown, a manifestation of developmental arrest when it persists, or an indication of psychological pathology or impairment. As we have noted previously, just as both male and female counselors can hold negative, stereotypic views of women, both heterosexual and lesbian/gay/bisexual counselors can exhibit internalized societal homophobia in the form of negative assumptions regarding sexual minority clients. Heterosexual counselors, however, face particular challenges in assimilating information and affirmation about populations with which they may have little (known) contact.

A heterosexual counselor may not realize, for example, that heterosexuality is simply one possible orientation out of several, or may firmly believe that heterosexuality is better than other forms of intimacy. Even when the awareness of a lesbian/gay/bisexual client's sexual orientation is present, counselors may hold stereotyped notions of lifestyle and behavior that not only may be inaccurate, but may serve to limit the options and choices of the client. The heterosexual counselor may not be comfortable with the client's sexual orientation or choices, and either may gloss over them and ignore critical lifestyle issues, or be so preoccupied with them that perspective on presenting issues is lost. Regardless of personal sexual orientation, the counselor also may be defensive about her or his therapeutic appropriateness, may be unwilling to refer the lesbian/gay/bisexual client to more appropriate resources, and may be defensive about her or his own sexual orientation and choices.

In terms of *knowledge* regarding sexual orientation, the societal invisibility of lesbian/gay/bisexual people, compounded by negative personal attitudes may have prevented a heterosexual counselor from having direct contact with or learning about lesbian or gay lifestyles or issues. The counselor may have little or no comprehension of the social, political, and legal realities faced by sexual minority clients, and may not understand the debilitating role that internalized oppression plays in mental health and adaptive functioning. The counselor may inappropriately assess normative coming out issues as pathology and plan interventions according to negative views of the client. For example, a client in the early phases of the coming out process often will express feelings of depression, frustration, self-hatred, and fear about being lesbian or gay. A counselor who interprets such feelings as justification for engaging in gay-aversive strategies aimed at changing the client's sexual orientation will do a severe disservice to an individual who is more likely seeking acceptance and affirmation. Because of general lack of knowledge about lesbian/gay/bisexual people, the heterosexual counselor also may be unable to determine how existing theoretical and procedural elements of therapy may apply differently to sexual minority clients. Career counseling, for example, that is focused on clarifying possible job choices based on a lesbian client's interests and abilities may completely overlook the confounding difficulty of a dual-career job search in which lesbian identity cannot be revealed (Fassinger, 1996).

In terms of intervention techniques and *skills* for working with sexual minority clients, it is likely that the counselor (regardless of sexual orientation) will have been trained in fairly traditional approaches to counseling, emphasizing a dyadic relationship and intrapsychic focus. The counselor may not understand that invisibility and isolation leave many lesbian/gay/bisexual clients mired in the same ignorance as the population as a whole, and may fail to adopt the important proactive educational and advocacy roles in which she or he may serve. Being inexperienced in or reluctant to use a wide variety of therapeutic strategies also can constrain effective counseling. For example, Gestalt empty chair techniques and role-playing can be extremely helpful in exploring and rehearsing lesbian/gay clients' coming out issues, and a counselor who is not competent or comfortable with such techniques loses a valuable therapeutic opportunity. Moreover, the counselor may not be aware of the critically important function of community resources and connections in working with lesbian/gay/bisexual people, and may not adequately serve as a referral and information source for sexual minority clients.

Incorporating Gender and
Sexual Orientation Into MCC Training

Attitudes

Incorporating consideration of gender and sexual orientation into MCC training can and must occur in myriad ways and at a number of levels. Just as competent multicultural counseling must begin with attitudinal self-examination and heightened self-awareness on the part of the counselor, effective training must similarly begin with self-examination on the part of educators and supervisors. We must engage in a process of self-reflection that is not only personal but programmatic, to determine how adequately we are incorporating the attitudinal examination, knowledge base, and skill training for competent multicultural counseling. In engaging in personal reflection, we also must remember that thoroughly educating ourselves about the ways in which sex matters in counseling does not occur simply through involvement in personal and professional relationships with women and lesbian/gay/bisexual people (see Gilbert, 1992). We must go beyond personal views and experiences to the scholarly literature in order to inform our work as educators and supervisors of students.

Programmatically, we must ask ourselves what cultural values and assumptions are implicit in our training programs as they currently are structured—course offerings, counseling populations to whom trainees are exposed, research encouraged and/or permitted by students and faculty, admissions and evaluation decisions, and the "culture" of the program. For example, do we consistently offer courses on some cultural groups but not others, creating an implicit hierarchy of diversity in our programs (e.g., race/ethnicity but not gender or sexual orientation)? Do we incorporate multicultural considerations into all of our courses and training, or do we protest that there is already too much to cover and that we simply cannot add more content (e.g., do we ignore gender or sexual orientation in discussing the applicability of theories to particular clients)? Are members of the program faculty or counseling center staff perceived or treated differently based on their cultural status (e.g., are men given more behavioral latitude or accorded more respect than women)? Are students whose research interests focus on sexual orientation or gender discouraged, hindered, or burdened with implicit assumptions regarding comparison groups (e.g., is a student permitted to study lesbians without a gay male or heterosexual comparison group)? Are several faculty or staff doing all of the training around diversity issues (e.g., enriching and teaching courses, offering workshops, raising diversity issues during meetings), while the other faculty/staff do the "regular" work? Are there some topics (e.g., admissions policies) that cannot be discussed openly among faculty and staff because they threaten to unleash arguments regarding diversity? If we ourselves cannot manage the personal and programmatic transformation necessary for an appropriate multicultural climate, we will not be effective at training our students despite our laudable intentions.

Assuming our success at creating attitudinal openness in ourselves and our programs, we then can begin the process of effective multicultural training. Again, because attitudinal examination and increased self-awareness make up the necessary first step, we must create experiential opportunities for students to engage in self-exploration in nonthreatening situations. Experiential exercises, guest speakers and panels, workshops, field activities, and support groups are all ways that awareness can begin. To mention a few examples: We might enlist an outside person to offer a half-day workshop on homophobia and its effects in counseling; we might have a panel of lesbians and gay men visit our career class to discuss ways in which their sexual orientation has affected their vocational decisions and choices; role-plays with a gender focus could be incorporated into our beginning counseling courses; or the university counseling center could provide a support group for women (and available to graduate students) who are juggling multiple roles. One recurring criticism of current MCC training is its focus on content, that is, teaching trainees about oppressed groups, but not about themselves (Reynolds & Pope, 1991). It is important that MCC training incorporate experiential models that focus on the *process* of becoming multiculturally competent, including an emphasis on self-knowledge, interpersonal relationships, and worldviews (Reynolds & Pope, 1991).

Knowledge

In terms of helping trainees to build a knowledge base for understanding gender and sexual orientation issues in counseling, we must ensure that students in our programs are learning all they can regarding the social, political, historical, and psychological contexts of clients vis-à-vis sexual orientation and gender. Some have argued that unless a therapist (male or female) has specific nonsexist training, she or he will be incapable of helping women make independent decisions and work toward their individual goals in a sexist society (Nickerson & Kremgold-Barrett, 1990). Similar arguments have been made that only extensive training in lesbian/gay/bisexual issues readies counselors to provide affirmative therapy to sexual minority clients, regardless of their own sexual orientation (Buhrke & Douce, 1991;

Fassinger, 1991). It is a lamentable reality, however, that despite the presence of large numbers of women and lesbian/gay/bisexual people in therapy—indeed, women are the largest segment of the population to seek therapy, and studies suggest that lesbian/gay people seek help at rates two to four times higher than heterosexuals (Rudolph, 1988)—the majority of training programs do not offer specialized coursework or formal training (either required or optional) in working with women or with sexual minority clients (Atkinson & Hackett, 1995; Buhrke, 1989; Buhrke & Douce, 1991; Gilbert, 1992; Mintz, Rideout, & Bartels, 1994; Nickerson & Kremgold-Barrett, 1990).

For example, Mintz et al. (1994) in a study of counseling and clinical psychology students found that only about 15% of these students had taken a graduate-level course on counseling women or the psychology of women. Of the students who had taken a course, 82.5% reported that it was an elective, and only 17.5% reported that the course was required in their program. Moreover, approximately 58% reported that no course was offered in their program. Even more alarming results were reported by Buhrke (1989) in regard to graduate-level training in issues of sexual orientation. In her sample of female counseling psychology students, Buhrke found that almost one-third reported no exposure at all to lesbian/gay issues during their doctoral training, and almost one-half had not (to their knowledge) seen lesbian/gay clients. More than 70% were in programs where no faculty were engaged in research on sexual minority issues, and most reported that their knowledge came from informal sources, such as friends and peers.

These results are even more disturbing in light of the fact that there is a rich literature concerning the psychology of women and gender, and a burgeoning scholarly literature exists in regard to sexual orientation as well (e.g., see Fassinger, 1991; Gilbert, 1992). Numerous books, chapters, journals, articles, guidelines, and other documents exist that provide excellent resources for building a knowledge base regarding gender and sexual orientation. For example, as we indicated previously, the "Principles Concerning the Counseling and Psychotherapy of Women" (Division 17 Committee on Women, 1979) and the subsequent article concerning the rationale and implementation of the principles (Fitzgerald & Nutt, 1986), the APA report titled "Bias in Psychotherapy With Lesbians and Gay Men" (Committee on Lesbian and Gay Concerns, 1990; Garnets et al., 1991), and several important reviews of counseling issues (e.g., Atkinson & Hackett, 1995; Fassinger, 1991; Gilbert, 1992) outline necessary areas of knowledge and provide resources concerning those populations. Trainees should be expected to be familiar with current literature and to undergo periodic self-examination regarding their progress in knowledge acquisition and their appropriateness in working with women and sexual minority clients. Unfortunately, this rarely seems to occur. The Mintz et al. (1994) study indicated that more than half of internship-level counseling and clinical psychology students had never heard of the principles for counseling women, despite their widespread circulation for more than a decade. It is even less likely that students will be familiar with the recent APA report on bias in psychotherapy with lesbians and gay men.

Given that formal training in the necessary knowledge base for effective therapeutic work around issues of gender and sexual orientation is not occurring, we include here some suggestions regarding the inclusion of this content in formal coursework. Practicum courses should address issues of gender and sexuality in both women and men, and provide specific training in feminist and gender aware therapies, as well as in gay-affirmative approaches to working with sexual minority clients (Atkinson & Hackett, 1995). In practicum assignments, for example, students might deliberately be paired with clients who differ from them in order to motivate developing their knowledge base for effective work (e.g., a heterosexual male trainee working with a lesbian client). Counseling courses should focus on general information regarding gender and sexual orientation, as well as on the specific clinical concerns that disproportionately affect female and sexual minority clients; for women, this could include eating disorders, depression, and sexual assault and abuse, and for lesbian/gay/bisexual clients this might include coming out and sexual concerns, stigmatization, depression, and substance abuse (Atkinson & Hackett, 1995; Fassinger, 1991; Gilbert, 1992). Class assignments might be built around increasing cultural awareness (e.g., taking a course topic and writing a paper about its applicability to women or lesbian/gay/bisexual people). Assessment courses need to train therapists who understand and can recognize the appropriate use of assessment inventories with female and sexual minority clients, as well as provide alternative strategies, such as an analysis of gender roles or lesbian/gay identity development (Atkinson & Hackett, 1995; Enns, 1993; Fassinger, 1991, 1992).

Traditional modes of learning, such as courses, books, conferences, and the like, can contribute to the trainee's knowledge base, and many of the works referenced in this chapter provide a useful starting point for those wishing to expand their knowledge (see the Appendix for a summary/checklist of these issues). Similar to addressing the attitudinal component of competency, experiential learning also should be utilized in building knowledge, including such activities as workshops, community involvement, exercises, and group encounters of various kinds. For example, trainees routinely might be assigned in their classes to attend a campus or community event regarding a population about which they know very little (e.g., a movie about lesbians or gay men), and class time devoted to sharing these experiences and discussing their relevance to course material. Experiential learning also is directly applicable to developing and practicing purposeful strategies (i.e., skills) for effective intervention.

Skills

Given that formal coursework often is lacking in building a knowledge base regarding issues of gender and sexual orientation, clinical supervisors must be prepared to assist trainees in developing these competencies. We note again that the state of training in these issues suggests that supervisors may be even more uninformed than are trainees, and it is critically important for supervisors to engage in the personal work of building an attitudinal, knowledge, and skill foundation to assist them in counseling their own clients, as well as in training others for effective intervention with female and sexual minority populations. The opportunity for budding counselors to work with someone who differs from them on one or more cultural variables can range from meaningless to deleterious without an appropriately trained supervisor who can further the trainee's development, and who is willing and able to use supervision to address these critical variables in the therapy relationship.

In terms of skill development, it would seem that the most important qualities that trainees must develop are therapeutic flexibility and the courage to try innovative, nontraditional approaches to client problems. Understanding which theories and strategies are particularly helpful in working with women and lesbians/gays is discussed in the APA task force reports and counseling guidelines previously mentioned. These documents also indicate some of the less traditional, advocacy roles that are helpful in working with these populations, for example assertiveness training with women or knowing community resources in working with lesbian/gay/bisexual clients.

Finally, we emphasize again the importance of climate in fostering essential work in building competency in multicultural counseling. Much has been written about the critical balance between challenge and support in creating an environment optimal for growth. In challenging our students to engage in the difficult, often painful process of self-examination, it is imperative that we also provide the support they need to do that. We must be willing to be open about our own struggles with these issues, we must be aware of resources that can help them, we must understand the limitations inherent in our own cultural locations and those of our training programs, and we must not be reluctant to refer trainees to outside help when necessary. It may be motivational to frame these issues as concerns regarding professional impairment. Current writing and ethical thinking in the area of multiculturalism suggest strongly that ignorance and lack of awareness severely impair our ability to counsel diverse clients effectively. It therefore becomes an ethical imperative to ensure that all of our students have done the necessary work that will enable them to be effective counselors for clients positioned in varying cultural locations. In order to illustrate the potential benefit of an effective training experience regarding gender and sexual orientation, we present a brief case example in the following section.

Dr. Peter Goodfellow is a White, heterosexual, 53-year-old male counselor in the Counseling Center at Any University. He has been a staff member for many years, is an affiliate of the graduate program in counseling at AU, and often serves as a supervisor in the practica for graduate counseling students. He is psychodynamic in theoretical orientation, and is liked by his supervisees for his effectiveness in helping them to examine themselves as counselors and in encouraging them to use the therapeutic relationship actively in counseling. He was trained many years ago in a traditional counseling program, but considers himself up to date because he subscribes to and reads several counseling journals, attends APA regularly, is fairly active in his state psychological association, and rarely misses a guest speaker or staff development session offered in the Counseling Center at AU.

This semester he is supervising Jane Kwan Doe, an Asian American, heterosexual, 26-year-old female doctoral student. Jane came to AU with a master's degree in counseling from another university, where she was trained in client-centered strategies and completed most of her practice requirements in a community mental health clinic working with families. Jane is eager to work with college students, and may seek a position in a college counseling center upon completing her degree. She considers herself to hold fairly traditional values in terms of relationships and families, but also sees herself as open-minded because she has experienced prejudice directly and knows what it is like to be judged according to stereotypes. This is her first practicum in the doctoral program at AU.

Jane's client is a 19-year-old White female who presents with anxiety, depression, relationship problems, and religious doubts. She is fairly reticent and vague in her initial sessions with Jane, and Jane is frustrated with "not getting anywhere" with her client. Goodfellow suspects that the client may be struggling with sexual identity concerns that she is afraid to reveal to Jane, because Jane has several times used masculine language in reference to the client's intimate relationship.

In his supervision with Jane, Goodfellow uses a supportive, probing style to help Jane see what assumptions she has been making about her client, and to help her explore alternative conceptualizations. The possibility that her client is a lesbian initially provokes panic in Jane, who claims that she has never known a "homosexual person" and wants to refer the client to a more "knowledgeable" counselor. Goodfellow helps Jane to explore her own attitudes about same-sex relationships, using his educational role to include accurate information where relevant (e.g., that Jane probably *has* known lesbian or gay people, but has not been aware of their sexual orientation because of secrecy and invisibility). Goodfellow encourages Jane to work with the client as an opportunity for professional growth, and provides resources (articles, books, bibliographies) to help her build a knowledge base for working with her lesbian client. They explore ways in which Jane can create a gay-affirmative climate in counseling and facilitate openness in her client (e.g., using gender-neutral language, asking directly about same-sex relationships).

As sessions proceed, Jane becomes increasingly knowledgeable, confident, and skilled in her work with her client, both supported and appropriately challenged by Goodfellow's patient and persistent probing and teaching. He encourages her to try new techniques (such as role-playing to rehearse the client's coming out to family), shows her how to use these strategies, and helps her to determine the positive and negative aspects of her interventions. In addition, Goodfellow encourages Jane to inquire directly and frequently about her client's reactions to specific interventions and to the counseling process, as a way for Jane to monitor her own professional impact and progress. Goodfellow is not afraid to address areas in which he feels that Jane's own gender or sexual orientation are impeding her effectiveness with her client, but he is respectful of her cultural location vis-à-vis those (and other) variables; for example, he helps her to recognize how her own notions of acceptable roles for women and expressions of sexuality are rooted in her cultural and family background, and how her interaction with her client reflects those values and worldviews. Goodfellow also encourages Jane to plan and direct supervision sessions actively so that they meet her needs as she perceives them.

One persistent problem with Jane's client, however, is that strong religious prohibitions operating in the client's life maintain her fears and secrecy, and prevent her from feeling comfortable about her lesbian identity. Jane, who has no experience with Christian dogma, feels unable to engage in debate about the Bible and tends to shift topics whenever her client raises religious questions. Goodfellow first helps Jane to recognize this pattern and then arranges for a joint consultation with Dr. Lily Lambda, a new junior faculty member in the AU doctoral program who is an open lesbian and has professional expertise in lesbian/gay/bisexual issues in counseling. In this consultation, Jane learns from Dr. Lambda how to use Gestalt empty chair techniques in helping lesbian/gay/bisexual clients to articulate and resolve conflicting religious ideological demands, and how to provide resources and referrals when appropriate. Jane is able to implement this new learning in her remaining sessions with her client and successfully connects the client with several community resources by the end of the semester. Jane states in her final supervision session that she has learned a great deal and that she is eager to seek out additional experiences working with sexual minority clients.

In examining Goodfellow's work with Jane, it is clear that he demonstrates genuine appreciation of the complexities of effective supervision around issues of gender and sexual orientation. He carefully balances challenge and support in his supervisory relationship with Jane, and he willingly reveals his own struggles and limitations. The consultation he arranges with Dr. Lambda is particularly revealing of his sensitivity to relevant attitudes, knowledge, and skills, as he transforms a seemingly minor supervisory event into a positive learning experience for all involved. First, even though he is disinterested and uninformed in anything religious and feels incompetent to offer Jane the very concrete help she needs in working with these issues, he is not afraid to own and share his professional limitations. Second, he wants to model for Jane a professional commitment to seeking consultation when necessary, and in choosing a lesbian junior colleague, he is hoping to demonstrate that expertise (or its lack) can exist across gender, sexual orientation, and level of counseling experience. Third, he chooses to meet with Dr. Lambda in her own office, cognizant of the power dynamics inherent in requesting that a junior female colleague come to a senior male colleague's office, particularly when it is she who is providing service. In his attempt to foster a climate in which areas of expertise are honored regardless of the hierarchical structures imposed by gender, sexual orientation, and professional position, Goodfellow has empowered Dr. Lambda in this encounter, as well as Jane, who now not only has had the experience of meeting a "homosexual person" (and expert besides), but also has witnessed a female (like herself) recognized for professional contributions. Finally, Goodfellow models in all of his supervision with Jane his professional commitment to continued growth and learning, and his openness to new techniques and ideas. Probably the best testimony to his effectiveness as a supervisor is Jane's eagerness to gain additional experience with populations and issues that she initially found threatening and difficult.

Conclusion

In transforming our curricula and training to address MCC effectively, a number of approaches and foci have been advocated, ranging from offering extra content courses to infusing multiculturalism throughout the curriculum and training (see Atkinson & Hackett, 1995; Fouad, Manese, & Casas, 1992). Fouad et al. (1992), in their recommendations for an integrated approach to implementing cross-cultural counseling competencies in the counseling curriculum, particularly emphasized including a multicultural perspective in courses on counseling theory and practice, professional development, psychological assessment, and human development within the sociocultural context. They further pointed out that an integrative approach would require reconceptualizing and revising existing syllabi to include multiple perspectives as well as including separate courses in multicultural counseling. A similar approach was advocated by Atkinson and Hackett (1995) in regard to training for competent work with populations who are diverse in terms of gender, sexual orientation, age, and disability. It should be apparent from the foregoing discussion that we, too, advocate that the study of gender and sexual orientation be thoroughly integrated into counselor training, both through infusion into existing curricular experiences, as well as through the addition of specialized courses and training. Sex *matters*. Issues of gender and sexual orientation are core to individuals' experiences of their worlds, and must be included in MCC training if we are to reach the goal of training both ourselves and others to understand and work competently with the different worlds we encounter in a multicultural society.

APPENDIX

We summarize here major questions for consideration by programs interested in developing or expanding attention to gender and sexual orientation in the training that they provide. For detailed discussion of training content and issues regarding gender and sexual orientation, we refer readers to Buhrke and Douce (1991) and Atkinson and Hackett (1995), who provide excellent outlines of knowledge and experiences crucial to training counselors who are competent in these areas.

Program Assessment Regarding Gender and Sexual Orientation: Questions to Consider

1. Competence of Educators and Supervisors

    Are all educators and supervisors (faculty, counseling center staff, and affiliates/adjuncts) in the program equipped with appropriate attitudes, knowledge, and skills necessary for effective training regarding gender and sexual orientation? Is each individual clearly engaged in a process of personal awareness, reflection, and education in these areas? Are educators and supervisors aware of their own cultural locations and culturally induced beliefs? Do they encourage respect for differences? Are they willing to recognize their own limitations in these areas? Do they demonstrate commitment to continued growth and learning regarding client diversity?

2. Program Structure and Content

    a. Courses and Curriculum: Is specific content regarding gender and sexual orientation infused into the current curriculum? Is specialized training in these areas offered as well? Has each course been examined for implicit bias in topics covered or course procedures? Have practica, as well as courses in theories, assessment, research design, vocational issues, group and family therapy, professional issues, and core psychology areas, been carefully scrutinized to ensure inclusiveness of gender and sexual orientation? Do course evaluations request feedback regarding the extent to which gender and sexual orientation have been adequately included in the course? Are training opportunities structured to address the attitudes, knowledge, and skills required for effective counseling of diverse clients? Are experiential as well as more traditional content approaches utilized in training? Are additional resources and training opportunities made known to students who wish further to develop their personal and professional competence in the areas of gender and sexual orientation?

    b. Client Populations: Are trainees expected to work with clients who differ from them in gender and sexual orientation? If it is difficult for trainees to find clients who differ from them in the campus population, are such opportunities sought in off-campus practicum sites? Are client issues related to gender and sexual orientation highlighted and used as teaching opportunities when they arise in case presentations and other practicum activities?

c. Research: Does research being produced by both faculty and students in the program reflect consideration of gender and sexual orientation in content and procedures? Are faculty and students sensitive to possible bias in wording of instruments, research questions being investigated, and methodologies used? Are there at least some faculty who have gender and sexual orientation as foci of their work (and, if not, are they being actively recruited)? Is faculty expertise in these areas recognized and utilized, by other faculty as well as students? Has administrative or institutional support of research been examined for possible bias related to gender and sexual orientation (and addressed if necessary)?

d. Admission, Advising, and Evaluation: Are female and (open) sexual minority students admitted to the program? Are female and sexual minority students able to find faculty mentors who are willing to work with them? Are all students evaluated equivalently in admissions and evaluation decisions? Is multicultural competence regarding gender and sexual orientation (including attitudinal openness) an important criterion in evaluations of student progress?

3. Climate

Does the program present an appropriate balance of challenge and support to trainees? Do educators and supervisors also feel both supported and appropriately challenged in the training environment? Are the unique experiences and perspectives of women and lesbian/gay/bisexual people clearly valued in the program? Is unbiased language regarding gender and sexual orientation an explicit requirement in all oral communication and written documents in the program? Are sexist and homophobic comments and jokes addressed if and when they occur? Are different family structures taken into account when planning social activities in the program? Does the program provide recognition, reward, or reinforcement for those who actively work toward personal and professional competence regarding gender and sexual orientation?

References

American Psychological Association (APA). (1975). Report of the Task Force on Sex Bias and Sex Role Stereotyping in Psychotherapeutic Practice. *American Psychologist, 30,* 1169-1175.

American Psychological Association, Task Force on Sex Bias and Sex Role Stereotyping in Psychotherapeutic Practice. (1978). Guidelines for therapy with women. *American Psychologist, 33,* 1122-1123.

Atkinson, D. R., & Hackett, G. (1995). *Counseling diverse populations.* Madison, WI: William C. Brown.

Belenky, M. F., Clinchy, B. M., Goldberger, N. R., & Tarule, J. M. (1986). *Women's ways of knowing: The development of self, voice, and mind.* New York: Basic Books.

Bem, S. L., & Bem, D. J. (1970). Training the woman to know her place: The power of a nonconscious ideology. In M. H. Garskof (Ed.), *Roles women play: Readings toward women's liberation* (pp. 84-96). Belmont, CA: Brooks/Cole.

Betz, N. E., & Fitzgerald, L. F. (1987). *The career psychology of women.* New York: Academic Press.

Board of Ethnic Minority Affairs, Task Force on Delivery of Services to Ethnic Minority Populations. (1991). *Guidelines for providers of psychological services to ethnic, linguistic, and culturally diverse populations.* Washington, DC: American Psychological Association.

Brod, H. (Ed.). (1987). *The making of masculinities—The new men's studies.* Boston: Allen & Unwin.

Broverman, I. K., Broverman, D. M., Clarkson, F. E., Rosenkrantz, P. S., & Vogel, S. R. (1970). Sex role stereotypes and clinical judgments of mental health. *Journal of Consulting and Clinical Psychology, 34,* 1-7.

Buhrke, R. A. (1989). Female student perspectives on training in lesbian and gay issues. *The Counseling Psychologist, 17,* 629-636.

Buhrke, R. A., & Douce, L. A. (1991). Training issues for counseling psychologists in working with lesbian women and gay men. *The Counseling Psychologist, 19,* 216-234.

Comas-Diaz, L. (1994). An integrative approach. In L. Comas-Diaz & B. Greene (Eds.), *Women of color: Integrating ethnic and gender identities in psychotherapy* (pp. 287-318). New York: Guilford.

Comas-Diaz, L., & Greene, B. (Eds.). (1994). *Women of color: Integrating ethnic and gender identities in psychotherapy.* New York: Guilford.

Committee on Lesbian and Gay Concerns. (1990). *Bias in psychotherapy with lesbians and gay men.* Washington, DC: American Psychological Association.

Conger, J. (1975). Proceedings of the American Psychological Association for the year 1974: Minutes of the annual meeting of the Council of Representatives. *American Psychologist, 30,* 620-651.

Cook, E. P. (1993). The gendered context of life: Implications for women's and men's career-life plans. *The Career Development Quarterly, 41,* 227-237.

Davenport, D. S., & Yurich, J. M. (1991). Multicultural gender issues. *Journal of Counseling and Development, 70,* 64-71.

Deaux, K. (1985). Sex and gender. In L. Porter & M. Rosenzweig (Eds.), *Annual Review of Psychology, 36,* 49-81.

Diamant, L. (Ed.). (1993). *Homosexual issues in the workplace.* Washington, DC: Taylor & Francis.

Division 17 Committee on Women, American Psychological Association. (1979). Principles concerning the counseling and therapy of women. *The Counseling Psychologist, 8,* 21.

Enns, C. Z. (1993). Twenty years of feminist counseling and therapy: From naming biases to implementing multifaceted practice. *The Counseling Psychologist, 21,* 3-87.

Espín, O. M. (1993). Feminist therapy: Not for or by White women only. *The Counseling Psychologist, 21,* 103-108.

Fassinger, R. E. (1991). The hidden minority: Issues and challenges in working with lesbians and gay men. *The Counseling Psychologist, 19,* 157-176.

Fassinger, R. E. (1992, March). *An inclusive model of lesbian identity formation: Implications for intervention.* Paper presented at the annual conference of the Association for Women in Psychology, Long Beach, CA.

Fassinger, R. E. (1996). Notes from the margins: Integrating lesbian experience into the vocational psychology of women. *Journal of Vocational Behavior 48,* 160-175.

Fitzgerald, L. F., Fassinger, R. E., & Betz, N. E. (1995). Theoretical advances in the study of women's career development. In W. B. Walsh & S. H. Osipow (Eds), *Handbook of vocational psychology* (2nd ed., pp. 67-109). Hillsdale, NJ: Lawrence Erlbaum.

Fitzgerald, L. F., & Nutt, R. (1986). The Division 17 principles concerning the counseling/psychotherapy of women: Rationale and implementation. *The Counseling Psychologist, 14,* 180-216.

Fouad, N. A., Manese, J., & Casas, J. M. (1992, August). Curricular and training approaches in implementing cross-cultural counseling competencies. In P. W. Sue (Chair), *Cross-cultural counseling competencies: Revision, expansion, and implementation.* Symposium conducted at the annual convention of the American Psychological Association, Washington, DC.

Garnets, L., Hancock, K. A., Cochran, S. D., Goodchilds, J., & Peplau, L. A. (1991). Issues in psychotherapy with lesbians and gay men. *American Psychologist, 46,* 964-972.

Garnets, L., & Kimmel, D. (1991). Lesbian and gay male dimensions in the psychological study of human diversity. In J. D. Goodchilds (Ed.), *Psychological perspectives on human diversity in America* (pp. 137-192). Washington, DC: American Psychological Association.

Gilbert, L. A. (1992). Gender and counseling psychology: Current knowledge and directions for research and social action. In S. D. Brown & R. W. Lent (Eds.), *Handbook of counseling psychology* (2nd ed.). New York: John Wiley.

Gonsiorek, J. C., & Rudolph, J. R. (1991). Homosexual identity: Coming out and other developmental events. In J. C. Gonsiorek & J. D. Weinrich (Eds.), *Homosexuality: Research implications for public policy* (pp. 161-176). Newbury Park, CA: Sage.

Good, G. E., Gilbert, L. A., & Scher, M. (1990). Gender aware therapy: A synthesis of feminist therapy and knowledge about gender. *Journal of Counseling and Development, 68,* 376-380.

Hare-Mustin, R. T., & Maracek, J. (1988). The meaning of difference: Gender theory, postmodernism, and psychology. *American Psychologist, 43,* 455-464.

Hoshmand, L.L.S.T. (1989). Alternate research paradigms: A review and teaching proposal. *The Counseling Psychologist, 17,* 3-79.

Hyde, J. S. (1991). *Half the human experience: The psychology of women* (4th ed.). Lexington, MA: D. C. Heath.

Kaschak, E. (1992). *Engendered lives.* New York: Basic Books.

Katz, J. H. (1985). The sociopolitical nature of counseling. In Cross-cultural counseling [Special issue]. *The Counseling Psychologist, 13,* 615-624.

Mintz, L. B., Rideout, C. A., & Bartels, K. M. (1994). A national survey of interns' perceptions of their preparation for counseling women and of the atmosphere of their graduate education. *Professional Psychology: Research and Practice, 25,* 221-227.

Nickerson, E. T., & Kremgold-Barrett, A. (1990). Gender-fair psychotherapy in the United States: A possible dream? *International Journal for the Advancement of Counselling, 13,* 39-48.

Pedersen, P. (Ed.). (1991). Multiculturalism as a fourth force in counseling [Special issue]. *Journal of Counseling and Development, 70,* 4-250.

Reynolds, A. L., & Pope, R. L. (1991). The complexities of diversity: Exploring multiple oppressions. *Journal of Counseling and Development, 70,* 174-180.

Rudolph, J. (1988). Counselors' attitudes toward homosexuality: A selective review of the literature. *Journal of Counseling and Development, 67,* 165-168.

Sherif, C. (1982). Needed concepts in the study of gender identity. *Psychology of Women Quarterly, 6,* 375-398.

Sue, D. W., & Sue, D. (1990). *Counseling the culturally different: Theory and practice* (2nd ed.). New York: John Wiley.

Tavris, C. (1991). The mismeasure of woman: Paradoxes and perspectives in the study of gender. In J. D. Goodchilds (Ed.), *Psychological perspectives on human diversity in America* (pp. 91-136). Washington, DC: American Psychological Association.

Unger, R., & Crawford, M. (1992). *Women & gender: A feminist psychology.* New York: McGraw-Hill.

Yoder, J. D., & Kahn, A. S. (1993). Working toward an inclusive psychology of women. *American Psychologist, 48,* 846-850.

5

Multicultural
Counseling Training

A COMPETENCY MODEL
AND NATIONAL SURVEY

Joseph G. Ponterotto

There is little debate regarding the need to train counselors more effectively for work with culturally diverse clients (Reynolds, 1995). The professional literature is now replete with reports of national committees (e.g., Sue, Arredondo, & McDavis, 1992) and professional associations (see Pedersen, 1995) attesting to the need to address multiculturalism in a comprehensive fashion in counseling programs.

Recent surveys have documented the growing attention being paid to multicultural issues in training programs. In their periodic national survey, Hollis and Wantz (1990, 1994) noted that new multicultural courses were being added to existing counseling curriculums at a rapid pace. Specifically, these authors estimated that 76 training programs added a multicultural course between 1989 and 1991, and another 27 programs added the course during the 1993-1995 period.

In a survey of APA accredited counseling psychology programs, Hills and Strozier (1992) found that 87% of programs offered a multicultural course, and 59% required that the course be completed by all program students. More recently, Quintana and Bernal (1995) surveyed APA accredited counseling psychology programs and found that 73% of programs offered one or more multicultural courses, and 42% required a multicultural course. (For a review and integration of multicultural training surveys in counseling, school, clinical, and community psychology, see Ponterotto & Alexander, 1996.)

Although counseling training programs in general can be credited with efforts to incorporate diversity training in the curriculum, most specialists believe that much more progress is needed before the mental health needs of a culturally diverse clientele are likely to be met (D'Andrea & Daniels, 1991; Mio & Morris, 1990; Reynolds, 1995; Sue et al., 1992). A recent survey of doctoral graduates in counseling, school, and clinical psychology found that only a small percentage felt "extremely" or "very" competent to work with racial/ethnic minority clients (Allison, Crawford, Echemendia, Robinson, & Knepp, 1994). The current status of multicultural training in counseling programs is well summarized by Quintana and Bernal (1995): "normative data from counseling psychology programs indicated that most programs are providing training that leads to, at best, multicultural sensitivity, but very few appear to be providing training that prepares practitioners to be multiculturally proficient" (p. 102).

Important questions to address at this point are (a) What are the characteristics of effective multicultural training? (b) Which multicultural competencies are training programs meeting currently, and which competencies are they not meeting? and (c) What would a model multicultural training program in counseling psychology "look like"?

This chapter integrates the literature on model multicultural training programs. It reviews the recently put forth Multicultural Competency Checklist (Ponterotto, Alexander, & Grieger, 1995), designed to assist training programs in their multicultural development efforts. Further, the chapter presents the results of an original national survey using the Checklist and designed to assess the current status of multicultural training in counseling. The survey results are discussed and linked to previous mail surveys on the status of multicultural training. The chapter ends with the presentation of an outline for a model multicultural training program.

Learning From Model Programs
in Multicultural Counseling Training

One method of identifying key components or characteristics of proficient multicultural training is to examine so-called model programs. By examining both unique and common characteristics of these programs, researchers can begin to delineate important components of "quality multicultural training."

Over the years, writers have attempted to identify, and at times describe, counseling training programs believed to be strong in the multicultural area. Table 5.1 presents reviews of Arredondo (1985), Ponterotto and Casas (1987), Heath, Neimeyer, and Pedersen (1988), Leung (1993), and Rogers, Wade, Hoffman, Borowsky, and Sirmans (1995), all of whom identify "model" programs vis-à-vis multicultural training.

The procedures used by the authors cited in Table 5.1 to identify model programs were often quite subjective in nature. The Arredondo (1985) and Leung (1993) selections were based on the authors' own networking and knowledge of various programs nationwide. In the Ponterotto and Casas (1987), Heath et al. (1988), and Rogers et al. (1995) articles, programs were nominated by "specialists" or "experts" in the field. Criticisms, however, have been raised in the definition of "multicultural counseling expert" used in some of the studies. For example, the 53 "experts" in the Heath et al. (1988) study were so identified for having published one or more articles in a given year in selected journals. The present author, as well as others focusing on multicultural counseling training, question whether having published one multicultural article constitutes expertise in the area. Parham (1993) has raised similar concerns with regard to identifying multicultural experts and model programs.

Nonetheless, the nomination surveys are still valuable in that they provide some information on multiculturally focused training programs. A review of the articles cited in Table 5.1 would reveal that stronger multicultural training programs incorporate or infuse multiculturalism throughout the curriculum (see Ponterotto et al., 1995). In fact, many multicultural counseling specialists believe that a fully infused and integrated model is necessary to prepare culturally proficient and competent clinicians, researchers, and administrators (e.g., D'Andrea & Daniels, 1995; LaFromboise & Foster, 1992; Margolis & Rungta, 1986; Ponterotto et al., 1995; Sue et al., 1992).

A Comprehensive
Model of Multicultural Training

Recently, a pragmatic guide to multicultural program development was put forth (Ponterotto et al., 1995). The pragmatic guide was organized along a simple checklist that program faculty could use to assess their development vis-à-vis multicultural training, and set both short- and long-range goals to meet the specified multicultural competencies. The Multicultural Compe-

Table 5.1 Model Program in Multicultural Counseling Training

Author	Model Programs
Arredondo (1985)	Boston University; Teachers College, Columbia University; University of California-Santa Barbara; California State University-Northridge; Syracuse University; University of Massachusetts, Amherst; Western Washington University, Bellingham
Ponterotto & Casas (1987) (Top 5)	Syracuse University; Boston University; Western Washington University, Bellingham; University of Hawaii; University of California-Santa Barbara
Heath et al. (1988) (Top 5)	Syracuse University; University of Hawaii; Teachers College, Columbia University; University of California-Santa Barbara; Western Washington University, Bellingham
Leung (1993)	University of Wisconsin, Madison; Fordham University; Ohio State University; University of Nebraska-Lincoln; University of Houston
Rogers et al. (1995)	Fordham University; University of Maryland, College Park; Ohio State University; University of California-Santa Barbara; Teachers College, Columbia University
Institutions cited in three or more articles	University of California-Santa Barbara; Syracuse University; Western Washington University-Bellingham, Teachers College, Columbia University
Institutions cited in two or more articles	Boston University; Fordham University; University of Hawaii; Ohio State University

tency Checklist is organized along six sections and 22 specific competencies. In their presentation of the checklist, Ponterotto et al. (1995) present a research-supported and/or conceptual rationale for the broad categories and for each of the 22 specific competencies. Many of these competencies were extracted from a review of the "model program" literature. The checklist sections and competencies are listed in the first column of Table 5.2.

In assessing the status of multicultural training in doctoral counseling programs, the competency checklist could prove useful for a number of reasons. First, the checklist is carefully thought-out and comprehensive, and it is rooted in the preferred infusion/integration model of training (see D'Andrea & Daniels, 1995; LaFromboise & Foster, 1992; Margolis & Rungta, 1986). Second, the checklist uses a forced-choice format, in which the competency is either met or not met. There is no Likert-type scale to indicate "well, it's partially met." Finally, a national survey of training programs using the checklist as the assessment instrument will help identify which competencies are being met on a national basis, and which are more resistant to development. Such information could lead to concrete suggestions for multicultural program development. The next section of this chapter turns to the national survey using the Ponterotto et al. (1995) multicultural competency checklist.

The Multicultural
Competency Checklist Survey

Sample and Procedure

During spring semester, 1995, a three-page survey was sent to Training Directors or targeted individuals at 63 APA accredited and 27 non-APA accredited doctoral programs in counseling psychology. The APA accredited programs were selected from the annual listing in the December 1994 issue of *American Psychologist* (Note: the 1994 listing included 64 programs, but 1 of the programs terminated during the 1995 year). The non-APA accredited programs were selected at random from the Hollis and Wantz (1994) Counselor Preparation listing. The majority of these programs were Counselor Education doctoral programs approved by the Council for Accreditation of Counseling and Related Educational Programs (CACREP). An attempt was made to sample non-APA accredited programs from diverse regions of the country.

It should be noted that some previous and often cited counseling surveys were limited to APA accredited counseling psychology programs (e.g., Hills & Strozier, 1992; Quintana & Bernal, 1995). The present survey also included non-APA accredited programs because expanded coverage will reveal a more accurate picture of doctoral level counseling training nationwide.

The survey was sent either to a faculty member known to the present author (in hopes of increasing response rate) or to the program's Director of Training. Returns were received from 66 of the 90 programs for an overall response rate of 73%. For APA accredited programs, 49 of 63 programs responded for a response rate of 78%. For non-APA accredited programs, 17 of the 27 programs responded for a response rate of 63%. Given this overall response rate was deemed satisfactory, no follow-up mailing was made.

Table 5.2 Percentage of Programs Meeting Competencies on the Multicultural
Competency Checklist

Competency	n^a	Percentage
Minority Representation		
1. At least 30% of faculty represent racial/ethnic minority populations	19	29
2. At least 30% of faculty are bilingual	11	17
3. At least 30% of students in the program represent racial/ethnic minority populations	22	33
4. At least 30% of support staff (e.g., secretarial staff, graduate assistant pool) represent racial/ethnic minority populations	19	29
Curriculum Issues		
5. The program has a required multicultural counseling course	59	89
6. The program has one or more additional courses in the area that are required or recommended (e.g., advanced multicultural counseling research seminar, or an advanced clinical issues course)	41	62
7. Multicultural issues are integrated into all coursework. All program faculty can specify how this is done in their courses. Furthermore, syllabi clearly reflect multicultural inclusion	38	58
8. A diversity of teaching strategies and procedures are employed in the classroom. For example, both cooperative learning and individual achievement approaches are utilized	59	89
9. Varied assessment methods are used to evaluate student performance and learning. For example, students complete both written assignments and oral presentations	62	94
Counseling Practice and Supervision		
10. Students are exposed to a multicultural clientele during fieldwork. At least 30% of clients seen by students are non-White	23	35
11. Multicultural issues are considered an important component of clinical supervision whether the supervision is conducted by program faculty or on-site supervisors. The program has a mechanism to monitor the quality of field supervision	48	73
12. The program has an active "Multicultural Affairs Committee" composed of faculty and students. The committee provides leadership and support to the program with regard to multicultural issues	13	20

Table 5.2 Continued

Competency	n^a	Percentage
Research Considerations		
13. The program has a faculty member whose primary research interest is in multicultural issues	57	86
14. There is clear faculty research productivity in multicultural issues. This is evidenced by faculty journal publications and conference presentations on multicultural issues	55	83
15. Students are actively mentored in multicultural research. This is evidenced by student-faculty coauthored work on multicultural issues and completed dissertations on these issues	53	80
16. Diverse research methodologies are apparent in faculty and student research. Both quantitative and qualitative research methods are utilized	58	88
Student and Faculty Competency Evaluation		
17. One component of students' yearly (and end of program) evaluations is their sensitivity to and knowledge of multicultural issues. The program has a mechanism for assessing this competency (e.g., relevant questions are included on student evaluation forms)	23	35
18. One component of faculty teaching evaluations is the ability to integrate multicultural issues into the course. Faculty are also assessed on their ability to make all students, regardless of cultural background, feel equally comfortable in class. The program has a mechanism to assess this competency (e.g., questions on student evaluations of professors)	12	18
19. Multicultural issues are reflected in comprehensive examinations completed by students	49	74
20. The program incorporates a reliable and valid paper-and-pencil or behavioral assessment of student multicultural competency at some point in the program	13	20
Physical Environment		
21. The physical surroundings of the Program Area reflect an appreciation of cultural diversity (e.g., art work [posters, paintings] is multicultural in nature and readily visible to students, staff, faculty, and visitors upon entering the Program Area, faculty offices, etc.)	30	46
22. There is a "Multicultural Resource Center" of some form in the Program Area (or within the Department or Academic Unit) where students can convene. Cultural diversity is reflected in the decor of the room and in the resources available (e.g., books, journals, films, etc.)	11	17

NOTE: a. Total survey respondents, $N = 66$.

Survey Instrument

Each targeted faculty member received an individualized cover letter requesting participation in the study along with a three-page survey. Pages 1 and 2 of the survey included the 22-item Multicultural Competency Checklist taken directly from the Ponterotto et al. (1995) article. Table 5.2 presents the competency checklist items. Respondents were asked simply to check which of the 22 competencies were either "met" or "not met" by the program. Respondents were told that "the checklist can be completed by an individual faculty member or, preferably, by more than one program faculty member reviewing the items together."

As can be seen in Table 5.2, the competency checklist is organized along six dimensions: Minority Representation (4 items), Curriculum Issues (5 items), Counseling Practice and Supervision (3 items), Research Considerations (4 items), Student and Faculty Competency Evaluations (4 items), and Physical Environment (2 items). The third page of the survey asked the specific name of the doctoral programs (e.g., counseling psychology, counselor education, counseling and personnel services, etc.), whether the survey was filled out by a single faculty member or by more than one faculty member working together, and whether the regular instructor of the multicultural counseling course was a core or adjunct faculty member. Finally, the respondent(s) were given the opportunity to nominate their program as a "Model Multicultural Training Program" in one or more of the six competency areas included in the checklist.

Results

In reviewing the results of this study, the reader is again reminded that a rationale for each of the 22 competencies is presented in Ponterotto et al. (1995). For example, in the "Minority Representation" category, the 30% figure was chosen for each of the items based on the "critical mass" literature. This body of literature notes that a minimal 30% representation rate of minority students is needed to reach a positive campus climate for these students (Green, 1988; Ponterotto, Lewis, & Bullington, 1990). It is recommended that the results presented below be read simultaneously with the Ponterotto et al. (1995) report.

In 86% of the programs responding, the survey was completed by a single faculty member. In 14% of returns, the survey was completed by two or more faculty working together. Chi-square tests were used to examine whether the frequency with which competencies were met or unmet varied by APA status of the program. All 22 chi-square tests were not significant, indicating no differential pattern in meeting the competencies across APA status. In other words, the competencies more likely to be met (or unmet) by the APA accredited programs were also the competencies more likely to be met (or unmet) by non-APA accredited programs.

The data in Table 5.2, therefore, is collapsed across both APA accredited and non-APA accredited programs. Looking at these collective results, the five competencies met most frequently by counseling doctoral programs were Item 9, "Varied assessment methods are used to evaluate student performance and learning. For example, students complete both written assignments and oral presentations" (met by 94% of programs); Item 5, "The program has a required multicultural counseling course" (89%); Item 8, "A diversity of teaching strategies and procedures are employed in the class-room. For example, both cooperative learning and individual achievement approaches are utilized" (89%); Item 16, "Diverse research methodologies are apparent in faculty and student research. Both quantitative and qualitative research methods are utilized" (88%); and Item 13, "The program has a faculty member whose primary research interest is in multicultural issues" (86%) (see Table 5.2).

The five competencies most infrequently met were Item 2, "At least 30% of faculty are bilingual" (17%); Item 22, "There is a Multicultural Resource Center of some form in the Program Area (or within the Department or Academic Unit) where students can convene. Cultural diversity is reflected in the decor of the room and in the resources available (e.g., books, journals, films, etc.)" (17%); Item 18, "One component of faculty teaching evaluations is the ability to integrate multicultural issues into the course. Faculty are also assessed on their ability to make all students, regardless of cultural back-ground, feel equally comfortable in class. The program has a mechanism to assess this competency (e.g., questions on student evaluations of professors)" (18%); Item 12, "The program has an active Multicultural Affairs Committee composed of faculty and students. The committee provides leadership and support to the program with regard to multicultural issues" (20%); and Item 20, "The program incorporates a reliable and valid paper-and-pencil or behavioral assessment of student multicultural competency at some point in the program" (20%).

Table 5.3 presents an overall ranking of the six competency areas. To arrive at these figures, the mean of the percentages for all the competencies making up the area was calculated. It is evident that the most frequently met competency area was Research Considerations (84%); whereas the least frequently met competencies fell in the Minority Representation cate-gory (27%).

Table 5.3 Ranking of Six Competency Categories Met by Programs

Category	Mean Percentage
Research considerations	84.3
Curriculum issues	78.4
Counseling practice and supervision	42.7
Student and faculty competency evaluation	36.8
Physical environment	31.5
Minority representation	27.0

NOTE: a. Total survey respondents, $N = 66$.

Survey respondents were also asked to self-nominate programs as "model training programs" in one or more of the six competency areas. Eighteen percent ($n = 12$) self-nominated in the minority representation category; 27% ($n = 18$) in the curriculum category; 12% ($n = 8$) in the practice and supervision category; 35% ($n = 23$) in the research category; 6% ($n = 4$) in the student and faculty evaluation component; and 6% ($n = 4$) in the physical environment category.

A final analysis examined the number of competency areas self-nominated by programs. Fifty-nine percent ($n = 39$) of programs did not nominate themselves as a model in any competency area; 14% ($n = 9$) self-nominated in one area; 8% ($n = 5$) self-nominated in two categories; 9% ($n = 6$) self-nominated in three areas; 6% ($n = 4$) self-nominated in four categories; 3% ($n = 2$) self-nominated in five areas; and 2% ($n = 1$) self-nominated in all six areas.

Survey respondents were also asked to indicate whether their multicultural counseling course(s) was usually taught by a core or adjunct faculty member. In 70% of programs, the course was taught by core faculty members; 2% of programs used adjuncts or related staff (e.g., counseling center staff); and 8% utilized both core and adjunct faculty (20% of programs did not respond to this item).

Survey Discussion

The discussion section of this chapter will take a closer look at the competency areas met and not met by programs with an eye toward providing program recommendations for meeting the more challenging competency areas. A glance at Table 5.3 will show that programs are doing a generally good job of meeting the "Research Considerations" competency. The mean rating across the four items comprising this group was 84%. Recent major reviews of the empirical literature (e.g., Atkinson & Lowe, 1995; Atkinson & Thompson, 1992; Leong, Wagner, & Tata, 1995; Ponterotto & Casas, 1991) attest to the explosion of research interest in this area over the past decade. It appears students and faculty in doctoral counseling programs are presenting and publishing multicultural research regularly, and they are incorporating both qualitative and quantitative methods in this effort (refer back to Table 5.2).

Naturally, the checklist survey results say nothing about the quality or utility of the growing research base in multicultural counseling. Nonetheless, it is now fair to say that multicultural counseling research has left its infancy stage and moved into a more solid, theory-driven adolescent period (see recent enlightening and penetrating discussion by Rowe, Behrens, & Leach, 1995). It is clear from the present survey results that research activity is the strongest multicultural competency currently being met by training programs nationwide.

Another strength of counseling doctoral programs nationwide vis-à-vis multicultural training, is the infusion of cultural issues throughout the curriculum (see Table 5.3). The five competencies constituting the "Curriculum Issues" area are being met, on average, by 78% of programs. Within this category, the majority of programs in the sample have a required multicultural course and utilize diverse teaching strategies and student evaluation procedures. Roughly one half of all responding programs have been able to infuse multicultural issues into all course work (refer back to Table 5.2).

The three competencies comprising the "Counseling Practice and Supervision" area are being met, on average, by 43% of sampled programs. Although a majority of the programs consider multicultural issues central to the supervision process, only a minority of programs are able to offer students exposure to a minority-based clientele during practicum and fieldwork. Furthermore, only a minority of programs have an organized committee to help advise and oversee multicultural program development (see Table 5.2).

The lack of exposure to minority clientele is, in part, a reflection of geographic region. In some university towns (particularly in the Midwest), culturally diverse clients represent numerical minorities. In such cases, training programs may need to engage in focused outreach efforts to the minority communities in the town or in nearby towns. It is likely that with commitment, effort, and networking, faculty can increase the diversity of sites used for practica and internships. Furthermore, as the demographic landscape of the entire country continues to reflect a more culturally and linguistically diverse population, exposure and experience with a culturally diverse clientele will naturally evolve (see demographic projections in Ponterotto & Casas, 1991).

Thirty-seven percent of responding programs meet the competency area titled "Student and Faculty Competency Evaluation" (see Table 5.3). A look back at the four competencies that make up this grouping (see Table 5.2) reveals that although a good majority of programs integrate multicultural issues into comprehensive examinations, relatively few programs include such issues on faculty and student evaluations. Furthermore, only one fifth of responding programs incorporate a reliable and valid objective measure of multicultural awareness/competence.

A Program/Department Multicultural Affairs Committee (see Competency 12 in Table 5.2) could be the vehicle for writing items for the faculty teaching evaluations and develop procedures for student multicultural evaluation. Furthermore, such a committee could take on the task of reviewing standardized multicultural competency assessment instruments for possible integration into evaluation and accountability efforts. Such instruments now receiving widespread national attention are the Multicultural Counseling Inventory (MCI), the Cross-Cultural Counseling Inventory (CCCI-R), the Multicultural Counseling Awareness Scale (MCAS), and the Multicultural Awareness/Knowledge/Skills Survey (MAKSS). These instruments have been the subject of comprehensive psychometric reviews (see Ponterotto, Rieger, Barrett, & Sparks, 1994; Ponterotto & Alexander, 1996; and Pope-Davis & Dings, 1995).

The two items comprising the "Physical Environment" category are met, on average, by 32% of responding programs. Almost one half of the programs have decorated the program/department area (including in-house training clinics) so that cultural diversity is duly reflected. One would think that this competency is one of the easiest to meet. Whereas some competency goals may take a number of years to meet (e.g., adequate minority faculty and student representation), creating a physically hospitable and welcoming environment could be a relatively short-term goal.

Very few programs have a "Multicultural Resource Center" of sorts in the program/department area. Given the space and budgetary confines of many programs, this result is not surprising. Nonetheless, a creative and resourceful Multicultural Affairs Committee (refer back to Competency 12 in Table 5.2) may want to consider working on this competency.

The biggest challenge to counseling programs nationwide with regard to the Ponterotto et al. (1995) competency infusion model is "Minority Representation." On average, only 27% of programs (see Table 5.3) are meeting the four competencies in this category (refer back to Table 5.2). A few observations can be made regarding this result. First, this category probably is the most accurate with regard to the completion of the surveys. For example, it is easy to count the number of minority faculty and determine whether this number satisfies the 30% critical mass figure. There is little room for error or exaggeration on these items. On the other hand, take Item 7, "Multicultural issues are integrated into all coursework": I was surprised that 58% of programs met this category. In my experience, in most programs there may be two or three faculty who work for this full integration, but it is uncommon for the full faculty to integrate multicultural issues into every course. Perhaps this response is accurate, or it may reflect some exaggeration on the part of some respondents.

A second observation regarding this finding is that the pool of prospective minority faculty is much smaller than the pool of majority-group faculty. Therefore, meeting the faculty representation category is challenging. The same could likely be said for the student representation category as well. Nonetheless, more and more counseling programs are hiring minority faculty. The strong student recruitment efforts begun in some programs a few years ago are paying off as more minority students reach the doctoral rank. In late April 1995, I made a few quick calls that revealed that the counseling psychology programs at New York University, Rutgers University, Fordham University, Temple University, University of Wisconsin-Madison, Penn State University, Virginia Commonwealth University, and New Mexico State University all hired full-time, tenure-tract minority scholars for fall 1995 academic appointments. Undoubtedly there were additional programs that successfully recruited minority faculty for fall 1995.

As more and more minority students are attracted to and accepted into counseling doctoral programs, the availability of doctoral-level counseling psychologists for all settings will increase. However, recruiting minority students and faculty will still need to be a priority if programs are to meet the minimal 30% critical mass requirement.

Comparison of Present Survey Results With Recent Surveys

It would be instructive to compare and integrate the present results with those found in the recent Hills and Strozier (1992) and Quintana and Bernal (1995) surveys. Although the surveys took different forms and asked different questions, there was enough overlap in training information gathered to allow for meaningful comparisons. It is important to remember that the two comparison studies only surveyed APA accredited programs, whereas the present survey included also non-APA accredited doctoral programs.

The survey response rates for the three studies were as follows: Hills and Strozier, 80%; Quintana and Bernal, 67%; and the present study, 73%. These are all in the satisfactory range for national mail surveys, and the rates are similar enough not to warrant speculative discussion as to differences.

A common area of inquiry across the surveys was whether a multicultural course was required of all students. Quintana and Bernal found that only 42% of programs held this requirement; Hills and Strozier reported that 59% held this requirement; and the present study found that 89% held this requirement. Although the inconsistency across studies was at first surprising, it is important to note that data for Hills and Strozier was collected in 1989, and data for Quintana and Bernal in 1991 (though the article was not published until 1995); whereas the present survey data was collected in 1995. The jump witnessed in the present study is therefore likely reflective of an increasing number of programs requiring a multicultural counseling course. For those advocating increased multicultural training, this finding is clearly a positive indication of progress.

With regard to the integration of multicultural issues into other counseling courses, each survey asked the question in a different manner, so direct comparisons are not recommended. Nonetheless, the results are instructive. Quintana and Bernal found that 88% of programs address minority issues in general courses. Hills and Strozier report that 63% of programs have units with a multicultural focus in from 1 to 13 other courses. The present study found that 58% of program integrate multicultural issues into *all coursework.*

With regard to minority representation among the faculty, Hills and Strozier found that, collectively, 11% of program faculty were non-White. Quintana and Bernal found that 22% of programs had minority faculty representation of 20% or more. Finally, the present survey found that 29% of programs reported a 30%+ minority faculty representation rate. Interestingly, Quintana and Bernal were using the general minority population as a comparison measure, selecting 20% representation as a critical point, whereas the present survey used a 30% cutoff figure working from research and theory in "critical mass."

Additional comparisons can be made between the Quintana and Bernal study and present survey. With regard to practicum training, Quintana and Bernal found that 66% of programs provide practica in community agencies serving minority populations. The present survey found that 35% of programs provide access to fieldwork sites where at least 30% of clientele is non-White. Here again, the different wording of the questions make a direct comparison unwise.

With regard to research of the faculty, Quintana and Bernal (1995) reported that 83% of programs include faculty "conducting research on minority issues" (p. 111). This is consistent with the findings of the present survey, which found that 86% of programs have a faculty member whose primary research interest is in multiculturalism, and that also found 83% of programs reporting clear faculty research productivity in multicultural issues as evidenced by journal publications and conference presentations. The two surveys taken in tandem support the relative strength of multicultural research training over other aspects of training.

Though incorporating different surveys and focusing on different aspects of training, the three surveys integrated here provide good insight into the status of multicultural training in APA accredited and non-APA accredited doctoral programs in counseling and counseling psychology. The results of the two surveys, taken together, reveal that, relatively speaking, multicultural research represents the strongest aspect of training, and minority representation the weakest.

Survey Limitations and Further Observations

This survey relied on a simple checklist methodology completed by in-house faculty. The limitations and threats to accuracy of this method are quite obvious. First, faculty may want the program to look good, and they may have given the program the benefit of the doubt on some checklist items. In the discussion section, I raised this question forcefully. Second, the faculty respondent may simply not know what each faculty member does in her or his class or supervision meeting, and thus may not be in a position to respond for the whole program. Such a situation could easily lead to reporting inaccuracies. It is important to remember that only 14% of returned surveys were completed by two or more faculty working together.

The survey was also limited in its breadth of coverage. It was clearly focusing on a narrow definition of multiculturalism, examining only racial/ethnic diversity. As one Program Director wrote on the survey: The competencies "say nothing about gender, disability, sexual orientation— only ethnicity." Future survey research may want to examine the broader definition of multiculturalism.

Although the survey did not include a section for respondents to write comments (a good idea for any replication/extension research), a number of faculty did add commentary to the checklist. A number of respondents highlighted that the checklist was stimulating and did or could serve as a valuable stimulus for faculty discussion. Two quotes in this vein follow: "The faculty really enjoyed completing the survey and it spurred *much* discussion"; and a "Very valuable checklist. I intend to bring it to the entire faculty."

Another faculty respondent, who is a women of color, voiced the following frustration:

> Great job on this article and checklist. In your chapter, could you address how uncomfortable it is to be a token or the only voice that speaks on behalf of multicultural counseling? The issue that the ACA (American Counseling Association) Multicultural Counseling Forum is dealing with is quite relevant here, i.e., what about training for educators who think they are aware, have knowledge and skills they do not possess?

A final observation revolves around current receptivity to the competencies, and efforts under way to meet them. A number of respondents indicated that they were working on specific competencies. Common statements written next to various items could be paraphrased as follows: "We are working hard on this competency but have not met it yet." I did get the sense that many programs were actively engaged in efforts to bolster multicultural aspects of training. Interestingly, this result is consistent with the Quintana and Bernal (1995) study, which found that 65% of their programs were in a "transitional" period of multicultural development, where the program is actively engaged in the process of improving its multicultural training.

A Model Multicultural
Training Program

In this final section of the chapter, we turn our attention to an outline of a model multicultural program in counseling. What would such a program "look like"? The checklist items in Table 5.2 provide the foundation for a model program. Such a program would have a critical mass of minority students and faculty, so that feelings of isolation or aloneness were minimized. Students and faculty would be exposed to multiple worldviews and different ways of knowing and learning. Faculty would consider multicultural issues as central to their mission as educators and researchers. Faculty would be involved in continuing education with regard to their own multicultural development. Finally, support and backing around multicultural issues would be evident among key administrators such as Chairpersons, Deans, Vice Presidents, and so on.

In regard to curriculum, a model program would infuse multicultural issues throughout the curriculum. To some degree, counseling training would be culture-centered (Pedersen & Ivey, 1994). Just as empathy and good listening skills are considered common to all counseling students and faculty, so too would be a sensitivity and awareness of the impact of culture, power, and oppression in today's multicultural society.

Multicultural and gender issues would be integrated into coursework, practica and internships, and research. Multiculturalism would not be limited to a separate course or an elective "add-on," but instead serve as a central component to the training process. Students and faculty would be held accountable for their competence in multicultural counseling.

Does a model multicultural training program currently exist? This is a difficult question to answer as even the stronger programs (see Table 5.1) acknowledge extensive room for improvement vis-à-vis multicultural training. All of the programs cited in Table 5.1 have unique strengths with regard to multicultural training. One of the programs cited multiple times in Table 5.1 is the University of California, Santa Barbara. In some ways, this program stands out among its peers and is worthy of closer scrutiny as we identify model programs.

Originally an APA-Accredited Counseling Psychology Program, the Santa Barbara Program has evolved into a Combined Program in Counseling/Clinical/School Psychology. Due to its long-term efforts and success in the multicultural training arena, the program was featured recently in a full-length article in *The Counseling Psychologist* (Atkinson, Brown, & Casas, 1996). The authors highlight that achieving ethnic parity in counseling psychology is both a moral and ethical imperative. Each year, the population becomes increasingly diverse culturally and linguistically, yet counseling programs continue to struggle to recruit sufficient numbers of minority students to help meet the mental health needs of a growing ethnic minority population.

Particularly with regard to recruiting and graduating racial/ethnic minority Ph.D.s, the Santa Barbara Program is indeed model. Recall that Table 5.3 highlights that "minority representation" is the competency category that most programs fail to meet. After a systematic 25-year effort to recruit minority students, the Santa Barbara Program now has reached a point where 54% of its students represent African American, Hispanic American, Asian American, and American Indian populations. Looking specifically at the counseling program, 72% of the students are ethnic minorities. Of the combined 10 program faculty, 1 is African American, 1 is Hispanic, and 1 is Asian American.

Atkinson et al. (1996) highlight two critical elements that were essential to their success in achieving ethnic parity. First, there must be a clear and explicit commitment to achieving ethnic parity in the program itself and in the larger institution. Second, there must be programmatic commitment to the value of ethnic diversity. The authors highlight the distinction between *diversity appreciation* and *diversity tolerance* (see also D'Andrea & Daniels, 1991). Clearly, the former attitude is essential if minority students and faculty are to feel truly valued and welcome at the university.

Ponterotto (1996) evaluated the Santa Barbara Program on the Multicultural Competency Checklist and found that it met 17 of the 22 competencies. Inasmuch as case study methodology can inform multicultural program development (see Ponterotto & Casas, 1991), the Atkinson et al. (1996) article serves as an excellent guide for counseling (and other professional) programs committed to long-term efforts to achieve ethnic parity in counseling training. This article is replete with successful strategies for recruiting, retaining, and empowering ethnic minority students and faculty.

Conclusion

This chapter has reviewed the current status of multicultural training in doctoral programs in counseling psychology and counselor education. The Multicultural Competency Checklist was introduced and served as the instrument for a new national survey of doctoral programs in counseling. The results of this survey were integrated with the results of previous national mail surveys, and a clearer picture of specific strengths and limitations vis-à-vis multicultural training was presented. The chapter closed with a brief outline of a "model" training program, and highlighted one specific program as strong, particularly with regard to achieving ethnic parity in counseling psychology. It is my hope that this chapter will stimulate further thinking, debate, and research on the relevance of culture in counseling training.

References

Allison, K. W., Crawford, I., Echemendia, R., Robinson, L., & Knepp, D. (1994). Human diversity and professional competence: Training in clinical and counseling psychology revisited. *American Psychologist, 49,* 792-796.

Arredondo, P. (1985). Cross-cultural counselor education and training. In P. Pedersen (Ed.), *Handbook of cross-cultural counseling and therapy* (pp. 281-290). Westport, CT: Greenwood.

Atkinson, D. R., Brown, M. T., & Casas, J. M. (1996). Achieving ethnic parity in counseling psychology. *The Counseling Psychologist, 24,* 230-258.

Atkinson, D. R., & Lowe, S. M. (1995). The role of ethnicity, cultural knowledge, and conventional techniques in counseling and psychotherapy. In J. G. Ponterotto, J. M. Casas, L. A. Suzuki, & C. M. Alexander (Eds.), *Handbook of multicultural counseling* (pp. 387-414). Thousand Oaks, CA: Sage.

Atkinson, D. R., & Thompson, C. E. (1992). Racial, ethnic, and cultural variables in counseling. In S. D. Brown & R. W. Lent (Eds.), *Handbook of counseling psychology* (2nd ed.; pp. 349-382). New York: John Wiley.

D'Andrea, M., & Daniels, J. (1991). Exploring the different levels of multicultural counseling training in counselor education. *Journal of Counseling and Development, 70,* 78-85.

D'Andrea, M., & Daniels, J. (1995). Promoting multiculturalism and organizational change in the counseling profession: A case study. In J. G. Ponterotto, J. M. Casas, L. A. Suzuki, & C. M. Alexander (Eds.), *Handbook of multicultural counseling* (pp. 17-33). Thousand Oaks, CA: Sage.

Green, M. F. (1988). *Minorities on campus: A handbook for enhancing diversity.* Washington, DC: American Council on Education.

Heath, A. E., Neimeyer, G. J., & Pedersen, P. B. (1988). The future of cross-cultural counseling: A Delphi poll. *Journal of Counseling and Development, 67,* 27-30.

Hills, H. I., & Strozier, A. L. (1992). Multicultural training in APA-approved counseling psychology programs: A survey. *Professional Psychology: Research and Practice, 23,* 43-51.

Hollis, J. W., & Wantz, R. A. (1990). *Counselor preparation 1990-92: Programs, personnel, trends* (7th ed.). Muncie, IN: Accelerated Development, Inc.

Hollis, J. W., & Wantz, R. A. (1994). *Counselor preparation 1993-95: Vol. 2. Status, trends, and implications* (8th ed.). Muncie, IN: Accelerated Development, Inc.

LaFromboise, T. D., & Foster, S. L. (1992). Cross-cultural training: Scientist-practitioner model and methods. *The Counseling Psychologist, 20,* 472-489.

Leong, F.T.L., Wagner, N. S., & Tata, S. P. (1995). Racial and ethnic variations in help-seeking attitudes. In J. G. Ponterotto, J. M. Casas, L. A. Suzuki, & C. M. Alexander (Eds.), *Handbook of multicultural counseling* (pp. 415-438). Thousand Oaks, CA: Sage.

Leung, S. A. (Chair). (1993, August). *Multicultural counseling competencies training in counseling psychology: Four case studies.* Symposium presented at the annual meeting of the American Psychological Association, Toronto.

Margolis, R. L., & Rungta, S. A. (1986). Training counselors for work with special populations: A second look. *Journal of Counseling and Development, 64,* 642-644.

Mio, J. S., & Morris, D. R. (1990). Cross-cultural issues in psychology training programs: An invitation for discussion. *Professional Psychology: Research and Practice, 21,* 434-441.

Parham, T. A. (1993). White researchers conducting multicultural counseling research: Can their efforts be "Mo betta"? *The Counseling Psychologist, 21,* 250-256.

Pedersen, P. B. (1995). Culture-centered ethical guidelines for counselors. In J. G. Ponterotto, J. M. Casas, L. A. Suzuki, & C. M. Alexander (Eds.), *Handbook of multicultural counseling* (pp. 34-50). Thousand Oaks, CA: Sage.

Pedersen, P. B., & Ivey, A. E. (1994). *Culture-centered counseling and interviewing skills: A practical guide.* Westport, CT: Praeger.

Ponterotto, J. G. (1996). Multicultural counseling in the twenty-first century. *The Counseling Psychologist, 24,* 259-268.

Ponterotto, J. G., & Alexander, C. M. (1996). Assessing the multicultural competence of counselors and clinicians. In L. A. Suzuki, P. Meller, & J. G. Ponterotto (Eds.), *Multicul-*

tural assessment: Clinical, psychological, and educational applications (pp. 651-672). San Francisco: Jossey-Bass.

Ponterotto, J. G., Alexander, C. M., & Grieger, I. (1995). A multicultural competency checklist for counseling training programs. *Journal of Multicultural Counseling and Development, 23,* 11-20.

Ponterotto, J. G., & Casas, J. M. (1987). In search of multicultural competence within counselor education programs. *Journal of Counseling and Development, 65,* 430-434.

Ponterotto, J. G., & Casas, J. M. (1991). *Handbook of racial/ethnic minority counseling research.* Springfield, IL: Charles C Thomas.

Ponterotto, J. G., Lewis, D. E., & Bullington, R. (Eds.). (1990). *Affirmative action on campus.* San Francisco: Jossey-Bass.

Ponterotto, J. G., Rieger, B. P., Barrett, A., & Sparks, R. (1994). Assessing multicultural counseling competence: A review of instrumentation. *Journal of Counseling and Development, 72,* 316-322.

Pope-Davis, D. B., & Dings, J. G. (1995). The assessment of multicultural counseling competencies. In J. G. Ponterotto, J. M. Casas, L. A. Suzuki, & C. M. Alexander (Eds.), *Handbook of multicultural counseling* (pp. 287-311). Thousand Oaks, CA: Sage.

Quintana, S. M., & Bernal, M. E. (1995). Ethnic minority training in counseling psychology: Comparisons with clinical psychology and proposed standards. *The Counseling Psychologist, 23,* 102-121.

Reynolds, A. L. (1995). Challenges and strategies for teaching multicultural counseling courses. In J. G. Ponterotto, J. M. Casas, L. A. Suzuki, & C. M. Alexander (Eds.), *Handbook of multicultural counseling* (pp. 312-330). Thousand Oaks, CA: Sage.

Rogers, M. R., Wade, J. C., Hoffman, M. A., Borowsky, S., & Sirmans, M. (1995, February). *A multimethod study of exemplary multicultural training in APA-accredited school and counseling psychology programs.* Paper presented at the annual Winter Roundtable on Cross-Cultural Psychology and Education, Teachers College, Columbia University, New York.

Rowe, W., Behrens, J. T., & Leach, M. M. (1995). Racial/ethnic identity and racial consciousness: Looking back and looking forward. In J. G. Ponterotto, J. M. Casas, L. A. Suzuki, & C. M. Alexander (Eds.), *Handbook of multicultural counseling* (pp. 218-236). Thousand Oaks, CA: Sage.

Sue, D. W., Arredondo, P., & McDavis, R. J. (1992). Multicultural counseling competencies and standards: A call to the profession. *Journal of Counseling and Development, 70,* 477-486.

6

Course Development
in Multicultural Counseling

Charles R. Ridley

Dorothy L. Espelage

Karen J. Rubinstein

Training professionals to give better service to multicultural populations has been firmly established as an important mission of graduate training programs. Numerous voices from minority professionals, nonminority professionals, professional and accrediting associations, credentialing agencies, and special interests groups join together in a unified chorus to promote this agenda. Clearly, the attention given to multicultural training has exploded over the past two decades. Perhaps the clearest evidence of this explosion is the mandate for graduate programs to provide multicultural training (American Psychological Association, 1986; Ridley, 1985).

One of the most popular ways to institute multicultural training is through a separate course on the subject. Today, many graduate training programs offer a separate course as their minimal offering in multicultural training. In a survey of American Psychological Association (APA) accredited counseling psychology programs, Hills and Strozier (1992) reported that the majority of programs had a primary course focused on multicultural issues. They also found that more than half of the programs required students to take at least one multicultural course.

Implementation of a multicultural course, despite its popularity, is not without its challenges. Ridley, Mendoza, and Kanitz (1994) singled out two problems facing educators who are responsible for multicultural training. First, multicultural training and counseling is still in its infancy. Therefore, decisions about what features to include in and exclude from courses are difficult. Second, many counselor educators were trained in an era when multiculturalism was not an integral part of graduate training. Consequently, they often lack the background and knowledge to function as subject matter experts.

In light of these problems, the purpose of this chapter is practical in nature: to assist counselor educators and supervisors in developing and preparing courses on multicultural counseling. We write this chapter out of concern for educators who are caught between the pressure to develop a meaningful multicultural course, on the one hand, and their lack of expertise and the embryonic state of the field, on the other. We also anticipate that experts in the field will benefit from our course conceptualization.

To achieve our objective, the chapter is organized into four major sections. The first section examines how a separate multicultural course fits into the overall curriculum. The second section explores the advantages and disadvantages of a separate course. The third section identifies and summarizes topical areas that could be included in a multicultural course. The fourth section describes helpful instructional resources.

How Does a Multicultural
Course Fit Into the Curriculum?

Copeland (1982) initially identified the single course as a multicultural training (MCT) design. Ridley, Mendoza, and Kanitz (1992) extended the "model to include program schemes that offer more than one course (perhaps two or three) but not enough courses to be considered a subspecialty" (p. 329). No matter how one defines a separate course design, there remains the larger issue of deciding how it fits into the total curriculum. Ultimately, counselor educators must be concerned about achieving meaningful training outcomes and meeting accreditation requirements.

Ridley, Mendoza, and Kanitz (1994) presented a framework that is helpful for conceptualizing the place of a multicultural course. Their framework is represented as a pyramid, consisting of five levels (see Figure 6.1). In ascending order, the five levels or stages are training philosophy, learning objectives, instructional strategies, program designs, and evaluation. Concerning the utility of the pyramid, Ridley, Mendoza, and Kanitz (1994) stated, "The pyramid construction is symbolic, illustrating that the process of developing an MCT program progresses in stages. Each stage builds on the integrity of preceding stages and forms a foundation for subsequent stages" (p. 231).

The first stage of the pyramid is training philosophy. It is the foundation and basis of training. The major issues involved in formulating an MCT philosophy are the following: motivations, theoretical framework for conceptualizing counseling and training, defining "multicultural," and scope of training. According to the authors, explicit attention to MCT philosophy is rare. Therefore, counselor educators must seek to make their philosophies explicit, coherent, and socially relevant.

The second stage involves learning objectives. The authors of the pyramid distilled 10 basic learning objectives: displaying culturally responsive behaviors, ethical knowledge and practice, cultural empathy, critiquing counseling theories for cultural relevance, developing culturally theoretical orientations, knowledge of normative characteristics, cultural self-awareness, knowledge of within-group differences, multicultural concepts and issues, and respecting cultural differences. The authors presented these objectives as options for training, but they did not consider them to be all-inclusive or mutually exclusive. They believe that the most important consideration in selecting learning objectives is their consistency with the training philosophy.

The third stage involves instructional strategies. The authors described 10 generic instructional strategies: didactic methods, experiential exercises, supervised practica/internships, reading assignments, writing assignments, participatory learning, modeling/observational learning, technology-assisted training, introspection, and research. By crossing the 10 instructional strategies with the 10 learning objectives, counselor educators can conceptualize a maximum array of strategies per each objective. They may also identify other methods that have not been previously used for a particular objective, and they are encouraged to expand both the objectives and strategies.

The fourth stage of the pyramid consists of program designs. The authors described six designs found in the literature. Copeland (1982) introduced four of these designs: separate course, area of concentration, interdisciplinary, and integration. Ridley et al. (1992) added the traditional program and workshop designs to this list. Designs may be implemented separately or

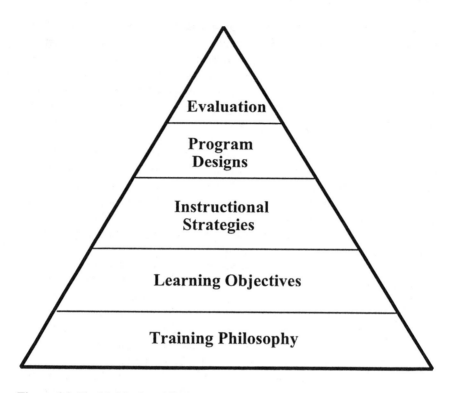

Figure 6.1. The Multicultural Counseling Training Program Development Pyramid

conjointly. To maximize the advantages and minimize the disadvantages of each design, the authors recommended combining a variety of designs. Moreover, they suggested that decisions made at this level must be guided by the program's training philosophy.

The fifth stage of the pyramid is evaluation. The authors described several barriers to effective evaluation: lack of clarity in training objectives, inadequate outcome measures, and research design problems. Evaluation is considered the most critical stage with respect to quality control and refinement of MCT. Evaluation is beneficial in providing a necessary feedback loop.

It should now be obvious that development of a multicultural course requires consideration of larger pedagogical issues. Any given course may serve a unique purpose, depending on how it is nested in a curriculum and training program. The purpose should be guided by the cogency of philosophy, specificity of learning objectives, linkages of learning objectives, instructional strategies and intended MCT outcomes, planful combination of the course with other program designs, and systematic evaluation of training. In short, every multicultural counseling course should be a means to a unique training end and not an end in itself.

The Relative Merits of the Separate Course Model

Once counselor educators determine how a multicultural course fits into the curriculum, they face some practical considerations. They should ask themselves this question: "To what extent can we successfully implement a course that meets our program objectives?" To answer this question, counselor educators should weigh the relative merits of the separate course model. Following is a discussion of the advantages and disadvantages of this design.

Advantages

1. Separate courses are relatively easy to infuse into an existing program (Copeland, 1982). This is especially true when the training program has a multicultural expert on its faculty. In such a situation, comparatively little effort or taxing of institutional resources is required. The faculty expert operates more or less independently in planning, teaching, and evaluating the course. The effort is not unlike that of faculty experts in any specialized field who develop and teach new courses.

2. This type of scheme assures coverage of the topic (Baruth & Manning, 1991). Although a single course may not provide enough training to foster multicultural counseling competency, it does guarantee that students gain exposure to the area (Ridley, Mendoza, & Kanitz, 1994). This is especially true if the course is required. In addition, a well-designed course can impart important information, provoke critical thinking, and begin to teach actual skills for use in multicultural contexts. A stimulating course also may motivate students to build on what they have learned and develop additional expertise in the area. Finally, a separate course may compensate for the lack of multiculturalism in other courses.

3. A separate course does not require total program evaluation (Baruth & Manning, 1991). Measuring training outcomes is always a great challenge. The challenge is more monumental when the outcomes are related to a total program. Ridley, Mendoza, and Kanitz (1994) developed a conceptual map for broadscale MCT evaluation, demonstrating the complexity of the pro-

cess. Evaluating a single course is more easily achieved and provides immediate feedback that can be used in course revision.

4. Employing a multicultural expert to teach a single course is not difficult for many programs (Baruth & Manning, 1991). Actually, programs have a variety of options to acquire the services of subject matter experts. Programs can hire faculty for tenure-line positions, employ adjunct or visiting faculty, retool an established professor, or contract with a scholar from another institution who could teach on a part-time bases. Ideally, each program should seek to hire its own resident expert.

Disadvantages

1. The major disadvantage of a separate course is its brevity and lack of depth (Reynolds, 1995). Although the course assures coverage of the topic, the content may be cursory, incomplete, or deficient. Several unintentional negative outcomes may result from superficial coverage (Ridley, Mendoza, & Kanitz, 1992, 1994). Programs may be at risk for being in violation of accreditation requirements. Midgette and Meggert (1991) assert that "offering a separate course in multicultural counseling does not meet minimum requirements to fulfill most standards" (p. 136). Trainees may learn to stereotype clients if only normative information is presented without adequate consideration of within-group differences. If the course focuses only on "knowledge and sensitivity," students may not learn any practical applications. If students do not learn multicultural skills, they may develop anxiety about the complexity of issues and avoid multicultural counseling.

2. A separate course may create counterproductive attitudes about multiculturalism. On the one hand, single, disjunctive courses may be viewed as ancillary (Baruth & Manning, 1991) or convey a sense of tokenism (Ridley et al., 1992). Brislin (1983) warned of the dangers of multicultural content becoming fringe interests. Hicks and Ridley (1979) sounded the call for "academic legitimacy." On the other hand, a single course may create the illusion of adequate training (Ridley et al., 1992). Both faculty and students may be co-opted into believing that the single course results in multiculturally competent counselors. This may be a case in which a little bit of knowledge makes a counselor dangerous, such as in the problem of counselors who stereotype based upon normative group data.

3. A separate course may not be required of all students (Baruth & Manning, 1991). If a program's commitment to MCT is marginal, some students may react with confusion and anger. They may find discrepancies between what they are taught in a multicultural course versus other courses that stress traditional theories and practice. One doctoral student expressed

anger that her multicultural course was an elective and came at the end of her program of studies. She lamented over her missed opportunities to have been more responsive to minority clients.

4. A separate course may place an unfair burden on the expert or invested faculty member. Because this design may represent low or marginal commitment, total faculty involvement may be lacking when it comes to multicultural initiatives. There is a tendency to foist all minority concerns onto the resident expert or minority faculty member without other members of the faculty sharing the ownership. One of the foremost scholars on multicultural counseling described how he felt unsupported by his own faculty, despite the wide recognition he receives in the profession.

Topical Areas

After examining the advantages and disadvantages of a separate multicultural course, counselor educators who adopt this model must select topics to cover. We have distilled from the literature nine topical areas that could be addressed in a multicultural course. Although we do not regard this list as exhaustive, we do believe it represents some of the most important topics. The nine topical areas are the following: rationale; racism, power, and prejudice; psychological assessment and diagnosis; therapy process variables and outcome goals; intervention strategies; multicultural counseling research; racial identity development; ethical issues in multicultural counseling; and normative group information.

The first author, Charles Ridley, covers each of these topics in his multicultural counseling course, but he gives varying degrees of attention to each topic. We recognize that the relative emphases on topics depends on a variety of factors. Prominent among these are the multicultural training philosophy, linkage with other courses in the curriculum and, as Reynolds (1995) pointed out, appropriateness and fit for students. Furthermore, as suggested by Ridley, Mendoza, and Kanitz (1994), educators can employ a variety of instructional strategies to facilitate learning in these content areas. Finally, we hope that our comments provide direction to develop lectures and generate classroom discussion.

Rationale

During the past 20 years, multiculturalism has become a powerful force in understanding not only the idiosyncratic nature of minority groups, but, more broadly, in understanding diversity among people in our complex social milieus. As such, multiculturalism examines both human differences and commonalities. Pedersen (1991) stated that multiculturalism may be viewed as a general theory and a "fourth force" in explaining human behavior. According to Pedersen, multiculturalism joins the ranks alongside the other three major forces: psychodynamic, behavioral, and humanistic perspectives. As a rationale for teaching multiculturalism, it can be argued that the perspective is itself a major theoretical framework for trainees to study. It also fosters opportunities for healthy critique of traditional theories of counseling.

Prejudice, Racism, and Power

Racism and prejudice are widespread. Yet these concepts are greatly misunderstood even among helping professionals. If counselors are to be effective in serving minority populations, it is imperative that they develop a better understanding of these concepts. They also need to come to terms with the mediating role power plays in perpetuating discriminatory behavior.

Prejudice. Racial, ethnic, and cultural prejudice arise in the form of preconceived judgments about individuals from selected groups—judgments, however, that are not based upon actual experience with the individuals who are prejudged. As such, prejudices are viewed as erroneous, generalized beliefs that tend to be inflexible in the face of disconfirming information. Prejudice lies in the attitudes and beliefs of individuals (Ponterotto & Pedersen, 1993).

Racism. Racism has been defined by Ridley (1995) as "any behavior or pattern of behavior that tends to systematically deny access to opportunities or privileges to members of one racial group while perpetuating access to opportunities and privileges to members of another racial group" (p. 28). Following this definition, racism—as opposed to racial prejudice—is the major source of harm to minority consumers. Racist actions may exist on an individual or institutional level, and may be either overt or covert. Further, racist behavior may be accompanied by race-based prejudices, in which case the racist act is intentional. On the other hand, racism may be unintentional. Here individuals are unaware of the deleterious effects of their behavior.

Power. Power of one group over another is the driving force behind racism. Jones (1981) states that "[racism] results from the transformation of race prejudice . . . through the exercise of power against a racial [or ethnic] group defined as inferior, by individuals and institutions with the intentional or unintentional support of the entire culture" (p. 28). White therapists and counselors are the major purveyors of power because of their disproportionate representation among the mental health professionals. This also means they are the greatest perpetrators of racism. At the same time, minority professionals also have the power vested in their positions. Although they may be well meaning, they often behave as unintentional racists. The power differential that exists between counselors of any race and minority consumers may result in inaccurate diagnoses, premature termination, inappropriate interventions, assignment to less qualified professionals, and unfavorable attitudes regarding treatment.

Psychological Assessment and Diagnosis

In mental health delivery systems, evidence suggests that racial and ethnic minority clients are likely to be informally assessed as pathological against the backdrop of the White majority cultural value system, more likely to score as severely psychopathological on assessment instruments, and more likely to receive inaccurate diagnoses reflective of more severe psychopathology than their majority-group member counterparts. In educational settings, minority students are more likely than White counterparts to receive lower estimates of measured intelligence (Helms, 1992).

A number of authors have elaborated on the difficulties of using standardized intellectual and personality instruments with ethnic minorities (Dana, 1993; Reynolds & Kaiser, 1990; Suzuki & Kugler, 1995). Suzuki and Kugler (1995) summarized the prominent areas of concern. These include (a) inappropriate test content, (b) inappropriate standardization samples, (c) examiner and language bias, (d) inequitable social consequences, (e) measurement of different constructs, (f) differential predictive validity, and (g) differences in test-taking skills.

In addition to the problems associated with psychological instruments, clinicians make judgmental and inferential errors that adversely affect consumers. Ridley (1995) highlighted some of the more prevalent of these errors: (a) fundamental attribution error, (b) diagnostic overshadowing, (c) confirmatory bias, (d) judgmental heuristics, (e) reconstructive memory, (f) overconfidence, and (g) attribution of paranoia.

To improve their multicultural assessment skills, clinicians must familiarize themselves with the aforementioned issues. Then they must check themselves to determine the extent to which they use tests appropriately or make judgmental and inferential errors. Once clinicians clear these hurdles, they can employ other assessment strategies. Concerning the use of standardized instruments, Ridley (1995) made the following recommendations for clinicians: (a) broaden their view of assessment, (b) particularize their assessments, (c) contextualize their assessments, (d) use multiple methods of data collection, and (e) interpret test scores cautiously. Suzuki and Kugler (1995) added the suggestions that clinicians consider the concept of cultural equivalence, demographic and environmental factors, racial identity and acculturation, the use of translated tests, and language issues. Concerning personal debiasing strategies, Ridley (1995) recommended the following for clinicians: (a) investigate alternative explanations of client behavior, (b) consider probability and base rate data, (c) use both confirmatory and disconfirmatory hypothesis testing strategies, and (d) delay decision making.

Therapy Process Variables and Outcome Goals

Counseling sessions consist of therapeutic processes and goals. In multicultural counseling, these variables take on greater complexity than in intracultural counseling. The assumptions that counseling techniques can be applied universally and that common therapeutic goals exist for all clients is due to the counselor's cultural encapsulation and denial of cultural differences. This assumption of universality has been challenged as a viable approach to counseling members of racial and ethnic minority groups. This is not to say, however, that basic counseling skills do not have utility for minority clients. Probably, counselors need a different paradigm in which they can combine basic skills with culturally responsive skills. This process must begin with an explicit, enlightened determination of the appropriateness of commonly utilized counseling processes and relevant goals (Sue & Sue, 1990).

For years, no attempt had been made to define the characteristics of a culturally skilled counselor. More recently, the culturally skilled counselor has been defined as possessing a tripartite set of competencies consisting of beliefs/attitudes (i.e., active awareness of personal assumptions regarding human nature and behavior change), knowledge (i.e., active attempts to understand the worldview of the client), and skills (i.e., active development and practice of culturally sensitive and relevant interventions) (Sue et al., 1982; Sue, Arredondo, & McDavis, 1992). Counselors who do not possess these competencies miss crucial opportunities to bridge gaps in communication concerning the relevance of cultural experience to the client's problems. This inevitably results in misunderstandings, distrust, and lack of rapport. Consequently, minority clients do not benefit from counseling in the same way as clients who hold similar cultural values and worldviews as the counselor.

Redefinition of therapeutic outcomes is also needed. Western notions of individual achievement and individual change, to the neglect of environmental change, is an example of a questionable outcome. Gelso and Fretz (1992) noted that these therapeutic goals may be inconsistent with the value systems of some racial and ethnic minority group members. In addition, process goals for within-session behaviors, including self-disclosure, exploration of feelings, and risk-taking, need to be reexamined in multicultural counseling contexts.

Ridley (1995) suggested that counselors and clients have unique expertise and should work collaboratively in setting therapeutic goals. Counselors have expert knowledge concerning psychological theory and therapeutic interventions, and clients are experts on their own problems, life circumstances, and worldviews. Collaboration takes on particular importance in multicultural counseling. Ridley identified three process goals: (a) establishing a working alliance, which includes attending to minority clients' mistrust of counselors; (b) explicitly exploring the racial dynamics between the counselor and client; and (c) obtaining a counseling agreement that clarifies roles and expectations for counseling. In addition, he identified three culturally relevant outcome goals: (a) resolution of racial victimization, (b) establishment of bicultural competence, and (c) building of assertive responses in reaction to racism.

Intervention Strategies

Effective intervention with racial and ethnic minority clients requires that counselors look beyond the universal perspective. A more advantageous approach involves counseling minority clients idiographically. This approach requires that counselors have cultural empathy (Ridley & Lingle, 1996); acknowledge normative information but not apply it indiscriminately; and develop individualized treatment plans, utilizing a range of interventions appropriate to the idiographic experience of each client. Therefore, the idiographic approach necessitates flexibility, and it challenges the assumption that fair treatment is equal treatment. According to Sue (1977), equitable treatment may be discriminatory. The idiographic approach to intervention supports the notion of differential but nondiscriminatory treatment (Ridley, 1995). Such differential and flexible usage of treatment interventions means that counselors have a broad repertoire of therapeutic responses and pay careful attention to cultural cues sent and received by the client. This approach will aid in determining which interventions are most appropriate. Another view endorses indigenous interventions (Atkinson & Lowe, 1995). Counselors using indigenous interventions conceptualize problems in a manner that is consistent with the client's belief system and compatible with the client's culture (Sue & Zane, 1987).

Multicultural Counseling Research

The foundation of any discipline is the body of research and scholarship upon which knowledge is advanced. In multicultural counseling, most of the knowledge base is conceptual in nature. However, there is a growing body of empirical literature. This, of course, bodes well for the specialty as scholars have become increasingly cognizant of the inability of the profession to adequately meet the needs of minority populations they serve (Ponterotto & Casas, 1991).

The history of multicultural counseling research is a short one, beginning in the late 1940s when some attention was given to the role of culture in counseling and psychotherapy. During that era, no empirical research was published. It was not until the 1960s that more systematic cross-cultural research began. At that point, the main focus was on client preferences regarding counselor race. The lack of research relating to cross-cultural treatment and diagnosis is strikingly evident. By the 1970s, a more prominent attention to counseling racial and ethnic minority clients research became discernible in the literature. The effects of race on a variety of client and counselor variables gained importance and became more carefully scrutinized (Atkinson, 1985).

This positive trend in cross-cultural research has continued well into the 1990s, where multicultural counseling research programs can be divided into five different topical areas: (a) variables pertinent to the racial and ethnic minority client, including behavior and social patterns, values, socio-psychological developmental trends of various minority groups, counselor preference and perceived effectiveness; (b) counseling process variables, including intervention techniques used with specific groups; (c) the effectiveness and relevance of traditional assessment techniques with multicultural populations; (d) variables involved in counselors' cultural biases and the implications for counseling outcome and client welfare; and (e) professional issues and development, including the development of multicultural counseling training programs (Ponterotto & Casas, 1991).

Despite the recent advances in cross-cultural counseling research, there remains a good deal of criticism. Ponterotto and Casas (1991), two prominent researchers in the field, have summarized these criticisms: (a) multicultural counseling research is not based upon a sound theoretical or structural foundation from which to evaluate research findings and/or the importance of various topics of study; (b) much of the multicultural counseling research is anecdotal and speculative, whereas little empirical data exist demonstrating the impact of a variety of variables on counseling outcome; (c) too much of the research continues to focus on specific counselor or client variables that affect the counseling process, while little attention is given to sociopolitical, historical, and developmental factors that may account for minority client behavior patterns both within and external to the counseling session; (d) differences within various racial and ethnic minority groups are largely ignored in favor of approaches that perpetuate stereotypes and generalizations; (e) a majority of the studies conducted are analogue studies, and college students are typically subjects, which makes the results less generalizable; and (f) methodology is often flawed because sample sizes are low and culturally biased assessment instruments are often utilized.

Racial Identity Development

The importance of within-group differences among counselors and clients has been given increased attention. Racial identity development has emerged as a major theoretical paradigm for conceptualizing within-group differences. The model mitigates the idea that racial group membership alone dictates how people will react in counseling, respond to specific interventions, or show preference for the type of counselor. In addition, racial identity is viewed as a model for conceptualizing the sociopolitical forces influencing the course of development and associated problems minority client's experience (Sue & Sue, 1990). Finally, the awareness of one's own racial identity development process is perceived as being imperative for all counseling trainees. This helps to focus the cultural dynamics involved in the counseling session on the counselor, together with the traditional focus on the client (Ponterotto & Pedersen, 1993).

A variety of models of racial/ethnic identity development have been proposed and widely researched. These models are useful in guiding trainees though the self-awareness process. They also help counselors to understand better the impact of race or ethnicity on the counseling process. The models are set forth in stages of development. Through the resolution of the conflicts presented at the various stages, individuals come to terms with themselves as racial and cultural beings. Early models of moral identity development have influenced the conceptualization of models of minority identity development (Atkinson, Morton, & Sue, 1993); race-specific, client-based models of minority identity development (Cross, 1971, 1978); and, most recently, majority counselor-based, White racial identity development models (Helms, 1984; Ponterotto, 1988).

Minority Identity Development Models. Cross (1971, 1978) and Sue and Sue (1990), among others, have constructed models of racial identity development. They describe a process whereby minority group members in the United States move from degrading themselves because of their minority group status to firmly accepting and celebrating their identities as racial and cultural beings. These models conceptualize minority individuals as moving from a stage of placing high value on the majority culture, while devaluing their own minority cultural experiences, through crises that challenge their attitudes. The crisis in identity precipitates individuals' acceptance of themselves as members of an oppressed group. Strong negative feelings begin to be expressed toward members of the majority culture. Then individuals begin to immerse themselves in their own culture and eventually emerge with a sense of racial and cultural pride. As individuals work through their crisis in identity, they may, at some point, devalue members of other minority groups. This may result from an overwhelming sense of immersion into their own culture. At the final stages of identity development, individuals begin to internalize positive attitudes toward their new identity, resolve conflicts between majority and minority cultures, actively attempt to eliminate all forms of oppression, and open themselves to constructive elements of the majority culture and to individuals from the dominant culture who are active in eliminating oppression of minority groups.

White Racial Identity Development Model. Helms (1984) and Ponterotto (1988) consider multicultural counseling as much a process of White counselors understanding their own cultural and racial development as it is understanding the racial identity development of minority clients. Common themes run through their models. Initially, counselors—many of whom had given little or no serious thought to issues of multiculturalism and oppression—begin to recognize the reality of individuals of other cultures. At this stage, they tend to evaluate minority group members according to dominant cultural standards. Eventually, feelings of guilt and shame for treating minority group members as inferior begin to surface as they realize the benefits of being White. They attempt to resolve the conflict either by avoiding contact with minorities or by trying to convince other Whites that minorities are not inferior. Those who avoid contact accept themselves as racist, and their previous conflictual feelings get transformed into racial anger and fear.

The alternative to accepting oneself as a racist is the further exploration and development of one's own racial identity. Progress is indicated by a dissatisfaction with racism in society, an unwillingness to be identified as racist, and a commitment to examining one's own possible contribution to racism. This process is accompanied by a search for a more positive White identity. The search involves efforts to become reeducated, to seek the guidance of others who have made an identity switch, and to educate and to change beliefs of other members of the dominant culture. When the new White racial identity is internalized, the individual seeks to learn about other cultural groups and eliminate oppression.

Helms (1984) proposed an integration of both minority racial identity development models and White identity development models. She suggested that the counseling process can be conceptualized as an interaction between members of two racial or cultural groups. Helms also recommended the development of culture-specific interaction models that describe the interaction in the counseling dyad. Her position is that benefits for the client can be maximized when interventions facilitate the racial identity development of both the client and counselor.

Ethical Issues in Multicultural Counseling

Ridley, Mendoza, and Kanitz (1994) suggested that ethical knowledge and practice, as it pertains to multicultural counseling, can be viewed on two levels. One level regards the provision of ethical training to counselor trainees, which includes training in multicultural counseling. The other level includes providing ethics training, which entails providing instruction in ethics issues pertinent to multicultural counseling.

Ethical training has been recognized by the American Psychological Association to include preparation of trainees to work competently with multicultural populations. Several authors have challenged the adequacy of the separate course model in meeting ethical requirements for training counselors to work with culturally diverse clients (Ridley, Mendoza, & Kanitz, 1994; Ibrahim & Arredondo, 1986). Ibrahim and Arredondo (1986) proposed the creation of standards for ethical training of counselors in working with clients of diverse backgrounds.

Training counselors in the multitude of ethical issues involved in multicultural counseling must include the development of moral and ethical awareness and problem solving. This task must go beyond mere familiarity with existing standards, for the current standards have been regarded as having questionable relevance to racial and ethnic minority groups. In addition, current guidelines do not guard against the cultural encapsulation of counselors. Cayleff (1986) suggests that failing to take into account the specific cultural worldviews of clients constitutes a violation of the principle involving a general respect for the rights and dignity of our clients. This argument could be taken a step farther: Failing to take a client's worldviews into account could actually cause harm occurring in the form of inappropriate conceptualization of the problem and ineffective treatment.

In a thoughtful chapter, Pedersen (1995) challenged counselors to distinguish between "fundamental" ethical principles and "discretionary" aspects of ethics. The former are non-negotiable and should not be compromised. They are not modifiable. Pedersen argues persuasively that the ethical guidelines of professional associations are discretionary and irresponsive to culturally diverse populations. His conclusion is the need for modification of these guidelines.

Another ethical consideration in multiculturalism pertains to research. Without well-conceived and tested interventions, professionals cannot be certain that they are delivering adequate service. Obviously, the larger ethical issue is welfare of the consumer. Recommendations for the inclusion of ethical guidelines in the area of multicultural research are as follows: delineation of a clear and culturally responsive theoretical perspective from which to base research, collaboration with members of minority groups under study, incorporation of within-group differences into research questions, and concern for promoting research that not only prevents harm to members of racial and ethnic minority groups but provides benefits as well (Ponterotto & Casas, 1991; Casas, Ponterotto, & Gutierez, 1986; Ibrahim & Arredondo, 1986).

Normative Group Information

Considerable attention in the literature is given to the most visible racial and cultural minority groups in this country. Often the focus is on African Americans, Asian Americans, Hispanic Americans, and Native Americans (e.g., Atkinson et al., 1993; Sue & Sue, 1990). Discussions typically center around dominant themes and characteristics of members of these respective groups. Other groups such as Southeast Asian immigrants or Puerto Ricans are sometimes described in the literature as well.

Ridley, Mendoza, and Kanitz (1994) identified knowledge of normative characteristics of cultural groups as one of their 10 learning objectives. Reynolds (1995), though signaling caution, corroborated this view:

> It is vital that a component of multicultural training include some cultural-specific content and information. Although many have expressed concerns about the dangers of focusing on cultural group differences (e.g., that can lead to stereotyping), it is vital that individuals understand that cultural differences exist and that they vary on an individual basis. (p. 320)

The assumption underlying the emphasis on knowledge of normative characteristics is that this enables counselors to understand members of the various groups better, and consequently to employ better clinical interventions. In teaching this topic, counselor educators should have two pressing concerns. First, they should encourage students to use normative characteristics as guidelines rather than as rigid rules in counseling. This will help students avoid the often cited problem of stereotyping clients. Second, educators need to help students integrate their knowledge of cultural groups into their interventions. Otherwise, they run the risk of not using the cultural data in a way that is beneficial to the client (Ridley, Mendoza, Kanitz, Angermeier, & Zenk, 1994).

Annotation:
Bibliography and Instructional Aids

An explosion of literature and instructional aids exists in the field of multicultural counseling. The proliferation of information makes it difficult to keep up with advances in the field, let alone determine which resources can most beneficially serve one's training needs. In this section, we annotate books and audiovisual aids. We have selected works that we believe are both representative of the field and reflect state-of-the-art thinking. Certainly, there was an element of subjectivity in deciding what to include and exclude. However, the spirit of our decisions was to assist counselor educators who are less entrenched in the field.

Atkinson, D. R., Morten, G., & Sue, D. W. (Eds.). (1993). *Counseling American Minorities: A Cross-Cultural Perspective* (4th ed.). Madison, WI: William C. Brown & Benchmark.

This book is intended to introduce both theory and practice of cross-cultural counseling to counselors and mental health practitioners. More than 20 well-known researchers and theorists in the field of cross-cultural counseling have contributed chapters addressing issues related to counseling the four major American minority groups: African Americans, American Indians, Asian Americans, and Latinos. The book is arranged in six sections.

The first section introduces cross-cultural terminology and highlights the importance of within-group differences among racial/ethnic minorities. This is followed by a lengthy discussion of how counseling has failed to meet the mental health needs of racial/ethnic minorities. The next four sections include a historical or sociological overview of each of the four racial/ethnic groups and a discussion of the pertinent issues related to counseling those groups. In each chapter, case examples are presented that require the reader to apply both theory and practice to a hypothetical cross-cultural counseling situation. This is a most useful instructional tool. A final chapter explores the future direction of cross-cultural counseling.

Boyd-Franklin, N. (1989). *Black Families in Therapy: A Multisystems Approach.* New York: Guilford.

This book should be required reading for every counselor-in-training. Case examples are used throughout the text, bringing to life and contextualizing the ever-important issues faced by Black families. Throughout the book, the author highlights the importance of letting go of stereotypes and viewing each Black family as a unique entity.

The text is divided into four sections. A section titled "The Cultural Context of Black, Afro-American Families" includes a discussion on racism, racial identification, skin color issues, Black extended family patterns, role flexibility and boundary confusion, and religion and spirituality. The next section explores the major treatment theories, issues, and interventions to be used with Black families. An emphasis is placed on the therapist's use of self to "join" with the family, or initiating of a therapeutic intervention by building a relationship with the family. Boyd-Franklin presents her own multisystems model as a framework for facilitating the joining or engaging with families. This model allows therapists to intervene at multiple levels, including individual, family, church, and community.

The next section deals with the diversity of familial structures, including single-parent Black families, Black middle-class families, and Black couples. Implications for training, supervision, and research are discussed in the last section.

Comas-Diaz, L., & Griffith, E. E. H. (Eds.). (1988). *Clinical Guidelines in Cross-Cultural Mental Health.* New York: John Wiley.

A number of psychiatrists and psychologists discuss a variety of topics related to working with clients from different ethnic and cultural backgrounds. The contributors represent a cross-section of academicians and clinicians who merge theory and practice, providing a framework for the development of cross-cultural skills. The book has three sections. The first section examines ethnosociocultural factors such as cultural identity and adjustment, ethnic diversity and values, language and psychotherapy, religion and politics in psychotherapy, and ethnocultural assessment. These issues are examined in the context of the therapeutic relationship, and implications for treatment are discussed.

The next section focuses on six ethnic groups: Afro-Americans, Mexican Americans, Puerto Ricans, Cubans, Southeast Asian Refugees, and West Indians. Each chapter begins with a historical perspective and follows with a delineation of important sociocultural factors that have implications for clinical practice. Between-group and within-group differences are emphasized. The book ends with a discussion of the limitations of current mental health practices.

Dana, R. H. (1993). *Multicultural Assessment Perspectives for Professional Psychology*. Boston: Allyn & Bacon.

This book methodically and carefully outlines an argument and rationale for the development of a multicultural model of assessment. An overview of the psychological services available for multicultural populations provides the groundwork for this argument. Minority groups' underutilization of the mental health services are attributed to a mental health system that embraces an Anglo-American worldview.

The next four sections discuss the identity, values, beliefs, and perceptions of four minority groups: African Americans, Asian Americans, Hispanic Americans, and Native Americans. A general outline of current approaches and uses of assessment is followed by an informative discussion of potential moderating variables (e.g., acculturation, ethnic identity) in the assessment of clients from the four minority groups. This leads to the final chapter, in which a flowchart for multicultural assessment practices is presented. Emphasis is placed on the awareness and incorporation of moderator variables and identification of confounds in assessment. Cultural validity is seen as an important imperative in the selection of measures and interpretation of findings. These considerations result in a culturally competent assessment.

Helms, J. E. (Ed.). (1990). *Black and White Racial Identity: Theory, Research, and Practice*. Westport, CT: Greenwood.

Scholars come together to discuss the importance and usefulness of racial identity models in understanding the behavior of Blacks and Whites. This book moves beyond the question of whether race or culture should be included in psychological theory and begins with the notion that psychological theory and practice must be guided by racially and culturally explicit models. The first section includes a review of several areas of research: racial identity terminology, Black racial identity theory, measurement of Black racial identity attitudes, and measurement of White racial identity develop-ment. The second section explores the psychological correlates of racial identity, including values, attitudes, and cognitive styles. In the last section, the impact of racial identity on the counseling process is discussed.

McGoldrick, M., Pearce, J. K., & Giordano, J. (Eds.). (1982). *Ethnicity and Family Therapy*. New York: Guilford.

This classic demonstrates that the family cannot be isolated from the larger context of culture. Contributors represent the fields of nursing, psychiatry, psychology, and social work. This book was a major breakthrough in the way in which clinicians and researchers conceptualize the impact of ethnicity on the family system. A conceptual overview of ethnicity and family therapy introduces the text and is followed by an ecological model of ethnic families. The contributors argue that family and ethnicity are inevitably linked and the goal of therapy should be to delineate this relationship, incorporating ethnic-ity into theories and models of family therapy.

The following 19 chapters provide a comprehensive discussion of the cultural background for 19 of America's ethnic groups (i.e., Black families, Irish families, Cuban families). Each chapter focuses on analyzing belief systems, values, cultural contexts, and religion and spirituality in each group. In addition, these factors are discussed in relationship to therapy process and outcome. Specific intervention strategies are discussed using actual case examples. The remaining chapters focus on myths or stereotypes of certain ethnic groups, followed by several intervention strategies for use with Vietnamese families and Chinese American families.

Pedersen, P. B. (Ed.). (1988). *Handbook of Cross-Cultural Counseling and Therapy* (2nd ed.). Westport, CT: Greenwood.

This book is definitely an encyclopedia of cross-cultural counseling and therapy. The 40 chapters are an attempt to condense the volumes of articles and books in this field. Paul Pedersen selected prominent authors and asked them to condense their ideas into short chapters. The final product is an exhaustive review of many issues in this broad field.

There are too many chapters to summarize. However, the book has five major sections: (a) Special Topics, (b) Alternative Research Methodologies, (c) Specific Client Populations, (d) Key Issues of Controversy, and (e) Guidelines for Education and Training.

Pedersen, P. B. (1994). *A handbook for Developing Multicultural Aware-ness* (2nd ed.). Alexandria, VA: American Counseling Association.

This book is easy to read and a must for counselors-in-training, counselors, supervisors, instructors, and mental health practitioners. Paul Pedersen arranges the book in three sections: awareness of culturally learned assumptions, knowledge of multicultural information, and multicultural skills. Rules of multiculturalism are outlined in the first chapter. Culture is described as broad, complex, and dynamic. This is followed by a chapter on the three-stage developmental progression from multicultural awareness to knowledge to skill. An enlightening discussion of 10 common cultural biases in dominant counseling theories follows. This section ends with a chapter that provides a number of exercises to help readers determine their implicit learned assumptions.

The next section covers multicultural information that should be incorporated into a counselor's knowledge base. Topics include: culture shock; racism, prejudice, and power; racial/ethnic identity development models; patterns of cultural systems; research in multicultural counseling; and ethical dilemmas of multicultural counselors. Skills for multicultural action are found in the last section of this book and include a discussion of Pedersen's triad training model and dimensions of multicultural skill training.

Pedersen, P. B., Draguns, J. G., Lonner, W. J., & Trimble, J. E. (Eds.). (1996). *Counseling Across Cultures* (4th. ed.). Thousand Oaks, CA: Sage.

Following the tradition of the first three editions, this completely updated and expanded classic should continue as one of the leading books in the field. Thirty scholars from racially and ethnically diverse backgrounds examine the cultural context of assessment and intervention with a focus on African Americans, Asian Americans, Hispanics, American Indians, refugees, and international students. Other topics covered are gender issues, ethics, cultural empathy, behavioral approaches, and the future of the field. In addition, the book discusses the effectiveness of intercultural counseling. The book has practical information for practitioners as well as thoughtful reflections for scholars and researchers. Students and counselors who have not read much in this area can get a good overview.

Ponterotto, J. G., Casas, J. M., Suzuki, L. A., & Alexander, C. M. (Eds.) (1995). *Handbook of Multicultural Counseling*. Thousand Oaks, CA: Sage.

This book provides the reader with the most recent advances and latest developments in multicultural theory, research, and practice. Leading scholars, as well as emerging scholars, provide a comprehensive summary of current, pressing issues in this field. The book is divided into seven sections.

Historical perspectives and professional issues are presented in the first section. This is followed by a discussion of theory and models of racial and ethnic identity development. Supervision and training issues are found in the next section. Section 4 consists of three chapters addressing practical strategies in multicultural counseling, including training models, interviewing, and assessment. Section 5 includes two research reviews of the role of ethnicity and race in counseling and psychotherapy. The last two sections of this edited book include a number of critical and emerging topics in multicultural counseling. Titles include (1) Indigenous Models of Mental Health Intervention, (2) Breakdown of Authority and Implications for Counseling Young African American Males, (3) Multicultural Organizational Development, (4) Intelligence and Personality Assessment, (5) Counseling Children and Adolescents in Schools, (6) Multicultural Health Counseling, (7) Career Development and Counseling, (8) Group Work, and (9) Culture and Families. This book is best used as a reference for the majority of issues in the theory, research, and practice of multicultural counseling.

Ridley, C. R. (1995). *Overcoming Unintentional Racism in Counseling and Therapy: A Practitioner's Guide to Intentional Intervention*. Thousand Oaks, CA: Sage.

This book is written for all mental health practitioners, regardless of their professional, racial, or cultural backgrounds. The dynamics and effects of racism in counseling and therapy are examined, with special attention given to the insidiousness of unintentional racism. The author argues persuasively that many practitioners sabotage their own therapeutic efforts, and in so doing perpetuate the very problems they seek to overcome. The book is organized into two major sections. The first section consists of six chapters that explore the nature, scope, history, and dynamics of racism in mental health delivery systems. The second section, which consists of five chapters, offers strategies and recommendations to overcome the counselor's unintentional racism. The book offers supporting clinical examples to help counselors gain insight into their therapeutic practices and modify their interventions.

Sue, D. W., & Sue, D. (1990). *Counseling the Culturally Different: Theory and Practice* (2nd ed.). New York: John Wiley.

This book integrates the most updated published research in the theory and practice of multicultural counseling. The book is divided into three sections. In the first, the authors provide readers with a conceptual framework to understand the minority experience and how counseling interacts with larger societal forces. This section includes (a) barriers to effective counseling, (b) communication styles, (c) sociopolitical considerations of mistrust in counseling, (d) racial/cultural identity development, (e) cross-cultural family counseling, (f) dimensions of worldviews, and (g) the culturally skilled counselor. The next section includes chapters that highlight the most important issues in counseling four specific minority groups: (a) American Indians, (b) Asian Americans, (c) Black Americans, and (d) Hispanic Americans. The final section includes 18 cases that are intended to portray common cross-cultural issues and dilemmas faced by counselors.

Audiovisual Aids

The following audiovisual materials are distributed by Microtraining Associates, an organization spearheaded by Dr. Allen Ivey, a leader in the field of microskills training and its application to multicultural counseling and therapy. For the past 30, years this organization has published and distributed books and videotapes to thousands of mental health professionals. A description of books and videotapes is outlined in an annual newsletter and a number of videotapes were selected and summarized from the 1996 newsletters. Not included below are videotapes from leading professionals in the field of multicultural counseling, including Teresa LaFromboise, Patricia Arredondo, Thomas Parham, and Paul Pedersen. Requests for materials and/or the annual newsletter may be directed to Microtraining Associates at 413-549-2630.

Ivey, A., & Shizuru, L. S. (Producers), Darby, G. E. (Director), & Pedersen, P. (Consultant). (1981). *Cross-Cultural Counseling: Clinical Case Examples* [Film]. Honolulu: The East-West Center. (Available from Microtraining Associates, Inc., P. O. Box 9641, North Amherst, MA 01059-9641).

This 52-minute videotape raises the issue of what roles culture plays in counseling and how assumptions underlying traditional theories of counseling may be inadequate in the multicultural context. Three case examples are used to illustrate how some microskills are more appropriate than others for multicultural counseling. In the first case, a White counselor and White client focus on the feelings and behaviors of the client, ignoring any impact of the client's decisions on other people. In the second case, a Japanese counselor and client demonstrate the importance of including other family members in the decision-making process. In the third case, another counselor-client dyad shows how the emphasis on relationships in traditional theories may be ineffective when a client wants more action out of the counseling process. These case examples are followed by a minilecture on multicultural issues.

Pope-Davis, D. B., Reynolds, A. L., & Vázquez, L. A. (1992). *Multicultural Counseling: Issues of Ethnic Diversity* [Film]. (Available from The University of Iowa Video Center, C-215 Seashore Hall, Iowa City, IA 52242, or call 1-800-369-4692).

This 28-minute video focuses on how ethnic and racial differences between counselor and client may impact the interpersonal process. Dr. Donald Pope-Davis encourages the viewer to consider the role played by culture in the presenting problem, the individuality of the client, and how cultural assumptions influence the worldviews of the counselor and client. Three vignettes are presented, including a Puerto Rican counselor-African American client, a White American counselor-Mexican American client, and a Black American counselor-Asian American client. A series of stimulating questions follow each vignette. Instructors can stop the video after each vignette and begin a discussion based on each question. These questions make this video an excellent instructional tool.

Sue, D. W. (1989a). *Barriers to Cross-Cultural Counseling* [Film]. (Available from Microtraining Associates, Inc., N. Amherst, MA 01059).

This is the first of a three-part lecture series, all of which include materials from *Counseling the Culturally Different* (Sue & Sue, 1990). In 75 minutes, Dr. Derald Wing Sue includes a discussion of those communication styles, culture-bound values, and class-bound values, implicit and explicit in counseling, that create conflict between culturally different counselors and clients. He argues that universal application of these counseling interventions contributes to minority groups underutilization of mental health services. Emphasis is placed on the development of culturally specific intervention strategies.

Sue, D.W. (1989b). *Minority Identity Development for Counseling* [Film]. (Available from Microtraining, Inc., P. O. Box 9641, North Amherst, MA 01059-9641).

This is the second lecture of a three-part lecture series. In 64 minutes, Dr. Derald Wing Sue presents the five stages of the racial cultural identity development model. Advantages of this model are proposed. First, it recognizes within-group differences in minority groups and sensitizes persons to those aspects of oppression, discrimination, and racism. Second, this model provides counselors with an excellent assessment tool that dictates specific, tailored or individualized interventions. Implications for counseling are outlined for each of the five stages.

Sue, D. W. (1990). *Culture-Specific Strategies in Counseling* [Film]. (Available from Microtraining Associates, Inc., P. O. Box 9641, North Amherst, MA 01059-9641).

This is the final lecture of a three-part series. A rationale for the use of culture-specific techniques is presented. Communication styles, both verbal and nonverbal, are different both between and within minority groups. Dr. Derald Wing Sue includes a detailed discussion on the role of proxemics, kinesics, paralanguage, and high-low context communication in cross-cultural counseling. Solid research studies support these notions.

Conclusion

Of the six models identified in the literature to integrate multicultural content into counseling training, the separate course persists as the most popular. Counselor educators who are responsible for developing and teaching multicultural counseling courses often face two major problems. They may lack expertise in the area due to their own traditional training. Guidance as to what topics to include in a course may also be unavailable to them. Much of their uncertainty is due to the embryonic state of the field.

This chapter was written to assist instructors of multicultural counseling courses. After setting the separate course model into the overall context of multicultural training, the relative merits of this model were discussed. Then nine topical areas deemed of importance to a multicultural course were presented. Finally, an annotation of selected books and audiovisual aids was provided. We believe this annotation should shorten and enhance the counselor educator's efforts to identify beneficial instructional resources.

To conclude, we anticipate several practical outcomes of our presentation. Obviously, we hope that counselor educators will incorporate our suggestions about topical areas and instructional resources into their courses. More important, we hope that they will design courses that are consistent with their programmatic philosophy, needs, and learning objectives. Programs that begin with a philosophy of multicultural training may very well move beyond our ideas about course content and instructional resources. We encourage such experimentation. To ascertain the effectiveness of courses and improve pedagogy, we also encourage the consistent evaluation of multicultural courses. Finally, we recommend the publication of quantitative and qualitative evaluation reports. If these steps are taken, we are confident that graduate training programs will be greatly enriched.

References

American Psychological Association. (1986). *Accreditation handbook* (Rev. ed.). Washington, DC: APA Committee on Accreditation and Accreditation Office.

Atkinson, D. R., & Lowe, S. M. (1995). The role of ethnicity, cultural knowledge, and conventional techniques in counseling and psychotherapy. In J. G. Ponterotto, J. M. Casas, L. A. Suzuki, & C. M. Alexander (Eds.), *Handbook of multicultural counseling* (pp. 387-414). Thousand Oaks, CA: Sage.

Atkinson, D. R., Morton, G., & Sue, D. W. (Eds.). (1993). *Counseling American minorities; A cross-cultural perspective* (4th ed.). Madison, WI: Brown & Benchmark.

Atkinson, D. R. (1985). A meta-review of research on cross-cultural counseling and psychotherapy. *Journal of Multicultural Counseling and Development, 13,* 138-153.

Baruth, L. G., & Manning, M. L. (1991). *Multicultural counseling and psychotherapy: A lifespan perspective.* Columbus, OH: Merrill.

Boyd-Franklin, N. (1989). *Black families in therapy: A multisystems approach.* New York: Guilford.

Brislin, R. W. (1983, August). *Cross-cultural studies in social psychology of relevance to ethnic group research: Examples and recommendations.* Paper presented at the annual meeting of the Psychological Association, Anaheim, CA.

Casas, J. M., Ponterotto, J. G., & Gutierez, J. M. (1986). An ethical indictment of counseling research and training: The cross-cultural perspective. *Journal of Counseling and Development, 64,* 347-349.

Cayleff, S. E. (1986). Ethical issues in counseling gender, race, and culturally distinct groups. *Journal of Counseling and Development, 64,* 345-347.

Comas-Diaz, L., & Griffith, E.E.H. (Eds.). (1988). *Clinical guidelines in cross-cultural mental health.* New York: John Wiley.

Copeland, E. J. (1982). Minority populations and traditional counseling programs: Some alternatives. *Counselor Education and Supervision, 21,* 187-193

Cross, W. E., Jr. (1971). The Negro-to-Black conversion experience: Toward a psychology of Black liberation. *Black World, 20*(9), 13-27.

Cross. W. E., Jr. (1978). The Thomas and Cross models of psychological Nigrescence: A review. *Journal of Black Psychology, 5*(1), 13-31.

Dana, R. H. (1993). *Multicultural assessment perspectives for professional psychology.* Boston: Allyn & Bacon.

Gelso, C. J., & Fretz, B. R. (1992). *Counseling psychology.* Fort Worth, TX: Harcourt Brace Jovanovich.

Helms, J. E. (1984). Toward a theoretical explanation of the effects of race on counseling: A Black and White model. *The Counseling Psychologist, 12,* 153-165.

Helms, J. E. (Ed.). (1990). *Black and White racial identity: Theory, research, and practice.* Westport, CT: Greenwood.

Helms, J. E. (1992). Why is there no study of cultural equivalence in standardized cognitive ability testing? *American Psychologist, 47*(9), 1083-1101.

Hicks, L., & Ridley, S. (1979). Black studies in psychology. *American Psychologist, 34,* 597-602.

Hills, H. I., & Strozier, A. L. (1992). Multicultural training in APA-approved counseling psychology programs: A survey. *Professional Psychology: Research and Practice, 23*(1), 43-51.

Ibrahim, F. A., & Arredondo, P. M. (1986). Ethical standards for cross-cultural counseling: Counselor preparation, practice, assessment, and research. *Journal of Counseling and Development, 64,* 349-352.

Ivey, A., Shizuru, L. S. (Producers), Darby, G. E. (Director), & Pedersen, P. (Consultant). (1981). *Cross-cultural counseling: Clinical case examples* [Film]. Honolulu: The East-West Center. (Available from Microtraining Associates, Inc., N. Amherst, MA 01059)

Jones, J. M. (1981). The concept of racism and its changing reality. In B. J. Bowser & R. G. Hunt (Eds.), *Impacts of racism on White Americans* (1st ed., pp. 27-49). Beverly Hills, CA: Sage.

McGoldrick, M., Pearce, J. K., & Giordano, J. (Eds.). (1982). *Ethnicity and family therapy.* New York: Guilford.

Midgette, T. E., & Meggert, S. S. (1991). Multicultural counseling instruction: A challenge for faculties in the 21st century. *Journal of Counseling and Development, 70,* 136-141.

Pedersen, P. (Ed.). (1988). *Handbook of cross-cultural counseling and therapy* (2nd ed.). Westport, CT: Greenwood.

Pedersen, P. B. (1991). Multiculturalism as a generic approach to counseling. *Journal of Counseling and Development, 70,*(1), 6-12.

Pedersen, P. B. (1994). *A handbook for developing multicultural awareness* (2nd ed.). Alexandria, VA: American Counseling Association.

Pedersen, P. B. (1995). Culture-centered ethical guidelines for counselors. In J. G. Ponterotto, J. M. Casas, L. A. Suzuki, & C. M. Alexander (Eds.), *Handbook of multicultural counseling* (pp. 387-414). Thousand Oaks, CA: Sage.

Pedersen, P. B., Draguns, J. G., Lonner, W. J., & Trimble, J. E. (Eds.). (1996). *Counseling across cultures* (4th ed.). Honolulu: University of Hawaii Press.

Ponterotto, J. G. (1988). Racial consciousness development among White counselors' trainees: A stage model. *Journal of Multicultural Counseling and Development, 16,* 146-156.

Ponterotto, J. G., & Casas, J. M. (1991). *Handbook of racial/ethnic minority counseling research.* Springfield, IL: Charles C Thomas.

Ponterotto, J. G., Casas, J. M., Suzuki, L. A., & Alexander, C. M. (Eds.). (1995). *Handbook of multicultural counseling.* Thousand Oaks, CA: Sage.

Ponterotto, J. G., & Pedersen, P. B. (1993). *Preventing prejudice: A guide for counselors and educators.* Newbury Park, CA: Sage.

Pope-Davis, D. B., Reynolds, A. L., & Vázquez, L. A. (1992). *Multicultural counseling: Issues of ethnic diversity* [Film]. (Available from The University of Iowa Video Center, C-215 Seashore Hall, Iowa City, IA 52242, or call 1-800-369-4692)

Reynolds, A. L. (1995). Challenges and strategies for teaching multicultural counseling courses. In J. G. Ponterotto, J. M. Casas, L. A. Suzuki, & C. M. Alexander (Eds.), *Handbook of multicultural counseling* (pp. 387-414). Thousand Oaks, CA: Sage.

Reynolds, C. R., & Kaiser, S. M. (1990). Test bias in psychological assessment. In T. B. Gutkin & C. R. Reynolds (Eds.), *The handbook of school psychology* (pp. 487-525). New York: John Wiley.

Ridley, C. R. (1985). Imperatives for ethnic and cultural relevance in psychology training programs. *Professional Psychology: Research and Practice, 16*(5), 611-622.

Ridley, C. R. (1995). *Overcoming unintentional racism in counseling and therapy: A practitioner's guide to intentional intervention.* Thousand Oaks, CA: Sage.

Ridley, C. R., & Lingle, D. W. (1996). Cultural empathy in multicultural counseling: A multidimensional process model. In P. B. Pedersen, J. G. Draguns, W. J. Lonner, & J. E. Trimble (Eds.). *Counseling across cultures* (4th ed., pp. 21-46). Thousand Oaks, CA: Sage.

Ridley, C. R., Mendoza, D. W., & Kanitz, B. E. (1992). Program designs for multicultural training, *Journal of Psychology and Christianity, 11*(4), 326-336.

Ridley, C. R., Mendoza, D. W., & Kanitz, B. E. (1994). Multicultural training: Reexamination, operationalization, and integration. *The Counseling Psychologist, 22*(2), 227-289.

Ridley, C. R., Mendoza, D. W., Kanitz, B. E., Angermeier, L., & Zenk, R. (1994). Cultural sensitivity in multicultural counseling: A perceptual schema model. *Journal of Counseling Psychology, 41(2),* 125-136.

Sue, D. W. (1977). Counseling the culturally different: A conceptual analysis. *Personnel and Guidance Journal, 55*(7), 422-425.

Sue, D. W. (1989a). *Barriers to cross-cultural counseling* [Film]. (Available from Microtraining Associates, Inc., N. Amherst, MA 01059)

Sue, D. W. (1989b). *Minority identity development for counseling* [Film]. (Available from Microtraining Associates, Inc., N. Amherst, MA 01059)

Sue, D. W. (1990). *Culture-specific strategies in counseling* [Film]. (Available from Microtraining Associates, Inc., N. Amherst, MA 01059)

Sue, D. W., Arredondo, P., & McDavis, R. J. (1992). Multicultural counseling competencies and standards: A call to the profession. *Journal of Counseling and Development, 70,* 477-486.

Sue, D. W., Bernier, J. E., Durran, A., Feinberg, L., Pedersen, P., Smith, E. J., & Vasquez-Nuttall, E. (1982). Position paper: Cross-cultural counseling competencies. *The Counseling Psychologist, 10*(2), 45-52.

Sue, D. W., & Sue, S. (1990). *Counseling the culturally different: Theory and practice* (2nd ed.). New York: John Wiley.

Sue, S., & Zane, N. (1987). The role of culture and cultural techniques in psychotherapy: A critique and reformulation. *American Psychologist, 42*(1), 37-45.

Suzuki, L. A., & Kugler, J. F. (1995). Intelligence and personality assessment: Multicultural perspectives. In J. G. Ponterotto, J. M. Casas, L. A. Suzuki, & C. M. Alexander (Eds.), *Handbook of multicultural counseling* (pp. 493-515). Thousand Oaks, CA: Sage.

7

A Systemic
Multicultural Curriculum Model

THE PEDAGOGICAL PROCESS

Luis A. Vázquez

Counseling programs have been described as maintaining the status quo in the United States. The status quo has often been described as White middle-class America (Midgette & Meggert, 1991). However, as minority populations are predicted to represent the majority of the population in the United States by the year 2000, the definition of the status quo must also change (Sue & Sue, 1990). Such changes demand that counseling programs diversify their curriculums. Over the past 25 years, the Council for Accreditation of Counseling and Related Educational Programs (CACREP) and the American Psychological Association (APA) have made it clear, through standards, that faculty and students are responsible for safeguarding the rights and personal dignity of their clients, supervisees, and those students under their instruction. In order to meet the training needs necessary to meet the demands of such standards, courses in counseling programs must be well organized to reflect the cultural diversity of society.

The counseling profession is in great need of literature on how to address diverse populations and the practice of counseling in the classroom. A few studies have documented that students representing groups of "minority status" have often felt alienated and many times invisible in the classroom (Atkinson, 1985; Fordham & Ogbu, 1986: Sotello & Turner, 1994). Due to lack of knowledge, interest, or, as many professors argue, lack of time to prepare appropriate literature inclusive of diversity, a multicultural curriculum is often not infused throughout the variety of counseling courses. Often, *one* course has been designated as the official multicultural education for students (Das, 1995). At first glance, the one course option sounds very practical. For one semester, the students are immersed in a literature of diversity that often includes culture, race, and gender. Such courses usually encourage students to explore their personal values and biases toward various cultural groups different from their own (Schaller & DeLaGarza, 1994).

Assignments take the role of experiential exercises individually and in a group. Students are asked to be "vulnerable" among their classmates in order to develop self-awareness. The intensity of such an experience and the knowledge shared often leave students with the desire to participate in an advanced course of diversity or else completely withdraw from the affirmation of diversity. In addition, students often begin to challenge other professors in various courses regarding how diversity directly relates to the subject matter presented in the classroom. These encounters are often met with resistance from the instructor or a superficial explanation as to the time allotted to teach the course that cannot possibly meet such demands or requests.

In general, two reactions are usually elicited by the faculty. For some faculty members there is a *conflict* with their own values and for others an *excitement* about exploring and taking risks. The former group of educators have historically taught courses in counseling programs that have reflected White middle-class society, with limited information related to other cultures, to race, or to gender. Information presented about groups different from White middle-class America has been deficient in nature (Sue & Sue, 1990), often depicting gross generalities and contributing to stereotypes for the various groups. The difficulties inherent in this kind of curriculum are the acknowledgment by current and past educators of their contributions to maintaining the status quo. Such courses may well be named "the stereotyping of ethnic groups." No educator has ever grown up in a nonsexist, nonracist, nonprejudiced, open, multilingual society. However, very few educators are willing to accept the fact that they along with many others have never been trained to work with populations of diversity. A strong ego, stubbornness, and privilege all contribute to maintaining a traditional White middle-class curriculum. This kind of role-modeling by professors breeds students with the same types of attitudes and privileges. These attitudes send the message that a multicultural curriculum is an abstract fad of temporary interest and lacking in any substance to add to our training in counseling.

If we were to acknowledge these issues publicly in our profession, many changes would have to occur. Educators resisting the changes in curriculum would have to participate in a process of change. Such a process would include self-examination of one's values, communication style, and an interdependence with individuals from diverse cultures (Ponterotto & Casas, 1987). For many educators, this process would be a very difficult and humbling experience. It is no wonder that, more times than not, there is a *designated* faculty member who teaches the single-course approach to multiculturalism. This approach can give the other faculty members a false sense of security and temporary relief from responsibility to multicultural issues until students begin to challenge them in class. The end result with this approach is educators who exist as *Multiculturally Impaired individuals.*

The latter group of educators usually has acknowledged the shortcomings of counseling programs in areas of diversity and counseling. This group of educators finds the challenge of developing a curriculum of diversity very exhilarating. They welcome the opportunity for self-exploration and see multiculturalism as everyone's responsibility, as well as their own in the program. These educators begin to question how they can model behaviors of affirmation of diversity for students and colleagues. They begin to acquire the role of learner as well as teacher when they empower students to share in the self-exploration process necessary in multicultural training. Due to lack of training from their own programs, these educators seek assistance from people of diversity from various cultures and begin to develop a library of information. These educators approach every course they teach from a multicultural point of view, exploring the similarities and differences within and between groups of diversity. The difficulty with this approach is in defining and incorporating the "what and how" of multiculturalism into the course.

There is an increasing amount of literature about what constitutes multiculturalism (D'Andrea, Daniels, & Heck, 1991; Pedersen, 1985; Sue, Arredondo, & McDavis, 1992), but very little has actually explored issues in curriculum development (McRae & Johnson, 1992). What kind of experiential exercises should be used? How do we use these exercises in a psychological, developmental approach to multicultural training? Regardless of the approach promoted within a counseling program—single course, infusion, or both—it requires the support of the existing faculty within the program.

The purpose of this chapter is to conceptualize the process that counseling programs must endure in diversifying current course requirements to meet current demands and standards of multiculturalism along with the dynamics involved with such a process. In addition, the following issues will be considered through a process of multiculturalism leading to a model titled The Multicultural Journey (Vázquez, 1995b): (a) definition of the counseling program's culture, (b) operationalization of a multicultural curriculum, (c) diverse methods of instruction, and (d) development of a syllabus representative of diversity.

The Process of Multiculturalism

We are committed to facilitating and training students in our counseling program in developing mutual respect and understanding among people of diverse backgrounds; sexual/affectional orientation; mental and physical disabilities; religious/spiritual beliefs; as well as other types of diversity.

This statement—in various forms—is often written as the philosophy/mission of counseling programs in an attempt to promote inclusion of groups often excluded. Obviously, the statement sounds very supportive and appears to relay the message that acceptance and affirmation, not just tolerance, are the norm. However, what does this statement mean to the faculty? How will such a philosophy/mission be implemented? What are the responsibilities of the faculty in this process? What are the demands of such a statement for curriculum development? Or, is this a politically correct statement that lacks commitment?

These questions are often asked as faculty begin to ask "what is" multiculturalism and "how to do" multiculturalism in the educational setting. As previously mentioned, this can be a very difficult process, because very few faculty—if any—have lived in a multiethnic, multiracial, multidisabled, nonsexist supportive environment. Yet the mission for counseling programs has been written and "the how to do" is left to be articulated and implemented by the counseling program faculty.

The task of implementing such a curriculum resembles a "journey" full of explorations, expectations, challenges, emotions, and changes. The journey may be exhilarating, troublesome, and exciting as well as painful. Let us travel through the process of one possible journey in the development of a model exploring experiences that faculty may endure in the development of a multicultural sensitive curriculum. The framework for this model originated as part of my participation with others at a midwestern university counseling center in an attempt to create a multiculturally sensitive environment (University of Iowa Counseling Service, 1993). Since this experience, I have modified the model to create a better understanding of faculty and curriculum development in relation to multicultural issues (Vázquez, 1995b).

The Program Culture

It seems logical that the first task among the faculty before deciding on a goal to affirm diversity is to reach a consensus regarding the definition of culture, because this definition will establish the base for the standard of training in the program. Culture may be conceptualized in a multitude of ways that lead to how people develop patterns of perceptions and organizations of the world that are common to a group of people and passed on either interpersonally or intergenerationally (Schaller & DeLaGarza, 1994). Each culture consists of customs, values, ideas, and skills. Inherent in each culture are different ways of communicating and of perceiving the world, along with ways to influence members of other cultures socially (Hecht, Andersen, & Ribeau, 1989). The possibilities for conflict immediately become apparent when deciding what culture is. However, the standard of measure used in assessing the culture of the program will rely on the faculty's consensus on the conceptualization, definition, and operationalization of the term *culture*.

Once this task has been accomplished, the faculty can begin to articulate the counseling program's culture. This task entails the examination of the goal of each course in a program and the values that are taught and reinforced not only in each course, but in the program as a whole. How these issues are communicated to the students and each faculty member in maintaining the current program's culture is of utmost importance in understanding the *power* of the current program culture. Due to the expertise that faculty members in the counseling field have acquired in relation to communication and facilitation throughout their own training, it seems that they are in the best position to reach a consensus in times of disagreement. The inherent assumption is that if any field can take the leadership in developing culturally sensitive training, it is the counseling field. Yet this has been approximately 15 years in the making with minimal results or agreement on what actually constitutes culturally sensitive training experiences (Midgette & Meggert, 1991). The question therefore remains: "What are the obstacles facing the development of a multicultural curriculum and training program?" These issues will be explored on the multicultural journey.

The Multicultural Journey

The multicultural journey consists of (a) goals/mission (aspirations) of the program, including target and scope, along with (b) the context of the differing situations encountered by individuals within the realm of the structure of the program and the interpersonal dynamics (see Appendix A).

Goals/Missions (Aspirations)

A goal is an aim or a purpose that the faculty has chosen to work toward and accomplish. In this case, the goal is to develop culturally sensitive training to ensure that students develop competence in working with diverse populations in order to meet the demands of the national counseling organizations and society. The goal must also be compared to the program's current goals, values, and how they differ or are similar to each other. This task presents great challenges in evaluating how the current counseling program has or has not accomplished the goal of becoming multiculturally sensitive. In addition, it requires the participation of all the faculty involved in the program.

The multicultural goals of the educational setting are directly related to the mission and aspirations to be achieved by its members. This process involves two steps in the facilitation of the goals to implement the mission of the program. These steps can be defined as the target and the scope of the goals to accomplish the mission.

Target

The target involves the implementation of the goals with a specific audience. This audience can be the students or the faculty. At the students' level, structural course considerations include a psychological, developmental sequencing of material with a flexibility for adjustment related to the students' understanding of issues of diversity. For example, the teaching of history, Western worldview, and self-awareness exercises for introspection, along with appropriate readings, is one possible sequence for a single course on diversity (Das, 1995). Such a sequence would lead to interpersonal interactions among students and further emphasize the goal of developing self-awareness and knowledge about diversity.

In addition, the concepts taught in the diversity course should be well integrated across the knowledge bases present in the traditional courses. For example, when teaching a course of counseling theories, the original author's worldviews should be presented within the historical context of the theories to afford the students a true understanding of the theory. Such a method of teaching will allow students to be critical examiners of the author's culture and how such theories impact our current culture of counseling. It is crucial that all the counseling courses in a program be developed with multiculturalism as their base. The incorporation of this perspective will affirm the importance of diversity in academics among the students, faculty, and the university community. Other issues include requirements and expectations in the classroom.

The Classroom. Every classroom develops and operates according to its own norms or acceptable patterns of behavior established by the instructor. "Don't challenge the instructor," for example. "This is not a place for self-awareness." "Sexist and ethnic/racial jokes are OK, this is not a politically correct class." "I will decide what constitutes racism." These norms are all too common in many organizations and university classrooms (Miller, 1987). Norms such as mutual respect, openness to differing worldviews, and a trusting environment must be established in order to explore culturally sensitive subjects. For example, appropriate self-disclose or self-monitoring behaviors from the instructor serve as a model for students. Having the students participate in experiential exercises related to exploration of other cultures can be very helpful. Also, creating outside assignments that facilitate interactions with students from diverse cultures, along with keeping a journal, can be very rewarding.

Without examples for students to follow, diversity is reduced to a "requirement" of readings with very little substance. From this perspective, many students acquire a superficial, politically correct rhetoric about diversity with very little commitment. Therefore, the faculty must play a major role in the process of affirming diversity.

The Faculty. Working with faculty in the same department as the target may involve challenging the policies of the program, feeling comfortable with conflict, and taking a stand against an issue that negatively affects diversity (Sue & Sue, 1990). This sounds very simple and direct, yet there are several issues that must be considered: for instance, commitment of faculty members to diversity, exploration of current policies, the facilitation of challenges for change, and the inclusion of people of color. Commitment to diversity by faculty members brings forth the inescapable process of self-examination. At this juncture, the faculty may react in several different roles related to the process of self-examination.

Through observations, interviews, and reviewing the literature related to the organizational development of diversity (Barón, 1992; McEwen & Roper, 1994; Simons, 1989), I have conceptualized several personality styles that participating voluntary or involuntary faculty adhere to in the development of a multicultural curriculum for their counseling program. The differing styles that may occur for the participants of the journey consist of Adventurer, Passenger, Tourist, Antagonist, and Wanderer.

Adventurers are excited about the process of self-exploration, often volunteering to share experiences and critically examining themselves as well as others. Adventurers have a high level of commitment to all issues related to oppression. Their energy level is quite high, even to the point of overwhelming themselves over the goals to be accomplished. On the other hand, Adventurers can find themselves frustrated over the lack of enthusiasm in other faculty members. The risk-taking behaviors of Adventurers are often interpreted as misguided or threatening by other faculty members. Adventurers often feel alienated and distanced from the status quo. They are often people of color, women, and White males with a strong commitment to diversity. Every group needs an Adventurer to challenge the status quo.

Passengers are people who appear to be in the midst of things yet do very little to volunteer or to answer questions related to diversity. They often appear to be undecided—riding the fence, so to speak. Passengers' diplomatic skills are very high, but without direction, except to relieve themselves of challenges imposed by other faculty members. Passengers will always be there physically, but not psychologically. A good vocabulary on diversity is consistent with Passengers lacking a commitment to anything related to diversity.

Tourists are faculty members who enjoy exploring new cultures, not to create change but to observe how other people think. These individuals will ask many questions—with little sensitivity—and will claim great privilege, expecting others to cater to their needs. They will often impose their own cultural views when interpreting the culture of others, leading to many stereotypical views of the cultures they experience. Tourists will participate in program changes only when they themselves are directly benefited, but not if any sacrifices are asked in return.

Antagonists are very outspoken, with a mission of maintaining the status quo. They will often repeat themselves about past successes and argue about reinventing the wheel. Antagonists often minimize the perceptions of individuals committed to diversity. Fairness without equality appears to be a central theme, as long as the Antagonist gets to define what fairness is for everyone else. No matter what is presented in the area of diversity, Antagonists will personalize the information and become very emotional, often without logic or openness to the ideas of others. Other faculty members may feel that their discussions about diversity are often sabotaged by the Antagonist, leading to frustration, irritation, and lack of progress.

A Wanderer will not commit to issues for a substantial length of time. The quest of finding oneself is at the core of this person's goal in life. Wanderers borrow from many different cultures without committing to any of them or examining their own culture. Paraphernalia from several different cultures can often be found in their offices. These faculty members attend activities for secondary gains, but only if invited by someone committed to diversity. They are often "politically correct" people. Wanderers can sound very convincing about their commitment to diversity, often resembling Adventurers. Once Wanderers are challenged about diversity, however, others soon find that there is very little substance and genuineness in their commitment— if there is any commitment.

Faculty members will operate from a dominant personality style, and at times may borrow a characteristic from another personality style that seems advantageous. Observing the interactions of these roles among faculty in counseling programs can be an exciting process in itself. Once these personality styles have been clearly delineated within the program's faculty, the process leads into the scope of the program.

Scope

The scope of a program includes an integration of such issues as the population to be targeted and the process the program will participate in to accomplish its goal of diversity. In other words, the scope can be defined as the extent of coverage given to moderator variables in relation to particular group(s): multiethnic, racial, gender, or sexual orientation. Moderator variables are such concepts as acculturation, worldview, and identity development (Dana, 1993). These variables distinguish within- and between-group differences and similarities in research and theory. Moderator variables can be used to guide instructors' presentations in class regarding researchers' interpretations of results in studies, methodological issues in research, conceptual interpretations of theories, assessment issues with diverse populations, and issues presented among the students in the classroom (Berry, Poortinga, Segall, & Dasen, 1992).

Targeting such a scope would be appropriate for any course in counseling/psychology programs. The difficulty often stated by professors is that gathering this kind of information is time-consuming and the material is often not found in "mainstream" journals. A second difficulty professors often mention is how they might integrate multicultural information into their lesson plans without diluting the "main" content.

Again, these are issues that need to be addressed in relation to the first step of the multicultural journey—in the program's mission of the program and its goals of multiculturalism. The members in the setting are expected to commit to this scope as part of the mission. Committing to diversifying the curriculum with information about groups of diverse cultural background results in expectations such as updating course syllabi, creating literature reviews, and consulting with individuals who have expertise in diversity. It also sends a message to students about the importance of these issues in research and practice.

Context

Structure

The context of the multicultural journey involves the interpersonal relationships that constitute the structure of the counseling program and the dynamics of these relationships. The concepts of social power and social influence can provide a framework for understanding the interpersonal dynamics of the program faculty. *Social power* is defined as a deliberately imposed social process that may lead to potential social influence (Henderson, 1981). There are four dimensions that can stand alone or together that define social power: dependence, intentionality, (in)equity, and role structure. Tedeschi and Lindskold (1976) explain the meaning of *dependency* as not having control of the physical or social environment or of the available information that another person controls in the environment. Within counseling programs, the issue of dependency is very important. Whoever controls information and has the power to decide on physical and social environmental changes will be a deciding factor in the development of a multicultural curriculum. The faculty member(s) with this dimension of social power controls information valuable to such issues as tenure and promotion of other faculty members, including the development of a multicultural physical environment and affirming other languages and other forms of diversity for the social milieu of the department. This would also include promoting and hiring diverse, bilingual support staff as well as faculty.

Intentionality is the deliberate actions of an agent to produce changes in the target person (Dahl, 1957). The faculty member(s) who hold this form of social power controls such things as the inclusion of diversity in evaluations of students and other faculty members. It is within this realm that the issue of diversity can be given "power" in a counseling program. If diversity is deliberately included as part of the tenure process, the teaching process, and the evaluation process, then it becomes part of the norm instead of the exception for all aspects of a counseling program. Such intentionality would impact the third form of social power, (in)equity.

The issue—*(in)equity*—is concerned with whether all parties receive outcomes equal to their inputs (Walster, Walster, & Berscheid, 1978). (In)equity is directly related to the responsibility that all faculty members have to contribute to the development of a curriculum of diversity. What often happens is that one or two faculty members become the "multicultural experts" and the other faculty members encourage these roles, thereby relieving themselves of responsibility for these issues. (In)equity occurs when the efforts of the "multicultural experts" are not rewarded through the tenure or merit process and when all the issues related to diversity that should include the faculty as a whole are directed at the one or two individuals. The last dimension, *role structure,* is discussed as a cluster of norms (rules of behavior) that help define the relationship and provide for task maintenance functions (Thibaut & Kelley, 1959). Role structure includes "knowing one's place." In other words, in every educational department there are different rules related to the age, gender, seniority in the program, ascribed or achieved power, and color of the faculty member(s).

Understanding the role structures of the different faculty members will enable faculty member(s) committed to diversity to actualize the reality of such a goal. For example, an older, White, male faculty member with seniority in the program and with ascribed power may believe that the counseling program should remain morally neutral, be normative (Western world values), and at the same time be ideal (all things beneficial to the majority population), so that when other faculty work to benefit students, it is done with the attitude that will allow "them" (people of diversity) to be more like the senior member, "status quo." These norms are formal social inventions that accomplish quite effectively what otherwise would require informal social influence—the exercise of personal power.

The ideal counseling program would include a physical and social environment celebrating diversity through art and professional development activities that disperse information about groups of diversity. The program would also include an evaluation criterion concerning diversity, related to tenure and teaching, with equal commitment and participation for all faculty members in the process of developing a multicultural program. Finally, the program would be a model through its role structure, affirming diversity for all the students through admission criteria and activities as well as through teaching. The ideal program is a goal to be actualized through the interpersonal dynamics of the faculty members in counseling programs.

Interpersonal Dynamics

Interpersonal dynamics include communication patterns (listening/validating/supporting), along with the length of time and the investment faculty members have in a program. Examining these dynamics through the concepts of social influence allow the faculty members a framework for conceptualizing the interpersonal dynamics in their counseling program.

Festinger and Raven (1959) define social influence as the informal ability individuals possess to effect a change in a person's cognition, attitude, or behavior based on the notion of free choice. These authors suggest three bases that create these changes in a person: informational influence, expert influence, and attraction influence. Informational influence is the transmission of knowledge to other persons that results in a permanent change in their cognitive structure. The exchange of empirical as well as theoretical information related to diversity is crucial in creating change in faculty members. Such information is pertinent to the academic cognitive training of faculty members. Types of shared information would include ethical guidelines; standards of providers; research related to moderator variables (acculturation, identity, worldview); multicultural theories of development and training—the list goes on. Educating the faculty with such information in order to form a base of support is consistent with much of cultural training of academia and the educational decision-making process.

A source is considered to have expert influence to the degree that the perceiving person accepts the source's messages as containing valid content (Hovland, Janis, & Kelley, 1953). Often the case in counseling programs, the "expert" is a faculty person of color relegated to one area of expertise. When the "expert" begins to share information about how multiculturalism can be implemented throughout various courses, the other faculty members begin to question the expertise of the faculty person. It is crucial to have not only credible faculty members, but also valid support for innovative ideas for multicultural curriculum development. The expertise needs to be shared among all the faculty members for multicultural curriculum development to be successful.

Influence through attractiveness means that a person accepts the viewpoint of those who have similar beliefs, opinions, and attitudes because they represent the norm (Festinger & Raven, 1959). For multiculturalism, attractiveness is directly related to faculty members who have a calling, a specific identity, or who view multiculturalism as part of a job function. Faculty members who have a calling are very much aware of the oppression of several groups and are committed to developing a social identity against oppression. These faculty members will not only defend their own groups against oppression, but will also accept the viewpoints of oppression in other groups. Faculty members with a specific identity will only support efforts to enhance multiculturalism as long as these apply only to their specific group identity—for instance, a woman faculty member wanting to deal only with issues related to gender, or faculty members wanting to focus only on a specific race or ethnicity. Faculty members who view multiculturalism as part of a job function will be impacted by attractiveness influence only if it is an issue of social status for their position in academia.

Ideally, all faculty members would develop a library of information—accessible to all other faculty members—that is related to diversity for each of the courses they teach, thereby developing the role of expert in each other and making the process of sharing information attractive to all involved in the development of a multicultural program curriculum, regardless of the expectations of those who have a calling, a specific identity, or a job function. It is evident, after considering the components of the multicultural journey along with the personality styles of the faculty, that developing a multicultural curriculum can be demanding, emotional, and challenging (see Appendix B).

Development of a Multicultural Curriculum

Students' Interests

Students take multicultural courses for a variety of reasons, including several that are practical. Specifically, they want to understand how issues of diversity relate to other groups that they may work with in different settings, they want to develop greater self-awareness about what their biases are in relation to other populations, or they take the course or courses because it is a requirement of the program. Obviously, with such immense demands on multicultural issues across the required areas of counseling, it would seem logical that students can best be served through the infusion of such material throughout all courses as well as focusing on specific themes in a single course on diversity (Das, 1995). The cooperation of faculty members is needed to accomplish this task.

Instructors' Interests

It is impossible and undesirable for instructors to ignore their own personal interests and values when planning and teaching a course (Chambers, Lewis, & Kerezsi, 1995). Instructors' theoretical biases and research experiences, coupled with their political and moral beliefs, all affect how topics are emphasized and what kind of text/readings they choose for the class. Students are usually very interested in learning about their instructors' research and ideas. It is therefore very important for instructors to acknowledge their approach to and beliefs about diversity and to balance course content with the presentation of diverse ideas. Instructors may wish to develop a basic list of objectives for each class, with such general themes as awareness, knowledge, or skills (Pedersen, 1985).

Awareness. Awareness would focus on the students' understanding of their own beliefs and values (McRae & Johnson, 1992). One way this could be accomplished is through exploring the assumptions made by the various authors within the subject area, comparing these assumptions with events occurring during the time and place the subject area was developed, and how the particular subject area applies to students' beliefs about themselves and others. This could be done through projects, class exercises, and videos that allow students to apply these issues to themselves.

Knowledge. This theme provides students with information about such within- and between-group differences as culture and gender in relation to a subject area (Sue & Sue, 1990). Various moderator variables—such as acculturation, worldview, identity, language—can be examined in relation to the subject area and how these subject areas are advantageous as well as disadvantageous to various diverse populations. In the area of psychodiagnostics, for example, the moderator variables can be used to show how psychodynamics affects assessment. In research, the exploration of various constructs and assumptions can be undertaken in relation to the cultural appropriateness or inappropriateness for the participants in the study (Das, 1995). When awareness and knowledge of diversity is well infused throughout the various courses, an integrated effort toward the development of skills becomes well established in research and practice.

Skills. The "how to" of awareness and knowledge is usually considered the greatest challenge for counseling programs (McRae & Johnson, 1992). Application is usually restricted to courses such as psychodiagnostics, to practica, and to applied research courses. The culmination of the culturally infused courses adds even more support to the culturally infused applied courses. Examples for developing skills can be presented through written outlines and videotapes in which students demonstrate their ability to conduct a multicultural assessment schemata (Pope-Davis, Reynolds, & Vázquez, 1992; Pope-Davis, Vázquez, Reynolds, & Prieto, 1994). Another example might involve the use of genograms for the exploration of culturally appropriate interventions (Vázquez, 1995a). Yet another example could involve demonstrations through a multicultural case presentation in which the instructor would assess for appropriate process and outcome in relation to the moderator variables for between- and within-group differences for diverse clients (Dana, 1993). Finally, the appropriateness of process and outcome research can be critiqued in relation to cultural considerations for diverse clients. Once these themes are well defined for each course, special consideration is given to the level of the course.

Course Level

One of the most difficult tasks encountered by instructors is to teach at the level that is most appropriate for the graduate students' level of preparation (Berger, 1994). Especially in the area of diversity, there is a considerable range of awareness, knowledge, and skills among the students. In general, the less well prepared students are, the more important it is to explore their levels of introspection and of openness to diversity issues. One example might consist of structured journal entries to be collected every 3 weeks. This assignment would keep the instructor informed of the students' attitudes and feelings about the issues presented in class. Well-structured group projects can also serve as a form of evaluation of competency in the subject area.

Once the class as a whole has reached a basic level of knowledge of the theories about diversity within the selected subject area, the instructor will be able to expand the content of the course to include a greater knowledge base in areas of research and practice. It is not unusual, however, for professors to be idealistic about their students' maturity and openness to diversity. Because many students have been well socialized to please the instructor and to avoid conflict in graduate school, guidelines that protect and direct the students' academic standing in class, whether controversial or not, can prove very beneficial in the organization of the course.

Course Organization

Two approaches are usually considered when organizing a course: a chronological/developmental approach and a topical approach (Berger, 1994). In a chronological/developmental approach, the instructor teaches the course from a progressive perspective. For example, in a single course on diversity the instructor might begin with a base of history leading to exercises in self-awareness to the understanding of other cultures' diverse perspectives, leading to the integration of these issues coupled with a demonstration of competence. Other courses in which the chronological/developmental approach may be useful include practica and ethics.

The topical approach allows a specific focus on course content, with an overriding theme of diversity. For example, when teaching a course in theory, students may be taught to view theories from a critical perspective of diversity. This can be accomplished by critiquing the cultural assumptions for each theory in relation to issues of wellness. The same process can be used throughout such courses as personality and assessment. For some courses, a combination of both approaches may be beneficial.

The Syllabus

The syllabus is presented on the first day of the class and contains important information about the course, such as what will be covered, what will be expected of the students, and how the students will be graded. This process helps students to plan accordingly and protects the instructor if questions arise about various aspects of the course—such as requirements, due dates, and so on. Because the first day of class sets the tone of the course for the rest of the academic term, the goals and objectives for the course must be clearly conceptualized before writing a syllabus. If clear statements made about the course goals and objectives include diversity, students come to view these issues as having great importance in their development as psychologists/counselors.

Course Goals

The counseling program's curriculum should incorporate an examination of current social-political trends with issues of theory, research, and practice of counseling (Das, 1995). A clear and precise philosophy about diversity must be articulated that will guide the development of the course syllabus. For each course, a search for historical truths must be evaluated along with the availability of research for issues about diversity (Das, 1995). The examination of these issues can be the base on which to build the material used for each course. This process will lead to the development of appropriate objectives.

Course Objectives

Objectives are developed to enhance and to support the goals of diversity for each course. Such objectives would include selecting the competencies and skills that students will be able to achieve in each course and how these objectives meet the demands of diversity (Midgette & Meggert, 1991). An objective for a research course might include examining the cultural assumptions in common constructs used in research: for example, examining such concepts as self-esteem or self-efficacy for their appropriateness with certain cultural groups. Another objective would include examining the instruments that operationalize these concepts and how responses from differing cultural groups may give the impression of low self-esteem or low self-efficacy, whereas the responses may actually connote culturally appropriate behaviors. For both of these examples, it is the process that is used for examining these concepts in relation to issues of diversity that is most important.

The ability of students to think critically in dealing with issues of research, especially in the area of diversity, is another area of utmost importance. Many of the historical research contributions by psychologists and counselors have provided the fuel for discrimination against persons of diversity (Sue & Sue, 1990). Only after carefully critiquing the studies have researchers found the lack of scientific rigor evident in the areas of methodology, instrumentation, and cultural stereotypical interpretations about the populations that were studied.

When the goals and objectives for the course have been established, methods of instruction need to be considered that will promote and enhance the writing of the syllabus. Such methods may include oral presentations, field trips to cultural activities, videotapes, class demonstrations, and research projects, to name a few.

The Writing of a Syllabus

The syllabus usually contains several parts. These include course goals and objectives, requirements, policy statements, calendar, evaluation, and other supplemental resources (Fernald, 1995). The course description should include the goal of the course and its objectives. For this section, the role of diversity should be well integrated into both the goal and objectives of the course. The infusion and inclusion of diversity in the syllabus will begin to set the norms from the first day of class. It will also send a message about the importance of diversity to the students.

The requirements section of the syllabus should include any required texts, reading packets, or other reading sources necessary for the class. The sources used for the course should be carefully scrutinized for the inclusion of diversity, regardless of the class, before the required reading list is chosen. An example given earlier in this chapter supports the importance of studying traditional theories of counseling by examining the cultural assumptions underlying these theories in order to provide an in-depth understanding for students in the application of such theories with groups of diversity. This will ensure consistency among the course goals and objectives.

The requirements section should also include descriptions of required projects, format of the exams, grading criteria, and contribution of each assignment to total course grade, along with the importance of class participation (Aikin, 1994). Policies regarding lack of student progress should follow the requirements section. Policy statements in a syllabus are similar to binding contracts. The instructor's policies should include specific language related to makeup exams, late papers, and issues related to special accommodations for students and student expectations of learning about diversity. For example, it is important that students understand and are informed about whether or not late assignments will be accepted and under what conditions. The policies will alleviate many misunderstandings about these issues between instructors and students.

The calendar includes the dates that have been set for the required readings, projects, and examinations. These dates serve as a method of organization for both the instructor and the students. Once the dates have been set for the requirements, it is imperative that they be examined for the appropriateness of sequencing the objectives to be taught, whether the syllabus has been developed based on a chronological/developmental or topic-oriented method. The sequencing of learning certain basic concepts is very important for the chronological/developmental approach, because these concepts build upon each other and examine the interactions across different domains of diversity. In the topical approach, learning the basic process of critiquing a content area for cultural assumptions is of utmost importance. For example, knowing how to critique the cultural assumptions inherent in differing theories of personality enriches an in-depth understanding of human development throughout the various personality theories presented by the instructor.

The examination format is directly related to the instructor's teaching methods and the goals and objectives of the course (Benassi & Fernald, 1993). Most instructors use a combination of evaluation methods. The evaluation methods should be consistent with the cultural values affirmed throughout the course. The evaluation of the understanding of diversity should be inclusive of the various modes of learning (visual, auditory, kinesthetic, and experiential), in order to provide well-rounded learning experiences for all students. Several methods have been used by instructors to meet the various modes of learning in relation to diversity. The following methods are examples used to assess multicultural competence in the areas of awareness, knowledge, and skills.

A traditional method that is often used is a multiple choice test based on the integration versus the "regurgitation" of the application of multicultural concepts to the subject area of the course. Another popular method involves the development of a literature review and the designing of a study to address an aspect of diversity in the subject matter of the course. The use of a multicultural genogram is increasingly gaining acceptance (Vázquez, 1995a). This method would allow students the opportunity to become aware of their own ethnicity or ethnicities; to compare them to the worldviews of their ancestors across three generations; and to examine areas of bias, limitation, and strength. The writing of position statements about the discussions of the readings from a clinical, research, or personal perspective as they relate to diversity can be very useful in creating further awareness.

Forms of evaluation used to assess competence in practice and application may include self-report measures as well as videotaped demonstrations, assessment interviews, and self-monitoring journals. Self-report measures such as the Multicultural Awareness-Knowledge-Skills Survey (MAKSS; D'Andrea et al., 1991); the Multicultural Counseling Inventory (MCI; Sodowsky, Taffe, Gutkin, & Wise, 1994); or the Multicultural Counseling Awareness Scale (MCAS-B; Ponterotto, Rieger, Barrett, & Sparks, 1994) can be used to develop goals and objectives for training between the supervisor and the supervisee in addressing areas of growth and further training in multicultural counseling.

The Interpersonal Process Recall (I.P.R.) is very useful for gaining new insights into the counselor's impact on diverse clients (Kagan, Krathwohl, & Miller, 1963). I.P.R. can be part of the evaluation process used when students participate in any interactions between themselves and diverse clients. For example, I.P.R. can be used in conjunction with a videotaped multicultural ecological assessment to assess a student's comfort level and ability to build a therapeutic relationship with a diverse client (H. Coleman, personal communication, November 30, 1995). The videotape can offer valuable information about the interpersonal process used by the student during the gathering of information related to the client's family, community, assets, interpersonal history, and self-perceptions. In addition, the student can integrate the information gathered by writing a comprehensive report with recommendations. As part of the evaluation of the report, emphasis is placed on the use of within-group moderator variables such as worldview, acculturation, and identity development as they relate to the recommendations and the assessment.

Another component that can be used for evaluation of competence involves the use of a journal that focuses on self-monitoring behaviors throughout the various practice assignments, addressing the questions of (a) what issues triggered a reaction? (b) where did this reaction come from? and (c) how did you deal with this reaction? The process of self-monitoring allows students to look for patterns of behaviors, discomfort/comfort, and biases when working with clients of diversity.

The methods of evaluation mentioned here are but a few suggestions of how to meet the objectives of a course. These tasks are used to enhance students' abilities to learn the content of the course and for self-evaluation of their understanding of the objectives of the course. Again, the methods of evaluating students are based on the goals and objectives of the class.

Conclusion

Counseling programs must go through dramatic changes to accomplish the goal of infusing diversity throughout their various curriculum requirements. Pedagogy that is philosophically based on issues of diversity will require faculty and student attitude changes. As evidenced in the multicultural journey, the combinations of the various aspects overlap each other, demanding strong skills in facilitation and consensus. Understanding the various personality styles discussed in this chapter can provide a framework for conceptualizing the interactions faculty members encounter, especially those faculty who perceive themselves as Adventurers without a strong social power base. A systemic, well-executed multicultural program of instruction will produce optimal multicultural training opportunities for students and faculty once the issues presented by the multicultural journey are challenged, acknowledged, and resolved among the faculty members.

The multicultural journey provides an awareness of structure and interpersonal dynamics that can be explored to alleviate barriers that impede diversity in educational development. The transcendence of multiculturalism from journey to curriculum development will prove to be a logical transition if it is established with support, commitment, and intentionality. The development of a well-integrated syllabus with goals that are well thought out and that are integrated with strong objectives will provide the substance needed for the use of various methods of instruction. Using this process of intentionality in the infusion of diversity into curriculum development will promote an academic atmosphere of learning and understanding in the field of counseling.

Faculty have a great influence in shaping the minds of future psychologists/counselors; it is our responsibility truly to understand the dynamics of oppression (McIntosh, 1989) and how our pedagogy directly contributes to the maintenance of such a system. The words of Socrates, "Know thyself," are more true now than ever before in the training of counselors/psychologists. Multiculturalism cannot be minimized to an isolated experience or a single course for students (Das, 1995). It must serve as the umbrella under which issues, groups, and interactions are practiced, taught, and researched. As faculty and instructors in psychology/counseling programs, it is our responsibility to educate our students with the most ethical, intellectual, and accountable experiences and information available in our profession. Merely examining the "what" of multiculturalism and not the "how" is ethically irresponsible to the students, the field of counseling, and ourselves as faculty. The responsibility of multiculturalism belongs to all of us in the field of education, beginning with the president and his or her administrators, to the deans of the departments, to the counseling program chairs, to the programs' faculty, and finally to the students. We have the responsibility of teaching students the process of acquiring knowledge, as well as of using that knowledge to promote diversity in human development. Diversity is a gift to be cherished and not a fear to be destroyed because of lack of knowledge.

APPENDIX A

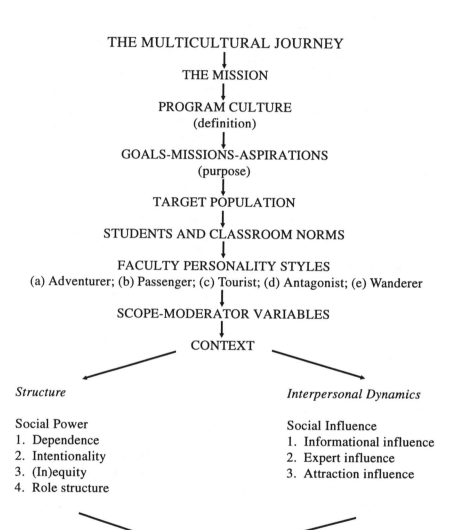

THE MULTICULTURAL JOURNEY

THE MISSION

PROGRAM CULTURE
(definition)

GOALS-MISSIONS-ASPIRATIONS
(purpose)

TARGET POPULATION

STUDENTS AND CLASSROOM NORMS

FACULTY PERSONALITY STYLES
(a) Adventurer; (b) Passenger; (c) Tourist; (d) Antagonist; (e) Wanderer

SCOPE-MODERATOR VARIABLES

CONTEXT

Structure

Social Power
1. Dependence
2. Intentionality
3. (In)equity
4. Role structure

Interpersonal Dynamics

Social Influence
1. Informational influence
2. Expert influence
3. Attraction influence

DEVELOPMENT OF THE MULTICULTURAL CURRICULUM

APPENDIX B

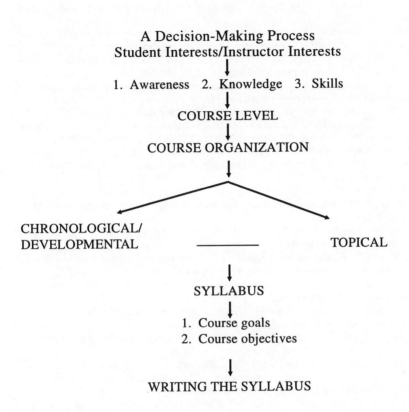

A Decision-Making Process
Student Interests/Instructor Interests

↓

1. Awareness   2. Knowledge   3. Skills

↓

COURSE LEVEL

↓

COURSE ORGANIZATION

↓

CHRONOLOGICAL/
DEVELOPMENTAL   ————   TOPICAL

↓

SYLLABUS

↓

1. Course goals
2. Course objectives

↓

WRITING THE SYLLABUS

1. Goals
2. Objectives
3. Requirements
4. Policy statements
5. Calendar
6. Evaluation
7. Supplemental resources

References

Aikin, J. (1994). *LA: Classroom manual: College of Liberal Arts.* Iowa City: University of Iowa.

Atkinson, D. R. (1985). A meta-review of research on cross-cultural counseling and psychotherapy. *Journal of Multicultural Counseling and Development, 13,* 138-153.

Barón, A., Jr. (1992). Valuing ethnic diversity: A day-long workshop for university personnel. *Journal of College Student Development, 33*(2), 178-180.

Benassi, V. A., & Fernald, P. S. (1993). Preparing tomorrow's psychologists for careers in academe. *Teaching of Psychology, 20,* 149-155.

Berger, K. S. (1994). *The developing person through the lifespan* (3rd ed.). New York: Worth.

Berry, J. W., Poortinga, Y. H., Segall, M. H., & Dasen, P. R. (1992). *Cross-cultural psychology: Research and applications.* New York: Cambridge University Press.

Chambers, T., Lewis, J., & Kerezsi, P. (1995). African American faculty and White American students: Cross-cultural pedagogy in counselor preparation programs. *The Counseling Psychologist, 23*(1), 43-62.

Dahl, R. A. (1957). The concept of power. *Behavioral Science, 2,* 201-218.

Dana, R. H. (1993). *Multicultural assessment perspectives for professional psychology.* Boston: Allyn & Bacon.

D'Andrea, M., Daniels, J., & Heck, R. (1991). Evaluating the impact of multicultural counseling training. *Journal of Counseling and Development, 70*(1), 143-150.

Das, A. K. (1995). Rethinking multicultural counseling: Implications for counselor education. *Journal of Counseling & Development, 74,* 45-52.

Fernald, P. S. (1995). Preparing psychology graduate students for the professoriate. *American Psychologist, 50*(6), 421-427.

Festinger, J.R.P., Jr., & Raven, B. (1959). The basis of social power. In D. Cartwright (Ed.), *Studies in social power.* Ann Arbor, MI: Institute for Social Research.

Fordham, S., & Ogbu, J. U. (1986). Black students' school success: Coping with the "burden of 'acting White.' " *The Urban Review, 18*(3), 177-206.

Hecht, M., Andersen, P., & Ribeau, S. (1989). The cultural dimension of nonverbal communication. In M. Asante & W. Gudykunst (Eds.), *Handbook of international and intercultural communication* (pp. 163-185). London: Sage.

Henderson, A. H. (1981). *Social power: Social psychological models and theories.* New York: Praeger.

Hovland, C. I., Janis, I. L., & Kelley, H. C. (1953). *Communication and persuasion.* New Haven, CT: Yale University Press.

Kagan, N., Krathwohl, D. R., & Miller, R. (1963). Stimulated recall in therapy using video tape: A case study. *Journal of Counseling Psychology, 10*(3), 237-243.

McEwen, M. K., & Roper, L. D. (1994). Incorporating multiculturalism into student affairs preparation programs: Suggestions from the literature. *Journal of College Student Development, 35,* 46-53.

McIntosh, P. (1989). White privilege: Unpacking the invisible knapsack. *Peace and Freedom,* pp. 10-12.

McRae, M., & Johnson, S. (1992). Toward training for competence in multicultural counselor education. *Journal of Counseling and Development, 70,* 131-141.

Midgette, T. E., & Meggert, S. S. (1991). Multicultural counseling instruction: A challenge for faculties in the 21st century. *Journal of Counseling & Development, 7*(1), 136-141.

Miller, F. A. (1987). *Moving a team to multiculturalism.* Unpublished manuscript. Cincinnati, OH.

Pedersen, P. (1985). *Handbook of cross-cultural counseling and therapy.* Westport, CT: Greenwood.

Ponterotto, J. G., & Casas, J. M. (1987). In search of multicultural competence within counselor education programs. *Journal of Counseling and Development, 65,* 430-434.

Ponterotto, J. G., Rieger, B. P., Barrett, A., & Sparks, R. (1994). Assessing multicultural counseling competence: A review of instrumentation. *Journal of Counseling and Development, 72,* 316-322.

Pope-Davis, D., Reynolds, A. L., & Vázquez, L. A. (1992). *Multicultural counseling: Issues of ethnic diversity* (Video workbook). (Available from The University of Iowa Video Center, C-215 Seashore Hall, Iowa City, IA 52242, or call 1-800-369-4692)

Pope-Davis, D., Vázquez, L. A., Reynolds, A. L., & Prieto, L. R. (1994). *Multicultural counseling: Issues of ethnic diversity* (Video workbook). (Available from The University of Iowa Video Center, c215 Seashore Hall, Iowa City, IA 52242, or call 1-800-369-4692)

Schaller, J., & DeLaGarza, D. (1994). Infusion of culture and gender issues in rehabilitation counselor education curricula. *Rehabilitation Education, 8*(2), 166-180.

Simons, G. F. (1989). *Working together: How to become more effective in a multicultural organization.* Los Altos, CA: Crisp Publications.

Sodowsky, G. R., Taffe, R. C., Gutkin, T. B., & Wise, S. L. (1994). Development of the Multicultural Counseling Inventory: A self-report measure of multicultural competencies. *Journal of Counseling Psychology, 41,* 137-148.

Sotello, C., & Turner, V. (1994). Guests in someone else's house: Students of color. *The Review of Higher Education, 17*(4), 355-370.

Sue, D., Arredondo, P., & McDavis, R. (1992). Multicultural counseling competencies and standards: A call to the profession. *Journal of Counseling and Development, 70,* 477-483.

Sue, D. W., & Sue, D. (1990). *Counseling the culturally different: Theory and practice* (2nd. ed.). New York: John Wiley.

Tedeschi, J. T., & Lindskold, S. (1976). *Social psychology: Interdependence, interaction, and influence.* New York: John Wiley.

Thibaut, J. W., & Kelley, H. H. (1959). *The social psychology of groups.* New York: John Wiley.

University of Iowa Counseling Service. (1993). *A framework for processing issues of diversity* (Presented at a weekly staff meeting, University of Iowa, Iowa City).

Vázquez, L. A. (1995a). *The multicultural genogram: A tool for instruction.* Manuscript in progress.

Vázquez, L. A. (1995b). *The multicultural journey: The process of developing a multicultural curriculum and program in counseling.* Manuscript in progress.

Walster, E., Walster, G. W., & Berscheid, E. (1978). *Equity: Theory and research.* Boston: Allyn & Bacon.

8

Toward Defining a
Multicultural Training Philosophy

Mark M. Leach
Michael A. Carlton

"Why do we need to talk about multiculturalism? All we do is teach stereotypes anyway." This quote from a colleague reflects the need to educate faculty about multicultural training programs, beginning with the training philosophy.

Psychology programs are giving increased attention to the importance of incorporating multicultural issues into training (e.g., D'Andrea & Daniels, 1991; Pedersen, 1987; Ponterotto, Casas, Suzuki, & Alexander, 1995; Ridley, 1985). Unfortunately, multicultural training at the graduate level has been unfocused and in need of direction (Ponterotto, Alexander, & Grieger, 1995). Numerous multicultural models are in existence that incorporate various multicultural philosophies, yet there is considerable variability in the inclusion and quality of multicultural training (Ridley, Mendoza, & Kanitz, 1994). Therefore, many current professionals are inadequately prepared to treat culturally diverse clientele (Baruth & Manning, 1991; Copeland, 1982;

Ridley, Mendoza, & Kanitz, 1992). Consequently, there has been frustration with the lack of a coherent structure in educating faculty about training philosophy, models, structure, and outcomes.

Graduate training programs have lacked direction in training multiculturally competent counselors for work with increasingly diverse populations (Bernal & Padilla, 1982; Chunn, Dunston, & Ross-Sheriff, 1983; Ridley, 1985). There are numerous reasons for this (see Ridley et al., 1994), but primarily, many educators were not multiculturally trained themselves and are not considered culturally competent. Although "culturally sensitive" procedures have been implemented, the philosophy of multicultural training has not been delineated in many counseling programs. Ridley et al. (1994) stated that "program developers must strive to make their own philosophies explicit, coherent, and socially relevant" (p. 231). To incorporate multicultural training programs without this foundation is analogous to "placing the cart before the horse."

We argue that until the philosophical groundwork for a multicultural training program has been laid in professional programs, it will be difficult, if not impossible, to expect students to become culturally competent. The need for multicultural training is clear to those faculty currently in the field, yet many faculty are still naive about or unfamiliar with the relevance of multicultural training. Many faculty view multiculturalism as directly related to external political correctness, against which there has been a backlash in recent years. It will therefore be difficult to create a multicultural training model until discussions regarding training philosophies are initiated. Some multicultural training programs are unlikely to succeed because a fundamental multicultural training philosophy is not embedded and defined in the program.

We would like to point out a few assumptions embedded within this chapter. First, multiculturalism is a philosophy and not a specialty area to be guided solely by historically oppressed racioethnic individuals. Second, multiculturalism is not merely about race and ethnic issues, but includes religion, gender, lifestyle, and many other sociopolitical factors. The crucial concern is a reliance on viewing the individual within a collective, as all behavior is contextual. Third, by enhancing one's existing knowledge through acquiring and imparting multicultural information, one becomes a better faculty trainer. Better training leads to better recruitment and retention of culturally diverse students, and society benefits from trained students competent in multicultural issues.

Arredondo (1994) stated, "My observation is that multiculturalism is not debatable; it is a given" (p. 308). Nevertheless, not everyone agrees about the urgency of incorporating cultural diversity into programs (e.g.,

Jones, 1990; Midgette & Meggert, 1991; Smith, 1982; Stricker, 1990; Troy, 1990). As a result, increasing faculty consideration of multiculturalism in all aspects of training programs has been frustratingly slow. Models outlining multicultural training formats are emerging (e.g., Ridley et al., 1994), yet most psychology programs that might benefit from more inclusive cultural program designs still use the single course format (Hills & Strozier, 1992).

Ridley et al. (1994) recently constructed a five-stage model (training philosophy, training goals, instructional strategies, program designs, and evaluation methods) that may be considered one of the most inclusive multicultural training models illustrated to date. At the base of their model is the training philosophy. Because of its comprehensiveness, the present authors have used the Ridley et al. (1994) model to generate ideas for this chapter. In essence, the purpose of this chapter is to further delineate the first level of the Ridley et al. (1994) model, the multicultural training philosophy. This will be accomplished by (a) discussing what constitutes a training philosophy, (b) delineating the values of some existing training models, (c) identifying the cultural appropriateness of existing training philosophies, and (d) discussing how to implement philosophical and programmatic change.

Why the Need for a
Training Philosophy?

The term *philosophy* has no clear, unbiased, universally accepted definition. It is perhaps this lack of a clear definition that contributes to the paucity of literature concerning training philosophies (Ridley et al., 1994). Yet philosophies are often considered to be an expression of a value judgment that will translate into a subjectively important act (Edwards & Pap, 1973). A training philosophy, then, is the directional guiding belief that a training program behaviorally follows.

A training philosophy sets the foundation from which Ridley et al.'s (1994) learning objectives, instructional strategies, program designs, and evaluative mechanisms are derived. Without it, a training program cannot exist and no training model can stand. It is this philosophical foundation that separates highly effective from less effective training programs, regardless of the specific philosophy. All training programs are philosophically based, but many of these philosophies are not explicitly stated. This leads to a vague but seemingly shared understanding that there is a collective belief system among program faculty (Adler, 1983).

Traditional
Training Philosophies

With the increasing emphases on multicultural counseling competencies (e.g., Bernal & Castro, 1994; Ponterotto & Casas, 1987; Pope-Davis & Ottavi, 1994; Pope-Davis, Prieto, Reynolds, & Vázquez, 1994), questions that all programs should periodically ask themselves are, "Who are our clientele?" and "How do our existing training philosophies relate to these populations?" Persico (1991) has raised the following point: "What social purpose is achieved by educating and training doctoral-level psychologists? We educate and train psychologists in order to ensure that a regular supply of competently trained clinicians is able to meet the mental health needs of the population" (p. 57).

Who, then, are ultimately our clientele? Some may argue that students are the clientele because of the direct relationship between faculty and students. However, our ultimate clientele is the community population. Atkinson, Morten, and Sue (1993), reporting on the 1990 U.S. Census, indicated that by the year 2000 more than one third of the U.S. population will be racioethnic minorities. With current immigration patterns and differential birth rates, White Americans will become a numerical minority by the year 2010. Many individuals from emerging diverse groups do not espouse traditional European American values and philosophies, which has resulted in a decrease in relevance of the "melting pot" theory. Through past and current sociopolitical "rights" movements, some diverse individuals are resisting the melting pot theory and maintaining their respective cultural ideologies. Traditional psychological counseling theories are socially based on the melting pot phenomena, whereas culturally sensitive theories tend to be amenable to more culture-specific values.

The reliance of traditional training models and theories of psychotherapy on Eurocentric, middle-class values and beliefs has been well documented (e.g., Katz, 1985; Pedersen, 1987; Sue & Sue, 1990). Many of these European-based models are couched in philosophies of individualism, dualism, logical positivism and structural determinism, pragmatism, control, nuclear patriarchal structures, intrapsychic phenomena, low-context, and are time- and space-bound. Many of our traditional theories lack an adequate inclusion of cultural influences, including differing values, beliefs about change, and worldviews. In addition, Eurocentric theories have been criticized as overlooking the sociopolitical realities of diverse cultural groups (e.g., racism, discrimination, oppression; see Atkinson & Hackett, 1995; Atkinson et al., 1993; Katz, 1985; Lee & Richardson, 1992; Locke, 1992; McFadden, 1994; Ponterotto & Casas, 1991; Ponterotto, Casas, et al.,

1995; Ponterotto & Pedersen, 1993; Sue & Sue, 1990). Further, many European American faculty overlook the fact that they, too, are culture-bound.

Some authors have argued that the Euro-American culture has had such a major influence on daily living that many individuals have difficulty teasing out culture specifics. This makes the task of delineating a training philosophy particularly difficult. Leong (1992) pointed out that, "Explaining cultural differences to any particular group is akin to describing water to the goldfish that has no knowledge of any other medium of existence" (p. 219).

Broader culturally based models often emphasize beliefs such as holism, collectivism, spirituality, sociopolitical influences, culture-specific values, lifestyles, and historical context more than do traditional Eurocentric perspectives (see Ivey, 1994; Paniagua, 1994; Sue & Sue, 1990). These beliefs are based on philosophical assumptions at times diametric to many prevalent models. Culturally sensitive models are no better or worse than traditional models, yet they may be more consistent with worldviews of many potential clients and students given the changing national and university demographics. Several authors (e.g., Sue, 1977; Sue & Zane, 1987) have indicated that minority groups are underrepresented in community mental health. One fairly consistent explanation is that minority group members may believe that White counselors will not share similar values and expectations. Therefore it is imperative that faculty trainers become familiar with and teach from multiple perspectives in order to increase clientele relevance.

In essence, traditional training programs have perpetuated existing theoretical bases of psychotherapy. Furthermore, many programs have incorporated and imparted philosophies that reflect Eurocentric organizational, theoretical, clinical, supervisory, and research models. For example, some departments are unwilling to include student input into faculty meetings (hierarchy, control), rely almost exclusively on traditional student testing practices (logical positivism), and focus primarily on traditional therapeutic models (intrapsychic reliance, individualism). An example may offer an overview:

Let us briefly look at general mental health practice. Let us assume that a client enters our office, receives counseling for 50 minutes, and leaves, with no further therapist-client contact until the next scheduled appointment. What are some of our assumptions? First, it is understood that the client must arrive at an unfamiliar, time- and space-bound setting to receive unfamiliar services. Further, the client is expected to begin discussing concerns quickly, particularly with the increased emphasis on short-term treatment models. The expectation of immediate expression is based on a Western idea of self-expression and openness, which is not necessarily consistent with other cultural groups. Finally, it is generally expected that the client is the change agent, and it is currently unlikely that the counselor and client discussed sociocultural and historical issues. Our traditional reliance on individualism and autonomy is extremely pervasive in traditional culture, as is the "Protestant" work ethic claiming that if you work harder you will achieve your goals. Given contextual constraints, the latter may not be an accurate assumption.

This office-visit scenario depicts a number of philosophical assumptions of many traditional models. These assumptions are perpetuated by training beliefs that hold that the client must arrive to see you within a constrained structure and must act in a specified manner to receive help. Consider a brief alternative: How might faculty view the idea that counseling can occur in a neutral or client-chosen setting for an extended period of time? This focal shift is already occurring in many applied settings, but is not usually discussed in academic settings.

Multicultural Training Philosophies

Some faculty seem to hold a belief that existing theoretical models can be applied to all individuals. Unfortunately, the extreme etic (universal) perspective is based in monoculturalism and cultural encapsulation (Wrenn, 1965, 1985), which has existed in psychology for years. Axelson (1993) recommended that the first step in effecting change is to become aware of hidden prejudice, whereas others (Bowser & Hunt, 1981; Carney & Kahn, 1984; Carter & Helms, 1992) suggested that White prejudice significantly inhibits counseling with non-Whites. Becoming aware of prejudice may effect philosophical change leading to culturally aware organizational and therapeutic models.

As outlined in McEwen and Roper (1994), Minnich (1990) has described four basic errors that are inherent in traditional models and, by extension, training programs. The first is *faulty generalization,* or the belief that because much of the literature has been established by one group, this group sets the standard for all other groups (universalization). The second is *circular reasoning,* or the idea that works derived from one group are universally appropriate for other groups. The third is *mystified concepts,* or the view that because values, attitudes, and notions are so embedded in "reality," they are rarely questioned. The fourth is *partial knowledge,* or the notion that, because of the first three errors, we will never achieve comprehensive knowledge.

These perspectives are understandable given that (a) most current faculty have not been trained in multicultural competencies and are not aware of a multicultural philosophy, and (b) multiculturalism has generally been allocated to a "minority" status within departments. Existing programmatic value systems often relegate multiculturalism to a specialty area, and it is our belief that until European culture is explicitly incorporated into multiculturalism, culturally sensitive theories will continue to receive specialty designation.

The implicit philosophy that models normed and based on a broad European heritage can be universally applied is currently misguided. We contend that it is imperative to revisit, with a multicultural perspective, theoretical models that were initially based on monocultural ideology. For example, Usher (1989) studied the multicultural relevance of Rogerian thought. Many of the first author's students attest that humanistic philosophy, specifically Rogerian beliefs, is culturally sensitive because of the emphases on egalitarianism, counselor facilitation of the client's discovery of meanings (e.g., "not imposing Eurocentric values"), and individual dignity (Corsini, 1984). Although many Rogerian concepts were found to be appropriate across cultures (e.g., humanitarianism), others (e.g., reliance on the individual as sole change agent) did not account for sociopolitical factors. Usher (1989), therefore, suggested that Rogerian approaches are biased toward European thought.

European thought in itself is not necessarily negative, particularly with many client types. However, more research needs to be established attending to the relevance of other models with non-Eurocentric beliefs for those clients who may desire less traditional models. Overall, our traditional training models based on White middle-class values and philosophies may not be appropriate with the "diversification of America" (U.S. Bureau of the Census, 1990). If we as trainers are to maintain training relevancy, we must begin to incorporate more culturally relevant models into our program. This will be explicated below, through multicultural training philosophies.

Creating Multicultural Training Philosophies

In the professional literature, little attention has been paid to multicultural training philosophies. Bernal and Padilla (1982) investigated clinical psychology training programs to determine their investment in multiculturalism. Information regarding racioethnically diverse faculty, coursework, practica, research, and language requirements were described in their findings, and philosophies were deduced from the responses and were extended. Responding to Korchin's (1980) belief that a separate ethnic psychology is not needed and inclusive models should be incorporated into programs for all students, Bernal and Padilla (1982) stated that a multicultural training philosophy must be in place for this to occur.

> The components include a concern for cultural sensitivity, a better under-
> standing of racism and its consequences for mental health, knowledge about
> the merits and dangers of customs of different cultures as they affect their
> members in terms of universal standards of mental health, an increase in
> opportunities for students to work with clients of ethnically similar and
> dissimilar backgrounds, and enlargement of the numbers of minority students
> and faculty. The multicultural training philosophy acknowledges that it is vital
> for trainees to have broad-based historical and cultural understanding of
> minority groups, to develop positive attitudes toward them, to gain theoretical
> knowledge and expertise in the scientific study of sociocultural variables, to
> become experienced in the application of primary, secondary, and tertiary
> preventive strategies that are culturally appropriate, and to be able to com-
> municate fluently in their client's language. (p. 786)

Expanding on Bernal and Padilla (1982), Ridley (1985) described imperatives for future psychological training programs. These include a written
commitment to diversity, inclusion of ethnic and cultural material into all
relevant coursework, assertive recruitment (and presumed retention) efforts,
hiring a multicultural expert to assist in the development of a multicultural
focus, and an ethnic-issues coordinator. Many of the imperatives were
derived from a "collective" philosophical base.

Echemendia and Congett (1991) explicitly stated portions of the Pennsylvania State University clinical psychology program philosophy. They emphasized multicultural training as generic training (Pedersen, 1991), as
reflected in the program's curricula. All courses included cultural diversity
issues that are clearly stated in the syllabi, and comprehensive exams included questions on diversity. Programmatic structural areas included allowing students to take culturally related courses outside of their program,
collaborative efforts with external agencies with minority clients, aggressive
and creative recruiting practices, and faculty/student collaboration continually to develop multicultural interests. Financial backing occurs for
faculty development and program administration by supportive university
offices.

Mirrored in these behavior efforts is the willingness of faculty and administration to incorporate multiculturalism into their collective program. In
order to do so, the administration and faculty need to be amenable to

questioning traditional programs and offering students and faculty experiences that may be construed as personally and professionally risky. For example, in order for students to engage in competent clinical work with culturally diverse populations, faculty must first be willing to act as culturally competent supervisors and consultants. It is presumed that many of the Penn State faculty engaged in multicultural (re)training. How a transition from ethnocentrism to multiculturalism was achieved was not elucidated, however.

Finally, Ridley et al. (1994) delineated a multicultural training philosophy consisting of four categories: (a) motivation for multicultural training, (b) theoretical frameworks for conceptualizing cultural variables in multicultural counseling and training, (c) definitions of multiculturalism, and (d) scope of multicultural training in terms of aspects of training programs delineated as targets of multicultural training intervention. Their recommendation that everyone in the respective programs discuss these areas—with the hope that discussion will lead to a formalized training philosophy—is admirable.

Through open discussion, faculty need to determine the appropriateness of their respective training programs for diverse populations. This should be accomplished within an atmosphere of respect for all perspectives. This is probably easier in theory than practice, because if there were a consistent willingness to be respectful, open, and honest about multicultural issues, then the need for the discussion itself might not exist. By asking the question of how appropriate their training is given the population, faculty can begin with their own training philosophy as reflected in their program mission statement.

Mission Statements

Mission statements are proactive statements outlining the direction of the program; they are not reactive statements outlining what the training program already does. They dictate where the program wants to go instead of the status quo. Mission statements reflect both formal and implied training goals and objectives, and state the purpose and focus of training at the respective institution. Therefore, mission statements should be updated periodically. No empirical evidence has compared mission statements to traditional training models or philosophies. We therefore solicited mission statements from a number of psychology programs nationally. Unfortunately, our perusal of mission statements indicated a failure of many programs reviewed to state their philosophies explicitly, except for general statements such as "adhere to the scientist-practitioner model." Little multicultural information was gleaned from the missions, although some reported statements such as "sensitive to diversity issues."

Little attention has been paid to the values, attitudes, and biases that govern the mission of the training program. In fact, many programs surveyed were not acutely aware of their respective mission statements, and some programs assumed that the statement was embedded in doctoral admissions information. Vaill (1989, p. 104) determined that "the literature seems to assume that members of an organization are 'informed about the mission' or 'inspired with the vision' in pretty much the same way that everyday communication occurs" (as cited in Kushner & Blum, 1994).

For example, does the mission statement reflect a commitment to diversity? An example of a mission statement recently submitted for adoption at our institution is an initial attempt at incorporating a multicultural belief system into the program. From there it is hoped that programmatic behavioral and organizational changes will occur.

> The Ph.D. program in Counseling Psychology is designed to train students in the use of developmental/educational, reventive, and remedial interventions for social change within the diverse context of contemporary society. Firmly rooted in the scientist-practitioner model, the program includes an organized sequence of courses, practica, and internships designed to enhance students' cultural competence in individual and group counseling, research, supervision, and teaching at the university level. Brief-term interventions are emphasized that focus on a person's assets and strengths regardless of the degree of disturbance. The program is organizationally integrated with the Department's graduate and undergraduate programs in Counseling Psychology, School Counseling, and Social and Rehabilitation Services to capitalize on training opportunities available in clinical supervision and the teaching of topical areas in which students have previously demonstrated competence. Students are expected to adhere to the highest ethical standards, including sensitivity to diverse values and cultures, and to examine sociopolitical influences on the individual and group from a multicultural perspective in which the person-environment interaction is emphasized. Graduates of the program have established careers in academia, community mental health agencies, Veterans Administration and university medical centers, public and private inpatient facilities, and private practice. (p. 2)

Programs will need to devise their own statements based on their specific emphases and needs. For example, the above mission statement does not include explicit language competencies (implicitly, English is presumed), while some training programs in other geographic regions may deem language a critical component. This mission statement is not intended to be valid for all programs, but is merely a way to begin incorporating an alternative philosophy.

Programmatic Philosophical Change

Sue (1991) indicated that valuing diversity is a slow, ongoing process that can be derailed at any time (Hunt, Bell, Wei, & Ingle, 1992; Massey, 1991; Santiago-Negron, 1991; Vaughn, 1991). Kushner and Blum (1994) discussed the need for assessing organizational receptivity to multicultural training. Through organizational analyses, they outlined several models that help determine an organization's willingness to address and implement multicultural issues. These are discussed through theoretical frameworks, conceptual models, and organizational analyses. It is beyond the scope of this chapter to discuss these models in detail, but the reader may want to become more familiar with these if future program multicultural implementation or enhancement is desired. A number of models have been proposed that discuss stages of multicultural development and organizational willingness to incorporate multiculturalism (e.g., D'Andrea & Daniels, 1991; Jackson & Hardiman, 1981; Jackson & Holvino, 1988; Massey, 1991).

Through an organizational analysis of counselor education programs, D'Andrea and Daniels (1991) have proposed a model utilizing two levels and four stages. An outline of this model is discussed below, with each stage followed by examples of characteristics, philosophies, and suggestions to move the department to a level more consistent with multicultural philosophies. In addition to D'Andrea and Daniels (1991), these philosophies were derived from numerous multicultural writers, including Persico (1991) and Ponterotto, Alexander, and Grieger (1995).

Level 1 (The Cultural Encapsulation Stage)

Stage 1: Cultural Entrenchment

Characteristics. Stage 1 is manifested by a virtually nonexistent multicultural program. At best, cultural stereotypes and traditional models are presented, and ethnocentrism is perpetuated. An assumption is that there are shared beliefs among faculty and students, and counseling is often described as objective and neutral. Obviously, contrasting worldviews are not discussed and there is often a naive sense that core counseling conditions such as empathy and genuineness transcend cultural boundaries and are sufficient for change.

PHILOSOPHIES

1. Clients have essentially the same concerns, regardless of culture.
2. Our theories are applicable to everyone, because behavior is behavior.
3. Culture has little influence on individuals and pathology. We all have an idea of that which is normal. Besides, we can't even define culture.
4. Some clients may need different approaches, but there are other people (e.g., minorities) who deal with that.
5. Our organizational structure has worked well. Why do we need to become more multicultural?
6. The basic clinical skills (e.g., empathy) are universal and transcend race and ethnicity.
7. Multiculturalism is just an extension of the political correctness movement.
8. The best person should be accepted and rewarded, period.
9. We are all human beings and all we would do is teach stereotypes anyway.
10. Multiculturalism might hurt our economic survival.
11. Everyone should assimilate (e.g., "We are all Americans").

Suggestions for Change. In Stage 1, educational organizations tend to perceive training from a monocultural perspective. There is a significant amount of discrimination, largely through resistance or unawareness. Some training programs will continue to resist a multicultural philosophy until a "critical mass" of students or faculty is in place or until professional legislation or accrediting boards begin to use cultural diversity as a criterion for continuation. These "bottom-up" and "top-down" approaches may be effective, but for vastly different reasons. Regardless of the type of approach taken, program developers must eventually decide whether to become proactive toward addressing and incorporating multiculturalism into their respective programs. At this stage, individual faculty can increase awareness of racism and sexism through educational programs (e.g., Corvin & Wiggins, 1989; Ponterotto, 1988) and departmental meetings. Alternatively, initial discussion with faculty around typologies of multiculturalism (Carter & Qureshi, 1995), worldviews (Ibrahim, 1991), or the individualism-collectivism constructs (Kim, Triandis, Kagitcibasi, Choi, & Yoon, 1994) could occur. These topics help focus the discussion on differing philosophical perspectives and assumptions instead of relying on discussions of racioethnic groups, because some faculty may respond negatively if multiculturalism is viewed specifically as a racioethnic issue.

Predominantly monocultural training environments tend to respond to external motivators such as legal, legislative, departmental, and political decrees (Jackson & Holvino, 1988). These top-down approaches are primarily externally based and may be the most resisted form of change. Professional mandates (e.g., APA Office of Ethnic Minority Affairs, 1993), legal obligations (Ridley, 1985; Ridley et al., 1994), and external political correctness (Pedersen, 1991) may be seen as confrontational or suppressive because of "academic freedom" or individual beliefs surrounding ethnocentrism. Imposing tolerance for diversity rather than internal motivations for change may lead to resistance within training programs.

Top-down approaches—though needed for any change to occur—may lead to more externally based, culturally sensitive training models and behaviors, but the individual and training philosophy may not change. There is a prevalent belief that ethnic minority affairs should be designated a specialty area, and the influence of outside forces does little to motivate intrinsic change. Nevertheless, a top-down approach is needed in order to make others aware of both multiculturalism as a whole and the need to include multiculturalism in training philosophies.

Stage 2: The Cross-Cultural Awakening Stage

Characteristics. Stage 2 programs adhere to many of the same philosophical assumptions as Stage 1 programs, but also realize that many traditional approaches are not always appropriate to diverse cultural groups. Yet few faculty are aware or committed enough to elaborate beyond the brief indications that not all approaches are appropriate. D'Andrea and Daniels (1991) indicated that most programs fall into this stage, while a smaller portion fall into the final two stages.

PHILOSOPHIES

1. Perhaps multiculturalism has a place because not all traditional approaches are applicable. We have people on the faculty who can teach multiculturalism.
2. Institutional racism probably occurs but not in our department. We just have a hard time recruiting minorities.
3. The students could benefit from seeing some diverse clients.
4. Social oppression isn't good but what can we do at the graduate level? The students need that information before they get to graduate school.
5. The students get a course in multicultural issues, and the instructor is an expert in that area.
6. Some of the faculty cover multicultural issues in their courses. This is evidenced by some course readings.

7. We believe that there are many between-group similarities and these should be covered more than the differences.
8. The demographic representation of clients and students is changing and we need to address this.
9. Most faculty fluctuate on being an affirmative action employer.

Suggestions for Change. In moving from Stage 1 to Stage 2, emphasizing a bottom-up approach may be beneficial. The bottom-up approach states that once a critical mass (e.g., 15%-30%, see Green, 1988; Kanter, 1977; Ponterotto, Lewis, & Bullington, 1990) is established by students and faculty, the relevancy and applicability of existing clinical models and research designs may be questioned. For example, the senior author consistently informs students to ask questions of cultural relevancy in all classes. Listed below are examples of questions students can ask of faculty during their training:

1. Would your hypotheses change regarding treatment if this client were Native American instead of European American?
2. What does the literature say about working with various Asian populations in group counseling?
3. During supervision, can you help me to see if there are any cultural transference issues with my client?

Obviously these questions are general, and culturally sensitive faculty trainers should have an understanding of increasingly important within-group variables such as acculturation level (e.g., LaFromboise, Coleman, & Gerton, 1993), racioethnic identity and consciousness (e.g., Helms, 1990, 1995; Phinney, 1990; Rowe, Behrens, & Leach, 1995; Sodowsky, Kwan, & Pannu, 1995), and cultural mistrust (Leach, Rowe, & Steward, 1995; Terrell & Terrell, 1984).

It is hoped that when some faculty are questioned they will (a) realize that course enhancement can be made and (b) actively seek out multicultural information and incorporate this information into their syllabi. Many historical changes in academia have occurred because of students questioning the status quo and expecting changes. Perhaps questioning faculty during courses, in program meetings, and in other venues may motivate some faculty to question a reliance on Eurocentric beliefs.

Students or faculty can request an ethnic coordinator (Ridley, 1985), a "Multicultural Affairs Committee" consisting of students and faculty, multiculturally relevant clinical supervision, additional multicultural coursework and multicultural practica, and research focusing on multicultural issues (Ponterotto, Alexander, & Grieger, 1995). It is at this stage that faculty can begin to redesign their mission statements, including philosophies consistent with multicultural frameworks. These allow for continued internal philosophical change.

Level 2 (The Conscientious Level)

Stage 3: The Cultural Integrity Stage

Characteristics. Stage 3 programs believe in the importance of multicultural courses and are considered to be in a transitional stage. More consistent attention is given to cultural diversity issues, and various faculty may devote small portions of their classes to cultural issues. Students are taught to increase their understanding of cultural issues through a variety of media and to work toward an understanding of personal biases, values, and more. Further, information about racioethnic groups, sociopolitical systems, and institutional barriers is discussed.

PHILOSOPHIES
1. We must maintain cultural integrity of clients, and students should consider gender, ethnicity, and class values.
2. Both faculty and students should be aware of their own values, prejudices, and attitudes regarding diverse clients. Most faculty can cite references (e.g., Atkinson et al., 1993; Pedersen, 1987; Sue & Sue, 1990) when discussing racioethnic values.
3. The faculty are willing to learn about "alternative" models derived from philosophies of Afrocentrism and feminism. We are aware of ontological, axiological, and cosmological differences and similarities between other cultural groups and our own.
4. The sociopolitical system, including academia, influences clients, students, and organizational structure. Most faculty can discuss how this is accomplished.
5. Most faculty can talk comfortably about racial issues and believe such discussion is necessary for effective training.
6. We believe it is necessary to achieve financial and political support from the Dean and other administrators to further multiculturalism. We have repeatedly effected change through constant efforts directed toward the administration.

Suggestions for Change. Movement toward multicultural environments is more likely to support change conditions such as "paradigm shifts, alternative worldviews, commitment from top management, interracial coalitions, a critical mass of organizational members with a change agenda, and worldwide socio-political changes" (Jackson & Holvino, 1988, p. 18). In Stage 3, more advanced training regarding multicultural issues can occur. For example, further development can occur through regional, national, and international workshops and institutes.

At this stage, further discussion can occur regarding issues such as sociopolitical influences on the departmental structure, student performance appraisal, recruitment and retention of diverse students and faculty, and support services and resources. It is at this point that faculty can begin discussing greater inclusiveness across disciplines. For example, proposals can be made regarding students receiving coursework in anthropology, sociology, and women's studies. Outcomes of the discussions regarding more inclusive training programs can be proposed to the Dean and other administrators. It is important to keep in mind that many of the proposed changes listed can occur without any additional revenue. Structural change can occur through philosophical change.

Stage 4: The Infusion Stage

Characteristics. Stage 4 programs adhere to a significant emphasis on multiculturalism. Interdisciplinary coursework is offered, a planned multicultural commitment to complement other areas of coursework is enacted, and multicultural training becomes more synonymous with generic counseling (Arredondo, 1994; Fukuyama, 1990; Ivey, 1994; Pedersen, 1991).

PHILOSOPHIES

1. We believe that both faculty and students have developed a wide variety of counseling approaches that are culturally sensitive.
2. Our program is not equipped to provide all multicultural material, and other disciplines (e.g., social work, anthropology, African American Studies) can offer valuable information.
3. Most faculty intentionally discuss cultural issues as part of every course. Most faculty members believe in the necessity of inclusion.
4. Most faculty believe in synergistic problem solving, interdependence, pluralism, and the development of all human potential.
5. Most faculty members can discuss nontraditional models such as Africentrism, feminism, and constructivism.
6. We believe in teaching culturally sensitive communication strategies and their relationship to traditional strategies.

7. Diversity is valued and faculty believe that they can continue to learn cultural issues from their students.
8. Faculty members can discuss the ontology, axiology, and cosmology of various cultural groups.

Suggestions for Change. Finally, in Stage 4 the philosophy of the department is consistent with the philosophy of multiculturalism. Numerous belief systems, pluralism, positive conflict, and alternative work structures are understood as determining a healthy and productive department. This is accomplished by aligning "internal mechanisms, mission, relations with the environment and the multicultural agenda of an organization (a macrosystems level intervention)" (Jackson & Holvino, 1988, p. 16). In essence, there is a belief in the integration between internal systems and the environment. Psychology is considered and taught on both a micro and macro level, and political, social, economic, and intrapsychic factors are integratively taken into account.

It is hoped that the belief statements will help counselor educators identify their existing training program philosophies. Once identified, it is hoped that interested counselor trainers will seriously and openly consider the level of multicultural commitment of their respective programs. As can be seen in the model, there is a progression from traditional to less traditional beliefs, from a strict hierarchy to more egalitarianism, from no awareness of sociopolitical systems to an incorporation of sociopolitical systems, and from significant resistance or unawareness to infusion.

As discussed earlier, change to multicultural philosophies requires long, arduous work. Persico (1991) discussed eight steps to creating a diverse institutional climate, with the first being the establishing of institutional commitment. Consistent with Persico's (1991) Step 1, Massey (1991) depicted a 5-year, 10-step staff development program for implementing multicultural curricula, with the first 1½ years focusing on philosophical awareness. General guidelines within the first step include the need that policies and procedures must be in place in order to create a culturally diverse climate. Ponterotto, Alexander, and Grieger (1995) recommend that a multicultural student organization be involved in all of these policy decisions in order to monitor and add input to the process. Policy needs include transcending the typical affirmative action policy, administrators reporting on their commitment to diversity, acceptance that policy makers will fail sometimes because of the years of policy being based on monoculturalism, acceptance that we all must learn, a faculty body consistent with the diversity of the general population, and an agreement that it is unacceptable not to achieve the goals.

Program Evaluation

What would a multiculturally based training program look like? Although little systematic training program evaluation has been implemented historically (Ridley et al., 1994) there are two articles that offer excellent evaluation perspectives on multicultural training programs. Based on an implicit "collective" philosophy, Ponterotto, Alexander, and Grieger (1995) offer a multicultural evaluation tool to help programs determine strength and deficiency areas. Six categorical training competency areas in this checklist include (a) minority representation, (b) curriculum issues, (c) counseling practice and supervision, (d) research considerations, (e) student and faculty competency evaluation, and (f) the physical environment. This checklist provides an excellent avenue for programs to define and evaluate cultural goals.

Describing additional evaluation components, Ridley et al. (1994) discuss three areas needing further study: (a) a lack of clarity in training objectives, (b) inadequate outcome measures, and (c) problems with research design strategies. From these categories faculty can begin to determine their cultural training efficacy, and hence their students' multicultural counseling competencies.

In order to move toward the visions of Ponterotto, Alexander, and Grieger (1995) and Ridley et al. (1994), it is our belief that for multicultural training to become generic training (Pedersen, 1991), programs will need to include the following:

1. additional cultural competence training for faculty (with administrative funding);
2. faculty willingness to accept and incorporate alternative belief systems;
3. mission statements reflecting an openness to cultural issues;
4. faculty familiarity with diverse teaching strategies (e.g., see Roberts et al., 1994);
5. multicultural research by faculty and culturally appropriate readings in all coursework;
6. culturally based practica; and
7. student selection of internship sites familiar with multicultural issues, with subsequent reports from internship programs regarding student cultural competency.

Although these may be programmatic goals and therefore evaluation components, movement toward these goals will be moderated by the program's philosophical stage(s) outlined above.

Consistently agreed-upon formal evaluation methods are virtually nonexistent. Further, it is unlikely that outcome congruity will pervade every program (short of external mandates), given the subjectivity of the multicultural field and individual departmental needs. Until universally agreed-upon outcome measures can be devised and validated, each department may need to construct outcome criteria consistent with its mission and goals. Future research should focus on developing comprehensive, culturally relevant instruments designed to assess departmental needs.

Using Massey (1991) as a foundation, departments must be willing

1. to devise a mission statement incorporating cultural issues;
2. to define objectives collaboratively, utilizing individuals from groups such as multicultural affairs committees and a women's studies programs—the objectives should cover the areas defined above and those outlined by Ponterotto, Alexander, and Grieger (1995) and Ridley et al. (1994);
3. to devise detailed outcome measures based on the specific objectives that can be verified—although not initially intended for use as a programmatic outcome measure, the Multicultural Awareness-Knowledge-Skills Survey (MAKSS; D'Andrea, Daniels, & Heck, 1991), is one example of an instrument that can be administered to faculty as a reference point for determining cultural competency; and
4. to reevaluate the objectives and progress during faculty meetings each academic term.

Future Challenges
for Multiculturalism

The multicultural field will continue to incur resistance until training programs can more clearly delineate the field from the concept of "political correctness" that often precludes the furthering of discussion. Politically correct behaviors may not be highly related to a multicultural philosophy, because some of these behaviors are often reactions to political climates or other external factors. Further, politically correct behaviors are often set prior to entering training programs or discussion at faculty meetings due to previous emotionally valenced experiences.

Two interesting phenomena seem to have occurred with the growing popularity of this field. First, many individuals experience visceral reactions associated with discussion of the movement. The first three "forces" within psychology (i.e., psychodynamism, behaviorism, humanism) do not seem to invoke strong emotional reactions for either faculty or students, and are typically left to rational debate. Acceptance of multiculturalism forces many trainers and students directly to confront (or deny) their own prejudices, values, and worldviews. Conversely, personal human prejudice rarely seems to enter into a debate on the efficacy of cognitive-behavioral approaches to the treatment of persons with anxiety disorders.

Second, the multicultural field seems to tap into a common human fear: the fear of the unknown. Because the field is still in its infancy, many academicians may perceive it as more nebulous than other subdisciplines. Most faculty were not trained in multicultural issues and may view this "force" with apprehensiveness. This is compounded by diverse groups attempting to maintain their cultural lifestyles, with subsequent programmatic unawareness as to how to work with individuals or groups not willing to assimilate fully into "American" culture. It is therefore incumbent upon the field to address these emotional reactions rather than fuel the perceived affective components often associated with personal notions of multiculturalism.

In order to accelerate departmental multicultural acceptance, there must be the recognition of majority group members as having cultural bases. Whites often do not perceive themselves as having a culture, and it is sometimes difficult for many majority group individuals to separate "American" culture from "White" culture. Discussion may allow for individual separation of culture from race and ethnicity as related to individuals.

Similarly, writers and instructors must begin to define their terms clearly. It is not uncommon to read manuscripts or listen to instructors who interchange the terms *race, ethnicity,* and *culture.* Confusion is then perpetuated by students who further misuse these terms. This may lead to the erroneously accepted idea that multicultural equals multiracial (ethnic). Departmental faculty members can begin to discuss multiculturalism in terms of alternative paradigms (e.g., worldviews, collectivism) that are less likely to lead to confusion and are considered less threatening than focusing primarily on racioethnic issues.

The lack of one prominent individual identified as spearheading the field of multiculturalism is yet another compounding factor in the field's acceptance among some faculty. From some educators' perspectives, the perceived leadership deficit makes it difficult for them to feel grounded in the cultural learning process. For some faculty and students, the existence of "one guiding theory" would provide a point of reference from which to move forward.

Furthermore, the field has been criticized for offering little information regarding practical applications for working with diverse cultures. However, empirical evidence regarding practical applications has been increasing. The challenge will be for culturally sensitive faculty members to assist other members at a starting point relevant to their subdisciplines.

A necessary challenge to the field will be discussion between majority and minority group faculty regarding their interlinking historical relationship. The contextual nature of prejudice, values, attitudes, and sociopolitical movements must be illuminated before training programs can fully incorporate multiculturalism.

Finally, faculty must understand that espousing a multicultural perspective does not mean renouncing previously conceived philosophies (e.g., behaviorism, psychodynamism, humanism), but understanding the limitations of these perspectives. Therefore, trainers are not relinquishing previously held beliefs but rather can be seen as enhancing their personal philosophical perspectives. It is hoped that this frame of reference will help some faculty feel less threatened by multiculturalism.

Conclusion

In her questionnaire, Adler (1983) proposed reasons for the paucity of multicultural issues discussed in organizations. Top arguments included a common language, denial, and assumed similarity. This chapter attempted to expand the philosophical framework with which to build multicultural programs. We offered examples of traditional and multicultural training philosophies, questions programs can ask to determine existing philosophies, discussion of mission statements, and a brief description of what multicultural training programs might include. It is hoped that through discussions within departments, faculty can begin to arrive at reasons and means for incorporating a multicultural training philosophy.

References

Adler, N. J. (1983). Organizational development in a multicultural environment. *The Journal of Applied Behavioral Science, 19,* 349-365.

American Psychological Association, Office of Ethnic Minority Affairs. (1993). Guidelines for providers of psychological services to ethnic, linguistic, and culturally diverse populations. *American Psychologist, 48*(1), 45-48.

Arredondo, P. (1994). Multicultural training: A response. *The Counseling Psychologist, 22,* 308-314.

Atkinson, D. R., & Hackett, G. (1995). *Counseling diverse populations.* Dubuque, IA: Brown & Benchmark.

Atkinson, D. R., Morten, G., & Sue, D. W. (1993). *Counseling American minorities* (4th ed.). Dubuque, IA: Brown & Benchmark.

Axelson, J. A. (1993). *Counseling and development in a multicultural society* (Rev. ed.). Monterey, CA: Brooks/Cole.

Baruth, L. G., & Manning, M. L. (1991). *Multicultural counseling and psychotherapy: A lifespan approach.* New York: Merrill.

Bernal, M. E., & Castro, F. G. (1994). Are clinical psychologists prepared for service and research with ethnic minorities? Report of a decade of progress. *American Psychologist, 49,* 797-805.

Bernal, M. E., & Padilla, A. M. (1982). Status of minority curricula and training in clinical psychology. *American Psychologist, 37,* 780-787.

Bowser, B. P., & Hunt, R. G. (1981). *Impact of racism on White Americans* (1st ed.). Beverly Hills, CA: Sage.

Carney, C. G., & Kahn, K. B. (1984). Building competencies for effective cross-cultural counseling: A developmental view. *The Counseling Psychologist, 12,* 111-119.

Carter, R. T., & Helms, J. E. (1992). The counseling process as defined by relationship types. *Journal of Multicultural Counseling and Development, 20*(4), 181-201.

Carter, R. T., & Qureshi, A. (1995). A typology of philosophical assumptions in multicultural counseling and training. In J. G. Ponterotto, J. M. Casas, L. A. Suzuki, & C. M. Alexander (Eds.), *Handbook of multicultural counseling* (pp. 239-262). Thousand Oaks, CA: Sage.

Chunn, J., Dunston, P., & Ross-Sheriff, F. (1983). *Mental health and people of color: Curriculum development and change.* Washington, DC: Howard University Press.

Copeland, E. J. (1982). Minority populations and traditional counseling programs: Some alternatives. *Counseling Education and Supervision, 21,* 187-193.

Corsini, R. J. (1984). *Current psychotherapies* (3rd ed.). Itasca, IL: F. E. Peacock.

Corvin, S. A., & Wiggins, F. (1989). An antiracism training model for White professionals. *Journal of Multicultural Counseling and Development, 17*(3), 105-114.

Counseling Psychology Program. (1995). *Ph.D. program in counseling psychology.* Hattiesburg, MS: University of Southern Mississippi.

D'Andrea, M., & Daniels, J. (1991). Exploring the different levels of multicultural counseling training in counselor education. *Journal of Counseling and Development, 70,* 78-85.

D'Andrea, M., Daniels, J., & Heck, R. (1991). Evaluating the impact of multicultural counseling training. *Journal of Counseling and Development, 70,* 143-150.

Echemendia, R. J., & Congett, S. M. (1991). Ethnic minority clinical training in a rural context: Pennsylvania State University. In H. Myers, P. Wohlford, L. P. Guzman, & R. Echemendia (Eds.), *Ethnic minority perspectives on clinical training and services in psychology* (pp. 91-96). Washington, DC: American Psychological Association.

Edwards, P., & Pap, A. (1973). General introduction. In P. Edwards & A. Pap (Eds.), *A modern introduction to philosophy: Readings from classical and contemporary sources* (3rd ed.). New York: Free Press.

Fukuyama, M. A. (1990). Taking a universal approach to multicultural counseling. *Counselor Education and Supervision, 30,* 7-17.

Green, M. F. (1988). *Minorities on campus: A handbook for enhancing diversity.* Washington, DC: American Council of Education.

Helms, J. E. (Ed.). (1990). *Black and White racial identity: Theory, research, and practice.* Westport, CT: Greenwood.

Helms, J. E. (1995). An update of Helms's White and people of color racial identity models. In J. G. Ponterotto, J. M. Casas, L. A. Suzuki, & C. M. Alexander (Eds.), *Handbook of multicultural counseling* (pp. 181-198). Thousand Oaks, CA: Sage.

Hills, H. I., & Strozier, A. L. (1992). Multicultural training in APA-approved counseling psychology programs: A survey. *Professional Psychology: Research and Practice, 23*(1), 43-51.

Hunt, J. A., Bell, L. A., Wei, W., & Ingle, G. (1992). Monoculturalism to multiculturalism: Lessons from three public universities. In M. Adams (Ed.), *Promoting diversity in college classrooms: Innovative responses for the curriculum, faculty, and institutions* (pp. 101-104). San Francisco: Jossey-Bass.

Ibrahim, F. A. (1991). Contribution of cultural worldview to generic counseling and development. *Journal of Counseling and Development, 70*(1), 13-19.

Ivey, A. E. (1994). *Intentional interviewing and counseling: Facilitating client development in a multicultural society* (3rd ed.). Pacific Grove, CA: Brooks/Cole.

Jackson, B., & Hardiman, R. (1981). *Organizational stages of multicultural awareness.* Unpublished manuscript.

Jackson, B. W., & Holvino, E. (1988). Developing multicultural organizations. *Journal of Religion and the Applied Behavioral Sciences, 9*(2), 14-19.

Jones, J. M. (1990). Invitational address: Who is training our ethnic minority psychologists, and are they doing it right? In G. Stricker, E. Davis-Russell, E. Bourg, E. Duran, W. R. Hammond, J. McHolland, K. Polite, & B. E. Vaughn (Eds.), *Toward ethnic diversification in psychology education and training* (pp. 17-34). Washington, DC: American Psychological Association.

Kanter, R. M. (1977). *Men and women of the corporation.* New York: Basic Books.

Katz, J. H. (1985). The sociopolitical nature of counseling. *The Counseling Psychologist, 13,* 615-624.

Kim, U., Triandis, H. C., Kagitcibasi, C., Choi, S., & Yoon, G. (Eds.). (1994). *Individualism and collectivism: Theory, method, and applications.* Thousand Oaks, CA: Sage.

Korchin, S. J. (1980). Clinical psychology and minority problems. *American Psychologist, 35*(3), 262-269.

Kushner, J. L., & Blum, L. (1994, August). *Assessing receptivity to multicultural training: An organizational analysis.* Paper presented at the 102nd annual convention of the American Psychological Association, Los Angeles.

LaFromboise, T., Coleman, H. L., & Gerton, J. (1993). Psychological impact of biculturalism: Evidence and theory. *Psychological Bulletin, 114*(3), 395-412.

Leach, M. M., Rowe, W., & Steward, R. (1995, August). *The multicultural mistrust scale: Rationale and description.* Paper presented at the 103rd annual convention of the American Psychological Association, New York.

Lee, C. C., & Richardson, B. L. (Eds.). (1992). *Multicultural issues in counseling: New approaches to diversity.* Alexandria, VA: American Association for Counseling and Development.

Leong, F.T.L. (1992). Guidelines for minimizing premature termination among Asian American clients in group counseling. *Journal for Specialists in Group Work, 17,* 218-228.

Locke, D. C. (1992). *Increasing multicultural understanding: A comprehensive model.* Newbury Park, CA: Sage.

Massey, I. (1991). Making and managing change. In I. Massey (Ed.), *More than skin deep: Developing anti-racist multicultural education in schools* (pp. 103-126). London: Hodder & Stoughton.

McEwen, M. K., & Roper, L. D. (1994). Incorporating multiculturalism into student affairs preparation programs: Suggestions from the literature. *Journal of College Student Development, 35,* 46-53.

McFadden, J. (Ed.). (1994). *Transcultural counseling: Bilateral and international perspectives.* Alexandria, VA: American Counseling Association.

Midgette, T. E., & Meggert, S. S. (1991). Multicultural counseling instruction: A challenge for faculties in the 21st century. *Journal of Counseling and Development, 70,* 136-141.

Minnich, E. K. (1990). *Transforming knowledge.* Philadelphia: Temple University Press.

Paniagua, F. A. (1994). *Assessing and treating culturally diverse clients: A practical guide.* Thousand Oaks, CA: Sage.

Pedersen, P. (1987). Ten frequent assumptions of cultural bias in counseling. *Journal of Multicultural Counseling and Development, 15*(1), 16-24.

Pedersen, P. B. (1991). Multiculturalism as a generic approach to counseling. *Journal of Counseling and Development, 70,* 6-12.

Persico, C. F. (1991). Creating an institutional climate that honors diversity. In G. Stricker, E. Davis-Russell, E. Bourg, E. Duran, W. R. Hammond, J. McHolland, K. Polite, & B. E. Vaughn (Eds.), *Toward ethnic diversification in psychology education and training* (pp. 55-63). Washington, DC: American Psychological Association.

Phinney, J. S. (1990). Ethnic identity in adolescents and adults: Review of research. *Psychological Bulletin, 108,* 499-514.

Ponterotto, J. G. (1988). Racial consciousness development among White counselor trainees: A stage model. *Journal of Multicultural Counseling and Development, 16,* 146-156.

Ponterotto, J. G., Alexander, C. M., & Grieger, I. (1995). A multicultural competency checklist for counseling psychology programs. *Journal of Multicultural Counseling and Development, 23,* 11-20.

Ponterotto, J. G., & Casas, M. (1987). In search of multicultural competence within counselor education programs. *Journal of Counseling and Development, 65,* 430-434.

Ponterotto, J. G., & Casas, J. M. (1991). In search of multicultural competence within counselor education programs. *Journal of Counseling and Development, 70,* 430-434.

Ponterotto, J. G., Casas, J. M., Suzuki, L. A., & Alexander, C. M. (Eds.). (1995). *Handbook of multicultural counseling.* Thousand Oaks, CA: Sage.

Ponterotto, J. G., Lewis, D. E., & Bullington, R. (1990). *Affirmative action on campus.* San Francisco: Jossey-Bass.

Ponterotto, J. G., & Pedersen, P. B. (1993). *Preventing prejudice: A guide for counselors and educators.* Newbury Park, CA: Sage.

Pope-Davis, D. B., & Ottavi, T. M. (1994). Examining the association between self-reported multicultural counseling competencies and demographic variables among counselors. *Journal of Counseling and Development, 72,* 651-660.

Pope-Davis, D. B., Prieto, L., Reynolds, A. L., & Vázquez, L. A. (1994). *Multicultural counseling: Issues of diversity. A training video.* Iowa City: University of Iowa, Audiovisual Center.

Ridley, C. R. (1985). Imperatives for ethnic and cultural relevances in psychology training programs. *Professional Psychology: Research and Practice, 16,* 611-622.

Ridley, C. R., Mendoza, D. W., & Kanitz, B. E. (1992). Program designs for multicultural training. *Journal of Psychology and Christianity, 11,* 326-336.

Ridley, C. R., Mendoza, D. W., & Kanitz, B. E. (1994). Multicultural training: Reexamination, operationalization, and integration. *The Counseling Psychologist, 22,* 227-289.

Roberts, H., Gonzales, J. C., Harris, O. D., Huff, D. J., Johns, A. M., Lou, R., & Scott, O. L. (1994). *Teaching from a multicultural perspective.* Thousand Oaks, CA: Sage.

Rowe, W., Behrens, J. T., & Leach, M. M. (1995). Racial/ethnic identity and racial conscious-
ness: Looking back and looking forward. In J. G. Ponterotto, J. M. Casas, L. A. Suzuki,
& C. M. Alexander (Eds.), *Handbook of multicultural counseling* (pp. 218-235).
Thousand Oaks, CA: Sage.

Santiago-Negron, S. (1991). Institutional change and leadership: Challenges in education. In
G. Stricker, E. Davis-Russell, E. Bourg, E. Duran, W. R. Hammond, J. McHolland,
K. Polite, & B. E. Vaughn (Eds.), *Toward ethnic diversification in psychology education
and training* (pp. 65-75). Washington, DC: American Psychological Association.

Smith, E. J. (1982). Counseling psychology in the marketplace: The status of ethnic
minorities. *The Counseling Psychologist, 10*(1), 61-68.

Sodowsky, G. R., Kwan, K. L., & Pannu, R. (1995). Ethnic identity in Asians in the United
States: Conceptualization and illustrations. In J. G. Ponterotto, J. M. Casas, L. A. Suzuki,
& C. M. Alexander (Eds.), *Handbook of multicultural counseling* (pp. 123-154).
Thousand Oaks, CA: Sage.

Stricker, G. (1990). Keynote address: Minority issues in professional training. In G. Stricker,
E. Davis-Russell, E. Bourg, E. Duran, W. R. Hammond, J. McHolland, K. Polite, &
B. E. Vaughn (Eds.), *Toward ethnic diversification in psychology education and training*
(pp. 3-8). Washington, DC: American Psychological Association.

Sue, D. W. (1991). A model for cultural diversity training. *Journal of Counseling and
Development, 70,* 99-105.

Sue, D. W., & Sue, D. (1990). *Counseling the culturally different: Theory and practice* (2nd
ed.). New York: John Wiley.

Sue, S. (1977). Community mental health services to minority groups: Some optimism, some
pessimism. *American Psychologist, 32,* 616-624.

Sue, S., & Zane, N. (1987). The role of culture and cultural techniques in psychotherapy: A
critique and reformulation. *American Psychologist, 37,* 1239-1244.

Terrell, F., & Terrell, S. (1984). Race of counselor, client, sex, cultural mistrust level, and
premature termination from counseling among Black clients. *Journal of Counseling
Psychology, 31,* 371-375.

Troy, W. G. (1990). Ethnic and cultural diversity and the professional psychology training
curriculum. In G. Stricker, E. Davis-Russell, E. Bourg, E. Duran, W. R. Hammond,
J. McHolland, K. Polite, & B. E. Vaughn (Eds.), *Toward ethnic diversification in psychology education and training* (pp. 179-187). Washington, DC: American Psychological
Association.

U.S. Bureau of the Census. (1990). *Statistical abstract of the United States: 1990* (110th ed.).
Washington, DC: Government Printing Press.

Usher, C. H. (1989). Recognizing cultural bias in counseling theory and practice: The case
of Rogers. *Journal of Multicultural Counseling and Development, 17,* 62-71.

Vaill, P. B. (1989). *Managing as a performing art.* San Francisco: Jossey-Bass.

Vaughn, B. E. (1991). The problem of organizational culture in achieving ethnic diversity in
professional psychology training: Implications for recruitment. In G. Stricker, E. Davis-
Russell, E. Bourg, W. R. Hammond, J. McHolland, K. Polite, & B. E. Vaughn (Eds.),
Toward ethnic diversification in psychology education and training (pp. 113-120).
Washington, DC: American Psychological Association.

Wrenn, C. G. (1965). The culturally encapsulated counselor. *Harvard Educational Review,
32,* 444-449.

Wrenn, C. G. (1985). Afterword: The culturally encapsulated counselor revisited. In
P. Pedersen (Ed.), *Handbook of cross-cultural counseling and therapy* (pp. 323-329).
Westport, CT: Greenwood.

9

Using the Multicultural Change Intervention Matrix (MCIM) as a Multicultural Counseling Training Model

Amy L. Reynolds

Over the past three decades, psychology, and in particular counseling psychology, has explored, discussed, and, to varying degrees, incorporated multicultural perspectives in its scholarly and applied work. The focus of the multicultural approach within psychology and counseling has significantly varied over time (Jackson, 1995). During the 1960s and 1970s, the literature focused on the inadequacies of psychology and mental health professionals to address the needs of people of color, most frequently Blacks (Peterson, 1967; Vontress, 1969, 1971; Wrenn, 1962). The writings in the 1970s and 1980s centered on the issues and perspectives of specific cultural groups, thus attempting to rectify the prior inadequacies of the literature to incorporate the voices of people of color (see Atkinson, Morten, & Sue, 1979; Attneave, 1969; Pedersen, Lonner, & Draguns, 1976; Sue, Allen, & Conway, 1981; Sue & Sue, 1971). This content focus (e.g., attention to increasing the multicultural knowledge of psychologists and counselors) has included expanding our understanding of within-group differences such as racial identity and acculturation (Carter, 1995; Choney, Berryhill-Paapke, & Robbins, 1995; Cross, 1971, 1991; Helms, 1990; Padilla, 1980; Phinney, 1990).

More recently, in the 1990s, psychology has highlighted multicultural training as an important emphasis within the profession. Journal articles, books chapters, and conference presentations and papers are increasingly addressing how to train multiculturally competent counselors effectively (Carney & Kahn, 1984; LaFromboise & Foster, 1992; Lopez et al., 1989; Parker, Valley, & Geary, 1986; Ridley, 1985; Ridley, Mendoza, & Kanitz, 1994). Specific training models and assessment tools are being developed and offered for training programs to consider (Christensen, 1989; D'Andrea & Daniels, 1991; D'Andrea, Daniels, & Heck, 1991; LaFromboise, Coleman, & Hernandez, 1991; Ponterotto, Rieger, Barrett, & Sparks, 1994; Sodowsky, Taffe, Gutkin, & Wise, 1994).

Although the increasingly complex and diverse multicultural literature within psychology has significantly affected the direction and focus of many psychology training programs, there are many who argue that not enough is being done to ensure that these programs incorporate multicultural perspectives in substantial ways (D'Andrea & Daniels, 1995; Ponterotto & Casas, 1987; Ridley, 1985; Sue, Arredondo, & McDavis, 1992; Sue & Sue, 1990). Having an ethical imperative within the profession (Burn, 1992; Casas, Ponterotto, & Gutierrez, 1986; LaFromboise & Foster, 1989) and the multicultural literature available does not guarantee that training programs effectively and meaningfully incorporate multicultural content or— more important—ensure that their graduates are multiculturally competent. Some psychologists contend that an organizational perspective is needed that helps training programs make the changes necessary for a genuine and meaningful multiculturalism (D'Andrea & Daniels, 1995; Davis-Russell, 1992; Johnson, 1992; Ponterotto, Alexander, & Grieger, 1995; Reynolds, 1995; Sue, 1995).

In order to understand the types of changes needed within counseling and psychology training programs to create more multiculturally sensitive and skilled counselors and psychologists, it is important to explore briefly what the literature says has been done and needs to be done. Although several surveys of training programs and their graduates have reported increases in the amount of multicultural training being done (Bernal & Castro, 1994; Hills & Strozier, 1992; Ponterotto & Casas, 1987; Wyatt & Parham, 1985), there is no guarantee that such training has led to counselors who are more effective counseling clients who are culturally different from themselves. Although there has been an increase in proposed training models and strategies (see Brooks & Kahn, 1990; Lefley, 1986; Mio, 1989; Parker et al., 1986; Ridley, Mendoza, & Kanitz, 1994), the lack of evaluation and research of these training efforts means that most counseling programs are using untested multicultural training efforts (Reynolds, 1995; Ridley, Mendoza, Kanitz, Angermeier, & Zenk, 1994).

Many writers have explored the various types of multicultural counseling training designs and strategies. According to Reynolds (1995), there are three types of multicultural training: (a) multicultural awareness and sensitivity; (b) unlearning oppression; and (c) multicultural awareness, knowledge, and skills. The purpose of the multicultural awareness and sensitivity training is for individuals to increase their tolerance or acceptance of cultural differences. Training that focuses on unlearning oppression highlights the realities of racism, sexism, heterosexism, and other forms of oppression. The goal of the third type of multicultural training is to enhance multicultural awareness, knowledge, and skills and to help individuals work more effectively with people who are culturally different from them. Another way to conceptualize this type of multicultural training is as multicultural competency-based training, which is the focus of a large percentage of the multicultural counseling training efforts (Reynolds, 1995).

Counseling programs have used a variety of means to infuse multicultural content into counseling courses. Copeland (1982) described several multicultural program designs: (a) separate course, (b) area of concentration model, (c) interdisciplinary approach, and (d) integration model. Although the single course method is frequently cited as the most common approach, it is also criticized for its inability to ensure multicultural competence among counselors and psychologists in training (LaFromboise & Foster, 1992; Margolis & Rungta, 1986; Midgette & Meggert, 1991). In the single course method, a program has only one multicultural course within the entire curriculum; it may or may not be required and it does not significantly infuse multicultural issues in the coursework. D'Andrea and Daniels (1995) highlighted four major concerns with the current conceptualization and implementation of the single multicultural counseling course: (a) these courses are typically not integrated into the overall curriculum, (b) there is rarely a coherent and robust conceptual framework that connects these courses with specific multicultural competencies that students can learn, (c) programs tend not to designate additional resources and personnel to encourage further development of multicultural competencies among students once a multicultural course has been introduced, and (d) these courses tend to take an intellectual approach rather than analyze the fundamental issues of oppression. These courses are not enough. A systems-based approach is necessary in order to create mental health service delivery that effectively meets the needs of traditionally underserved and underrepresented clientele (D'Andrea & Daniels, 1995; Sue, 1995).

Importance of Institutional
and Organizational Change

Although the increased focus on multicultural training within the counseling and psychology professions is encouraging, such educational efforts are not enough (D'Andrea & Daniels, 1995). If the counseling profession truly wants to change and genuinely wants to incorporate multiculturalism, there must be more emphasis on institutional and organizational change. According to Carter (1995), often the paradigms used to understand the role of race in psychotherapy "inflict the burden of change on those who are racially or culturally different, rather than on the individuals or systems that provide mental health services" (p. 44). Some studies have shown that counseling programs do not necessarily lack the motivation or interest to incorporate multiculturalism; however, many need guidance and direction to support their efforts (Ponterotto et al., 1995). Whenever possible, use of diverse disciplines and perspectives and innovative models within the multicultural counseling training efforts is highly valuable and only strengthens the viability of the training effort (Copeland, 1982). D'Andrea and Daniels (1995) stated that strategies are needed within the profession that can help counseling professionals "move beyond their own ethnocentric ways of thinking and behaving" (p. 21).

Despite the many efforts of training programs to incorporate multicultural content into their curriculum, many psychologists continue to perceive the efforts of training programs as monocultural (D'Andrea & Daniels, 1995; Hills & Strozier, 1992; Sue, Arredondo, & McDavis, 1992; Wyatt & Parham, 1985). Sue (1995) asserted that training programs, as subsystems within the larger university system, must be part of a more system-based change effort that utilizes the principles of organization development and, more specifically, multicultural organization development. Other psychologists have articulated the need for an organizational or institutional perspective.

According to Johnson (1992), "the leaders of today's institutions of higher education are challenged to revise not only their curricula, but also their organizational processes" (p. 32). Davis-Russell (1992) recommended seven actions be undertaken in order to create an institution that recognizes and embraces cultural diversity: (a) establishing institutional commitment, (b) creating a culturally diverse faculty, (c) creating a culturally diverse administration, (d) creating a culturally diverse student body, (e) creating student-faculty support, (f) generating financial aid funds, and (g) broadening the core curriculum. Although Johnson (1992) emphasized an organizational perspective, he also stressed that "accommodating diversity becomes a personal development issue for every member of an educating organization" (p. 34).

Even within an organizational or institutional perspective, there are varied approaches. D'Andrea and Daniels (1995) offered a model for encouraging change in professional associations that is currently being used to infuse multiculturalism into the American Counseling Association. Four strategies are central to their model: (a) mobilization, (b) education, (c) organizational approaches, and (d) institutionalizing. Mobilization involves creating forums so that voices of the rank-and-file membership of professional associations can be heard. Education strategies offer cultural content knowledge as well information about how organizations change. Organizational approaches focus on gaining feedback and recommendations from the membership about needed changes and future directions within the organization. Finally, institutionalizing involves formalizing these recommendations by creating resolutions that must be voted on by the leadership bodies of professional association. D'Andrea and Daniels (1995) believe that by creating change within professional associations we can more effectively transform the profession.

Ponterotto et al. (1995) suggested the use of another organizational strategy—a multicultural competency checklist for counseling training programs. Their checklist has 22 items focused on six major areas, including minority representation, curriculum issues, counseling practice and supervision, research considerations, student and faculty competency evaluation, and physical environment. Training programs can use the checklist to assess their current multicultural efforts and to set future goals and plans. According to Ponterotto et al. (1995), "the process required to complete the whole checklist is in and of itself a valuable exercise for the program" (p. 17).

Utilizing Multicultural Organization Development in Training Programs

Counseling psychology's roots are based in values and beliefs that support and encourage embracing of individual and cultural differences. These values are the foundation for the incorporation of multiculturalism into our training programs. Utilizing the growing knowledge base of multicultural organization development (MCOD) (see Jackson & Hardiman, 1981; Jackson & Holvino, 1988; Katz, 1989) provides additional values and beliefs as well as some tools that can be used to put those beliefs into action. MCOD experts emphasize some specific values that counseling psychology would do well to incorporate into its training programs. Some of these values include (a) believing in multicultural organizations as a possibility and necessity, (b) understanding the cyclical nature of change, (c) being prepared for people and systems to be upset by any change efforts and embracing their reactions and even their defenses as a natural and healthy part of the process, and (d) being sure that change efforts, in order to be successful, go beyond superficial measures and are systematically designed as organizational and cultural change efforts (Jackson & Hardiman, 1981; Katz, 1989).

According to Pope (1995), "paradigmatic shifts are essential . . . to create genuine and lasting multicultural campus environments. Changing our worldview is a necessary and first step to create new practices and strategies which will restructure and transform our campuses" (p. 233). It is vital that we believe that our training programs can truly incorporate multicultural awareness, knowledge, and skills at their core; that they can become multicultural. This belief is the first step in the process of creating change. However, we must realize that, as Katz (1989) stated, organizations do not become multicultural overnight. Creating multicultural environments is a process that requires expertise, focused reflection, commitment, specific competencies, and purposeful action (Pope & Reynolds, 1995). Katz (1989) highlighted the importance of organizations studying their belief systems and using them to support their change efforts.

It is not enough to value diversity and change: We must gather the knowledge and tools that will allow us to transform our beliefs into action. Because the field of MCOD is still in the process of knowledge production (Pope, 1993a), it is difficult to provide much more than a sketch of the various routes to achieving the goal of a multicultural organization. The first step in achieving that goal is to have a clear picture of what you are striving for: An image of a multicultural environment is needed. In 1981, Jackson and Hardiman offered the following description of a multicultural organization:

> A multicultural organization reflects the contribution and interests of diverse cultural and social groups in its mission, operations, and . . . service delivery; acts on a commitment to eradicate social oppression in all forms within the organization; includes the members of diverse cultural and social groups as full participants, especially in decisions that shape the organization; and follows through on broader external social responsibilities, including support

of efforts to eliminate all forms of social oppression and to educate others in multicultural perspectives. (p. 1)

Translating this vision into the various aspects and culture of a psychology training program means that the faculty must provide their time, energy, and other resources (e.g., monetary, human, etc.). Ultimately this requires "creating an openness to all diverse cultures and people, to distributing power and decision-making, and to eradicating social injustice" (Pope, 1995, p. 236). This change will not occur without a commitment to alter how the program or department functions. This commitment would be visible in the following ways: redefinition of what it means to be an effective and ethical psychologist; extensive recruitment and retention efforts; multicultural curriculum; and faculty development programs and activities that increase multicultural awareness, knowledge, and skills.

Transforming an academic department into an environment that truly integrates the values and beliefs of multiculturalism is a challenging task. Some multicultural experts believe that unless there are interventions that focus on the organization as a system, long-term change cannot happen (Cummings & Huse, 1989; Jackson & Holvino, 1988; Sargent, 1983). Although increasing numbers of psychology training programs have attempted to integrate multicultural issues, there appears to be a lack of systemic multicultural change efforts. In addition, many of the training programs seem to focus on content information about the various underrepresented groups and have not fully included the oppression or social justice agenda in their teaching efforts. For counseling programs to integrate multicultural issues effectively, they must utilize systemic and systematic approaches that examine the underlying organizational structure of the program and social justice issues (Katz, 1989; Pope, 1995; Sue, 1995). According to Pope (1995) and others (Driscoll, 1990; Jackson & Holvino, 1988; Sue, 1995), multicultural organization development (MCOD) provides a framework for long-term multicultural systems change and addresses social justice issues.

Multicultural Change
Intervention Matrix (MCIM)

The Multicultural Change Intervention Matrix (MCIM), developed by Pope (1993b), is an example of an alternative conceptual model that was developed from an organization development perspective and initially utilized to explore multicultural issues in higher education, yet is quite applicable as an approach to multicultural counseling training. The MCIM is based on systemic planned change and multicultural organization development (MCOD) literature that provides a framework for understanding the change efforts, interventions, and/or activities that may be used to address multicultural issues (Pope, 1993b).

The MCIM consists of two major dimensions. One dimension identifies three possible targets of intervention: (a) individual, (b) group, and (c) institution. In an academic context, change can be targeted for individuals or groups of students or faculty in a program as well as for a department or institution. The second dimension of the matrix identifies two levels of intervention: (a) first-order change and (b) second-order change. The basis of first- and second-order change comes from the family systems literature in the work of Watzlawick, Weakland, and Fisch (as cited in Lyddon, 1990). Lyddon applied Watzlawick et al.'s work to a broader counseling context and Pope (1993b) expanded it to fit her multicultural change model. According to Lyddon, first-order change is "change without change," or change in a system that does not generate systemic or structural change. Lyddon describes second-order change as "change of change" that incorporates any change that significantly transforms the structure of a system.

It is possible, according to Lyddon (1990), to alter the structure of an individual, group, or institution—such as adding new members to a group—without changing the core structure, thus maintaining the original system or status quo. This is considered first-order change. When change occurs that creates a transformation in the actual definition or makeup of the structure of the individual, group, or institution, it is considered second-order change.

As shown in Figure 9.1, the MCIM offers six different ways to perceive and structure multicultural change efforts. According to Pope (1995), "by increasing one's understanding of the range of targets and goals that may be used in multicultural training, one can more easily expand the types of activities, strategies, and tools considered" (p. 243). By exploring these six cells of the MCIM, it is possible to increase, expand, and/or alter one's multicultural training options. Although much of the description of these possible change efforts is taken from the work of Pope (1995), additional information about applications in a counseling or academic context has been included.

Cell A change efforts (first-order change—individual) typically focus on education at the awareness, knowledge, or skill level. This type of educational effort is often content oriented and may include information on various racial or other cultural groups. Within a counseling training program, some examples might include: sharing information on cross-cultural communica-

TARGET OF CHANGE	TYPE OF CHANGE	
	1ST ORDER CHANGE	2ND ORDER CHANGE
INDIVIDUAL	A Awareness	B Paradigm Shift
GROUP	C Membership	D Restructuring
INSTITUTION	E Programmatic	F Systemic

Figure 9.1. The Multicultural Change Intervention Matrix

SOURCE: From *An Analysis of Multiracial Change Efforts in Student Affairs,* by R. L. Pope, 1993a. (Doctoral dissertation, University of Massachusetts at Amherst, 1992). *Dissertation Abstracts International, 53-10,* 3457A. Used with permission.

tion or data on the presenting concerns or treatment outcomes of various racial groups, describing the economic and social conditions for a particular cultural group, or providing a brief antiracism presentation. These interventions would most likely occur within a classroom context, although it is possible that they may occur within the context of a relationship such as between a professor and a student or a supervisor and a student. In that situation, it might involve the professor or supervisor discussing these issues with a student, providing information, offering her or his perspective, and/or challenging the student's point of view.

A Cell B change effort (second-order change—individual) is typically aimed at the cognitive restructuring level suggesting worldview or paradigm shifts. Kuhn describes the concept of paradigm shift (as cited by Kuh, 1983) as a "radical change in the way in which the world is viewed" (p. 1). Pope (1993b) believes that these worldview or paradigm shifts demand more intensive, interactive, or experiential interventions that move beyond content about various cultural groups. In other words, these shifts mean moving beyond awareness. Often these efforts focus more on process, with the goal of challenging an individual's underlying cultural assumptions or beliefs. Some examples within an academic context might include a prolonged and extensive consciousness-raising retreat focused on individual growth and change and experientially oriented (i.e., individuals would examine their belief/thought systems in a self-challenging manner). Within an individual relationship between student and faculty member, it might involve a more active and challenging stance on the part of the professor or supervisor, in which the student is compelled to reexamine her or his worldview, assumptions, or values.

A Cell C change effort (first-order change—group) involves changing group membership by increasing the number of individuals from underrepresented groups without altering the purpose, goals, or norms of the group. Interventions in this cell focus more on numbers than on exploring the underlying group values and the structural dynamics of the group (e.g., norms, organizational structure, criteria for membership). Most recruitment efforts would be considered Cell C interventions, because they traditionally focus on increasing the number of individuals from an underrepresented group without assessing the environment's policies and practices and without modifying expectations and services for members of those groups. Within a counseling psychology program, a Cell C effort might involve attempts to increase the number of students of color without changing the communication norms or the curriculum of the program. In other words, if a program focuses more on recruitment than retention, its efforts are more likely to be first-order.

Cell D change efforts (second-order change—group) focus on the underlying values and practices of a group rather than on increasing the amount of diversity within an environment. This type of change involves examining the group makeup, norms, values, and goals prior to changing the group. In the case of a counseling psychology program, the group could be faculty, students, or both. By focusing on the structural level, a program could consider complete reformation and restructuring with new goals and members. In order for this effort to be successful, members of underrepresented groups (returning and new) must be involved in this process of self-reflection and planned change. For example, a program could host a retreat for all counseling students and faculty to reexamine and reformulate the philosophy, values, and goals of the counseling program, including multicultural training efforts. A consultant could be brought in to work with the faculty to examine their own beliefs plus the culture and values of the program. This approach would require that a program and its individual faculty reexamine its entire philosophy, purpose, and practices. Davis-Russell, Forbes, Bascuas, and Duran (1991) emphasized the importance of creating a multicultural learning community that involved students, faculty, and administrators within psychology preparation programs.

A Cell E change effort (first-order change—institution) typically entails a programmatic intervention at the institutional or departmental level that considers multicultural issues without changing the underlying values and structure of the institution. Hiring a faculty member whose explicit or implicit responsibility is to address the concerns of students of color or to incorporate multicultural issues into the curriculum would be considered a first-order change, because it is probably not likely to transform the underlying institutional dynamics, values, or priorities. Adding a multicultural course to the curriculum of a counseling program without changing how students are evaluated throughout the program or what is considered a competent and effective psychologist in training will probably not create institutional change.

More intrusive interventions that involve evaluation of all institutional or organizational values, goals, and methods are typically used in Cell F change efforts (second-order change—institution). Upon examination, these underlying structures can be infused with multicultural values and efforts. Some examples within a counseling psychology program would include requiring all faculty to infuse multicultural content into all aspects of the curriculum and evaluating students on their ability to work effectively across cultures, as well as linking faculty merit and promotion decisions to faculty members' ability to incorporate multiculturalism into their teaching.

Although these six cells of the MCIM involve separate and unique types of interventions, "their relationship with each other is fluid and dynamic" (Pope, 1995, p. 244). Without some work at the awareness level, a paradigm shift within an individual is probably not possible. If there is no recruitment, retention efforts are not needed. Finally, "programmatic efforts may be a necessary precursor to the development of systemic change" (Pope, 1995, p. 244). Pope (1995) conceptualized dotted lines between the various cells as an illustration of the interconnection among and between types of interventions and targets of change. By focusing on the interconnection and encouraging use of all six levels and targets of multicultural interventions, it is more likely that the counseling and psychology profession can become more multicultural in all ways. According to Pope (1995),

> while the dualistic nature of our society might encourage readers to assume that second-order change is "better" than first-order change since it creates long-term and structural transformation, it is vital that all six types of change efforts be seen as a valuable and necessary part of the multicultural training process. (p. 244)

The MCIM emphasizes exploring change at the individual, group, and institutional levels, which some multicultural experts argue is necessary in order truly to infuse multiculturalism in a counseling program (LaFromboise & Foster, 1992). The MCIM can be used to design the goals and activities of an individual course or to restructure an entire counseling curriculum. The first step in using this matrix would be as a tool to conceptualize and assess the type and level of multicultural training efforts currently being used in a counseling program. Once the initial assessment is completed, faculty can identify what types of training are typically missing and what can be done to expand and enhance their multicultural initiatives.

According to Pope (1993a), utilizing a method of systemic planned change efforts, like MCOD, to create multicultural change may not only assist with the necessary goal setting but also will identify methods of implementation. Much of the multicultural training offered in counseling programs typically focuses solely on changing individual students without examining whether the faculty or the program itself also might need to change. Without information that examines the targets and levels of multicultural training, it is increasingly difficult to make informed and effective decisions about what interventions will help create multiculturally competent counselors.

Multicultural Change
Intervention Matrix (MCIM): An Illustration

In order to understand how the MCIM can be used within counseling and psychology training programs, it is important to use concrete and current examples to illustrate its potential effectiveness. Consider the typical training program and how it incorporates multicultural issues at the individual, group, and institutional levels. As has been established, most training programs utilize the single course approach to multicultural education, which is most likely a Cell A change effort (first-order change—individual), although that depends on how the course is structured and implemented. If multiculturalism is not infused into all courses, it is less likely that students will have to struggle on a personal or worldview level with what it means to work with clients and individuals who are culturally different from them. Without that struggle, they may be less likely to understand their biases and weaknesses in working with individuals who are culturally different from them. On the group level, although many training programs attempt to attract and recruit a diverse student body, it is probably much less common for those programs to invest time and energy into examining the group norms and organizational structures within the program. Unless programs institute a thorough assessment of the environment's effect on individuals from underrepresented groups, it will be difficult to create second-order change on the group level. Finally, from an institutional or organizational perspective, most training programs do not move beyond first-order change. For example, when faculty of color are hired, it may be seen as their implicit or explicit responsibility to address multicultural issues. Unless all faculty members are invested in multicultural issues, students are less likely to consider multicultural competencies as core competencies. The underlying policies and procedures of the training program must be examined and possibly changed if true multicultural change is desired.

Although the typical training program has its limits in terms of current multicultural change efforts, it is possible to imagine what the ideal training program would look like and to describe it using the MCIM. First and foremost, an exemplary training program is not one that is perfect and has accomplished all the requisite multicultural tasks; rather, it is one that is firmly committed to the process of becoming a multicultural organization and training multiculturally competent psychologists and counselors. On the individual level, the ideal program would have a single course focused on multicultural issues, plus have multiculturalism infused and integrated into all of the required *and* elective courses. Such integration would require that faculty work closely together, examining their assumptions and their course designs. The practicum or practice-oriented courses would need to emphasize the application of the multicultural awareness, knowledge, and skills with a diverse clientele. It would be advantageous for each new cohort of students to experience a retreat or some other intensive group-oriented process that would encourage them to examine themselves on a very personal level. This personal reflection is important to their self-assessment of their awareness, knowledge, and skills for working with clients who are culturally different from them. In order to achieve this goal, it is vital that the faculty also have experienced this type of process and be able to address these issues and their own shortcomings openly and honestly. In an ideal program, students and faculty would be evaluated on their ability to incorporate and apply multicultural learnings. Thorough assessments of the climate and of students' perceptions of the faculty and multicultural content would be ongoing. An advisory board of students, faculty, alumni, and community members could be created to oversee and provide input to the program regarding their multicultural efforts. Ideally, the students and faculty would be diverse in cultural identity, values, and perspectives. While for many programs the ideal might seem like an unreasonable goal or expectation, it is important that training programs set goals and develop plans that cause them to reach beyond their expectations. There are so few models of exemplary training programs that we need to use our imagination and not be limited by attitudes or resources. The goal of making the counseling and psychology profession accessible to all is far too important to be set aside.

Summary and
Need for Research

Despite the increased attention to multicultural issues in the counseling profession, the "profession's viability and relevance in the future will largely depend on the manner in which it reflects a genuine commitment to multicultural counseling in its training programs, service delivery strategies, and research efforts today" (D'Andrea & Daniels, 1995, pp. 21-22). According to Sue (1995), "our ability to influence organizational dynamics represents the next multicultural counseling frontier" (p. 474). This chapter offered a promising framework, the Multicultural Change Intervention Matrix (MCIM), that can assist counseling and psychology training programs in their efforts to incorporate multicultural awareness, knowledge, and skills in meaningful, systemic, and systematic ways.

The MCIM is a new model, and significant research must be undertaken before it is clear that it is a valid and useful conceptualization of multicultural change efforts. The underlying philosophy, the definition of the various cells, and its ability to be used as a codifying tool for understanding how institutions create multicultural change must be further studied.

The MCIM has possibilities as a training model that can be incorporated as a way of infusing multiculturalism in counseling and psychology training programs. Pope (1995) stated that the MCIM can be used for assessment, strategic planning, and curricular transformation. The theoretical perspectives of MCOD and the application possibilities of the MCIM offer the counseling and psychology profession the opportunity for a new paradigm. According to Pope (1995), "thirty years is a long time to allocate time and resources for methods which have proven inconsistent and ineffective" (p. 247). The profession needs to move beyond the values of multiculturalism and to create and evaluate effective strategies, tools, and methods for ensuring that multicultural competencies are being taught to the next generation of mental health providers.

References

Atkinson, D. R., Morten, G., & Sue, D. W. (Eds.). (1979). *Counseling American minorities: A cross-cultural perspective* (3rd ed.). Madison, WI: Brown & Benchmark.

Attneave, C. (1969). Therapy in trial settings and urban network intervention. *Family Process, 8,* 192-210.

Bernal, M. E., & Castro, F. G. (1994). Are clinical psychologists prepared for service and research with ethnic minorities? Report of a decade of progress. *American Psychologist, 49,* 797-805.

Brooks, G. S., & Kahn, S. E. (1990). Evaluation of a course in gender and cultural issues. *Counselor Education and Supervision, 30,* 66-76.

Burn, D. (1992). Ethical implications in cross-cultural counseling and training. *Journal of Counseling and Development, 70,* 578-583.

Carney, C. G., & Kahn, K. B. (1984). Building competencies for effective cross-cultural counseling: A developmental view. *The Counseling Psychologist, 12,* 111-119.

Carter, R. T. (1995). *The influence of race and racial identity in psychotherapy: Toward a racially inclusive model.* New York: Wiley Interscience.

Casas, J. M., Ponterotto, J. G., & Gutierrez, J. M. (1986). An ethical indictment of counseling research and training: The cross-cultural perspective. *Journal of Counseling and Development, 64,* 347-349.

Choney, S. K., Berryhill-Paapke, E., & Robbins, R. R. (1995). The acculturation of American Indians. In J. G. Ponterotto, J. M. Casas, L. A. Suzuki, & C. M. Alexander (Eds.), *Handbook of multicultural counseling* (pp. 73-92). Thousand Oaks, CA: Sage.

Christensen, C. P. (1989). Cross-cultural awareness: A conceptual model. *Counselor Education and Supervision, 28,* 270-289.

Copeland, E. J. (1982). Minority populations and traditional counseling programs: Some alternatives. *Counselor Education and Supervision, 21,* 187-193.

Cross, W. E. (1971). The Negro-to-Black conversion experience: Toward a psychology of Black liberation. *Black World, 20,* 13-27.

Cross, W. E. (1991). *Shades of Black: Diversity in African American identity.* Philadelphia: Temple University Press.

Cummings, T. G., & Huse, E. F. (1989). *Organization development and change* (4th ed.). St. Paul, MN: West.

D'Andrea, M., & Daniels, J. (1991). Exploring the different levels of multicultural counseling training in counselor education. *Journal of Counseling and Development, 70,* 78-85.

D'Andrea, M., & Daniels, J. (1995). Promoting multiculturalism and organizational change in the counseling profession: A case study. In J. G. Ponterotto, J. M. Casas, L. A. Suzuki, & C. M. Alexander (Eds.), *Handbook of multicultural counseling* (pp. 17-33). Thousand Oaks, CA: Sage.

D'Andrea, M., Daniels, J., & Heck, R. (1991). Evaluating the impact of multicultural counseling training. *Journal of Counseling and Development, 70,* 143-150.

Davis-Russell, E. (1992). Preparing institutions for cultural diversity. In S. D. Johnson & R. T. Carter (Eds.), *Addressing cultural issues in an organizational context* (pp. 8-12). Teachers College Winter Roundtable Edited Conference Proceedings, New York, NY.

Davis-Russell, E. D., Forbes, W. T., Bascuas, J., & Duran, E. (1991). Ethnic diversity and the core curriculum. In R. Peterson, J. McHolland, R. Bent, E. Davis-Russell, G. Edwall, K. Polite, D. Singer, & G. Stricker (Eds.), *The core curriculum in professional psychology* (pp. 147-151). Washington, DC: American Psychological Association.

Driscoll, A. (1990). [Untitled comprehensive examination paper]. Unpublished manuscript. University of Massachusetts at Amherst.

Helms, J. E. (Ed.) (1990). *Black and White racial identity: Theory, research, and practice.* Westport, CT: Greenwood.

Hills, H. I., & Strozier, A. L. (1992). Multicultural training in APA-approved counseling psychology programs: A survey. *Professional Psychology: Research and Practice, 23,* 43-51.

Jackson, B. W., & Hardiman, R. (1981). *Description of a multicultural organization: "A vision."* Unpublished manuscript, University of Massachusetts at Amherst.

Jackson, B. W., & Holvino, E. (1988). Developing multicultural organizations. *Journal of Applied Behavioral Science and Religion, 9,* 14-19.

Jackson, M. L. (1995). Multicultural counseling: Historical perspectives. In J. G. Ponterotto, J. M. Casas, L. A. Suzuki, & C. M. Alexander (Eds.), *Handbook of multicultural counseling* (pp. 3-16). Thousand Oaks, CA: Sage.

Johnson, S. D. (1992). The cultural dilemma of educating organizations. In S. D. Johnson & R. T. Carter (Eds.), *Addressing cultural issues in an organizational context* (pp. 32-34). Teachers College Winter Roundtable Edited Conference Proceedings, New York, NY.

Katz, J. (1989). The challenge of diversity. In C. Wollbright (Ed.), *Valuing diversity* (pp. 1-22). Bloomington, IN: Association of College Unions-International.

Kuh, G. D. (Ed.). (1983). *Understanding student affairs organizations* (New Directions for Student Services, Vol. 23). San Francisco: Jossey-Bass.

LaFromboise, T. D., Coleman, H.L.K., & Hernandez, A. (1991). Development and factor structure of the Cross-Cultural Counseling Inventory-Revised. *Professional Psychology: Research and Practice, 22,* 380-388.

LaFromboise, T. D., & Foster, S. L. (1989). Ethics in multicultural counseling. In P. B. Pedersen, W. J. Lonner, & J. E. Trimble (Eds.), *Counseling across cultures* (3rd ed.; pp. 115-136). Honolulu: University of Hawaii Press.

LaFromboise, T. D., & Foster, S. L. (1992). Cross-cultural training: Scientist-practitioner models and methods. *The Counseling Psychologist, 20,* 472-489.

Lefley, H. P. (1986). Evaluating the effects of cross-cultural training: Some research results. In H. P. Lefley & P. Pedersen (Eds.), *Cross-cultural counseling for mental health professionals* (pp. 49-71). Springfield, IL: Charles C Thomas.

Lopez, S. R., Grover, K. P., Holland, D., Johnson, M. J., Kain, C. D., Kanel, K., Mellins, C. A., & Rhyne, M. C. (1989). Development of culturally sensitive psychotherapists. *Professional Psychology: Research and Practice, 20,* 369-376.

Lyddon, W. J. (1990). First- and second-order change: Implications for rationalist and constructivist cognitive therapies. *Journal of Counseling and Development, 69,* 122-127.

Margolis, R. L., & Rungta, S. A. (1986). Training counselors for work with special populations: A second look. *Journal of Counseling and Development, 64,* 642-644.

Midgette, T. E., & Meggert, S. S. (1991). Multicultural counseling instruction: A challenge for faculties in the 21st century. *Journal of Counseling and Development, 70,* 136-141.

Mio, J. S. (1989). Experiential involvement as an adjunct to teaching cultural sensitivity. *Journal of Multicultural Counseling and Development, 17,* 38-46.

Padilla, A. M. (Ed.). (1980). *Acculturation: Theory, models, and some new findings.* Boulder, CO: Westview.

Parker, W. M., Valley, M. M., & Geary, C. A. (1986). Acquiring cultural knowledge for counselors in training: A multifaceted approach. *Counselor Education and Supervision, 26,* 61-71.

Pedersen, P., Lonner, W. J., & Draguns, J. G. (1976). *Counseling across cultures.* Honolulu: University of Hawaii Press.

Peterson, R. A. (1967). Rehabilitation of the culturally different: A model of the individual in cultural change. *Personnel and Guidance Journal, 45,* 1001-1007.

Phinney, J. S. (1990). Ethnic identity in adolescence and adulthood: A review of research. *Psychological Bulletin, 108,* 499-514.

Ponterotto, J. G., Alexander, C. M., & Grieger, I. (1995). A multicultural competency checklist for counseling training programs. *Journal of Multicultural Counseling and Development, 23,* 11-20.

Ponterotto, J. G., & Casas, J. M. (1987). In search of multicultural competence within counselor education programs. *Journal of Counseling and Development, 65,* 430-434.

Ponterotto, J. G., Rieger, B. P., Barrett, A., & Sparks, R. (1994). Assessing multicultural counseling competence: A review of instrumentation. *Journal of Counseling and Development, 72,* 316-322.

Pope, R. L. (1993a). An analysis of multiracial change efforts in student affairs (Doctoral dissertation, University of Massachusetts at Amherst, 1982). *Dissertation Abstracts International, 53-10,* 3457A.

Pope, R. L. (1993b). Multicultural organization development in student affairs: An introduction. *Journal of College Student Development, 34,* 201-205.

Pope, R. L. (1995). Multicultural organization development: Implications and applications for student affairs. In J. Fried & Associates, *Shifting paradigms in student affairs: Culture, context, teaching, and learning.* Lanham, MD: American College Personnel Association.

Pope, R. L., & Reynolds, A. L. (1995). *Multicultural competencies in student affairs: Integrating multicultural knowledge, awareness, and skills.* Manuscript submitted for publication.

Reynolds, A. L. (1995). Challenges and strategies for teaching multicultural counseling courses. In J. G. Ponterotto, J. M. Casas, L. A. Suzuki, & C. M. Alexander (Eds.), *Handbook of multicultural counseling* (pp. 312-330). Thousand Oaks, CA: Sage.

Ridley, C. R. (1985). Imperatives for ethnic and cultural relevance in psychology training programs. *Professional Psychology: Research and Practice, 16,* 611-622.

Ridley, C. R., Mendoza, D. W., & Kanitz, B. E. (1994). Multicultural training: Reexamination, operationalization, and integration. *The Counseling Psychologist, 22,* 227-289.

Ridley, C. R., Mendoza, D. W., Kanitz, B. E., Angermeier, L., & Zenk, R. (1994). Cultural sensitivity in multicultural counseling: A perceptual schema model. *Journal of Counseling Psychology, 41,* 125-136.

Sargent, A. G. (1983). Affirmative action: A guide to systems change for managers. In R. A. Ritvo & A. Sargent (Eds.), *NTL Manager's Handbook* (pp. 223-237). Arlington, VA: NTL Institute.

Sodowsky, G. R., Taffe, R. C., Gutkin, T. B., & Wise, S. L. (1994). Development of the Multicultural Counseling Inventory: A self-report measure of multicultural competencies. *Journal of Counseling Psychology, 41,* 137-148.

Sue, D. W. (1995). Multicultural organization development: Implications for the counseling profession. In J. G. Ponterotto, J. M. Casas, L. A. Suzuki, & C. M. Alexander (Eds.), *Handbook of multicultural counseling* (pp. 474-492). Thousand Oaks, CA: Sage.

Sue, D. W., & Sue, D. (1990). *Counseling the culturally different: Theory and practice* (2nd ed.). New York: John Wiley.

Sue, S., & Sue, D. W. (1971). Chinese-American personality and mental health. *Amerasia Journal, 2,* 39-49.

Sue, S., Allen, D. B., & Conway, L. (1981). The responsiveness and equality of mental health care to Chicanos and Native Americans. *American Journal of Community Psychology, 6,* 137-146.

Sue, D. W., Arredondo, P., & McDavis, R. J. (1992). Multicultural counseling competencies and standards: A call to the profession. *Journal of Counseling and Development, 70,* 477-486.

Vontress, C. E. (1969). Counseling the culturally different in our society. *Journal of Employment Counseling, 6,* 9-16.

Vontress, C. E. (1971). *Counseling Negroes: Series 6. Minority groups and guidance*. Boston: Houghton Mifflin.

Wrenn, C. G. (1962). The culturally encapsulated counselor. *Harvard Educational Review, 32*, 444-449.

Wyatt, G., & Parham, W. (1985). The inclusion of culturally sensitive course materials in graduate school and training programs. *Psychotherapy, 22*, 461-468.

10

A Multicultural Immersion Experience

FILLING A VOID IN MULTICULTURAL TRAINING

Donald B. Pope-Davis

Cynthia Breaux

William M. Liu

Much of the current training in multicultural counseling has focused on increasing personal awareness and enhancing cultural knowledge and information, with the hope that students will have the capacity to integrate what they have learned so that their cultural competence will be reflected in their clinical skills and ability. Of these essential elements, knowledge has received the greatest attention in the research literature. Recent findings suggest that knowledge acquisition is not sufficient for adequate training in multicultural counseling, and they criticize the lack of emphasis on experiential training (McRae & Johnson, 1991; Merta, Stringham, & Ponterotto, 1988; Ridley, Mendoza, & Kanitz, 1994; Wehrly, 1991). Experiential training is defined by Ridley et al. (1994) as "exercises that provide occasions for trainees to personally experience immersion in a culture different from their own" (p. 263). This form of experiential training may be fundamental to multicultural counseling, because such in vivo experiences may provide the basis for reducing prejudice and racism.

This chapter will briefly review the current state of multicultural training, describe current methods of training, and discuss components of immersion and theories of prejudice reduction to determine which experiential exercises might be most useful for training. Based upon this overview, this chapter will then outline an immersion project for use in multicultural training as a means of addressing the experiential element judged essential by Ridley et al. (1994) and others.

Current Status of Training

Most of the research literature on the current status of training focuses on counseling, clinical, and school psychology doctoral programs. Bernal and Castro (1994) compared the findings of their 1990 survey of 96 APA-accredited clinical programs with a similar survey conducted in 1980 by Bernal and Padilla (1982). They found a 20% increase in the number of programs offering minority-related courses, and 17% more programs requiring minority-related courses for the doctorate. Eighty-six percent of the programs reported minority content being included in existing courses. There was a 24% increase in placing clinical trainees in community mental health agencies that serve minority clients. Furthermore, 10% more programs reported that faculty were engaged in minority mental health research. These positive findings were overshadowed by extant deficiencies found by Bernal and Castro (1994). For example, 39% of the clinical programs continued to have no minority-related courses, 74% of programs did not require any minority course for completion of the doctorate, and 47% had no clinical faculty conducting minority mental health research.

A 1988 survey of APA-approved counseling psychology programs regarding multicultural counseling training was conducted by Hills and Strozier (1992). Forty-three of the 49 respondents indicated they had at least one multicultural course; 31 included multiculturally focused content in other courses. Fifty-nine percent of the programs required their students to take at least one course to receive their doctorate. In 45% of the programs, students could plan a multicultural subspecialty. More recently, Ponterotto conducted a 1995 survey of 63 APA accredited and 27 non-APA accredited doctoral programs in counseling psychology. He found that 89% of the programs had a required multicultural counseling course, in contrast to the 59% found by Hills and Strozier (1992), indicating an improvement in requirements in the 7 years between surveys.

Notable in the previous studies are the differing number of requirements in multicultural training between the counseling and clinical programs. These differences may account in part for the findings of Pope-Davis, Reynolds, Dings, and Nielson (1995) in a survey of 344 graduate students from 131 APA-approved clinical and counseling psychology programs. They found that counseling psychology students rated themselves as more multiculturally competent than did clinical psychology students in three of the four multicultural competency areas of knowledge, awareness, skills, and relationship. Regarding multicultural course requirements, counseling psychology students had completed an average of 1.6 multicultural counseling courses, whereas clinical psychology students had completed an average of 0.09, representing a difference of almost one standard deviation. Counseling psychology students also reported more multicultural supervision than did clinical psychology students.

Directors of 121 doctoral and nondoctoral school psychology programs responded to a survey assessing multicultural training by Rogers, Ponterotto, Conoley, and Wiese (1992). Results indicated that 40% of the programs did not offer specific courses in minority issues nor did they include multicultural content in core school psychology courses. Furthermore, one third of the programs provided limited access to minority children during field training. These results were found despite the fact that 90% of the respondents indicated that multicultural training was essential.

A 1990 survey of APA members regarding multicultural training by Allison, Crawford, Echemendia, LaVome, and Knepp (1994) yielded interesting results. The 259 participants had received PhDs, PsyDs, or EdDs from counseling or clinical psychology programs. Only one quarter of the participants had taken a course focusing on the provision of services to diverse populations in their training programs. About one-half indicated that their supervision for therapy cases "never" or "infrequently" addressed cultural issues. Almost 93% reported working with African American clients during their practicum or internship training. However, the modal response for exposure to other groups, "e.g., Native Americans, Black Hispanics, Hispanics, gays, lesbians, bisexuals, and individuals with a sensory impairment" (Allison et al., 1994, p. 795) was zero.

Training Methods

Most multicultural training programs emphasize the knowledge component of competency (Lewis & Hayes, 1991; McRae & Johnson, 1991) via lectures, reading materials, and videos. For example, Mio and Morris (1990) propose a course in which general cultural issues and four specific minority groups are examined in a lecture, reading, and video format followed by student presentations. Sue and Sue (1990), however, contend that awareness of minority issues should be stimulated at not solely a cognitive level. Rather, they suggest, courses should contain affective and consciousness-raising components. Furthermore, Lloyd (1987) suggests didactically disseminated information may be used by students in a generalized way to form stereo-typical judgments about clients rather than to allow for clients' individual differences.

Several proposed developmental models take the emotional element of acquiring cultural sensitivity into account by treating training as a developmental process. The idea behind these models is that trainees will require tasks appropriate to their movement through different developmental stages. According to Atkinson, Morten, and Sue (1993), Carney and Kahn in 1984 were the first to advance a developmental model of training in cross-cultural counseling. Their model consists of five stages of identity development with corresponding training exercises. For example, in Stage 2 of their model, when the trainee is still employing ethnocentric counseling approaches despite dawning awareness of cultural issues, the trainer provides information about alternative worldviews, ethnocentrism, and barriers to cross-cultural counseling.

Sabnani, Ponterotto, and Borodovsky (1991) integrate the White racial identity development models of Helms (1984), Hardiman (1982), and Ponterotto (1988) to form the basis of their cross-cultural training model. The posited stages through which the counselor moves are (1) lack of awareness of self as a racial being; (2) interaction with members of other cultures; (3) breakdown of former knowledge regarding racial matters; (4) pro-minority stance; (5) pro-White, antiminority stance; and (6) internalization. Similar to Carney's and Kahn's model, they propose training tasks appropriate for each stage of development. For example, in the stage in which the trainee takes a pro-minority/antiracism stance, two of the training tasks are role-playing exercises and minority student panels (Sabnani et al., 1991). The tasks are accompanied by goals and correspond to the beliefs/attitudes, knowledge, and skills delineated by Sue, Arredondo, and McDavis (1992). One of the novel ingredients of this developmental training model is the inclusion of in vivo exposure to non-White ethnic groups and races. For example, one of the tasks in Stage 2 is "tours to other communities" (Sabnani et al., 1991, p. 87). The model also includes simulated and actual counseling experiences between members of different cultures.

Many other models also use simulated or classroom experiences involving intercultural contact. One of these, the Partners Program (Mio, 1989), matches students in a multicultural counseling course with immigrant students for the semester's duration. Mio (1989) assessed whether students participating in this program were more culturally sensitive than those who did not participate by the use of independent judges who evaluated student papers and final exam grades. He reported support for the idea that pairing people of different cultures promoted cultural sensitivity.

The Minnesota Multiethnic Counselor Education Curriculum (MMCEC) (Johnson, 1982, cited in McRae & Johnson, 1991) included input from psychologists who were African Americans, Asian Americans, Hispanic Americans, and American Indians. The curriculum also included interviews with clients representing different racial and ethnic groups, and exercises to apply practically the knowledge learned. According to McRae and Johnson (1991), Johnson later developed a two-part graduate course, the first section concentrating on knowledge acquisition and the second on laboratory exercises designed to increase intercultural communications skills.

Two other models are designed around simulating intercultural counseling. The triad training model (Pedersen, 1977, 1994) is a videotaped role-play that divides counselor trainees into teams of three. One trainee acts as the counselor, one the "anticounselor" or "procounselor," and one the client. The "anticounselor" closely matches the client culturally and "is deliberately subversive in attempting to exaggerate mistakes by the counselor during the interview" (Pedersen, 1994, p. 44). In this way, according to Pedersen (1994), the anticounselor forces the counselor to be more aware of the client's perspective. The "procounselor" is similarly culturally matched with the client, but emphasizes the positive messages between client and counselor (Pedersen, 1994). The more recent version of the triad training model does not specifically have a multicultural focus and includes both anticounselor and procounselor roles. According to Atkinson et al. (1993), several researchers "have provided research evidence that counselors who participate in triad training increase their ability to interact empathically, genuinely, and with understanding of affective communication" (p. 325).

Culture-specific counseling (Nwachuku & Ivey, 1991) also uses simulated counseling as a multicultural training tool. This model was presented by the authors as a 3-hour workshop appropriate for incorporation into a multicultural counseling course (Nwachuku & Ivey, 1991). The first step in this approach is for an individual or group from a targeted culture to examine key values and aspects of the culture, focusing on emic helping styles and problem-solving strategies. The second step is to generate training materials based on this analysis. The core of the workshop includes (a) a lecture by an individual or group representing the targeted culture, (b) a presentation of an effective training tape (ETT) and an ineffective training tape (ITT), and (c) a role-playing practice session with videotaped vignettes (Nwachuku &

Ivey, 1991). The authors contend that this training model has the potential for widespread use, suggesting feminist counseling and gay counseling as examples of applications.

Simulating culture shock was the purpose of an exercise for cross-cultural training proposed by Merta et al. (1988). Their 3-hour, two-part activity includes both cognitive and behavioral components. The cognitive component consists of a group discussion followed by a lecture explaining culture shock and positive cultural adjustment. The behavioral component consists of scripted exchanges between an interviewee (the counseling trainee) and an interviewer (of a differing culture). This exchange is designed to subject the interviewee to cultural differences to which she or he will experience some degree of culture shock. The exchange is witnessed by students observing via a one-way mirror. A confederate of the interviewer, who is of the same culture, explains cultural incongruencies occurring in the interaction to the observing students. A discussion involving both participants and observers follows.

Theory

One drawback to all the training methods reviewed is they do not meet the "immersion" component proposed by Ridley et al. (1994). There may be essential reasons for direct, prolonged, in vivo contact with a culture different from that of the trainees. To understand why this may be true, it is helpful to consider cognitive concepts explored by researchers in areas other than counseling, such as social psychologists.

According to Stephan (1987), a substantial number of investigations propose that contact situations among members of different groups are expected to improve intergroup relations, a concept known as the contact hypothesis. This hypothesis has been applied in many areas, such as academic and international relations. The jigsaw technique (Aronson & Osherow, 1980) is a well-known school application of the contact hypothesis in which students work together in multiethnic groups, employing peer teaching. A similar technique is the teams-games-tournament (TGT) (DeVries, Edwards, & Slavin, 1978), which introduces elements of interdependence and competition to peer teaching.

Results of these studies and others like them indicate that cooperation in multiethnic groups improves intergroup relations (Stephan, 1987). Certain conditions have been specified under which contact should occur for relations to improve (e.g., equal status, accepting social atmosphere, etc.; Rothbart & Lewis, 1994; Stephan, 1987). One of the elements shared by most of the techniques based on the contact hypothesis is a longer duration than laboratory studies (Stephan, 1987). An important question is raised by the short duration of many of the techniques used in multicultural counseling training, such as the employment of culture shock in the Merta et al. (1988) study. Because of the brevity of the exercise, are participants left with a negative impression due to experiencing culture shock without a sufficient period of adaptation?

Bruschke, Gartner, and Seiter (1993) investigated this hypothesis in a study using BAFA BAFA, a popular classroom simulation game. In BAFA BAFA, students are divided into two imaginary cultures, "Alpha" and "Beta." Members of the Alpha culture are instructed in the language and customs of their culture only. The same is done with Beta members. Each "culture" then visits the other and experiences the difficulties of interacting with members of an unfamiliar culture (Bruschke et al., 1993). A thorough debriefing follows. When Bruschke et al. (1993) assessed the use of BAFA BAFA in courses at two large Western universities, they found the simulation increased students' ethnocentrism and dogmatism in contrast to courses not using BAFA BAFA. They attributed the outcome to a lack of time to adjust following the culture shock.

Although the classroom techniques applying the contact hypothesis are longer in duration than culture shock techniques and have been said to improve intergroup relations, they do not necessarily result in a reduction in prejudice. Rothbart and John (1985) argue that the effects of intergroup contact on stereotypic beliefs depend upon two stages: (a) contact occurring in a way that challenges existing group stereotypes and (b) disconfirming information that *must be generalized from specific group members to the group as a whole*. For group stereotypes to change, they argue, disconfirming information must be associated with the most prototypical group members. The contact hypothesis provides for the first stage, but not necessarily for the second. "Even if favorable interactions are generated in the first stage, there is still the difficult task of generalization to the group as a whole" (Rothbart & Lewis, 1994, p. 373).

To explain their position, Rothbart and John (1985) present a cognitive processing model. The model assumes that people cognitively categorize social groups based on visible attributes of a person, such as gender or race. Attributes of a social category consist of episodes stored in memory that a person most strongly associates with that category. For example, someone asked to describe a fraternity member will remember instances of specific fraternity males, whose attributes are then integrated into a single impression, a prototype. For a new episode to become associated with a category depends on the goodness-of-fit between that category and the episode (Rothbart & John, 1985). So if, for instance, a man who holds a stereotype of sorority women as empty-headed husband-seekers encounters a sorority woman who is a physics major, she may not activate his category for sorority women. Instead, she may be more prototypic of the category Science Major and the episode will be associated with that category. In the same way, when we are thinking of the category Birds, the prototype that comes to mind is typically not a penguin.

This idea of social categorization has been supported in the literature, notably in a study by Royle (1983) examining the effects of integrating women into the Marine Corps. Royle found that male members of the Marine Corps continued to harass women in general, but not those belonging to their own group. The author concluded that the female Marine Corps members were seen as individuals and that change in attitude toward women as a class had not occurred.

Rothbart and John (1985) assert that it is possible for stereotypic beliefs to change "when disconfirming information is embedded in an episode that otherwise represents a good fit to the stereotypic category" (p. 91). When applied to multicultural counseling training, where are these episodes most likely to occur—in the classroom, where students may not be able to generalize from their simulation partners (usually other college students) to the cultural group, or in an in vivo situation where the trainee is immersed in the targeted culture?

In addition, for negative traits to be cognitively disassociated from a social group, several instances of intergroup contact are necessary (Rothbart & John, 1985). Ironically, according to Rothbart and John, the more unfavorable the trait, the fewer the number of instances required for confirmation and the greater the number of instances necessary for disconfirmation. These assertions support the previous arguments for experiential exercises of longer duration.

The necessity of including experiential exercises involving intercultural contact in multicultural training has been supported in the literature (Merta et al., 1988; Ridley et al., 1994; Wehrly, 1991). It appears that the type of contact has important implications for the quality and success of training. Based on the cognitive processing model proposed by Rothbart and John (1985) and the contact hypothesis, (a) contact should result in the reduction of prejudice through generalizing attributes of specific individuals to the cultural group, and (b) the contact should be of sufficient duration to accommodate adjustment following culture shock. To accomplish this, it appears that the most valuable experiential exercise would be one of longer duration involving in vivo contact.

Multicultural
Immersion Experience (MIE)

Much of the multicultural training literature has focused on identifying multicultural competencies (Sue et al., 1992) that counselors should possess as a means of better responding to the needs of culturally different groups. In light of findings that show placement in minority related agencies is increasing (Allison et al., 1994; Bernal & Padilla, 1982), yet courses and experiences related to these populations is still relatively small (Bernal & Castro, 1994; Rogers et al., 1992), it seems important to develop a means to assist counselors in developing a more diverse and integrated worldview. Although "in-class" exercises are a step in the right direction, a critical component that is often absent from this training literature is how to encourage counseling students to begin actually to experience different cultures on a firsthand basis. Such an experience would enhance traditional educational methods, such as role-playing, and make the immediacy of the multicultural experience a reality. Individuals would have the opportunity not only to test and evaluate what they have read and learned about different cultural groups, but to experience how these cultural groups define and experience themselves on a daily basis.

In an attempt to encourage such an activity, the Multicultural Immersion Experience (MIE) was developed. This activity is intended to be used as part of a multicultural course and is most effective if completed over an academic semester. The components and assignments in the MIE are designed to combine cognitive and affective experiences (Sue & Sue, 1990) in order to make the MIE more integrated and applicable.

Phase I

Students are required to identify a group they perceive to be culturally different from themselves (e.g., Mexican American, African American, gay, lesbian, or bisexual groups or organizations) in the university or surrounding communities. The understanding is that the student will become involved or *immersed* in that group for the entire semester (or duration of the course), attending group or individual meetings, social gatherings, presentations, discussions, and so forth, that the group is involved in. Identification of the groups and organizations that students want to be immersed in can be refined through individual meetings with the instructor to ensure that the student is going to be challenged.

Students' involvement in groups and organizations may have multiple benefits. For example, according to Arredondo et al. (1996), counselors who are multiculturally aware and competent are involved with these diverse groups in order to balance the classroom and clinical setting. Counselors then may gain added information about groups that would help in evaluating the usefulness of certain clinical tools (e.g., MMPI), or acquire knowledge about the nuances of a particular community that would assist them later on.

Prior to immersing themselves, counselors should be assessed on their overall multicultural competency. Instruments such as the Multicultural Counseling Inventory (MCI; Sodowsky, Taffe, Gutkin, & Wise, 1994), the Multicultural Counseling Awareness Scale (MCAS-B; Ponterotto et al., 1993), or the Multicultural Awareness-Knowledge-Skills Survey (MAKSS; D'Andrea, Daniels, & Heck, 1991) can be used for this purpose. This assessment would provide a baseline report on the counselor's overall efficacy prior to the immersion experience. This assessment can be kept by the counselor-in-training or given to the instructor or supervisor. Later, the assessment can be given again to see if there are any changes in the counselor's multicultural competency. The assessment should also be a part of the students' final report on their experiences. Specifically, this can be a way for the students to reflect upon their experiences and any personal changes made.

As part of the immersion experience, students should write a short auto-biography that specifically includes issues of oppression, race, class, and gender. Students can then tie in their personal history with the group they expect to interact with. Arredondo et al. (1996) point out that skilled and aware counselors should be able to understand how their culture has inter-acted with other cultures. Specifically, the student can begin an initial exploration as to how the differences in culture might relate to the counseling experience. Students can offer any stereotypes that they might have (e.g., Rothbart & John, 1985), where they might have learned them, and how they impact the potential counseling relationship. Similarly, students can write honestly about the anxieties they are feeling at the time, and the possible source of these anxieties. The student should also be able to provide a brief history of the group (e.g., racial, gender, religious affiliation) in the area and on campus. This will provide the student with a historical background of the group, the changes in the surrounding area that have affected it, and any changes in its mission over time. It is to be expected that many students will find this portion of the immersion experience to be cumbersome, but it is believed that this pre-immersion preparation not only provides a deeper understanding of the organization and culture, but helps to challenge the assumption that students can use the organizations' members to teach them everything they need. In essence, this is a step to help students become active participants rather than passive learners. Students will be required to write out their assumptions about the group after the experience, as well.

During the initial phase, students should also be able to identify someone who will serve as a liaison or sponsor to their immersed group. This liaison or sponsor should be willing to discuss his or her own cultural views, orientation/perspectives, and worldview with the student. The liaison should also be willing to attend class at the end of the semester as part of an open discussion that will occur.

Phase II

During the immersion experience, the students are required to keep a journal. The journal can vary in length, and can be daily or weekly. This journal will be turned in at the end of the semester. The journal should reflect the cognitive and affective experiences of the student, and honestly address any feelings of anxiety or discomfort that may be associated with the immersion. For example, students may find that they do not see themselves as homophobic, yet they are reluctant or feel anxious about being seen in public with the groups' members. Journal entries can also allow students to write out questions that may arise and that can be addressed in class or used as a source of reflection.

Students should enter the group as willing participants who are interested in becoming part of the group. That means that students should not state at the first group meeting they are doing this exercise as part of a course assignment and will be there only in order to "observe." This rationalization not only places students outside the group, but also provides an effective excuse for not dealing with their own feelings and cognitions; in effect, it provides a shield and prevents any real "immersion" from occurring. Such statements may come from the student as an attempt to maintain some type of power and authority over the group, and the immersion experience becomes strictly ethnographic and anthropological. Students should not deceive group members about how they actually came to be in the group, but they also should not make it part of their identity in the group. A problem that may arise in the MIE is multiple students going to the same group. The instructor can either not allow it or see that students minimize their contact with each other.

As part of the course, the students should be willing to engage in the various activities of the group. This may be accomplished by allowing students to take a lab section or discussion section concomitantly with the multicultural course. In the classroom, students should be able to engage in discourse pertaining to their experience, and, specifically, how it is affecting them and how it could potentially affect the counseling relationship. This would also provide an opportunity to discuss questions that occurred during their experience.

Phase III

Throughout the semester, students should also be preparing for a presentation. Over the course of the last few weeks, the instructor should arrange for the sponsor or liaison and/or other members of each immersed group to participate in a roundtable discussion with the rest of the class. The discussion can take two different formats, depending on the size of the class and the similarity of the topic to be discussed. One format could consist of one group at a time engaged in a class discussion, while the other format could consist of more than one group with similar interests and/or orientations in a similar discussion. The student(s) who selected the group should facilitate this discussion. Debriefing after each discussion with the class is encouraged. As Merta et al. (1988) pointed out, after a cultural shock of some type, insufficient processing time can often lead to lingering negative effects that can potentially reduce the effectiveness of the MIE.

The final product for the course should include reflections from the competency assessment tools (e.g., MCI, MCAS-B, MAKSS) and any differences that may have occurred, comments on the journal entries (e.g., comments to students' earlier statements or contemplation on remarks made by the instructor), and an integration of their autobiography and historical analysis. Most important, students need to reflect on their experience and to discuss changes that occurred. Other projects for students may be to design a syllabus for a potential course on that particular group that should include topic areas and readings. In addition, students in the course can provide an executive summary (e.g., two pages, front and back) on their immersed group that includes help- and health-related resources that would be useful for other counselors.

Summary and Other Reflections

Sue et al. (1992) remind us of projections made by the 1990 U.S. Census, such as, by the year 2000 more than one third of the population will consist of racial and ethnic minorities, and by 2010 White Americans will be in the minority, making up approximately 48% of the population. It is, therefore, not unreasonable to assume that there will be greater numbers of racial and ethnic minorities to counsel, and there will likely be more counselors of color. Given this potential reality, the multicultural counseling literature must begin to include and discuss issues relating to the cultural competence of counselors of color.

Arredondo (1994) states, "One of the fundamental problems with the majority of literature is the exclusive emphasis on the ethnoracial minority cultures as the focus of multicultural counseling training" (p. 310). She calls for an expanded view of multicultural counseling, claiming that "us and them" thinking results from the predominant assumption that multicultural counseling involves White counselors with persons of color. Similarly, Atkinson (1994) asserts, "With very few exceptions, the general framework for developing a multicultural counseling training program . . . appears to be directed exclusively toward the training of European American counseling psychologists" (p. 303). Although he claims this is understandable, he also states, "ethnocentrism is not the exclusive domain of European Americans" (p. 303).

Arredondo (1994) and Atkinson (1994) make important points, but perhaps there is a more compelling argument for expanding the largely White-counselor focus of multicultural counseling training: The multicultural counseling training literature appears to mirror society's habit of considering racial, ethnic, and other groups of diversity to be invisible. In the spirit of inclusion, it would seem to be the responsibility of counseling training programs to meet the needs of trainees of diversity as conscientiously as those of White trainees. To assume that a trainee who is Black can competently counsel a person who is gay simply because both share a history of oppression does a disservice to both trainee and counselee. Thus, multicultural counseling training exercises and experiences *must* take into account a variety of counselor/client combinations.

References

Allison, D. W., Crawford, I., Echemendia, R., LaVome, R., & Knepp, D. (1994). Training in clinical and counseling psychology revisited. *American Psychologist, 49,* 792-796.

Aronson, E., & Osherow, N. (1980). Cooperation, prosocial behavior, and academic performance: Experiments in the desegregated classroom. In L. Bickman (Ed.), *Applied social psychology annual.* Beverly Hills, CA: Sage.

Arredondo, P. (1994). Multicultural training: A response. *The Counseling Psychologist, 22,* 308-314.

Arredondo, P., Toporek, R., Brown, S., Jones, J., Locke, D. C., Sanchez, J., & Stadler, H. (1996). *Operationalization of the multicultural competencies.* New York: Association for Multicultural Counseling and Development.

Atkinson, D. R. (1994). Multicultural training: A call for standards. *The Counseling Psychologist, 22,* 300-307.

Atkinson, D. R., Morten, G., & Sue, D. W. (1993). *Counseling American minorities: A cross-cultural perspective* (4th ed.). Madison, WI: Brown & Benchmark.

Bernal, M. E., & Castro, F. G. (1994). Are clinical psychologists prepared for service and research with ethnic minorities. *American Psychologist, 49,* 797-805.

Bernal, M. E., & Padilla, A. M. (1982). Status of minority curricula and training in clinical psychology. *American Psychologist, 37,* 780-787.

Bruschke, J. C., Gartner, C., & Seiter, J. S. (1993). Student ethnocentrism, dogmatism, and motivation: A study of BAFA BAFA. *Simulation and Gaming, 24,* 9-20.

Carney, C. G., & Kahn, K. B. (1984). Building competencies for effective cross-cultural counseling: A developmental view. *The Counseling Psychologist, 12,* 111-119.

D'Andrea, M., Daniels, J., & Heck, R. (1991). Evaluating the impact of multicultural counseling training. *Journal of Counseling and Development, 70,* 143-150.

DeVries, D. L., Edwards, K. J., & Slavin, R. E. (1978). Biracial learning teams and race relations in the classroom: Four field experiments using teams-games-tournaments. *Journal of Educational Psychology, 70,* 356-362.

Hardiman, R. (1982). *White racial identity development: A process oriented model for describing the racial consciousness of White Americans.* Unpublished doctoral dissertation, University of Massachusetts, Amherst.

Helms, J. E. (1984). Towards a theoretical explanation of the effects of race on counseling: A Black and White model. *The Counseling Psychologist, 12,* 153-165.

Hills, H. I., & Strozier, A. L. (1992). Multicultural training in APA-approved counseling psychology programs: A survey. *Professional Psychology: Research and Practice, 23,* 43-51.

Johnson, S. D. (1982). *The Minnesota Multiethnic Counselor Education Curriculum: The design and evaluation of an intervention for cross-cultural counselor education.* Unpublished doctoral dissertation, University of Minnesota, Minneapolis.

Lewis, A. C., & Hayes, S. (1991). Multiculturalism and the school counseling curriculum. *Journal of Counseling and Development, 70,* 119-125.

Lloyd, A. P. (1987). Multicultural counseling: Does it belong in a counselor education program? *Counselor Education and Supervision, 26,* 164-167.

McRae, M. B., & Johnson, S. D. (1991). Toward training for competence in multicultural counselor education. *Journal of Counseling and Development, 70,* 131-135.

Merta, R. J., Stringham, E. M., & Ponterotto, J. G. (1988). Simulating culture shock in counselor trainees: An experiential exercise for cross-cultural training. *Journal of Counseling and Development, 66,* 242-245.

Mio, J. S. (1989). Experiential involvement as an adjunct to teaching cultural sensitivity. *Journal of Multicultural Counseling and Development, 17,* 38-46.

Mio, J. S., & Morris, D. R. (1990). Cross-cultural issues in psychology training programs: An invitation for discussion. *Professional Psychology: Research and Practice, 21,* 434-441.

Nwachuku, U. T., & Ivey, A. E. (1991). Culture-specific counseling: An alternative training model. *Journal of Counseling and Development, 70,* 106-111.

Pedersen, P. B. (1977). The triad model of cross-cultural training. *Personnel and Guidance Journal, 56,* 94-100.

Pedersen, P. (1994). Simulating the client's internal dialogue as a counselor training technique. *Simulation and Gaming, 25,* 40-50.

Ponterotto, J. G. (1988). Racial consciousness development among White counselor trainees: A stage model. *Journal of Multicultural Counseling and Development, 16,* 146-156.

Ponterotto, J. G. (1995, August). Multicultural counseling training: A competency model and national survey. In D. B. Pope-Davis (Chair), *Becoming multiculturally competent— Strategies for changing curricula, training, and supervision.* Symposium conducted at the annual meeting of the American Psychological Association, New York City.

Ponterotto, J. G., Rieger, B. P., Barrett, A., Harris, G., Sparks, R., Sanchez, C. M., & Magido, D. (1993). Development and initial validation of the Multicultural Counseling Awareness Scale (MCAS). In *Measurement and testing: Multicultural assessment.* Ninth Buros-Nebraska Symposium, Lincoln, NE.

Pope-Davis, D. B., Reynolds, A. L., Dings, J. G., & Nielson, D. (1995). Examining multi-cultural counseling competencies of graduate students in psychology. *Professional Psychology: Research and Practice, 26,* 322-329.

Ridley, C. R., Mendoza, D. W., & Kanitz, B. E. (1994). Multicultural training: Reexamina-tion, operationalization, and integration. *The Counseling Psychologist, 22,* 227-289.

Rogers, M. R., Ponterotto, J. G., Conoley, J. C., & Wiese, M. J. (1992). Multicultural training in school psychology: A national survey. *School Psychology Review, 21,* 603-616.

Rothbart, M., & John, O. P. (1985). Social categorization and behavioral episodes: A cognitive analysis of the effects of intergroup contact. *Journal of Social Issues, 41,* 81-104.

Rothbart, M., & Lewis, S. (1994). Cognitive processes and intergroup relations: A historical perspective. In P. G. Devine, D. L. Hamilton, & T. M. Ostrom (Eds.), *Social cognition: Impact on social psychology.* San Diego, CA: Academic Press.

Royle, M. H. (1983). *Factors affecting the integration of women into the Marine Corps.* Unpublished doctoral dissertation, Claremont Graduate School, Claremont, CA.

Sabnani, H. B., Ponterotto, J. G., & Borodovsky, L. G. (1991). White racial identity development and cross-cultural counselor training: A stage model. *The Counseling Psychologist, 19,* 76-102.

Sodowsky, G. R., Taffe, R. C., Gutkin, T. B., & Wise, S. L. (1994). Development of the Multicultural Counseling Inventory: A self-report measure of multicultural competen-cies. *Journal of Counseling Psychology, 41,* 137-148.

Stephan, W. G. (1987). The contact hypothesis in intergroup relations. In C. Hendrick (Ed.), *Group processes and intergroup relations.* Newbury Park, CA: Sage.

Sue, D. W., Arredondo, P., & McDavis, R. J. (1992). Multicultural counseling competencies and standards: A call to the profession. *Journal of Counseling and Development, 70,* 477-486.

Sue, D. W., & Sue, D. (1990). *Counseling the culturally different: Theory and practice.* New York: John Wiley.

Wehrly, B. (1991). Preparing multicultural counselors. *Counseling and Human Development, 24,* 1-24.

11

Cultural Ambience

THE IMPORTANCE OF A CULTURALLY AWARE LEARNING ENVIRONMENT IN THE TRAINING AND EDUCATION OF COUNSELORS

Alberta M. Gloria

Donald B. Pope-Davis

It is estimated that by the year 2000, one of every three people in the United States will be a person of color (Highlen, 1994). Composed of numerous different racial, ethnic, and cultural groups and subgroups, the United States is dynamic in context and scope. As such, diversity issues of bilingual education and domestic partner benefits to increased racial and ethnic populations (Uba & Sue, 1991; U.S. Department of Commerce, 1991) are at the core of our financial and educational institutions, communities, and homes on a daily basis.

As a result of changes in societal demographics, many questions have been raised about multicultural issues in higher education: Is a diversity course or courses a reasonable requirement for a degree? Who should finance such a requirement? Who will recruit, retain, and pay the instructors who are qualified to teach these classes that infuse diversity? Will faculty lose their academic freedom? Will faculty need to be retrained to become competent in diversity and multicultural issues? How will the university tenure process reflect multicultural issues and competencies? Why is it necessary to learn about lifestyles different from White values and/or beliefs? Ultimately, one question exists: Is it necessary to define, understand, and appreciate the differences of all people instead of identifying and focusing on their similarities? That is, why not bring individuals together based on commonalities instead of distinguishing individuals based on racial, ethnic, or cultural differences?

The struggle for multiculturalism in academia is a recent phenomenon. In the 1960s, individuals protested the unavailability of educational opportunities, challenging "the questionable relevance and apparent elitism of the higher education system" (Perisco, 1990, p. 56). These views paralleled the assertions by leaders of the civil rights movement that American society was essentially racist. This assertion was grounded in historical realities in which White Americans had denied voting opportunities and equal access to education, and had discriminated against individuals on the basis of their color, class, and gender (Perisco, 1990). As a result, many social, political, and higher education institutions began to examine ways to honor and respect cultural diversity.

According to Sue and Sue (1990), infusing diversity within an institution requires an economic, social, political, and moral commitment. Unfortunately, attention to diversity has primarily been a function of changing demographics, rather than an innate or personal need to seek personal knowledge, growth, or understanding. Furthermore, Sleeter and Grant (1994) have pointed out that as need for cultural understanding grows, subsequent misunderstanding and resentment follows.

Counselor education and psychology programs have attempted to answer some of these questions by attending to both diversity and multicultural issues (Ponterotto, Alexander, & Grieger, 1995). Highlen (1994) has asked a timely and appropriate question: "Will psychology as a science and as a profession be able to meet the demands that this changing demographic composition and accompanying cultural pluralism will pose?" (p. 91). Governing bodies of these academic programs have recognized that ignoring the demographic and cultural changes occurring in the United States would be tantamount to covering their eyes and ears and denying the world around them.

In particular, considering changes in society is important in the therapeutic relationship between counselors and their clients. A counselor cannot expect his or her clients to adapt to the counselor's frame of reference. Instead, the counselor needs to adjust to and work within the client's worldview (Atkinson, Morten, & Sue, 1993), and be skilled at attending, functioning, and acting in a culturally appropriate and ethical manner.

Although attention to knowledge, skills, and abilities (Sue, Arredondo, & McDavis, 1992; Pedersen, 1994) as well as the multicultural competencies of counselors (Pope-Davis & Ottavi, 1994; McRae & Johnson, 1991) is important, the training and learning environment also needs to address, model, and reinforce a cultural environment that honors and includes both diversity and multiculturalism. Without institutional support, the student-in-training is in essence being educated about diversity in an environment in which there is little personal and professional commitment to diversity. Choosing to ignore attitudes, behaviors, and experiences that do not honor or support diversity is to assume that they do not affect the learning environment. Furthermore, it also communicates hidden messages that different groups of people are not valued or respected (Gonzalez, 1994).

The charge of creating a multicultural climate and environment, however, is problematic and complex. The concept of multiculturalism has been plagued with difficulties due to its definition and meaning (Pedersen, 1991). Grant and Millar (1992) have identified that an unclear definition of multicultural education has allowed critics either to ignore multicultural education or to view it is as a construct without credibility. That is, given the lack of a unified and accepted definition, multicultural education and training is often believed to address only the needs of students of color or some single aspect of diversity. In addition, educators, administrators, and institutional personnel have not adopted a single, unified plan for multicultural education and training; different conceptual views and approaches have emerged (Sleeter & Grant, 1994). Thus, one reason why programs have been slow to provide comprehensive multicultural training for students has been a lack of a defining purpose and/or standardized commitment to multicultural education (D'Andrea & Daniels, 1991).

Rather than address multiculturalism as an attempt to incorporate culturally different individuals into White society or as an attempt to learn from a distance about culturally different people, Gibson (1976) identified multiculturalism as the everyday human experiences in which individuals function in diverse contexts and settings. Similar to Pedersen's (1991) conceptualization of multiculturalism as the fourth force of psychology, every experience can be seen as a multicultural experience. The term *multiculturalism* will therefore be used to identify educational and training practices in which trainees address race, culture, ethnicity, language, socioeconomic status, gender, lifestyle, age, religion, and ability.

The focus of this chapter is not to address the manner in which multiculturalism is to be defined, taught, or assessed. Rather, it is to discuss the subtle aspects of the cultural and learning environment in which counselors-in-training are taught. In doing so, this chapter will highlight events that have implications for the cultural milieu of the university and the counseling training and learning environment. Four different cultural ambiences or environments will be examined and discussed: (a) the college/university environment, (b) the student training and learning environment, (c) the classroom/curriculum environment, and (d) the faculty environment.

College/University Environment

"Institutions that have shaped academic culture are relatively homogeneous by class, race, ethnicity, and gender. The values they emphasize . . . are those congenial to a White, male, middle-class orientation" (Menges & Exum, 1983, p. 136). Thus, beliefs, behaviors, or values that differ from sanctioned academic norms are often considered deviant or abnormal. Furthermore, individuals who differ are often thought to be inadequately prepared or unmotivated for academia. All too frequently the motivation and commitment of students are questioned when they have family and/or financial obligations that require time and energy away from academic responsibilities (Choi-Pearson & Gloria, 1995; Fiske, 1988). An environment that attempts to assimilate all of its members to one model of appropriate student behavior inherently does not value or respect diversity or attend to individual differences.

A plethora of empirical and conceptual research exists that describes the difficulties and struggles faced by students of color (Cervantes, 1988; Choi-Pearson & Gloria, 1995; Ponterotto, 1990; Wright, 1987), gay and lesbian students (Slater, 1993), disabled students (West, Kregel, Getzel, & Zhu-Ming, 1993), women students (Hudson & O'Regan, 1994), and nontraditional students (Lacefield & Mahan, 1988) in higher education. This phenomenon has been identified by many researchers as "culture shock" (Fiske, 1988; Gunnings, 1982; Madrazo-Peterson & Rodriguez, 1978; Vasquez, 1982). Fiske (1988) suggests that people from marginalized communities who enter predominately White institutions experience a shock that ranges from subtle or not-so-subtle discrimination, to the "loneliness and tensions inherent in finding their way in institutions built around an alien culture" (p. 29). This feeling of alienation and isolation is often the result of being one of a few individuals of a minority community.

Often, the process of assimilating into the university culture is quite difficult as the students are pulled away from sociocultural and familial support, producing a great deal of stress (Cervantes, 1988). Quite frequently, psychological stress emerges when these trainees are caught in an identity crisis of having to choose between their own culture and that of the White university (Ortiz & Arce, 1983). Unfortunately, the choice results in the feeling of being caught in the middle. That is, students want to be loyal and identify with their own cultural community, while at the same time there is pressure to "fit in" with the middle-class, White, male value system in order to succeed within the academic and university environment (Cervantes, 1988).

For example, Chicano/Chicana students might receive negative feedback for behaving "too Mexican" in their academic department, residence hall, or personal setting, yet also be shunned by their Chicano/Chicana social support system for being "too Anglo" (Casas & Vasquez, 1989). Furthermore, as discussed by Ruiz and Casas (1981),

> The very same behaviors which are appropriate in the Anglo classroom may nonetheless create disharmony if generalized inappropriately to the Chicano culture. The Chicano student who questions his elders assertively at home as he does professors at school could be perceived as aggressive and insolent rather than as a "good student." (p. 193)

Another example includes a single-parent student whose parental responsibilities require him or her to be absent from academic activities. The frequent message of "you are in academia now," sends the subtle message that students are expected to conform. Furthermore, as noted earlier, given that nonattendance is often regarded as lack of motivation or ability or as an unwillingness to cooperate (Choi-Pearson & Gloria, 1995; Fiske, 1988), this student is subtly told that personal needs and culture are not as important as the academic culture.

Students must therefore perform a balancing act of maintaining their cultural values and identity while at the same time attempting to integrate themselves into the existing majority university environment. Smith (1985) identifies this as the out-group/in-group phenomenon experienced by many students of different cultural communities.

The lack of role models and individuals who are willing to serve as role models for students of color (Fiske, 1988; Olmedo, 1990), gay and lesbian students (Fassinger, in press), nontraditional students, and other students from marginalized communities also serves to create a culturally depleted environment. For instance, in an analysis by the Hispanic Association of Colleges and Universities ("Closing the Hispanic Faculty Gap," 1995), the faculty-to-student ratio for White students was 1 to 24, followed by a 1-to-54 ratio for African American students, and a 1-to-76 ratio for Hispanic students. Although there is a small percentage of available racial/ethnic faculty mentors, White faculty who choose not to mentor students of color send detrimental messages to students. First, students of color are told that their needs and concerns are no different than those of White students, thereby discounting their differences and cultural being. Subsequently, students are also told that only racial/ethnic faculty can mentor racial/ethnic students.

Faculty who choose not to mentor nontraditional students send similar messages. These students are often passed over for younger "traditional" students. Nontraditional students are covertly told that, given their life experiences, they do not need help in managing graduate school or understanding academia. Students may feel helpless and unimportant because they do not "fit" into academia.

Furthermore, gay or lesbian students are often not reflected in academia. Given the often inhospitable atmosphere, gay or lesbian faculty may not feel comfortable in identifying as such. As a result, Fassinger (in press) points out that this is damaging to lesbians and gays who feel that they do not have information sources or role models. Also, lack of role models covertly sends the message that the environment may not be welcoming for gays or lesbians. Again, the ambience of the learning environment and the messages sent to the students of an inhospitable cultural learning environment subtly occurs.

Student Training and Learning Environment

Issues of alienation (Fields, 1988), isolation (Ponterotto, 1990), cultural incongruence (Fiske, 1988; Choi-Pearson & Gloria, 1995), and not being self-reflected in the university environment (Fields, 1988) are but a few of the difficulties experienced by students of differing cultural communities in higher education. As these issues are raised, the White academic culture often feels threatened when the cultural ambience of the academic learning environment in which all students are being trained is examined. As such, a "defensive learning environment" occurs that is not welcoming to a cultural ambience that is different from the (academic) status quo. This fear is often exhibited when a department resists participating in training or a self-study of diversity or when students are opposed to supporting activities that honor differences.

Similar to the incongruence faced at the university level, trainees encounter the problem of balancing culture at the department or program level. Choi-Pearson and Gloria (1995) reported a cultural incongruence of racial/ethnic students as they experienced stress, confusion, and dissonance about belonging to an academic culture incongruent with their own cultural attitudes, beliefs, and behaviors. Other researchers have reported similar findings of feelings of not "fitting in" (Cervantes, 1988; Fields, 1988). The problem involves the conflict in knowing how to balance participation in two different cultures without "stepping on toes" or of "juggling two cultures" (Fiske, 1988, p. 29). For example, given the important of deference to "elders" in many racial/ethnic groups (Sue & Sue, 1990), it is not unusual for students of color to question the appropriateness of knocking on a professor's door, giving a professor feedback, or calling a professor by his or her first name (Choi-Pearson & Gloria, 1995). When individuals in the environment are not aware of or do not act on this incongruence, students receive the message that their culture is not as important as the academic culture that already exists in the training environment. These students may feel as if they do not have options and feel helpless in the environment.

Specifically investigating perceptions of minority graduate students regarding their graduate education, Cervantes (1988) conducted interviews with 29 racial/ethnic doctoral students (15 Chicano/Latino, 8 Black, and 6 Asian) over 2 academic years. Comments reflected the need for students to be integrated and act like the majority group of students as it "is the only chance you will have to be accepted" (p. 35). Expressing similar feelings, another student stated, "People want me to strip my identity in order to remain here" (p. 37). In addition, another student experienced similar pressures: "It is expected that you talk and act in a certain way. . . . So I can act like a White person, and I can talk intellectually, so I am not as discriminated against as people who have an accent" (p. 37). Each of these statements reflects the lack of cultural congruity that is often experienced by ethnic minority students in higher education. As one student said, "people seem different here. . . . I feel very intimidated" (p. 37). As a result of these comments, Cervantes concluded that feelings of alienation and isolation are common concerns among minority students.

DeFreece (1987) labeled similar feelings of isolation, withdrawal, and cultural alienation as "nonentitlement" (p. 570), or feeling as if one is not welcomed in higher education due to cultural or ethnic differences. She also pointed out that "these feelings are intensified if the minority student is also a woman" (p. 570). Women of color confront a double devaluation as a result of their gender and race (Stein, 1994). In general, given that academia has primarily been male-dominated, female trainees may feel misunderstood and devalued within academia. Similarly, nontraditional female students may encounter even more intense feelings of not being welcomed in higher education.

Gunnings (1982) indicated that "setting aside the variables of race or culture, one can see that all students of higher education must deal daily with stress-provoking components. Consider, for example, the strains and tensions that accompany course examinations, the difficulties of keeping up with the academic standards of the institution, and financial difficulties" (p. 14). Unfortunately, however, training settings have been criticized for maintaining the status quo and not reflecting diversity issues and the differential needs of students (Highlen, 1994; Pedersen, 1991). Subsequently, students from marginalized communities find it necessary to balance or juggle two competing and often disparate cultures in an environment that provides little to no support.

Classroom/Curriculum Environment

Though the student training environment and cultural ambience is often not open to or accepting of change and diversity in accommodating differential needs (Choi-Pearson & Gloria, 1995; Ponterotto, 1990), another student-centered arena resistant to change is the classroom and/or curriculum. In order to attend to changing societal need, as well as to prepare counselors adequately regarding issues of diversity, there is a need for the creation of an environment in which dialogue about multiculturalism can be address throughout all academic, professional practice, and social experiences. This has particular implications for faculty, who not only train counselors but also provide the content and the learning environment for their academic courses.

Infusing or incorporating issues of diversity, which may or may not have a primary focus within the class content, has been equated with losing academic freedom within one's own classroom. *Infusion* is perhaps one of the most feared words for academicians. This fear may come from unknown changes that may be required, to fear that the faculty does not know how to change a course they have been teaching for many years. Academic freedom is an important concept that allows each individual instructor to identify materials that are pertinent for the students' growth and knowledge. Although faculty may fear retribution from the "cultural infusion police," it is the faculty's ethical responsibility to prepare their students to address competently the needs and issues of today's diverse society (Altmaier, 1993; American Psychological Association, 1992). In order to do so, Scott (1994) suggests that faculty first learn more about the relationship of multiculturalism and diversity issues to their discipline and course content.

Whether diversity is integrated on the surface or at the core of the curricula, both overt and covert messages are sent to counselors-in-training about the commitment and importance of diversity within that setting. For instance, what messages are sent when an instructor of ethics does not feel the need to address the "Guidelines for Providers of Psychological Services to Ethnic, Linguistic, and Culturally Diverse Populations" (American Psychological Association, 1993) If the instructor inappropriately rationalizes that these guidelines are more suitably addressed in the multicultural class, students are in essence being told that issues of diversity need be addressed only when the client is visibly or audibly recognizable as an individual from a marginalized community. Furthermore, students are told that multicultural issues need be addressed only outside of core courses. As such, training programs may inadvertently encourage their students to make subjective judgments about who are "multicultural" clients and who are not.

Other academic courses that initially seem to have a less obvious need for addressing diversity or multiculturalism are research methodology and statistics. An instructor may easily identify research methodology or statistics as independent from the conceptual understanding of diversity. Yet as indicated by Marín and Marín (1991), knowledge of subject characteristics and core beliefs and values is imperative in the collection of data, analyses to be utilized, and interpretation of results. Knowledge of multicultural issues is of utmost importance in accurately and sensitively researching and reflecting different populations, as researchers consistently call for more culturally sensitive and appropriate investigations (Casas & Atkinson, 1981; Marín & Marín, 1991; Parham, 1989).

Other courses in which individual cultural differences need to be taken into consideration are assessment-related courses. For instance, Dana (1993) stresses the importance of understanding how to administer, score, and interpret instruments for different cultural populations. As the majority of standardized instruments are normed on White middle-class individuals, it seems evident that more than one chapter or one class period is needed to understand the differential applications of the assessment instruments. Unfortunately, when a limited amount of time is earmarked for addressing diversity, this allows for and inadvertently promotes the continuance of the status quo.

For each of these classes, the multicultural class is both assumed and expected to be the only arena necessary to address diversity (Ponterotto et al., 1995). Quite frequently, training programs inadvertently maintain this atmosphere as the conceptualization of diversity issues is secondary and operationalized as an appendage to other more important training information (D'Andrea & Daniels, 1991). That is, only one course for multicultural issues is provided, in which all information thought to be necessary for multicultural competency is provided. Furthermore, this conveys the belief that "how to be multicultural" can both be taught and learned in one academic course.

Choi-Pearson and Gloria (1995) reported that, within the classroom setting, graduate students of color were uncomfortable when they were asked by the instructor to "give the ethnic point of view" (p. 4). Sedlacek (1983) identified the request of a minority point of view to be insensitive. No one individual can speak for his or her entire culture—nor may want to. This request may place the student in an uncomfortable and alienating situation in front of the entire class. It is important to consider that teaching *about* multiculturalism is a need of a changing society. However, teaching *from* a multicultural perspective is just as necessary. For instance, Lou (1994) identifies the need to teach all students as equally as possible because unconscious differential treatment and class activities can alienate, isolate, hurt, and be uncomfortable for students. Grading class participation or having students call attention to themselves is based on individualistic and competitive values. These values, however, may not be in congruence with those values of cooperation, unity, or humbleness often held by other cultural groups such as American Indians (Peregoy, 1993) or Chicanos/Latinos (Sue & Sue, 1990).

Faculty Environment

The cultural environment of faculty is often very similar to the cultural environment of students. Hall (1990) refers to an environment of "benign neglect" (p. 109) in which individuals inadvertently forget to attend to diversity and do nothing but propose to respond openly to discrimination issues. That is, diversity issues are given "lip service" in which no actions or behaviors are enacted to support the diversity rhetoric. Strickland (1995) identifies that departments and faculty often speak favorably of diversity, yet do not act and react with the same efficiency or effectiveness.

There is also growing evidence that faculty of color experience severe marginalization. Research has indicated that minority faculty frequently feel "unwelcomed, unappreciated, and unwanted," both socially and professionally (Johnsrud, 1993, p. 7). Quite often, minority faculty believe that their colleagues feel that they were hired as a result of affirmative action policies. Unfortunately, faculty subsequently feel pressure to prove continually that they are worthy of their positions or appointments (Luz Reyes & Halcon, 1988). Often, faculty of color feel they must work twice as hard as their White counterparts to prove themselves (Stein, 1994). Taylor (1995) identified that academic institutions endorse subtle organizational arrangements that selectively weed out diverse faculty through alienation, isolation, and racism. Similarly, sexism, ageism, and homophobia result in the same selective weeding of faculty. Such an inhospitable environment diminishes any positive gains made and denies that a diversified cultural ambience is important.

Although most faculty experience the pressure of producing scholarly research, most women and faculty of color also experience additional requests to provide services for department and university committees (Carnegie Foundation for the Advancement of Teaching, 1990) as well as for their respective cultural communities (Johnsrud, 1993). Community activities that are considered educational training or consultation are often considered nonacademic, and their academic relevance is called into question (Banks, 1984). That is, these community and university service activities are rarely factored into retention, promotion, and tenure decisions. Providing a review process in which credit/merit is given "for specialties, competencies, and unique offerings to the university should be incorporated at all universities" (Hall, 1990, p. 110). Without such a tenure process, the system is monoculturally conceptualized.

Most academic institutions place the greatest emphasis on scholarly research, followed by teaching, and then community service. Thus, work within diverse community settings is generally not considered within the retention, promotion, and tenure process of tenure-track professors. Faculty of color, however, are asked and often assigned to serve on university and department committees; are called by their respective communities to provide consultant, counseling, and professional services; and are sought out by diverse students (in and out of their department) for mentorship and thesis/dissertation advisement (Menges & Exum, 1983; Stein, 1994). These services are invaluable to the respective communities but require a significant time commitment that is rarely acknowledged in the tenure process. Olmedo (1995) best summarizes this process with the simple yet poignant statement, "[The] reason they hire you is the reason they fire you."

Scholarly research is consistently identified as the key to retention, promotion, and tenure. Unfortunately, minority faculty research is often devalued or dismissed if it is nonmainstream or perceived to be self-serving (Luz Reyes & Halcon, 1988). Grant and Millar (1992) found that scholars of color indicated that their work is frequently not accepted as solid scholarship. They further state that this "academic ethnocentrism and elitism act[s] to limit multicultural education research" (p. 9). Beyond limiting the research field, it also affects the learning environment when the department proposes to embrace diversity yet does not support its faculty when they conduct multicultural research. This incongruence may inadvertently convey to both faculty and students that it is not acceptable to pursue a multicultural research agenda. Again, both the faculty and students are indirectly informed of the need to be the same or to assimilate into the academic cultural milieu.

Perhaps Olmedo (1990) most succinctly depicts the need for the tenure process to reflect and support diversity. Olmedo states,

> If cultural diversity is an important value of the institution then this value should be properly reflected in the institution's criteria and standards for retention and promotion of faculty. This means that recognition of cultural diversity and minority issues should permeate the typical criteria pertaining to research activities, teaching, professional service, and service to the institution. (p. 103)

In providing a training and learning atmosphere for counselors, it is imperative that its faculty have a sense of fairness and comfort of the review procedure to honor cultural diversity. If faculty of color do not feel comfortable in the environment or with the tenure process, it would seem difficult for other faculty and students to be comfortable as well.

Recommendations

As universities, colleges, departments, and programs become more multiculturally aware and sensitive, they become more effective in providing a diversified arena in which *all* their members can participate (Katz, 1989). In providing a cultural ambience or cultural learning environment for counselors-in-training, it is imperative to realize that diversity is a reality and is more than a value system. Hard work is thus necessary for acting and reacting in ways that support our words and beliefs about diversity. Most important, commitment is the key to providing a culturally sensitive, congruent, and comfortable environment for each student (Guzman, 1991). Only in a learning environment of varied perspectives, such as creativity, critical thinking, problem solving, and openness to multiculturalism, will students appreciate and embrace all aspects of diversity (Manning & Coleman-Boatwright, 1991).

There have been numerous suggestions for enhancing the retention of students and faculty as well as for promoting multiculturalism and diversity within a training program (Choi-Pearson & Gloria, 1995; Guzman, 1991; Persico, 1990; Scott, 1994; Vaughn, 1990). Although the following recommendations may overlap with previous suggestions, these recommendations are specific to creating and supporting a culturally aware training and learning environment for counselors-in-training as well as for faculty.

1. Move away from the concept of a "traditional student." As demographics change, so will the student cohorts within the training program. Maintaining the belief that all students will learn, think, act, and react in the same manner is inappropriate as well as irrational.

2. Actively attend and bolster all students within the academic program equally. The department as a whole and faculty as individuals need to take responsibility for the personal and academic success of *each* student.

3. Provide continuing education for faculty regarding issues of multiculturalism and diversity in order for them to have the skills, knowledge, attitudes, and understanding infuse their curricula.

4. Provide ongoing training seminars to increase multicultural awareness and decrease defensiveness in faculty and students toward issues of multiculturalism and diversity.

5. Provide more than one multicultural course within an academic training program. A series of multicultural and diversity courses will, as well as infusing multiculturalism into all courses, provide an environment that transmits a message of commitment to diversity issues.

6. Teach multiculturalism from a multicultural perspective. Provide different learning activities and options within the classroom that are respectful and accommodate different cultures and ways of being.

7. Examine personal cultural perspectives, biases and prejudices, which may interfere with the ability to teach all students as equally as possible.

8. Avoid admitting students or hiring faculty as tokens. That is, it is not only the number of students from marginalized communities that provides for a diverse environment, it is the reorganization and restructure of attitudes about and behavior toward a welcoming cultural environment.

9. Avoid questioning or placing faculty in an environment in which they need to work twice as hard to be perceived as equal to White faculty colleagues. Furthermore, recognize both racial/ethnic and nonracial/nonethnic research as legitimate and academically relevant.

10. Restructure the tenure system to reflect multicultural competencies and community activities as academically relevant.

11. Provide opportunities for feedback from students, faculty, and staff regarding the multicultural ambience of the learning and training environment.

12. In creating an environment that is multiculturally focused, be careful not to become "culturally encapsulated." That is, continually provide learning experiences and actively work toward a culturally welcoming environment.

13. Examine and modify both the overt and covert policies and procedures that serve to create the illusion that equality exists in the learning and training environment.

14. Take personal and professional responsibility for creating, teaching, and supporting multiculturalism within academic classrooms, research agendas, and learning environments.

15. Speak, think, act, react, and interact multiculturally, because every interaction *is* multicultural.

Conclusion

In striving toward a culturally aware learning and training environment, the issue of assessment is an important consideration. That is, how does a training program know that a culturally sensitive ambience has been established? Although there is no simplistic answer to this query, Ponterotto et al. (1995) provide an initial answer. These authors developed a Multicultural Competency Checklist (MCC) that identifies cultural goals and objectives that directly affect the cultural ambience of the learning and training environment. For instance, the MCC assesses the different components of minority representation, curriculum issues, professional practice and supervision, research considerations, student and faculty competency evaluation, and physical environment. Training programs can utilize the MCC as an assessment guide as they move toward enhancing and maintaining a cultural environment.

Furthermore, given the changing dynamics of the cultural environment of training programs, evaluation of the cultural atmosphere needs to be ongoing. Unfortunately, there is a tendency to believe that "no news is good news." That is, if faculty or students do not raise diversity issues or concerns, then the cultural ambience is assumed to be satisfactory. Within this cultural ambience, however, feedback or opinions may not be given due to the potential for repercussions or the lack of comfort within the environment. In this situation, a culturally unwelcoming environment perpetuates itself. Program students and faculty may then falsely believe that they have reached a point at which no change or evaluation of the environment is needed.

To avoid this cultural encapsulation, Pedersen (1994) cautions that we do not accept the following culturally biased assumption:

We already know all of our assumptions. In an era of diminishing resources we need to recognize the danger of a closed, biased, and culturally encapsulated system that promoted domination by an elitist group representing a special point of view. If we are unwilling or unable to challenge our assumptions, we will be less likely to communicate effectively with persons from other cultures. (p. 50)

It is only with continued attention, effort, and awareness that a culturally sensitive ambience can be created for the academic, social, and personal success of all its members.

References

Altmaier, E. M. (1993). Role of Criterion II in accreditation. *Professional Psychology: Research and Practice, 24,* 127-129.

American Psychological Association. (1993). Guidelines for providers of psychological services to ethnic, linguistic, and culturally diverse populations. *American Psychologist, 48,* 45-48.

American Psychological Association. (1993). Ethical principles of psychologists and code of conduct. *American Psychologist, 47,* 1597-1611.

Atkinson, D. R., Morten, G., & Sue, D. W. (1993). *Counseling American minorities: A cross-cultural perspective.* Madison, WI: Brown & Benchmark.

Banks, W. M. (1984). Afro-American scholars in the university: Roles and conflicts. *American Behavioral Scientist, 27,* 325-339.

Carnegie Foundation for the Advancement of Teaching. (1990). Women faculty excel as campus citizens. *Change, 22,* 39-43.

Casas, J. M., & Atkinson, D. R. (1981). The Mexican American in higher education: An example of subtle stereotyping. *Personnel and Guidance Journal,* 473-476.

Casas, J. M., & Vasquez, M. J. T. (1989). Counseling the Hispanic client: A theoretical and applied perspective. In P. B. Pedersen, J. G. Draguns, W. J. Lonner, & J. E. Trimble (Eds.), *Counseling across cultures* (3rd ed., pp. 153-175). Honolulu: University of Hawaii Press.

Cervantes, O. F. (1988). The realities that Latinos, Chicanos, and other ethnic minority students encounter in graduate school. *Journal of La Raza Studies,* 33-41.

Choi-Pearson, C. P., & Gloria, A. M. (1995, Spring). "From the back seat of the bus": Perspectives and suggestions from racial/ethnic graduate students. *American Psychological Association Graduate Student Newsletter, 7,* pp. 1-5.

Closing the Hispanic faculty gap. (1995, January-February). *Hispanic Association of Colleges and Universities Newsletter,* pp. 1, 7.

Dana, R. H. (1993). *Multicultural assessment perspectives for professional psychology.* Boston: Allyn & Bacon.

D'Andrea, M., & Daniels, J. (1991). Exploring the different levels of multicultural counseling training in counselor education. *Journal of Counseling and Development, 70,* 78-85.

DeFreece, M. T. (1987). Women of color: No longer ignored. *Journal of College Student Personnel, 28,* 570-571.

Fassinger, R. E. (in press). From invisibility to integration: Lesbian identity in the workplace. *Career Development Quarterly.*

Fields, C. (1988). The Hispanic pipeline: Narrow, leaking, and needing repair. Change, 20, 20-27.

Fiske, E. B. (1988). The undergraduate Hispanic experience: A case of juggling two cultures. *Change, 20,* 29-33.

Gibson, M. A. (1976). Approaches to multicultural education in the United States: Some concepts and assumptions. *Anthropology and Education Quarterly, 7,* 7-18.

Gonzalez, J. C. (1994). Once you accept, then you can teach. In *Survival skills for scholars: Teaching from a multicultural perspective* (No. 12, pp. 1-16). Thousand Oaks, CA: Sage.

Grant, C. A., & Millar, S. (1992). Research and multicultural education: Barriers, needs, and boundaries. In C. A. Grant (Ed.), *Research and multicultural education: From the margins to the mainstream.* Washington, DC: Falmer Press.

Gunnings, B. B. (1982, October). Stress and the minority student on a predominately White campus. *Journal of Non-White Concerns,* pp. 11-16.

Guzman, L. P. (1991). Incorporating cultural diversity into psychology training programs. In H. F. Myers, P. Wohlford, L. P. Guzman, & R. J. Echemendia (Eds.), *Ethnic minority perspectives on clinical training and services in psychology* (pp. 67-70). Washington, DC: American Psychological Association.

Hall, C.C.I. (1990). Qualified minorities are encouraged to apply: The recruitment of ethnic minority and female psychologists. In G. Stricker, E. Davis-Russell, E. Bourg, E. Duran, W. R. Hammond, J. McHolland, K. Polite, & B. E. Vaughn (Eds.), *Toward ethnic diversification in psychology education and training* (pp. 105-111). Washington, DC: American Psychological Association.

Highlen, P. S. (1994). Racial/ethic diversity in doctoral programs of psychology: Challenges for the twenty-first century. *Applied and Preventive Psychology, 3,* 91-108.

Hudson, S. A., & O'Regan, J. (1994). Stress and the graduate psychology student. *Journal of Clinical Psychology, 50,* 973-977.

Johnsrud, L. K. (1993). Women and minority faculty experiences: Defining and responding to diverse realities. In J. Gainen & R. Boice (Eds.), *Building a diverse faculty: New directions for teaching and learning* (pp. 3-16). San Francisco: Jossey-Bass.

Katz, J. (1989). The challenge of diversity. In C. Woolbright (Ed.), *Valuing diversity* (pp. 1-22). Bloomington, IN: Association of College Unions-International.

Lacefield, W. E., & Mahan, J. M. (1988). Factors influencing satisfaction of non-traditional students within mainstream graduate programs. *Educational Research Quarterly, 12,* 36-50.

Lou, R. (1994). Teaching all students equally. In H. Roberts, J. C. Gonzales, O. D. Harris, D. J. Huff, A. M. Johns, R. Lou, & O. L. Scott, *Survival skills for scholars: Teaching from a multicultural perspective* (pp. 28-45). Thousand Oaks, CA: Sage.

Luz Reyes, M. L., & Halcon, J. J. (1988). Racism in academia: The old wolf revisited. *Harvard Educational Review, 58,* 229-314.

Madrazo-Peterson, R., & Rodriguez, M. (1978). Minority students: Perceptions of a university environment. *Journal of College Student Personnel, 17,* 259-263.

Manning, K., & Coleman-Boatwright, P. (1991). Student affairs initiatives toward a multicultural university. *Journal of College Student Development, 32,* 367-374.

Marín, G., & Marín, B. V. (1991). *Research with Hispanic populations.* Newbury Park, CA: Sage.

McRae, M. B., & Johnson, S. D. (1991). Toward training for competence in multicultural counselor education. *Journal of Counseling and Development, 70,* 131-135.

Menges, R. J., & Exum, W. H. (1983). Barriers to the progress of women and minority faculty. *Journal of Higher Education, 54,* 123-144.

Olmedo, E. L. (1990). Minority faculty development: Issues in retention and promotion. In G. Stricker, E. Davis-Russell, E. Bourg, E. Duran, W. R. Hammond, J. McHolland, K. Polite, & B. E. Vaughn (Eds.), *Toward ethnic diversification in psychology education and training* (pp. 99-104). Washington, DC: American Psychological Association.

Olmedo, E. L. (1995, August). In *Mentoring women and people of color for leadership in organized psychology: Solutions and strategies.* Symposium conducted at the meeting of the 103rd Annual Conference of the American Psychological Association, New York City.

Ortiz, V., & Arce, C. H. (1983). Language orientation and mental health status among persons of Mexican descent. *Journal of Hispanic Behavioral Sciences, 6,* 127-143.

Parham, T. A. (1989). Cycles of psychological nigresence. *The Counseling Psychologist, 17,* 187-226.

Pedersen, P. B. (Ed.). (1991). Multiculturalism as a fourth force in counseling [Special issue]. *Journal of Counseling and Development, 70,* 4-250.

Pedersen, P. B. (1994). *A handbook for developing multicultural awareness* (2nd ed.). Alexandria, VA: American Counseling Association.

Peregoy, J. J. (1993). Transcultural counseling with American Indians and Alaskan natives: Contemporary issues for consideration. In J. McFadden (Ed.), *Transcultural counseling: Bilateral and international perspectives.* Alexandria, VA: American Counseling Association.

Perisco, C. F. (1990). Creating an institutional climate that honors diversity. In G. Stricker, E. Davis-Russell, E. Bourg, E. Duran, W. R. Hammond, J. McHolland, K. Polite, & B. E. Vaughn (Eds.), *Toward ethnic diversification in psychology education and training* (pp. 55-63). Washington, DC: American Psychological Association.

Ponterotto, J. G. (1990). Racial/ethnic minority and women students in higher education: A status report. *New Directions for Student Services, 52,* 45-59.

Ponterotto, J. G., Alexander, C. M., & Grieger, I. (1995). A multicultural competency checklist for counseling training programs. *Journal of Multicultural Counseling and Development, 23,* 11-20.

Pope-Davis, D. B., & Ottavi, T. M. (1994). Examining the association between self-reported multicultural counseling competencies and demographic variables among counselors. *Journal of Counseling and Development, 72,* 651-654.

Ruiz, R. A., & Casas, M. J. (1981). Culturally relevant and behavioristic counseling for Chicano college students. In P. B. Pedersen, J. G. Draguns, W. J. Lonner, & J. E. Trimble (Eds.), *Counseling across cultures* (pp. 181-202). Honolulu: University of Hawaii Press.

Scott, O. L. (1994). Including multicultural content and perspectives in your courses. In H. Roberts, J. C. Gonzales, O. D. Harris, D. J. Huff, A. M. Johns, R. Lou, & O. L. Scott, *Survival skills for scholars: Teaching from a multicultural perspective* (pp. 46-59). Thousand Oaks, CA: Sage.

Sedlacek, W. E. (1983). Teaching minority students. In J. H. Cones, J. F. Noonan, & D. Janha (Eds.), *Teaching advanced students: New directions for teaching and learning* (pp. 39-50). San Francisco: Jossey-Bass.

Slater, B. R. (1993). Violence against lesbian and gay male college students. In Campus violence: Kinds, causes, and cures [Special issue]. *Journal of College Student Psychotherapy, 8,* 177-202.

Sleeter, C. E., & Grant, C. A. (1994). *Making choices for multicultural education: Approaches to race, class, and gender.* New York: Macmillan.

Smith, E.M.J. (1985). Ethnic minorities: Life stress, social support, and mental health issues. *The Counseling Psychologist, 13,* 537-579.

Stein, W. J. (1994). The survival of American Indian faculty. *Thought and Action: The NEA Higher Education Journal, 10,* 101-114.

Strickland, B. (1995). In *Mentoring women and people of color for leadership in organized psychology: Solutions and strategies.* Symposium conducted at the meeting of the 103rd Annual Conference of the American Psychological Association, New York City.

Sue, D. W., Arredondo, P., & McDavis, R. J. (1992). Multicultural counseling competencies and standards: A call to the profession. *Journal of Counseling and Development, 70,* 477-486.

Sue, D. W., & Sue, D. (1990). *Counseling the culturally different: Theory and practice* (2nd ed.). New York: John Wiley.

Taylor, D. (1995, August). In *Mentoring women and people of color for leadership in organized psychology: Solutions and strategies.* Symposium conducted at the meeting of the 103rd Annual Conference of the American Psychological Association, New York City.

Uba, L., & Sue, S. (1991). Nature and scope of services for Asian and Pacific Islander Americans. In N. Mokuau (Ed.), *Handbook of social services for Asian and Pacific Islanders* (pp. 3-19). Westport, CT: Greenwood.

U.S. Department of Commerce. (1991, March 11). *Bureau of the Census News* (CB 91-100). Washington, DC: U.S. Department of Commerce.

Vasquez, M.J.T. (1982). Confronting barriers to the participation of Mexican American women in higher education. *Hispanic Journal of Behavioral Sciences, 4,* 147-165.

Vaughn, B. E. (1990). The problem of organizational culture in achieving ethnic diversity in professional psychology training: Implications for recruitment. In G. Stricker, E. Davis-Russell, E. Bourg, E. Duran, W. R. Hammond, J. McHolland, K. Polite, & B. E. Vaughn (Eds), *Toward ethnic diversification in psychology education and training* (pp. 113-120). Washington, DC: American Psychological Association.

West, M., Kregel, J., Getzel, E. E., Ming, Z., Ipsen, S. M., & Martin, E. D. (1993). Beyond section 504: Satisfaction and empowerment of students with disabilities in higher education. *Exceptional Children, 59,* 456-467.

Wright, D. J. (1987). Minority students: Developmental beginnings. *New Directions for Student Services, 38,* 5-21.

PART III

Multicultural Supervision

12

Multiculturalism as a Context for Supervision

PERSPECTIVES, LIMITATIONS, AND IMPLICATIONS

Gerald L. Stone

Clinical supervision is judged to be an important activity by many professional psychologists (see Stoltenberg & Delworth, 1987) and professional organizations (e.g., American Psychological Association, 1986). Recent articles and books in professional psychology and counseling point to multiculturalism as an important context for supervision (e.g., Leong, 1994). Various arguments have been put forward to substantiate the importance of cultural contextualism in the education of psychological practitioners. Some argue that changing demography (moving to a situation of multiple minorities in terms of U.S. population statistics) and the inadequacy of traditional training dictate that multicultural education is the obvious thing to do. Others claim that the use of a multicultural approach is the "right thing to do" because of professional mandates (American Psychological Association, 1993) and practice guidelines (Sue, Arredondo, & McDavis, 1992). Ridley, Mendoza, and Kanitz (1994) have summarized these arguments as well as other more psychological motivations for multicultural training. Whatever the nature of the argument, I assume that most educational and psychological activities including clinical supervision involve cultural considerations. As one colleague put it, "It (multiculturalism) just *is*. Deal with it." In a sense, this chapter is one way of "dealing with it."

The problem of "dealing with it" as it pertains to supervision in a multicultural context is that the literatures linking multiculturalism and supervision are rare. Moreover, the multiculturalism literature is voluminous, yielding a "Tower of Babel" experience for most professionals who attempt to read it. The challenge is to translate these various voices of multiculturalism into coherent perspectives with implications for supervisory practice. A critical examination of these perspectives is made in hope of fostering an attitude of reflection and inquiry concerning multicultural supervision. In accomplishing these goals, I will describe and examine the cultural difference and cultural affiliation perspectives and their relevant supervisory implications. Before undertaking these translations, it is critical to discuss the definitional dilemma surrounding the inclusiveness or exclusiveness of the terms *multicultural* and *supervision*.

Conceptual Issues

Part of the dilemma lies with terminology often associated with these two constructs. Controversial terms like *race, culture,* and *ethnicity* are frequently used as static categories that are interchangeable, resulting in confusion (see Johnson, 1990). For example, a recent book titled *Social and Biological Aspects of Ethnicity* (Chapman, 1993) reports that worldwide patterns of genetic variation suggest that there are no discrete boundaries between so-called races. Ho (1995) described the problem of cultural boundaries in an era of cultural contact and the dynamic process of enculturation to many cultures. And all of the arguments beg the question of what qualifies as a cultural focus and what does not.

In terms of cultural focus, those identified as inclusives or exclusives regarding the definition of multiculturalism would probably agree to some extent that cultural factors are important in most psychological counseling and training activities. They disagree about the focus. Inclusives adopt a broad and international approach to defining *multicultural* that often includes the ambiguous terms of *race, ethnicity, nationality, social class, religion, gender, affectional orientation, age, disability,* and more. As such, psychologists and counselors would deal with several overlapping minority groups including not only racial and ethnic minorities, but women, gays, lesbians, bisexuals, the hearing impaired, and, most of all, individuals affiliated with several special populations.

There are others, the exclusives, who prefer to restrict the focus to the "visible racial ethnic minority groups" in the United States, including African Americans, American Indians, Asian Americans, and Hispanics and Latinos. The exclusives argue that an overinclusive definition reduces racial and ethnic concerns to a "false consciousness" of garden variety human difference, thereby masking racism and injustice and allowing counseling professionals to avoid dealing with the "race issue."

A view adopted in this chapter is that inclusives and exclusives got it right and wrong because they are focusing on different types of minority populations. Both are correct in viewing most counseling activity as involving cultural factors. The inclusives consider a diversity of minority groups including groups ("autonomous minorities" and "immigrant minorities") that may be victims of prejudice but are not subordinated groups in a system of rigid stratification, whereas the exclusives limit their discussion to "caste-like minorities" who have experienced involuntary incorporation into society and have been relegated to subordinate status (see typology of minority groups in Ogbu, 1983). Thus, inclusives are prone to treat autonomous minority groups (Jews) in a similar fashion to caste-like minorities (African American), because these groups simply represent individual differences. Little recognition of the difference in quality of power relations is sufficiently acknowledged in an inclusive definition. On the other hand, exclusives do focus on power relations of caste-like minorities, but fail to acknowledge sufficiently that other cultural factors are worthy of multicultural inquiry. Both definitions would benefit from the perceptive analysis of minority groups by Ogbu (1983) and the reality of multiple cultural identities (see Ho, 1995).

Supervision, perhaps less controversial, also is a term that occasionally suffers from cycles of inflation and deflation. Some discuss supervision as part of a curriculum, whereas others tend to confuse training (with many components) with supervision. What activities are properly designated as supervisory activities? Do these activities include role-playing, reading, group discussion? Or are activities restricted to the supervisor-supervisee relationship? Is the focus of supervision on personal growth and development of the supervisee, skill acquisition, case management, or client change? To a large extent, the specific definition of *supervision* (as well as of *multicultural*) used in this chapter will emerge as each perspective is elaborated. Generally speaking (see Holloway, 1992), supervision is an interpersonal process that typically involves a more experienced clinician ("master") with oversight and evaluative responsibility for a less experienced clinician(s) ("apprentice") who shares educational and therapeutic goals. The educational goal primarily concerns the growth and development of professional competence in the trainee, although educational benefits are often obtained by the supervisor. Therapeutically, supervisor and supervisee collaborate to ensure the welfare of the client. This collaboration often takes place in a multicultural context involving supervisees and supervisors who are affiliated in different ways with different (or similar) cultural groups.

The Approach

As indicated earlier, this chapter is structured to focus on a critical examination of multiculturalism and the generation of recommendations for multicultural supervision. The chapter has two major parts and follows a common format. The parts are composed of two multicultural perspectives, labeled cultural difference and cultural affiliation. These two perspectives seem to represent major voices in multiculturalism, and in one sense, represent a continuum of multicultural awareness. That is, at one end of the continuum is a focus on external differences (cultural difference), while the opposite end is represented by internal differences (cultural affiliation). Although the continuum does not need to be value-laden with developmental expectations of moving from an external to an internal orientation, it does appear that many contemporary multicultural writers in psychology and counseling favor a developmental approach to these two perspectives on multicultural awareness from externalism (cultural difference) to internalism (cultural affiliation).

The same format is followed in discussing each perspective. The perspective is defined conceptually through an analysis of selected literatures and by example. Definition is followed by a critical commentary focusing on the problem and controversies. The next section translates the multicultural perspective into implications for supervision through the use of examples and application of a generic learning model emphasizing the experiential learning cycle developed by Kolb (1984) and extended to counseling and supervision by Abbey, Hunt, and Weiser (1985). The phases of experiential learning include concrete experience, reflective observation, abstract conceptualization, and active experimentation. That is, begin with the concrete experience of multicultural supervision; then reflect on the experience, conceptualize it, and take some action such as recommendations for multicultural supervision practice. For our purposes, I have consolidated some phases (reflective observation and abstract conceptualization become a reflection phase) and added others (learning set representing prior learning [multicultural training] needed to perform a task [multicultural supervision]; see Gagne & Paradise, 1961), resulting in a learning set-experience-reflection-action model of linking multiculturalism to supervision. Finally, after an examination of perspectives, the chapter provides a summary through an application of an experiential learning model to this chapter.

Cultural Difference Perspective

Definition

The first multicultural perspective to gain widespread popularity in the psychological and counseling literatures was termed cultural difference (e.g., McGoldrick, Pearce, & Giordano, 1982; Sue & Sue, 1990). Cultural difference has been usually conceptualized as an anthropological or a sociological construct. The anthropological description uses cultural referents, pertaining to "patterned regularities" related to different cultural groups including customs, language, traditions, beliefs, and values. These patterned regularities are assumed to be more or less shared by individuals belonging to these groups. The anthropological approach is often associated with an international definition of multiculturalism in which cultural differences are discussed in relationship to cultural regions and cross-cultural contact. For example, the counseling of international students (see Essandoh, 1995; Pedersen, 1991a) presents one kind of cross-cultural situation faced by psychological counselors (e.g., adjustment may be easier when a student visits a country from the same cultural region—an Iowan [North America] visiting England [Europe]).

Although some of the multicultural counseling work does touch on an international cultural difference perspective, including the aforementioned counseling of international students as well as Fulbright or other programs for fostering cultural exchanges of faculty (e.g., Hood, 1993; McWhirter, 1988; O'Neil, 1993; Skovholt, 1988; Stadler, 1995), by far most of the attention in counseling has focused on the sociological approach. While the cultural anthropology-based approach dealt with international cultures, the sociologically based writers were focused on the four groups of oppressed minorities in the United States—American Indians, Asian Americans, African Americans, and Hispanic Americans. These ethnic, racial, and cultural groups share a common experience of oppression, including involuntary incorporation—of American Indians (forced onto reservations), of Asian Americans (forced into concentration camps during World War II), of African Americans (forced into slavery), and of Hispanic or Latino Americans (forced from power in the Southwest)—into U.S. society and relegation to subordinate status. Historically, interest in these groups by psychologists and counselors was stimulated by the human rights movement of the 1960s and 1970s and the resulting question of the usefulness of mental health services for these groups. For example, S. Sue and associates (Sue, Allen, & Conway, 1975; Sue & McKinney, 1975; Sue, McKinney, Allen, & Hall, 1974) found that these four groups underutilized traditional mental health services.

Two major theoretical assumptions underlie the cultural difference philosophy: cultural determinism and cultural hegemony. Cultural determinism, the belief that human behavior is simply a response to cultural stimuli (strong form), leads to the following cultural difference logic: (a) people belong to different cultural groups; (b) people, as members of different cultural groups, share the same culture; (c) therefore, the counseling interventions need to be appropriate to the specific culture. Cultural hegemony elaborates the cultural difference logic by specifying the nature of the "difference," namely, difference definitions are linked to the privileged culture of White males in the United States and the resulting oppression of other individuals who do not share this privileged culture.

Commentary

There are a number of problems and controversies that emerge from the strong form of the cultural difference logic. One general, unfortunate consequence has been the view of culture as an obstacle to overcome in counseling practice rather than an opportunity to enhance practice. A few clarifying examples may help. In the domain of statistics, this obstacle/opportunity question is related to earlier attempts by researchers to remove the "obstacle" of human difference by assigning these differences to the error term or using so-called homogenous male samples rather than including human differences as valued independent variables. In mental health services, the obstacle of cultural differences was removed by assuming one approach fits all, namely, traditional mental health models based on the majority culture. In order to view culture as an enhancement opportunity, not only do we have to move beyond denial (assigned to the meaninglessness of an error term) and hegemony (one form fits all), but we must address the new challenges that have arisen. The newer culture-as-obstacle challenges have emerged as reactions to the implementation of the cultural difference program. Guilt and political correctness (see Pedersen, 1991b) may appear to respond to cultural differences in a respectful way, but the underlying theme is to experience culture as a threat and to respond with self-preoccupation (guilt) or self-protection (orthodoxy of respect). Guilt often arises in White supervisees and supervisors as they become aware of the history of racism and its continued prevalence in a society dominated by White people. Guilt can also arise in minority supervisees and supervisors in response to the increasing needs of their respective minority communities (e.g., "I have some question about your brotherhood with Black people, given how preoccupied you are with making it in a White world."). Whatever the source, guilt is a normative response and can have motivating properties in dealing with cultural issues, but preoccupation with guilt deflects attention away from learning about culture, including one's own culture, to pursuing personal goals of salvation, absolution, and forgiveness. Political correctness is a complex response to cultural differences and multicultural training. On the one hand, sensitive supervisors have tried to create respectful learning environments by eliminating offensive language and behavior, raising the issues of racism and oppression, and working to meet the standards of accrediting organizations. On the other hand, extremism in the pursuit of an orthodoxy of respect, regardless of the good intentions of White or minority supervisors, has little virtue if it results in a new oppression through censorship of alternative points of view. Unfortunately, it is not always clear that political correctness of the dogmatic kind leads to open discussions of diversity issues. Here again we see the deflection away from the volatile issues of diversity and racism to a self-protective veneer of polite language from a "good person trying to do the right thing."

Specific consequences flow from the notions about cultural groups. If knowledge of individuals is determined by cultural group membership, then judgments about individuals are readily made on the basis of knowledge about a group. There is danger of overgeneralization and ethnic stereotyping when individuals are limited in their self-definition to external reference groups. Although many writers are aware of these stereotyping tendencies, our literature often speaks of stereotypes. For example, in response to a special issue on culture and counseling, reactants underscored the problems of ethnic stereotypes. In responding to a paper on White students' reactions to African American faculty (see Chambers, Lewis, & Kerezi, 1995), Lee (1995) states: "However, to leave the reader with the idea that all White students are inherently racists and that all African American faculty think, feel, and behave in radically different ways from their White counterparts is, to my way of thinking, dangerous scholarship" (p. 80). In response to another paper concerned with Hispanic immigrants, Arbona (1995) responds:

> Smart and Smart (1995) also suggest that Hispanics' preference for "closer familial and societal relationships" and their belief that "*la vida es dura*" may isolate them in their barrios and alienate them from "support from Anglo-dominated schools, work settings, health care, and other support agencies" (p. 32). In my view, this characterization of Hispanic cultural values and attitudes is also stereotypical and simplistic, because it totally disregards the impact that contextual factors, such as economic resources, level of education, and quality of available support services, may have in Hispanics' help-seeking behaviors. (p. 76)

These issues are related to a larger dilemma of an emic (particularistic) versus etic (universalistic) approach to education and training. Briefly, the emic approach is the one most closely associated with the cultural difference perspective, in which attention is focused on culture-specific education and training that is not universally applicable nor generalizable to members of other cultural groups. Etic approaches are generic yet culturally sensitive. They are based on the assumption that it is useful to develop counseling models and theories that reflect universal aspects of human life while considering cultural factors and avoiding cultural hegemony, stereotyping, and particularism (e.g., Sodowsky, Taffe, Gutkin, & Wise, 1994; Speight, Myers, Cox, & Highlen, 1991). Though most writers try to balance these approaches because the either/or resolution is unsatisfactory, the current resolutions give primary emphasis to an emic approach in order to rectify the effects of cultural hegemony.

Strong emic approaches to practice can lead to an unfortunate particularism. In crafting unique practices for more than 100 different ethnic groups, the approach tends to take on the negative consequences of a cookbook mentality in which food types are replaced by cultural stereotypes. Recipes easily become stereotyped practices (e.g., match counselor or client on preference—female counselor with female client) without careful evaluation. For example, Fowler and Wagner (1993) found evidence in which dissimilarity between counselor (male) and client (abused female) facilitated client change.

In summary, the strong cultural difference program is an externalistic approach, preoccupied with between-group differences and focused on a particularist approach to education, training, and supervision. The approach has promoted the awareness of the importance of cultural factors in counseling and supervision, resulting in consciousness raising about the effects of cultural hegemony in and the development of knowledge, practices, policies, and personnel that are more culturally sensitive. There are also some problems with a strong cultural differences orientation—defensive reactions and stereotyping—that are primarily a consequence of its strengths. The reliance on cultural group membership as an individual's definition helps identify culture as a potent context for understanding in counseling and supervision, but also has the effect of neglecting the individual.

Implications for Supervision

The cultural difference perspective has been translated into a massive literature on multicultural and cross-cultural training (e.g., Ridley, Mendoza, & Kanitz, 1994; Triandis, Brislin, & Hui, 1988), but few articles have been devoted to multicultural supervision (see review in Leong & Wagner, 1994). The fundamental assumption of multicultural training based on cultural differences is the development of a culturally sensitive (Ridley, Mendoza, Kanitz, Angermeier, & Zenk, 1994) and skilled counselor (Sue & Sue, 1990). But how does one translate all this information about cultural differences into appropriate supervisory practices fostering a culturally sensitive and skilled counselor? Without an adequate research base, we could look to other literatures for implications about supervision such as multicultural counseling (e.g., Coleman, Wampold, & Casali, 1995) and draw suggestive links between the impact of cultural factors in the counseling process to the process of supervision. Another approach is to emphasize experiential learning (see Abbey et al., 1985; Kolb, 1984). Begin with the concrete experience of multicultural supervision (see example below) and then reflect, conceptualize, and make some recommendations. My example is drawn from my experience as a clinical supervisor for an intern, a White woman (Mary).

Mary had come to the internship with a great deal of academic experience in women's studies. The writings of Carol Gilligan had been a major influence on her. During our supervision time, she would bring up issues about the supervision she was conducting with a practicum student. One day, she mentioned, "You know, we sure do supervise differently. I seem to be much more concerned about how the issue affects the relationship, and you, more concerned about solving the problem." I thought about that comment and talked about it a long time afterward in case conferences and group supervision with both male and female students from different cultural groups. Eventually, Mary completed a dissertation and an empirical article on the topic (Johnson & Stone, 1989) and studied with Carol Gilligan at Harvard.

This example illustrates a common experiential process for my growth and development in understanding cultural differences. As the example illustrates, the process begins with (a) a *learning set* (or the prior learning and capabilities needed to perform a task; Gagne & Paradise, 1961) fostered, in the example of Mary, by her prior experiences of women's studies and my reading in the area, and (b) *experience* through my exposure to a female supervisee. These experiences led to (c) *reflection* and analysis in individual and group supervision. Finally, the observations led to (d) *action,* including empirical inquiry. This process is similar to the experiential learning cycle (concrete experience-reflective observation-abstract conceptualization-active experimentation) developed by Kolb (1984) and extended to counseling and supervision by Abbey et al. (1985).

Based on this process, several recommendations can be made about multicultural supervision. The recommendations are related to each phase of the experiential learning process including learning set, experience, reflection, and action. The learning set recommendation is a basic assumption of all training programs committed to developing culturally sensitive and skilled counselors and psychologists. That is, valuing of and respect for cultural differences permeates the entire training program, including all courses and practica (see LaFromboise & Foster, 1992). Thus the clinical supervision component of the training program is not required to carry the full burden of multicultural training resulting in the placement of culturally unprepared students in an agency with culturally different clients and/or supervisors. Furthermore, supervisors are also part of the cultural competence education equation, necessitating the continuing education of supervisors about what it means to be a culturally competent practitioner. A basic assumption of multicultural supervision is that the student and the supervisor have had sufficient prior exposure to multicultural training so as to possess the capabilities to develop an effective supervisory environment through which the trainer and trainee can learn more about cultural factors in therapeutic practice. The learning set assumption is a set of prior and integrated multicultural educational experiences, providing the new supervisee with the set (capabilities) to learn. Many writers have discussed these integrated multicultural instructional and experiential components (e.g., Ridley, Mendoza, & Kanitz, 1994; Sabnani, Ponterotto, & Borodovsky, 1991) that provide a learning set for multicultural supervision.

The second phase of the process emphasizes concrete experience. Most of the research on multicultural supervision (see Stoltenberg, McNeill, & Crethar, 1994), including racial and ethnic minority trainees (Cook & Helms, 1988; Fukuyama, 1994; McRoy, Freeman, Logan, & Blackmon, 1986; Vander Kolk, 1974), have defined it as a supervisor-supervisee relationship in which cultural differences are examined through cross-cultural dyads. Of course, a good argument could be made that cultural factors affect counseling and supervision with culturally similar clients and supervisors and that a more inclusive approach would address these issues. For the trainee with an appropriate learning set, there is little substitute for exposure to diverse client populations and supervisors who have expertise in multicultural issues. Beyond simple placement and exposure, the process of supervision needs to focus systematically on multicultural issues. For example, in supervision, the viewing of a videotape of a counseling session with culturally different (or similar) clients should involve (as a matter of course) the exploration of cultural reactions and cognitions (see explanation of cultural schemata in Ridley, Mendoza, Kanitz, Angermeier, & Zenk, 1994) and interpretation of clinical impressions through alternative cultural worldviews (Ibrahim, 1991).

These systematic components of supervision dedicated to multicultural factors lead to the more reflective recommendations. As noted, the direct experience of cultural issues through exposure to diverse (or similar) client populations needs to be reflected upon in a systematic manner through individual supervision, but perhaps more important, systematic attention to these factors could benefit from group supervision activities. For example, structured interventions in group supervision could include case presentations to a panel of culturally diverse professionals, using a culturally diverse consultant for language or worldview expertise, and so forth. It seems imperative when more and more counseling or supervisory situations involve students from collectivist cultures that supervision not be limited to individualistic modes. More attention needs to be directed at enhancing group supervision (see Holloway & Johnson, 1985), including ensuring that the composition of the group is diverse, participants have an adequate learning set, leaders have expertise, and the process of group supervision is planned to provide an integrated and systematic focus on multicultural issues. Too often, if group supervision lacks experts and prepared students, or depends on whatever comes forward in case presentations and discussion, the result will be to avoid cultural factors.

The last phase is about action. After reflecting on cross-cultural experiences, it is time to take some type of action. The action can take many forms, from sharing with your peers about what your cross-cultural (or personal cultural) experiences were like, to more active projects involving social justice and giving something back to the community (e.g., assisting with various peer counseling programs for minority students on campus). Serious consideration should be given to structuring an action component for multicultural supervision that emphasizes research. Whether the research component is translated into traditional formats—dissertations, publications, and professional presentations—or into required thought-piece papers at the conclusion of supervision, it is imperative for solid cognitive work to be done in order to consolidate the experiential-based observations (see Coleman, in press). These consolidated works can provide the sorely needed beginnings of studies and databases for evaluating the ever-increasing models and theories about cultural differences and provide some information for application and policy changes for mental health work with culturally diverse clients.

Cultural
Affiliation Perspective

Definition

The cultural affiliation perspective represents a second wave of popular perspectives in the literature. One impetus for the development of the cultural affiliation conceptualization was as a possible explanation for the growing awareness of within-group differences and the mixed findings about race and preference for counselors (e.g., Helms, 1984). Whereas the cultural difference paradigm emphasized the anthropological interests of group membership and a shared culture, cultural affiliation perspectives are more psychologically oriented. The affiliation construct represents the degree to which the individual associates with his or her cultural group, the dominant culture, or both. There are at least three forms of cultural affiliation. One form, racial or ethnic identity (e.g., Helms, 1990, 1994), defines cultural affiliation in terms of racial or ethnic identity theory. (Of course, identity theory work is not restricted to racial and ethnic minorities, but includes identity models for women [Downing & Roush, 1985; Peck, 1986], gay men and lesbians [Gonsiorek & Rudolph, 1991; Troiden, 1989], and more general minority identity models [see Atkinson, Morten, & Sue, 1979].) A second form, acculturation (e.g., Berry, 1984; Padilla, 1980) is more concerned with the psychological and sociological aspects of the adaptation process of one group, for example Hispanic or Latino immigrants, to the rules and behaviors of another group, White Americans in the United States. A more idiographic form includes theoretical positions of subjective culture (Triandis, 1972), cultural schemata (Ridley, Mendoza, Kanitz, Angermeier, & Zenk, 1994), internalized culture (Ho, 1995), and worldviews (Ibrahim, 1991).

The racial and ethnic identity model literature is ever-changing and expanding at such a rate that describing it is like trying to describe a moving target through an album of past still photographs that captured the target for a moment, but no longer. For example, current racial identity models grew out of the civil rights and racial-group empowerment ("Black Power") movements, resulting in the stage-model of Black racial identity proposed by Cross (1971, 1978) and refined by Cross and associates (Cross, 1991; Cross, Parham, & Helms, 1991; Hall, Cross, & Freedle, 1972), and operationalized, researched, and elaborated by Helms and Parham (e.g., 1990a, 1990b; Parham, 1989; Parham & Helms, 1981). From these earlier works, Helms's stage-wise Black racial identity theory (Helms, 1990) has expanded into a racial identity model for all people of color (see Helms, 1994), a model of White racial development (Helms, 1984, 1990), a model of Black and White interaction (Helms, 1984), and transformed from a developmental stage process model to an evolutionary ego-identity status circumplex model (Helms & Piper, 1994). Given the many alternative models of racial identity, controversies (e.g., Rowe & Atkinson, 1995; Rowe, Bennett, & Atkinson, 1994; Thompson, 1994), and continued change and refinement of existing models, no attempt is made to cover all the nuances of the various models. For our purposes, a basic overview of the converging themes will suffice.

These themes involve a converging of attention on a common focus and process. The focus is on the psychological meaning of the experience of membership in an oppressed (or dominant) group. Typically, the process that captures these meanings is an evolutionary process, a progression of the growing awareness of the experience of oppression (or experience of benefiting from oppression) often characterized by stages, phases, types, or ego status. These "stages" involve distinct and measurable attitudes toward important reference groups, such as the self-identified group(s) of affiliation and the relevant dominant-nondominant group(s) with which the affiliation group is in contact. Progression for the member of an oppressed group, is often described in "stages" (see Helms, 1994) as movement from dependence on the dominant culture for self-definition and devaluation of one's own cultural group (conformity); through a period of confusion and ambivalence (dissonance); to an active rejection of the dominant culture, combined with an idealization of one's own cultural group (immersion/emersion). Following this resistance and immersion phase, development continues with a positive commitment to one's own group (internalization), and finally, one is able to integrate and accept one's own cultural values while being able to be an empathetic collaborator with members of other relevant dominant and nondominant groups (integrated awareness). For a member of the dominant group (benefits from the oppression; Helms, 1990), progression ("stage" in parentheses) ranges from unawareness of alternative cultural viewpoints (contact) to a multicultural perspective (autonomy). Beginning with a monocultural point of view (contact), a person from the dominant group encounters persons from different and nondominant groups, and through these encounters initiates a journey through a process of reevaluation and exploration (disintegration), idealization of dominant culture and denigration of nondominant groups (reintegration), intellectualized acceptance of the person's own group and awareness of others (pseudo-independence), introspective appraisal and working on a nonaggressive cultural identity (immersion/emersion), and finally, comes to an internalization of a multicultural perspective that values diversity (autonomy).

Of course, there are also a number of points on which culture-identity development models diverge, including number of reference groups (e.g., Atkinson et al., 1979), developmental nature of the progression (e.g., hierarchical and sequential stages [Helms, 1990] versus types [Rowe et al., 1994], and ego status [Helms, 1994]), and different conceptualizations of identity development (see Rowe et al., 1994).

Other writers use a different cultural affiliation framework to understand within-group differences. These writers focus on acculturation (see Berry, 1984; Padilla, 1980; Smart & Smart, 1995) as a process of psychological change as a consequence of exposure to a new culture. Historically, the psychological approach to acculturation emerged from a cultural level of analysis (e.g., cultural anthropology) that described changes in cultural groups as a result of their interaction (see Rogler, Cortes, & Malgady, 1991). Typically, there are three phases of acculturation described as contact, conflict, and adaption. Contact can occur through visitation of foreign students or immigrants to the United States, in which foreign students or immigrants leave behind a way of life that is familiar and adapt to another culture. Through contact can come conflict based on efforts to retain a strong connection to one's own cultural group while pursuing a positive adjustment to the more salient and dominant cultural group. The adaptation phase refers to the actions and experiences that are linked to acculturation, either as changes in preexisting cultural beliefs and practices or as acculturative stress experienced when acculturation tasks overwhelm one's ability to cope. Ways of adapting include assimilation, rejection, integration, and deculturation. Assimilation refers to a unidirectional process of moving away from the preexisting cultural identity and into the dominant cultural identity. Rejection points to the withdrawal from the larger host society. Integration suggests that it is possible to maintain cultural integrity within the larger society without losing one's membership in the culture of origin or becoming solely identified with the larger society. Deculturation refers to feelings of alienation and high levels of acculturative stress; persons have lost connection with both their culture of origin and their host culture. Similar modes of adaption have been described as outcomes of second culture acquisitions (see La-Fromboise, Coleman, & Gerton, 1993). In other words, an individual becomes assimilated, marginalized, bicultural/multicultural, or alienated.

A final cultural affiliation approach—distinguishing cultural differences within a particular cultural group—emphasizes an idiographic stance (see Allport, 1961). There are several variants of the idiographic approach. For example, the subjective culture construct is more focused on shared cognitive patterns and responses from members of a cultural group than on understanding individualized worldviews. Yet the fundamental focus of an idiographic stance is on the internalized psychological meanings individuals create in response to their cultural group memberships. Individuals are not merely understood as representatives of external cultural groups of which they are members nor are they understood by cultural-level constructs of internalized norms or cognitive maps. Rather, individuals are conceptualized as participating in aspects of many different cultural groups from which they gain information, organize it, and generate meaning from the information in unique ways. The emphasis on the individual is not necessarily a slide into solipsism, because we all learn about the world from normative information stimulated from our interactions occurring in particular cultural contexts. Many times normative and psychological information will be a good fit, but we respond and process such normative information through our personal framework of meanings generated from our participation in these cultural groups.

An example from my consultation experience at The University of Iowa during the multiple homicide tragedy (see Stone, 1993) emphasizes the importance of an idiographic understanding. In the aftermath of the shootings on campus, the University was concerned about the impact of the tragedy on international students, especially the Chinese student community because one of the victims and the shooter were Chinese. As the campus coordinator of psychological emergency services, I contacted the office that served international students and was directed to the liaisons for the various Chinese Student Associations. I contacted the individuals designated and offered psychological services and debriefing opportunities, but they politely declined, indicating that the Chinese community would prefer to deal with matters in their own community. I was taught to respect the strengths and wisdom of indigenous communities and wished them well. Later, as I was speaking to a class on crisis intervention, several Chinese students asked why

I did not keep asking the liaisons about services. After much discussion, it was pointed out to me how it is culturally appropriate (at least in this student's worldview) in the Chinese community to decline politely, and failure to recognize or to be culturally sensitive to this point may have excluded some of the Chinese students from beneficial services. A student finally said: "You know, we Chinese, are not the same." From this comment, I checked this particular student's interpretation out with a variety of Chinese students and faculty. What I found was an array of different responses. Some said, "That student in class is simply a very Westernized Chinese student. The Chinese way is to take care of their own in a foreign land." Others, concurring with the student in class, stated, "You should have been more direct"; while another Chinese student, overhearing this discussion, whispered to me: "Directness would not be polite."

In the above example, we have the classic example of political correctness gone wrong. While I was preoccupied with displaying an orthodoxy of respect (respect that no means "no" in terms of the decline of the liaison), I failed to recognize the continuum of differences within the Chinese community. One needs to assess the cultural understanding of the individual ("You know, we Chinese, are not the same"). In terms of the cultural affiliation model, the use of an acculturation (Suinn, Rickard-Figueroa, Lew, & Vigil, 1987) and/or worldview (individualism vs. collectivism; Triandis, 1989) perspective would have countered a stereotyping tendency. To rely on individual representatives (liaisons or individual students) of a heterogeneous cultural group for institutional decisions leads to misunderstandings and in some cases the lack of beneficial intervention.

Commentary

What to make of this rich yet confusing literature from the cultural affiliation perspective? As with the cultural difference perspective, there is no lack of controversy. The racial identity form of cultural affiliation has been taken to task about its terminology, conceptualization, and research support. Terms such as *race, ethnicity,* or *nationality* are often arbitrary. Race, a salient classification for many identity theories, lacks a consensual definition (see Yee, Fairchild, Weizman, & Wyatt, 1993) and does not reflect the tendency of individuals of different "races" to self-identify with many overlapping cultural groups (see Reynolds & Pope, 1991). In a recent study (Pope-Davis, Stone, & Nelson, 1996), we found that when graduate students of color were given an open-ended question, they used 53 different terms (e.g., ranging from Cape Verdean to Eurasian-Chinese-Jewish) to signify their cultural identification. Many racial identity theories do not capture the realities of bi- or multicultural identities (see LaFromboise et al., 1993; Poston, 1990). There is growing acknowledgment of the need to define racial factors (see Helms, 1994), and there is no disputing the fact that racial identity models ensure that the concept of race (skin color) has a sociopolitical history. In the United States that reality is one of subordination, racism, and oppression for people of color. It is not only an interesting human difference, but a difference associated with an oppressive power relationship.

Another term that has given fits to identity theorists is the conceptualization of identity progression. The word *developmental,* with its emphasis on hierarchical sequential stages, does not easily fit the descriptions of arrested development (Helms, 1984) or a movement back and forth between stages (Parham, 1989). Research (e.g., Bennett, Behrens, & Rowe, 1993; Swanson, Tokar, & Davis, 1994; Tokar & Swanson, 1991) has not been supportive of the stages in the White racial identity model (Helms, 1984; 1990). Recent work (e.g., Helms, 1994) has moved away from the restrictive developmental conceptualization.

An emerging controversy has to do with the framework one uses to think about the progression of the dominant cultural group (see Rowe & Atkinson, 1995; Rowe et al., 1994; Thompson, 1994). The critics question conceptualizing White Racial Identity Development (WRID) as primarily concerned with Whites' attitudes toward people of color with little attention to their own cultural group. This happens, according to the critics, because racial and ethnic identity theorists have used the oppressive minority identity development model as a common reference point. That is, whereas people of color develop attitudes toward their racial-group membership, Whites develop attitudes not about their racial group per se, but—given the use of the oppressive identity model—the focus is on developing attitudes about racial and ethnic groups. These critical writers have proposed another model, one adapted from Phinney's (1989) work on stages of ethnic identity. The debate is good and healthy because we need alternatives to investigate in controversial areas where feelings are strong, but the debate also casts cultural affiliation into Black-White terms without acknowledging the ambiguities of racial terms, the reality of multiple cultural identities, and the unfortunate consequences of a Black-White hegemony in multicultural education (e.g., Mio & Iwamasa, 1993).

The acculturation and idiographic approaches also have problems. Both approaches, although developed to account for within-group differences, can easily degenerate into simplicities. For instance, acculturation is often situation specific and multidimensional (see Keefe & Padilla, 1987; Padilla, 1980). Individuals may vary in the amount to which they are acculturated on various traits, or, the extent to which an individual shows evidence of trait acculturation will depend on the situation. In the previous example concerning Chinese students, it may be that acculturated students in a group of Chinese students will retain native traits ("polite rejection of request"), but in a class of White Americans will adopt characteristics of the host society (e.g., "Be more direct."). Moreover, acculturation theorists have tended to focus on the minority cultural group without due regard to the dominant cultural groups or host culture. Such a limited focus becomes a hegemony of the host culture, with the implicit view that the minority cultures have the problems and need fixing while the dominant culture becomes a silent partner in pathologizing the ways of the "other."

The idiographic approach (as many minority identity models and psychological acculturation concepts) does a good job of bringing within-group differences into focus, but these cultural affiliation modes of interpretation tend to concentrate on the individual at the expense of the reality of the interactional world. Since the cognitive renaissance in psychology, there has been a tendency to shift the emphasis from an interpersonal world (e.g., Kurt Lewin) to an intrapersonal perspective (e.g., the information processing perspective of cultural schemata; see Ridley, Mendoza, Kanitz, Angermeier, & Zenk, 1994). This shift may not bode well for psychological counseling and supervision, representing interpersonal processes. The idiographic shift has not gone unnoticed. Identity model and acculturation theorists have recognized the tendency to concentrate on only one participant, the minority person (see Berry, 1993; Helms, 1984). These writers encouraged researchers to focus on the interaction of "stage"-related attitudes (identity models) or ethnic minority and dominant cultural groups.

Implications for Supervision

Most of the work of translating the cultural affiliation perspective into supervision has used cross-cultural dyads and "developmental" models of supervision (see Holloway, 1987, 1992; Stoltenberg et al., 1994; Worthington, 1987) for understanding these dyadic interactions. The instantiation of a cultural affiliation approach for supervision can be seen in the early developmental work on multicultural training (Carney & Kahn, 1984), the Black and White interaction model of Helms (1984, 1990), and extensions to supervision by Cook (1994) and to family therapy by Gushue (1993), and cross-cultural supervision research (e.g., Cook & Helms, 1988; Fukuyama, 1994). Unfortunately, much of the writing has been about racial minorities as supervisees and Whites as supervisors, although more recent research points to reactions of White students to African American teachers (e.g., Chambers et al., 1995). Thus, one way of exploring the supervisory implications is to adopt an interactive perspective in which the dynamics of multicultural supervision can be examined. For example, in an extension of Helms's (1990) interactive model, she argues that the dynamics of social dyads (including supervision) can be understood as the interaction of racial identity "stages." These interactive "stages" can be parallel (supervisor/supervisee at similar stage), progressive (supervisor at least one stage ahead of supervisee), regressive (supervisee at least one stage ahead of supervisor), or crossed (supervisee and supervisor at affectively opposite stages). Given an understanding of the type of racial identity stage (status) match, supervisors and supervisees could discuss racial issues in terms of the racial identity model and likely predict the affective dynamics that would occur around such discussions. For instance, a progressive supervisory relationship may be well suited for the definition of supervision (mentor/mentee relationship), whereas a regressive one may shift responsibilities in a potential role-reversal phenomenon (mentee to mentor). Of course, lacking any data, it could be that the regressive relationship is more productive because it corrects the previous history of powerlessness of the mentee if the mentee is a racial minority and the supervisor is White. On the other hand, it may provide further exploitation if the minority supervisee is responsible for educating the supervisor about cultural issues.

As before, I will draw on the experiential learning model for supervisory implications. This example is based on my clinical supervisory responsibility for a female intern from Puerto Rico.

Norma, another intern, was also in supervision with me. In watching her videotapes I noticed how "lifeless" her responding was to many of her clients, but how energetic and responsive she was in communicating with some of her colleagues in Spanish. Since our agency had been offering psychological services in Spanish for more than 10 years, I had occasion to talk with my Hispanic/Latino colleagues about their different emotional tone when speaking in their second language as opposed to their mother tongue. From these conversations, I asked Norma to conduct some interview sessions in Spanish with Spanish-speaking clients and to be supervised by a bilingual supervisor. She shared one of those tapes with me and I observed an enhanced emotional intensity. As our supervision progressed, I asked her to switch to her mother tongue when describing some of her emotional reactions to her clients. Since I did not speak Spanish, I consulted these same bilingual colleagues for translations. I found her therapy and supervision to improve in emotional engagement and intensity under these conditions. Once again I reflected on these encounters and sat on a Committee of a doctoral student whose study concerned emotional intensity in a second language.

The experiential learning process with Norma began with a *learning set* fostered by her experience in second-language acquisition and my more indirect experience in an agency that had offered bilingual services for a number of years. The *concrete experience* was gained through exposure to a female intern from Puerto Rico, and was followed by *reflection* in individual and group supervision and *action* including empirical inquiry (e.g., dissertation).

The implications for supervision based on cultural affiliation (as opposed to cultural difference) are much more internally focused. As indicated earlier, the learning set implications direct our attention to the entire training context rather than to considering supervision as only an isolated component in developing cultural competence. But the cultural affiliation implications are not so much about course or book knowledge obtained from the training program prior to supervision, as the extent of personal knowledge emerging from personal exploration of one's own cultural identity and related values and biases. Unless the training program provides presupervisory activities (e.g., role-playing—Pedersen's, 1977, triad counselor training approach), consciousness-raising discussions about personal values and beliefs, and supervisors who are aware of cultural affiliation models and personally experienced in their own identity development, it is doubtful that supervisors and supervisees are prepared to engage in productive work in terms of supervisee cultural affiliation progression and cross-cultural client work.

As alluded to earlier, it is important to expose supervisees to the experience of being supervised by a culturally different supervisor (as well as a culturally similar supervisor). It is also time to expand (as much as possible) the supervisory experience from the traditional pairing of White supervisor and minority supervisee. These traditional pairings reinforce the past history of power inequality and foster mistrust (see Watkins, Terrell, Miller, & Terrell, 1989). If programs lack nondominant-culture supervisors, we need to move into the community and use these resources. It is vitally important that pairings involve people of color in supervisory roles with culturally nondominant and dominant supervisees. Through these pairings, identity models, acculturation theory, and/or idiographic perspectives can provide a useful focus for discussing cultural differences, personal attitudes, racism, and the contribution of these factors in client conceptualization and counselor-client interactions.

After the cultural experience and exploration of personal attitudes via cultural affiliation modes, it is time for reflection. Group supervision is an ideal process in which to analyze trainees' journals (see Lopez et al., 1989) about their cultural experience, and how each trainee attributes meaning to particular cultural phenomena. Group supervision provides a context for addressing dilemmas in culturally impacted counseling and/or supervision: "At what point did you judge race to be a factor? Why?" Is it possible to focus on the supervisory relationship or case management per se without addressing the sociopolitical experience of race within a Black-White supervision dyad? Whose responsibility is it to bring the race issue into focus? And what about "White" culture (whatever that term means)? How do we help "White" students (whatever that term means) or members of the dominant society talk about their culture when they say, "I have no culture, I'm from California."

Finally, and most critically, action in the form of research is desperately needed. So much theory, so little data. Speculation, experience, and advocacy are no replacement for careful experimentation. We need these trainee journals about cultural experiences as well as systematic evaluation of competing models of White racial identity development.

Summary

To end this chapter, the experiential learning model was applied again. I submitted this work (learning set) to a panel of my colleagues, some of whom were people of color, who had extensive multicultural experience. They read the chapter and provided feedback. The concrete experience of reading their feedback led to a summarization of reflections (reflection) and recommendations (actions).

A few of the panel comments include the following:

Boy, you are long on theory, short on application.

You know, a bit of arrogance flavors your writing . . . like, you are above the fray, shooting from the hip.

So, what do you recommend.

With colleagues like these, who share this kind of feedback, it is difficult to avoid multicultural issues (or to "deal with it" as stated earlier). But I agree, for the most part, with those comments. First, "the long on theory, short on applications" statement accurately reflects the content of the chapter because it is not highly prescriptive or technique oriented given the state of the art of multiculturalism as well as multicultural supervision. The second statement, "flavor of arrogance," is hard to digest, but partially emerges undoubtedly from my privileged status as a member of a dominant culture group (i.e., what others refer to as a White savior syndrome). I hope that is not the only explanation, because my intention was to wrestle with controversial issues, provide some critical reflection, and draw some implications for supervisory practice. Although the writing may have soapbox tendencies, the resolution of these controversies is not clear to me. What is clear to me (at least most of the time), is that these political and highly charged controversies need to be lifted from the darkness of the basement and exposed to the sunshine of hearty and healthy debate. Although the "arrogance" comment renews my understanding of the role of caution in advocacy, it does not deter me from pursuing critical inquiry. Too often, we have become uncritical cheerleaders or polite reactants—concerned more about guilt and reactions of others—than oppositional-type characters like former President Harry Truman ("show me").

The last comment moves me to reiterate recommendations from earlier sections for your reflection. The first recommendation, elaborated above in response to the "arrogance" comment, has to do with an attitude of discovery, exploration, and critical thinking, as opposed to political correctness, in approaching multicultural issues. The next four recommendations are related to the experiential model of learning phases used in this chapter—learning set, concrete experience, reflection, and action.

The preceding recommendations based on the experiential learning model made clear that supervision is only one component in multicultural training and cannot carry the full burden. Multicultural training and personal work must precede and follow supervision. Besides the concrete experience of being supervised within a cross-cultural or similar cultural dyad and challenged to address cultural issues, more emphasis needs to be put on the process of group supervision and action research. In closing, we have discovered that multiculturalism is a pervasive yet confusing reality for supervisors and supervisees. It is time we "deal with it"—study it, experience it, talk about it, and do something about it.

References

Abbey, D. S., Hunt, D. E., & Weiser, J. C. (1985). Variations on a theme by Kolb: A new perspective for understanding counseling and supervision. *The Counseling Psychologist, 13,* 477-501.

Allport, G. W. (1961). *Pattern and growth in personality.* New York: Holt, Rinehart & Winston.

American Psychological Association. (1986). *Accreditation handbook* (Rev. ed.). Washington, DC: APA Committee on Accreditation and Accreditation Office.

American Psychological Association, Office of Ethnic Minority Affairs. (1993). Guidelines for providers of psychological services to ethnic, linguistic, and culturally diverse populations. *American Psychologist, 48*(1), 45-48.

Arbona, C. (1995). Culture, ethnicity, and race: A reaction. *The Counseling Psychologist, 23,* 74-78.

Atkinson, D. R., Morten, G., & Sue, D. W. (1979). A minority identity development model. In D. R. Atkinson, G. Morten, & D. W. Sue (Eds.), *Counseling American minorities: A cross-cultural perspective* (4th ed.). Madison, WI: Brown & Benchmark.

Bennett, E. K., Behrens, J. T., & Rowe, W. (1993, August). *The White Racial Identity Scale: Validity and factor structure.* Paper presented at the meeting of the American Psychological Association, Toronto.

Berry, J. W. (1984). Psychological adaption of foreign students. In R. Samuda & A. Wolfgang (Eds.), *Intercultural counseling and assessment* (pp. 235-248). Toronto: Hogrefe.

Berry, J. W. (1993). Ethnic identity in plural societies. In M. E. Bernal & G. P. Knight (Eds.), *Ethnic identity: Formation and transformation among Hispanics and other minorities* (pp. 271-296). Albany: SUNY Press.

Carney, C. G., & Kahn, K. B. (1984). Building competencies for effective cross-cultural counseling: A developmental view. *The Counseling Psychologist, 12,* 111-119.

Chambers, R., Lewis, J., & Kerezi, P. (1995). African American faculty and White American students: Cross-cultural pedagogy in counselor preparation programs. *The Counseling Psychologist, 23,* 43-62.

Chapman, M. (Ed). (1993). *Social and biological aspects of ethnicity.* Oxford, UK: Oxford University Press.

Coleman, H.L.K. (in press). Portfolio assessment of multicultural counseling competency. *The Counseling Psychologist.*

Coleman, H.L.K., Wampold, B. E., & Casali, S. L. (1995). Ethnic minorities' ratings of ethnically similar and European counselors: A meta-analysis. *Journal of Counseling Psychology, 42,* 55-64.

Cook, D. A. (1994). Racial identity in supervision. *Counselor Education and Supervision, 34,* 132-141.

Cook, D. A., & Helms, J. E. (1988). Visible racial/ethnic group supervisees' satisfaction with cross-cultural supervision as predicted by relationship characteristics. *Journal of Counseling Psychology, 35,* 268-274.

Cross, W. E., Jr. (1971). The Negro-to-Black conversion experience. *Black World, 20,* 13-27.

Cross, W. E., Jr. (1978). The Thomas and Cross models of psychological nigrescence: A review. *Journal of Black Psychology, 5,* 13-31.

Cross, W. E., Jr. (1991). *Shades of Black: Diversity in African American identity.* Philadelphia: Temple University Press.

Cross, W. E., Jr., Parham, T. A., & Helms, J. E. (1991). The stages of Black identity development: Nigrescence models. In R. C. Jones (Ed.), *Black psychology* (pp. 319-338). Berkeley: University of California Press.

Downing, N. C., & Roush, K. L. (1985). From passive acceptance to active commitment: A model of feminist identity development for women. *The Counseling Psychologist, 13,* 695-709.

Essandoh, P. K. (1995). Counseling issues with African college students in U.S. colleges and universities. *The Counseling Psychologist, 23,* 348-360.

Fowler, W. E., & Wagner, W. C. (1993). Preference for and comfort with male versus female counselors among sexually abused girls in individual treatment. *Journal of Counseling Psychology, 40,* 65-72.

Fukuyama, M. (1994). Critical incidents in multicultural counseling supervision: A phenomenological approach to supervision research. *Counselor Education and Supervision, 34,* 142-151.

Gagne, R. M., & Paradise, N. E. (1961). Abilities and learning sets in knowledge acquisition. *Psychological Monographs, 75*(Whole No. 18).

Gonsiorek, J. C., & Rudolph, J. R. (1991). Homosexual identity: Coming out and other developmental events. In J. C. Gonsiorek & J. D. Weinrich (Eds.), *Homosexuality: Research implications for public policy* (pp. 161-176). Newbury Park, CA: Sage.

Gushue, G. V. (1993). Cultural identity development and family assessment: An interaction model. *The Counseling Psychologist, 21,* 487-513.

Hall, W. S., Cross, W. E., Jr., & Freedle, R. (1972). Stages in development of Black awareness: An exploratory investigation. In R. J. Jones (Ed.), *Black psychology.* New York: Harper & Row.

Helms, J. E. (1984). Toward a theoretical explanation of the effects of race on counseling: A Black and White model. *The Counseling Psychologist, 12,* 153-165.

Helms, J. E. (1990). *Black and White racial identity: Theory, research, and practice.* Westport, CT: Greenwood.

Helms, J. E. (1994). Racial identity and career assessment. *Journal of Career Assessment, 2,* 199-209.

Helms, J. E., & Parham, T. A. (1990a). The Black racial identity scale (Form RIAS-B). In J. E. Helms (Ed.), *Black and White racial identity: Theory, research, and practice* (pp. 245-247). Westport, CT: Greenwood.

Helms, J. E., & Parham, T. A. (1990b). The relationship between Black racial identity attitudes and cognitive attitudes and cognitive styles. In J. E. Helms (Ed.), *Black and White racial identity: Theory, research, and practice* (pp. 119-131). Westport, CT: Greenwood.

Helms, J. E., & Piper, R. E. (1994). Implications of racial identity theory for vocational psychology. *Journal of Vocational Behavior, 44,* 124-138.

Ho, D.Y.F. (1995). Internalized culture, culturocentrism, and transcendence. *The Counseling Psychologist, 23,* 4-24.

Holloway, E. L. (1987). Developmental models of supervision: Is it development. *Professional Psychology: Research and Practice, 18,* 209-216.

Holloway, E. L. (1992). Supervision: A way of teaching and learning. In S. D. Brown & R. W. Lent (Eds.), *Handbook of counseling psychology* (2nd ed.; pp. 177-214). New York: John Wiley.

Holloway, E. L., & Johnson, R. (1985). Group supervision widely practical and poorly understood. *Counselor Education and Supervision, 24,* 332-340.

Hood, A. B. (1993). A Fulbright counseling psychologist in a rebellious Soviet Republic. *The Counseling Psychologist, 21,* 635-642.

Ibrahim, F. A. (1991). Contribution of cultural worldview to generic counseling and development. *Journal of Counseling and Development, 70,* 13-19.

Johnson, M., & Stone, G. L. (1989). Logic and nurture: Gender differences in thinking about psychotherapy. *Professional Psychology: Research and Practice, 20,* 123-127.

Johnson, S. C. (1990). Toward clarifying culture, race, and ethnicity in the context of multicultural counseling. *Journal of Multicultural Counseling and Development, 18,* 41-50.

Keefe, S. E., & Padilla, A. M. (1987). *Chicano ethnicity.* Albuquerque: University of New Mexico Press.

Kolb, D. A. (1984). *Experiential learning.* Englewood Cliffs, NJ: Prentice Hall.

LaFromboise, T. D., & Foster, S. L. (1992). Cross-cultural training: Scientist-practitioner model and methods. *The Counseling Psychologist, 20,* 472-489.

LaFromboise, T., Coleman, H.L.K., & Gerton, J. (1993). Psychological impact of biculturalism: Evidence and theory. *Psychological Bulletin, 114,* 395-412.

Lee, C. C. (1995). Reflections of a multicultural road warrior: A response to Smart and Smart; Chambers, Lewis, and Kerizsi; and Ho. *The Counseling Psychologist, 23,* 79-81.

Leong, F.T.L. (1994). Cross-cultural supervision: Emergence of the cultural dimension: The roles and impact of culture on counseling and supervision [Special section]. *Counselor Education and Supervision, 34,* 114-116.

Leong, F.T.L., & Wagner, N. M. (1994). Cross-cultural counseling supervision: What do we know? What do we need to know? *Counselor Education and Supervision, 34,* 117-131.

Lopez, S. R., Grover, K. P., Holland, D., Johnson, M. J., Kain, C. D., Kanel, K., Mellins, C. A., & Rhyne, M. C. (1989). Development of culturally sensitive psychotherapists. *Professional Psychology: Research and Practice, 20,* 369-376.

McGoldrick, J., Pearce, J. K., & Giordano, J. (Eds.). (1982). *Ethnicity and family therapy.* New York: Guilford.

McRoy, R. G., Freeman, E. M., Logan, S. L., & Blackmon, B. (1986). Cross-cultural field supervision: Implications for social work education. *Journal of Social Work Education, 22,* 50-56.

McWhirter, J. J. (1988). Implications for the Fulbright Senior Scholar Program for Counseling Psychology. *The Counseling Psychologist, 16,* 307-310.

Mio, J. S., & Iwamasa, F. (1993). To do, or not to do: That is the question for White cross-cultural researchers. *The Counseling Psychologist, 21,* 197-212.

O'Neil, J. M. (1993). A counseling psychologist in Russia as a Fulbright scholar: "James in wonderland." *The Counseling Psychologist, 21,* 643-652.

Ogbu, J. V. (1983). Minority status and schooling in plural societies. *Cooperative Education Review, 27,* 168-190.

Padilla, A. M. (Ed.). (1980). *Acculturation: Theory, models, and some new findings* (pp. 47-84). Boulder, CO: Westview.

Parham, T. A. (1989). Cycles of psychological Nigrescence. *The Counseling Psychologist, 17,* 187-226.

Parham, T. A., & Helms, J. E. (1981). The influence of Black students' racial identity attitudes on preference of counselor's race. *Journal of Counseling Psychology, 28,* 250-257.

Peck, T. (1986). Women's self-definition in adulthood: From a different model. *Psychology of Women Quarterly, 10,* 274-284.

Pedersen, P. B. (1977). The triad model of cross-cultural counselor training. *Personnel and Guidance Journal, 56,* 94-100.

Pedersen, P. B. (1991a). Counseling international students. *The Counseling Psychologist, 19,* 10-58.

Pedersen, P. B. (1991b). Multiculturalism as a generic approach to counseling. *Journal of Counseling and Development, 20,* 6-12.

Phinney, J. S. (1989). Stages of ethnic identity development in minority group adolescents. *Journal of Early Adolescence, 9,* 34-49.

Pope-Davis, D. B., Stone, G. L., & Nelson, D. (1996). *Survey of minority graduate students in counseling psychology.* Manuscript submitted for publication.

Poston, W. C. (1990). The biracial identity development model: A needed addition. *Journal of Counseling and Development, 69,* 152-155.

Reynolds, A. C., & Pope, R. L. (1991). The complexities of diversity: Exploring multiple oppressions. *Journal of Counseling and Development, 70,* 174-180.

Ridley, C. R., Mendoza, D. W., & Kanitz, B. E. (1994). Multicultural training: Reexamination, operationalization, and integration. *The Counseling Psychologist, 22,* 227-289.

Ridley, C. R., Mendoza, D. W., Kanitz, B. E., Angermeier, L., & Zenk, R. (1994). Cultural sensitivity in multicultural counseling: A perceptual schema model. *Journal of Counseling Psychology, 41,* 125-136.

Rogler, L. H., Cortes, D. E., & Malgady, R. G. (1991). Acculturation and mental health status among Hispanics: Convergence and new directions for research. *American Psychologist, 46,* 585-597.

Rowe, W., & Atkinson, D. R. (1995). Misrepresentation and interpretation: Critical evaluation of White racial identity development models. *The Counseling Psychologist, 23,* 364-367.

Rowe, W., Bennett, S. K., & Atkinson, D. R. (1994). White racial identity models: A critique and alternative proposal. *The Counseling Psychologist, 22,* 129-146.

Sabnani, H. B., Ponterotto, J. G., & Borodovsky, L. G. (1991). White racial identity development and cross-cultural training: A stage model. *The Counseling Psychologist, 19,* 76-102.

Skovholt, T. M. (1988). Searching for reality. *The Counseling Psychologist, 16,* 282-287.

Smart, J. F., & Smart, D. W. (1995). Acculturative stress: The experience of the Hispanic immigrant. *The Counseling Psychologist, 23,* 25-42.

Sodowsky, G. R., Taffe, R. C. Gutkin, T. B., & Wise, S. L. (1994). A self-report measure of multicultural competencies. *Journal of Counseling Psychology, 41,* 137-148.

Speight, S. L., Myers, L. J., Cox, C. I., & Highlen, P. S. (1991). A redefinition of multicultural counseling. *Journal of Counseling and Development, 70,* 29-36.

Stadler, H. A. (1995). Learning from "the struggle": A U.S. counseling psychologist in South Africa. *The Counseling Psychologist, 23,* 315-323.

Stoltenberg, C. D., & Delworth, U. (1987). *Supervising counselor and therapists.* San Francisco: Jossey-Bass.

Stoltenberg, C. D., McNeill, B. W., & Crethar, H. C. (1994). Changes in supervision as counselors and therapists gain experience: A review. *Professional Psychology: Research and Practice, 25,* 416-449.

Stone, G. L. (1993). Psychological challenges and responses to a campus tragedy: The Iowa experience. *Journal of College Student Psychotherapy, 8,* 259-271.

Sue, D. W., & Sue, D. (1990). *Counseling the culturally different: Theory and practice* (2nd ed.). New York: John Wiley.

Sue, D. W., Arredondo, P., & McDavis, R. J. (1992). Multicultural competencies and standards: A call to the profession. *Journal of Counseling and Development, 70,* 477-486.

Sue, S., Allen, D., & Conway, L. (1975). The responsiveness and equality of mental health care to Chicanos and Native Americans. *American Journal of Community Psychology, 45,* 111-118.

Sue, S., & McKinney, H. (1975). Asian Americans in the community mental health care system. *American Journal of Orthopsychiatry, 45,* 111-118.

Sue, S., McKinney, H., Allen, D., & Hall, J. (1974). Delivery of community health services to Black and White clients. *Journal of Consulting Psychology, 42,* 794-801.

Suinn, R. M., Rickard-Figueroa, K., Lew, S., & Vigil, P. (1987). The Suinn-Lew Asian Self-Identity Acculturation Scale: An initial report. *Educational and Psychological Measurement, 7,* 401-407.

Swanson, J. L., Tokar, D. M., & Davis, L. E. (1994). Content and construct validity of the White Racial Identity Attitude Scale. *Journal of Vocational Behavior, 44,* 198-217.

Thompson, C. E. (1994). Helm's White racial identity development (WRID) theory: Another look. *The Counseling Psychologist, 22,* 645-649.

Tokar, D. M., & Swanson, J. L. (1991). An investigation of Helms (1984) model of White racial identity development. *Journal of Counseling Psychology, 38,* 296-301.

Triandis, H. C. (1972). *The analysis of subjective culture.* New York: John Wiley.

Triandis, H. C. (1989). The self and social behavior in differing cultural contexts. *Psychological Review, 96,* 506-520.

Triandis, H. C., Brislin, R. W., & Hui, H. C. (1988). Cross-cultural training across the individualism-collectivism divide. *International Journal of Intercultural Relations, 12,* 269-289.

Troiden, R. R. (1989). The formation of homosexual identities. *Journal of Homosexuality, 17,* 43-73.

Vander Kolk, C. (1974). The relationship of personality, values, and race to anticipation of the supervisory relationship. *Rehabilitation Counseling Bulletin, 18,* 41-46.

Watkins, C. E., Jr., Terrell, F., Miller, F. S., & Terrell, S. L. (1989). Cultural mistrust and its effects on expectational variables in Black client-White counselor relationships. *Journal of Counseling Psychology, 36,* 447-450.

Worthington, E. L., Jr. (1987). Changes in supervision as counselors and supervisors gain experience. *Professional Psychology: Research and Practice, 18,* 186-208.

Yee, A. H., Fairchild, H. H., Weizman, F., & Wyatt, G. E. (1993). Addressing psychology's problems with race. *American Psychologist, 48,* 1132-1140.

13

Multicultural Counseling Supervision

CENTRAL ISSUES, THEORETICAL CONSIDERATIONS, AND PRACTICAL STRATEGIES

Michael D'Andrea

Judy Daniels

The multicultural movement is having a tremendous impact on the counseling profession. The rising attention this area has received over the past decade has led Pedersen (1990) to refer accurately to multiculturalism as the "fourth force" in counseling and psychology. This "fourth force" is stimulating greater awareness of the importance of developing a broad range of multicultural counseling competencies when working with clients from diverse cultural, ethnic, and racial backgrounds.

Most of this attention has been aimed at understanding the cultural dimension of counseling; much less is known about what is commonly referred to as multicultural or cross-cultural supervision. Because it is readily agreed that counselor supervision is a critical part of the practitioner's ongoing professional development, this chapter has been designed to explore a number of important issues related to multicultural supervision.

AUTHORS' NOTE: Special thanks are extended to Dr. Thomas Parham, president of the Association of Black Psychologists, for his consultative assistance in preparing this chapter.

In examining these issues, we have directed particular attention to four questions that are central in a discussion about multicultural supervision:

1. What is multicultural counseling?
2. What is multicultural supervision?
3. What are some of the important issues and challenges that multicultural supervisors typically face in their work?
4. What strategies can supervisors implement to promote more effective multicultural supervision in the future?

By addressing these questions in the following sections of this chapter, it is hoped that the reader will gain a greater understanding of this newly developing area in the counseling profession.

What Is
Multicultural Counseling?

Multicultural counseling is both a professional movement and a distinct area of study and practice. As a professional "movement," multicultural counseling emerged in response to a combination of factors, including

1. the rapid cultural diversification of the United States;
2. a growing awareness that the traditional individual-remedial-intrapsychic counseling paradigm is not a particularly efficacious model to use to promote the psychological well-being of persons from diverse cultural, ethnic, and racial backgrounds; and
3. an increasing understanding of the need for practitioners to develop new ways of working with culturally diverse clients in the 21st century (Atkinson, Morten, & Sue, 1993; Sue & Sue, 1990).

Clearly, the rapidly changing demography of the United States is a key factor in the multicultural counseling movement's increasing influence and acceptance in the profession.

Upon examining the changing demography of this country, it has been predicted that by the year 2010 every major metropolitan area in the United States—with the exception of Milwaukee, Wisconsin—will be composed of a majority of persons who come from non-White, non-European backgrounds. It has been noted further that by 2020, the majority of persons living in the United States will come from what have ironically been referred to in the past as "minority group backgrounds." This "minority majority" will be primarily composed of persons who are currently classified as African Americans, Asian Americans, Latinos/Latinas, Native Americans, and individuals from diverse Pacific Island groups (U.S. Bureau of the Census, 1993).

Researchers have investigated the implications of this demographic transformation for the counseling profession. In this regard, it has consistently been noted that persons from non-White, non-European backgrounds tend to underutilize traditional counseling and psychotherapeutic services (Cheung & Snowden, 1990; Magoon, 1988; Sue, 1988). The underutilization of traditional psychotherapeutic services by persons from non-White, non-European backgrounds should not be particularly surprising when one considers that counseling and psychotherapy emerged from a predominately White, Western perspective and worldview.

As a result, the notion of going to a relative stranger (e.g., professional counselor) to discuss openly highly personal problems is a generally accepted method of receiving help for many persons from White European backgrounds in the United States. Yet this concept of "professional helping" is frequently viewed as an uncomfortable and unnatural way of getting personal assistance by many individuals from diverse cultural, ethnic, and racial backgrounds. These research findings suggest that if counselors are to have a greater impact on clients from diverse backgrounds, they will need to develop and implement counseling strategies that reflect greater cultural-specificity and responsivity.

It has also been reported that, when they do seek help from professional counselors and therapists, non-White individuals demonstrate unusually high premature dropout rates. In terms of these attrition rates, it was noted that one out of two non-White, non-European clients dropped out of counseling after the first session when they were matched with a White counselor/therapist. This sharply contrasted with the one out of five White clients who reportedly dropped out of counseling after the first session when they were matched with a White therapist/counselor (Sue, 1988; Sue & Sue, 1990).

Researchers have indicated that these three trends (i.e., the cultural transformation of the United States; the underutilization of traditional counseling services by culturally diverse client populations; and the high premature dropout rates among non-White, non-European persons) represent serious threats to the future viability of the counseling profession (Daniels & D'Andrea, in press).

The rapid diversification of the United States has also stimulated a great deal of theoretical and empirical work in multicultural counseling. By providing practitioners with an expanded knowledge base related to the work they do with persons from culturally diverse backgrounds, multiculturalism has emerged as a distinct area of study and a disciplined approach to counseling practice. This new area has gained increased professional legitimation with the recent publication of a set of 38 competencies that defines what it means to be a culturally competent counselor. These competencies have been operationalized and are listed in three main categories— multicultural awareness, knowledge, and skills (Arredondo et al., 1996; Sue, Arredondo, & McDavis, 1992).

The competencies have been specifically designed to clarify the types of multicultural awareness, knowledge, and skills counselors need to acquire to work effectively with persons from the five major racial-cultural groups in the United States (i.e., Africans/Blacks, Asians, Caucasians/Europeans, Hispanics/Latinos, and Native Americans/Indigenous peoples; Arredondo et al., 1996). These competencies have been formally endorsed by the Association for Multicultural Counseling and Development (AMCD) and represent the standards that practitioners are expected to uphold when providing counseling services in an ethical and professional manner to persons in diverse client populations.

What Is
Multicultural Supervision?

Multicultural supervision and *cross-cultural supervision* are relatively new terms in the profession. They are often used interchangeably to describe the process whereby counseling practitioners collaborate with other counseling experts in ways that enhance their overall understanding and effectiveness in working with culturally different clients. Because both terms stimulate a variety of images about the purpose and practice of supervision, it is important that supervisors and supervisees/counselors have a clear understanding of what they mean.

Leong and Wagner (1994) have taken time to outline the differences between these two terms. According to these researchers, "cross-cultural counseling supervision is defined as a supervisory relationship in which the supervisor and the supervisee are from different cultural groups (e.g., White supervisor-Black supervisee, Asian American supervisor-White supervisee, Black supervisor-Hispanic supervisee, and so forth)" (p. 118).

In contrast, multicultural supervision refers to those supervisory and/or counseling situations that are affected by multiple cultural factors. Some examples of multicultural supervision include but are not limited to the following situations:

1. A White supervisor provides clinical supervision with a White super-
   visee/counselor who is working with Asian, African American, Hispanic/
   Latino, or Native American clients.
2. A White supervisor is responsible for the clinical supervision of several
   counselors including a White supervisee, an African American supervisee,
   and an Asian American supervisee. Each of these supervisees/counselors
   serves a predominately White client population, although there is a small
   percentage of African American and Asian American clients who seek counseling services from the agency in which the supervisor and the super-
   visees/counselors are employed.

As these examples suggest, the "multi" dimension of "multicultural supervision" refers to those situations in which supervisors and supervisees are
involved in examining a variety of cultural/ethnic/racial issues pertinent
to effective counseling with clients from diverse backgrounds (Leong &
Wagner, 1994).

In light of the rapid cultural diversification of the United States, it is
suggested that the term *cross-cultural supervision* represents too narrow a
construct for the types of supervisory challenges professionals will be
presented with in the coming years. Given this nation's changing
demographics, supervisors will soon find it a rare occasion when only two
cultural factors (i.e., a White supervisor working with an African American
supervisee/counselor who provides counseling services to only African
American clients) are relevant concerns for the supervision process. Consequently, the term *multicultural supervision* is thought to reflect more accurately the complex challenges counselor supervisors and supervisees face
in their work.

The following section examines a number of important issues related to
multicultural supervision. By presenting these issues, it is hoped that supervisors and supervisees will gain a better understanding of the numerous
challenges that emerge when one addresses cultural considerations in the
supervisory process. In the final section of this chapter, a number of action
strategies for improving the current state of multicultural supervision are
discussed.

What Are the Central Issues and
Dynamics Associated With Multicultural Supervision?

Developing counseling competence should be viewed as an ongoing
process in which practitioners continually strive to build on the foundational

knowledge and skills they originally acquired in preservice training. Counselor supervision is an important aspect of the practitioner's ongoing professional development. As such, supervisors and supervisees need to be aware of the overall goals and purposes of supervision. Bradley (1989) presents three generic goals that are thought to be applicable to most counseling supervision situations. According to Bradley (1989), counselor supervision involves

1. providing an environment and experiences that facilitate the counselor's personal and professional development,
2. fostering the development of more effective counseling and consultation skills, and
3. increasing the overall accountability for the quality of professional counseling services clients receive.

Although multicultural supervision embraces these broad supervisory goals, it directs particular attention to the ways in which the supervisor's, supervisee's, and client's level of ethnic-racial identity development impacts both the counseling and the supervision processes.

Understanding Ethnic and Racial Identity Development Issues in Supervision

Counselors and psychologists are becoming increasingly aware of the ways in which a person's ethnic-racial identity development affects his or her overall psychological functioning. The terms *ethnic identity development* and *racial identity development* refer to the way individuals view themselves as cultural/ethnic/racial beings. From a psychological perspective, multicultural counselors and supervisors believe that these factors represent important considerations that need to be addressed in an open and explicit manner during supervision.

Researchers have directed much attention to various issues related to ethnic and racial identity development over the past 20 years. As a result, several theoretical frameworks have emerged that have tremendous relevance for the work counseling practitioners and supervisors do. This includes Cross's (1971, 1995) model of Black racial identity development, Kim's (1981) model of Asian-American identity development, the minority identity development (MID) model (Atkinson et al., 1993), and various White identity development models (Hardiman, 1982; Helms, 1995; Helms & Carter, 1990; Ponterotto & Pedersen, 1993).

In the past, counseling practitioners have utilized these developmental models for a better understanding of some of the unique psychological within-group differences that exist among clients from the same cultural, ethnic, and racial backgrounds. It is suggested, however, that the description of the "stages" and "statuses" that make up these theoretical models can also be used

1. to assess the supervisor's and supervisee's own level of ethnic-racial identity development, and
2. to gain insights into some of the challenges and dynamics that are likely to occur during supervision, in part, as a result of the complementary or conflicting nature of the supervisor's and supervisee's level of ethnic-racial identity development.

Being able to assess at which stage(s) of ethnic-racial identity development supervisors and supervisees are likely to be operating is a critical consideration in understanding the process of multicultural supervision. It is important, therefore, that supervisors and supervisees/counselors take the time to consider how their own ethnic-racial identity development and level of multicultural competence impacts their views of counseling and supervision. By reviewing the characteristics of the stages that make up the various ethnic and racial identity development models mentioned above, supervisors and supervisees can begin to assess their own level of functioning in these areas. A set of self-assessment strategies, which supervisors and supervisees may also find helpful for evaluating their own level of multicultural competence, is presented later in this chapter.

We have taken time here, however, to outline the characteristics associated with three stages of the minority identity development (MID) model (Atkinson et al., 1993) and three White Racial Identity Ego Stages/Statuses (Cook, 1994; Helms, 1995). This is done to provide the reader with a general idea of their descriptive value in the supervision process.

Minority Identity Development (MID): The Conformity, Resistance/Immersion, and Synergetic Stages

Persons from non-White minority groups who are operating at the *Conformity Stage* demonstrate an unequivocal preference for the values and norms of the dominant White-Western group in the United States. In contrast, they manifest negative and self-depreciating attitudes about their own ethnic-racial background as well as about persons from other non-White minority groups. Supervisors and supervisees operating at this stage are likely to prefer working with White professionals, because they consider minority counselors and supervisors to be generally less qualified and competent than their White counterparts.

At the *Resistance/Immersion Stage,* individuals are characterized by their strong positive feelings and pride in their cultural background. These positive characteristics are accompanied by a heightened sense of distrust and dislike for White Americans. In contrast to Conformity Stage persons, supervisors and supervisees at the Resistance/Immersion Stage are inclined to demonstrate a strong preference for working with members of their own group or another minority group. A generalized distrust of White persons represents a major challenge that White supervisors should be prepared to address when supervising persons at the Resistance/Immersion Stage.

Individuals who have developed to the *Synergistic Stage* are characterized by a sense of self-fulfillment in terms of their own cultural/ethnic/racial identity. They reflect a high level of regard for themselves and their cultural group. Unlike persons at the Resistance/Immersion Stage, however, Synergistic Stage individuals are "not characterized by a blanket acceptance of all values and norms of their minority group" (Ponterotto & Pedersen, 1993, p. 49).

These persons are also often noted to be socially active in their communities. This activism is rooted in a desire to eliminate various forms of oppression and discrimination that negatively affect persons in their cultural group as well as members of other oppressed minority groups in the United States.

When working with Synergistic Stage individuals, supervisors are encouraged to initiate discussions about the cultural dimension of counseling to learn from their supervisee's views of multiculturalism. Also, by acknowledging the positive interrelationship between counseling and social action (D'Andrea, 1995; Lewis & Lewis, 1989), supervisors are able explicitly to communicate their respect for the Synergistic Stage supervisee's commitment to this form of activism.

White Racial
Identity Stages/Statuses

At the *Contact Stage,* White persons do not consider race to be a distinguishing factor in a person's psychological development. Instead, individuals at this stage/status focus on the "common humanity" of all persons.

They tend to embrace the notion that there is only one important race—the human race. Supervisors and supervisees operating at the Contact Stage are not likely to analyze counseling dynamics from a cultural perspective. Some may even demonstrate resistance to the suggestion that cultural, ethnic, and racial issues are important factors that need to be addressed in the counseling process.

In contrast, persons operating at the *Pseudo-Independence Stage* have developed a broader understanding of the ways in which race, ethnicity, and culture affect one's psychological development. However, discussions about racial differences tend to occur only when they are interacting with persons of color. These discussions are often characterized by generalized (and sometimes inaccurate) assumptions about various racial groups. Supervisors and supervisees/counselors functioning at the Pseudo-Independence Stage recognize the cultural biases inherent to counseling theories but lack the knowledge of how to adapt traditional counseling approaches to better meet the unique needs and worldviews of culturally different clients (Cook, 1994).

Persons at the *Autonomy Stage/Status* are much more knowledgeable about the ways in which racial and cultural factors influence one's development. Supervisors and supervisees operating at this stage are frequently motivated to discuss the cultural biases that underlie many traditional counseling theories and techniques. They also effectively utilize their multicultural awareness and knowledge to develop and implement culturally responsive supervision and counseling strategies in their work (Cook, 1994).

Different Combinations, Interesting Challenges

It is instructive to consider some of the challenges that are likely to ensue when supervisors and supervisees/counselors who are operating at different stages of these developmental models are matched together in supervision. For instance, a non-White Conformity Stage supervisee is likely to find comfort in working with a Contact Stage supervisor, who generally ignores the racial and cultural dimensions in counseling and supervision. This same supervisee is likely to be frustrated, however, when Autonomy Stage supervisors insist on discussing racial and cultural issues within the context of supervision.

In contrast, supervisees functioning at the Resistance/Immersion Stage are likely to be very frustrated when matched with White supervisors operating from the Contact Stage. The Contact Stage supervisor's general cultural naïveté and lack of sensitivity to racial differences sharply conflict with the Immersion Stage supervisee's heightened interest and pride in ethnic-racial issues.

When persons at the Synergetic and Autonomy Stages are matched together, their expansive understanding and high level of respect for cultural diversity represent very different conditions under which supervision can be done. In this sort of supervisory situation, a great deal of mutual learning about multicultural counseling is likely to occur for both the supervisee and the supervisor.

The scenarios described above involve White supervisors who work with non-White supervisees/counselors. Although these sorts of supervisory dyads do exist, White supervisors usually work with White supervisees. Given the fact that the vast majority of practicing supervisors and supervisees/counselors in the United States come from White European backgrounds, it is disturbing to note that very little discussion has focused on the White supervisor's role in promoting the multicultural counseling competence of White supervisees. In attempting to stimulate discussion of this important issue, we describe some of the dynamics that might result when White supervisors and supervisees who are functioning at different stages of racial identity development are matched together in supervision.

For example, White supervisors who are functioning at the Contact Stage/Status may be put off by the Autonomy Stage supervisee's expressed interest in and questions about the cultural dimension of counseling. In contrast, because White supervisees functioning at the Pseudo-Independence Stage have developed an increased level of multicultural awareness and knowledge, they are often more receptive to learning about culturally specific counseling approaches from supervisors who are operating at the Autonomy Stage/Status.

Because the Autonomy Stage/Status is characterized by persons who have an expansive multicultural knowledge base, much in-depth learning about this topic can occur when the supervisor and supervisee are both functioning at this stage. When matched together in supervision, Autonomy Stage supervisors and supervisees can use their collective knowledge to analyze multicultural counseling dynamics in much more sophisticated terms than persons who are operating at the other stages of the White racial identity development models (Cross, 1995; Helms, 1995). Supervisory sessions that are composed of supervisors and supervisees who are both operating at the Autonomy Stage are encouraged to focus on two particular issues in supervision:

1. Assessing the environmental context: Particular time and energy should be directed toward analyzing how the client's environmental contexts (e.g., family, school, workplace) affect his or her psychological health and cultural well-being.

2. Empowerment counseling strategies: Supervisors and supervisees should work together to identify the types of counseling strategies that are likely to be most effective in terms of promoting clients' levels of personal empowerment and psychological well-being. McWhirter's (1994) "empowerment counseling" framework and Ivey's (1995) model of "personal liberation counseling" provide supervisors and supervisees with many practical ideas and strategies that are particularly relevant in these areas.

These scenarios have been presented to increase the reader's recognition of some of the ways in which ethnic-racial identity development theories might be utilized in multicultural supervision. Supervisors and supervisees are strongly encouraged to review these developmental models in more detail to gain a greater understanding of their potential use in counseling and supervision.

Stages of Multicultural Supervision: Focusing on the Supervisees' Level of Multicultural Counseling Competence

In reviewing the literature related to multicultural supervision, Leong and Wagner (1994) discussed several supervisory models that reflect similarities with the above-mentioned ethnic-racial identity development frameworks. This includes a description of Carney and Kahn's (1984) stages of multicultural counselor development. In this model, Carney and Kahn focus on various types of supervisee characteristics that are commonly manifested in multicultural supervision meetings and suggest ways that supervisors might effectively help increase the supervisee's level of multicultural counseling competence during these meetings.

At Stage 1 of Carney and Kahn's (1984) model, supervisees possess little knowledge about multicultural counseling. The supervisor's primary task at this stage is to encourage supervisees to explore ways that they themselves, as well as their clients, have been impacted by being a member of a particular cultural, ethnic, and racial group. Leong and Wagner (1994) stated that this sort of cultural awareness-building activity should be done within a highly structured and supportive supervisory environment.

Supervisees at Stage 2 demonstrate an increased awareness and knowledge about cultural, ethnic, and racial issues. However, they usually manifest a very limited understanding of the ways in which both the client's and the counselor's level of ethnic-racial identity development affect the counseling process. Supervisors would do well to help these supervisees (a) increase their familiarity with various ethnic-racial identity development theories, (b) help them begin to assess where their clients and they themselves are functioning according to these models, (c) initiate discussions about the types of dynamics that might ensue when the counselor and client are operating at different (or the same) stages of ethnic-racial identity development, and (d) foster supervisees' awareness and confidence in using culturally specific counseling interventions with their clients (Sue & Zane, 1987). This latter recommendation might be accomplished, in part, by having supervisors

1. give specific examples of the ways in which traditional counseling approaches can be modified to complement the values and worldviews of culturally-different clients, and
2. provide information about some of the indigenous helping methods that continue to be used by persons in various cultural, ethnic, and racial groups in the United States (Atkinson et al., 1993; Sue & Sue, 1990).

At Stage 3, supervisees exhibit conflicting emotions about working with culturally different clients. These feelings are commonly linked to a heightened sense of dissonance that is generated when

1. supervisees are genuinely interested in working in a more culturally-responsive, sensitive and respectful manner with their clients, but
2. feel trapped by the limits of their own professional training, which encourages the use of traditional counseling strategies and approaches that are culturally biased and often conflict with the values and worldviews of persons from diverse cultural backgrounds (Carter, 1991).

When working with Stage 3 supervisees, supervisors are encouraged to acknowledge their awareness of this dilemma and be supportive of the frustrations that supervisees may experience in attempting to resolve this dissonance. Support in this regard includes providing opportunities that facilitate the acquisition of new, culturally responsive counseling skills (Sue, 1988).

According to Carney and Kahn (1984), Stage 4 supervisees are in the process of developing a new professional identity as multicultural counselors. These supervisees/counselors are noted to exhibit a heightened aware-ness of their own ethnic-racial identity as well as an understanding their client's development in this area. Counselors at Stage 4 are much more knowledgeable about cultural issues and have developed a broader repertoire of multicultural counseling skills than supervisees at the preceding stages.

When working with Stage 4 counselors, supervisors should assist them in developing a more comprehensive understanding of the impact and inter-relationship among various contextual factors (e.g., the client's gender, cultural background, socioeconomic standing, etc.). Supervisors would do well to encourage Stage 4 supervisees to make their own decisions regarding the cultural appropriateness of their counseling approaches and to discuss their reasoning for making these decisions during supervision meetings.

Finally, in Stage 5, supervisees are noted to take a more activistic posture by using their knowledge of multiculturalism to advocate for the rights of persons from diverse ethnic-racial groups. This sort of advocacy can be effectively and productively done in a variety of settings in which culturally diverse clients normally develop (e.g., in family, school, employment, com-munity-agency settings). When working with these supervisees, Leong and Wagner (1994) recommended that "the supervisor now becomes more and more of a consultant than an educator. The supervisor's role is to guide supervisees' efforts toward areas where they can more effectively help create social change" (p. 125).

Carney and Kahn's (1984) model of counselor development provides an practical way of thinking about several important issues related to multicul-tural supervision. This model directs particular attention to

1. the supervisee's level of multicultural counseling competence,
2. the types of supervisory strategies and tasks that are likely to foster further development in this area, and
3. the various roles supervisors might play when supervising counselors who are operating at different stages of the model.

The issues raised in Carney and Kahn's framework overlap sugges-tions made by other multicultural supervision researchers and theorists in the past (Bernard & Goodyear, 1992; Fukuyama, 1994; Vasquez & McKinley, 1982). It is interesting to note that most of the work done in this area has largely focused on supervisor's role in promoting the supervisee's level of multicultural competence. Another important but often overlooked issue involves the supervisor's own level of multicultural supervision competence.

Considering the Supervisor's
Level of Multicultural Competence

Ideally, multicultural supervision should be conducted by persons who have developed a broad awareness and knowledge base in multicultural counseling. Unfortunately, this is usually not the case. Because the multicultural counseling movement is a relatively new force in the profession, few counselor supervisors have received formal training in this area. Thus, without any formal training in multicultural supervision, they are likely to have

1. the same level of multicultural competence as many of their White supervisees, and
2. less cultural awareness and knowledge than many non-White, culturally different supervisees/counselors whom they are expected to supervise.

Recently, a number of researchers have raised questions about the supervisor's lack of multicultural competence in the supervisory process (Brown & Landrum-Brown, 1995; Fukuyama, 1994; Priest, 1994). The following discussion examines some of the issues that are related to these questions. A set of action strategies designed to increase the supervisor's multicultural effectiveness is also presented.

This discussion is based on two assumptions about the current state of counselor supervision in general and multicultural supervision in particular. First, it is suggested that the majority of counselor supervisors in the United States is more advanced than their supervisees in terms of their generic understanding of the content and process of counseling. Second, it is strongly asserted that this assumption should not be made about supervisors' level of multicultural counseling or supervision.

Given the newness of multicultural supervision and the lack of training that supervisors have received in this area, it is understandable why many (if not most) counselor supervisors simply do not possess the competencies that are necessary for them to serve as informed and knowledgeable role models in multicultural supervision sessions. Paradoxically, one of the interesting contradictions in doing multicultural supervision at the present time is that many culturally diverse supervisees are likely to have a greater understanding of the cultural dimension of counseling than their supervisors.

This paradox is complicated by the fact that the process of supervision has traditionally been based on an inherent power differential between the supervisor and the supervisee. That is, in supervision, there is usually an explicit or implicit understanding that the supervisor's role includes acting as a expert consultant, supporter, and evaluator of supervisees who, in contrast, are considered to be less experienced and knowledgeable about counseling processes. Because this power differential continues to be perpetuated in the profession, many supervisors are likely to have difficulty making the adjustments necessary to work with supervisees who are as knowledgeable—perhaps even more knowledgeable—about multicultural counseling issues as themselves.

Recognizing that this power differential is also likely to undermine the supervisees' willingness to challenge their supervisor's thoughts about multicultural counseling issues, it is very important that supervisors take the initiative to

1. assess their own level of multicultural competence;
2. foster a collaborative relationship with those supervisees who share a similar level of multicultural competence; and
3. actively solicit information, suggestions, and advice from those culturally diverse supervisees whose level of multicultural awareness and knowledge exceeds their own.

Taking the initiative of fostering a more coequal, collegial relationship with supervisees who possess a greater understanding of multicultural counseling issues is a radical departure from the traditional notion of supervision. Traditionally, the overall effectiveness and value of counselor supervision has been implicitly linked to the supervisor's level of counseling competence and experience (Glatthorn, 1990). Thus when supervisors recognize the limits of their own multicultural competence and make an effort to consult with their supervisees to develop a better understanding of the ways in which cultural factors might impact counseling and supervision, they risk making themselves professionally vulnerable in the process.

This sort of professional vulnerability is rooted in one of the profession's myths about counselor supervision. Basically, this myth suggests that "competent" supervisors should be able to help foster their supervisees' professional development by effectively assessing and discussing all aspects of the work supervisees do with their clients. Unfortunately, some supervisors feel pressed to live up to this unrealistic expectation and, as a result, end up providing guidance and information about multicultural issues even when they have marginal experience or knowledge about this area of counseling.

What Action Strategies Can
Professionals Implement to Promote
the Effective Practice of Multicultural Supervision?

Counselor supervisors need to have specific ideas about the types of things they can do to overcome this sense of professional vulnerability and help improve the current state of multicultural supervision. A number of practical action strategies are listed below that supervisors may find helpful in addressing these needs. Several additional recommendations are made regarding the actions our national professional association, the Association for Counselor Education and Supervision (ACES), might take to promote the development of culturally competent supervisors in the future.

First, to increase their level of multicultural supervision competence, supervisors need to demonstrate a sincere willingness and a genuine commitment to developing the types of awareness, knowledge, and skills that are necessary to become more effective multicultural supervisors. This first step is an essential prerequisite for professionals to take in attempting to move beyond their present level of understanding of multicultural supervision.

Starting from this important commitment, counselor supervisors should take time to assess their own level of multicultural competence. The following set of questions can be used as a guideline in evaluating one's competency level in this area. These questions are specifically designed to help supervisors consider themselves in relation to the three areas of multicultural competence that were approved by the Association for Multicultural Counseling and Development (AMCD) (Arredondo, et al., 1996; Sue et al., 1992). The questions listed below have been developed to help supervisors direct particular attention to their own level of multicultural counseling awareness, knowledge, and skills. It is recommended that supervisors take time to answer all of the following questions in the order they are presented.

1. Using the models described earlier in this chapter as a guide, at what level of ethnic-racial identity development would I currently assess myself to be functioning?
2. How are the characteristics of this stage reflected in my current approach to multicultural supervision?
3. How would I rate my level of understanding of the following terms: *culture, ethnicity,* and *race?*
4. What is my understanding of the ways in which cultural, ethnic, and racial factors influence the counseling process?
5. How would I rate my understanding of the ways in which cultural, ethnic, and racial factors influence the supervision process?

6. How would I rate my knowledge of persons from diverse cultural, ethnic, and racial backgrounds?

7. What sort of formal training have I had that supports my knowledge and understanding of multicultural counseling and supervision?

8. What sort of other experiences have I had that support my knowledge and understanding of multicultural counseling and supervision?

9. How would I rate my ability to provide cultural-specific counseling services for clients from diverse backgrounds?

Supervisors are likely to gain new insights about their own level of multicultural supervision competence by taking time to complete this sort of self-assessment. By identifying their own multicultural strengthens and limitations in this way, counselor supervisors can more intentionally and productively implement the following action strategies.

1. Counselor supervisors should plan on attending workshops and presentations that are specifically designed to promote an understanding of multicultural counseling and supervision. Such presentations are increasingly available at state, regional, and national counseling association conferences and conventions.

Attending professional development workshops that address issues related to multicultural counseling and supervision is an excellent way to nurture one's development in these areas.

2. Supervisors should actively seek out and consult with the numerous "cultural ambassadors" who are available in everyone's local community. In talking about "cultural ambassadors," we are referring to those persons who are acknowledged role-models within their communities. This may include but certainly is not limited to consulting with religious leaders, political representatives, persons who have successfully developed economic endeavors that promote their group's cultural pride, and elderly persons who are viewed as respected leaders within their cultural communities.

Although these ambassadors possess a wealth of knowledge about their cultural community, counselors and supervisors have been slow to tap into this wisdom in ways that would increase their own level of multicultural competence.

3. When working directly with their supervisees, counselor supervisors should take time to clarify the strengths and limitations of their own counseling and supervision approaches. Typically, many supervisors have developed a broad range of generic counseling competencies but are often limited in terms of their knowledge and experience in counseling persons from diverse cultural backgrounds.

Supervisors are thought to be acting in an ethical manner when they let their supervisees know that, though they possess many supervisory strengths, they are also aware of their limitations when it comes to issues related to multicultural counseling. This is especially important to do when working with non-White supervisees who may have a greater level of understanding of cultural, ethnic, and racial issues than the supervisor. Supervisors should emphasize their interest and commitment to learn about multicultural issues from other persons and especially from their non-White and culturally diverse supervisees.

It is also important to point out that addressing multicultural issues in supervision will often necessitate an increased level of collaboration between the supervisor and supervisee. Consequently, they will need to work together as coequals in striving to attain a better understanding of the types of multicultural counseling strategies that will most effectively meet the needs of clients from diverse ethnic-racial backgrounds.

On a broader scale, it is suggested that professional counseling associations would do well to support those multicultural researchers and theorists who are directing time and energy toward increasing our understanding of this new area of supervision. Offering small research grants and other forms of fiscal support would help defray some of the costs associated with implementing new research initiatives in this area. The Association for Counselor Education and Supervision (ACES) is the most obvious professional counseling association that should take a leading role in addressing these recommendations.

It is further recommended that the leaders in ACES should convene a special ad hoc committee that would be responsible for developing a set of multicultural supervision competencies for the profession. These competencies should be designed to provide supervisors and supervisees with a clear idea of the goals and objectives of multicultural supervision. The existing list of multicultural counseling competencies, which has been approved by AMCD, would be a important resource to refer to when developing a set of multicultural supervision guidelines and standards in this regard.

Recognizing that very few supervisors received any sort of formal training in multicultural supervision in the past, it is important that ongoing professional development institutes be developed in this area. To initiate this sort of project, representatives from ACES and AMCD could work together to outline a set of regional training strategies that are specifically designed to promote a host of multicultural supervision competencies among the current and next generation of counselor supervisors. It has been stressed that this sort of regional training project is necessary to help combat the perpetuation of institutionalized counseling and supervision practices that are both eth-nocentric and unintentionally racist in nature (D'Andrea, 1995).

In conclusion, this chapter has attempted to address a number of questions related to the practice of multicultural supervision. Given the demographic transformation that is occurring in the United States, it is emphasized that supervisors and counselors will be increasingly pressed to provide culturally responsive services in a competent and sensitive manner in the future. It is suggested that the manner in which supervisors and counselors respond to this challenge will have a significant impact on their own effectiveness and the overall viability of the counseling profession in the 21st century.

References

Arredondo, P., Toporek, R., Brown, S. P., Jones, J., Locke, D. C., Sanchez, J., & Stadler, H. (1996). Operationalization of the multicultural counseling competencies. *Journal of Multicultural Counseling and Development, 24,* 42-78.

Atkinson, D. R., Morten, G., & Sue, D. W. (Eds.). (1993). *Counseling American minorities: A cross-cultural perspective* (4th ed.). Dubuque, IA: Brown & Benchmark.

Bernard, J. M., & Goodyear, R. K. (1992). *Fundamentals in clinical supervision.* Needham Heights, MA: Allyn & Bacon.

Bradley, L. J. (Ed.). (1989). *Counselor supervision: Principles, process, and practice* (2nd ed.). Muncie, IN: Accelerated Development.

Brown, M. T., & Landrum-Brown, J. (1995). Counselor supervision: Cross-cultural perspectives. In J. G. Ponterotto, J. M. Casas, L. A. Suzuki, & C. M. Alexander (Eds.), *Handbook of multicultural counseling* (pp. 263-286). Thousand Oaks, CA: Sage.

Carney, C. G., & Kahn, K. B. (1984). Building competencies for effective cross-cultural counseling: A developmental view. *The Counseling Psychologist, 12*(1), 111-119.

Carter, R. T. (1991). Cultural values: A review of empirical research and implications for counseling. *Journal of Counseling and Development, 70,* 164-173.

Cheung, F. K., & Snowden, L. R. (1990). Community mental health and ethnic minority populations. *Community Mental Health Journal, 26,* 277-291.

Cook, D. A. (1994). Racial identity in supervision. *Counselor Education and Supervision, 34*(2), 132-141.

Cross, W. E. (1971). The Negro-to-Black conversion experience: Toward a psychology of Black liberation. *Black World, 20,* 13-19.

Cross, W. E. (1995). The psychology of nigrescence: Revising the Cross model. In J. G. Ponterotto, J. M. Casas, L. A. Suzuki, & C. M. Alexander (Eds.), *Handbook of multicultural counseling* (pp. 93-122). Thousand Oaks, CA: Sage.

D'Andrea, M. (1995, April). *RESPECTFUL counseling: An integrative framework for diversity counseling.* Paper presented at the meeting of the American Counseling Association, Denver, CO.

Daniels, J., & D'Andrea, M. (in press). *Ameliorating ethnocentrism in the counseling profession.* Pacific Grove, CA: Brooks/Cole.

Fukuyama, M. A. (1994). Critical incidents in multicultural counseling supervision: A phenomenological approach to supervision research. *Counselor Education, 34*(2), 142-151.

Glatthorn, A. A. (1990). *Supervisory leadership: Instruction to instructional supervision.* Glenview, IL: Scott, Foresman.

Hardiman, R. (1982). *White identity development: A process oriented model for describing the racial consciousness of White Americans.* Unpublished doctoral dissertation, University of Massachusetts, Amherst.

Helms, J. E. (1995). An update of Helms' White and people of color racial identity models. In J. G. Ponterotto, J. M. Casas, L. A. Suzuki, & C. M. Alexander (Eds.), *Handbook of multicultural counseling* (pp. 181-198). Thousand Oaks, CA: Sage.

Helms, J. E., & Carter, R. T. (1990). Development of the White Racial Identity Inventory. In J. E. Helms (Ed.), *Black and White racial identity: Theory, research, and practice* (pp. 67-80). Westport, CT: Greenwood.

Ivey, A. E. (1995). Psychotherapy as liberation: Toward specific skills and strategies in multicultural counseling and therapy. In J. G. Ponterotto, J. M. Casas, L. A. Suzuki, & C. M. Alexander (Eds.), *Handbook of multicultural counseling* (pp. 53-72). Thousand Oaks, CA: Sage.

Kim, J. (1981). *Process of Asian-American identity development: A study of Japanese American women's perceptions of their struggle to achieve positive identities.* Unpublished doctoral dissertation, University of Massachusetts, Amherst.

Leong, F.T.L., & Wagner, D. A. (1994). Cross-cultural counseling supervision: What do we know? What do we need to know? *Counselor Education and Supervision, 34*(2), 117-131.

Lewis, J. A., & Lewis, M. D. (1989). *Community counseling.* Pacific Grove, CA: Brooks/Cole.

Magoon, T. M. (1988). *1987/88 college and university counseling center data bank.* College Park: University of Maryland Counseling Center.

McWhirter, E. H. (1994). *Counseling for empowerment.* Alexandria, VA: American Counseling Association.

Pedersen, P. B. (1990). The multicultural perspective as a fourth force in counseling. *Journal of Mental Health Counseling, 12,* 93-95.

Ponterotto, J. G., & Pedersen, P. B. (1993). *Preventing prejudice: A guide for counselors and educators.* Newbury Park, CA: Sage.

Priest, R. (1994). Minority supervisor and majority supervisee: Another perspective of clinical reality. *Counselor Education and Supervision, 34*(2), 152-158.

Sue, D. W., Arredondo, P., & McDavis, R. J. (1992). Multicultural counseling competencies and standards: A call to the profession. *Journal of Counseling and Development, 70,* 477-486.

Sue, D. W., & Sue, D. (1990). *Counseling the culturally different: Theory and practice* (2nd ed.). New York: John Wiley.

Sue, S. (1988). Psychotherapeutic services for ethnic minorities: Two decades of research findings. *American Psychologist, 43,* 301-308.

Sue, S., & Zane, N. (1987). The role of culture and cultural techniques in psychotherapy: A critique and reformulation. *American Psychologist, 42,* 37-45.

U.S. Bureau of the Census. (1993). *Statistical abstract of the United States.* Washington, DC: Government Printing Office.

Vasquez, M. J., & McKinley, D. L. (1982). Supervision: A conceptual model: Reactions and an extension. *The Community Psychologist, 10*(1), 59-63.

14

Facilitating Multicultural Competency in Counseling Supervision

OPERATIONALIZING A PRACTICAL FRAMEWORK

Madonna G. Constantine

The development and establishment of well-articulated (a) ethical guidelines for psychological practice with a range of culturally diverse clients (American Psychological Association, 1993); (b) multicultural competencies and standards for the counseling profession (Sue, Arredondo, & McDavis, 1992); (c) conceptual models of multicultural training (e.g., Ridley, Mendoza, & Kanitz, 1994); and (d) applied models of assessing multicultural counseling competency (e.g., Coleman, 1996) have made it possible for mental health professionals to consider and implement a wide range of traditional and nontraditional approaches in working with culturally diverse individuals. With respect to individual counseling supervision, there is a paucity of information that identifies and highlights salient issues and approaches in developing multicultural knowledge, awareness, and skills in a supervisory context.

Generally, little is known about the specific impact(s) of various cultural factors on individual supervision relationships (Cook & Helms, 1988). Much of the previous literature on multicultural counseling supervision has out-lined conceptual models (e.g., Morgan, 1984; Tyler, Brome, & Williams, 1991) and theories (e.g., Bernard & Goodyear, 1992) that lack empirical evidence for their assertions (Leong & Wagner, 1994). Most of the empirical research that does exist (e.g., Cook & Helms, 1988; Hilton, Russell, & Salmi, 1995; Vander Kolk, 1974) has historically emphasized only the variable of race or ethnicity when defining the existence of a multicultural supervision relationship (Leong & Wagner, 1994).

In the supervision literature, the terms *multicultural* and *cross-cultural* have often been used interchangeably to denote cultural differences (primari-ly racial or ethnic differences) between a supervisor and supervisee (Leong & Wagner, 1994). However, individual supervision pairings are typically multicultural in that there are many different types of cultural group mem-berships represented in these dyads (Bernard, 1994; Fukuyama, 1994). It is only in recent years that increasing attention has been paid to the potential impact of various cultural group memberships (e.g., race/ethnicity, sex/gender, sexual orientation, religious affiliation, physical ability, etc.) on both the presenting issues of clients and on the professional and personal ex-periences of supervisees.

One of the primary goals of counseling supervision is to facilitate the development of therapeutic competence in a supervisee (Loganbill, Hardy, & Delworth, 1982). The process through which such competence is achieved depends, for example, on the values, worldviews, beliefs, and actions of both the supervisor and the supervisee in the context of their relationship. In past years, much of what has constituted clinical supervision has consisted of counselor "skill building" and the identification and implementation of therapeutic techniques that were believed to be effective in alleviating client distress; multicultural diversity issues were virtually ignored or minimized. In supervision relationships, the goal of facilitating therapeutic competence in a supervisee will never be fully achieved if critical cultural issues with respect to clients, supervisees, and even supervisors are not acknowledged, discussed, and explored. Sadly, many applied and academic training programs continue to regard the development of multicultural awareness, knowledge, and skill with respect to both counseling and supervision as an optional endeavor.

Priest (1994) asserted that many current counseling supervisors were educated and trained prior to the development of multicultural training models; he also questioned how these supervisors might gain expertise related to multicultural issues in order to provide multiculturally competent counseling and supervision. Bernard (1994) discussed the need for more empirical verifications of multicultural supervision experiences or interactions. In an attempt to advance the knowledge and practice of multicultural supervision through empirically based research, I sought to ascertain information from predoctoral intern supervisees and their individual clinical supervisors about various issues related to their supervision relationship. More specifically, in the form of an exploratory study, I proposed to (a) identify the extent to which multicultural differences were present in their dyadic supervision relationship; (b) determine the degree to which intern supervisors had received formal academic training in multicultural counseling and, thus, were experienced in providing an appropriate level of supervision related to multicultural issues; (c) solicit perceptions from interns and their supervisors about the extent to which multicultural issues were discussed and addressed in their supervision relationships; and (d) identify ways that interns and their supervisors believed their supervision relationship could have been enhanced with regard to multicultural issues. It was my hope that this information would help me develop a practical framework that could be used to facilitate multicultural competency in supervision and even counseling relationships.

The Study's
Participants and Procedure

The potential respondents were predoctoral psychology interns (and their supervisors) at American Psychological Association (APA)-accredited internship sites in professional psychology with five or fewer internship slots. This procedure was implemented in order to reduce the likelihood that a supervisor would serve as an individual supervisor to more than one intern at a particular site and, thus, rate the supervisee with whom the supervisor felt most comfortable or successful in providing multicultural supervision. Within this restricted target population, 22 internship training programs were randomly selected for participation in the study.

Internship training directors at the chosen sites were sent survey packets and asked to distribute a packet to each of their interns and the corresponding individual clinical supervisor. The packets were mailed to internship sites after a seemingly appropriate length of time to establish a supervision relationship (i.e., 3-6 months after the start of the internship, depending on the site). Each packet was coded by supervisory pairing and included a cover letter explaining the purposes of the study, a postage-paid return envelope, and a two-page questionnaire. The questionnaire consisted of a demographic section and a series of open-ended questions related to the respondents' experiences in providing counseling to specific cultural populations and their experiences in their current counseling supervision relationship.

A total of 170 surveys (85 pairs) were mailed to internship sites, and two internship sites returned a total of 8 surveys unopened. Out of the possible remaining 162 surveys, 93 (52 from interns and 41 from supervisors) were completed and returned, resulting in a response rate of 57.4%. Out of the completed surveys that were returned, 60 questionnaires were matched intern and supervisor pairings. These 30 pairs were included in the present study. The remaining unmatched surveys were not included in the data analyses. No follow-up phone calls or mailings were conducted.

Study participants represented a variety of job/internship settings. Twelve respondents (40.0%) worked in a hospital, eight (26.7%) in a university counseling center, four (13.3%) in a community mental health center, four (13.3%) in a medical school, and two (6.7%) in a correctional facility.

Results of the Study

Demographic Characteristics of Respondents

The frequencies and percentages of the demographic characteristics of interns and supervisors by sex, race/ethnicity, religious affiliation, sexual orientation, marital status, and physical disability are listed in Table 14.1 (the percentages for some demographic categories may not total 100% due to missing data). In a comparison of each intern-supervisor dyad, it was noted that all 30 of the supervisory pairs were composed of individuals who were culturally dissimilar on at least two of the demographic variables included in Table 14.1. The mean age of supervisors was nearly 47 years, and the interns' mean age was 34 years. Supervisors reported an average of almost 16 years of counseling experience, whereas the supervisees' reported average was 6 years of counseling experience.

Training and Experience in
Counseling Diverse Populations

Participants were asked to provide information about their level of training with regard to multicultural issues. Nine interns (30.0%) and 21 supervisors (70.0%) stated that they had never completed a multicultural or cross-cultural counseling course; 11 interns (36.7%) and 4 supervisors (13.3%) reported that they had completed one such course; and 10 interns (33.3%) and 5 supervisors (16.7%) stated that they had completed two or more multicultural or cross-cultural counseling courses.

Table 14.1 Demographic Characteristics

SEX	Supervisors		Supervisees	
Male	10	(33.3%)	12	(40.0%)
Female	18	(60.0%)	17	(56.7%)
RACE	**Supervisors**		**Supervisees**	
White	27	(90.0%)	21	(70.0%)
Black	2	(6.7%)	0	
Asian-American	0		2	(6.7%)
Hispanic	1	(3.3%)	1	(3.3%)
Native American	0		1	(3.3%)
Other/Biracial	0		5	(16.7%)
RELIGIOUS AFFILIATION	**Supervisors**		**Supervisees**	
Catholic	2	(6.7%)	6	(20.0%)
Protestant	4	(13.3%)	1	(3.3%)
Jewish	5	(16.7%)	1	(3.3%)
Unitarian	3	(10.0%)	1	(3.3%)
Quaker	3	(10.0%)	0	
Baptist	0		1	(3.3%)
Agnostic	1	(3.3%)	2	(6.7%)
Other	5	(16.7%)	11	(36.7%)
SEXUAL ORIENTATION	**Supervisors**		**Supervisees**	
Heterosexual	25	(83.3%)	25	(83.3%)
Lesbian	4	(13.3%)	0	
Gay Male	0		1	(3.3%)
Bisexual	1	(3.3%)	4	(13.3%)
MARITAL STATUS	**Supervisors**		**Supervisees**	
Single	6	(20.0%)	5	(16.7%)
Married	17	(56.7%)	18	(60.0%)
Cohabitant	1	(3.3%)	4	(13.3%)
Divorced	3	(10.0%)	2	(6.7%)
Widowed	1	(3.3%)	1	(3.3%)
Other	2	(6.7%)	0	
PHYSICAL DISABILITY	**Supervisors**		**Supervisees**	
No	30	(100.0%)	29	(96.7%)
Yes	0		1	(3.3%)

NOTE: The percentages for some demographic categories may not total 100% due to missing data.

Respondents were also asked to indicate, over the course of their counseling career, the average percentage of clients on their caseload who tended to be culturally different from them with respect to sex, racial/ethnic group membership, and sexual orientation. Both supervisors and supervisees reported that an average of nearly 41% of their clients at any given time were likely to represent the opposite sex. Supervisors indicated that an average of 9% of their clients tended to be racially or ethnically different from them, whereas supervisees reported an average of nearly 12%. Supervisors also reported that approximately 10% of their clients tended to be gay, lesbian, or bisexual clients, while supervisees reported an average of about 12%. In addition, when asked to estimate the total number of persons with physical disabilities they have seen in counseling over the course of their career, supervisors indicated a mean of nearly 20 clients and interns reported an average of about 7 clients.

The Supervision Relationship

Respondents were asked to indicate the mean number of hours they had spent in supervision thus far with their current individual supervisor or intern. Interns reported an average of about 26 hours and supervisors reported an average of 32 hours. Participants were also asked to state the percentage of their current supervision time spent discussing or exploring multicultural issues. Supervisors reported spending about 15% of their supervision time addressing such issues, and interns reported an average of nearly 14%.

Supervisors were asked to respond to two open-ended questions about their relationship with their supervisee. For these open-ended items, some respondents did not provide answers while others gave one or more responses. In the first question, supervisors were asked to indicate the ways their supervision relationship could be enhanced in general. Their answers, including the number of supervisors who gave the particular response, were as follows: more time with intern supervisee ($n = 5$); more self-disclosure on the part of the intern ($n = 4$); more processing of the supervision relationship ($n = 4$); relationship is fine/needs no improvement ($n = 4$); more audio- or videotapes by intern ($n = 3$); intern could have more grounding in psychodynamic theory ($n = 3$); match supervisor and intern by theoretical orientation ($n = 3$); and intern and supervisor could spend less time on administrative issues ($n = 2$). Interns, in response to the same questions, reported more time with supervisor ($n = 6$); supervisor could offer more feedback ($n = 6$); more processing of the supervision relationship ($n = 5$); match supervisor and intern by theoretical orientation ($n = 3$); relationship is fine/needs no improvement ($n = 3$); supervisor could be more accepting of intern's abilities ($n = 2$); supervisor could spend less time discussing his or her personal issues ($n = 2$); and supervisor could increase level of intern accountability ($n = 1$).

Respondents were also asked to indicate the ways their supervision relationship could have been more enhanced, specifically with regard to multicultural (MC) issues. Supervisors provided the following responses: more ethnic minority clients for intern ($n = 6$); more processing of supervisor's and intern's racial differences ($n = 4$); MC focus not necessary/don't care much about MC issues ($n = 4$); more exploration of intern's ethnic background ($n = 3$); intern could bring up MC issues more ($n = 3$); more readings in MC area for both supervisor and intern ($n = 2$); never thought about MC issues before ($n = 2$); and relationship is fine/needs no improvement ($n = 2$). Interns, in providing responses to the same questions, noted the following: supervisor seemed reluctant to bring up and discuss MC issues ($n = 12$); more processing of supervisors' and interns' cultural differences ($n = 4$); more discussion of racial and ethnic minority perspectives ($n = 4$); have more ethnic minority clients ($n = 3$); have a supervisor of a different race ($n = 3$); no ethnic minority clients thus far in my internship, so multiculturalism is not an issue ($n = 2$); and relationship is fine/needs no improvement ($n = 1$).

Discussion of the Study's Results

The results of this exploratory study identified several salient issues related to multicultural issues in supervision relationships. First, each of the relationships between supervisors and supervisees was found to be multicultural in that respondents were culturally different on at least two demographic dimensions. Pedersen (1991) states that every encounter between a counselor and a client represents a multicultural interaction when differences exist. It is important that a broad range of cultural variables (not solely race/ethnicity) be identified in acknowledging the presence of a multicultural supervision relationship. Failure to discuss or explore the potential plethora of important demographic variables that may be present in supervision relationships may adversely affect the quality, content, process, and outcome of such relationships.

Seventy percent of the supervisors in this study had not completed a formal multicultural or cross-cultural counseling course, whereas 70% of the intern supervisees reported that they had completed at least one such course. Midgette and Meggert (1991) questioned the degree to which counseling supervisors were familiar with multicultural issues with regard to counseling their own clients. Bernard (1992) asserted that it would not be illogical to expect that supervisors might experience difficulty in providing competent multicultural supervision if they have not taken coursework in either multicultural counseling or supervision. If supervisors are not appropriately trained to work with a range of cultural populations their professional effectiveness may be greatly diminished, and this phenomenon may result in inadvertent harm to both supervisees and clients. Priest (1994) highlighted the need for counseling supervisors to educate themselves in the areas of multicultural counseling and supervision through coursework, practical experiences, research activities, and memberships in professional organizations, so that they may develop sensitivity and competency in working with a variety of culturally diverse populations. Such recommendations may serve as critical means in helping supervisors to secure appropriate levels of competence with regard to multicultural issues.

Supervisors and interns reported having spent an average of nearly 15% of their current supervision time addressing or discussing multicultural issues, and some respondents reported that their supervision relationship could have been more enhanced if they had spent more time processing their relationship with regard to their cultural differences. Several supervisees, however, reported that they felt their supervisors seemed reluctant to bring up issues of multicultural diversity in the context of their relationship. Helms (1994) pointed out that significant, provocative constructs like race and ethnicity are frequently ignored or minimized by individuals who may feel uncomfortable or ill-equipped to deal with racial or ethnic differences in the context of counseling or supervision relationships. Cook (1994) asserted that although either member of a supervisory dyad may introduce a discussion of cultural differences, a supervisor's response to such discussion is pivotal in determining the extent to which these issues will be processed in their relationship. It seems important to note that because of the power dynamics inherent in supervision relationships, it should be a supervisor's responsibility to serve as the catalyst in facilitating discussions of multicultural issues with a supervisee (Priest, 1994). It is possible that some supervisors' reluctance to explore such issues in the context of their supervision relationships may be related to their lack of formal training in dealing with a myriad of diverse populations.

Relatedly, some supervisors in this exploratory study indicated that they did not feel multicultural issues were important; some others asserted that they had not thought much about issues of multicultural diversity. Serious questions are thus raised with respect to how supervisors might be educated to deal with issues of multicultural diversity if they are unable (or unwilling) to see the importance of such issues in their lives and in the lives of their supervisees and clients. Cook (1994) discussed the possibility of a parallel process occurring between a client and therapist in a counseling session and between a supervisee and supervisor in supervision with regard to a lack of acknowledgment of racial differences in the context of these relationships. She further asserted that if supervisors do not feel that multicultural diversity issues are important to discuss in supervision relationships, supervisees may discern that it is not safe or appropriate to raise such issues in supervision or in their therapy relationships. This unwillingness to process and explore such vital issues may contribute to miscommunication, "hidden" agendas, and feelings of disconnection and resentment in the supervision relationship, the sum total of which may ultimately result in clients being underserved.

Based on the findings of this exploratory study, I offer a few recommendations with regard to supervision and counseling relationships. First, supervisors must find ways to augment their levels of sensitivity and competence in working with multicultural populations, particularly with supervisees and clients. Bernard (1994) asserts that supervisors should, at the very minimum, be as multiculturally competent as their supervisees. Professional development opportunities through peer supervision, workshops, conferences, and reading materials may be reasonable avenues for supervisors to pursue in order to expand their awareness, sensitivity, and competence in working with a wide range of cultural groups.

Second, graduate programs in applied psychology must take the initiative in evaluating their own successes, or lack thereof, in integrating multicultural counseling concepts into all aspects of their curricula, training, and supervision. Obtaining feedback from current students and recent graduates about their perceptions of their programs' efforts to facilitate multicultural competence might provide useful information to these programs about ways to improve their ability to provide multicultural training in didactic and applied curricula. In addition, data from clients about a therapist's effectiveness as it relates to multicultural sensitivity and competency in the context of the counseling relationship might provide useful information about whether or not a therapist, and possibly his or her supervisor, demonstrates true multicultural competence.

Third, empirical research that examines the intersection of various demographic variables (e.g., race/ethnicity, sex, socioeconomic status, etc.) on supervision relationships is critical. Research that focuses on the impact of such variables in supervision relationships would provide valuable data-based information about the ways that cultural dimensions may interact in their relationships.

Despite some limitations of this exploratory study (e.g., response bias, limited generalizability of findings), the results led to the development of a practical framework for increasing supervisors' and supervisees' competency in addressing multicultural issues in the context of their supervision relationships. In the next section of this chapter, I will discuss the framework and will present a case example that illustrates the use of this framework in a supervision relationship.

Facilitating Multicultural Competency in Supervision Relationships: Operationalizing a Practical Framework

Although the importance of acknowledging a range of demographic variables or identities in supervision (and even counseling) relationships has been established, it is often the case that many individuals are reluctant to explore issues of multicultural diversity in such relationships. In particular, the study's results, which were presented in the previous section of this chapter, revealed that some supervisees perceived their supervisors as reticent to bring up issues of multicultural diversity in the context of their relationship. Perhaps this phenomenon exists because of some supervisors' discomfort with these issues or because some supervisors believe that multicultural diversity issues are unimportant. Some supervisors may even question the extent to which the raising of such issues in supervision reflects their "own issues and needs" versus the issues and needs of their supervisees. An additional issue for some supervisors may be their concern that "calling attention" to cultural differences in the supervision relationship may feel "disrespectful," particularly if the supervisee is a visible ethnic/racial group member.

To facilitate the active discussion of salient cultural issues in the supervision relationship, the framework proposed here involves the use of semi-structured questions that aid participants in (a) identifying their cultural group identities and (b) acknowledging the extent to which these identities influence their interactions in both supervision and counseling relationships. Ideally, the framework should be introduced fairly early in the supervision relationship because it may be quite effective in establishing rapport between supervisors and supervisees, and in highlighting the importance of attending to multicultural issues in supervision relationships. In developing this framework, it was my hope that its use would not only increase supervisors' and supervisees' awareness and discussion of their own cultural differences, but would also have an impact on both supervisors' and supervisees' clients by increasing these counselors' knowledge of and skill in working with diverse clients.

In using the framework in supervision, supervisors and supervisees discuss and explore their responses to a series of questions related to their individual cultural identities. These questions are as follows:

1a. What are the main demographic variables (e.g., race/ethnicity, gender, sexual orientation, age, socioeconomic status, etc.) that make up my cultural identities?

1b. What worldviews (e.g., assumptions, biases, values, etc.) do I bring to the supervision relationship based on these cultural identities?

2a. What value systems, based on my demographic identities, are inherent in my approach to supervision?

2b. What value systems, based on my demographic identities, underlie the strategies and techniques I use in supervision?

3a. What knowledge do I possess about the worldviews of supervisors/supervisees who have different cultural identities from me?

3b. What skills do I possess for working with supervisors/supervisees who have different cultural identities from me?

4a. What are some of my struggles and challenges in working with supervisors/supervisees who are culturally different from me?

4b. How do I address or resolve these issues?

5. In what ways would I like to improve my abilities in working with culturally diverse supervisors/supervisees?

Although the framework was initially developed for use in the early stages of the supervision relationship, it can also be used on an ongoing basis to help supervisors and supervisees continue their discussion of multicultural differences. For example, with some minor modifications the framework can be successfully integrated into a case conceptualization format by supervisees as they discuss their clients' presenting concerns in supervision. The framework could allow supervisees (a) to identify and understand relevant cultural, contextual information (e.g., race/ethnicity, sex, social class, worldviews, etc.) related to their clients' presenting issues; and (b) to understand how their own and their clients' demographic identities may interact to potentially affect counseling goals, process, and outcomes. Additional questions and issues related to multicultural diversity issues may be incorporated into the framework by either supervisors or supervisees, depending on the goals of the supervision relationship.

The following case example illustrates the use of the framework in a counseling supervision situation.

Lisa (a pseudonym) is a 38-year-old, married, White, female second-year doctoral student who was a practicum student at a university counseling center. She was being supervised at her clinical placement by a 36-year-old, single, African American female staff psychologist.

The first two supervision meetings between Lisa and her supervisor were spent establishing rapport, discussing Lisa's practicum goals, and assessing Lisa's developmental and competency levels with respect to conducting psychotherapy. Lisa delineated two primary practicum goals: (a) processing dynamic issues in the therapeutic relationship in a more active fashion; and (b) "being more genuine and present" in counseling relationships. She described herself as "a psychodynamic therapist who would like to expand my orientation to include more humanistic perspectives." She also reported herself to be proficient in working with a wide range of psychological problems. When asked by her supervisor about her experience in working with culturally diverse populations, Lisa replied, "I really don't make distinctions between Whites and other people. We're all Americans. I believe that people are people, and should not be seen as belonging to a certain race."

Lisa's supervisor then encouraged her to discuss her background and experience in interacting with a broad range of diverse populations including, but not limited to, people of color, gay/lesbian/bisexual individuals, men, and persons with disabilities. Lisa admitted that her interactions with such populations were quite limited as she had historically been "more comfortable and effective counseling White, heterosexual, middle-class women like myself." As Lisa explored her feelings related to being ineffective in working with various cultural populations, she became tearful and acknowledged that she compensated for her ineffectiveness by ignoring cultural issues in counseling rather than identifying their importance.

Although Lisa demonstrated a moderate level of competency in working with Whites who had myriad emotional and psychological concerns, her supervisor noted major shortcomings in Lisa's competency to work with several types of multicultural populations that presented with psychological concerns. For example, Lisa was unable to discuss how she might work differently with a gay male client who was experiencing romantic relationship issues versus a heterosexual client who presented with romantic relationship concerns. She was also unable to articulate basic "etic" concepts related to working with various ethnic and racial groups. Despite feeling initially frustrated with herself for her lack of knowledge and experience in dealing with diversity issues, Lisa made a commitment to explore cultural issues in further detail over the course of her supervision sessions.

In their third meeting, Lisa's supervisor introduced the aforementioned framework in their supervision relationship in order to facilitate Lisa's level of multicultural competency. Lisa and her supervisor spent most of this meeting sharing their responses to the questions included in the framework; they both emerged from this session with a clearer sense of each other's values, worldviews, therapeutic working styles, and more. Lisa also claimed that she felt better understood by her supervisor because of their ability to discuss their cultural similarities and differences in the context of the supervision relationship.

Lisa came to the next supervision meeting stating that the framework had begun to affect her conceptualizations of and work with clients. She discussed how she felt particularly successful with one of her clients after an intervention in which she acknowledged and processed an "obvious" cultural issue with this client; Lisa stated that the client felt very understood and validated by her, and seemed to be feeling increasingly comfortable with her as a therapist as a result of this intervention. Lisa and her supervisor agreed to incorporate regularly many of the questions included in the framework as a means of consistently discussing issues related to multicultural diversity with respect to each of Lisa's clients. They blended some of these questions into their case conceptualization format in supervision, and found that this method enabled them to keep cultural diversity issues in the forefront of their discussions of clients. They also believed that the framework led to the identification and development of many successful, culturally appropriate interventions. By the end of their supervision relationship, Lisa reported that she had achieved and "exceeded" her two primary practicum goals and felt encouraged to continue working on augmenting her competency in working with a wide range of culturally diverse clients.

Other supervisors and supervisees who have utilized this framework thus far have found that it was very effective in helping them to identify and process issues of cultural diversity in both supervision and counseling relationships. Although I have received qualitative feedback about the effectiveness of the framework in facilitating multicultural competency in supervision relationships, it will be important to obtain empirically based information related to assessing the feasibility and effectiveness of the framework. It is my hope that this framework, or even similar types of interventions, may be adopted by supervisors for use in supervision dyads in order to increase the frequency or intensity of discussing salient multicultural supervision issues.

References

American Psychological Association. (1993). Guidelines for providers of psychological services to ethnic, linguistic, and culturally diverse populations. *American Psychologist, 48*(1), 45-48.

Bernard, J. M. (1992). Training master's level counseling students in the fundamentals of clinical supervision. *The Clinical Supervisor, 10,* 133-143.

Bernard, J. M. (1994). Multicultural supervision: A reaction to Leong and Wagner, Cook, Priest, and Fukuyama. *Counselor Education and Supervision, 34*(2), 159-171.

Bernard, J. M., & Goodyear, R. K. (1992). *Fundamentals in clinical supervision.* Needham Heights, MA: Allyn & Bacon.

Coleman, H.L.K. (1996). Portfolio assessment of multicultural counseling competency. *The Counseling Psychologist, 24,* 216-229.

Cook, D. A. (1994). Racial identity in supervision. *Counselor Education and Supervision, 34*(2), 132-141.

Cook, D. A., & Helms, J. E. (1988). Visible racial/ethnic group supervisees' satisfaction with cross-cultural supervision as predicted by relationship characteristics. *Journal of Counseling Psychology, 35,* 268-274.

Fukuyama, M. A. (1994). Critical incidents in multicultural counseling supervision: A phenomenological approach to supervision research. *Counselor Education and Supervision, 34*(2), 142-151.

Helms, J. E. (1994). How multiculturalism obscures racial factors in the therapy process: Comment on Ridley et al. (1994), Sodowsky et al. (1994), Ottavi et al. (1994), and Thompson et al. (1994). *Journal of Counseling Psychology, 41*(2), 162-165.

Hilton, D. B., Russell, R. K., & Salmi, S. W. (1995). The effects of supervisor's race and level of support on perceptions of supervision. *Journal of Counseling and Development, 73*(5), 559-563.

Leong, F.T.L., & Wagner, N. M. (1994). Cross-cultural counseling supervision: What do we know? What do we need to know? *Counselor Education and Supervision, 34*(2), 117-131.

Loganbill, C., Hardy, E., & Delworth, U. (1982). Supervision: A conceptual model. *The Counseling Psychologist, 10,* 3-42.

Midgette, T. E., & Meggert, S. S. (1991). Multicultural counseling instruction: A challenge for faculties in the 21st century. *Journal of Counseling and Development, 70,* 136-141.

Morgan, D. W. (1984). Cross-cultural factors in the supervision of psychotherapy. *Psychiatric Forum, 12*(2), 61-64.

Pedersen, P. B. (1991). Multiculturalism as a generic approach to counseling. *Journal of Counseling and Development, 70*(1), 6-12.

Priest, R. (1994). Cross-cultural supervision: An examination of clinical reality. *Counselor Education and Supervision, 34*(2), 152-158.

Ridley, C. R., Mendoza, D. W., & Kanitz, B. E. (1994). Multicultural training: Reexamination, operationalization, and integration. *The Counseling Psychologist, 22,* 227-289.

Sue, D. W., Arredondo, P., & McDavis, R. J. (1992). Multicultural counseling competencies and standards: A call to the profession. *Journal of Counseling and Development, 70,* 477-486.

Tyler, F. B., Brome, D. R., & Williams, J. E. (1991). *Ethnic validity, ecology, and psychotherapy: A psychological competence model.* New York: Plenum.

Vander Kolk, C. J. (1974). The relationship of personality, values, and race to anticipation of the supervisory relationship. *Rehabilitation Counseling Bulletin, 18*(1), 41-46.

15

The Supervision Relationship in Multicultural Training

Rocío P. Martínez

Elizabeth L. Holloway

It has largely been agreed that an effective multicultural training needs to be placed at the core of the counseling curriculum (Ivey, 1987, p. 169). In the past decade, multicultural training efforts have increased awareness, sensitivity, and commitment to the development of pluralistic educational programming and mental health delivery systems (D'Andrea & Daniels, 1991; Midgette & Meggert, 1991; Speight, Myers, Cox, & Highlen, 1991). A few cross-cultural supervision research studies have suggested that the supervisory relationship has the potential to translate counselors' multicultural theoretical knowledge to actual practice (Cook & Helms, 1988; Peterson, 1991; Ryan & Hendricks, 1989).

Carney and Kahn (1984) suggested that the knowledge base obtained in cross-cultural counseling courses can be reinforced in the skill domain through the use of role-playing and video simulations requiring students to respond to problems presented by members of different cultural groups (p. 114). Ivey (1987) suggested that the use of "counselor intentionality" involves "an extention [*sic*] of original thinking in intentionality and cultural expertise" (p. 170). This method requires that counselors learn "to integrate an understanding of individual multicultural differences so that they might deliberately use various counseling techniques or approaches" that are effective in working cross-culturally (Ivey, 1987, p. 170).

In spite of the use of these experiential techniques in training, the specific role of supervision in multicultural training models has not been fully described and there are few studies that have specifically investigated the cross-cultural correlates of supervision (Leong & Wagner, 1994). Comprehensive multicultural training requires structural changes at the institutional, curriculum, and instructional levels. The supervision process is one of the avenues whereby cultural expertise can be developed because, ideally, behaviors can be observed, analyzed, and evaluated in a safe and individualized relationship. Supervision of the student's clinical practice provides an opportunity for the supervisor to examine counselor behavior in action and for the trainee to demonstrate the attitude and skills demanded of multicultural contexts. The supervisor's challenge is to create a teaching-learning context that will enhance the supervisee's skill in constructing relevant pluralistic frames of reference from which to devise effective change strategies for the client.

The supervisor is strategically positioned at the final stages of the student's training and is gatekeeper to a student's entry to the profession. It therefore seems important to identify supervision approaches that work in conjunction with multicultural training models. In this chapter we will first describe multicultural training models in relation to supervision. We will then use the framework, Systems Approach to Supervision (SAS; Holloway, 1995), to describe how the principles of multicultural training may be applied in the supervisory context. The relationship of supervision will be our focus because it is the core element of the SAS model and because it is our opinion that relationship development is particularly salient in multicultural training. To illustrate the application of the SAS model, we will analyze a training case in supervision related to cross-cultural learning and competence.

Supervision in Multicultural
Training Models

In spite of the use of instructional methodologies and experiential techniques in training, the specific role of supervision in multicultural training models has not been fully described, and there are few studies that have specifically investigated the cross-cultural correlates of supervision. Among the existing approaches to multicultural supervision there are few clinical, research, and theoretical models that emphasize issues of race, ethnicity, and culture.

The developmental models of supervision have been used as a foundation for several of the multicultural training models. In 1982, Vasquez and McKinley expanded Loganbill, Hardy, and Delworth's (1982) model to include the dimension of ethnicity and trainees' multicultural identity to each of the three stages. The first stage promoted growth and awareness of multiculturalism. In the second stage, the supervisor offered clarification between class and cultural issues, and encouraged the expression of emotional concerns and negative feelings. Finally, the integration stage helped the trainees to develop a multicultural identity that viewed cultures objectively in terms of negative and/or positive values. Similarly, Carney and Kahn (1984) argued that a developmental process was involved in building competencies for cross-cultural counseling. They described five stages of development for training counselor psychologists in pluralistic counseling skills. These are (a) unawareness, (b) beginning awareness, (c) conscious awareness, (d) consolidated awareness, and (e) transcendent awareness. Their model suggested a high degree of structure and clear direction provided by the supervisor at its early stages. At the later stages, a decrease in structure and greater responsibility will be taken by the trainees.

Other training models have focused primarily on using supervision to teach a knowledge base for cultural awareness and sensitivity. For example, Morgan's (1984) clinical model of cross-cultural supervision expects the supervisor to be aware of multicultural issues, to address them early in supervision, and to help trainees examine their own sociocultural background. Cook's (1994) racial identity model is applied to supervision by a process of exploring the inclusion or exclusion of racial issues when the supervisor and supervisee exhibit various racial identity attitudes. Racial identity theories (Helms, 1984) included two models, the People of Color Racial Identity and the White Racial Identity. According to Cook, the racial identity ego described in these models is related to the manner in which racial issues are addressed in supervision. Within the supervisory relationship both participants might approach the relationship with awareness of racial issues in therapy and supervision and/or with disregard and ignorance. In either case there are implications for the supervisory relationship, multicultural training, and service delivery. Peterson (1991) stressed the supervisor's dual role of helping trainees explore their own and their clients' attitudes regarding race and ethnic diversity, while also clarifying institutional policy. He stressed four levels of interaction that are important to supervision: the client or family, the therapist, the supervisor, and the institution. The process of supervision between supervisors and therapists of culturally and linguistically different background is parallel to the cross-cultural psychotherapy interaction between client and therapist. Attitude similarity rather than membership similarity ensured counseling and supervision success.

A more comprehensive program of training has been proposed by Parker, Valley, and Geary (1986). Their approach consists of a combination of assessment, review of the literature, personal involvement, and development of small group projects. The assessment of cultural knowledge involves an examination of the students' multicultural history, comfort level in multicultural settings, personal beliefs about cross-cultural issues, and knowledge of ethnic minority cultures. A review of the literature is acquired as part of a multicultural training course offering information about lifestyles, customs, traditions, language patterns, values, and histories of different groups. The use of role-playing, modeling, and microtraining recommended instructional techniques for skill acquisition.

Many of the training models have been criticized for their lack of attention to the relation between interpersonal dynamics of the supervisor and supervisee and the issues involved in discussing racial and ethnic differences within the context of a one-on-one teaching relationship (Leong & Wagner, 1994). Empirical studies of relationship of supervision have addressed some of these issues (Cook & Helms, 1988; McRoy, Freeman, Logan, & Blackmon, 1986; Remington & DaCosta, 1989). McRoy et al. (1986) studied the dynamics of race and power. They found that both trainees and supervisors identified more potential problems than benefits in cross-cultural supervisory relationships. For example, Black and Hispanic supervisors experienced lack of acceptance of their authority and competence by their White trainees. There are relevant implications for cross-cultural supervision, especially in the areas of racial attitudes, patterns of thinking and problem solving, and cultural value systems. Cook and Helms (1988) studied the race factor in supervisory relationships. Their empirical study factor analyzed the responses of 225 subjects to the Barrett-Lennard (1962) Relationship inventory to determine the relationship dimensions that supervisees felt characterized their supervision experiences. The results indicated that a relationship of "caring" was the most critical dimension in the development of culturally sensitive attitudes and behaviors.

Arguments for the importance of the supervisory relationship in cross-cultural competencies can be found in the literature (Ryan & Hendricks, 1989; Vargas, 1989). For example, Vargas argued that supervision is a safe place where trainees are able to uncover their vulnerabilities in order to attain a more mature self-understanding when working across cultures. She discussed three cultural issues and their implications for both therapeutic and supervisory relationships. The first issue, cultural countertransference, is evidence that the cultural factors of the client are being overemphasized in the assessment of the client's diagnosis and severity of problem. The second issue, cultural manifestations of the parallel process, is essentially the projection of the cultural issues in the counseling relationship into the supervisory relationship. The third issue deals with the interaction between the cultural context and the therapist's narcissistic experience.

Ryan and Hendricks (1989) also explored the implications of cultural differences and their impact in the supervisory relationship. Specifically, the areas of cognitive orientation, motivation orientation, communication styles, value orientation, and sensory orientation were examined in relationship to Asian and Hispanic trainees. Recommendations for ethnic-sensitive supervision included (a) awareness of differences in cognitive value, motivation, and sensory values as well as communication styles; (b) open discussions of racial content and experiences in direct services including feelings , attitudes, and values; (c) setting mutually agreeable expectations for the supervision learning process; and (d) recognition of social and cultural differences and an invitation to openness and development of self-awareness.

It is evident from these training models that supervision has often been considered the place where the development of the competent multicultural practitioner could occur. However, the training models stop short of providing a framework for the practice of supervision. They do not provide a bridge between principles of multicultural training and the practice of supervision as guided by a more comprehensive model of supervision. Because practicum and internship experiences confront the trainee with the challenge of integrating theory, research, and practice knowledge, the supervised clinical experience provides a unique opportunity to teach the skills of translating cross-cultural knowledge to interventions with diverse clients. The relationship between the supervisor and trainee becomes a place for both participants to acknowledge and discuss not only their clients', but—just as important— their own worldviews. The Systems Approach to Supervision (SAS) offers a systematic framework for discussion of cross-cultural cases. In particular, SAS emphasizes the critical factors of the relationship that create a learning environment that supports these sensitive and challenging discussions.

The Systems Approach to Supervision

The goal of supervision[1] is the enhancement of the student's effective professional functioning, and the interpersonal nature of supervision provides an opportunity for the supervisee to be fully involved toward that end. Supervision is the establishment of an ongoing relationship in which the supervisor designs specific learning tasks and teaching strategies related to the supervisee's development as a professional. SAS offers a systematic framework for integrating cultural aspects into the process of learning to be a culturally competent professional. The supervisor must build a learning environment that empowers trainees to examine openly their own values, attitudes, knowledge, and skills relevant to multicultural practice competency. In this way, supervisees are empowered in the process of acquiring attitudes, skills, and knowledge for independent, effective professional practice. This process of empowerment through relationship is a challenge relevant to all aspects of a multicultural training program and it is a fundamental value of the SAS model. The assumptions of the SAS model are the following:

- The goal of supervision is to provide an opportunity for the supervisee *to learn* a broad spectrum of professional attitudes, knowledge and skills in an effective and supportive manner.
- Successful supervision occurs within the context of a complex *professional relationship* that is ongoing and mutually involving.
- The supervisory relationship is the primary context for facilitating the *involvement of the learner* in reaching the goals of supervision. The essential nature of this interpersonal process bestows power on both members as they form the relationship.
- For the supervisor, both the *content and process* of supervision become an integral part of the design of instructional approaches within the relationship.
- As the supervisor teaches, the trainee is further empowered by (a) acquiring the skills and knowledge of the professional work and (b) gaining knowledge through experiencing and articulating interpersonal situations. (Holloway, 1995, p. 6)

There are seven factors in the SAS model. In Figure 15.1, the seven factors are represented as wings connected to the body of supervision, the relationship. The Tasks and Functions are used to describe the supervision process in terms of "the what of supervision" or what the teaching topic is, and "the how of supervision" or how the supervisor is teaching. These two factors are represented in the foreground of the interaction and together create the "process matrix" that describes the intersection of Task and Function as it occurs in the interaction. The contextual factors Supervisor, Trainee, Client, and Institution contain the various characteristics that have been empirically identified as correlates of supervision process and outcome. Any or all of these factors may be influential in the participants' attitudes and behaviors in the process. The relationship is the core factor and governs the process of the supervision interaction. This depiction is the foundation of the Systems Approach to Supervision (SAS).

As a system, this model has been designed to suggest that each wing can be examined independently of the others and then also examined in the context of a particular item and/or all items. It is understood that the components of the model are also part of a dynamic process in that they mutually influence one another and are highly interrelated. The process is influenced by each of the factors and, reciprocally, the process itself influences the factors.

Through a process of describing and mapping the interaction, SAS provides a heuristic tool to examine the supervision session. The multiple factors that may be influential in the supervision situation can be systematically considered. Being aware of "the big picture," the supervisor is able to access strategies and attitudes during supervision that will enhance the learning environment for a particular supervisee. With knowledge of the whole system, deliberate choices can be made by both supervisor and supervisee within the context of specific relevant supervisory factors.

Imagine this picture spinning in light, creating shadows on a screen. The projected images would reflect the idiosyncratic patterns of task, function, and the contextual factors as specifically relevant to the moment-to-moment interactions of the supervisor and trainee. A detailed examination of the screen would provide up-to-date information about (a) the nature of the task, (b) what function the supervisor was carrying out, (c) the character of the relationship, and (d) what contextual factors were relevant to the process. The graphic model is used to identify anchor points in this complex process and to encourage supervisors to discover and name the most salient factors in a particular piece of work.

The SAS provides a common language of supervision that is relevant to supervisors and educators of different theoretical and cultural points of view. The model provides a systematic guide for supervisors to ask questions about what they think, what they do, and how what they do affects multicultural learning. Nevertheless, it is important to recognize that one of the limitations of any system is the individuals who enact the process and the fact that trainers are often in the process of developing their own awareness, knowledge, and skills in the multicultural area. The limitations of trainers in terms of cultural worldview and life experiences presents real challenges in the supervision context. Often White, middle-class counselor-educators have reported "having very limited personal or professional experience interacting with culturally different persons" (D'Andrea & Daniels, 1991, p. 81). Trainers who have gained their knowledge from a particular cultural worldview with limited exposure to and appreciation for other cultural worldviews

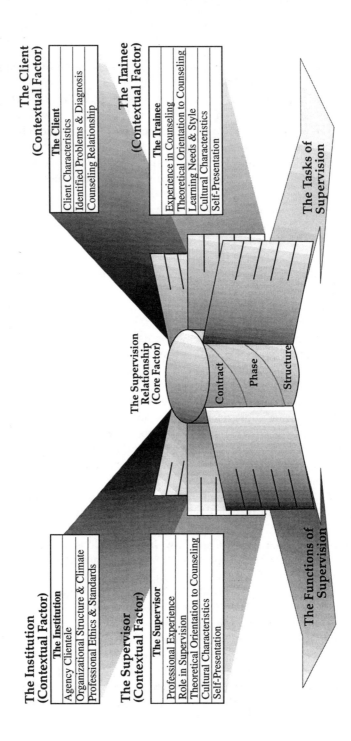

The Client
(Contextual Factor)

The Client
Client Characteristics
Identified Problems & Diagnosis
Counseling Relationship

The Trainee
(Contextual Factor)

The Trainee
Experience in Counseling
Theoretical Orientation to Counseling
Learning Needs & Style
Cultural Characteristics
Self-Presentation

The Institution
(Contextual Factor)

The Institution
Agency Clientele
Organizational Structure & Climate
Professional Ethics & Standards

The Supervisor
(Contextual Factor)

The Supervisor
Professional Experience
Role in Supervision
Theoretical Orientation to Counseling
Cultural Characteristics
Self-Presentation

The Supervision
Relationship
(Core Factor)

Contract

Phase

Structure

The Tasks of
Supervision

The Functions of
Supervision

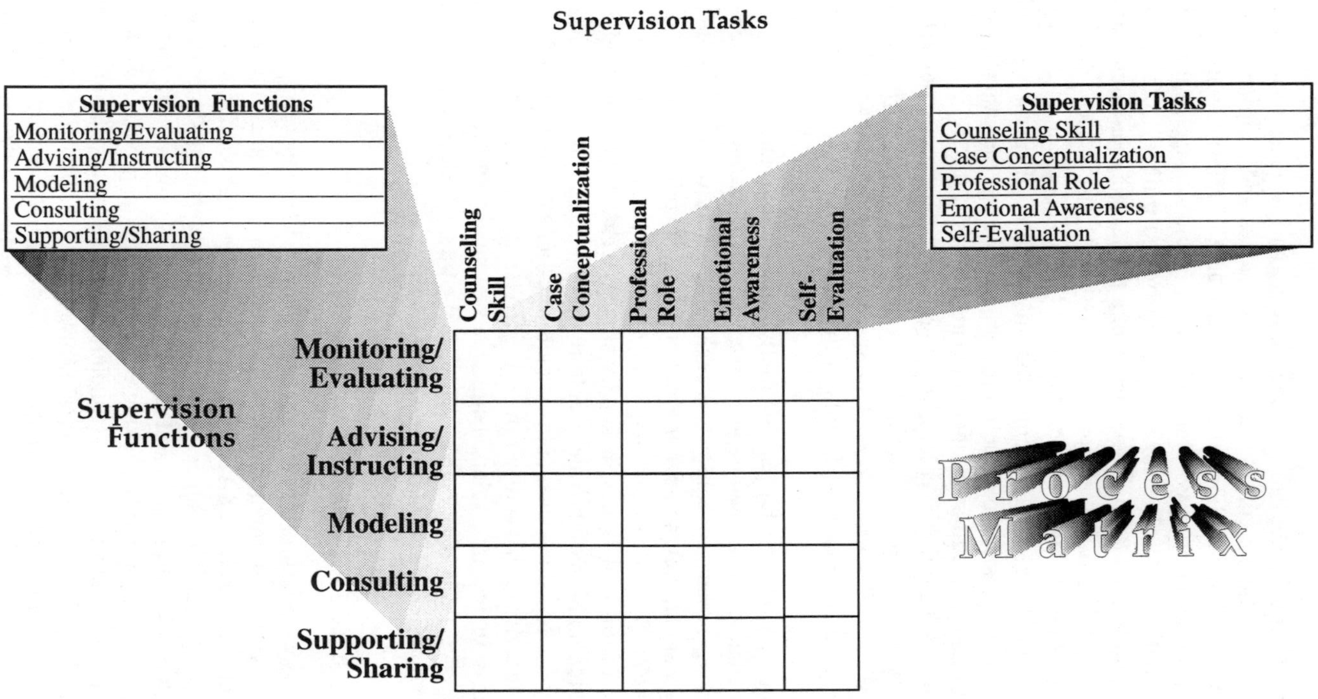
Supervision Tasks
Supervision Functions
Monitoring/Evaluating
Advising/Instructing
Modeling
Consulting
Supporting/Sharing
Supervision Tasks
Counseling Skill
Case Conceptualization
Professional Role
Emotional Awareness
Self-Evaluation
Counseling Skill
Case Conceptualization
Professional Role
Emotional Awareness
Self-Evaluation
Supervision Functions
Monitoring/ Evaluating
Advising/ Instructing
Modeling
Consulting
Supporting/ Sharing
Process Matrix

Figure 15.1. The Systems Approach to Supervision: Tasks, Functions, and Contextual Factors

NOTE: From *Clinical Supervision: A Systems Approach* (pp. 58-59), by E. L. Holloway, 1995, Thousand Oaks, CA: Sage. Copyright 1994 by Sage Publications. Reprinted with permission.

may interpret client behavior and experiences with a narrow filter. Disregarding the individual client's cultural heritage and values and/or interpreting the client's behavior with a limited contextual frame of reference are then part of the supervision process. These elements would surface in the cultural characteristics and values of the supervisor and trainee factors (see Figure 15.1, highlighted bands). For instance, a trainee may encounter opposition on the trainer's part to integrating issues of culture and ethnicity. Trainers or supervisors may feel threatened and inadequate in providing advising, teaching, and/or consultation because of personal and professional limitations in cross-cultural competency. On the other hand, trainees who feel cross-culturally incompetent may resist the trainer's suggestions. Threat and anxiety over lack of cultural competencies are powerful feelings that will likely emerge in the supervisory relationship (Mueller & Kell, 1972). By not attending to these feelings, the supervisor may ignore or diminish the salience of cultural factors in the trainee's professional development.

The supervision relationship, a potentially collaborative and supportive learning environment, can encourage a systematic exploration of multicultural counseling issues. In contrast, a reckoning of cultural issues in a "case-driven manner," often under conflict or crisis, can potentially become overwhelming and compartmentalized. Such case-driven rather than systematic infusion of cultural issues in supervision prevents a broader understanding and recognition of the role of culture in counseling and supervision. It is the very act of asking questions of culture as an expected part of the process of supervision that will ultimately uncover the deeper meaning of cultural factors in learning relationships. A systematic multicultural approach to supervision is critical in developing the trainee's deep experience and empathy for clients in *a pluralistic society.*

Dimensions of the Supervision Relationship

The supervisory relationship[2] is a relational context for rehearsing some of the culturally relevant themes and skills needed for clinical competence in cross-cultural counseling. SAS identifies three essential elements in the relationship and process of supervision: (a) the interpersonal structure of the relationship—the dimensions of power and involvement, (b) phases of the relationship—relational development specific to the participants, and (c) the supervisory contract—the establishment of a set of expectations for the tasks and functions of supervision (Holloway, 1995, p. 49). The interpersonal structure includes the constructs of power and involvement, both of which are enacted in the supervisory relationship. Because of the larger social issues of power that dominate cross-cultural relations, our focus is on the "Interpersonal Structure" factor (see Figure 15.1, highlighted on Relationship factor) of the relationship as defined by the model. Power and involvement are helpful constructs in understanding the nature of the supervisory relationship in relation to multicultural issues.

From a Eurocentric perspective, a worldview that has dominated Western institutional structures, power has been viewed as a vehicle of control and dominance. To be powerful is to wield influence and to control resources and information. In the helping professions, power has often been viewed pejoratively because the concept of control and dominance has seemingly been antithetical to the tenets of mutuality and unconditional positive regard. This interpretation limits the ability of power in constructing a mutually empowering relationship (Holloway, 1995).

Dunlap and Goldman (1991), in a review of the historical roots of power in educational settings, concluded that power has essentially been regarded as "power over" or domination. Earlier on, Follett (1941) introduced the concept of "power with," a concept that was pluralistic and representative of an ever-evolving process of human interaction. Her conception of power offers an alternative that is based on involvement and mutual influence. This basis for power is more consistent with psychotherapy and supervision in which the intent is not to control, but rather to empower individuals to exercise self-control and determination. Power as a vehicle in constructing a mutually empowering relationship is a contrasting view to the traditional Eurocentric perspective that conceives of power as a vehicle of control and dominance (Holloway, 1995). In the case of the multicultural relationship, power and involvement are indeed crucial to the development of trust and, ultimately, mutuality. Building trust and mutuality in the context of the cross-cultural counselor-client relationship is one of the greatest challenges. The ethnic minority in the United States may enter the counseling relationship anticipating another potential experience of "power over" and domination. Multicultural counseling and training developed in the spirit of self-determination, similar to feminist approaches to therapy. Western generic counseling values were perceived as a type of controlling force.

Leary's (1957) theory of interpersonal relations places power in a relational system that includes an *involvement* or affiliation dimension that, in his view, every relationship has by definition. Involvement might also be referred to as intimacy that includes "attachments," the degree to which each person uses the other as a source of self-confirmation (Miller & Rogers, 1976). Affiliation influences the exercise and effect of power in the dyadic relationship and is crucial in creating more individualized versus more role-bound or stereotypic relationships. Both participants determine the distribution of power or the degree of attachment to one another (Morton, Alexander, & Altman, 1976).

Supervision is a formal relationship in which the supervisor's task includes imparting expert knowledge, making judgments of trainees' performance, and acting as a gatekeeper to the profession. Formal power, or power attributed to the position, rests with the supervisor, and in this regard the supervisory relationship is a hierarchical one. However, the exercise of power cannot be accomplished independently. The mutually influential process of relationship and the ongoing interaction among individuals allow for a shared influence to emerge. The relationship is the container of dynamic process in which the supervisor and supervisee negotiate a personal way of utilizing a structure of power and involvement that accommodates the trainee's progression of learning. Power may take very different forms depending on the personal and institutional resources available and the type of involvement of the individuals (Holloway, 1995). This interpersonal structure of relationship becomes the basis for the process by which the trainee will acquire knowledge and skills (Holloway, 1995, p. 48).

The Multicultural Relationship in the SAS Model

The basis for power in the SAS conception of relationship is consistent with the role of power in psychotherapy, "where the intent is not to control, but rather to empower individuals to exercise self-control and determination" (Holloway, 1995, p. 51). Thus the notion of power through involvement is central to the interpersonal structure of the supervision relationship. The degree of relational influence potential will determine the degree of social bonding and thus the persuasiveness of the relationship. As the relationship develops, the participants will utilize more personally relevant interpersonal, psychological, and differentiated information to make predictions of each others' behavior and thus reduce interpersonal uncertainty. Nonetheless, the relationship takes on a unique character that can be defined by power and involvement; the participants bring their own cultural history and interpersonal style. These cultural and interpersonal factors influence how the supervisor and trainee ultimately present themselves in forming their new relationship (see Figure 15.1: Supervisor and Trainee Contextual Factors).

As the trainee integrates multicultural knowledge and skills within the context of the relationship of supervision, a progression toward a collaborative learning alliance evolves. Supervisor and the supervisee are "responsible for establishing a relational structure that is flexible enough to accommodate the trainee's particular professional needs in an intense, collaborative learning alliance" (Holloway, 1995, p. 48). It appears that a parallel between this relationship and the counselor-client relationship can be drawn in multicultural training.

"The current focus of multicultural training is on 'knowing what,' or learning about the specific differences between cultural groups, versus 'knowing how,' or the process of learning how to interact with the culture" (Johnson, 1987). Developing the ability to apply cultural knowledge in a relationship with a person from another culture is part of the domain of skill development in multicultural training. Integrating information about a particular culture into applied interactions becomes a real challenge to most helpers. Sue (1981) argued that "the dynamics of the relationship involve issues of power and control, acceptance, trust, and positive and negative perceptions about racial ethnic groups" (p. 131). Supervisors and supervisees bring to the relationship of supervision their own interpersonal style. Their style of teaching and learning in supervision will be influenced by their individual and cultural characteristics. These historical and contemporary cultural experiences will shape the process of supervision, as will the process form the relationship structure. This interpersonal structure will uniquely determine the participants' engagement in the process.

In the supervision relationship, the supervisor exercises the guiding function of evaluation and support within the structure of the professional relationship. As McRae and Johnson (1991) emphasize, "Supervision of counselor trainees needs to include discussions of cultural values, attitudes, and stereotypes as they surface in the counseling relationship" (p. 135). The supervisory relationship is similar to the expert model of intervention, because it provides the trainee with a supportive relationship in which learned cultural-specific knowledge can be applied within a context in which formative and summative evaluation is available.

A series of basic assumptions about how people learn and change their behavior are challenged by the intercultural supervisor-trainee therapeutic relationship. Multicultural training models such as the specific culture training model allow for an exploration of the basic assumptions of the helping relationship across cultures (Nwachuku & Ivey, 1991). The process of supervision is enacted within that relationship; similarly, the process of intercultural communication is enacted within the supervisor-trainee relationship at the various training stages. Trainees have the potential of being sensitized to cultural issues in the safety of the supervision relationship and then translating this understanding and experience to their work in the counseling relationship. For example, trainees may consult with their supervisor on alternative support systems in the client's community or famil—the Shaman in the case of the Hmong, the *Curandera* in the case of Hispanics.

It is interesting to compare the roles of pro- and/or anti-counselor in the triad model of cross-cultural counselor training (Pedersen, 1977) to that of the supervisor role in the SAS model. The supervisory relationship is described as hierarchical because "the supervisor's task includes imparting expert knowledge, making judgments of trainees' performance, and acting as a gatekeeper to the profession" (Holloway, 1995, p. 50). In the case of the triad model, the pro- or anti-counselor offers trainees the expert knowledge regarding the target culture in question, providing trainees with suggestions about their performance during the cross-cultural counseling role-playing. Neimeyer, Fukuyama, Bingham, Hall, and Mussenden (1986) found that "participants in the anti-counselor role plays reported feeling less competent and more confused than those in the pro-counselor role plays" (p. 439). It appears that the counselors in this study were less comfortable dealing with confrontation of self in multicultural counseling situations. Indeed, the anti-counselor may be an unequal exercise of power.

The SAS model suggests that "the mutually influential process of relationship and the on-going interaction process between individuals allow for a shared influence to emerge" (Holloway, 1995, p. 50). Power is a property of the relationship and not of one individual or the other; power occurs within the context of a relationship (Hinde, 1979). In supervision the relationship is built on "power with" and genuine openness to learning the differences and commonalities of the participants' cultural views. This approach to teaching the skills of multicultural competence can enhance communication and an understanding of one's own and the supervisor's worldviews. Consequently, institutional cultural bias may be addressed within the context of supervision. Ivey's (1977) approach concurs with this point of view; he described the culturally effective individual as "an effective communicator in more than one cultural context" (p. 20) and asserted that interpersonal effectiveness was accomplished only if cultural knowledge was applied to counselor communications and interventions.

SAS emphasizes the structure of the relationship to teach the trainee skills for working with the culturally different client. Moreover, the interpersonal structure of the supervision relationship is based on the development of power with or mutuality through involvement.

Now we will turn to a cross-cultural training case that illustrates the dynamic relationships and perceptions of trainees in a group consultation on supervision. The consultation group serves as a social system in which self-perceptions as well as perceptions of culturally different clients and their social systems can be explored.

Group Consultation on Supervision

The cross-cultural training of supervisors can take place in the context of a consultation group focused on the practice of the supervisor membership. Teaching supervision in the consultation group can be done using the SAS framework as a common language for describing supervisory events and to analyze the multilayered relationships of supervision. The supervisor's decision making is enhanced in the process of discussion in the consultative group, and the group format offers a variety of possibilities and advantages for the cross-cultural learning process.

Case examples discussed in the consultation group are relevant to three relationship contexts: (a) the counseling relationships of the counselor-trainees or counselor-client dyads; (b) the supervisory relationships that exist in the supervisor-trainee dyads; and (c) the consultative group, which is the group of supervisors who meet with a trainer to discuss and learn about the practice of supervision (Holloway, 1995, p. 162). Using the SAS model as a reference point in case discussions allows us to identify the sources of the dilemma and to understand how various factors interrelate and how they influence the three relational contexts mentioned earlier. Indeed, a "multilayered analysis penetrates each relationship and enhances the opportunity to recognize the context in which each issue emerges and how it influences other contexts" (Holloway, 1995, p. 163). The group consultation may deal with any of the roles or issues that emerge in these three related contexts. Not only is multiple feedback part of this context, but the collective function of a consultative group offers counselors who are supervisors an arena in which issues of power and culture are encountered and confronted collectively. These in themselves call for collaborative and group-oriented intervention strategies that are possibly in harmony with the cross-cultural experience of non-Western groups (Sue & Sue, 1990).

Case Study: The Missing Connection[3]

The Supervisor's Dilemma. The supervisor was concerned that she was not equally involved with both of her trainees and wondered if her differential supervisory treatment was a cultural phenomenon.

The Clinical Service Setting. The trainees were seeing their first clients in a practicum setting. They had been meeting with the supervisor for a period of 2 months of counseling training. The supervised clinical training included case conceptualization and intervention strategies in the counseling process.

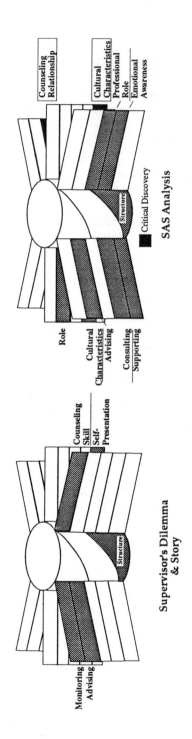

Supervisor's Dilemma
& Story

Monitoring
Advising

Counseling
Skill
Self-
Presentation

Structure

SAS Analysis

Role

Cultural
Characteristics
Advising

Consulting
Supporting

Structure

Critical Discovery

Counseling
Relationship

Cultural
Characteristics
Professional
Role
Emotional
Awareness

340

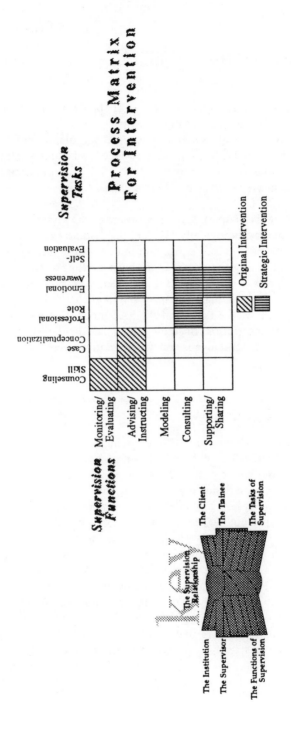

Figure 15.2. Case Study: SAS Analysis in Supervision Consultation

NOTE: From *Clinical Supervision: A Systems Approach* (p. 169), by E. L. Holloway, 1995, Thousand Oaks, CA: Sage. Copyright 1994 by Sage Publications. Reprinted with permission.

Role-playing and videotaped client sessions were the primary methods of training.

The Supervisor. The supervisor was a Hispanic woman with considerable clinical experience. She was highly respected both within her agency and in the larger professional community. As an expert in multicultural counseling, she was often asked to be a consultant on race and ethnic relations to a variety of organizations. The supervisor had integrated cultural issues as part of her philosophical views in the practice of supervision.

The Trainees. The supervisor was working with two trainees. Lily was very dynamic and psychologically minded. She had no experience in counseling prior to entering a master's program in counseling. Marge was at the same stage of her training program, but had been working at a residential treatment center for a number of years. Both trainees were European Americans, but Marge, who was bilingual in Spanish and English, had lived in Latin cultures. Figure 15.2 shows the factors of the SAS model that were identified in the supervisor's description of their dilemma, the consultation process as reflected in the SAS analysis, and the recommended process matrix interventions.

The Supervisor's Story

My supervision is very different with these two trainees. With Lily, I find myself filled with enthusiasm and anticipation for the process between us, whereas with Marge it is like pulling teeth. I am very directive. I experience myself asking one question after another and then telling her how I think about counseling. Yet with all of this work, I don't hear from her, not in a real sense. I hadn't expected this from Marge; although she is not Latina, she knows my language and has lived in a culture similar to mine. I had expected a greater affinity between us. There are times when we speak in Spanish, and yet even then there is a barrier, a lack of feeling involved with her, whereas Lily seems to think the way I do about a relationship. What I worry about the most is the comparing that I am doing. I find myself wishing that Marge would be more like Lily. I don't know if she has good skills because I can't seem to get her involved in supervision. Maybe this is her way of dealing with relationships. You know, sometimes I feel that I want to talk more about her family history to try to figure out why she won't connect with me. I am so disappointed because I really think that she has potential and there is so much more we could do.

The Consultation

The group was surprised at this contrast in these two trainees, but more specifically at the lack of connection that the supervisor felt with Marge. The group was composed primarily of majority culture counselors. They began to focus on Marge. What interpersonal or self-presentation factors were getting in the way of her being in supervision? What were her learning needs? Maybe because she had been practicing, she wasn't feeling as needy for supervision. What, really, was her level of experience? Was she hiding her anxiety about not being as competent as her supervisor might think given her previous counseling experience? Maybe it was acceptable not to be very engaged with the trainee; maybe that connection wasn't a necessary part of the empowerment of the trainee. What were the supervisory factors here? Was the supervisor expecting too much of the relationship and of the linguistic or possible cultural connection? Maybe her expectations were too high? Finally, the group centered on the structure of the relationship as related to the cross-cultural factors.

The SAS Analysis

The consultation group acknowledged that the relationship was the center of the difficulty. Three aspects of the relationship were discussed: the contract between the participants, the phase of the relationship, and the interpersonal structure. The supervisor had been careful in laying out her assumptions about and perspective on supervision to both of her trainees. She had invited them to discuss any aspects of this with her and to share their own thoughts and feelings about the cross-cultural aspects of their relationship in supervision. Both trainees were encouraged to examine their own sociocultural backgrounds and worldviews as part of their involvement in a cross-cultural supervisory relationship. Moreover, the supervisor noted the importance of clarifying cultural issues and encouraged the expression of emotional concerns and negative feelings as part of the multicultural supervisory process. Yet the structure of the relationship itself had taken different forms in the two cases, and the group first asked her to chart where she felt most comfortable in a supervisory relationship with regard to power and involvement. She felt that both culturally and professionally she valued mutual engagement and shared power, power that would be most characterized by using a consulting or supporting function with her trainees. In other words, she liked to minimize the distance between herself and her trainee while still maintaining the role and responsibility of the supervisor. When she characterized the relationship of each of her two trainees using power and involvement, she discovered that with Lily she had a professional relationship that fit these ideals, whereas with Marge she felt forced to use functions such as advising and monitoring, resulting in a more controlling use of power or "power over" and with, at best, a neutral affiliation or involvement. She also realized that the more she tried to create situations in which she would be more connected with Marge, the more Marge pulled away. Finally, in desperation, she would start giving advice and that seemed to alleviate Marge's anxiety, but she felt herself greatly discouraged. She felt that as supervisor, she wasn't living up to her model and was being too authoritative.

This vignette illustrates the integration of cultural issues into the supervisory relationship through a redefinition of the use of power and involvement in the interaction. The supervisor, being a member of a minority group, understood the importance of treating the interaction in supervision as a cross-cultural one. The cultural characteristics, worldview, and assumptive world of the supervisor were laid out early in the supervisory relationship as part of a working contract. Yet the notion of power and interactional style was not presented in such a clear manner. It was assumed that both trainees would respond to the hierarchical supervisory relationship in a similar way. In reality, however, the cultural characteristics of "Marge" and her past experiences with cross-cultural issues and power needed to be addressed as part of the initial phase of the supervisory relationship.

The consultative group wondered if the supervisor had expressed these feelings of being disconnected and of not knowing what Marge thought about the clinical issues that were facing her and how she experienced the supervisory relationship. The supervisor recognized that this type of intervention would in and of itself demand a greater connection with Marge because it dealt with the immediacy of the situation.

The supervisor was concerned about her expectations for supervision and began to question whether those expectations were realistic in the context of a Eurocentric view. At issue was whether it was appropriate for her to expect a more connected relationship in supervision. Could this trainee learn the necessary skills in a more distant relationship? The ramifications for the trainee of not making warm and substantial connections in the counseling relationship were of critical concern. The supervisor watched the development of the counseling relationship closely to see if the trainee would establish a similar interpersonal structure with the client. With her clients, Marge was reserved but inviting in her manner. Nonetheless, Marge seemed to be challenged by one of her clients, who continuously denied having any problems. As Vargas (1989) suggests, the cultural manifestations of the parallel process are a reflection of the supervisor-trainee relationship and mimic the dynamics between the trainee and the client in terms of the inability to connect in a significant manner in both relationships. The supervisor began to question once again the cross-cultural issues that had been operating. Was the trainee not connecting because she did not value the supervisor's expertise as a woman and a Hispanic? Indeed, the supervisor experienced a lack of acceptance of her authority and competence by the trainee. She wondered about her previous assumptions in terms of areas of convergence with the trainee. If cultural differences could be overcome by focusing on areas of convergence, she did not trust her ability to judge similarity of experiences in this particular supervisory relationship. She also asked herself if she was not switching to a referent base of power because she saw the supervisor as different in attitudes and values. The issues of culture, gender, and role were all possible factors in understanding the trainee's lack of involvement in supervision.

The supervisor began to discuss these issues with the trainee in a consultative manner and within the context of worldview. She began the conversation in a very general, almost academic sense, but eventually the discussion began to focus on the personal experiences each of them had in developing their values and goals as professionals. A supportive atmosphere allowed for the evolving of sharing of personal and professional experiences. The supervisor proceeded to show the trainee a videotaped session in which both of them had participated and suggested that they discuss their impressions. Further involvement was achieved through modeling of a positive interaction and a mutually engaging process of understanding.

Finally, the trainee revealed that she felt uncomfortable with the supervisor because she perceived the latter as very powerful and knowledgeable and she resented that power. Her experience in Latin cultures had not been entirely positive; although she was drawn to the openness among people, her contrasting reserve made her feel intimidated and unseen. She left the country feeling unaccepted and resentful in spite of her host family's efforts to make her feel a part of things. She acknowledged that being with her supervisor reminded her of this experience. She felt inadequate to form a relationship with the supervisor and was afraid that the supervisor would also find her inadequate. Through this discussion, both the trainee and the supervisor began to form a relationship that was more meaningful, more connected, and more sensitively attuned to the differences between them.

In this case study, the supervision interaction was a safe place to uncover vulnerabilities for the attainment of a more mature self-understanding. However, the lack of recognition of social and cultural differences early in the process of supervision affected the possibility of developing a mutually engaging relationship. Attitude similarity was quickly assumed by the supervisor, because cultural similarities were taken for granted due to this trainee's experiences in the minority culture.

Solomon (1986) argued that, historically, minorities in the United States have experienced disempowerment and oppression. In our example, a Caucasian trainee had the experience of having been placed in a minority context while living overseas. Conflict in values and assumptions that arose in the case example reflect the importance of the cultural dimension and cross-cultural differences in supervision from a contextual and historical perspective. According to Tyler, Brome, and Williams (1991), the supervisor and supervisee explore cultural differences in supervision and attempt to transcend them by focusing on areas of convergence. The SAS model uses the relationship as a focal point whereby the dimensions of cultural characteristics and differences are explored. In this example, the supervisor perhaps assumed that the trainee had not viewed her as an expert in the field. On the contrary, the case shows that the trainee was quite intimidated by the expertise of the supervisor's level of experience, preventing the trainee from relating in terms of mutuality.

Conclusions

Training for effective communication in supervision is a multifaceted and multilayered process. Multiculturalism is an important perspective that has seldom been addressed within the supervisory context itself. When supervisors and trainees examine their own cultural values and assumptions, self-awareness and knowledge grow, helping the relationship develop into a mutually engaging process. The consultation group offers a unique opportunity for studying the supervisory relationship in a systematic fashion, integrating the knowledge base and skill development relevant for a cross-cultural clientele. The collaborative learning alliance is the relational structure that promotes learning of the profession. In the case study, the collaborative learning alliance was experienced by the supervisor at the consultation group and transferred to the trainee at the supervisory sessions. Furthermore, this collaboration can be transferred into the counseling relationship with the cross-cultural client. In this manner, the supervisory relationship serves as a rehearsal of culturally relevant attitudes and beliefs needed for cross-cultural competency.

The goal of developing a collaborative learning alliance sets the tone for the exploration of multicultural counseling issues in a nonpolitical and nonstereotypic manner. Power occurs within the context of a relationship; therefore, the dynamics of power and involvement are critical elements in creating an environment that engenders the trust and mutuality for discussing these highly sensitive issues. With such a learning relationship, supervisors and trainees can be encouraged to become aware of their own racial-ethnic issues, biases, and potential countertransference issues.

Cross-cultural supervision has identified a variety of common problems, such as "overinterpreting the influence of culture, underinterpreting the influence of culture, avoiding cultural issues, and fear of being labeled as a racist" (Leong & Wagner, 1994, p. 121). Solomon (1986) argued that there are limited theories of human behavior and clinical supervision that give clear guidelines as to what to expect or what to do in cross-cultural cases. Indeed, these are common concerns in cross-cultural supervision that can be addressed in the context of a relationship that offers a collaborative approach to teaching and learning. Vargas (1989) said, "the supervisor's job is to make supervision a safe place where trainees are able to express their vulnerability and in this way achieve more mature self-understanding" (cited in Leong & Wagner, 1994, p. 122). Therefore, it is in the context of the collaborative learning alliance that the relationship can culminate in the development of a multiculturally competent practitioner. Unfortunately, many supervisors may have a tendency to exclude interpersonal dynamics in their discussions of race and ethnicity because of the vulnerability and hypersensitivity of these topics in society in general. It is hoped that the SAS model, based on principles of a "power-with" relational structure can provide a heuristic framework that encourages the development of multicultural competence in counselors and their supervisors.

Notes

1. This section has been adapted from *Clinical Supervision: A Systems Approach* (pp. 1-7), by E. L. Holloway, 1995, Thousand Oaks, CA: Sage. Copyright 1994 by Sage Publications. Reprinted with permission.

2. This section has been adapted from *Clinical Supervision: A Systems Approach* (pp. 41-42), by E. L. Holloway, 1995, Thousand Oaks, CA: Sage. Copyright 1994 by Sage Publications. Reprinted with permission.

3. The case "Missing the Connection" is from *Clinical Supervision: A Systems Approach* (pp. 168-170), by E. L. Holloway, 1995, Thousand Oaks, CA: Sage. Copyright 1994 by Sage Publications.

References

Barrett-Lennard, G. T. (1962). Dimensions of the therapist response as causal factors in therapeutic change. *Psychological Monographs Applied, 76*(Whole No. 562).

Carney, C. G., & Kahn, K. B. (1984). Building competencies for effective cross-cultural counseling: A developmental view. *The Counseling Psychologist, 12,* 111-119.

Cook, D. A. (1994). Racial identity in supervision. *Counselor Education and Supervision, 34,* 132-141.

Cook, D. A., & Helms, J. E. (1988). Visible racial/ethnic group supervisees' satisfaction with cross-cultural supervision as predicted by relationship characteristics. *Journal of Counseling Psychology, 35,* 268-274.

D'Andrea, M., & Daniels, J. (1991). Exploring the different levels of multicultural counseling training in counselor education. *Journal of Counseling and Development, 70,* 78-85.

Dunlap, D., & Goldman, P. (1991). Rethinking power in schools. *Educational Administration Quarterly, 27,* 5-29.

Follett, M. P. (1941). The meaning of responsibility in business management. In H. C. Metcalf & L. Urwick (Eds.), *Dynamic administration: The collected papers of Mary Parker Follett* (pp. 141-166). London: Pitman.

Helms, J. E. (1984). Toward a theoretical explanation of the effect of race on counseling: A Black and White model. *The Counseling Psychologist, 12*(4), 153-165.

Hinde, R. A. (1979). *Towards understanding relationships.* New York: Academic Press.

Holloway, E. L. (1995). *Clinical supervision: A systems approach.* Thousand Oaks, CA: Sage.

Ivey, A. E. (1977). Cultural expertise: Toward systematic outcome criteria in counseling and psychological education. *Personnel and Guidance Journal, 55,* 296-302.

Ivey, A. E. (1987). Cultural intentionality: The core of effective helping. *Counselor Education and Supervision, 26,* 168-172.

Johnson, S. D. (1987). Knowing that versus knowing how: Toward achieving expertise through multicultural training for counseling. *The Counseling Psychologist, 15,* 320-331.

Leary, T. (1957). *Interpersonal diagnosis of personality: A theory and a methodology for personality evaluation.* New York: Ronald Press.

Leong, F.T.L., & Wagner, N. S. (1994). Cross-cultural counseling supervision: What do we know? What do we need to know? *Counselor Education and Supervision, 34,* 117-131.

Loganbill, C., Hardy, E., & Delworth, U. (1982). Supervision: A conceptual model. *The Counseling Psychologist, 10,* 3-42.

McRae, M. B., & Johnson, S. D. (1991). Toward training for competence in multicultural counselor education. *Journal of Counseling and Development, 70,* 131-135.

McRoy, R. G., Freeman, E. M., Logan, S. L., & Blackmon, B. (1986). Cross-cultural field supervision: Implications for social work education. *Journal of Social Work Education, 22,* 50-56.

Midgette, T. E., & Meggert, S. S. (1991). Multicultural counseling instruction: A challenge for faculties in the 21st century. *Journal of Counseling and Development, 70,* 136-141.

Miller, F. E., & Rogers, L. E. (1976). *Explorations in interpersonal communication.* Beverly Hills, CA: Sage.

Morgan, D. W. (1984). Cross-cultural factors in the supervision of psychotherapy. *Psychiatric Forum, 12*(2), 61-64.

Morton, T., Alexander, C., & Altman, I. (1976). Communication and relationship definition. In G. Miller (Ed.), *Explorations in interpersonal communication* (pp. 105-125). Beverly Hills, CA: Sage.

Mueller, W. J., & Kell, B. L. (1972). *Coping with conflict: Supervising counselors and psychotherapists.* Englewood Cliffs, NJ: Prentice Hall.

Neimeyer, G. J., Fukuyama, M. A., Bingham, R. P., Hall, L.E., & Mussenden, M. E. (1986). Training cross-cultural counselors: A comparison of the pro-counselor and anti-counselor triad models. *Journal of Counseling and Development, 64,* 437-439.

Nwachuku, U. T., & Ivey, A. E. (1991). Culture specific counseling: An alternative training model. *Journal of Counseling and Development, 70,* 106-111.

Parker, W. M., Valley, M. M., & Geary, C. A. (1986). Acquiring cultural knowledge for counselors in training: A multifaceted approach. *Counselor Education and Supervision, 26,* 61-71.

Pedersen, P. B. (1977). The triad model of cross-cultural training. *Personnel and Guidance Journal, 56,* 94-100.

Peterson, F. K. (1991). Issues of race and ethnicity in supervision: Emphasizing who you are, not what you know. *The Clinical Supervisor, 9,* 15-31.

Remington, G., & DaCosta, G. (1989). Ethnocultural factors in resident supervision: Black supervisor and White supervisees. *American Journal of Psychotherapy, 43*(3), 398-404.

Ryan, A. S., & Hendricks, C. O. (1989). Culture and communication: Supervising the Asian and Hispanic social workers. *The Clinical Supervisor, 7*(1), 27-40.

Solomon, B. (1986). Power: The troublesome factor in cross-cultural supervision. *Smith College Journal, School for Social Work, 10,* 27-32.

Speight, S. L., Myers, L. J., Cox, C. I., & Highlen, P. S. (1991). A redefinition of multicultural counseling. *Journal of Counseling & Development, 70,* 29-36.

Sue, D. W. (1981). *Counseling the culturally different: Theory and practice.* New York: John Wiley.

Sue, D. W., & Sue, D. (1990). *Counseling the culturally different: Theory and practice* (2nd ed.). New York: John Wiley.

Tyler, F. B., Brome, D. R., & Williams, J. E. (1991). *Ethnic validity, ecology, and psychotherapy: A psychosocial competence model.* New York: Plenum.

Vargas, L. A. (1989, August). *Training psychologists to be culturally responsive: Issues in supervision.* Paper presented at a symposium at the 97th Annual Convention of the American Psychological Association, New Orleans.

Vasquez, M.J.T., & McKinley, D. L. (1982). Supervision: A conceptual model: Reactions and an extension. *The Counseling Psychologist, 10*(1), 59-63.

16

Postmodern Supervision

A MULTICULTURAL PERSPECTIVE

Roberto Cortéz González

This chapter presents a postmodern reconceptualization of multicultural clinical supervision that integrates and extends Interpersonal Process Recall (I.P.R.; Kagan, 1976, 1980), the discrimination model (Bernard, 1979, 1981, 1989; Bernard & Goodyear, 1992; Lanning, 1986), and live supervision (Bernard & Goodyear, 1992; Boscolo & Cecchin, 1982; Haley, 1976; Hardy, 1993; Lowenstein & Reder, 1982; McDaniel, Weber, & McKeever, 1983; Montalvo, 1973; Roberts, 1983; Selvini Palazzoli, Boscolo, Cecchin, & Prata, 1980; Sperling et al., 1986). First, the convergent influences that contributed to the evolution of this particular style of postmodern supervision are described and discussed. Second, applications

AUTHOR'S NOTE: Correspondence should be sent to Roberto Cortéz González, Ph.D.; Associate Professor; Educational Psychology and Special Services, College of Education; The University of Texas at El Paso; El Paso, TX, 79968-0567.

to supervision are provided. In this section, appreciative inquiry (Barrett & Cooperrider, 1990; Cooperrider, 1990; Cooperrider & Srivastva, 1987; Srivastva, Fry, & Cooperrider, 1990) is presented as a postmodern extension of I.P.R. *Supervisor-as-partial-learner,* which allows for the "mutual expertise" of supervisor, supervisee(s), and client(s), is proposed as a postmodern extension of the discrimination model. "Language of affect" is also reconceptualized from the viewpoint of postmodern, multicultural clinical practice. Third, some implications for multicultural relevance are explored. Ethical issues are considered throughout all three sections.

Convergent Influences

Postmodernism

For the purposes of this chapter, *postmodernism* refers to paradigms based upon a consciousness of multiple belief systems and multiple perspectives. In contrast, *modernism* refers to paradigms based upon rational, objective/positivist/empirical traditions (Borgmann, 1992; Efran, Lukens, & Lukens, 1988; Flew, 1984; Gergen, 1985, 1991a, 1991b; O'Hara & Anderson, 1991). *Paradigm* refers to "a central overall way of regarding phenomena . . . [and] may dictate what type of explanation will be found acceptable" (Flew, 1984, p. 261). Postmodernism rejects the epistemological assumptions of mainstream social science and its research over the past three decades (Rosenau, 1992). *Epistemology* refers to "the nature and derivation of knowledge, the scope of knowledge, and the reliability of claims to knowledge" (Flew, 1984, p. 109).

In the social sciences, postmodernism is a reaction to uncritical confidence in objective knowledge, the Enlightenment heritage, and the methodological suppositions of modern science. Rosenau explains that postmodernism is more than just another novel academic paradigm: A new and different movement is coalescing into a broad-gauged reconceptualization of how we experience and explain the world around us. She adds, "In its most *extreme* formulations, postmodernism is revolutionary; it goes to the very core of what constitutes social science and radically dismisses it. In its more *moderate* proclamations, postmodernism encourages substantive redefinition and innovation" (p. 4, italics in original). Extreme postmodernism deconstructs modernity. Rosenau's user-friendly glossary of terms defines *deconstruction* as "a postmodern method of analysis. "Its goal is to undo all constructions. Deconstruction tears a text apart, reveals its contradictions and assumptions; its intent, however, is not to improve, revise, or offer a better version of the text" (p. xi). Rosenau further differentiates *skeptical* postmodernists from *affirmative* postmodernists (italics in original) as two broad general orientations in relation to the social sciences. The skeptical orientation is inspired by Continental European philosophies and offers a pessimistic assessment of the postmodern age as one of fragmentation, disintegration, malaise, and meaninglessness. The affirmative orientation is more indigenous to Anglo-North American culture than to the Continent, and has a more hopeful, optimistic view of the postmodern age.

In psychotherapy, postmodern paradigms may be subsumed under narrative approaches, which concern themselves with the stories people create and tell to make sense of their worlds (Penn, 1991; Sarbin, 1986). Narrative approaches are proposed as a viable alternative to the positivist paradigm, in which scientific explanations for human behavior are respected as the only acceptable source of genuine knowledge (Flew, 1984; Gergen, 1973; Sarbin, 1986). Human predicaments and attempted resolutions are central considerations in narratives, and depart from the mechanistic objective of uncovering context-free laws of behavior. Mechanistic models are based on supposedly known processes such as drives, instinct, libidinal energy, cognitions, reinforcement, and mental states (Flew, 1984; Sarbin, 1986). Therapy, however, is an inquiry into clients' self-narratives. The literary quality of therapeutic renderings is emphasized. Gergen and Gergen (1986) write that the most essential ingredient of narrative accounting (or storytelling) is its capacity to structure events in such a way that they demonstrate, first, a connectedness or coherence, and second, a sense of movement or direction through time. To succeed as a narrative, goal states or valued endpoints must be established, and events must be selected and arranged in such a way that the goal state is rendered more or less probable. A description of events unrelated to the goal state detracts from or dissolves the sense of narrative. The establishment of endpoints and selection of events become guidelines in narrative therapy. Three prototypical narrative forms have been identified (Gergen & Gergen, 1984). *Progressive narratives* are those in which progress toward the goal is enhanced. *Regressive narratives* are those in which progress toward a goal is impeded. *Stability narratives* are those in which no change occurs. Narrative approaches to therapy strive to facilitate progressive narratives for clients.

Some postmodern, narrative therapies use a social constructionist framework (e.g., Berger & Luckmann, 1966; Gergen, 1973, 1985, 1991a, 1991b; McNamee & Gergen, 1992). Social constructionism views meanings and understandings of the world as developed through social interaction (Gergen, 1985), and arose, in part, because attempts to render accurate understandings of absolute, objective truths in psychology have not been established (Guerin, 1992; Scarr, 1985). Implicitly and explicitly, social constructionism challenges the normative foundations of psychological knowledge. Gergen (1985) asserts that a network of social agreements, rather than empirical evidence, form the basis for conclusions based on the positivist paradigm. Other narrative approaches use a constructivist framework (e.g., Mahoney, 1989, 1993; Meichenbaum, 1994; Meichenbaum & Fong, 1993; von Glasersfeld, 1984). Constuctivism is founded on the idea that humans actively construct their personal realities and create their own representational models of the world (Meichenbaum & Fong, 1993). A burgeoning literature on postmodern approaches has appeared. Some publications have originated in the marriage and family therapy field (Andersen, 1987, 1991; Anderson, 1991; Anderson & Goolishian, 1988; Doherty, 1991; Hoffmann, 1990, 1991; Laird, 1989; O'Hara & Anderson, 1991; Parry, 1991; Sluzki, 1992; White & Epston, 1990). Other publications have addressed feminism in family therapy (Weingarten, 1991) and in psychology (Hare-Mustin & Maracek, 1988), lesbian and gay families (Laird, 1993), religious identification (Kudlac, 1991), career development and vocational psychology (Richardson, 1993), and cultural issues (González, Biever, & Gardner, 1993, 1994; González, North, Ricks, & Biever, 1992; Howard, 1991).

Modernist therapies used with multicultural clients tend to view the therapist as the expert who conceptualizes the case from a given theoretical perspective that makes normative assumptions regarding what is and is not "healthy behavior" (González et al., 1994). In contrast, postmodern practitioners are becoming skeptical of elaborate theoretical orientations (Doherty, 1991). The lack of precise scientific knowledge about the origins of mental disorders has also given rise to alternative, postmodern reconceptualizations of therapy, with emphasis placed on new narratives and metaphors for understanding one's life and improving skills for negotiating meaning (Gergen, 1991b). Doherty (1991) writes that the goal of postmodern therapy is to enable clients to find new meanings in their life situations and to "restory" their problems in ways that free them from the mesmerizing power of the dominant culture. Such liberation is vital when working with multicultural clients. Universal psychological structures in individuals and systemic interactions in families become superseded by social and historical contexts from which clients can derive multiple meanings. This multiplicity of perspectives seemingly is shared by postmodernism and multiculturalism. Social constructions of reality have been and can be oppressive to minority individuals, and therefore personal constructions of reality merit as much attention when relational issues are addressed in therapy. The multicultural perspective's

recognition of diversity within groups also promotes personal constructions as a legitimate counterpart to social constructionism in postmodern
therapy. Thus, affirmative postmodernism and multiculturalism in clinical
practice are a combination of *both* conventional *and* alternative conceptualizations.

Modern and postmodern perspectives in psychology recently have been
the topic of vigorous debate (Denner, 1995; Gergen, 1994, 1995; Mente,
1995; Russell & Gaubatz, 1995; Smith, 1994, 1995; White & Wang, 1995).
The intent of these interchanges is to stimulate further dialogue rather than
to arrive at a conclusion once and for all. Although Gergen (1985) attempts
to keep social constructionism and constructivism as separate, the two terms
have been used interchangeably (Efran et al., 1988; Mahoney, 1989), which
can create some confusion. Along these lines, there appear to be conflicting
versions of the origins of constructivism (Meichenbaum & Fong, 1993; von
Glasersfeld, 1984). Both social constructionism and constructivism are
postmodern paradigms.

Several authors have pointed out the contradictions of postmodern
therapies (Coale, 1992; Efran & Clarfield, 1992; Efran et al., 1988; Held,
1990; Minuchin, 1991). Held (1990) questions the epistemological rigor and
intellectual integrity of multiple realities and what makes for more effective
therapy. She asserts, "the view that we cannot, under any circumstances,
know an independent reality is itself, paradoxically, a reality claim" (p. 181).
Minuchin (1991) takes issue with postmodern therapists who deny the
legitimacy of their own clinical expertise to avoid the appearance of control,
thereby anointing themselves as the new crew of experts. He warns of
therapists who risk clinical irrelevance by getting too wrapped up in abstrac-
tions about the subjectivity of all truths. He also raises the ethical issue of
impairment among postmodern therapists, "wounded healers" who, like
some of their modernist practitioner counterparts, often are reluctant to seek
help for themselves and their relationships. At times, postmodernists can
resemble some of their modernist counterparts in a few other ways: a lack of
basic "people skills" and a failure to practice what they preach, which does
not prevent the disparagement of those not of their ideological clique. Efran
et al. (1988) admonish that "those who make their living being experts on
the implications of language [in narrative therapy] ought to think twice
before taking too many liberties with it" (p. 34). Efran and his colleagues
caution against using postmodernism as a means of trifling with established
words and meanings. Coale (1992) is concerned that, "The emphasis on
language as *the* mechanism for changing meaning is a contradiction of the
. . . position that all reality is non-objective and, therefore, that there is room

for many ways of understanding and doing anything" (p. 23, italics in original). She does not see language as any less instrumental than behavioral interventions and adds that, in many circumstances, nonverbal interventions (such as art therapy) can be more effective than language in facilitating change. Sensory impaired people (i.e., blind or deaf), for whom language functions differentially, may also have other mechanisms for changing meaning. Efran and Clarfield (1992) write that the postmodern idea that hierarchy can be eliminated in therapy is absurd and counterproductive. "To act as if all views are equal and that we—as therapists—have no favorites among them undercuts the very sort of frank exchange we want and expect to have with our clients" (p. 208). If postmodernists do not squarely and courageously face this underside of themselves, the chronic risk is that of rigid paradigmatic stratification that is the antithesis of postmodernism.

Walsh (1993) offers a succinct critique of the acceptance of multiple realities:

> A serious danger . . . lies in the assumption that all views presented are equally valid and that they are honest and accurate representations of the [given] experience. Such assumptions become problematic where an individual or family distorts or denies experience and events, such as alcohol abuse, sexual abuse, or suicide. (p. 33)

Coyne (1985) writes of external forces that really affect our clients' lives, forces that cannot be ignored or deconstructed. For example, Hacker (1992) addresses the conditions that perpetuate the disenfranchisement of African Americans in the United States, conditions that cannot be dismissed by the intellectual posturing of deconstruction. Bass and Davis (1988) warn survivors of sexual abuse about attempts to perpetuate the invalidation of a survivor's experience, the confusion and distress about what was real that can ensue, and the need to develop the capacity to trust one's inner voice (see pp. 116-117). Gilligan and Noel (1995) discuss listening and being heard as an intensely relational act. Their work with adolescent females revealed the paradox of adolescents' separating off parts of themselves in relationships to stay in those relationships. The adolescent females held back, so that there was a socially constructed reality that discounted their personal experience of reality. The adolescents believed that if their inner worlds were brought into relationships, then no one would want to be with them. For the adolescents, there was a difference between what was said and what seemed to be.

The disengagement of adolescent females has direct implications for supervision and training issues. When the social construction of clinical reality is superimposed on a personally constructed clinical reality that is different, it is as if that personally known reality does not exist. A false presentation of self occurs when one disconnects from the truth of one's own experience. From a postmodern stance, the challenge for supervisors will be to not override supervisees' own knowledge, which undermines supervisees' sense of trusting what they know and feel. Minimizing the confusing relational realities between supervisor and supervisee will, it is hoped, decrease any similar confusions embedded in the supervisees' clinical practice with clients. Supervisees can feel like they are being "force fed" when social constructionism alone is used in postmodern supervision, which can impede supervisees' clinical efficacy and development as a therapist. Using *both* social constructionism *and* constructivism offers a more comprehensive approach to minimizing confusing relational realities in postmodern supervision than using either paradigm alone.

Interpersonal Process Recall

Originally a model of human communication, Interpersonal Process Recall (I.P.R.; Kagan, 1976, 1980) has evolved into the most widely known supervision model for reviewing a videotape of a counseling session (Bernard & Goodyear, 1992). In a summary of research and development in I.P.R., Kagan (1980) describes the essence of his approach:

> If a person is videotaped while he or she is relating to another and is then shown the recording immediately after the interaction, the person is able to recall thoughts and feelings in amazing detail and depth. . . . Usually there [is] some self-evaluation as well as a detailed *narrative* of the impact on the person of the "other" he or she has been relating with. If a remote control stop-start switch [is] given to the people so that they could stop and start the play-back at will, usually a wealth of understanding about some of their underlying motives, thoughts, and feelings during the inter-personal transaction [can] be verbalized by them. (p. 262, emphasis added)

If a person views the videotape with the help of someone trained in how to encourage the viewer to verbalize and elaborate on that which is recalled during the viewing, the recall process works more reliably, and more information about underlying thoughts and feelings can be facilitated. Kagan (1980) refers to the facilitator's role as that of an active, *inquiring colleague* (p. 263, italics in original).

When used as a way of reviewing an audiotape or videotape of a counseling session, I.P.R. becomes a process of learning by self-discovery, by self-teaching. Optimally, supervisees will experience I.P.R. as a nonjudgmental approach. The model has a phenomenological basis. Kagan (1980) writes, "Truly people are the best authority on their own dynamics and the best interpreter of their own experience" (pp. 279-280). Facilitative questions, called inquirer leads, include leads that inspire affective exploration, approaches that encourage cognitive examination, questions about body sensations, getting at images, questions that help search out expectations, explorations into each other's mutual perceptions, leads into associations, and checking out unstated agendas (Harris & Werner, n.d.).

Kagan (1980) also presents the theoretical constructs of interpersonal communication that he added to the I.P.R. model. In the context of therapy and in everyday interactions, two basically opposed states—the need for people and the fear of people—manifest themselves in a variety of behaviors. People can be the most potent source of satisfaction for each other and the most potent source of pain for each other. Fear of people usually clusters around four basic themes: (a) "the other person will hurt me," or (b) "the other person will incorporate or seduce me." Similarly, people fear (c) hurting others or (d) incorporating others. The individual's movement toward and away from others may be summarized as an attempt to find a balance between the pain of boredom and deprivation when contact is too distant and the experience of anxiety when interpersonal contact is too close. A primary manifestation of this approach-avoidance dynamic is the socially learned habit of behaving diplomatically. People have an almost uncanny ability to hear each other's most subtle messages, though they acknowledge and label only a small part of what they perceive and what they usually react to. Kagan calls this almost universal characteristic "feigning of clinical naïveté," and contends that "the reluctance to label messages honestly is based on an unwillingness to become *that* involved with the other" (p. 275, italics in the original). The purpose of I.P.R., then, is to provide supervisees with a safe haven for their perceptions and reactions. The supervisor's role becomes that of a facilitator to stimulate the awareness of the supervisee beyond the point at which it operated during the therapy session (Bernard & Goodyear, 1992).

For me, a postmodern extension of I.P.R. is the approach to organizational consultation known as appreciative inquiry (Barrett & Cooperrider, 1990; Cooperrider, 1990; Cooperrider & Srivastva, 1987; Srivastva et al., 1990). Appreciative inquiry moves from "telling it like it is" to "telling it as it may become" (Srivastva et al., 1990). Especially with systems divided by conflict and caught in defensive perception, there is "an invitation to see anew, to facilitate the learning of new knowledge, to create scenarios of future action, and to overcome areas of rigidity" (Barrett & Cooperrider, 1990, p. 224). Anticipatory realities are used to become a guiding image for the future (Cooperrider, 1990).

I.P.R.'s inquirer role, though leading to narrative recall, may appear too linear and too modern in its "self-discovery" for some postmodernists. I.P.R.'s phenomenological basis, and supervisees' post hoc verbalizations of their underlying motives, thoughts, and feelings, also may rely excessively on innate processes for some postmodernists. Yet I.P.R. allows for supervisees' personal constructions of clinical realities to be voiced. In addition, many I.P.R.-based questions can be extended into the generation of anticipatory realities in clinical supervision.

The Discrimination Model

The discrimination model is so called because a dominant characteristic is the identification and action upon choice points in the supervisory process of supervisees (Bernard, 1979). Supervisors use a cognitive map to track the focus of supervision and to determine the best supervisory vehicle for accomplishing supervision goals (Bernard & Goodyear, 1992). Three basic foci of supervision (process skills, conceptualization skills, and personalization skills) and three basic roles of supervisors (teacher, counselor, and consultant) allow nine different choice points from which a supervisor can respond to a supervisee.

Process skills refer to the counselor's behaviors that are most readily observable. The overt implementation of such skills include

> (a) ability to open an interview smoothly, (b) competence in the use of reflections, probes, restatement, summaries or interpretations, (c) helping clients say what is on their minds, (d) using nonverbal communication to enhance verbal communication, (e) successfully implementing intervention strategies, and (f) achieving interview closure. (Bernard, 1979, pp. 61-62)

Process skills involve therapeutic technique and strategy. Most supervisees learn such skills early in their training. These skills follow a continuum of difficulty. A supervisor evaluating from a process perspective attends to the execution, rather than the choice of, those skills and strategies of the supervisee (Bernard, 1979).

In contrast to process skills, conceptualization skills pertain to most of the supervisee's covert behaviors. The deliberate thinking and case analysis by the trainee is not always observable to the supervisor. Conceptualization skills include

> (a) the ability to understand what the client is saying, (b) the skill in identifying themes in the client's messages, (c) the skill to recognize appropriate and inappropriate goals for the client, (d) skill in *choosing* strategies that are appropriate to the client's expressed goals, and (e) skill in recognition of even subtle improvement by the client. (Bernard, 1979, p. 62, italics in the original)

Two distinct kinds of thinking included are the conceptualization done *in the counseling session* and the conceptualization done *between sessions*. The supervisor looks for both levels of conceptualization in the trainee.

Personalization skills are the third basic focus of supervisors who use the discrimination model. As the label suggests, these skills refer to the more personal aspects of the supervisor's learning, and include overt and readily observable behaviors as well as behaviors that are subtle and more difficult to identify. Personalization skills include

> (a) the counselor's comfort in assuming some authority in the counseling relationship and taking responsibility for his or her specialized knowledge and skills, (b) the ability of the counselor to hear challenges by the client or feedback from the supervisor without becoming overly defensive, (c) the ability to be comfortable with the counselor's own feelings and attitudes, as well as those of the clients, and (d) the ability to have a fundamental respect for the client. (Bernard, 1979, pp. 62-63)

Personal growth opportunities abound for both supervisor and supervisee when the focus is on personalization skills.

Lanning (1986) adds a fourth focus of supervision, professional behaviors, to the original model. Professional behaviors refer to a supervisee's behaviors that reflect an ability to adhere to commonly accepted principles of professional practice. These behaviors include being on time for appointments, maintaining confidentiality, being able to effect an appropriate referral, and maintaining appropriate personal relationships with clients.

Supervisor's styles are influenced by the roles they choose. Bernard (1979, 1994) describes three different roles and their purposes. Supervisor-as-teacher is the most common role for supervisors to take with beginning counselors. In the teacher role, the supervisor takes responsibility for knowing what the supervisee needs to do or learn, be it a new technique, a new intervention, or another direct suggestion about the counselor's work. Also in the teacher role, the supervisor acknowledges the rightness or wrongness of a particular counselor strategy. Supervisor-as-counselor emphasizes the interpersonal or intrapersonal dynamics of the trainees. In the counselor role, most often the supervisor's concern is the personal growth of the supervisee. Supervisor-as-consultant is the most common role for supervisors with advanced counselor trainees. In the consultant role, the supervisor encourages supervisees to think on their own and to trust their own insights. Authority for what transpires in the session is equally shared.

The discrimination model allows for flexibility of supervisor roles and foci and is situation specific. In supervision, that which transpires moment to moment as most salient opens itself up to moderate, affirmative postmodern possibilities. The model's focus on personalization skills attends to supervisees' personally constructed narratives of their training experiences. Supervisor-as-counselor provides a check on supervisees' being "force fed" the supervisor's social construction of clinical realities by respecting supervisees' personal constructions of clinical realities. Likewise, supervisor-as-consultant takes into consideration supervisees' personally constructed narratives. The cognitive map that supervisors use to track the focus of supervision and determine the best supervisory vehicle for accomplishing supervision goals may assume too much of an objective world for some postmodernists. In the counselor role, supervisors will have to ensure that they do not end up doing therapy with supervisees (Pope & Vasquez, 1991). Moreover, supervisors will have to ensure that they remain appropriate about self-disclosure and not exploit the dependency of the supervisee. Bernard and Goodyear (1992) discuss the strengths and weaknesses of the discrimination model. First, more than most models that have addressed supervisor roles, the model is rooted in technical eclecticism that frees the user to be broadly flexible in responding to the supervisee. However, a possible limitation is that it is not driven by any theoretical approach. Second, the discrimination model is concerned with the *training* aspects of supervision. The complementary limitation is that, in its original form, the model does not directly ensure quality of client care. To overcome this limitation, Lanning (1986) added the fourth function of supervision, professional behaviors, to the original model. Third, the model has extensive empirical support (see Bernard & Goodyear, 1992, p. 46, for a complete listing of references). The quantitative research results supporting the utility of the model may, however, be rejected by some postmodernists. Fourth, explicit training in the model is discussed (Bernard, 1981) in conjunction with I.P.R. (Bernard, 1989). As a postmodern extension of the model, the role of *supervisor-as-partial-learner* is discussed in the Applications to Supervision section below. With explicit attention to supervisor-as-partial-learner, informed uncertainty is shared equally among supervisors, supervisees, and clients—and allows for a "mutual expertise" that has a moderate, affirmative postmodernist tone.

Live Supervision

Live supervision represents a paradigm shift from either individual or group supervision that consists of two essential differences: The distinction between therapy and supervision seems less pronounced than in traditional supervision, and the role of the supervisor is significantly changed to include both coaching and co-therapist dimensions (Bernard & Goodyear, 1992). Live supervision is a hallmark of family therapy programs. Montalvo (1973) offers one of the earliest descriptions of live supervision: The supervisor watches the session, usually behind a one-way mirror, and intervenes upon the session to guide the supervisee's behavior at the moment that action is happening. Live supervision assumes that there is always a significant gap between a therapist's self-report about a case and what is actually observed to happen. It also assumes that strategies based on what is actually observed to be happening require some correction while on course. The supervisor attempts to guide the therapist to consider the uniqueness of the presenting problem and the individual perspectives of the participants in creating circumstances that help them to change (Montalvo, 1973). With live supervision, the relations among supervisor, supervisee, and clients become threaded perspectives of a reality that moves and is moved by shifts in the perspective of all participants. These patterns of interaction are the emphasis in systemic approaches. The recursive nature of these patterns is described here momentarily. The variety of perspectives in live supervision is one source of postmodern clinical practice.

Models of live supervision by Montalvo (1973) and Haley (1976) have been described as supervisor-guided (Roberts, 1983). Haley (1976) calls live supervision the most effective form of supervision, and also the most expensive for a training institution or clinic. Like Montalvo, Haley states the need for supervisors and supervisees to clarify ahead of time what their relationship is and what the purpose of supervision is. "The supervisor must be able to adapt to a relationship with an experienced colleague, to a student who is experienced but not in the particular approach being taught, or to a student who has never done any therapy at all" (Haley, 1976, p. 192). Haley suggests a contract of agreement, similar to Montalvo. Live supervision protects clients from incompetence and allows for the teaching of how to do therapy at the moment when the therapist is doing just that.

Other models of live supervision, such as that developed by the Milan Centre for Family Therapy (Boscolo & Cecchin, 1982; Selvini Palazzoli et al., 1980), have been described as collaborative in nature (Roberts, 1983). Sperling and colleagues (1986) have also presented the collaborative team as a method of supervision and training. In the collaborative team approach, the supervisor's role is primarily that of a teacher who gradually turns over the reins of power and control to the supervisees themselves (Sperling et al., 1986). Supervisees as well as supervisor can phone in to the therapists during the live session, can provide each other with feedback, and can contribute to case conceptualization.

On both supervisor-guided and collaborative teams, case conceptualization stems primarily from systems theory. Briefly, systemic frameworks emphasize transactions between individuals, and interdependence between and among persons, rather than the individual characteristics of clients as the primary therapeutic focus (Huber, 1994). Individual motivation and intention are of secondary importance. Even when attention is zeroed in on a single person, that person's actions are analyzed in terms of how they affect and shape the actions of other members of the relationship system, as well as how other members' actions reciprocally affect and shape the individual's actions. Space considerations limit extensive discussion of systems theory here; useful introductions include Goldenberg and Goldenberg (1991), McGoldrick, Pearce, and Giordano (1982), and Walsh (1993). Multiple theoretical approaches to supervision are addressed by McDaniel et al. (1983).

Relevant to the present discussion are the closely related supervision procedures and the circular and reflexive therapeutic questions developed by the Milan team (Boscolo, & Cecchin, 1982; Cecchin, 1987; Selvini Palazzoli et al., 1980; Penn, 1982; Tomm, 1985, 1987). In their strategic/systemic approach, symptoms are viewed as communication acts embedded in interaction patterns of repetitive sequences between persons. The goal is to interrupt rigid feedback cycles, change symptom maintaining sequences, and shift perspectives to enable more empowered positions. Originally, the Milan team used a pre-session, session, inter-session, conclusion of session, post-session format. In the pre-session, all known data concerning the clients is elaborated upon and hypotheses formed that will be tested during the encounter with clients. During the session, the co-therapists try to elicit information from the clients and create observable interactions among various members of the family. The live supervisor intervenes as necessary. The inter-session discussion examines new data that has been elicited, and decisions are made about eventual interventions. The conclusion of the session entails the co-therapists rejoining the clients to make a prescription. Circular questioning and circular questions form the interview style. By *circularity,* Selvini Palazzoli et al. (1980) mean "the capacity of the therapist to conduct his [*sic*] investigation on the basis of feedback from the family in response to the information he [*sic*] solicits about relationships" (p. 8). The therapist asks questions in order to become "coupled" with the family in a coevolutionary process of systemic exploration to understand the system and facilitate therapeutic change (Tomm, 1985). The shift in perspective produced by the strategic/systemic approach, and the therapist's knowing that he or she does not know the answer to such questions, gives rise to postmodern, narrative approaches to therapy and supervision.

The main asset of live supervision—its capacity for getting closer to actual clinical happenings rather than self-reports about them—does not make it any more foolproof than any other arrangement involving humans (Montalvo, 1973). In view of the confluence of the feminist, constructionist/constructivist, and cultural relativist movements, Hardy (1993) articulates 10 questions, reflections, and future directions of live supervision, particularly as the family therapy field approaches an epistemological shift from structuralism and positivism to postmodernism and relativism. The full impact of these epistemological shifts has yet to be realized (Hardy, 1993). Moreover, the confluence of the above movements in live supervision beyond the family therapy field is yet to be realized.

Multiculturalism

Pedersen (1990) offers a broad definition of culture that recognizes the following variables: ethnographic (ethnicity, nationality, religion, language usage); demographic (age, gender, place of residence); status (social, economic, educational factors); affiliations (formal memberships, informal memberships). Encounters among supervisor(s), supervisee(s), and client(s) become multicultural interactions when differences exist among the variables recognized above. These potential multiple dimensions are endowed with moderate, affirmative postmodern discourse. Discourse refers to "a system of statements, practices, and institutional structures that share common values" (Hare-Mustin, 1994, p. 19).

If multiculturalism is to be more than a passing trend in the mental health professions, many training programs will be pressed to expand the traditional format of therapist-client training dyads. Multicultural clientele may be less individualistic, and may be more effectively served in therapy with members of the varying human systems that are significant in their lives and relevant to clients' presenting issues. Linzer (1984), for example, writes about the third- and fourth-generation effects in Jewish families of survivors of the Holocaust. Individual therapy for a grandchild or great-grandchild of such a survivor may not be the most effective mode of treatment (see also Bauman, 1995). For largely individually trained practitioners, paradigmatic shifts into systemic orientations and epistemological shifts within systemic orientations may become more necessary than ever before. The ongoing challenge will be to work from both individual psychology and systems interactions. Among the ethical issues that will arise are the interdependence of personal responsibility (Yalom, 1980), especially from a multicultural perspective (Steele, 1990,), and environmental determinism (Huber, 1994). The recognition of culture as dynamic (Pedersen, 1990), with alternate cultural identities replacing one another in salience, opens up into a postmodern view of understandings within therapy and supervision as always changing. Pedersen neglects to mention sexual orientation among the variables in his broad definition of culture, a variable that has postmodern multicultural clinical applications (González et al., 1994).

The convergent influences identified above represent an explicit articulation of the concepts that contribute to my postmodern, multicultural clinical supervision. This blending of paradigms and epistemologies sets the tone, or mood, for what I do as a supervisor. Yet it would be inaccurate to refer to this blending as an integrated framework. Richardson (1993) describes framework as connoting "a kind of scaffold or structure for organizing knowledge, questions, and so forth. . . . It is useful for organizing 'knowledge out there' and implies an independence or disconnection between the knower and the known" (p. 427). In contrast to such a framework, she proposes a "location of study" as "a point of view, a perspective of the knower in relation to what is known. . . . What can be known from any particular location is admittedly affected by the location of the knower" (p. 427). In postmodern terms, this location is sometimes referred to as "situated knowledge." The applications to supervision presented below illustrate my location, or situated knowledge, at this writing. With respect to multiculturalism, I locate myself as a moderate, affirmative postmodernist. Modernist variables such as race, culture, ethnicity, gender, demographics, and socioeconomic status are irreducible categories of human existence that cannot be deconstructed. Objective social and political structures of oppression *do* exist outside the realities created—or glossed over—by language. Sometimes these realities are perpetuated by socially constructed, dominant discourses that serve as smoke screens to disguise inequities (Hare-Mustin, 1994), or by indirect talk—coded, politically laden, and sarcastic language— that aims to silence others (Capper, 1995). I shy away from extreme, skeptical postmodern discourse that becomes too hobbled by its own language to be able to exercise the spirit of reconceptualizations about how we experience the world around us. In the context of supervision, the task becomes one of engendering an environment in which supervisees, clients, and supervisor can all voice and own the truth of their respective experiences.

Applications
to Supervision

To the fullest extent possible, I strive to identify and to reinforce each supervisee's individual strengths, and to help supervisees' confidence levels increase regarding their abilities as therapists. Concurrently, I make it immediately clear to my supervisees that client welfare comes first, supervisees' training needs come second (Pope & Vasquez, 1991). Criteria for supervisee evaluation is handed out to first-time supervisees. I agree with Bernard (1992) that supervisors have a professional mandate to judge the competence of their supervisees; we heighten the threat of the evaluation process by denying its centrality to the supervision process. Thus, though I find some postmodern ideas appealing, I retain my so-called modernist roots for supervisee evaluation purposes. I always provide excerpts from Bernard's (1979) discrimination model—pre-highlighted for supervisees' reading convenience—to make explicit the primary basis of my supervisory work, thereby reducing somewhat supervisees' anxiety and tension. I also provide a handout on "Often Used Inquirer Leads" from I.P.R. (complied by Abigeli Harris & Donald Werner, n.d.). With the discrimination model and I.P.R. handouts, supervisees know where I am coming from as a supervisor right from the start.

In addition to basic guidelines of live supervision provided by Montalvo (1973), Haley (1976), and the Milan team, I add the three following points, based on my own experiences with live supervision: First, we are all vulnerable when having our therapy work observed from behind a one-way mirror. Second, whatever is said behind-the-mirror is understood as fair game for repetition in the presence of the observed therapists during intersessions and post-sessions; "back-biting behind-the-mirror" with positive connotation to one's face will not be tolerated. Third, as a supervisor, I will "catch" supervisees if I have to—especially beginning therapists, without thinking any less of them, should occasions arise when they find themselves in over their heads with clients—by calling in to the therapy room and giving an explicit directive or by walking in after receiving advance permission from the supervisees through calling ahead. These three *human considerations,* when coupled with theoretical aspects of live supervision, engender additional mutual respect and support on a live supervision team. Come what may, at least a common language is established up front in terms of what I am on the lookout for as a supervisor.

I further agree with Bernard (1992) that theoretical compatibility between supervisor and supervisee is unnecessary. In particular, I want my supervisees to know from which theory they are conceptualizing and intervening with a client. I also want supervisees to be aware of the ideologies of various theories (Lakin, 1988), especially in terms of judgments about normality, maturity, adjustment, and what is deemed optimal, good, or bad. Clients' concerns may be viewed from multiple perspectives: primarily biological, failures in development, uncontrollable social and economic factors, personal moral crises (Lakin, 1988), limiting self-narratives (White, 1994), or family systems interactions. Respectively, supervisee interventions can become referrals for biological restoration (i.e., evaluation for medication), enhancement of insight and self-understanding, societal change (if possible), moral realignment (Lakin, 1988), restorying a self-narrative (White, 1994), or a systems-level intervention (Cecchin, 1987; Penn, 1982; Tomm, 1985, 1987). The ongoing ethical challenge is for supervisors and their trainees to be aware of the value positions they take and communicate to their clients (Lakin, 1988). Bernard (1992) contends that supervisors are responsible for helping supervisees to scrutinize different theories and to begin to identify the theory (or theories) that fit into the supervisee's own clinical style, cultural context, and personal vision. Based on the discrimination model, this theoretical scrutiny entails the supervisor-as-consultant focusing on conceptualization skills. By encouraging supervisees to develop their own visions of clinical reality, I am extending from my modernist foundations into a moderate, affirmative postmodernism.

When supervisees ask about my theoretical orientation in therapy, I tell them that I have a strong cognitive-behavioral and social learning foundation, with an intensive year of psychodynamic training and supervision training from my pre-doctoral internship, plus 1½ years of post-doctoral supervision in systems theory and postmodern, narrative approaches. I share my unfolding orientation so that supervisees can discern how I have kept in my clinical repertoire those experiences that have felt comfortable, natural, and reliable for me, and that I honestly believe are useful, ethical means for engaging clients with a minimum of clinical affectation.

I bring into my therapy and clinical work a willingness to attend to clients' personal psychology, family dynamics, and social reality (Aponte, 1991). Through this complex process, which can fit into a moderate, affirmative postmodern framework with a multicultural perspective, innovations and re-substantiation of therapy and supervision can occur. Included in these postmodern considerations are (a) *supervisor-as-partial-learner,* (b) language usage and paradigm choice, (c) supervisees' expression of strong affect in supervision, (d) attention to client nonverbal behaviors, and (e) attention to client verbal statements.

Supervisor-as-Partial-Learner

As a postmodern extension of Bernard's roles of supervisor-as- teacher, -counselor, and -consultant, I propose a fourth role: *supervisor-as-partial-learner.* This fourth role is an outgrowth of my own practical experience and reflects my emergent, situated knowledge. Supervisor-as-partial-learner represents my own style, cultural context, and personal vision. Extensive dialogues, readings, deconstructions and reconstructions, critical thinking (Ruggiero, 1990), and other deliberations have contributed to this current, professional self-narrative. Supervisor-as-partial-learner, during live supervision behind-the-mirror, means that the most I can arrive at is a partial truth about what I am observing in supervisee-client interactions. I agree with Pope and Vasquez (1991) that (a) the supervisor bears ultimate responsibility—both ethically and legally—for the services that supervisees provide, and (b) the supervisor must clearly, frankly, and promptly communicate to the supervisee his or her assessment of strengths, weaknesses, and development. Therefore, I cannot abdicate the role of "expert" altogether (Anderson & Goolishian, 1992). I can partially understand the multicultural nuances among myself, my supervisees, and our clients. In live supervision, pre-, inter-, and post-sessions allow for a further exchange of understandings among team members that enables a "mutual expertise." During individual and group supervision as well, I can partially know. From a moderate, affirmative postmodernism, the integrated authorial intentions of supervisor, supervisee, and client enhance each other; we are "mutual experts" and share center stage together.

Often, I have been surprised by supervisees' direct requests for feedback on how smoothly they have opened and closed an interview, on how skillful they appear in identifying themes in client narratives or choosing interventions appropriate with clients' goals, on how clearly they seem to hear client challenges, and how nondefensively they visibly respond to those challenges. Supervisor-as-partial-learner, in response to supervisees' requests for feedback, means that I can accommodate such requests with an informed uncertainty (Minuchin, 1991) that provides an opportunity for mutual examination with supervisees to discuss if what I observed validates the supervisees' experience. I can address and own what seems to me to be happening in a session. With informed uncertainty as a frame of reference, supervisor-as-partial-learner allows my observations and feedback to be questioned—not deconstructed, which offers no practical, alternative observations—by supervisees regarding the validity of the supervisees' and clients' interactional experiences. Informed uncertainty allows for a full-hearted exchange of possibilities (Minuchin, 1991)—"mutual expertise." In contrast, "feigning clinical naïveté" (Kagan, 1980) can be disengaging and hinder collaboration, can undermine beginning supervisees' clinical development, and can diminish supervisees' trust in getting an honest response (Efran & Clarfield, 1992) from supervisors. Supervisor-as-partial-learner facilitates collaboration between "mutual experts." When supervisees request direction from me about conducting interviews, identifying narrative themes, or dealing effectively with client challenges, I move into supervisor-as-teacher, focusing respectively on process, conceptualization, and personalization skills. In the teacher role, I am hierarchical, which provides the unequivocal support my supervisees ask for at such moments.

A second meaning of supervisor-as-partial-learner is that, because of extensive classroom teaching, I will not separate my working knowledge of developmental psychology; individual, group, and systemic therapies; career counseling; cognitive therapy; ethics; and multiculturalism from the context of supervision and therapy, because the use of informed uncertainty about various topics from those subjects is what serves to validate progressive narratives for supervisees and clients. Few postmodern readings appear to make explicit room for including a working knowledge of such subjects. In the role of partial learner, informed uncertainty about various topics and subject matters allows for innovation and resubstantiation among receptive supervisees and clients. For example, a partial list of topical handouts I have given to clients, either directly or through supervisees, includes "Coping With Depression" (Beck & Greenberg, 1974), "How to Use a Condom ('rubber')" (Maryland State Department of Health and Mental Hygiene, 1987), "Reactions to Divorce and Child Development" (Hodges, 1986), and "Read This Before Coming Out to Your Parents" (Sauerman, 1984). Rather than presenting such handouts as a totalizing view, I invite clients to consider what, if anything, fits for them. I would not be 100% participatory (Efran et al., 1988) in supervision and therapy if I did not use my working knowledge of various subject matters and relevant topics within such subjects.

As a third meaning of supervisor-as-partial-learner, I can genuinely learn from my supervisees without pretending that power differentials do not exist. For example, some of my supervisees have been teachers in public schools. They can inform me about formal procedures, common practices, and informal attitudes that school personnel sometimes display toward students, parents, and referrals to therapy. Supervisees are invited to share such expertise during supervision. Other supervisees have more practical knowledge than I do about certain cultural subgroups. On one live supervision team, a young client who was "gang-bait" was referred for therapy by a local elementary school counselor. A team member happened to work in another school district on gang prevention activities. This supervisee took me on a personally guided tour of the most prominent locales for graffiti-sprayed walls and fences in San Antonio's West Side. Learning the meanings of turf-gang and street-gang symbols was like deciphering hieroglyphics! We took a drive down the client's street and saw a boarded-up house on the same block, riddled with graffiti. During live supervision, the team behind-the-mirror heard firsthand of the pressures the client was under to join a gang. From the supervisee's tour and the young client's narrative, I gained a much deeper appreciation of the pervasiveness of gangs, their worldviews, and their multiple messages. On my regular drive home after that tour, I noticed graffiti on bus stops, building walls, and utility boxes on telephone poles that I had not tuned into before.

In Texas, master's-level certified psychologists can conduct psychological assessment under the supervision of doctoral-level licensed psychologists. Some of my doctoral-level supervisees had earned their livelihoods for many years by assessing intelligence and personality. Their extensive knowledge of response patterns on various instruments by certain multicultural client subgroups was helpful to teammates and myself. At times, I had to coax reticent supervisees to state what they knew from such paradigms, to remind them that, despite some postmodernists' proclamations that assessment and diagnosis reify pathology, these were also tools of our trade. I am well aware of the historical abuses of assessment and diagnosis when practiced on ethnic and racial minorities, but since these tools are not going to be discontinued, it behooved us to be informed about them (see Jones & Thorne, 1987, for further discussion). The richness is in allowing for as many narratives as possible.

As a fourth meaning of supervisor-as-partial-learner, occasionally supervisees bring onto my supervisory caseload ongoing clients who are new to me. Sometimes supervisees ask me to join them as a new co-therapist with these ongoing clients. Especially with ongoing clients who appear "stuck," I can ask a circular or reflexive question of my co-therapist in the presence of the client(s) that creates generative shifts. For example, as a new co-therapist on an ongoing case, in the presence of the client, I can ask my co-therapist a reflexive, process-interruption question to expose the current process (Tomm, 1987), "Does [client's name] seem less depressed to you than before?" Such a question can curtail the client's depressing process and, it is hoped, facilitate self-healing. It is asked as if the co-therapists were gossiping in the presence of the client (Haley, 1976; Penn, 1982; Tomm,

1985). Also, it is asked in a way that separates the behavior from the client so as to minimize the reification of pathology. Dependent on the context, of course, another question I could ask my co-therapist about the same client is, "Is [client's name] depressive behavior reducing faster than you thought might have happened?" This circular, temporal difference question focuses on a difference between category differences at two points in time, in this instance, between the past and the present (Tomm, 1985). However, the question is also asked in such a way that there is an embedded suggestion of differences between the present and future (supervisor-as-partial-learner focusing on conceptualization skills). A less systemic flavored, I.P.R.-based question could be followed up from one of the co-therapists to the client, "What is it like for you to hear us talking about you in this way?" Thus, supervisor, supervisee, and client share center stage together, partially learning from each other, sharing their "mutual expertise."

Supervisor-as-partial-learner has the potential to create an atmosphere where all involved can participate as fully engaged partners. Nobody (a) has to be the sole expert, (b) has to masquerade as being in a one-down position, or (c) has to pretend to buy into a socially constructed clinical reality that contradicts their personally constructed clinical reality. Participants also retain personal responsibility for decisions to withhold any "mutual expertise" that they can contribute to the clinical interaction. A climate can be established that energizes and empowers those who share in the therapeutic endeavor. This infinitely fascinating, dynamic approach is but one viable means of providing postmodern, multicultural clinical supervision.

Language Usage and Paradigm Choice

For multilingual persons, language use may vary according to context. Rodriguez (1982) writes of his bilingual family's use of Spanish as the language of intimacy, English as the language of public life. Spanish can become the "language of affect" for some Hispanic clients in therapy. Sometimes a supervisee does not speak Spanish, and it appears the bilingual clients' usage of Spanish is imminent. In one instance, a young mother and her elementary school-age child were referred by the child's teacher. During the first session, written informed consent and confidentiality procedures were explained in English, which the mother spoke and read fluently. Initially, the mother's public demeanor was polite and cooperative. When the co-therapists asked for her understanding of the teacher's referral of the child to us, the mother visibly struggled to contain her emotions. The mother's response began, "*Dijo* . . ." ("[the teacher] said . . ."), then she caught herself. I called in to the monolingual English-speaking co-therapists, "Repeat after me, *¿'Dijo qué?'* " ("[the teacher] said what?"). With this prompt, the mother finished her reply in Spanish. I then called in to the co-therapists, "Now, matter-of-factly ask her to repeat in English what she just said." The mother was welcomed to use Spanish first whenever she wanted, as long as she had repeated her words to the co-therapists in English. This bilingual accommodation worked for both the clients and the supervisees.

In a subsequent session, the mother described her child's teacher as *sangrona,* an idiomatic Spanish adjective that roughly translates into *cold-blooded*—but the nuance gets lost in translation. As a bilingual supervisor-as-partial-learner, I had a working knowledge of the idioms she was using. However, I did not know what they meant for her. Using a circular, categorical context question, I instructed the co-therapists to ask, "When your child's teacher is behaving like a *sangrona,* what does the teacher do?" Such a question asks about the relationship of idiomatic meaning and action (Tomm, 1985). The relationship of action to meaning was addressed by asking the mother, "When the teacher does things that are *sangrona,* what does that mean to you?" A question introducing a hypothesis to reveal recursiveness (Tomm, 1987) then followed: "When the teacher gets *sangrona,* and you get angry, what does your child do at school? at home?" A future-oriented question to highlight potential consequences (Tomm, 1987) was, "What do you think would happen if you continued to see the teacher as *sangrona?*" These inquiries (supervisor-as-consultant focusing on conceptualization skills), using both English and idiomatic Spanish in the same sentences, were spoken in "Tex-Mex." In a later session, once the therapeutic relationship had been established, a nonsystemic question was asked of the mother, "Who else do you get angry with?" There seemed to be a pattern in her relationships that became problematic for her. When she admitted that there was, she was invited to return, alone, for some brief individual therapy. She acknowledged that the school and her child were not the only problems, and was amenable to personal psychological interventions. Part of this paradigmatic shift entailed co-therapists not getting caught up in family secrets (Karpel, 1980), especially if her child or other family members were likely to rejoin the therapy at another time. Another option was for someone else to see the mother individually.

Marcos and Urcuyo (1979) write that constant self-initiated language switching can be a deliberate attempt by bilingual clients to escape from important feelings and experiences. Language switching as a form of resistance (Marcos & Urcuyo, 1979) was resubstantiated with the mother in the above instance by recognizing that "language of affect" other than English is not uncommon for those who are bilingually active. Furthermore, language switching may be reconceptualized from resistance to an acknowledgment that such switching is a way of life for many bilingual Spanish-speakers in the Southwestern United States. The above mother's self-narrative reflects such a way of life, and when acknowledged conveys respect for the client.

In supervision, one task is to process with monolingual English-speaking supervisees any personally constructed awkwardness they may feel about these various kinds of language usage (supervisor-as-counselor and -partial-learner focusing on personalization skills). Bilingual client/monolingual therapist differences may be inevitable, although this need not impede therapeutic effectiveness. Nevertheless, cultural and linguistic nuances of clients' constructions of their worlds may be missed by monolingual service providers. Some supervisees seem to get frustrated that such clients do not learn to speak English, and it becomes useful to examine how this apparent frustration affects supervisees' interaction with their clients (supervisor-as-counselor and -partial-learner focusing on personalization skills). A second supervisory task is not to play favorites toward supervisees who can speak Spanish and/or Tex-Mex with me (supervisor-as-teacher focusing on professional behavior). A third supervisory task is openly to address paradigmatic shifts back and forth between systemic and individually oriented therapies (supervisor-as-teacher focusing on conceptualization skills). A fourth supervisory issue is to arrange, when possible, for one bilingual team member to translate simultaneously from English to Spanish behind-the-mirror while a bilingual co-therapist remains with the clients in the therapy room.

Supervisee's Expression of Strong Affect in Supervision

Hardiman, Jackson, and Kim (n.d.) have an exercise called "Growing Up Racially/Ethnically" that explores culture-specific messages one received while growing up. Among other topics, the exercise touches upon the expression of strong feelings, especially anger and affection, as socially conditioned differentially across cultures. As a supervisor, my multiculturally relevant experiences of supervisees' expression of strong affect includes times when they have cried during supervision. I can count on one hand the number of times it happened over the years. Generally (and thankfully), the supervisory environment has felt safe enough for supervisees to shed tears. Weeping occurred in different circumstances. In one situation, during a pre-session on a live-supervision team, the supervisee was clearly overextended and excessively fatigued. The supervisee was concerned with making a good impression on me (I believe there is no credible way to deny one's power as a supervisor in such an instance), but was simply overscheduled with commitments (frequently, I feel compassion for motivated graduate students who inadvertently overload themselves). Fortunately, this supervisee had no clients scheduled yet on my supervisee caseload. The opportunity arose for the team to generate some anticipatory realities as a guiding image of the future (Cooperrider, 1990), among them (a) stay on the team, but behind-the-mirror, without client contact; (b) stay on the team and see clients; (c) rejoin the team later after a certain number of commitments decreased; (d) drop the team and sign up in another semester (supervisor-as-consultant focusing on professional behavior). I invited the supervisee to act in the interests of the supervisee's self-care and wellness, believing that any move to treat oneself better seemed to me to be a more memorable lesson than anything that could be learned on my team (supervisor-as-teacher and -partial-learner focusing on personalization skills). The final decision was left up to the supervisee to decide what was best (supervisor-as-consultant and -partial-learner focusing on professional behavior), who chose option (d). The challenge for me was to respect the emotional expression through the tears of the supervisee's initial frustration without judging it pejoratively. The generating of several options shifted the context from making a good impression on me to getting into the habit of taking care of oneself early on as the supervisee entered a challenging profession (supervisor-as-teacher focusing on professional behavior).

In another instance, I served as a co-therapist and individual supervisor with a male supervisee in an ongoing group. During one post-session, the supervisee told me he was angry with a male group member who, during the session, was angry and frustrated himself. Several group members had offered empathy, encouragement, and advice to this one male group member—all of which he appeared to ignore. I had asked the client what he heard the other group members telling him. I also asked the other group members what they believed their fellow client had heard. My co-therapist uncharacteristically had remained silent during this part of the session. In the post-session, I was surprised that the supervisee was angry because I had noted no traces of anger during the group session. I asked the supervisee about the source of his anger (supervisor-as-consultant and supervisor-as-partial-learner focusing on personalization skills). He replied that the male group member rejected all help and appeared to enjoy being miserable. Using I.P.R.-based inquirer leads, I then asked the supervisee what it was, if anything, about a helpless-appearing male that angered him (supervisor-as-counselor and supervisor-as-partial-learner focusing on personalization skills). Then I became an appreciative inquirer to explore with the supervisee on seemingly possible responses in the future (supervisor-as-consultant and supervisor-as-partial-learner focusing on conceptualization skills, process skills, and professional behavior). Other times, I have found it useful to provide supervisees with a condensed handout on "blaming the victim" (Ryan, 1971) when the supervisee's level of frustration with clients seems to intensify (supervisor-as-teacher and -partial-learner focusing on concep-tualization and personalization skills). With culturally different and especial-ly lower-income clients, supervisees can revert to victim blaming when narratives in therapy stabilize or when client worldviews challenge the sensibilities of supervisees. Victim blaming on the part of the supervisee, of course, facilitates a regressive narrative with clients.

On the one hand, in the two examples above, I contextualized to clinical supervision the supervisee's expression of strong affect. On the other hand, I focused on more generalized patterns of behavior by inviting the supervisee in the first situation to acquire the habit of treating oneself better, and by asking the supervisee in the second instance about his usual reactions to helpless-appearing males. Attention to *both* contextual *and* generalized (i.e., context-free) demeanor of the supervisees embodied a moderate, affirmative postmodernism. In addition, *both* appreciative inquiry *and* I.P.R.-based inquiry were used as supervisory tools. Also, I always have found it extreme-ly valuable to explore with supervisees productive, therapeutic responses for those moments when, inevitably, their sensibilities are challenged by clients' worldviews.

Attention to Client Nonverbal Behaviors

Sometimes clients' gender role socialization and cultural background is revealed when their body language and body movement are observed in live supervision. From a collaborative team stance, my supervisees are welcome to point out these nonverbals. The richness of these behind-the-mirror observations enhances the therapy work we do. In one situation, the clients were a Mexican American family consisting of an elementary school-aged boy and his grandparents. The grandparents had adopted him after one parent deserted him and the other, custodial parent was murdered. The grandfather's tender gaze toward his grandson was tempered by a stiff, seated body posture. During the session, the grandfather sat with arms folded across his chest; otherwise, he never moved, physically. He let his wife and grandson do almost all the talking, but was clearly present and engaged in the session. From behind-the-mirror, my team could not see what the co-therapists in the room could plainly see—the frequency with which the grandfather's eyes welled up with tears. During an inter-session consultation, the co-therapists in the room alerted my team about the grandfather's unshed tears. Out of respect for the grandfather's bereavement and his need to be strong— *fuerte*—for his family, we deliberately did nothing about the grandfather's powerful nonverbals. Rodriguez (1982) defines *fuerte* as "not physical strength as much as inner strength, character" (p. 128). The co-therapists in the room could clearly see that the grandfather was doing all he could to maintain his composure, as was "proper" for him to do (Rodriguez, 1982). The grandfather declined an invitation to be seen for an individual session, and we did not press it (supervisor-as-consultant focusing on process skills and professional behavior).

This example illustrates cultural and contextual bases for supervision and therapy where nonverbals provide a key opportunity to intervene—or not intervene—as the case may be (see Sue & Sue, 1990, for further discussion about the role nonverbal communication plays with multicultural clientele). When interventions based on nonverbal behavior generate new narratives that consider gender role and ethnic socialization, then postmodern multicultural clinical work happens. Yet as with the grandfather in the example above, ethical behavior encourages retaining sight of clients' abilities to act in their own best interests in keeping with their cultural self-definition (Cayleff, 1986).

Attention to Client Verbal Statements

Gender socialization can be reflected in supervisees' responses to clients' verbal statements. One live supervision team I had was all female supervisees. I was doing conjoint couples therapy with one of the supervisees when the husband turned to me in the therapy session and, man-to-man, said to me: "The mistake I made was in letting my wife go out and get a job in the first place." The murmurings of the team members literally reverberated through the one-way mirror! During the post-session, we as a team discussed the supervisees' reactions. They were offended by what they construed as the husband's sexist remark. I warned the supervisees that there would be times when they would have their personal sensibilities offended by their multicultural clients' statements (supervisor-as-teacher focusing on conceptualization skills). I used I.P.R. inquiries to ask the supervisees what it was like to have been offended so (supervisor-as-counselor and -partial-learner focusing on conceptualization skills). Team members expressed their multiple points of view. These multiple expressions lent themselves to a moderate, affirmative postmodernist extension: namely, an appreciative inquiry of the possible ways that supervisees could respond in the future when their personal sensibilities were offended by clients during a therapy session (supervisor-as-consultant and -partial-learner focusing on process, conceptualization, and personalization skills).

These supervisory interventions and dialogues can be applied to perceived racist, homophobic, and other seemingly prejudicial client statements. Multiple supervisory roles and foci, integrated with a progression from I.P.R.'s self-discovery learning to appreciative inquiry's generation of anticipatory realities, allowed supervisees to learn on both personal and socially constructed clinical narratives. I began with where the supervisees were at that moment of behind-the-mirror murmuring, processed it with them, and then changed the context to generate new perspectives on when our personal sensibilities are assaulted by culturally different clients.

Implications for Multicultural Relevance

Postmodernism can hardly be talked about as if it were a single symbolic monolith (Russell & Gaubatz, 1995, p. 390). I agree with Hollinger (1994) when he states, "Coming to terms with postmodernism does not mean throwing out everything in the classic body of writings, but finding new ways to make old and new ideas work together in specific contexts" (p. 186). Likewise, Bauman (1993) acknowledges that, "A sufficient residue of modern sentiments has been imparted to all of us by training" (pp. 33-34). The supervisory style represented here retains the vestiges of my modernist-based training. The complex process of my extension into postmodern multicultural clinical supervision encompasses, but is not limited to case conceptualizations derived from (a) *both* modernism *and* postmodernism, (b) *both* social constructionism *and* constructivism, (c) *both* psychology *and* family therapy, (d) *both* circular *and* lineal causalities (Dell, 1986), (e) *both* in the counseling session *and* between sessions (Bernard, 1979); with supervision that is (f) *both* hierarchical *and* collaborative, (g) *both* traditional *and* live; with supervisees who are (h) *both* master's *and* doctoral level, (i) *both* male *and* female, (j) *both* so-called Hispanic *and* so-called Anglo; with myself as (k) *both* co-therapist *and* behind-the mirror; with clients who are (l) *both* children *and* adults, (m) *both* male *and* female, who speak in (n) *both* English *and* Spanish with combined permutations contingent upon their everyday language. The intricacies of movement within and between these multiple views represents a dance more than a stance. This dance is part of my current, professional self-narrative, and—in moderate, affirmative postmodern terms—reflects my emergent, situated knowledge. Excluding multiculturalism for a moment, of the other convergent influences that have contributed to my particular style of clinical supervision (postmodernism, I.P.R., the discrimination model, and live supervision), I.P.R. has demonstrated the most multicultural relevance thus far. I.P.R. has been widely applied (in teaching; family therapy; medical, pharmacy, and law schools; hospitals; secondary schools; agencies and prison personnel programs) in several countries (United States, Canada, Australia, Sweden, Denmark, Norway, Puerto Rico, & Israel) (Kagan, 1980).

Another moderate, affirmative postmodern tone is found in my presentations of (a) appreciative inquiry as an extension of I.P.R., (b) supervisor-as-partial-learner as an extension of the discrimination model, and (c) the resubstantiations of "mutual expertise" in supervision and (d) "language of affect" among bilingual and multilingual clientele. In multicultural clinical practice, the emphasis is placed equally on the impressions that are found in both the *personal* and *social* experiences of both clinician and client (Axelson, 1993, p. 3, italics in the original). For me, this equally placed emphasis lends itself to a "mutuality of expertise" between clinician and client, where neither pretends to be in a one-down position. "Language of affect" has multicultural relevance, in that clients can be minimally pathologized for using their everyday language(s) as a means of revealing their way of life in therapy.

Other, self-identified postmodernists should be asked about their own particular styles of supervision. Furthermore, it is important to ask to what extent, if any, are psychiatric evaluation and psychotropic medication, standardized assessment and diagnosis, and 12-step programs and hypnosis admissible in others' postmodern clinical activities. If a client is amenable to any of the aforementioned practices, it becomes incumbent upon me to respect such a worldview and to be willing to incorporate those practices into my clinical activities with those particular clients. In addition, other self-identified postmodernists should be asked about their views on quantitative and qualitative research methodologies, because perspectives will vary (Scarr, 1989). Inquirers have the right to straightforward answers to these questions, especially if this information is not provided up front.

Among my convergent influences, postmodernism's multicultural relevance will demand the most ongoing attention. Benhabib (1992), for example, mentions multiculturalism, feminism, and postmodernism as paradigms that have grown out of the decline of modernist epistemology. She deliberates whether the meta-philosophical premises of postmodernism are compatible with the normative content of feminism, not just as a theoretical position but as a theory of women's struggle for emancipation. Part of her concern is that the Enlightenment and modernist principles to which postmodernists should bid farewell are by no means clear. Using the phrase "strong version of postmodernism" (p. 213), she states that a strong postmodern style undermines the feminist commitment to women's agency and sense of selfhood, to the reappropriation of women's own history in the name of an emancipated future, and to the exercise of radical social criticism which uncovers gender "in all its endless variety and monotonous similarity" (p. 229). She writes that feminist theory can ally itself with the strong version of postmodernism only at the risk of incoherence and self-contradictoriness. Ultimately, she disagrees that postmodernism and feminism are conceptual and political allies. Her conclusions are food for thought.

From a multicultural perspective, the full impact of affirmative postmodernism, indigenous to Anglo-North American culture (Rosenau, 1992), may be of limited utility to diverse groups in the United States. For instance, how does the "magical realism" discourse of Latino peoples, as exemplified in literature (e.g., Anaya, 1994; García Marquez, 1976/1991; Nichols, 1987), and the closely related spiritual narratives of Mexican American Roman Catholic clients (González, 1994; González et al., 1994) pertain to an Anglo-centric paradigm? In addition, postmodernism as a reaction to the Enlightenment heritage may be of limited applicability to Spanish-speaking peoples. The Enlightenment scarcely penetrated beyond the intellectual circles of Spain and her American colonies (Fuentes, 1992; Gay, 1966), chiefly because of obstruction by the Inquisition. The modern world criticized by Continental European skeptical postmodernists, or by Anglo-North American affirmative postmodernists, was never the modern world of the overwhelming majority of the Spanish-speaking (Johnson, 1991), among other peoples. Postmodern discourse is rarely heard among construction laborers or low-income housing residents (Russell & Gaubatz, 1995). "Third World affirmative postmodernism" already has been described as inconsistent (Rosenau, 1992), but then, so have the constructs of multicultural positivists (Helms, 1994).

After several years of university teaching, clinical practice, and supervision on the predominantly Hispanic and lower-income West Side of San Antonio, Texas, I disagree that the modern world is rapidly waning (Srivastva et al., 1990) or dead (Hoffmann, 1991). As I write from El Paso, Texas—with daily views of the impoverished outskirts of the city of Juárez, Mexico, as I drive in to work—I accept that pockets of postmodernism exist, as do pockets of appalling premodern poverty. San Antonio's West Side contains the 11th most poverty-stricken census tract in the United States (Flores, 1995), while El Paso County has an estimated 72,750 people residing in *colonias* that lack clean drinking water and adequate sewage systems (Self, 1995). Aware of such economic distress, I find further dialogue consisting of endless abstract speculations about postmodernism inappropriate for me. I am interested in any practical application postmodernism has with multicultural clients, and in keeping my own backyard clean. I uphold the value that clinical work with disenfranchised and lower-income clients is a fundamentally human encounter, with little place for the clinician's intellectual posturing and the supervisor's proselytizing of paradigms. I find myself expanding into a postmodern orientation beyond those of the Continent and Anglo-North America. The more I am exposed to readings on postmodernism, to other self-identified postmodern clinical practitioners, and to lower-income and culturally diverse clients, the more I prefer using *both* constructivism *and* social contructionism in my therapy and supervision work. Constructivism allows for a retention of personal responsibility than can balance social constructionism from deteriorating into political manipulation and/or oppressive conspiracies of silence.

Mindful of the potential limitations of applying postmodernism to diverse peoples, there are also enormous possibilities. Years ago, "the cultural construction of clinical realities" elicited cross-cultural clients' explanations of what brought them into therapy (Kleinman, Eisenberg, & Good, 1978). In the present-day Southwestern United States, millions of *mestizos*—so-called Hispanics descended from a mingling of peoples (European and indigenous), cultures (Spanish and indigenous), and religions (Roman Catholic and indigenous)—have no contradiction in the duality of life as bilingual and bicultural (sometimes multicultural) persons (United States Catholic Conference, 1991). Native Americans, also, can be *both* Christians *and* members of their tribes and be complete persons in mind, body, and soul (United States Catholic Conference, 1991). The Southwest is but one place where local narratives are manifested in more than one language and cultural tradition. Such manifestations potentially can be akin to an affirmative, moderate postmodernism, with the recognition that there can be no culture without language and rituals (United States Catholic Conference, 1991). But in the Southwest and elsewhere, as we reach the second millennium, the technological advances presumed to have created the postmodern world (Gergen, 1991b) may be matched by the proliferation of an eschatological revival, giving rise to a throwback to the Romantic Age's notion of the soul.

Huston Smith (1989) writes that it took confrontations between cultures to bring home the fact that people see the world differently, but that the pendulum has swung too far in the direction of multiplicity. "Multiple views, yes; multiple realities, no. . . . Even if reality were no more than the sum of all . . . multiple realities . . ., that sum would stand as the inclusive reality which would not itself be multiple" (pp. 234-235). He adds that "it is impossible that any one system has all the truth. Other voices should be listened to" (p. 240). In the context of supervision and therapy, I believe the most preferable resonance is when nobody—supervisor, supervisee, or client—owns center stage alone, as with the musical conversations of a string quartet. Yet achieving collaborative resonance in clinical work on a consistent basis is unlikely—even a string quartet has a first violinist/conductor.

Among the ongoing ethical issues regarding postmodern multicultural clinical practice are (a) Can supervisors and supervisees automatically assume the right to define clients' presenting problems in terms of their own therapeutic orientation? (Huber, 1994), and (b) Should primary responsibility for defining how change should occur rest with the supervisor, the supervisee, or the client(s)? (Corey, Corey, & Callanan, 1993). Given the multiplicity of perspectives, Bauman (1993) opines that the few but tested and trustworthy ethical rules we have are not made for the measure of our present times of *"strongly felt moral ambiguity"* (p. 21, italics in the original). However one wishes to conceptualize the times we live in, a casual disregard or deconstruction of ethical codes is unwarranted.

Optimally, I prefer that supervisees find it permissible to be imperfect with regard to multiculturalism and postmodernism. Supervisees are permitted to struggle with these paradigms and are invited to be frank with their responses. They are allowed to reveal ignorance and misunderstanding. Overall, my task in supervision, as in therapy, is to assess what contingencies hinder or facilitate *both* personal *and* social constructions that enable generative shifts in perspective, meanings, interpretations, evaluations, and explanations. With these narrative approaches, I integrate a multicultural perspective in which cultural differences can be rooted in the preferred stories habitually entertained by ethnic, class, racial, and cultural groups—and individuals within those groups. I encourage my supervisees to consider the differing stories that we all learn as part of our socialization in different cultures (Howard, 1991). It is hoped that supervisees will not experience guilt for what they accept or believe, but will take personal responsibility for accepting as much as they can, and challenge themselves to examine socially constructed, oppressive attitudes and beliefs that they uncritically may have bought in to. Part of this entails respecting clients' modern narratives, and the premodern experience of those who live in poverty. After client welfare, it becomes a matter of the meanings that supervisees construe of their multicultural supervision and therapy experiences. "The fruit of a tree shows the care it has had" (Sirach, 27:6).

References

Anaya, R. A. (1994). *Bless me, Ultima.* New York, Warner Books.
Andersen, T. (1987). The reflecting team: Dialogue and meta-dialogue in clinical work. *Family Process, 26,* 415-428.

Andersen, T. (1991). *The reflecting team: Dialogues and dialogues about the dialogues.* New York: Norton.

Anderson, H. D. (1991, October). *"Not knowing": An essential element of therapeutic conversation.* Paper presented at the Annual Conference of the American Association of Marriage and Family Therapy, Dallas, TX.

Anderson, H. D., & Goolishian, H. A. (1988). Humans systems as linguistic systems: Preliminary and evolving ideas about the implications for clinical theory. *Family Process, 27,* 371-393.

Anderson, H. D., & Goolishian, H. A. (1991, January). *New directions in systemic therapy: A language systems approach.* Symposium presented at the Texas Association of Marriage and Family Therapy, Dallas, TX.

Anderson, H. D., & Goolishian, H. A. (1992). The client is the expert: A not-knowing approach to therapy. In S. McNamee & K. J. Gergen (Eds.), *Therapy as social construction* (pp. 23-39). London: Sage.

Aponte, H. J. (1991). Training on the person of the therapist for work with the poor and minorities. *Journal of Independent Social Work, 5,* 23-39.

Axelson, J. A. (1993). *Counseling and development in a multicultural society.* Pacific Grove, CA: Brooks/Cole.

Barrett, F. J., & Cooperrider, D. L. (1990). Generative metaphor intervention: A new approach for working with systems divided by conflict and caught in defensive perception. *The Journal of Applied Behavioral Science, 26,* 219-239.

Bass, E., & Davis, L. (1988). *The courage to heal: A guide for women survivors of child sexual abuse.* New York: Harper & Row.

Bauman, Z. (1993). *Postmodern ethics.* Cambridge, MA: Blackwell.

Bauman, Z. (1995). *Life in fragments: Essays in postmodern morality.* Cambridge, MA: Blackwell.

Beck, A. T., & Greenberg, R. L. (1974). *Coping with depression.* New York: Institute for Rational Living.

Benhabib, S. (1992). *Situating the self: Gender, community, and postmodernism in contemporary ethics.* New York: Routledge.

Berger, P. L., & Luckmann, T. (1966). *The social construction of reality.* Garden City, NY: Doubleday.

Bernard, J. M. (1979). Supervisor training: A discrimination model. *Counselor Education and Supervision, 19,* 60-68.

Bernard, J. M. (1981). Inservice training for clinical supervisors. *Professional Psychology, 12,* 740-748.

Bernard, J. M. (1989). Training supervisors to examine relationship variables using I.P.R. *The Clinical Supervisor, 7,* 103-112.

Bernard, J. M. (1992). The challenge of psychotherapy-based supervision: Making the pieces fit. *Counselor Education and Supervision, 31,* 232-237.

Bernard, J. M. (1994). Receiving and using supervision. In H. Hackney & S. Cormier (Eds.), *Counseling strategies and interventions* (4th ed.; pp. 169-189). Boston: Allyn & Bacon.

Bernard, J. M., & Goodyear, R. K. (1992). *Fundamentals of clinical supervision.* Boston: Allyn & Bacon.

Borgmann, A. (1992). *Crossing the postmodern divide.* Chicago: University of Chicago Press.

Boscolo, L., & Cecchin, G. (1982). Training in systemic therapy at the Milan Centre. In R. Whiffin & J. Byng-Hall (Eds.), *Family therapy supervision* (pp. 153-165). New York: Grune & Stratton.

Capper, C. A. (1995, October). *Discourses of dysfunction: Being silenced and silencing.* Paper presented at the University Council for Educational Administration Annual Convention, Salt Lake City.

Cayleff, S. E. (1986). Ethical issues in counseling gender, race, and culturally distinct groups. *Journal of Counseling and Development, 64,* 345-347.

Cecchin, G. (1987). Hypothesizing, circularity, and neutrality revisited: An invitation to curiosity. *Family Process, 26,* 405-413.

Coale, H. W. (1992). The constructivist emphasis on language: A critical conversation. *Journal of Strategic and Systemic Therapies, 11,* 12-26.

Cooperrider, D. L. (1990). Positive image, positive action: The affirmative basis of organizing. In S. Srivastva, D. L. Cooperrider, & Associates (Eds.), *Appreciative management and leadership: The power of positive thought and action in organizations* (pp. 91-125). San Francisco: Jossey-Bass.

Cooperrider, D. L., & Srivastva, S. (1987). Appreciative inquiry in organizational life. In W. A. Pasmore & R. W. Woodman (Eds.), *Research in organizational change and development* (Vol. 1, pp. 129-169). Greenwich, CT: JAI.

Corey, G., Corey, M. S., & Callanan, P. (1993). *Issues and ethics in the helping profession* (4th ed.). Pacific Grove, CA: Brooks/Cole.

Coyne, J. C. (1985). Toward a theory of frames and reframing: The social nature of frames. *Journal of Marital and Family Therapy, 11,* 337-344.

Dell, P. (1986). In defense of "lineal causality." *Family Process, 25,* 513-521.

Denner, B. (1995). Stalked by the postmodern beast. *American Psychologist, 50,* 390-391.

Doherty, W. J. (1991). Family therapy goes postmodern. *Family Therapy Networker, 15*(5), 37-42.

Efran, J. S., & Clarfield, L. E. (1992). Constructionist therapy: Sense and nonsense. In S. McNamee & K. J. Gergen (Eds.), *Therapy as social construction* (pp. 200-217). London: Sage.

Efran, J. S., Lukens, R. J., & Lukens, M. D. (1988). Constructivism: What's in it for you? *Family Therapy Networker, 12*(5), 27-35.

Flew, A. (1984). *A dictionary of philosophy* (rev. 2nd ed., rev.). New York: St. Martin's.

Flores, V. (1995, June 18). West Side growth seen stunted by lack of official attention. *San Antonio Express News,* pp. 1A, 14A.

Fuentes, C. (1992). *The buried mirror: Reflection on Spain and the New World.* Boston: Houghton Mifflin.

García Marquez, G. (1991). *One hundred years of solitude.* New York: HarperCollins. (Original work published 1976)

Gay, P. (1966). *Age of enlightenment.* New York: Time, Inc.

Gergen, K. J. (1973). Social psychology as history. *Journal of Personality and Social Psychology, 26,* 309-320.

Gergen, K. J. (1985). The social constructionist movement in modern psychology. *American Psychologist, 40,* 266-275.

Gergen, K. J. (1991a). The saturated family. *Family Therapy Networker, 15*(5), 27-35.

Gergen, K. J. (1991b). *The saturated self: Dilemmas of identity in contemporary life.* New York: Basic Books.

Gergen, K. J. (1994). Exploring the postmodern: Perils or potentials? *American Psychologist, 49,* 412-416.

Gergen, K. J. (1995). Postmodern psychology: Resonance and reflection. *American Psychologist, 50,* 394.

Gergen, K. J., & Gergen, M. J. (1986). Narrative form and the construction of psychological science. In T. R. Sarbin (Ed.), *Narrative psychology: The storied nature of human conduct* (pp. 22-44). New York: Praeger.

Gergen, M. M., & Gergen, K. J. (1984). The social construction of narrative accounts. In K. J. Gergen & M. M. Gergen (Eds.), *Historical social psychology* (pp. 173-189). Hillsdale, NJ: Lawrence Erlbaum.

Gilligan, C., & Noel, N. (1995, April). *Cartography of a lost time: Women, girls, and relationships* (Workshop sponsored by the Austin Women's Psychotherapy Project, Austin, TX).

Goldenberg, I., & Goldenberg, H. (1991). *Family therapy: An overview* (3rd ed.). Pacific Grove, CA: Brooks/Cole.

González, R. C. (1994, August). Multiculturalism and social constructionism: An overview. In J. M. Georgoulakis (Chair), *Multiculturalism in therapy: Social constructionist applications.* Symposium conducted at the American Psychological Association Annual Convention, Los Angeles.

González, R. C., Biever, J. L., & Gardner, G. T. (1993). Multiculturalism and social constructionism: Made for each other. In S. D. Johnson, Jr., R. T. Carter, E. I. Sicalides, & T. R. Buckley (Eds.), *Training for competence in cross-cultural counseling and psychotherapy: The 1993 Teachers College Winter Roundtable edited conference proceedings* (pp. 7-12). New York: Columbia University, Teachers College.

González, R. C., Biever, J. L., & Gardner, G. T. (1994). The multicultural perspective in therapy: A social constructionist approach. *Psychotherapy, 31*(3), 515-524.

González, R. C., North, M.-W., Ricks, K. A., & Biever, J. L. (1992). Language and social context in a cross-cultural workforce. In S. D. Johnson, Jr., & R. T. Carter (Eds.), *Addressing cultural issues in an organizational context: The 1992 Teachers College Roundtable edited conference proceedings* (pp. 62-72). New York: Columbia University, Teachers College.

Guerin, B. (1992). Behavioral analysis and the social construction of knowledge. *American Psychologist, 47,* 1423-1432.

Hacker, A. (1992). *Two nations: Black and White, separate, hostile, unequal.* New York: Charles Scribner's Sons.

Haley, J. (1976). *Problem-solving therapy: New strategies for effective family therapy.* San Francisco: Jossey-Bass.

Hardiman, R., Jackson, B., & Kim, J. (n.d.). *Growing up racially/ethnically* [multicultural exercise]. Amherst, MA: New Perspectives, Inc.

Hardy, K. V. (1993). Live supervision in the postmodern era of family therapy: Issues, reflections, and questions. *Contemporary Family Therapy, 15,* 9-20.

Hare-Mustin, R. T. (1994). Discourses in the mirrored room: A postmodern analysis of therapy. *Family Process, 33,* 19-35.

Hare-Mustin, R. T., & Maracek, J. (1988). The meaning of difference: Gender theory, postmodernism, and psychology. *American Psychology, 43,* 455-464.

Harris, A., & Werner, D. (n.d.). *Often used inquirer leads* [handout]. Available from Dr. Roberto Cortéz González.

Held, B. S. (1990). What's in a name? Some confusions and concerns about constructivism. *Journal of Marital and Family Therapy, 16,* 179-186.

Helms, J. E. (1994). How multiculturalism obscures racial factors in the therapy process: Comment on Ridley et al. (1994), Sodowsky et al. (1994), Ottavi et al. (1994), and Thompson et al. (1994). *Journal of Counseling Psychology, 41,* 162-165.

Hodges, W. (1986). *Interventions for children of divorce.* New York: John Wiley.

Hoffmann, L. (1990). Constructing realities: An art of lenses. *Family Process, 29,* 1-12.

Hoffmann, L. (1991). A reflexive stance for family therapy. *Journal of Strategic and Systemic Therapies, 10,* 4-17.

Hollinger, R. (1994). *Postmodernism and the social sciences: A thematic approach.* Thousand Oaks, CA: Sage.

Howard, G. S. (1991). Culture tales: A narrative approach to thinking, cross-cultural psychology, and psychotherapy. *American Psychologist, 46,* 187-197.

Huber, C. H. (1994). *Ethical, legal, and professional issues in the practice of marriage and family therapy* (2nd ed.). New York: Merrill.

Johnson, P. (1991). *The birth of the modern: World society 1815-1830.* New York: Harper-Collins.

Jones, E. E., & Thorne, A. (1987). Rediscovery of the subject: Intercultural approaches to clinical assessment. *Journal of Consulting and Clinical Psychology, 55,* 488-495.

Kagan, N. (1976). *Influencing human interaction.* Mason, WI: Mason Media.

Kagan, N. (1980). Influencing human interaction—Eighteen years with I.P.R. In A. K. Hess (Ed.), *Psychotherapy supervision: Theory, research, and practice* (pp. 262-286). New York: John Wiley.

Karpel, M. A. (1980). Family secrets: I. Conceptual and ethical issues in the relational context. II. Ethical and practical considerations in therapeutic management. *Family Process, 19,* 295-306.

Kleinman, A., Eisenberg, L., & Good, B. (1978). Culture, illness, and care: Clinical lessons from anthropologic and cross-cultural research. *Annals of Internal Medicine, 88,* 251-258.

Kudlac, K. E. (1991). Including God in the conversation: The influence of religious beliefs on the problem-organized system. *Family Therapy, 18,* 277-285.

Laird, J. (1989). Women and stories: Restorying women's self-constructions. In M. McGoldrick, C. M. Anderson, & F. Walsh (Eds.), *Women in families: A framework for family therapy* (pp. 427-450). New York: Norton.

Laird, J. (1993). Lesbian and gay families. In F. Walsh (Ed.), *Normal family processes* (2nd ed.; pp. 282-328). New York: Guilford.

Lakin, M. (1988). *Ethical issues in the psychotherapies.* New York: Oxford University Press.

Lanning, W. (1986). Development of the supervisor emphasis rating form. *Counselor Education and Supervision, 25,* 191-196.

Linzer, N. (1984). *The Jewish family: Authority and tradition in modern perspective.* New York: Human Sciences Press.

Lowenstein, S. F., & Reder, P. (1982). Trainees' initial reactions to live family therapy supervision. In R. Whiffin & J. Byng-Hall (Eds.), *Family therapy supervision* (pp. 115-129). New York: Grune & Stratton.

Mahoney, M. J. (1989). Holy epistemology! Construing the constructions of the constructivists. *Canadian Psychology/Psychologie Canadienne, 30,* 187-188.

Mahoney, M. J. (1993). The postmodern self in psychotherapy. *Journal of Cognitive Psychotherapy: An International Quarterly, 7,* 241-250.

Marcos, L. R., & Urcuyo, L. (1979). Dynamic psychotherapy with the bilingual patient. *American Journal of Psychotherapy, 33,* 331-338.

Maryland State Department of Health and Mental Hygiene. (1987). *How to use a condom (rubber)* (Stock No. 6-23) [pocket-sized pamphlet].

McDaniel, S. H., Weber, T., & McKeever, J. (1983). Multiple theoretical approaches to supervision: Choices in family therapy training. *Family Process, 22,* 491-500.

McGoldrick, M., Pearce, J. K., & Giordano, J. (Eds.). (1982). *Ethnicity and family therapy.* New York: Guilford.

McNamee, S., & Gergen, K. J. (Eds.). (1992). *Therapy as social construction.* London: Sage.

Meichenbaum, D. (1994, May). *Treating patients with post-traumatic stress disorder: A cognitive-behavioral approach* (Workshop sponsored by the Institute for the Advancement of Human Behavior, New Orleans, LA).

Meichenbaum, D., & Fong, G. T. (1993). How individuals control their own minds: A constructive narrative perspective. In D. M. Wegner & J. W. Pennebaker (Eds.), *Handbook of mental control* (pp. 473-490). Englewood Cliffs, NJ: Prentice Hall.

Mente, D. (1995). Whose truth? Whose goodness? Whose beauty? *American Psychologist, 50,* 391.

Minuchin, S. (1991). The seductions of constructivism. *Family Therapy Networker, 15*(5), 47-50.

Montalvo, B. (1973). Aspects of live supervision. *Family Process, 12,* 343-359.

Nichols, J. T. (1987). *The Milagro beanfield war.* New York: Ballantine.

O'Hara, M., & Anderson, W. T. (1991). Welcome to the postmodern world. *Family Therapy Networker, 15*(5), 19-25.

Osterhoudt, R. G. (1973). On Keating on the competitive motif in athletics and playful activity. In R. G. Osterhoudt (Ed.), *The philosophy of sport* (pp. 192-198). Springfield, IL: Charles C Thomas.

Parry, A. (1991). A universe of stories. *Family Process, 30,* 37-54.

Pedersen, P. (1990). The multicultural perspective as a fourth force in counseling. *Journal of Mental Health Counseling, 12,* 93-95.

Penn, P. (1982). Circular questioning. *Family Process, 21,* 267-280.

Penn, P. (1991). Letters to ourselves. *Family Therapy Networker, 15*(5), 43-45.

Pope, K. S., & Vasquez, M.J.T. (1991). *Ethics in psychotherapy and counseling: A practical guide for psychologists.* San Francisco: Jossey-Bass.

Richardson, M. S. (1993). Work in people's lives: A location for counseling psychologists. *Journal of Counseling Psychology, 40,* 425-433.

Roberts, J. (1983). Two models of live supervision: Collaborative team and supervisor-guided. *Journal of Strategic and Systemic Therapies, 2,* 68-83.

Rodriguez, R. (1982). *Hunger of memory.* New York: Bantam Books.

Rosenau, P. M. (1992). *Post-modernism and the social sciences: Insights, inroads, and intrusions.* Princeton, NJ: Princeton University Press.

Ruggiero, V. R. (1990). Beyond feelings: A guide to critical thinking (3rd ed.). Mountain View, CA: Mayfield.

Russell, R. L., & Gaubatz, M. D. (1995). Contested affinities: Reaction to Gergen's (1994) and Smith's (1994) postmodernisms. *American Psychologist, 50,* 389-390.

Ryan, W. (1971). *Blaming the victim.* New York: Random House.

Sarbin, T. R. (Ed.). (1986). *Narrative psychology: The storied nature of human conduct.* New York: Praeger.

Sauerman, T. H. (1984). *Read this before coming out to your parents.* Los Angeles: Parents & Friends of Lesbians and Gays, Inc. [booklet]. (An updated brochure is available from PFLAG-Philadelphia, P. O. Box 176, Titusville, NJ 08560.)

Scarr, S. (1985). Constructing psychology. Making facts and fables for our times. *American Psychologist, 40,* 499-412.

Scarr, S. (1989). Constructivism and socially sensitive research. *American Psychologist, 44,* 849.

Self, B. (1995, October 22). Colonias cost taxpayers $500 million. *El Paso Times,* pp. 1A, 14A.

Selvini Palazzoli, M., Boscolo, L., Cecchin, G., & Prata, G. (1980). Hypothesizing—circularity—neutrality: Three guidelines for the conductor of the session. *Family Process, 19,* 3-12.

Sluzki, C. E. (1992). Transformations: A blueprint for narrative changes in therapy. *Family Process, 31,* 217-230.

Smith, H. (1989). *Beyond the post-modern mind.* Wheaton, IL: Theosophical Publishing House.

Smith, M. B. (1994). Selfhood at risk: Postmodern perils and the perils of postmodernism. *American Psychologist, 49,* 405-411.

Smith, M. B. (1995). About postmodernism: Reply to Gergen and others. *American Psychologist, 50,* 393-394.

Sperling, M. B., Handen, B. L., Miller, D., Schumm, P., Pirrotta, S., Simons, L. A., Lysiak, G., & Terry, L. (1986). The collaborative team as a training and therapeutic tool. *Counselor Education and Supervision, 25,* 183-190.

Srivastva, S., Fry, R. E., & Cooperrider, D. L. (1990). Introduction: The call for executive appreciation. In S. Srivastva, D. L. Cooperrider, & Associates (Eds.), *Appreciative management and leadership: The power of positive thought and action in organizations* (pp. 1-33). San Francisco: Jossey-Bass.

Steele, S. (1990). *The content of our character: A new vision of race in America.* New York: HarperCollins.

Sue, D. W., & Sue, D. (1990). *Counseling the culturally different: Theory and practice* (2nd ed.). New York: John Wiley.

Tomm, K. (1985). Circular interviewing: A multifaceted clinical tool. In D. Campbell & R. Draper (Eds.), *Applications of systemic family therapy: The Milan approach* (Vol. 3, pp. 33-45). Orlando, FL: Grune & Stratton.

Tomm, K. (1987). Interventive interviewing: Part II. Reflexive questioning as a means to enable self-healing. *Family Process, 26,* 167-183.

United States Catholic Conference (Producer). (1991). *On fire with faith* [Videotape]. (Available from the Office for Publishing and Promotion Services, United States Catholic Conference, Washington, D.C.).

von Glasersfeld, E. (1984). An introduction to radical constructivism. In P. Watzlawick (Ed.), *The invented reality* (pp. 17-39). New York: Norton.

Walsh, F. (1993). Conceptualization of normal family processes. In F. Walsh (Ed.), *Normal family process* (2nd ed.; pp. 3-69). New York: Guilford.

Weingarten, K. (1991). The discourses of intimacy: Adding a social constructionist and feminist view. *Family Process, 30,* 285-305.

White, D., & Wang, A. (1995). Universalism, humanism, and postmodernism. *American Psychologist, 50,* 392-393.

White, M. (1994, March). *Therapeutic conversations as collaborative inquiry* (Workshop sponsored by the Austin Child Guidance Center, Austin, TX).

White, M., & Epston, D. (1990). *Narrative means to therapeutic ends.* New York: Norton.

Yalom, I. D. (1980). *Existential psychotherapy.* New York: Basic Books.

17

Cross-Cultural Supervision

ISSUES FOR THE WHITE SUPERVISOR

Margaret L. Fong

Suzanne H. Lease

As the United States becomes more ethnically diverse, the supervision triad of client, counselor, and supervisor will most likely contain persons of differing racial/ethnic backgrounds who are confronting problems and concerns in a complex social environment. Currently, and perhaps for some time to come, the vast majority of supervisors in this triad will be White and members of the majority culture. In the spring of 1995, we conducted an informal poll of counseling psychology and counselor education training programs as to the racial composition of faculty supervisors. We learned that few programs have more than one or two ethnic/racial minority supervisors. In fact, many programs have no minority faculty providing supervision! There is often increased opportunity to be supervised by a minority practitioner when completing an off-campus practicum or internship, but this does not seem to occur in any planned or structured manner.

Although receiving supervision provided by a White counselor appears to be the rule rather than the exception, literature that examines the effects of race, identity, and awareness when a White supervisor works with either a racial/ethnic minority supervisee or supervises a trainee working with a minority client is extremely sparse. Leong and Wagner (1994) conducted a comprehensive review of the literature on cross-cultural supervision. They identified only three empirical studies that address cross-cultural supervision, and only two of these focus on White supervisors with minority supervisees. Vander Kolk (1974) and Cook and Helms (1988) studied perceptions of minority supervisees with White supervisors. Their results suggest that race is an issue in supervision with respect to expectations of supervisor's levels of empathy, congruence, and respect (Vander Kolk, 1974) and perceived supervisor liking (Cook & Helms, 1988). Both studies are limited to perceptual data from the supervisee, ignoring supervisee behavior and all supervisor, client, and supervision process variables. In fact, to date, empirically supported information is not available about the process of cross-cultural supervision or how the White supervisor's own racial identity, cultural values and biases, and unexamined racial attitudes affect the minority supervisee or the supervisee's work with minority clients.

Given this paucity of information, how can the White supervisor provide supervision in a manner consistent with the AMCD multicultural counseling competencies and standards (Sue, Arredondo, & McDavis, 1992) and the Association for Counselor Education and Supervision (ACES) (1990) standards for counseling supervision? This is the dilemma that challenges us, both White counseling psychologists with training, experience, and some expertise in multicultural counseling and supervision. This chapter is structured to guide the White supervisor in conducting cross-cultural supervision. Drawing on the cross-cultural counseling and supervision literature and our experience, we will focus on issues relevant to the White supervisor, including supervision process dynamics, and then describe appropriate multicultural supervision interventions.

Issues for the White Supervisor

Although there is a lack of empirical literature, a number of authors have presented their views about the supervisor in multicultural supervision settings (see Leong & Wagner, 1994, for a comprehensive review). A consistent theme in the literature is the critical role of the supervisor in promoting cultural awareness; in identifying cultural influences on client behavior, counselor-client interactions, and the supervisory relationship; and in providing culture-sensitive support and challenge to the supervisee. Our response, however, would be, "Easier said than done." A number of historic, cultural, and role-related issues affect White supervisors' attempts to provide effective cross-cultural supervision. These include unintentional racism, power dynamics, trust and the supervisory alliance, and communication issues.

Unintentional Racism

Ridley (1995) asserts that many counselors are well intentioned, have sincere motivations to help, endorse ethical principles, yet engage in racist counseling practices (p. 10). He terms this "unintentional racism," noting that "racism is what people do, regardless of what they think or feel" (p. 10). He lists assuming that good intentions make one automatically helpful, traditional clinical training, and cultural tunnel vision as some of the factors in racist counseling practices. Extending this to supervision, the White supervisor may often engage in similar unintentional racism.

Bernard and Goodyear (1992) suggest that even as the supervisee must explore the cultural meaning of worldview, experience, and identity in the therapy session, so must the supervisor explore these same issues in the supervisory relationship. However, they and other authors (e.g., Bradshaw, 1982; Fong, 1994) have noted that supervisors, uncomfortable or uninformed about cultural issues, often ignore or avoid cultural issues in supervision. Both White racial identity models (Rowe, Bennett, & Atkinson, 1994; Helms, 1990; Ponterotto, 1988) and the concept of White privilege (McIntosh, 1988) provide explanations for such behavior.

White Racial Identity. Racial identity relates to how one feels, thinks, and behaves in regard to oneself, one's own racial group, and members of other racial groups (Helms, 1990). Generally, White racial identity models conceptualize White racial identity as a developmental process by which White individuals move from a position of unawareness about the impact of race and themselves as racial beings, to a consciousness and valuing of their own Whiteness, while simultaneously valuing members of other races and working to eliminate oppression in all forms (Sabnani, Ponterotto, & Borodovsky, 1991). To date, Helms's work has been the subject of the majority of the empirical investigations and has most closely examined the interactions of individuals with differing racial attitudes. Helms (1994) describes evolving White identity ego statuses of contact, disintegration, reintegration, pseudo-independence, immersion/emersion, and autonomy.

The less evolved White identity statuses of contact, disintegration, reintegration, and pseudo-independence seem most related to supervisor avoidance and minimalization of cultural issues in supervision. White supervisors in the contact ego status likely received little formal training on cultural issues, the cultural values embedded in current counseling theories and techniques (Ridley, 1995; Sue & Zane, 1987), and the diversity of world-views (Ibrahim, 1991), and they can be considered culturally encapsulated (Wrenn, 1962). Supervisors at this level of awareness minimize and ignore racial issues that may have an impact on the minority supervisee or client, and they avoid the affect around these issues. If both supervisor and super-visee share these attitudes, client concerns about racial issues may never be raised and resolved. If the supervisee is at a more advanced level and attempts to bring racial issues into the supervisory discussions, he or she may not be heard.

Supervisors in the disintegration status may be acknowledging conflicting feelings about being White and may be realizing that the counseling tech-niques they were taught are not always effective with minority clients. Likewise, they may have been rejected in a previous attempt to supervise a minority individual and thus may have concluded that there is little that the differing races can do together. This attitude of hopelessness may be com-municated to the White supervisee working with a minority client so that the trainee becomes discouraged, does not pursue meaningful issues in therapy, and fails to be effective with the client. If supervisors functioning from the disintegration ego status are working with minority trainees, they may be guarded and defensive, and they may communicate this same sense of hopelessness about the effectiveness of their work with the trainees.

White supervisors in the reintegration status may have dealt with their conflict in the previous identity status by altering their belief system to one that views minority individuals with fear, anger, and dislike and views Whites as racially superior. Supervisors with these attitudes may have negative feelings toward minority individuals but experience dissonance over this because it violates training program philosophies and perceptions of self as a humanistic counselor and good supervisor. Supervisors at this stage of racial consciousness may try to hide or deny their feelings, but they may unconsciously display them through nonverbal communication when working with their supervisees. They may attend less to their minority supervisee's work and to process issues, be less available to the supervisee, and be less forthcoming with help. If the supervisee is working with a minority client, the supervisor might have difficulty attending to the details of the particular case and facilitating the resolution of any difficulties the trainee may have with the client. The supervisors may also subtly convey their negative attitudes about the client to the trainee and thus shape the trainee's own racial attitudes. Trainees with more evolved attitudes of racial identity may lose respect for the supervisor when reintegration attitudes are exhibited.

Supervisors working from the pseudo-independent status question their previous beliefs about minority inferiority and begin to see the role of Whites in perpetuating racism. Rowe et al. (1994), who emphasize a cognitive approach to racial identity, have a similar consciousness status, the "dissonant type," in which individuals are "open to new information because it might reduce their uncertainty (about racial issues), but lack the commitment to the ideas they might express" (p. 137). These supervisors may feel they understand racial issues, but do so primarily on a cognitive level, not on an affective level. Thus, they still might interpret minority supervisee or minority client behaviors through the lens of White standards rather than attending to alternative perspectives. Supervisors at this level would find it difficult to deal with affective resistance from either the client or the trainee and might resort to cognitive analyses of cultural issues.

Because many White supervisors have at best limited multicultural experience and knowledge, we suspect that the above descriptions of supervisors at the less evolved statuses are reflective of current cross-cultural supervision practice. Our conclusion is supported by the recent findings of Pope-Davis and Ottavi (1994) that White counselors affiliated with university counseling centers scored lower on measures of cultural awareness and cultural knowledge than ethnic minority counselors, and by the findings of Mintz, Bartels, and Rideout (1995) that psychology interns reported mediocre preparation for counseling ethnic minority clients.

Helms (1990) also proposed an interaction model that examined the relationship of clients and counselors at differing stages of racial consciousness. Dyads may share similar racial attitudes (parallel) or diametrically opposed attitudes (crossed). She suggests the relationships may be progressive if the counselor is at a more advanced level than the client or regressive if the counselor is behind the client in development of a racial identity. Cook (1994; Cook & Helms, 1988) has extended this model to explore supervisory interactions from this perspective, but does not focus on the White supervisor.

White Privilege. White privilege as posited by McIntosh (1988) is defined as the unearned benefits that White individuals can count on receiving every day, without even being aware that such benefits exist. These include not being questioned or viewed suspiciously every day because of one's race; seeing one's values and history validated and reinforced in the media and popular culture; not having to be the representative of the entire White race in groups or discussions about racial issues; and not having to worry about being targeted by police, employers, or anyone else due to race. Being the recipient of White privilege allows one to neglect or be oblivious to anything outside of the dominant White culture without fear of repercussions.

In the supervision setting, White privilege could manifest itself in the ignorance of other cultures' worldviews (Ibrahim, 1991) and the automatic acceptance of the White culture's values and goals as the accepted reference standard, thereby making the minority supervisee's or the minority client's actions look deviant by comparison. It could also manifest itself in the White supervisor's lack of awareness of the daily hassles involved with being a member of a nondominant group and in the supervisor's difficulty empathizing with experiences of oppression. The lack of awareness and empathy could block effective work with minority supervisees or supervisees working with minority clients.

Bernard and Goodyear (1992), in a discussion of the dangers of assumed similarity between supervisor and supervisee, noted that "supervisors can mistakenly assume that trainees identify with them culturally as well" (p. 198). That assumption can be heightened by the lack of conscious awareness of White privilege and can result in the unintentional imposition of White cultural values, which permeate modern counseling theories and strategies, onto the trainee. Because White privilege is inherent in and reinforced by the dominant culture, it gives White supervisors considerable power over whether even to discuss the impact of race and the benefits that accompany Whiteness that are in direct relation to the costs that accompany non-Whiteness. That power can be additive with the power already vested in the supervisor role, making it difficult, if not impossible, for the supervisee to question or comment on topics related to race unless the supervisor has indicated a willingness to process the issue.

Power Dynamics

Power is the ability to control ourselves and others (Ridley, 1995). Hart (1982) and Robiner (1982) noted that the supervisory relationship has traditionally been seen as hierarchical, with an innate power differential between supervisor and supervisee. This power differential remains in all current models of supervision in which the supervisor is viewed as having both expertise and the responsibility for evaluating the supervisee (Fong, 1994).

As Ridley (1995) so succinctly states about counselors, "it takes power to behave like a racist" (p. 21). Because the history of ethnic and race relations in the United States is one of power differentials, White paternalism, and racial minority oppression, minority supervisees may bring high levels of caution to supervision with the White supervisor (Brown & Landrum-Brown, 1995). Brown and Landrum-Brown suggest that the specific power dynamics of perceived paternalism and oppression on the part of the supervisor and potential internalized racial oppression on the part of the supervisee need to be carefully managed. We suspect that the White supervisor frequently ignores this power dynamic and variously perceives the minority supervisee or the supervisee's minority client as reluctant to disclose, resistant to feedback, unwilling to analyze his or her own behavior critically, or, conversely, as dependent or acquiescent. Notice that all of these perceptions place the locus of the problem on the supervisee or client, usually with that individual found to be deficient. Such negative perceptions can interfere with the quality of supervision and may result in the supervisor becoming more directive and controlling than normal, thus further distancing the supervisee or client.

Brown and Landrum-Brown (1995) emphasize the impact of minority supervisees' internalized racial oppression on supervision power dynamics. Defining internalized racial oppression as the psychosocial reactions to internalized stereotypes and negative messages, they identify strategies used to manage oppression, such as system beating, denial of racial heritage, or avoidance or rejection of White systems. They note, "for a supervisee, it [system beating] might involve manipulating the supervisor's guilt regarding racism in order to avoid certain training experiences" (Brown & Landrum-Brown, 1995). Again, this approach combined with a supervisor's avoidance of racial issues would preclude effective supervision. Likewise, pride and the desire not to fit into negative stereotypes of inadequacy may interfere with the minority supervisee asking for or being the recipient of needed help from the White supervisor.

Trust and Vulnerability

Issues of trust and vulnerability also interact with the issues of power and racial oppression in the cross-cultural supervisory relationship. Trust can be an essential ingredient for overcoming student anxieties about supervision. Olk and Friedlander (1992) attribute supervisee anxiety to the role of supervisee, which requires multiple roles that can consist of opposing behaviors. For example, during supervision sessions supervisees must view themselves as learners, ready to reveal their flaws and deficits and to receive feedback from the supervisor, while at the same time presenting themselves as competent for the purpose of evaluation. Likewise, supervisees may be encouraged to discuss personal issues bearing on their counseling, yet not have the freedom from judgment available in standard counseling relationships. Clearly, the supervisee must be able and willing to be in a vulnerable position, trusting the supervisor. This perspective is supported by a recent study of 123 counselor trainees conducted by Ladany and Friedlander (1995). They proposed that actions taken by the supervisor in the context of a strong working alliance could minimize trainee role difficulties. Results supported their hypothesis and suggested that the significant component of the working alliance for reducing trainee role conflict was a strong emotional bond (defined as mutual caring, liking, and trusting) between the trainee and supervisor.

As mentioned in previous sections, there are many barriers to the formation of such trust when the White supervisor provides cross-cultural supervision. Without this trust, it will be difficult for supervisees to expose themselves in order to gain useful feedback. If this trust does not occur, it is likely the supervisees will engage in resistant behaviors, hiding their work, delaying bringing in tapes that may show both good and bad work with their clients, and wanting to focus more on the content of what they are doing with their clients than on any deeper process issues during the supervision session.

A number of authors have suggested that the historical mistreatment of minorities has fostered a perception of all European Americans as potentially racist and not to be trusted (Priest, 1991; Sue & Sue, 1993; Trimble, 1988). Terrell and associates (Nickerson, Helms, & Terrell, 1994; Watkins & Terrell, 1988; Watkins, Terrell, Miller, & Terrell, 1989) have examined the concept of cultural mistrust in Black client-White counselor interactions. They found that those clients higher in mistrust were less likely to seek help and had lower expectations for the therapeutic encounter. Specifically, the clients viewed the counselors as less credible and less able to help them with issues of general anxiety, shyness, dating difficulties, and feelings of inferiority. If one extrapolates these results to the supervisory relationship, then Black supervisees who are more culturally mistrusting may have lower expectations of gain from the White supervisor and less inclination to reveal affective concerns in the supervision sessions. This would interfere in the development of the working alliance, which in turn assists in reducing anxiety in supervision.

The findings of both Vander Kolk (1974) and Cook and Helms (1988), cited earlier as the only empirical cross-cultural supervision studies with a White supervisor, support the importance of trust and the working alliance, particularly the strong emotional bond component. Vander Kolk found Black students expected their supervisors to be less empathic, respectful, and congruent than did White students. Cook and Helms identified factors that related to satisfaction of minority supervisees in cross-cultural supervision. In order of importance these were perceived supervisor liking, perceived emotional discomfort, perceived conditional interest, and perceived conditional liking.

Communication
Issues

Another factor that affects the supervisory relationship is a difference in communication styles between supervisor and supervisee. Sue and Sue (1990) summarized differences in linguistic styles among the differing ethnic groups and noted that the White style is typically characterized by loud and rapid speech, quick responding, direct task-oriented focus, head nods and other nonverbal markers, and prolonged eye contact when listening but less when speaking. These characteristics are not universal. Sue and Sue (1990) noted that the communication patterns of many Native Americans, Asian Americans, and Hispanic Americans are characterized by softer, slower speech, less direct eye contact, and an indirect approach to issues. These characterizations are generalizations only; there are substantial within-group differences based on gender, age, acculturation, SES, and a host of other factors. Nevertheless, because the supervisory process is based on clear communication, misinterpretations of verbal and nonverbal signals could inhibit that process. For example, a supervisee who makes minimal eye contact with the supervisor who has greater authority might be doing so out of respect for the supervisor. For the White supervisor who is used to direct eye contact, the supervisee might be seen as afraid, resistant to supervision, or having interpersonal difficulties of his or her own (depression, low self-esteem) that will need to be addressed before the supervisee begins work with clients. The White supervisor who is unaware of the possible cultural differences in communication styles may draw inappropriate conclusions about the supervisee and then pursue those conclusions to the detriment of the supervisory relationship. In a similar example, a supervisee who values a more indirect approach when discussing client concerns and eschews a direct approach as impolite and embarrassing may be viewed by the supervisor as timid and lacking good clinical instincts.

Twohey and Volker (1993) discussed gender issues in counseling supervision and speculated that communication difficulties might occur in supervision because of two different gender voices, one of care and one of justice. They propose that there has been a bias in counseling supervision toward the "male" voice of justice, which ignores or demeans the voice of care. We suggest there is a similar phenomenon of a bias toward the White voice in supervision that could devalue communication not conveyed in the culturally defined "normal" communication patterns. Because analysis of counseling responses, reporting of counseling actions, and supervision interactions—all verbal communications—are the primary bases for evaluation of the supervisee by the supervisor, these communication biases can seriously impact the student's grade and progress in training.

It may seem that we have painted a bleak picture of the cross-cultural supervision process when the supervisor is White—a picture of a process fraught with perils and rarely leading to a successful outcome. Yet for each of the issues raised, we recognize a variety of supervision strategies aimed at different aspects of the supervision process, and we suggest professional development strategies for the White supervisor.

Multicultural Supervision Interventions for the White Supervisor

In the previous section we described issues of racial identity, unexamined attitudes of White privilege, trust, power, and communication that we think can be barriers to provision of effective cross-cultural supervision by the White supervisor. In doing so, we also indirectly identified factors that seem to minimize such barriers. These include supervisor multicultural awareness and knowledge, a nonracist sense of White identity or consciousness, sensitivity to power and oppression in the supervisory relationship, attention to the development of trust in the supervisory relationship, and flexibility in communication styles. The first two factors could be characterized as "within" the supervisor and thus must be part of supervisors' professional development for cross-cultural supervision. The latter three factors are aspects of the supervision process that the supervisor should foster and develop by intentional supervision interventions in both individual and group supervision formats. We present interventions from the supervision and multicultural literature that seem to have potential to promote sensitive, effective cross-cultural supervision. However, we must caution that currently there are no empirical studies in the literature of cross-cultural supervision techniques.

Supervisor Professional Development

All supervisors, regardless of racial/ethnic background, need to seek professional development in the knowledge and skills of cross-cultural supervision. The ACES (1990) counseling supervision standards specify this in Standard 4.1, noting, the "supervisor demonstrates knowledge of individual differences with respect to gender, race, ethnicity, culture, and age and understands the importance of these characteristics in supervisory relationships" (p. 30). Likewise, Bernard (1994) states, "supervisors must be at least as multiculturally competent as their supervisees, and ideally, more so" (p. 170). Unfortunately, many White supervisors belong to a generation of professionals who completed training programs before multicultural counseling was emphasized (Pope-Davis & Ottavi, 1994). In fact, for many the assumption in training was that existing counseling and supervision theories and techniques were "generic," appropriate for all (Ridley, 1995).

Assessment of Competence. A first step in improving cross-cultural supervision would be a careful assessment by White supervisors of their own levels of multicultural knowledge and their individual White racial identity statuses. Several self-report instruments are available for self-assessment of multicultural counseling knowledge. The Multicultural Counseling Inventory (MCI; Sodowsky, Taffe, Gutkin, & Wise, 1994) provides an indication of self-perceived multicultural competencies in four different aspects: skills, knowledge, awareness, and relationship. Ponterotto and associates (Ponterotto et al., 1993) developed the Multicultural Counseling Awareness Scale (MCAS), which also measures self-perceived skills and awareness, but from the perspective of the respondent's beliefs about culturally sanctioned behavior rather than familiarity with multicultural counseling facts.

White racial identity can also be evaluated by self-report instruments. The White Racial Identity Inventory (Helms & Carter, 1990) contains items based on the Helms (1990) model of racial identity. It is designed to assess the individual's current cultural awareness and behaviors and then place the individual in a specific status (stage) of identity development. Based on a cognitive schema model of White racial consciousness, the Oklahoma Racial Attitudes Scales (Bennett, Behrens, & Rowe, 1993; Rowe et al., 1994) provide an alternative way to determine the individual's type of White racial consciousness.

The process of assessment itself should heighten the White supervisor's awareness of multicultural aspects of counseling and supervision. Outcomes of this assessment would include (a) identification of level of racial consciousness and (b) areas of multicultural knowledge that need further development.

Development Plan. Based on the assessment of competence, a professional development plan might include activities such as reading professional literature, attending continuing education seminars, consultation with more multiculturally competent colleagues, and initiating a White racial consciousness group. The plan should also include supervision.

Just as therapy is not generic, counseling supervision is not generic. The White supervisor needs specific competency in multicultural counseling supervision. All supervisors-in-training should work with supervisees from racial/ethnic groups other than their own and receive supervision of their cross-cultural supervision. Likewise, experienced supervisors without specific training in multicultural supervision will need to seek focused supervision of their supervision with a multicultural emphasis to meet gaps in experience and education. Peer supervision groups (Borders, 1991) would be one useful format for this, as a group of supervisors could focus on shared learning and assessment of cross-cultural supervision.

Interventions for Individual Supervision

We support models that advocate supervision as a method to assist multicultural counselor development (see Leong & Wagner, 1994, for a review of these models). These models view the supervisor as promoting the supervisee's growth by challenging cultural assumptions and encouraging mutual discussion of cultural aspects of counseling and supervision. This section and the one that follows, on group supervision interventions, assume that the White supervisor has achieved an adequate White racial consciousness and some competence in multicultural counseling. As Bernard (1994) strongly states, "The supervisor and his or her level of racial identity development will, in the great majority of cases, determine the sophistication of the discourse in supervision about racial issues" (p. 163).

Including a Cultural Perspective. A number of supervision techniques have been proposed to ensure that the cultural dimension is addressed, but none have research support (Bernard & Goodyear, 1992; Leong & Wagner, 1994). Both the administrative, structural aspects of individual supervision and the session content should have a multicultural perspective. Early in the supervisory process the White supervisor should provide planned discussion of culture and the culture of counseling. In addition, as part of forming the working alliance, the supervisor would initiate open exploration of supervisee and supervisor cultural backgrounds. These early discussions not only clearly signal that racial and ethnic concerns are legitimate parts of supervision, but also discourage either the supervisor or supervisee from making assumptions about each other based on race.

The methods of supervision also need structure. The required use of videotape (rather than audiotape) recordings of the supervisee's counseling sessions is recommended—because visual recording allows observation and discussion of vital, nonverbal cultural components. A review of all the clinical forms used for supervision—such as intake sheets, case management or case planning forms, and other written supervision reports—is needed. To what extent do each require the student to evaluate the cultural dimensions of their counseling? Likewise, supervisor and supervisee evaluation forms need to assess the cross-cultural aspects of counseling and supervision.

Addressing Power Dynamics. The White supervisor should consider interventions to share power or to empower the supervisee as ways of modifying the power imbalance. Evaluation of the supervisee is one aspect of the power imbalance. Bernard and Goodyear (1992) advocate that an open, structured evaluation process with clearly stated performance goals; objective evaluation forms; and planned, frequent feedback be developed. This helps reduce ambiguity and supervisee concerns that the White supervisor will make arbitrary evaluations. At the beginning of supervision, the supervisor discusses all aspects of evaluation and encourages supervisee questions and concerns. The supervisor should explain formative evaluation versus summative evaluation, and describe the supervisee's role in each.

The supervisor might consider ways to emphasize a collaborative approach to learning rather than the traditional hierarchial supervisor role. Although developmental models of supervision emphasize that beginning counselors need a structured, supportive approach in supervision, structure does not necessitate hierarchy. Collaboration can occur in seeking out additional resources, role-playing, planning counseling strategies in the session, and in ongoing evaluation by carefully incorporating both supervisee and supervisor inputs. For example, the supervisor could ensure that in reviewing a counseling tape the supervisee and supervisor each discuss identified strengths and weaknesses. The first author sets aside time at the end of each session for both supervisor and supervisee to think over the session and then discuss any "unfinished business."

Building Trust. We noted earlier the importance a strong emotional bond (i.e., mutual caring, liking, and trusting) has on minority supervisee's expectations and perceptions of the White supervisor. Based on her review of positive supervision critical incidents in supervision reported by minority interns, Fukuyama (1994) emphasizes that over time an open, supportive relationship builds minority supervisee trust. As part of this support, the White supervisor must consistently demonstrate respect and acceptance of cultural differences. This includes, Fukuyama notes, not stereotyping supervisees or their clinical cases. The interventions described above in "Including a Cultural Perspective" would also build trust.

As part of building trust in cross-cultural supervision, cultural mistrust must be addressed. One mode of addressing the mistrust based on racial differences and expectations is to discuss the meaning of race; its impact on supervisor, supervisee, and client; and experiences of oppression, directly in the supervisory session. Ellis and Robbins (1993) noted that it was vitally important for supervisors to address issues of cultural bias and oppression when they become salient. Of course, this requires cultural knowledge and multicultural awareness on the part of the White supervisor.

Clarifying Communication. Many of the interventions we have covered to this point have consisted of supervisor verbal communications, such as "to discuss" or "to explore." However, we earlier described communication as one of the factors that could impede cross-cultural supervision. This strong reliance in supervision on verbal communication makes continuous efforts to clarify communication essential.

One approach is to evaluate communications during the supervision process in ways that do not rely solely on the supervisor's perceptiveness. Videotaping supervision sessions, followed by careful review of the tape by the supervisor to identify patterns of communication and possible miscommunications, is valuable. Portions of the tape can then be shared with the supervisee, exploring each person's observations of potential cultural and individual differences in style, nonverbals, and more. Building in several ways to gather feedback about communication during supervision is also important. In discussing the expectations for supervision, the White supervisor can suggest a ground rule that when either participant is confused or uncertain about what is being discussed, or objects, or disagrees, that this be expressed at the time of occurrence. Because, culturally, some ethnic minority supervisees may consider that such a direct communication with a teacher would be disrespectful, several modes of expression should be encouraged; for example, by immediate discussion, by a brief written feedback form that is completed at the end of each session, or during a debriefing period at the end of the supervision session. The debriefing period was previously discussed in this section as a method to address power dynamics. The session feedback form consisting of two open-ended questions—"What was most helpful in supervision today?" "What seemed unclear or unhelpful in supervision today?"—has been used by the first author both with practicum supervisees and for supervision with beginning supervisors. Of course, none of these interventions will be effective if the supervisor does not respond in an open manner that encourages exploration or does not accept various communication styles as valid.

With respect to communication, Twohey and Volker (1993) noted that it was important for supervisors to be aware of both gender voices as they worked with their supervisees. Similarly, listening to both the White supervisor's voice and the cultural voice of the supervisee allows multiple perspectives of the interaction to be viewed and facilitates the conscious choice of the perspective that best fits the trainee's needs (Ellis & Robbins, 1993). The ability to listen for the cultural perspective again necessitates awareness of cultural values and worldviews by the White supervisor, bringing this section of the chapter back full circle to where it began.

Group Supervision Interventions

Group supervision can provide a rich context for assisting the multicultural counseling development of students and enhancing the cross-cultural supervision skills of the supervisor. All supervision groups, irrespective of purpose (e.g., assessment supervision, therapy supervision) or type of student (e.g., rehabilitation, counseling psychology), should address multicultural aspects. We discourage designating a specific "multicultural counseling supervision group." Ideally, the group of students will be diverse in respect to culture, gender, and age, as will the clients they are presenting in supervision.

Many of the interventions described for individual supervision can be adapted for group supervision, and we encourage the White supervisor to apply them. In this section, however, we describe interventions that specifically use group process as an integral part of the intervention. Perhaps the most essential perspective to be understood is how carefully the supervisor must attend to the group process aspects of group supervision, such as informal group leadership, the development of group norms, the development of cohesion and trust, and group collaboration in learning. Frequently the group consists of the White supervisor, mostly White counseling students, and one or two minority students. The potential for lack of cultural sensitivity and the acceptance of White, majority cultural norms for evaluation of clients and counseling interventions is great. The White supervisor needs to consider this reality carefully and approach group supervision as another form of cross-cultural supervision.

Creating a Sensitive Climate. In effective group supervision sessions, supervisees feel sufficiently safe to present their counseling tapes or case plans and to risk self-disclosure of mistakes or uncertainties. Supervisees need confidence that other group members and the supervisor will not reject them, humiliate them, or be disrespectful. Often, students fear being "singled out" as deficient or different. As the minority supervisee is often one of the few or the only minority counselor in the group, he or she is in a particularly vulnerable, socially isolated position. Group safety, as well as trust, must be deliberately fostered by the supervisor.

A number of approaches assist with setting the climate. In the first session, these may include a planned getting-acquainted exercise that will allow group members to see similarities and differences among the group members; a discussion of supervision goals, including expanded multicultural competency; and setting group ground rules similar to those described for individual supervision. In our department, faculty have adopted a diversity statement that affirms our intent that faculty, students, and staff treat all individuals with sensitivity and respect. This statement can be included in the course syllabus and read and discussed in the first session.

Another approach that sets a norm for participation and encourages diversity in thinking is the frequent use of round-robins to elicit student response and comments. In the round-robin each student in turn is expected to share an observation, possible intervention, or the type of response desired. The "mandatory" nature of this round-robin provides students with permission to make responses and balances out domination by a few students, resulting in a richer discussion. A built-in pass option in the round-robin does allow for students who wish to remain silent on a given topic.

Including a Cultural Perspective. We encourage the use of experiential exercises, particularly in the early sessions, to emphasize the importance of the multicultural components of counseling and of a diversity of perspectives. In addition, the student sharing and collaboration that occur in experiential exercises will enhance the development of group trust and cohesion needed for group supervision. Preli and Bernard (1993) developed a series of group exercises to engage counseling students, particularly the "White middle-class trainee," in multicultural aspects of therapy. Although intended for a multicultural counseling course, they seem very relevant for early sessions of group supervision prior to student case study or treatment planning topics. They use as an opener the "name game," which has students give their name and ethnicity, which is repeated around the group by each next person. This is followed by a discussion of how it felt to identify by ethnic group. Preli and Bernard note this exercise desensitizes students to mentioning ethnicity in the group and reveals intragroup differences, an important multicultural concept.

To further emphasize family and cultural interactions, Preli and Bernard (1993) use three exercises: the student structured interview, genogram presentations, and home video presentations. All of these activities have the students sharing with other group members. Arnold (1994) also uses a group exercise about families to develop "multiethnic consciousness." Students are given a structured set of six questions to answer verbally about their families. This is followed by a discussion of the influence of ethnicity on family structure, rules, communication patterns, and interactions. Arnold noted that "students gained an immediate understanding of the variations among families . . . and ethnic differences" (p. 144).

Group supervision is an ideal format for learning clinical decision making, and many supervision groups emphasize a case study or case management approach. Ridley (1995) views clinical decision making as an important source of unintentional racism, noting that counselor decisions such as making diagnoses, referrals, and treatment plans; suggesting termination; reporting abuse; and interpreting test data are all subject to preexisting stereotypes and the counselor's worldview. Written assignments and oral case studies for group supervision need to include consideration of client cultural aspects to help students learn to take a broader perspective in clinical decisions. The supervisor should ensure that multicultural concerns are addressed by all students for all clients. It is harmful to look to the single minority student in the group to carry the burden of speaking for minority issues and clients, a practice reported by Cook (1994) as common in group supervision.

We end this chapter with a caution. The reader may decide after reading to this point that we see cultural issues as the central focus for every supervision session or as *the* key variable in supervisor or supervisee behavior. This is not the case. Numerous authors (e.g., Bernard, 1994; Fukuyama, 1994; Leong & Wagner, 1994) have warned about overemphasizing cultural diversity issues in circumstances in which other variables are more cogent. To quote Fukuyama (1994), "sometimes the supervisor is trying too hard to be 'politically correct' " (p. 148). What we are strongly advocating is that multicultural issues in supervision, long neglected, receive proper attention. If this is to happen, White supervisors will need to modify current supervision practice. This chapter has highlighted issues in cross-cultural supervision and proposed many interventions that could assist White supervisors in meeting this challenge.

References

Arnold, M. S. (1994). Ethnicity and training marital and family therapists. *Counselor Education and Supervision, 33,* 139-147.

Association for Counselor Education and Supervision. (1990). Standards for counseling supervisors. *Journal of Counseling and Development, 69,* 30-32.

Bennett, E. K., Behrens, J. T., & Rowe, W. (1993, August). *The White Racial Identity Scale: Validity and factor structure.* Paper presented at the meeting of the American Psychological Association, Toronto.

Bernard, J. M. (1994). Multicultural supervision: A reaction to Leong and Wagner, Cook, Priest, and Fukuyama. *Counselor Education and Supervision, 34,* 159-171.

Bernard, J. M., & Goodyear, R. K. (1992). *Fundamentals of clinical supervision.* Boston: Allyn & Bacon.

Borders, L. D. (1991). A systematic approach to peer group supervision. *Journal of Counseling and Development, 69,* 248-252.

Bradshaw, W. H., Jr. (1982). Supervision in Black and White: Race as a factor in supervision. In M. Blumenfield (Ed.), *Applied supervision in psychotherapy* (pp. 199-220). New York: Grune & Stratton.

Brown, M. T., & Landrum-Brown, J. (1995). Counselor supervision: Cross-cultural perspectives. In J. G. Ponterotto, J. M. Casas, L. A. Suzuki, & C. M. Alexander (Eds.), *Handbook of multicultural counseling* (pp. 263-286). Thousand Oaks, CA: Sage.

Cook, D. A. (1994). Racial identity in supervision. *Counselor Education and Supervision, 34,* 132-141.

Cook, D. A., & Helms, J. E. (1988). Visible racial/ethnic group supervisees' satisfaction with cross-cultural supervision as predicted by relationship characteristics. *Journal of Counseling Psychology, 35,* 268-274,

Ellis, M. V., & Robbins, E. S. (1993). Voices of care and justice in clinical supervision: Issues and interventions. *Counselor Education and Supervision, 32,* 203-212.

Fong, M. L. (1994, April). Multicultural issues in supervision. *ERIC Digest* (EDO-CG-94-14). Greensboro, NC: ERIC Clearinghouse on Counseling and Student Services.

Fukuyama, M. A. (1994). Critical incidents in multicultural counseling supervision: A phenomenological approach to supervision research. *Counselor Education and Supervision, 43,* 142-151.

Hart, G. M. (1982). *The process of clinical supervision.* Baltimore, MD: University Park Press.

Helms, J. E. (Ed.). (1990). *Black and White racial identity: Theory, research, and practice* Westport, CT: Greenwood.

Helms, J. E. (1994). Racial identity and career assessment. *Journal of Career Assessment, 2,* 199-209.

Helms, J. E., & Carter, R. T. (1990). Development of the White Racial Identity Inventory. In J. E. Helms (Ed.), *Black and White racial identity: Theory, research, and practice* (pp. 67-80). Westport, CT: Greenwood.

Ibrahim, F. A. (1991). Contribution of cultural worldview to generic counseling and development. *Journal of Counseling and Development, 70,* 13-19.

Ladany, N., & Friedlander, M. L. (1995). The relationship between the supervisory working alliance and trainees' experience of role conflict and role ambiguity. *Counselor Education and Supervision, 34,* 220-231.

Leong, F.T.L., & Wagner, N. M. (1994). Cross-cultural supervision: What do we know? What do we need to know? *Counselor Education and Supervision, 34,* 117-132.

McIntosh, P. (1988). *White privilege and male privilege: A personal account of coming to see correspondences through work in women's studies.* Wellesley, MA: Wellesley College, Center for Research on Women.

Mintz, L. B., Bartels, K. M., & Rideout, C. A. (1995). Training in counseling ethnic minorities and race-based availability of graduate school resources. *Professional Psychology: Research and Practice, 26,* 316-321.

Nickerson, K. J., Helms, J. E., & Terrell, F. (1994). Cultural mistrust, opinions about mental illness, and Black students' attitudes toward seeking psychological help from White counselors. *Journal of Counseling Psychology, 41,* 378-385.

Olk, M., & Friedlander, M. L. (1992). Role conflict and ambiguity in the supervisory experiences of counselor trainees. *Journal of Counseling Psychology, 39,* 389-397.

Ponterotto, J. G. (1988). Racial consciousness development among White counselor trainees: A state model. *Journal of Multicultural Counseling and Development, 16,* 146-156.

Ponterotto, J. G., Rieger, B. P., Barrett, A., Harris, G., Sparks, R., Sanchez, C. M., & Magido, D. (1993, September). Development and initial validation of the Multicultural Counseling Awareness Scale (MCAS). In *Measurement and testing: Multicultural assessment.* Ninth Buros-Nebraska Symposium, Lincoln, NE.

Pope-Davis, D. B., & Ottavi, T. M. (1994). Examining the association between self-reported multicultural counseling competencies and demographic variables among counselors. *Journal of Counseling and Development, 72,* 651-654.

Preli, R., & Bernard, J. M. (1993). Making multiculturalism relevant for majority culture graduate students. *Journal of Marital and Family Therapy, 19,* 5-16.

Priest, R. (1991). Racism and prejudice as negative impacts on African American clients in therapy. *Journal of Counseling and Development, 70,* 213-215.

Ridley, C. R. (1995). *Overcoming unintentional racism in counseling and therapy: A practitioner's guide to intentional intervention.* Thousand Oaks, CA: Sage.

Robiner, W. N. (1982). Role diffusion in the supervisory relationship. *Professional Psychology, 13,* 258-267.

Rowe, W., Bennett, S. K., & Atkinson, D. R. (1994). White racial identity models: A critique and alternative proposal. *The Counseling Psychologist, 22,* 129-146.

Sabnani, H. B., Ponterotto, J. G., & Borodovsky, L. G. (1991). White racial identity development and cross-cultural counselor training: A stage model. *The Counseling Psychologist, 19,* 76-102.

Sodowsky, G. R., Taffe, R. C., Gutkin, T. B., & Wise, S. L. (1994). Development of the Multicultural Counseling Inventory (MCI): A self-report measure of multicultural competencies. *Journal of Counseling Psychology, 41,* 137-148.

Sue D., & Sue, D. W. (1993). Ethnic identity: Cultural factors in the psychological development of Asians in America. In D. R. Atkinson, G. Morten, & D. W. Sue (Eds.), *Counseling American minorities: A cross-cultural perspective* (4th ed.; pp. 199-210). Dubuque, IA: Brown & Benchmark.

Sue, D. W., & Sue, D. (1990). *Counseling the culturally different: Theory and practice* (2nd ed.). New York: John Wiley.

Sue, D. W., Arredondo, P., & McDavis, R. J. (1992). Multicultural counseling competencies and standards: A call to the profession. *Journal of Counseling and Development, 70,* 477-486.

Sue, S., & Zane, N. (1987). The role of culture and cultural techniques in psychotherapy: A critique and reformulation. *American Psychologist, 42,* 37-45.

Trimble, J. E. (1988). Stereotypic images. American Indians and prejudice. In P. Katz & D. Taylor (Eds.), *Eliminating racism and prejudice* (pp. 210-236). Elmsford, NY: Pergamon.

Twohey, D., & Volker, J. (1993). Listening for the voices of care and justice in counselor supervision. *Counselor Education and Supervision, 32,* 189-197.

Vander Kolk, C. J. (1974). The relationship of personality, values, and race to anticipation of the supervisory relationship. *Rehabilitation Counseling Bulletin, 18,* 41-46.

Watkins, C. E., Jr., & Terrell, F. (1988). Mistrust level and its effects on counseling expectations in Black client-White counselor relationships: An analogue study. *Journal of Counseling Psychology, 35,* 194-197.

Watkins, C. E., Jr., Terrell, F., Miller, F. S., & Terrell, S. L. (1989). Cultural mistrust and its effects on expectational variables in the Black client-White counselor relationships. *Journal of Counseling Psychology, 36,* 447-450.

Wrenn, C. G. (1962). The culturally encapsulated counselor. *Harvard Educational Review, 32,* 444-449.

Author Index

Abbey, D. S., 266, 271, 272
Adler, N. J., 186, 204
Aikin, J., 176
Alexander, C., 336
Alexander, C. M., 17, 112, 122, 151, 184, 194, 198, 200, 201, 202, 210, 243
Allen, D., 62, 268
Allen, D. B., 209
Allison, D. W., 229, 235
Allison, K. W., 112
Allport, G. W., 277
Altmaier, E. M., 249
Altman, I., 336
Alvarez, M., 31
Anaya, R. A., 378
Andersen, P., 163
Andersen, T., 353
Anderson, H. D., 353, 367
Anderson, W. T., 351, 353
Angermeier, L., 64, 147, 211, 271, 273, 275, 280
Aponte, H. J., 366
Aranalde, M. A., 21
Arbona, C., 270
Arce, C. H., 246

Arnold, M. S., 402
Aronson, E., 232
Arredondo, P., xi, 9, 69, 111, 113, 140, 161, 210, 212, 230, 235, 236, 239, 244, 264, 293, 305, 310, 388
Arredondo, P. M., 145, 146, 185, 199
Arter, J. A., 46
Atkinson, D. R., 13, 15, 16, 17, 32, 33, 38, 48, 52, 55, 89, 90, 93, 99, 100, 105, 106, 121, 127, 128, 141, 142, 143, 146, 147, 160, 187, 198, 209, 230, 231, 239, 244, 250, 274, 275, 276, 279, 291, 295, 296, 301, 389
Attneave, C., 209
Axelson, J. A., 189, 377
Ayers, L. R., 47

Banks, W. M., 252
Barón, A., Jr., 166
Barrett, A., 44, 122, 177, 210
Barrett, F. J., 351, 357, 358
Barrett-Lennard, G. T., 328
Bartels, K. M., 99, 391
Baruth, L. G., 135, 136, 184

Bascuas, J., 218
Bass, E., 355
Bauman, Z., 364, 376, 380
Beck, A. T., 368
Behrens, J. T., 121, 197, 279, 397
Belenky, M. F., 87
Bell, L. A., 194
Bem, D. J., 84
Bem, S. L., 84
Benassi, V. A., 177
Benhabib, S., 377
Bennett, E. K., 279, 397
Bennett, S. K., 275, 389
Berger, K. S., 173, 174
Berger, P. L., 352
Bernal, M. E., 112, 115, 123, 124, 126, 185,
    187, 190, 191, 210, 228, 235
Bernard, J. M., 302, 311, 317, 318, 350, 356,
    357, 358, 359, 360, 361, 365, 366,
    367, 389, 392, 396, 398, 399, 402,
    403
Bernier, J. E., 61, 69, 75
Berry, J. W., 32, 35, 168, 274, 276, 280
Berryhill-Paapke, E., 210
Bersheid, E., 169
Betancourt, H., 67
Betz, N. E., 92
Biever, J. L., 353
Bingham, R. P., 338
Blackmon, B., 273, 328
Blum, L., 193, 194
Borders, L. D., 398
Borgmann, A., 351
Borodovsky, L. G., 12, 230, 272, 389
Borowsky, S., 113
Boscolo, L., 350, 361, 362
Bowser, B. P., 189
Boyd-Franklin, N., 148
Bradley, L. J., 295
Bradshaw, C., 62
Bradshaw, W. H., Jr., 389
Brislin, R. W., 20, 136, 271
Brod, H., 86
Brome, D. R., 311, 346
Brooks, G. S., 211
Broverman, D. M., 88
Broverman, I. K., 88
Brown, M. T., 127, 303, 392, 393
Bruschke, J. C., 233

Buhrke, R. A., 98, 99, 106
Bullington, R., 118, 197
Burn, D., 16, 210

Caffarella, E. P., 51
Caffarella, R. S., 51
Callanan, P., 380
Campbell, J., 49
Campbell, L., 20
Canabal, I., 67
Capper, C. A., 364
Carney, C. G., 189, 210, 230, 280, 300, 301,
    302, 325, 327
Carskaddon, G. A., 52
Carter, M., 51
Carter, R. T., 64, 74, 189, 195, 210, 212,
    295, 301, 397
Casali, S. L., 271
Casas, J. M., 105, 113, 121, 122, 127, 128,
    142, 146, 151, 161, 184, 187, 210,
    246, 250
Casas, M. J., 246
Castro, F. G., 187, 210, 228, 235
Cayleff, S. E., 145, 375
Cecchin, G., 350, 361, 362, 366
Cervantes, O. F., 245, 246, 248
Cervantes, R. C., 21
Chambers, R., 269, 280
Chambers, T., 172
Chapman, M., 264
Cheung, F. K., 63, 76, 292
Choi, S., 195
Choi-Pearson, C. P., 245, 246, 247, 248,
    249, 251, 254
Choney, S. K., 210
Christensen, C. P., 210
Chunn, J., 185
Clarfield, L. E., 354, 355, 368
Clarkson, F. E., 88
Clinchy, B. M., 87
Coale, H. W., 354
Cochran, S. D., 91
Coleman, H., 69, 178
Coleman, H. L. K., 45, 53, 197, 210, 271,
    274, 277, 310
Coleman-Boatwright, P., 253
Collins, A., 46, 47, 56
Comas-Diaz, L., 88, 95, 148

Conger, J., 90
Congett, S. M., 191
Conoley, J. C., 229
Conway, L., 209, 268
Cook, D. A., 61, 62, 63, 65, 66, 273, 280,
    296, 298, 310, 311, 317, 318, 325,
    327, 328, 388, 391, 394, 403
Cook, E. P., 86, 92
Cooperrider, D. L., 351, 357, 358, 373
Copeland, E. J., 132, 133, 135, 184, 211, 212
Corey, G., 380
Corey, M. S., 380
Cormier, L. S., 45
Cormier, W. H., 45
Corsini, R. J., 190
Cortes, D. E., 276
Corvin, S. A., 195
Costantino, G., 19, 21
Cox, C. I., 270, 325
Coyne, J. C., 355
Crawford, I., 112, 229
Crawford, M., 89, 94
Crethar, H. C., 273
Cross, W. E., Jr., 15, 143, 144, 210, 275,
    295, 299
Cuellar, I., 21, 30
Cummings, T. G., 215

DaCosta, G., 328
Dahl, R. A., 169
Dana, R. H., 139, 149, 167, 173, 250
D'Andrea, M., 52, 69, 112, 113, 114, 128,
    161, 177, 184, 194, 196, 202, 210,
    211, 212, 213, 222, 236, 244, 251,
    292, 297, 308, 325, 331
Daniels, J., 52, 112, 113, 114, 128, 161, 184,
    194, 196, 202, 210, 211, 212, 213,
    222, 236, 244, 251, 292, 325, 331
Darby, G. E., 153
Das, A. K., 160, 165, 172, 173, 175, 179
Dasen, P. R., 168
Davenport, D. S., 86
Davis, L., 355
Davis, L. E., 279
Davis-Russell, E., 210, 212, 218
Deaux, K., 86
DeFreece, M. T., 248
DeLaGarza, D., 160, 163

Delworth, U., 263, 311, 327
Denner, B., 354
Desai, L., 51
DeVries, D. L., 232
Diamant, L., 90
Diaz-Guerrero, R., 71
Diaz-Soto, L., 75, 76
Dings, J. G., 122, 229
Doherty, W. J., 353
Douce, L. A., 98, 99, 106
Downing, N. C., 274
Draguns, J. G., 21, 151, 209
Driscoll, A., 215
Dunlap, D., 335
Dunston, P., 185
Duran, E., 218

Echemendia, R., 112, 191, 229
Edwards, K. J., 232
Edwards, P., 186
Efran, J. S., 351, 354, 355, 368
Eisenberg, L., 379
Ekman, P., 71
Ellis, M. V., 399, 400
Enns, C. Z., 88, 94, 95, 100
Epston, D., 353
Espín, O. M., 87, 88
Essandoh, P. K., 267
Exum, W. H., 245, 252

Fairchild, H. H., 65, 278
Fassinger, R. E., 89, 90, 92, 96, 99, 100, 246
Fernald, P. S., 176, 177
Festinger, J. R. P., Jr., 170, 171
Fields, C., 247, 248
Fisch, 216
Fiske, E. B., 245, 246, 247, 248
Fitzgerald, L. F., 87, 88, 92, 93, 94, 95, 99
Flew, A., 351, 352
Flores, V., 378
Follett, M. P., 335
Fong, G. T., 353, 354
Fong, M. L., 389, 392
Forbes, W. T., 218
Fordham, S., 160
Foster, S. L., 69, 113, 114, 210, 211, 219,
    272

Fouad, N. A., 105
Fowler, W. E., 270
Fox, D. B., 47
Freedle, R., 275
Freeman, E. M., 273, 328
Fretz, B. R., 141
Friedlander, M. L., 393
Fry, R. E., 351
Fuentes, C., 378
Fujino, D. C., 76
Fukuyama, M. A., 61, 199, 273, 280, 302, 303, 311, 338, 399, 403

Gagne, R. M., 267, 272
García Marquez, G., 378
Gardner, G. T., 353
Garnets, L., 89, 90, 91, 99
Gartner, C., 233
Gaubatz, M. D., 354, 376, 378
Gay, P., 378
Geary, C. A., 210, 328
Gelso, C. J., 141
Gergen, K. J., 351, 352, 353, 354, 379
Gergen, M. J., 352
Gergen, M. M., 352
Gerton, J., 197, 277
Getzel, E. E., 245
Gibson, M. A., 244
Gilbert, L. A., 86, 87, 88, 89, 97, 99, 100
Giles, T. R., 45
Gilligan, C., 355
Giordano, J., 150, 267, 362
Glatthorn, A. A., 304
Gloria, A. M., 245, 246, 247, 248, 249, 251, 254
Goldberger, N. R., 87
Goldenberg, H., 362
Goldenberg, I., 362
Goldman, P., 335
Gonsiorek, J. C., 90, 274
Gonzalez, J. C., 244
González, R. C., 353, 364, 378
Good, B., 379
Good, G. E., 88, 94
Goodchilds, J., 91
Goodyear, R. K., 302, 311, 350, 356, 357, 358, 360, 361, 389, 392, 398, 399
Goolishian, H. A., 353, 367

Grant, C. A., 243, 244, 252
Grant, S. K., 48
Green, M. F., 118, 197
Greenberg, R. L., 368
Greene, B., 88
Grieger, I., 17, 112, 184, 194, 198, 200, 201, 202, 210, 243
Griffith, E. E. H., 148
Guerin, B., 353
Gunnings, B. B., 245, 249
Gunnings, T., 62, 63
Gushue, G. V., 281
Gutierez, J. M., 146, 210
Gutkin, T. B., 9, 52, 61, 177, 210, 236, 270, 397
Guzman, L. P., 253, 254

Hacker, A., 355
Hackett, G., 89, 90, 93, 99, 100, 105, 106, 187
Halcon, J. J., 252
Haley, J., 350, 361, 365, 369
Hall, C. C. I., 251, 252
Hall, J., 62, 268
Hall, L. E., 338
Hall, W. S., 275
Hancock, K. A., 91
Hansen, J., 47
Hardiman, R., 194, 213, 214, 230, 295, 372
Hardy, E., 311, 327
Hardy, K. V., 350, 363
Hare-Mustin, R. T., 87, 353, 363, 364
Harris, A., 365
Harris, L. C., 21
Hart, G. M., 392
Hayes, S., 229
Heath, A. E., 113
Hecht, M., 163
Heck, R., 52, 161, 202, 210, 236
Held, B. S., 354
Hellman, S., 53
Helms, J., 21
Helms, J. E., 13, 14, 61, 62, 63, 65, 66, 67, 68, 72, 74, 75, 139, 143, 144, 145, 149, 189, 197, 210, 230, 270, 273, 274, 276, 279, 280, 281, 295, 296, 299, 310, 311, 317, 325, 327, 328, 378, 388, 389, 391, 394, 397

Henderson, A. H., 168
Hendricks, C. O., 325, 328, 329
Herbert, E., 47
Herman, T. L., 47
Hernandez, A., 53, 210
Hicks, L., 136
Highlen, P. S., 242, 243, 249, 270, 325
Hills, H. I., 111, 115, 123, 124, 132, 186, 210, 212, 228
Hilton, D. B., 311
Hinde, R. A., 338
Ho, D. Y. F., 264, 265, 275
Hodges, W., 368
Hoffman, M. A., 113
Hoffmann, L., 353, 378
Hofstede, G., 68, 70, 71
Hollinger, R., 376
Hollis, J. W., 111, 115
Holloway, E. L., 45, 48, 266, 273, 280, 326, 330, 334, 335, 336, 337, 338, 339
Holvino, E., 194, 195, 199, 200, 213, 215
Hood, A. B., 267
Hoshmand, L. L. S. T., 87
Hough, J. C., 21
Hovland, C. I., 170
Howard, G. S., 353, 380
Hu, L. T., 76
Huber, C. H., 362, 364, 380
Hudson, S. A., 245
Hui, H. C., 271
Hunt, D. E., 266
Hunt, J. A., 194
Hunt, R. G., 189
Huse, E. F., 215
Hyde, J. S., 89

Ibrahim, F. A., 64, 145, 146, 195, 273, 275, 390, 392
Ihle, G. M., 13
Ingle, G., 194
Ito, J., 62
Ivey, A., 153
Ivey, A. E., 28, 64, 127, 188, 199, 231, 232, 300, 325, 326, 337, 338
Ivey, M. B., 28, 64
Iwamasa, F., 278

Jackson, B., 13, 194, 372
Jackson, B. W., 194, 195, 199, 200, 213, 214, 215
Jackson, J. S., 20
Jackson, M. L., 209
Jacobson, C. K., 21
James, A., 53
Janis, I. L., 170
Jasso, R., 21
Jenal, S. T., 73, 74
John, O. P., 233, 234, 236
Johnson, M., 272
Johnson, P., 378
Johnson, R., 273
Johnson, S., 161, 172
Johnson, S. C., 264
Johnson, S. D., 12, 210, 212, 213, 227, 229, 231, 244, 337
Johnson, S. D., Jr., 70
Johnsrud, L. K., 251, 252
Jones, A., 63
Jones, E. E., 369
Jones, J. M., 186

Kagan, N., 178, 350, 356, 357, 368, 377
Kagitcibasi, C., 195
Kahn, A. S., 87, 88
Kahn, K. B., 189, 210, 230, 280, 300, 301, 302, 325, 327
Kahn, S. E., 211
Kaiser, S. M., 139
Kanitz, B. E., 3, 45, 64, 132, 133, 135, 136, 137, 145, 146, 147, 184, 185, 210, 211, 227, 264, 271, 272, 273, 275, 280, 310
Kanter, R. M., 197
Karpel, M. A., 371
Kaschak, E., 94
Katz, J., 213, 214, 215, 253
Katz, J. H., 5, 15, 16, 75, 88, 94, 187
Keefe, S. E., 279
Kell, B. L., 334
Kelley, H. C., 170
Kelley, H. H., 169
Kelly, G., 28
Kelly, G. D., 12
Kerezsi, P., 172, 269
Kim, J., 295, 372

Kim, U., 195
Kimmel, D., 89, 90
Kinzie, J. D., 21
Kleinman, A., 379
Klonoff, E., 67
Kluckhohn, F., 68, 70, 75
Knepp, D., 112, 229
Kohatsu, E. L., 67
Kolb, D. A., 266, 271, 272
Korchin, S. J., 191
Krathwohl, D. R., 178
Kregel, J., 245
Kremgold-Barrett, A., 88, 89, 98, 99
Kudlac, K. E., 353
Kugler, J. F., 139, 140
Kuh, G. D., 217
Kurtines, W., 21
Kushner, J. L., 193, 194
Kwan, K. L., 13, 197
Kwan, K. L. K., 13

Lacefield, W. E., 245
Ladany, N., 393
LaFromboise, T., 197, 277, 279
LaFromboise, T. D., 53, 56, 69, 75, 113,
    114, 210, 211, 219, 272
Lai, E. W. M., 21, 32, 33
Laird, J., 353
Lakin, M., 366
Landrine, H. A., 67
Landrum-Brown, J., 303, 392, 393
Lanning, W., 350, 359, 360
LaVome, R., 229
Leach, M. M., 121, 197
Leary, T., 335
Lee, C. C., 187, 269
Lefley, H. P., 211
Leong, F. T. L., 32, 33, 38, 121, 188, 263,
    271, 293, 294, 300, 302, 311, 326,
    328, 347, 388, 398, 403
Leung, S. A., 113
Lew, S., 21, 278
Lewin, K., 280
Lewis, A. C., 229
Lewis, D. E., 118, 197
Lewis, J., 172, 269
Lewis, J. A., 297
Lewis, J. F., 21

Lewis, M. D., 297
Lewis, S., 232, 233
Lindholm, K. J., 30, 31
Lindskold, S., 168
Lingle, D. W., 141
Linzer, N., 363
Li-Repac, D., 20
Lloyd, A. P., 230
Locke, D. C., 61, 187
Logan, S. L., 273, 328
Loganbill, C., 311, 327
Lonner, W. J., 151, 209
Lopez, S. R., 67, 210, 283
Lou, R., 251
Lowe, S. M., 121, 141
Lowenstein, S. F., 350
Luckmann, T., 352
Lukens, M. D., 351
Lukens, R. J., 351
Luz Reyes, M. L., 252
Lyddon, W. J., 216

Madrazo-Peterson, R., 245
Maeroff, G. I., 55
Magids, D. M., 52
Magoon, T. M., 292
Mahan, J. M., 245
Mahoney, M. J., 353, 354
Malgady, R. G., 19, 21, 276
Manese, J., 105
Manning, K., 253
Manning, M. L., 135, 136, 184
Maracek, J., 87, 353
Marcos, L. R., 371
Margolis, R. L., 113, 114, 211
Marín, B. V., 250
Marín, G., 250
Maruyama, M., 32
Massey, I., 194, 200, 202
Matsui, S., 32
Matsumoto, D., 71
McConahay, J. B., 21
McDaniel, S. H., 350, 362
McDavis, R. J., xi, 9, 69, 111, 140, 161, 210,
    212, 230, 244, 264, 293, 310, 388
McEwen, M. K., 166, 189
McFadden, J., 187
McGoldrick, J., 267

McGoldrick, M., 150, 362
McIntosh, P., 179, 389, 391
McKeever, J., 350
McKinley, D. L., 302, 327
McKinney, H., 62, 268
McNamee, S., 352
McNeill, B. W., 273
McRae, M. B., 12, 161, 172, 227, 229, 231,
     244, 337
McRoy, R. G., 273, 328
McWhirter, E. H., 300
McWhirter, J. J., 267
Meggert, S. S., 12, 136, 159, 164, 175, 186,
     211, 316, 325
Meichenbaum, D., 353, 354
Meijer, C., 76
Mendoza, D. W., 3, 45, 64, 132, 133, 135,
     136, 137, 145, 146, 147, 184, 185,
     210, 211, 227, 264, 271, 272, 273,
     275, 280, 310
Menges, R. J., 245, 252
Mente, D., 354
Mercer, J. R., 21
Merta, R. J., 227, 232, 233, 234, 238
Messcik, S., 56
Meyer, C. A., 46
Midgette, T. E., 12, 136, 159, 164, 175, 186,
     211, 316, 325
Millar, S., 244, 252
Miller, F. A., 165
Miller, F. E., 335
Miller, F. S., 282, 394
Miller, R., 178
Minnich, E. K., 189
Mintz, L. B., 99, 100, 391
Minuchin, S., 354, 367, 368
Mio, J. S., 112, 211, 229, 230, 231, 279
Mohatt, G. V., 75
Molinaro, K., 61, 70
Montalvo, B., 350, 361, 363, 365
Morgan, D. W., 311, 327
Morris, D. R., 112, 229
Morten, G., 13, 15, 143, 147, 187, 209, 230,
     244, 274, 291
Morton, T., 336
Mueller, W. J., 334
Mukherjee, S., 20
Mussenden, M. E., 338
Myers, L. J., 270, 325

Navarrete, C., 47, 55, 56
Neighbors, H. W., 20
Neimeyer, G. J., 113, 338
Nelson, D., 279
Nichols, J. T., 378
Nickerson, E. T., 88, 89, 98, 99
Nickerson, K. J., 394
Nielson, D., 229
Noel, N., 355
North, M.-W., 353
Nutt, R., 87, 88, 93, 94, 95, 99
Nwachuku, U. T., 231, 337

Ogbu, J. U., 160
Ogbu, J. V., 265
O'Hara, M., 351, 353
Olarte, S., 20
Olk, M., 393
Olmedo, E. L., 246, 252, 253
O'Neil, J., 55
O'Neil, J. M., 267
O'Regan, J., 245
Ortiz, V., 246
Osherow, N., 232
Ottavi, T. M., 187, 244, 391, 397

Padilla, A. M., 21, 30, 31, 32, 35, 185, 190,
     191, 210, 228, 235, 274, 276, 279
Paniagua, F. A., 188
Pannu, R., 13, 197
Pap, A., 186
Paradise, N. E., 267, 272
Parham, T. A., 113, 250, 275, 279
Parham, W., 210, 212
Paris, S. G., 47
Parker, W. M., 210, 211, 328
Parry, A., 353
Paulson, F. L., 46, 48
Paulson, P. P., 46
Pearce, J. K., 150, 267, 362
Peck, T., 274
Pedersen, P., 83, 153, 161, 172, 184, 187,
     198, 209, 231, 363, 364
Pedersen, P. B., 5, 12, 15, 16, 32, 34, 61,
     111, 113, 127, 138, 143, 146, 150,
     151, 188, 191, 196, 199, 201, 231,

244, 249, 255, 267, 269, 282, 290, 295, 297, 316, 338
Penn, P., 352, 362, 366, 369
Peplau, L. A., 91
Peregoy, J. J., 251
Persico, C. F., 187, 194, 200, 243, 254
Peterson, F. K., 325, 327
Peterson, R. A., 209
Phinney, J. S., 13, 21, 197, 210, 279
Piper, R. E., 275
Plake, B., 21
Ponterotto, J. G., 12, 13, 17, 44, 45, 52, 54, 55, 69, 75, 76, 112, 113, 114, 115, 118, 121, 122, 128, 138, 142, 143, 144, 146, 151, 161, 177, 184, 187, 188, 194, 195, 197, 198, 200, 201, 202, 210, 212, 213, 227, 229, 230, 236, 243, 245, 249, 250, 255, 272, 295, 297, 389, 397
Poortinga, Y. H., 168
Pope, K. S., 360, 365, 367
Pope, R. L., 84, 87, 95, 98, 214, 215, 216, 217, 219, 220, 222, 279
Pope-Davis, D. B., 122, 154, 173, 187, 229, 244, 279, 391, 397
Poston, W. C., 279
Prata, G., 350
Preli, R., 402
Priest, R., 303, 311, 317, 394
Prieto, L., 173, 187

Quintana, S. M., 112, 115, 123, 124, 126
Qureshi, A., 195

Raven, B., 170, 171
Reder, P., 350
Remington, G., 328
Reynolds, A. C., 278
Reynolds, A. L., 84, 87, 95, 98, 111, 112, 136, 137, 146, 154, 173, 187, 210, 211, 214, 229
Reynolds, C. R., 139
Ribeau, S., 163
Richardson, B. L., 187
Richardson, M. S., 353, 364
Richardson, T. Q., 61, 70, 75, 76
Rickard-Figueroa, K., 21, 278

Ricks, K. A., 353
Rideout, C. A., 99, 391
Ridley, C. R., 3, 4, 16, 25, 45, 48, 55, 64, 71, 131, 132, 133, 135, 136, 137, 138, 139, 140, 141, 145, 146, 147, 152, 184, 185, 186, 192, 196, 197, 201, 202, 210, 211, 227, 228, 232, 234, 264, 271, 272, 273, 275, 280, 310, 389, 390, 392, 397, 403
Ridley, S., 136
Rieger, B. P., 44, 122, 177, 210
Robbins, E. S., 399, 400
Robbins, R. R., 210
Roberts, H., 201
Roberts, J., 350, 361, 362
Robiner, W. N., 392
Robinson, L., 112
Robinson, T., 319
Rodriguez, M., 245
Rodriguez, R., 370, 375
Rogers, C. R., 12
Rogers, L. E., 335
Rogers, M. R., 113, 229, 235
Rogler, L. H., 19, 21, 276
Ronnestad, M. H., 48
Roper, L. D., 166, 189
Rosen, A. M., 20
Rosenau, P. M., 351, 378
Rosenkrantz, P. S., 88
Ross-Sheriff, F., 185
Rothbart, M., 232, 233, 234, 236
Roush, K. L., 274
Rowe, W., 121, 197, 275, 276, 279, 389, 391, 397
Royle, M. H., 234
Rudolph, J., 99
Rudolph, J. R., 90, 274
Ruggiero, V. R., 367
Ruiz, R. A., 246
Rungta, S. A., 113, 114, 211
Russell, R. K., 311
Russell, R. L., 354, 376, 378
Ryan, A. S., 325, 328, 329
Ryan, W., 374

Sabnani, H. B., 12, 13, 230, 272, 389
Salgado de Snyder, N., 21
Salmi, S. W., 311

Sanchez, C. M., 52
Santiago-Negron, S., 194
Sarbin, T. R., 352
Sargent, 215
Sauerman, T. H., 368
Scarr, S., 353, 377
Schaller, J., 160, 163
Scher, M., 88
Scopetta, M. A., 21
Scott, O. L., 249, 254
Seagull, A. A., 63
Sedlacek, W. E., 251
Segall, M. H., 168
Seiter, J. S., 233
Self, B., 378
Selvini Palazzoli, M., 350, 361, 362
Sherif, C., 86
Shizuru, L. S., 153
Shukla, S., 20
Simek-Downing, L., 28
Simek-Morgan, L., 64
Simons, G. F., 166
Simpkins, G., 62, 63
Sirach, 380
Sirmans, M., 113
Skovholt, T. M., 48, 267
Slater, B. R., 245
Slavin, R. E., 232
Sleeter, C. E., 243, 244
Sluzki, C. E., 353
Smart, D. W., 270, 276
Smart, J. F., 270, 276
Smith, E. J., 186
Smith, E. M. J., 246
Smith, H., 379
Smith, M. B., 354
Snowden, L., 63, 76
Snowden, L. R., 292
Sodowsky, G. R., 5, 9, 13, 21, 24, 32, 33,
    52, 61, 69, 177, 197, 210, 236, 270,
    397
Solomon, B., 346, 347
Sotello, C., 160
Spandel, V., 46
Sparks, R., 44, 122, 177, 210
Speight, S. L., 270, 325
Sperling, M. B., 350, 362
Srivastva, S., 351, 357, 378

Stadler, H. A., 267
Steele, S., 364
Stein, W. J., 248, 252
Stephan, W. G., 232, 233
Steward, R., 197
Stoltenberg, C. D., 263, 273, 280
Stone, B., 55
Stone, G. L., 272, 277, 278
Stricker, G., 186
Strickland, B., 251
Stringham, E. M., 227
Strodtbeck, F., 68, 70, 75
Strozier, A. L., 111, 115, 123, 124, 132, 186,
    210, 212, 228
Sue, D., 12, 13, 14, 15, 16, 31, 62, 63, 64,
    85, 89, 92, 95, 140, 143, 144, 146,
    152, 159, 160, 166, 172, 175, 187,
    188, 198, 210, 230, 235, 243, 248,
    251, 267, 271, 291, 292, 301, 339,
    375, 394, 395
Sue, D. W., x, 5, 9, 13, 14, 24, 31, 44, 48,
    49, 61, 62, 63, 64, 69, 75, 85, 89, 92,
    95, 111, 112, 113, 140, 141, 143,
    144, 146, 147, 152, 154, 155, 159,
    160, 161, 166, 172, 175, 187, 188,
    194, 198, 209, 210, 212, 215, 222,
    230, 235, 238, 243, 244, 248, 251,
    264, 267, 271, 274, 291, 292, 293,
    301, 305, 310, 339, 375, 388, 394,
    395
Sue, S., 19, 32, 34, 36, 62, 76, 142, 188,
    209, 242, 268, 292, 301, 390
Suinn, R. M., 21, 278
Suzuki, L. A., 139, 140, 151, 184
Swanson, J. L., 279
Szapocznik, J., 21

Taffe, R. C., 9, 52, 61, 177, 210, 236, 270,
    397
Takeuchi, D. T., 76
Tarule, J. M., 87
Tata, S. P., 121
Tatum, B., 76
Tavris, C., 87
Taylor, D., 252
Tedeschi, J. T., 168
Terrell, F., 197, 282, 394

Terrell, S., 197
Terrell, S. L., 282, 394
Thibaut, J. W., 169
Thomas, C. W., 21
Thompson, C. E., 16, 48, 121, 275, 279
Thompson, C. E. F., 73, 74
Thorne, A., 369
Tierney, R., 51, 53
Tokar, D. M., 279
Tomm, K., 362, 363, 366, 369, 370, 371
Triandis, H. C., 195, 271, 274, 278
Trimble, J. E., 75, 151, 394
Troiden, R. R., 274
Troy, W. G., 186
Tuescher, K., 53, 55
Turner, V., 160
Twohey, D., 395, 400
Tyler, F. B., 311, 346

Uba, L., 242
Unger, R., 89, 94
Urcuyo, L., 371
Usher, C. H., 190

Vaill, P. B., 193
Valley, M. M., 210, 328
Vander Kolk, C., 273, 311, 388, 394
Vargas, L. A., 328, 345, 347
Vasquez, M. J., 302
Vasquez, M. J. T., 245, 246, 327, 360, 365, 367
Vaughn, B. E., 194, 254
Vázquez, L. A., 154, 162, 163, 173, 177, 187
Vigil, P., 21, 278
Vogel, S. R., 88
Volker, J., 395, 400
von Glasersfeld, E., 353, 354
Vontress, C. E., 16, 63, 209

Wade, J. C., 113
Wagatsuma, Y., 30
Wagner, D. A., 293, 294, 300, 302
Wagner, N. M., 271, 311, 388, 398, 403
Wagner, N. S., 121, 326, 328, 347
Wagner, W. C., 270

Walsh, F., 355, 362
Walster, E., 169
Walster, G. W., 169
Wampold, B. E., 45, 271
Wang, A., 354
Wantz, R. A., 111, 115
Watkins, C. E., Jr., 282, 394
Watzlawick, 216
Weakland, 216
Weber, T., 350
Wehrly, B., 227, 234
Wei, W., 194
Weingarten, K., 353
Weiser, J. C., 266
Weizmann, F., 65, 278
Werner, D., 365
West, M., 245
White, D., 354
White, M., 353, 366
Wiese, M. J., 229
Wiggins, F., 195
Wiggins, G., 45, 47, 53, 55
Williams, D., 20
Williams, J. E., 311, 346
Williams, R. L., 21
Wise, S. L., 9, 52, 61, 177, 210, 236, 270, 397
Wolf, K., 46, 55
Woodle, J., 20
Worthington, E. L., Jr., 280
Wrenn, C. G., 15, 189, 209, 390
Wright, D. J., 245
Wyatt, G, 210, 212
Wyatt, G. E., 65, 278

Yalom, I. D., 364
Yee, A. H., 65, 278
Yoder, J. D., 87, 88
Yoon, G., 195
Yurich, J. M., 86

Zane, N., 32, 34, 36, 142, 188, 301, 390
Zane, N. W. S., 76
Zenk, R., 64, 147, 211, 271, 273, 275, 280
Zhu, M., 245

Subject Index

Academia:
    cultural ambience of, 242-256
    gender and sexual orientation in, 106-107
    See also Courses; Training; Universities
Academic freedom, 249
Accredited programs:
    of APA, 111-112, 115, 119, 123,
        131-132, 228-229, 312
    of CACREP, 159
Acculturation, 21, 30, 32
    cultural affiliation and, 274, 276-277
    phases of, 276-277
    research focus on, 210
Acculturative stress, 21, 30, 31, 32, 35
ACES. *See* Association for Counselor
        Education and Supervision
Achieved credibility, 32, 34
Action, in experiential learning, 272, 282,
    283
Adaptation, in acculturation, 276-277
Advocacy:
    political ideology and, 16-18
    supervision and, 302
Affect:
    language of, 370-372, 377

strong, 372-374
Affiliation:
    cultural, 274-283
    supervision and, 335
Affirmative action, 76
Affirmative postmodernists, 352
African Americans:
    as a caste-like minority group, 265
    assessment bias and, 20
    contact with, during training, 229
    course content on, 146
    faculty-to-student ratio for, 247
    oppression of, 268
    See also Blacks
Alienation, of students, 247, 248
Amae, 32, 34
Ambience. *See* Cultural ambience
Ambivalence, in oppressed groups, 275
AMCD. *See* Association for Multicultural
        Counseling and Development
American Counseling Association (ACA), 4,
    15, 213
American perspective:
    distinct from White culture, 203
    metaculture of, 68

status quo of, 159, 160, 161
American Psychological Association:
    accredited programs of, 111-112, 115,
        119, 123, 131-132, 228-229, 312
    guidelines of, xi, 4-5
    on culture, 31, 69, 250
    on ethics, 145
    on gays and lesbians, 90, 99
    on gender bias, 89
    on women, 99
    standards of, 159
Anger, 14, 373-374
Anthropology, and cultural difference, 267
Anticounselor, 231, 338
Appreciative inquiry, 357, 373, 374, 377
Approach-avoidance dynamic, 357
Arrogance, 284
Ascribed credibility, 32, 34
Asian Americans:
    assessment bias and, 19-20
    communication style of, 395
    course content on, 146
    identity development model for, 295
    oppression of, 268
    See also Chinese Americans; Japanese
        Americans
Assessment, of clients:
    bias in, 18-20, 91
    courses on, 139-140, 250
    emic perspective in, 22, 28-39
    etic perspective in, 18-28
    multicultural instruments for, 21
    pitfalls of, 19, 139
    qualitative approach to, 21-22
    recommendations for, 139-140
    structured, 19-20
    unstructured, 20
    workshop on, 22-28
Assessment, of MCC:
    by checklists, 113-126, 201, 213, 255,
        293, 305-306
    by portfolios, 43-57
    by structured instruments, 52, 53, 56,
        122, 236, 397
Assimilation, 35, 246. *See also* Acculturation
Association for Counselor Education and
        Supervision (ACES):
    recommendations for, 305, 307
    standards of, 388, 396

Association for Multicultural Counseling
        and Development (AMCD), 293, 305
    recommendations for, 307
    standards of, xi, 388
Assumptions:
    in assessment, workshop on, 23
    in the office visit, 188-189
    on knowing our assumptions, 256
    on supervision, 272, 392
    on training philosophies, 185
    on universality, x, 140, 141, 189, 270
    unlearning of, 15
Attitudes, MCC domain, 9, 69
    course content on, 140
    gender and, 92-93, 97-98
    meaning of, 92
    sexual orientation and, 95-96, 97-98
    training and, 97-98
    See also Awareness
Attraction influence, 171
Audiovisual materials, 153-155. *See also*
        Videotapes
Autonomous minorities, 265
Autonomy stage, of identity development,
        276, 298, 299
Awareness, MCC domain, 10-11
    course content on, 140
    in course objectives, 172
    individuals, change, and, 216
    portfolios and, 44, 48, 49
    training and, 75-76
    See also Attitudes

BAFA BAFA simulation, 233
Beliefs, MCC domain, 9, 10. *See also*
        Attitudes; Awareness
Bias:
    in assessment, 18-20, 91
    in diagnosis, 94
    in research, 86-88
    in therapy, 88-89, 91
Bilingual language switching, 370-372, 377
Bilingual services, 282
Bisexuals, 84, 90
    contact with, during training, 229
    knowledge about, 96
    rates of, in therapy, 99
    See also Sexual orientation

Black racial identity theory, 275
Blacks:
    identity development of, 295
    racial process models and, 64
    Whites, cultural affiliation, and, 279-280
    See also African Americans
Bottom-up approach, to change, 195, 197

CACREP (Council for Accreditation of
    Counseling and Related Educational
    Programs), 159
Calendar, course, 176-177
Caption, portfolio, 47
Career counseling, and sexual orientation, 96
Case-driven approach, to supervision, 334
Case examples:
    for assessment workshop, 23
    for emic perspective, 29-30
    for experiential learning cycle, 271-272,
        281-282
    for supervision, 321-323, 339-346
Case studies:
    for emic perspective, 28-39
    for gender and sexual orientation,
        102-105
Caste-like minorities, 265
Change, in training programs:
    first- vs. second-order, 216-219, 220-221
    Multicultural Change Intervention
        Matrix and, 215-222
    need for, 210, 212-213
    organizational development for, 213-215
    philosophies and, 194-200
Chicano students, 246
Chinese Americans:
    assessment bias and, 20
    ideographic approach with, 277-278, 280
Chronological approach, in courses, 174, 176
Circular questioning, 362-363, 369-370, 371
Circular reasoning, 189
Civil rights movement, 62, 243, 275
Classrooms:
    cultural ambience of, 249-251
    norms in, 165
Client-as-problem, 84
Climate, in building MCC, 101, 107, 200,
    401-402
Clinical supervision. *See* Supervision

Clinical vs. counseling training, 229
Collaboration:
    course content on, 141
    in supervision, 304, 307, 334, 336-337,
        346-347, 362, 399
Collective approaches, 94. *See also*
        Collaboration; Group approaches
Collectives, individuals within, 185
Collectivist cultures, 24, 273
Colleges. *See* Academia; Universities
Comfort level, with differences of others, 9
Coming-out issues, 96
Common humanity, 297. *See also*
        Universality assumption
Communication styles, 395-396, 400-401.
        See also Language; Nonverbal
        behavior
Community service, and cultural ambience,
        252
Competence statements, in portfolios, 47
Competencies. *See* Multicultural counseling
        competencies
Conceptualization skills, 358-359
Concrete experience, in experiential
        learning, 272, 282, 283
Conformity stage, of identity development,
        275, 296, 298
Conscientious level, in programmatic
        change, 198-200
Constructivism, 353, 354
Consultant, supervisor as, 302, 360
Contact hypothesis, 232-234
Contact stage, of identity development, 276,
        297-298, 299, 390
Context stripping, in research, 86-87
Cooperation, in multiethnic groups, 232
Council for Accreditation of Counseling and
        Related Educational Programs
        (CACREP), 159
Counseling supervision. *See* Supervision
Counseling trends, 292. *See also*
        Demographics
Counseling vs. clinical training, 229
Counselor, supervisor as, 360
Counselor-as-problem, 84
Counselor Effectiveness Rating Scale, 52
Counselor intentionality, 325-326
Courses:
    audiovisual materials for, 153-155

calendar for, 176-177
cultural ambience in, 249-251
development of, 131-156, 173-178, 181
for multicultural immersion, 235-238
goals of, 175
instructional methods for, 133, 175,
  230-238
instructional resources for, 147-155
in the total curriculum, 132-135
level of, 173-174
objectives of, 172-173, 175
on assessment, 250
on gender and sexual orientation, 99,
  100, 106
on statistics, 250
organization of, 174
purpose of, 134-135
requirements of, 176
separate, model of, 135-137, 211, 220,
  251
stereotyping by, 160
student evaluation in, 118, 119, 122,
  177-178
student responses to, 43-44
supervision and, 313-314, 316
surveys of, 111-112, 119, 120, 124,
  131-132
syllabus for, 174, 176-178
texts for, 147-153
topics covered by, 137-147
See also Faculty; Portfolios; Students;
  Training
Credibility, 32, 34
Cross-Cultural Counseling Inventory-R, 53,
  56, 122
Cross-cultural perspective, 39
  dyads in, 280-281
  in programmatic change, 196-198
  in training models, 230
  See also Etic perspective
Cross-cultural supervision, 293-294, 311
  White supervisors and, 387-403
  See also Supervision
Crying, during supervision, 372-373
Cultural affiliation, 274-281
  experiential learning and, 281-283
  forms of, 274-275
  See also Cultural difference perspective
Cultural ambassadors, in communities, 306

Cultural ambience, of training programs,
  242-245, 255-256
  for faculty, 247, 249, 250, 251-253
  for students, 245-251
  in classroom and curriculum, 249-251
  recommendations for, 253-255
  See also Climate; Environment
Cultural determinism, 268
Cultural difference perspective, 267-271
  experiential learning and, 271-274
  See also Cultural affiliation
Cultural empathy, 141
Cultural encapsulation, 194-198
Cultural entrenchment, 194-196
Cultural hegemony, 268
Cultural identity:
  cultural affiliation and, 279
  self-exploration in, 8, 9-15
  workshop on, 22-28
Cultural incongruence, 247-249
Cultural integrity, 198-199
Cultural mistrust, 394, 399
Culture:
  as obstacle vs. opportunity, 268
  complexity of, 83, 84
  course content on, 75-77, 146-147
  cultural difference and, 268-269
  emic perspective on, 28-39
  ethnicity and, 203
  etic perspective on, 18-28
  immersion experience and, 232-238
  internalized values of, 67-68
  MCC movement and, 62-65
  motivational model of, 68
  observational levels and, 72-74
  of training programs, 163-164
  operational definition of, 64
  personality characteristics and, 68
  program development and, 163
  psychological characteristics and, 65-66
  race and, 61, 64, 67, 70, 203, 264
  research implications of, 72-75
  societal classifications and, 65-66
  terminology and, 65-71
Culture conflict, 16, 19, 30, 32-33
Culture shock, 232, 233, 234, 245
Curriculum:
  cultural ambience in, 249-251
  development of, 132-134, 171-180

models of, 126-127
students' interests and, 171-172
survey of, 118, 119, 120, 121
See also Courses; Faculty; Students;
    Training

Deconstruction, definition of, 351
Deep-cultural self-empathy, 12-13
Deficit model, for guiding interventions, 62,
    63
Demographics:
    changes in, 238-239, 242-243, 263,
        291-292
    of supervision, 313, 318
Dependency, in social power, 168-169
Depression:
    acculturation and, 31, 32-33, 34
    assessment of, 20, 21
Developmental models:
    cultural affiliation and, 276, 279, 280
    supervision and, 295-304, 327
    training and, 143-145, 230
    See also Identity development
Deviations, misinterpretation of, 19
Diagnosis:
    bias in, 94
    course content on, 139-140
*Diagnostic and Statistical Manual of Mental
    Disorders IV (DSM-IV)*, 19
Diaries. *See* Journal diaries
Differential treatment, ix, x, 141
Disabled individuals, in academia, 245
Disconfirming information, and stereotypes,
    233-234
Discourse, and postmodernism, 363
Discrimination model, of supervision,
    358-361, 365-375
Discriminatory treatment, ix, 141
Disintegration stage, of identity
    development, 276, 390
Dissonance stage, of identity development,
    275
Diversity:
    as a gift, 179
    overemphasis on, 403
    postmodernism relevance to, 379-380
    See also Culture; Race
Diversity appreciation, 128

Diversity tolerance, 128
Diversity training, 75-77, 112, 127-128
    cultural ambience and, 243-244, 253
    curriculum and, 160, 178-179
    needed for all trainees, 239
    See also Supervision; Training
Domains, of MCC, 9-11
    course content on, 140
    gender and, 92-95, 97-102
    MCC conceptualizations and, 69
    meanings of, 92
    portfolios and, 44, 49
    sexual orientation and, 95-102
Dominant society:
    cultural affiliation and, 275, 276
    cultural norms of, 16, 19, 139
    metaculture of, 68
    supervision and, 284
    See also American perspective;
        Eurocentrism; Whites
Dropout rates, in counseling, 292
*DSM-IV (Diagnostic and Statistical Manual
    of Mental Disorders IV)*, 19

Education. *See* Courses; Training;
    Universities
Educators. *See* Faculty
Emic perspective, 28-39
    cultural difference and, 270
    etic perspective and, 22, 39
Emotion competence, 71
Emotions:
    generational differences and, 33
    self-exploration and, 12, 14
Empathy:
    cultural, 141
    cultural affiliation and, 275
    self, 12-13
Empowerment, of clients, 63
Environment, of training programs, 118,
    122. *See also* Climate; Cultural
    ambience
Epistemology, definition of, 351
Equal access, x
Equal treatment, ix, x, 141
Ethics:
    course content on, 145-146
    in research, 146

in supervision, 307, 351, 366, 367, 380
in training, 179, 249
Ethnic groups:
  as euphemism for race, 67
  concept of, 66-67
  MCC movement and, 62-63
  stereotyping of, by courses, 160
Ethnic identity:
  assessment of, 21
  cultural affiliation and, 274, 275
  development of, 143-145, 279, 295-300
  self-exploration in, 8, 9-15
  supervision and, 295-300
  workshop on, 22-28
Ethnicity:
  concept of, 67, 264
  distinct from race and culture, 203
  racism and, 13
Ethnocentrism, 68, 239
Etic, imposed, 22, 28
Etic perspective, 18-28
  cultural difference and, 270
  emic perspective and, 22, 39
Eurocentrism, 187-188, 190
  power and, 335
  supervision and, 335, 344
Evaluation:
  of faculty, 118, 119, 122
  of portfolios, 53-54, 55-56
  of students, 116, 118, 119, 122, 177-178
  of training programs, 134, 135-136, 155-156, 201-202, 255
  See also Assessment
Evidence, in portfolios, 47, 48-52
Exclusiveness, of multicultural concept, 264-265
Experiential learning, 98, 100, 121-122, 227, 230
  Partners Program for, 230-231
  supervision and, 266, 271-274, 281-284, 326, 402
  theory of, 232-234
  See also Immersion experience
Expert influence, 170-171
Experts:
  (in)equity and, 169
  on training programs, 113
  partial learning and, 368, 377

External differences. *See* Cultural difference perspective
External motivations, for MCC, 4-18

Faculty:
  academic freedom of, 249
  advocacy and, 17-18
  as program target, 164, 165-167
  change interventions and, 219, 220, 221
  cultural ambience for, 247, 249, 250, 251-253
  evaluations of, 118, 119, 122
  in curriculum development, 172-178
  influence of, 179
  in program development, 160-161, 163-171
  interests of, 172-173
  minority representation of, 123, 124, 126, 127
  multiculturally impaired, 161
  organizational change and, 215
  personality styles of, 166-167
  self-examination by, 161
  social influence of, 170-171
  social power and, 168-170
  training philosophies and, 185, 186, 189, 191-200, 203-204
Fair treatment, 141
Families:
  acculturation and, 32-39
  role conflicts in, 31, 33
Family assessment, 24
Family therapy, live supervision in, 361
Faulty generalization, and training, 189, 190
Feedback:
  portfolios and, 54
  supervision and, 367-368
Feminism:
  postmodernism and, 377-378
  therapy and, 94
  See also Gender; Sexual orientation

Gays, 84, 90, 96
  contact with, during training, 229
  in academia, 245
  rates of, in therapy, 99
  See also Sexual orientation

Gender, 84-85
  as determinant of life experiences, 86
  ideologies on, 85-89, 92-95
  role conflict and, 31, 96
  training on, 97-107
  verbal statements and, 375-376
  voices of, 395, 400
  See also Feminism; Men; Sexual
    orientation; Women
Gender aware therapy, 94
Gender bias:
  in diagnosis, 94
  in research, 86-88
  in therapy, 88-89
Generational conflict, and acculturation, 32,
    33-34, 35
Gestalt empty chair techniques, 96
Goals:
  in course content, 140, 141
  in portfolios, 51
  of courses, 175
  of portfolios, 47
  of training programs, 164-168, 201,
    218
Group approaches:
  for women, 94
  in supervision, 339-346, 401-403
  See also Collaboration; Live supervision
Group comparisons. *See* Etic perspective
Guilt, 14, 269

Heterosexism, 84, 90, 95. *See also* Sexism;
    Sexual orientation
Heterosexuals, 84
  as the norm, 87, 89, 95
  rates of, in therapy, 99
  See also Sexual orientation
Higher education. *See* Universities
Hispanic Americans:
  communication style of, 395
  contact with, during training, 229
  course content on, 146
  faculty-to-student ratio for, 247
  oppression of, 268
Homophobia, 90, 95. *See also* Sexism;
    Sexual orientation
Homosexuals. *See* Gays; Lesbians; Sexual
    orientation

Identity development:
  course content on, 143-145
  cultural, 279
  ethnic, 143-145, 279, 295-300
  models of, 144-145, 275, 279, 295-298
  racial, 143-145, 275, 279, 281, 295-300,
    327
  self-exploration and, 8, 9-15, 13
  self-report instruments for, 397
  sexual, 91
  stages of, 275-276, 296-299, 389-391
  supervision and, 295-300, 319-320, 327,
    389-391
Ideographic approaches, 39
  course content on, 141
  cultural affiliation and, 274-275,
    277-278, 280
  See also Emic perspective
Ideologies, nonconscious:
  on gender, 85-89, 92-95
  on sexual orientation, 85, 89-92, 95-96
Ideologies, political, 15-18
Immersion experience:
  MIE program for, 235-238
  theory and, 232-234
  See also Experiential learning
Immersion stage, of identity development,
    275, 297, 298
Immigrants:
  as minorities, 265
  course content on, 146
  experiential training and, 230-231
  See also Acculturation; Acculturative
    stress
Imposed etic, 22, 28
Inclusiveness, of multicultural construct,
    264-265
Indigenous interventions, 141-142
Individualism, 68
Individualism-collectivism, 70-71
Individuality, and emic perspective, 28
Individualized treatment, 141
(In)equity, in social power, 169
Influence, social, 170-171
Information. *See* Knowledge
Informational influence, 170
Infusion, 199-200, 249. *See also* Integrated
    model
Inquiring colleague, 356

Institutions:
    changes in, 212-215, 216, 218-221
    in Multicultural Change Intervention
        Matrix, 216, 218-219, 220-221
    in Systems Approach to Supervision, 330
Instructional methods, 133, 175, 230-238.
        See also Courses; Training
Instructional resources, 147-155
Instructors. *See* Faculty
Intake interview, 22
Intake summary, 22-25
Integrated awareness, 276
Integrated model, of training, 105, 112, 113,
        114, 126-127
    change intervention and, 219, 221
    cultural ambience and, 249-251
    program development and, 178-179
    supervision and, 318
    survey of, 121, 124
    See also Courses; Training
Intelligence, assessment of, 21, 369
Intentionality:
    in social power, 169
    of counselors, 325-326
Internal differences. *See* Cultural affiliation
Internalization:
    of cultural values, 67-68
    of one's own group, 275
    of oppression, 90
Internal motivations, for MCC, 4-18
International perspective, 267
Internship programs, survey of, 312-319.
        See also Supervision; Training
Interpersonal Process Recall (IPR):, 178,
        356-358
    application of, 365, 370, 373, 374, 375,
        376
    relevance of, 376-377
Interrater reliability, in portfolio evaluation,
        56
Intervention:
    course content on, 141-142
    deficit model for, 62, 63
    indigenous, 141-142
    in supervision, 337, 398-403
    in training, 215-222
    sexual orientation bias in, 91
Intimate relationships, and therapy bias, 91
Involuntary incorporation, 268

Involvement, in supervision, 334, 335, 336,
        344
IPR. *See* Interpersonal Process Recall
Isolation, of students, 248

Japanese Americans, 29-39
Jews, as an autonomous minority group,
        265
Jigsaw technique, 232
Journal diaries:
    for student evaluation, 178
    in immersion experiences, 237

Knowledge, MCC domain, 9, 10-11, 69
    course content on, 140
    gender and, 93-94, 98-101
    in course objectives, 172-173
    individuals, change, and, 216
    meaning of, 92
    portfolios and, 44, 48, 49
    sexual orientation and, 91, 96,
        98-101
    training and, 75, 76, 98-101, 227
Knowledge, partial, 189
Knowledge influence. *See* Informational
    influence

Language:
    diversity in, 64
    for facilitating change, 354-355
    gender voices of, 395, 400
    styles of, in supervision, 395-396
    switching of, 370-372, 377
Latino Americans, 268. *See also* Hispanic
        Americans
Learning environment, 247-249. *See also*
        Courses; Curriculum; Training
Learning objectives, 48, 133
Learning set, in experiential learning, 272,
        282, 283
Lesbians, 84, 90, 96
    contact with, during training, 229
    in academia, 245
    rates of, in therapy, 99
    See also Sexual orientation
Live supervision, 361-363, 365-376

Masculinity, of groups, 68
MCC. *See* Multicultural counseling competencies
MCIM. *See* Multicultural Change Intervention Matrix
MCOD (multicultural organization development), 213-215, 216
MCT (multicultural training). *See* Training
Melting pot theory, 187
Men:
    gender voice of, 395
    heterosexual, as a standard, 87
    values of, in academia, 245, 246, 248
Metaculture, 68
MIE (Multicultural Immersion Experience), 235-238
Minnesota Multiethnic Counselor Education Curriculum, 231
Minnesota Multiphasic Personality Inventory 2 (MMPI-2), 19
Minority identity development (MID) models, 144, 145
    supervision and, 295, 296-297, 298-299
Minority majority, 291-292
Minority representation, in training programs, 126, 127, 201
    change interventions and, 218
    survey of, 118, 122-123, 124
Missions, of training programs, 164-168, 192-194, 202
MMPI-2 (Minnesota Multiphasic Personality Inventory), 19
Modalities, of MCC, 49
Model training programs, 112-113, 120, 126-128, 221
Moderator variables, in training programs, 167-168
Modernism, definition of, 351
Monocultural practices, x
Motivation, for MCC, 4-18
    examples of, 8
    political ideology and, 15-18
    self-explorations and, 8, 9-15
Motivation, for training, 133, 192
Motivational model, of group functioning, 68
Multicultural, meaning of, 133
Multicultural Awareness-Knowledge-Skills Survey, 52, 122, 177, 202, 236

Multicultural Change Intervention Matrix (MCIM), 215-220
    illustration of, 220-221
    research needed on, 222
Multicultural competencies movement, 62-65
Multicultural Competency Checklist, 113-115, 201
    cultural ambience and, 255
    organizational change and, 213
    survey using, 115-126
Multicultural counseling, nature of, 291-293
Multicultural Counseling Awareness Scale, 52, 122, 177, 236, 397
Multicultural counseling competencies (MCC):
    checklists of, 113-126, 201, 213, 255, 293, 305-306
    criteria for, 52, 293
    emic perspective on, 28-39
    etic perspective on, 18-28
    meanings of, 64, 69-71
    philosophical perspectives on, 4-18
    portfolios for, 43-57
    position paper on, x-xi, 15, 44, 48, 69
    progressive nature of, 51
    self-exploration as fundamental to, 15
    true test of, 45
    See also Domains; Supervision; Training
Multicultural Counseling Inventory, 52, 122, 177, 236, 397
Multicultural Immersion Experience (MIE), 235-238
Multiculturalism:
    advocacy for, 16-18
    as a fourth force, 83, 244, 290
    as an umbrella, 179
    as a philosophy, 185
    beyond race and ethnic issues, 185
    meaning of, 70-71, 76, 125, 264-265
    meaning of, and training, 162-163, 192, 244
    process of, 162-163
    rationale for, 137-138
Multicultural journey, in program development, 163, 164-171, 180
Multiculturally impaired individuals, 161

Multicultural organization development (MCOD), 213-215, 216
Multicultural supervision, 293-294, 311
   multicultural counseling and, 291-293
   White supervisors and, 387-403
   See also Supervision
Multicultural training. *See* Training
Multilingual language switching, 370-372, 377
Mystified concepts, and training, 189

Narrative approaches, to therapy, 352
Native Americans:
   communication style of, 395
   contact with, during training, 229
   course content on, 146
   oppression of, 268
Negative emotions, and self-exploration, 14
Nonconscious ideologies. *See* Ideologies, nonconscious
Nontraditional students, 245
Nonverbal behavior, 374-375, 395
Normative groups, course content on, 146-147

Objectives:
   of courses, 172-173, 175
   of training programs, 202
Observation levels, 72-75
Obstacle, culture as, 268
Oklahoma Racial Attitudes Scales, 397
Openness, to self-examination, 9
Opportunity:
   compared to equal access, x
   culture as, 268
Oppression:
   by nonconscious ideologies, 85-86
   cultural difference and, 267-268
   internalization of, 90
   power dynamics and, 392-393
   racial identity and, 275-276
   unlearning of, 211
Organizational change, 212-215, 216, 218-221
Outcomes, course content on, 140, 141
Overpathologizing bias, 20

Pairings, supervisory. *See* Supervision relationship
Paradigm, definition of, 351
Parent-child relationships, and acculturation, 32, 33-34
Partial knowledge, and training, 189
Partial-learner, supervisor as, 360-361, 367-370, 377
Particularism, 270. *See also* Emic perspective
Partners Program, 230-231
Paternalism, 392
People, need for and fear of, 357
People of Color Racial Identity model, 327
Personality:
   assessment of, 369
   of faculty, 166-167
   of groups, 68
Personalization skills, 358, 359
Philosophy, multiculturalism as, 185
Philosophy, of MCC, 4-18
   emic perspective on, 28-39
   etic perspective on, 18-28
Philosophy, of training, 133, 155, 178
   changes in, stages of, 194-200
   definition of, 186
   implementation of, 194-204
   lists of, 195, 196-197, 198, 199-200
   multicultural, 189-204
   need for, 184-186
   traditional, 187-189
Physical environment, of training programs, 118, 122, 201
Physical vs. psychological symptoms, 31
Political correctness:
   cultural affiliation and, 278
   cultural difference and, 269
   training programs and, 202, 403
Political ideology, 15-18
Portfolios:
   concerns about, 54-55
   development of, 47-54
   evaluation of, 53-54, 55-56
   evidence in, 47, 48-52
   nature of, 46-47
   need for, 43-46
Position paper (1982), on MCC, x-xi, 15, 44, 48, 69
Postmodernism, nature of, 351-356

Postmodern supervision:
  applications of, 365-376
  convergent influences on, 350-365
  relevance of, 376-380
Power:
  race and, 138-139, 328, 392-393, 399
  social, 168-170
  supervision, and, 303-304, 317, 328,
    344-345, 347
  supervision, postmodernism, and, 368,
    372
  supervision, SAS model, and, 334-336,
    338
  supervision, White supervisors, and,
    392-393, 399
  training and, 163
Power distance, in groups, 68
Practicum courses:
  change intervention and, 221
  on gender and sexual orientation, 100
  portfolios for, 52
  surveys of, 124
Prejudice, 138, 233, 234. *See also* Racism
Prior learning. *See* Learning set
Process issues, 38-39, 140
Process skills, 358
Procounselor, 231, 338
Professional associations, organizational
    change in, 213
Professional behavior focus, 359
Professional development, for supervisors,
    396-398
Professional identity, 5-18, 301
Programs, educational. *See* Courses;
    Curriculum; Training
Progressive narratives, 352
Pseudo-independence stage, of identity
    development, 276, 298, 391
Psychoculture, 73 (table)
Psycho-domain, 72-74
Psychodynamic needs, assessment of, 21
Psychological characteristics, race, and
    culture, 65-66
Psychological race, 66
Psychological vs. physical symptoms, 31
Psychology:
  cultural affiliation and, 274, 275
  of identity development, 295
  See also Identity development

Psychorace, 66, 73 (table)

Race:
  course content on, 75-77
  cultural affiliation and, 278-279
  culture and, 61, 64, 67, 70, 203, 264
  ethnicity and, 203
  MCC movement and, 62-65
  observational levels and, 72-74
  power and, 138-139, 328, 392-393, 399
  psychological characteristics and, 65-66
  research implications of, 72-75
  societal classifications and, 65-66
  terminology and, 65-71
Racial identity:
  assessment of, 21
  course content on, 143-145
  cultural affiliation and, 274, 275, 279,
    281
  development of, 143-145, 275, 279, 281,
    295-300, 327
  racism and, 13
  research focus on, 210
  self-exploration in, 8, 9-15
  self-report instruments for, 397
  sociopolitics and, 13
  supervision and, 295-300, 327, 389-391
  workshop on, 22-28
Racial prejudice, 138. *See also* Prejudice;
    Racism
Racism:
  assessment of, 21
  compared to prejudice, 138
  course content on, 138-139
  definition of, 389
  identity and, 13
  MCC movement and, 63
  power and, 138-139, 328
  unintentional, 389-392
Rationale, for multiculturalism, 137-138
Reflection. *See* Self-exploration
Regressive narratives, 352
Reintegration stage, of identity
    development, 276, 390-391
Research:
  content focus of, 209-210
  criticism of, 142-143
  cultural ambience for, 252-253

ethics in, 146
gender bias in, 86-88
in training programs, 107, 118, 120-121, 124-125, 142-143, 201, 250
program areas of, 142
Resistance stage, of identity development, 297, 298
Retraining, motivation for, 4, 8
Role models, for students, 246
Role playing, 96, 231-232, 325
Roles:
acculturation and, 31, 33
multiple, in women, 94-95. *See also* Gender
of supervisors, 302, 358, 359-361, 367-370, 377
Role structure, in social power, 169-170

SAS. *See* Systems Approach to Supervision
Schizophrenia, and assessment bias, 20
Scope, of training programs, 167-168
Self-assessment, in supervision, 304, 305-306, 397. *See also* Portfolios
Self-empathy, 12-13
Self-exploration:
by faculty, 161
change interventions and, 217, 218, 221
in experiential learning, 272, 282, 283
in supervision, 357
in training, 97-98
of gender and sexual orientation, 98, 101
of identity, 8, 9-15, 296, 397
portfolios and, 55
primary goal of, 14
workshop on, 22-28
Sensitivity, and self-empathy, 12-13
Sensory impairment, 229
Sex, as a cultural force, 84. *See also* Gender; Sexual orientation
Sexism, 84, 92, 375. *See also* Heterosexism; Homophobia
Sexual orientation, 84-85
identity development in, 91
ideologies on, 85, 89-92, 95-96
therapy bias in, 91
training on, 91, 96, 97-107
See also Gender
Simulation methods, 231-232, 233, 325

Single parents, students as, 246
Skeptical postmodernists, 351-352
Skills, as foci of supervision, 358-360
Skills, MCC domain, 9, 10-11, 69
course content on, 140
gender and, 94-95, 101-102
in course objectives, 173
individuals, change, and, 216
meaning of, 92
portfolios and, 44, 48, 49
sexual orientation and, 96, 101-102
training and, 75, 101-102
Social categorization, 233-234
Social consciousness, 16
Social constructionism, 352-353, 354, 356
Social dyads, 281
Social influence, 170-171
Socialization:
acculturation and, 33-34
awareness of, 69
sociodemographic variables and, 60-61
Social power, 168-170. *See also* Power
Societal classifications, 65-66
Societal systems, negotiating of, 63
Sociocultural perspective, 74 (table)
Sociodemographic variables, and socialization, 60-61
Socio-domain, 72-74
Sociology, and cultural difference, 267
Sociopolitical perspective, 13, 15-18
Sociorace, 65, 66, 74 (table)
Stability narratives, 352
Standardized instruments:
inadequacy of, 19-20, 139-140, 250
usefulness of, 369
Standards:
of ACA, 15
of ACES, 388, 396
of AMCD, xi, 388
of APA, 159
of CACREP, 159
See also Accredited programs
Statistics courses, 250
Stereotyping:
assessment and, 19
by courses, 160
cultural difference and, 269
disconfirming information and, 233-234
gender and, 86

See also Bias
Strong affect, and supervision, 372-374
Structured assessment, 19-20. *See also
    names of assessment instruments*
Students:
    alienation of, 247, 248
    as program targets, 164-165
    change interventions and, 217, 218,
        220-221
    cultural ambience for, 245-251
    evaluation of, 116, 118, 119, 122,
        177-178
    interest of, and curriculum development,
        171-172
    minority representation of, 123, 126, 127
    multicultural advocacy and, 17-18
    nontraditional, 245
    role models for, 246
    training philosophies and, 185,
        194-200
Supervision, 263-264
    action strategies for, 306
    advocacy and, 302
    case-driven approach to, 334
    case examples of, 321-323, 339-346
    cultural affiliation and, 274-283
    cultural difference and, 267-274
    demographics of, 313, 318
    discrimination model of, 358-361,
        365-375
    ethics in, 307, 351, 366, 367, 380
    experiential learning and, 266, 271-274,
        281-284, 326, 402
    frameworks for, 319-323, 329-346
    identity development and, 295-300,
        319-320, 327, 389-391
    IPR and, 356-358, 365, 370, 373, 374,
        375, 376-377
    live, 361-363, 365-376
    MCC facilitated by, 300-308, 315-323,
        363-365, 388-389, 396-403
    MCC facilitated by, SAS, and, 331-346
    meaning of, 265-266
    models of, 326-329, 356-363
    multicultural concept and, 264-265
    nature of, 293-295, 330
    portfolios and, 52
    postmodern, 350-380

    recommendations for, 272-274, 282-283,
        284, 305-308, 315-316, 318-319,
        396-403
    research needs on, 310-312
    skills in, 358-360
    stages of, 300-302, 327
    supervisee's competence in, 300-302
    supervisor's competence in, 303-308, 397
    survey of, 312-319
    Systems Approach (SAS) to, 329-346
    videotapes and, 356-357
    See also Supervision relationship;
        Training
Supervision relationship:
    collaboration in, 304, 307, 334, 336-337,
        346-347, 362, 399
    framework for, 319-323
    group approaches in, 339-346, 401-403
    human considerations in, 365-366
    interventions in, 337, 398-403
    involvement in, 334, 335, 336, 344
    models applied to, 365-376
    mutual expertise in, 368, 377
    pairings in, 293-294, 298-300, 304, 311,
        328
    power in, 303-304, 317, 328, 344-345,
        347
    power in, and postmodernism, 368, 372
    power in, and SAS model, 334-336, 338
    power in, and White supervisors,
        392-393, 399
    professional development for, 396-398
    strong affect in, 372-374
    supervisor's roles in, 302, 359-360
    supervisor's roles in, as partial-learner,
        360-361, 367-370, 377
    survey of, 312-319
    Systems Approach (SAS) to, 329-346
    theoretical compatibility in, 366
    trust in, 393-394, 399-400
    vulnerability in, 393-394
    White supervisors, interventions for,
        396-403
    White supervisors, issues for, 388-396,
        399
    See also Supervision; Training
Surveys:
    of supervision programs, 312-319

of training programs, 111-112, 113-126, 131-132, 228-229
Syllabus, course, 174, 176-178
Symptoms:
cultural meanings of, 20
psychological vs. physical, 31
Synergistic stage, of identity development, 297, 299
Systems Approach to Supervision (SAS), 329-336
case study of, 339-346
factors in, 330-334
multicultural relationship and, 336-339

Targets:
of change, 216-219
of training programs, 164-167, 187, 192
Teacher, supervisor as, 359-360
Team approaches. *See* Collaboration; Group approaches
Teams-games-tournament technique, 232
Technology, for portfolios, 49
Textbooks, 147-153
Therapeutic outcome goals, 140, 141
Therapeutic processes, 140
Therapy bias, 88-89, 91
Time competence, 71
Top-down approach, to change, 195, 196
Topical approach, in courses, 174, 176-177
Training:
case study of, 102-105
changes in, and MCIM, 215-222
changes in, and MCOD, 213-215
changes in, and philosophy of, 194-200
changes in, need for, 210, 212-213
clientele of, 187
clinical vs. counseling, 229
context of, 168-171
course development for, 173-178, 181
cultural ambience of, 242-256
culture of, 163-164
curriculum development for, 171-180
development of, as a journey, 163, 164-171
diversity. *See* Diversity training
effectiveness of, 210-211
emic perspective and, 28-39

environment of, 118, 122
ethics in, 179, 249
etic perspective and, 18-28
evaluation of, 134, 135-136, 155-156, 201-202, 255
experiential, 98, 100, 121-122, 227, 230-231, 232-238
goals of, 164-168, 201, 218
immersion, 235-238
implementation of, 194-204
instructional strategies in, 133, 230-238
intervention in, 215-222
learning objectives in, 133
missions of, 164-168, 192-194, 202
model programs for, 112-113, 120, 126-128, 221
models of, 132-134, 215-222, 230-233
models of, and supervision, 326-329
models of, five-stage, 186
models of, four-stage, 194-200
models of, integrated. *See* Integrated model
models of, triad, 231
motivation for, 133, 192
objectives of, 202
on gender, 97-107
on sexual orientation, 91, 96, 97-107
philosophy of. *See* Philosophy, of training
political correctness and, 202
power in, 163
program development for, 133-134, 159-171, 211
program development for, stages of, 186, 194-200
scope of, 167-168
social influence in, 170-171
supervision confused with, 265
surveys of, 111-112, 113-126, 131-132, 228-229
targets of, 164-167, 192
See also Courses; Faculty; Students; Supervision
Triad training model, 231
Trust, in supervision, 393-394, 399-400

Uncertainty avoidance, in groups, 68

Underutilization, of counseling services, 292
Unintentional racism, 389-392
Universality assumption, x, 140, 141, 189,
        270. *See also* Etic perspective
Universities:
    changes needed in, 212
    cultural ambience in, 245-256
    multicultural advocacy in, 17
    See also Academia; Courses
University of California, Santa Barbara, 127
University of Iowa, 277-278
University of Nebraska-Lincoln, 17-18
Unlearning:
    of assumptions, 15
    of oppression, 211
Unstructured assessment, 20

Verbal statements, and gender, 375-376
Videotapes, for training and supervision,
        231, 325, 356-357, 398, 400, 402
Visible racial and ethnic groups (VREGs):
    exclusiveness and, 265
    MCC movement and, 62-63
Vision, for organizational change, 215
Voices, of gender, 395, 400
VREGs. *See* Visible racial and ethnic groups
Vulnerability, in supervision, 393-394

Western perspective, 188-189. *See also*
        American perspective; Eurocentrism
White privilege, 391-392
White Racial Identity Inventory, 397

White Racial Identity model, 327
Whites:
    as mental health standard, 62, 87
    as minority Americans, 238-239, 291-292
    assessment bias and, 16, 19, 20, 21
    as status quo or norm, 159, 160, 161,
        239, 250
    as supervisors, 388-403
    Blacks, cultural affiliation, and,
        279-280
    communication style of, 395
    distinct from American culture, 203
    faculty-to-student ratio for, 247
    guilt feelings of, 269
    identity development of, 144-145, 230,
        279, 295, 297-300
    Japanese Americans and, 30, 32
    norm of, in academia, 245-246, 247
    paternalism of, 392
    power of, 139
    prejudice of, 189
    training philosophies and, 189, 190, 203
    unintentional racism by, 389-392
White savior syndrome, 284
Women:
    culture elements dominated by, 68
    gender, ideology, and, 86-89, 92-95
    in academia, 245, 248-249, 252
    multiple roles of, 94-95
    rates of, in therapy, 99
    stereotypes of, 234
Workshop, on assessment, 22-28

About the Contributors

Cynthia Breaux is a doctoral candidate in the Counseling Psychology Program at the University of Maryland. She received her undergraduate and master's degrees from California Polytechnic State University where she received the Outstanding Graduate Student award in psychology. She has conducted research in the areas of utilization of counseling services by diverse racial/ethnic groups and stress in therapists who specialize in persons with HIV disease.

Michael A. Carlton is a doctoral student in the Counseling Psychology Program at the University of Southern Mississippi. His interests include rehabilitation counseling, minority group process, and research related to persons with disabilities and to minority identity development.

Hardin L. K. Coleman (Ph.D., Stanford University), is Assistant Professor in the Department of Psychology at the University of Wisconsin-Madison. His two areas of research are (a) assessment of multicultural and school counselor competence and (b) strategies for coping with cultural diversity. He is involved in the preparation of school and community mental health counselors to work with culturally diverse populations.

Madonna G. Constantine is Assistant Professor in the Counseling Psychology program at Temple University in Philadelphia. She has published and presented in the areas of racial and ethnic psychology, and the training and supervision of psychologists. She has also served as a consultant to numerous universities, organizations and corporations across the United States in the area of multicultural counseling, training,

and supervision; women's health issues; and college student development. She received her Ph.D. in Counseling Psychology from the University of Memphis.

Michael D'Andrea is Associate Professor in the Department of Counselor Education at the University of Hawaii, Manoa. He has published extensively in the areas of multicultural counseling and human development counseling. He is a coauthor of the Multicultural Counseling Awareness, Knowledge and Skills Scale (MAKSS), which has been identified as the most widely used instrument of its type in the United States. He received his Ed.D. in Human Development Counseling from Vanderbilt University.

Judy Daniels is Associate Professor in the Department of Counselor Education at the University of
Hawaii, Manoa. She cofounded and was the first state
president of the Hawaii Association for Multicultural
Counseling and Development and of the Hawaii Association for Counselor Education and Supervision. Her
research and scholarly interests are in the areas of
multicultural counseling; diversity training, with a
particular focus on homeless children and their families; and developmen-
tal psychology. She received her Ed.D. from Peabody College of Vanderbilt University.

Dorothy L. Espelage is a third-year doctoral student
in the Counseling Psychology Program at Indiana
University. Her major research interests include assessment and evaluation in multicultural counseling,
violence prevention, and intervention planning for
women with eating disorders. For the past 2 years, she
has led an evaluation team on a CDC-funded grant
assessing the impact of a multimedia violence preven-
tion program. In addition, she currently is a project coordinator of an
NIH-funded grant that focuses on the measurement of coping strategies in
families. She is completing an APA-approved pre-doctoral internship at
the Durham Veterans Administration Medical Center. She holds an M.A.
in Clinical Psychology from Radford University.

Ruth E. Fassinger is Associate Professor in the Counseling Psychology Program at the University of Maryland at College Park and an affiliate faculty member
in Women's Studies. Her areas of interest include the
psychology of women and gender, particularly
women's career development; issues of sexuality and
sexual orientation; the history of psychology; group
psychotherapy; and research methodology. She is a
licensed psychologist in Maryland and maintains a psychotherapy practice
specializing in women's and gender issues, particularly vocational issues,

sexual identity, and sexual abuse and violence. She consults frequently for local, state, and national organizations regarding issues of gender, work, sexuality, and mental health. She received her Ph.D. in Psychology from Ohio State University.

Margaret L. (Peggy) Fong (Ph.D., Arizona State University) is Professor and Chairperson, Department of Counseling, Educational Psychology and Research at The University of Memphis. Her areas of scholarship are assessment of mental disorders and counselor training and supervision. She has extensive multicultural training experiences in Hawaii, Florida, Tennessee, East Asia, and Germany.

Alberta M. Gloria is Assistant Professor in the Counseling Psychology Program at the University of Wisconsin–Madison. A former faculty member at the University of Utah, she has published and presented in areas related to educational issues for racial/ethnic students in higher education and professional practice issues for counselors in training. She received her doctoral degree in Counseling Psychology from Arizona State University and her master's from the University of Tennessee in industrial/organizational psychology.

Roberto Cortéz González (Ph.D., Stanford University) is Associate Professor in the Department of Educational Psychology and Special Services at the University of Texas at El Paso. He has taught and supervised at the graduate level since 1987. He is licensed in Texas as a psychologist and as a marriage and family therapist. He has served as a multicultural consultant to the American College Testing Service, the Department of Veterans Affairs, and to universities, school districts, social service agencies, and clinical practitioners. In recent years, he has explored narrative and postmodern approaches to therapy and supervision. He continually appraises the strengths and limitations—as well as the pretensions—of such approaches, especially with low-income and Spanish-speaking clientele.

Janet E. Helms is Professor of Psychology at the University of Maryland-College Park, where she is also Chair of the President's Commission on Ethnic Minority Issues. She is an affiliate of the Counseling Center at the University of Maryland and the Women's Studies Program, and is a licensed practitioner in the District of Columbia and Maryland. She has written many empirical and theoretical articles and chapters on the topics of race, culture, and gender identity  development, including "A Race is a Nice Thing to Have." Her forthcoming book with Donelda Cook is *Using Race and Culture in Counseling and Psychotherapy.*

 **Elizabeth L. Holloway** is Professor in the Department of Counseling Psychology and Director of the Educational and Psychological Training Center at the University of Wisconsin-Madison. She has a long career in the research, teaching, and practice of clinical supervision. She has recently published a book that describes her model for the training and practice of supervision. It has evolved from her experience in working with practicing supervisors and educators in the United States, Great Britain, Israel, Europe, and Asia. She is a leader in professional training issues, as evidenced by her writings, research awards, and keynote addresses on supervision and professional training in many parts of the world.

Phoebe Y. Kuo-Jackson is a third-year doctoral student in Counseling Psychology at the University of Nebraska-Lincoln. She received her M.A. in 1992 from California State University-Northridge. Her research and applied interests include ethnic and racial identity development, bicultural identity and competence, adolescent development, minority issues, and women's issues.

Mark M. Leach is Assistant Professor in the Department of Psychology at the University of Southern Mississippi. His professional interests include racioethnic identity and consciousness, cultural mistrust, multicultural training and philosophy, and counselor development. He received his Ph.D. from the University of Oklahoma.

Suzanne H. Lease is Associate Professor in the Department of Counseling, Educational Psychology and Research at The University of Memphis. Her teaching and research interest areas include multicultural counseling, career development, and gay and lesbian counseling issues. She received her Ph.D. from Southern Illinois University at Carbondale.

William M. Liu is a doctoral student in Counseling Psychology at the University of Maryland at College Park. He also works with the Asian American Studies Project at UMCP and teaches Asian American studies at UMCP and at the University of Maryland at Baltimore County. His research interests include racial and ethnic identity issues among Asian Pacific Americans,

multicultural competency and theory, and social class issues. He received his M.A. in counseling and college student personnel administration at the University of Maryland at College Park.

Gary J. Loya is a third-year doctoral student in Counseling Psychology at the University of Nebraska-Lincoln. He received his M.S. from Eastern Washington University. His heritage is biracial, born of mixed Mexican/Anglo parentage. His research and applied interests include multicultural counseling competencies, biracial identity formation and bicultural issues, and substance abuse counseling.

Rocío P. Martínez is a doctoral candidate in Counseling Psychology at the University of Wisconsin-Madison. She has served as a predoctoral intern psychologist at the UW-Madison's University Counseling and Consultation Services, and has worked as an Assistant Dean of Students at Purdue University. She has also worked as a counselor for the Community Mental Health at the UW-Madison Residence Halls, and as a consultant to the Minority Gifted Research Institute of both the University of Wisconsin and Purdue University.

Joseph G. Ponterotto is Professor, Counseling Psychology Program, Graduate School of Education at Fordham University-Lincoln Center, New York City. His research interests are reflected in his recent books: *Handbook of Multicultural Assessment: Clinical, Psychological, and Educational Applications* (1996); *Handbook of Multicultural Counseling* (Sage, 1995); *Preventing Prejudice: A Guide for Counselors and Educators* (Sage, 1993); the *Handbook of Racial/Ethnic Minority Counseling Research* (1991); and *Affirmative Action on Campus* (1990).

Donald B. Pope-Davis is Associate Professor in the Counseling Psychology Program, Department of Counseling and Personnel, at the University of Maryland, College Park. He is currently on the editorial boards of *The Counseling Psychologist* and the *Journal of Counseling and Development,* and an Ad Hoc reviewer for *Professional Psychology: Research and Practice.* He is the author of numerous texts and articles in the areas of multicultural counseling competencies, training, and education. He received his Ph.D. in Counseling Psychology from Stanford University.

Amy L. Reynolds is Assistant Professor of Counseling Psychology at Fordham University, Lincoln Center, New York. She received her doctorate in Counseling Psychology from The Ohio State University and worked for several years as a staff psychologist at The University of Iowa Counseling Service prior to becoming a faculty member. Her research interests and publications emphasize multicultural counseling,

training, and supervision; lesbian, gay, and bisexual issues; and feminist psychology.

Tina Q. Richardson, Ph.D., is Assistant Professor in Counseling Psychology in the Department of Education and Human Services at Lehigh University. She is a graduate of the Counseling Psychology Program at the University of Maryland. Her research interests include multicultural issues in counselor training, White racial identity development, gender identity development, and counseling women.

Beth Sperber Richie is a staff counselor at the University of Maryland Counseling Center and a consultant in private practice. Her current research and practice interests include women's career development and achievement, gender and racial diversity issues in organizations, eating disorders, sexual assault and harassment, and adult survivors of trauma. She received her Ph.D. in Counseling Psychology from the University of Maryland at College Park.

Charles R. Ridley is Associate Professor and Director of Training in the Counseling Psychology Program at Indiana University. Previously, he was a consulting psychologist in private industry and taught at the University of Maryland and the Graduate School of Psychology, Fuller Theological Seminary. His research and scholarly interests include multicultural counseling and training, the integration of psychology and theology, and organizational consultation. He has written *Overcoming Unintentional Racism in Counseling and Therapy: A Practitioner's Guide to Intentional Intervention* (Sage, 1995). He received his Ph.D. from the University of Minnesota.

Karen J. Rubinstein is a third-year doctoral student in the Counseling Psychology Program at Indiana University and Assistant to the Director at the Center for Human Growth, the university's counseling training facility. Her major research interests are in multicultural counseling, the effects of diversity training on organizational consultants, and the impact of organizational culture on racial and ethnic minority group members. She has coauthored and presented many papers on these topics at national and regional conferences. She holds an M.S.Ed. in Mental Health Counseling from the University of Miami.

...PETENCIES

...Professor in ...partment of ...Educational Psychology, University of ...braska-Lincoln. A first-generation immigrant from India, she does research on acculturation, ethnic identity, and adjustment difficulties of Asians in the United States; worldview differences; multicultural counseling competencies; and multicultural instrument development. At her university, she is an active member of the faculty senate, advocating for its ideals of faculty governance and academic freedom. She is the author of *Multicultural Assessment in Counseling and Clinical Psychology* (1996).

Gerald L. Stone is Professor in the College of Education and Director of the University Counseling Service at The University of Iowa. His interests include mental health policy in higher education, crisis and trauma work on campus, and psychotherapy with college students.

Luis A. Vázquez is Assistant Professor in Counseling Psychology in the Department of Counseling and Educational Psychology at New Mexico State University. Areas of special interest and research include acculturation and acculturative stress, identity development, and the organizational development of diversity in educational settings. His greatest interest is the "empowering" focus versus the "deficit" focus of research on diverse populations. He has published in the areas of acculturation and educational development, and has developed multicultural training videos used across the country in counseling programs. He received his doctorate in Counseling Psychology from the University of Iowa. He has also served as a consultant to higher education, school districts, and agencies in their multicultural development and policies.

PREPARING A BOOK PROSPECTUS

If you have an idea for a book in this series, and would like to submit it for consideration, we encourage you to develop a prospectus. The prospectus for a book focuses on the author's thoughts and helps to guide the series editor and publisher. Whereas an outline deals with the content and organization of a book, a prospectus emphasizes the rationale: why it is being written and for whom.

Here are some suggestions you might find useful as you prepare your prospectus for the Multicultural Aspects of Counseling series. Feel free to add items and respond in the style most representative of you and your project.

About the Project

Rationale: What is your purpose in writing the book? What are the goals you have for it?

Coverage: What topics do you plan to include? Are there topics that other people in the field might expect but that you don't plan to include? If so, why?

Approach: Will your treatment be "broad brush" or comprehensive? Will it be applied, a report of your own research program, a review of the research literature, theoretical, or some combination of these approaches? What aspects of your book will distinguish it from recent books treating the same or similar topics?

Apparatus/ Specifications: Describe any components of the book you plan to include to augment the textual discussions (for example, cases, flow charts, summaries, annotated bibliography, glossary). What length manuscript, including bibliography, do you anticipate? What types and amounts of illustrations (figures, tables) do you anticipate?

Schedule: When do you expect to have your first draft completed? When do you expect to have your final manuscript ready? Please be realistic in planning your schedule.

Author: What experience, background, or other qualifications do you bring to the project that make you uniquely qualified to undertake it? Please attach a current vita.

About the Market

Primary
Audience:

What is the primary market for the book? Professionals in what specific fields and subfields? Graduate and/or undergraduate students in what specific disciplines or programs? What associations, specific divisions of professional organizations, or key journals would provide targeted mailing lists for promoting your book?

Secondary
Audience:

Are there other audiences that might be interested in the book, but to a lesser degree? Please be as specific as possible in describing audiences for the book.

The Outline

The outline may be in a formal style or more informal with chapter titles followed by descriptions of contents. Most important is sufficient detail to give the publisher and series editor an accurate impression of the nature of your manuscript.

We prefer to deal with the prospectus rather than a manuscript, at least initially. The series editor and publisher will review the prospectus and decide whether we could or should add your book to our series. If we do not think the proposed book is appropriate for the series, we will inform you of our decision within six or eight weeks. If we decide the proposed book might fit within the scope of the series, we will request the manuscript, or two or three representative sample chapters, so that one or more of our editorial board members or academic advisors might review it.

The decision to offer to publish a manuscript is made by the publisher's editorial review committee based on the series editor's recommendation, as well as reviews by the series editorial board and academic advisors. The complete review usually requires three to four months.